CHILDREN &
YOUNG PEOPLE'S
WORKFORCE

Kate Beith

Debbie
Morrison

Kath Bulman

Sharina Forbes

Sue Griffin

Penny Tassoni

www.pearsonschoolsandfe.co.uk

✓ Free online support
✓ Useful weblinks
✓ 24 hour online ordering

0845 630 44 44

Part of Pearson

Heinemann is an imprint of Pearson Education Limited, Edinburgh Gate, Harlow, Essex, CM20 2JE

www.pearsonschoolsandfecolleges.co.uk

Heinemann is a registered trademark of Pearson Education Limited

Text © Kate Beith, Kath Bulman, Sharina Forbes, Sue Griffin, Penny Tassoni 2010
Typeset by Phoenix Photosetting
Original illustrations © Pearson Education Ltd 2010
Illustrated by Phoenix Photosetting/Harriet Stanes
Cover design by Woodern Ark
Picture research by Susie Prescott
Cover photo © Peter Dazeley/Getty

The rights of Kate Beith, Kath Bulman, Sharina Forbes, Sue Griffin, Penny Tassoni to be identified as authors of this work
have been asserted by them in accordance with the Copyright, Designs and Patents Act 1988.

First published 2010

14 13 12 11
10 9 8 7 6 5 4

British Library Cataloguing in Publication Data
A catalogue record for this book is available from the British Library

ISBN 978 0 435 03132 9

Acknowledgements
Pearson Education Ltd would like to thank Claire Dickinson for providing all information and features relating to Functional Skills in this book. Special thanks are due to the staff and children of The Old Station Nursery in Faringdon, Oxfordshire: Makaton Symbols and Line Drawings of Signs are reproduced with permission from The Makaton Charity (www.makaton.org).

The author and publisher would like to thank the following individuals and organisations for permission to reproduce photographs:

Studio8/Pearson Education (p1); Pearson Education Ltd/ Studio 8. Clark Wiseman (p5, p6); Banastock/Imagestate (p6); Pearson Education Ltd/ Studio 8. Clark Wiseman (p13); Catchlight Visual Services/Alamy (p13); Christoph Martin /Lifesize/Getty Images (p13); © Photodisc. 1999 (p13); Huntstock inc/Alamy (p14); Picture Partners/ Alamy (p19); Image Source/Alamy (p20); UK Stock Images Ltd/Alamy (p23); Stockbyte/Thinkstock (p24); Studio 1one/Shutterstock (p25); Polka Dot/Thinkstock (p26); Pearson Education Ltd/Tudor Photography (p27); Studio8/Pearson Education (p29); Stockbyte/Thinkstock (p33); Scott Indermaur/ Workbook Stock/ Getty Images (p34); Fuse/Getty Images (p36); © Tomasz Markowski/ Shutterstock (p37); Bananastock/Thinkstock (p38); Pearson Education Ltd/Mindstudio (p39); Studio8/Pearson Education (p45); Studio8/Pearson Education (p47, p49); Pearson Education Ltd/Jules Selmes (p50); Pearson Education Ltd/Studio 8. Clark Wiseman (p51); Pearson Education Ltd/Ian Wedgewood (p56); Pearson Education Ltd/Studio 8. Clark Wiseman (p59); Pearson Education Ltd/Jules Selmes (p63); Studio8/Pearson Education (p67); Picture Partners/Alamy (p69); Studio8/Pearson Education (p73); Anna Marlow/Pearson Education (p75); © Pearson Education Ltd/Tudor Photography (p77, p78); © Pearson Education Ltd/Jules Selmes (p80, p.81, p83, p84, p85); © Pearson Education Ltd/ Tudor Photography (p87, p88); © Pearson Education Ltd/Jules Selmes (p89); © Pearson Education Ltd/Tudor Photography (p90, p92); Ace Stock Ltd/Alamy (p93); Pearson Education Ltd/Lisa Payne Photography (p95); Anna Marlow/Pearson Education (p98); Robert A Pears/iStock Exclusive/Getty Images (p100); Pearson Education Ltd/Gareth Boden (p104); Altrendo Images/Getty Images (p105, p115); Pearson Education Ltd/Ian Wedgewood (p107 bottom); Studio8/ Pearson Education (p110); Pearson Education Ltd/Jules Selmes (p117); Imagebroker/Alamy (p119); Retna UK (p122); Anna Marlow/Pearson Education (p123); Studio8/Pearson Education (p124); Pearson Education Ltd /Jules Selmes (p127); Pearson Education Ltd/Gareth Boden (p129); vladm/Shutterstock (p130); Rob Marmion/Shutterstock (p134); Bananastock/Imagestate (p136); Bob Ebbeson/Alamy (p138); John Callan/Rex Features (p141); Angela Hampton Picture Library/ Alamy (p146); Rayes/Photodisc/Thinkstock (p148); photodisc. Kevin Peterson (p152); Andrew Fox/Alamy (p153); © Pearson Education Ltd/Tudor Photography (p155); Anna Marlow/Pearson Education (p157); istockphoto/Thinkstock (p161); Wildscape/Alamy (p165); Paul Doyle/Alamy (p170); GustoImages/Science PhotoLibrary (p177); iStockphoto/Thinkstock (p179); Studio8/Pearson Education (p181); Pearson Education Ltd. Stuart Cox (p182); Studio8/Pearson Education/ cropped (p184); Nigel Riches. www.imagesource.com (p186); Studio8/Pearson Education (p187); Anna Marlow/Pearson Education (p189, p.198); Studio8/ Pearson Education (p199, p201); Anna Marlow/Pearson Education (p204, p206, p209); Pearson Education Ltd/Gareth Boden (p213); Studio8/Pearson Education (p214); Pauline Cutler/Bubbles Photolibrary/Alamy (p219); Bananastock/Imagestate (p223); Bananastock/Imagestate (p225); Heide Benser/Corbis (p236); Mike Booth /Alamy (p241); Crea8tive Images/Shutterstock (p242 top); Hannamariah/ Shutterstock (p242 bottom); istockphoto/Thinkstock (p243 top); D Hurst/ Alamy (p243 middle); Dusan Zidar/Shutterstock (p243 bottom); Susie Prescott (p246); Pearson Education Ltd/Gareth Boden (p249); Chris Schmidt/ istockphoto (p250); JLP/Jose L Pelaez/Corbis (p258); Ian Wedgewood/Pearson Education Ltd (p261); Pearson/Clarke Wiseman (p267); Ariel Skelley/Blend Images/Corbis (p269); Leila Cutler/Alamy (p275); Pearson Education Ltd/Gareth Boden (p276); Studio8/Pearson Education (p277); ©Pearson Education Ltd/ Jules Selmes (p279); Tetra images/Getty Images (p285); Harcourt Education Ltd/Jules Selmes (p287); DK Images (p289); Ian Boddy/Science Photo Library (p290, p293, p.295); Studio8/Pearson Education (p297) George Doyle/Stockbyte/Thinkstock (p300); Colin Cuthburt/Science Photo Library (p306); Mediscan/Medical-on-line/Alamy (p309); DK Images (p310, p311, p314, p316, p317, 318); MIXA/Getty Images (p320); George Doyle/Stockbyte/Thinkstock (p326); Barros & Barros/The Image Bank/Getty Images (p342); Kablonk!RF/Golden Pixels LLC/Alamy (p345); Photofusion/Alamy (p347); © Pearson Education Ltd/Jules Selmes (p356); SW Productions/White/Photolibrary (p356); Frank Siteman/Science Faction/Getty Images (p357); Universal Images Group/Diverse Images/Getty Images (p359); Lawrence Migdale/Science Photo Library (p359); Joti/Science Photo Library (p364); Anna Marlow/Pearson Education (p366); Bananastock/Imagestate (p368); Forster Forest/Shutterstock (p371); Jules Selmes/ Pearson Education Ltd (p372); Alex Griffiths/Alamy (p375); istockphoto/Thinkstock (p377); Liquid Library/Jupiter Images/Getty Images/Thinkstock (p387); Studio8/Pearson Education (p392); Hemera/Thinkstock (p399 top); Msheldrake/Shutterstock (p399 bottom); Bananastock/Thinkstock (p400); Pixland/Thinkstock (p406); Inclusive Technology Ltd (p414); Lord and Leverett/Pearson Education Ltd (p417); Jules Selmes/ Pearson Education Ltd (p419, p421); istockphoto/Thinkstock (p423); Jupiter Images/Bananastock/Thinkstock (p428); Shutterstock/Christopher Parypa (p430); Adrien Sherratt/Alamy (p433); Anna Marlow/Pearson Education (p435); iStockphoto/Thinkstock (p440); Masha Z/Shutterstock (p446); Christopher Robbins/Valueline/Thinkstock (p450); Tamara Lackey/fstop/Corbis (p453); Pearson Education Ltd. Studio 8 (p458).

Every effort has been made to contact copyright holders of material reproduced in this book. Any omissions will be rectified in subsequent printings if notice is given to the publishers.

Websites
The websites used in this book were correct and up to date at the time of publication.

Pearson Education Limited is not responsible for the content of any external internet sites. It is essential for tutors to preview each website before using it in class so as to ensure that the URL is still accurate, relevant and appropriate. We suggest that tutors bookmark useful websites and consider enabling learners to access them through the school/college intranet.

Contents

Introduction

Welcome to this book and congratulations if you are studying for the Level 2 Certificate for the Children and Young People's Workforce. Although you have chosen a profession that is hard work it will bring you a lot of rewards!

This is a very exciting time to be studying for an early years qualification and there are now plenty of opportunities to progress further if you want to. It is good news that a variety of professional organisations have been involved in developing the new Level 2 Certificate and have made it clear that a high standard of work is expected of people working with children and young people in our challenging world.

This book is based upon a qualification that carefully considers the needs of the children and young people you will be working with and has been written by a group of experienced authors with a range of early years experience who understand how important it is to develop diverse skills when working with children. It is our aim to support you in developing your role as an early years professional, ensuring that you are able to support children or young people in a supervised capacity.

We hope that you find all the information and activities challenging and enjoyable and that when you have achieved the Certificate you are inspired to continue your studies as an early years professional.

Structure of the Level 2 Certificate

The Certificate is made up of a number of different units of assessment which sit within the QCF (Qualifications and Credit Framework). When you complete a unit successfully you will gain a certain number of credits. In order to complete the full Level 2 Certificate, you need to get a total of 35 credits. Your tutors and assessors will be able to explain in more detail what is required.

Credits

The credit value of each unit indicates the size of the unit and approximately how long it will take to achieve. Credit is based on how long an average learner would take to complete a unit, and 1 credit is roughly equal to 10 hours of learning, including time spent in class or group sessions, practical work, assessments or independent study.

Unit structure

Each unit has several learning outcomes and each of these is broken down into a number of assessment criteria. All the learning outcomes of the unit have to be assessed in order for you to complete the unit.

This example is taken from Unit MU 2.4 Support children's and young people's health and safety.

Learning outcome	Assessment criteria
2. Be able to recognise risks and hazards in the work setting and during off-site visits	2.1 Explain why a safe but challenging environment is important for children and young people
	2.2 Identify the differences between risk and hazard
	2.3 Identify potential hazards to the health, safety and security of children or young people in the work setting
	2.4 Contribute to health and safety risk assessment in areas of the work setting and for off-site visits

The Level 2 Certificate overview

The Certificate is made up of three groups of units:

- Skills for Care and Development (SfCD) Shared Nucleus Units: these are common to everyone working in the care and development sector.

- Level 2 Core Units: these are units that are common to everyone working with children and young people aged 0–19.

- Optional Units: these units are more specialist and tend to relate to specific areas of work with children or young people.

Everyone taking this qualification needs to complete all the units in the first two groups, and then choose a number of optional units to make the full credit total of 35. There are about 15 optional units of different credit sizes, covering many specialist areas such as disability or work with babies. What is available to you will depend on your interest and what is being offered by your centre or training provider. Your assessor will be able to provide more details of these.

List of Core units at Level 2

The Unit Reference numbers used in this book refer to the original numbers created by the Sector Skills Councils responsible for developing the units. Awarding organisations, such as CACHE, City and Guilds or Edexcel, may use a different numbering system.

Unit Reference No.	Unit title	Credit value
	SfCD Shared Nucleus Units	
SHC 21	Introduction to communication in health, social care or children's and young people's settings	3
SHC 23	Introduction to equality and Inclusion in health, social care or children's and young people's settings	2
SHC 22	Introduction to personal development in health, social care or children's and young people's settings	3
	Level 2 Core units	
TDA 2.1	Child and young person development	2
MU 2.2	Contribute to the support of child and young person development	3
TDA 2.2	Safeguarding the welfare of children and young people	3
MU 2.4	Contribute to children's and young people's health and safety	3
TDA 2.9	Support children's and young people's positive behaviour	2
MU 2.8	Contribute to the support of positive environments for children and young people	3
MU 2.9	Understand partnership working in services for children and young people	2
PEFAP 001	Paediatric emergency First Aid	1
MPII 002	Managing paediatric illness and injury	1
TDA 2.7	Maintain and support relationships with children and young people	3

Assessment of the Level 2 Certificate

Your awarding organisation, such as CACHE, Edexcel or City & Guilds will allow you to be assessed using a range of different methods, based on the learning outcomes and assessment criteria in the unit. Your assessor or tutor will provide you with help and support throughout the assessment process. Some common assessment methods are described below but others may be used as well:

- knowledge, understanding and skills that you demonstrate through your practice in a work setting and that are observed directly by your assessor

- evidence from an expert witness who may be an experienced practitioner who has worked alongside you, or others with suitable backgrounds who can vouch for your practice

- questions (oral and written) and professional discussion, usually with your assessor, which allows you to talk about what you know

- assignments and projects of different types including child studies

- assessment of your work products such as plans, displays, child observations, materials you have made to support children

- tests

- recognised prior learning.

Sometimes your awarding organisation will insist on a specific method such as a test or an assignment. Again your tutor or assessor will provide you with help and support to decide the best approach.

How to use this book

This book contains all the core units you need to complete your Level 2 Certificate and is divided into 3 sections:

1. Shared Nucleus units

2. Level 2 Core units

3. Optional units (includes 5 of the most popular optional units)

All the chapters are matched closely to the specifications of each unit in the syllabus and follow the unit learning outcomes and assessment criteria — making it easy for you to work through the criteria and be sure you are covering everything you need to know.

Key features of the book

Key terms — simple definitions of some of the more complex terms or pieces of jargon used in the book

Over to You — short task to enhance your understanding of a piece of information (e.g. internet research or a practical idea you could introduce in your setting).

Case study — real-life scenario exploring key issues to broaden your understanding of key topics; demonstrates how theory relates to everyday practice and poses reflective questions.

Best practice checklist — a checklist of key points to help you remember the main underpinning knowledge in a unit.

Skills builder — short activity linked thematically to the unit, specifically designed to develop your professional skills.

Getting ready for assessment — an activity to help you generate evidence for assessment of the unit.

Functional Skills — highlights where content in the unit enables you to apply Functional Skills in the broad areas of English, ICT and Maths — matched to the latest (2009) FS Standards at Level 1. The tips and explanations given show how Functional Skills can be contextualised to work in early years and will be of particular benefit to learners on Apprenticeship programmes.

Check your knowledge — at the end of each unit, these questions will help you consolidate your understanding and ensure you are ready to move on to the next unit.

Working life — some core units in the book end with a full-page magazine-inspired feature covering a key issue or topic, with expert guidance relating to problems that may be encountered in your working life. Contains the following 'mini-features':

- **My Story** — a practitioner's personal account; sometimes inspirational or uplifting, other times sharing a problem

- **Ask the Expert** — Questions and answers relating to working practice

- **Viewpoint** — topical issues discussed around the wider issues of childcare.

SHC 21

Introduction to communication

As a member of a team working with children effective communication is essential to ensure that you can all work together to create the best provision for the children and young people you are working with.

Learning outcomes

By the end of this unit you will:

1. understand why communication is important in the work setting

2. be able to meet the communication and language needs, wishes and preferences of individuals

3. be able to reduce barriers to communication

4. be able to apply principles and practices relating to confidentiality at work.

Understand why communication is important in the work setting

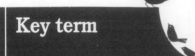

Key term

Communication: a way of exchanging information, either verbally (through speaking), in written form or non-verbally (including body language)

In a team working with children and young people, effective **communication** is essential to ensure that you all work together to create the best provision for them. In this unit you will look at what communication is, find different ways of communicating and how to break down any barriers to effective communication. You will also find out how to ensure that confidentiality is an important part of your daily communication at work.

You will have heard a great deal about how important communication is when you are working with children and young people. As an early years practitioner, the way you communicate with adults will also affect the quality of care provided for the children. You can learn how to be very clear in your communication so that everyone around you understands what it is you are trying to say or do.

Communication takes many different forms, from talking to letters and memos. Sometimes you may find it difficult to convey what you want to say, but it is important that you develop these skills in order to communicate effectively.

Why people communicate

There are many different reasons why people communicate. It is worth taking time to think about what these might be before you find out how to develop your communication skills.

Carefully look at the following list to see the different reasons people might communicate.

People communicate to:

- give information
- receive information
- give instructions
- receive instructions
- discuss a situation
- make a point or outline a concern
- express a need
- negotiate
- develop learning.

Over to You

List the different forms of communication you are involved in during one day in your setting, such as telling a parent about their child's day, listening to your manager in a team meeting or talking to a child while playing together.

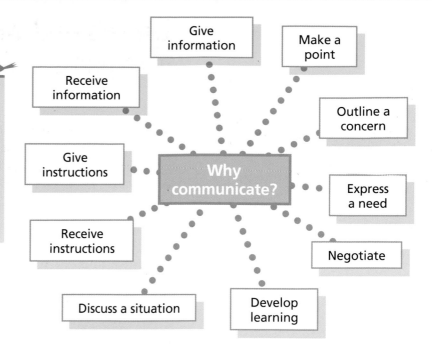

Figure 1: Why people communicate

Communications in your setting

There will be a range of reasons for people in your setting to communicate. This communication may take place between adults or children. Table 1 gives some of the reasons that adults and children in your setting may communicate.

Table 1: Reasons for communication

Reason for communication	Who may be involved
To give parents information about the daily activities of the setting including routines, visits and activities	Manager, parents, early years practitioners
To communicate child's progress in their learning	Early years teachers/practitioners/adults
To inform parents of incidents such as accidents and illnesses	Early years practitioners/managers/parents
To inform practitioners about child's life at home	Parents/early years practitioners
To lead an activity with children, such as storytelling or cooking	Early years practitioners/children
To encourage positive behaviour	Early years practitioners/children
To give instructions to children so that they understand what is required of them in routines and activities such as emergency practices and outings	Early years practitioners/children
To share information about children	Early years teams/parents
In regular team meetings about daily running of setting	All team practitioners
To inform parents and staff about emergencies such as closures because of weather conditions	All team practitioners
When mentoring or discussing performance management of team members	Manager/early years practitioner
To provide training about aspects of early years	Manager, visiting professionals

Case study:
Communicating with parents

At Brownhill Children's Centre Jo leads a room for children aged two to three years. She has written in the home communication book belonging to Lika, one of the children in her room, that she has had a very happy day and particularly enjoyed the cooking activity. Jo also includes a photo of Lika involved in cooking gingerbread men biscuits. Lika's mum has been very worried that she has not settled in well, but she does not pick her up at the end of the day. The next morning, Jo makes sure that she talks to Lika's mum in more detail about how well her daughter is settling in. Lika's mum seems relieved and thanks Jo for sending a note and photo home for her. She tells Jo that she and Lika have chatted about what she was doing in the photo.

1. What do you think are Jo's reasons for writing in the home communication book about Lika's day?

2. Why do you think that Jo puts a photo in the book?

How effective communication affects all aspects of your work

In your setting, **effective communication** is at the centre of everything you do. There will be many different aspects of your role for which you will need to be able to communicate well. Effective communication will make your role work and will enable you to develop your role as a practitioner working with children and young people.

Look at the diagram below to consider aspects in your role that may need you to communicate effectively.

Key term

Effective communication: communication in which the right message is both sent and received

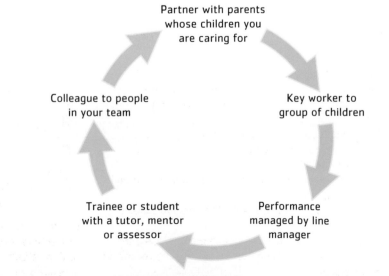

Figure 2: Aspects of your role that may need you to communicate effectively

Over to You

Think about a time when you could have communicated more effectively with a child or adult in your setting. Read the four points of effective communication. What do you think you could have done to make the communication more effective? Record how you would communicate if this situation arose again.

Functional Skills English: Writing

By completing this task you could develop your writing skills by writing a diary account of how you feel the communication went, why you were communicating and what you learnt from this communication.

Effective communication is a two-way process. The person communicating has to send the right message, but also needs to make sure that it is being correctly received and understood by the other person or people. Communication involves talking or verbal communication, and non-talking or non-verbal communication.

To communicate effectively you will need to:

- be very clear about what you are trying to say
- ensure that the person you are talking to understands what you are saying to them
- try to consider the other child's or adult's point of view
- have a rapport with the child or adult you are communicating with.

If people are given clear information they will be more likely to understand your point of view or the message that you are trying to deliver.

Communicating effectively is not always easy. You should always feel that you can seek support if you need advice to help you communicate, whether with a child or with an adult.

The benefits of effective communication

If you communicate effectively three major aspects of your work will benefit. They are:

- your relationship with the children
- your relationship with colleagues
- your relationship with parents.

Table 2 shows how effective communication can benefit these three main areas of your work with young children.

Table 2: The benefits of effective communication

Effective communication	Benefits
With children • Talk at their level, ensuring you have eye contact • Give them time to absorb what you are saying • Encourage them to restate what you have said • Use **open-ended questions** • Try to understand their point of view • Use age-appropriate language • Be consistent • Use pictorial communication, such as visual timetabling • Use positive body language • Ensure that you show respect by the way you talk and where you talk • When you are communicating in a group, ensure that it is of a size and at a time that are appropriate for the age of the children	 Children will feel respect and develop trust in you, and thus feel able to communicate with you. This will also have a positive effect on their engagement in their learning and development, as they will feel safe in their environment

Table 2: The benefits of effective communication (contd.)

Effective communication	Benefits
With parents • Ensure that you have a range of effective communication methods with parents such as face to face, telephone, email, and home communication books • Use the parents' preferred names • Be very clear about what you are saying • Respond as quickly as you can to any communication from a parent • Show them that you know their child and respect them as the main carers • Be careful to choose the right form of communication and adapt accordingly • Ensure that a parent with a second language or a communication need has the means to understand, such as an interpreter • Show respect and confidentiality as to where you communicate • Give the parent time to absorb information and answer • Use positive body language to show that you are listening	Adults will feel respected and that you value their children. Your relationship will develop positively if parents feel you are prepared to give them time and to listen to them. The child's learning and development will also benefit if the important adults in their life can communicate effectively about them 
With colleagues • Always communicate regularly and find out how you are expected to communicate with different colleagues • Communicate in the right place, e.g. if it is a sensitive issue, choose a confidential area • Be clear about what you want to say • Ensure that the other person understands what you are saying • Give the other person time to listen and respond • Use positive body language to show you are listening • In formal meetings always stick to the point and try to be concise • Always avoid being emotive when you communicate • If you are communicating via email or other written forms, make sure your language is professional and that you can ensure that your communication has been received • Use positive body language • Although you may not agree, always try to understand your colleague's point of view	 Effective communication will create an effective team. You will have the basis for a professional working relationship that will benefit the learning and development of each child and also help you to develop professionally

Observing an individual's reactions

When you communicate with children or adults it is important that you take into account what each individual is feeling and what they want to say. You can do this by carefully observing a variety of reactions. Some adults or children are confident enough to express themselves verbally, but for some you may only be able to gauge their response by observing their facial expressions, body language or what they do not say. It is therefore important that you develop the skills to 'read' children and adults by understanding their non-verbal as well as their verbal reactions.

Observing reactions: some points to bear in mind

- You will discover that individual reactions may relate to personality, culture or religion.

- Sometimes you will have to adapt the way you communicate because of the way a child or adult reacts to you.

- It is important that you observe a range of different reactions so that you know how to respond to a child or adult.

- You need to understand that children or adults express what they may not be able to put in words in a variety of ways. This may be as simple as lowering their eyelids with embarrassment or biting a lip through nervousness.

- You also need to be aware that expressions can have different meanings for different cultures.

Case study:
Understanding other cultures

Joan is a key worker in a nursery class and has a three-year-old Nepalese child Santosh to care for. The family have come straight from Nepal. Joan knows that she will need to understand the family's culture and so talks to a representative from the local Nepalese community. She discovers that Nepalese people sometimes shake their heads from side to side when they agree. She is glad that she has found this out as Santosh often does this when she speaks to him or when he cannot find the words he needs. Joan soon realises that Santosh is actually saying yes, perhaps to the offer of a story or a snack!

1. How does Joan's research help her to develop her communication with Santosh?

2. How do you think Joan can support other children and the adults in the class about the fact that Santosh sometimes shakes his head from side to side when he means yes?

Non-verbal reactions

Here are some of the non-verbal reactions that you might have to read when communicating.

Facial expressions

How often have you heard someone say that they know what someone is feeling because of the look on his or her face? This is often true, as facial expressions can be a way of finding out how someone feels. Facial expressions can also accompany talk: for example, a child or adult might knit their eyebrows if they are puzzled about something, and tight lips may mean that someone is angry about something. This will obviously vary from person to person and from culture to culture.

Eye contact refers to a person's behaviour while looking — whether they look you in the eye or not. People may have intense eye contact because they are trying to understand you. However, some cultures or people may avoid eye contact when they do not understand or agree with you, want to avoid showing their feelings or fear negative feedback.

People may have intense eye contact because they are trying to understand you

Body language

Can you remember being told as a teenager that you looked 'moody'? This is because your body language can often indicate your attitudes and emotions.

- If the person you are communicating with has arms crossed tightly over their chest, this may indicate anger or tension.

- If they lean forward with separated arms and legs, this can communicate warmth and friendliness.

- Indifference to your communication may be expressed through shoulder shrugs, raised arms, and outstretched hands.

- Clenched fists and hunching may convey anger.

- Slouched shoulders may convey a lack of confidence.

- A posture with the shoulders back in a relaxed position makes it more likely that others will view you as self-confident.

When observing an adult's or child's reactions to your communication, think about the items in the checklist opposite.

Your body language can say a lot

Best practice checklist: Reactions to communication

✓ If you communicate from too far away, then an adult or child may react indifferently to you

✓ If you go too close to a child or adult, you may observe an embarrassed or uncomfortable reaction

✓ Rules for proximity vary in different cultures and ethnic groups so you will want to find out about this when communicating with a variety of people

Gestures

Think of someone you know really well. You will probably know that if they make certain movements with their hands they are perhaps embarrassed or unhappy. It is important that you learn to observe and understand as much as you can about the gestures of the adults and children you are communicating with.

● People often use gestures such as head and hand movements to reveal or conceal feelings. They can use them to add emphasis, to illustrate points, and to manage turn-taking.

● A nod may encourage others to continue talking by nodding from time to time, whereas some gestures such as scratching your head or face indicate impatience or indifference.

Touch

Touch is an important part of non-verbal communication but you have to be sensitive as to how people use touch and observe how people use accompanying gestures. For example, to get your attention an adult may touch your arm while saying 'Excuse me'.

- If you observe carefully, you will see that a touch you think is firm may be actually kind, such as a hand on a shoulder or a handshake.

- It is also important to know that for some cultures touch is not appropriate.

Voice tone

Are their times when you know a relative or friend is unhappy with you just by the tone of their voice? Voice tone is an important part of understanding how a child or adult is communicating with you.

Reactions can vary and a quiet voice that indicates nervousness in one adult may just be a natural tone of voice in another. Make sure that you observe each individual's tone of voice as well as their physical reactions, so that you can interpret them clearly.

Getting ready for assessment

You will communicate with both adults and children individually and in groups. It is obviously more difficult to observe reactions to your communications from a group of people.

To help you find out about group communications, try to observe a children's group time or a meeting. Listed below are some tips to help you observe and find out what people are thinking or feeling. You could write up your notes as evidence for assessment. Ensure that you do not use real names.

- Who says the most?
- Who says the least?
- How do adults or children take turns to speak?
- Who talks to each other?
- How are interruptions handled?
- Do adults or children put up with two or more people talking at once?
- How do the group react to moments of silence?
- Are open-ended questions used?

Be able to meet the communication and language needs, wishes and preferences of individuals

In the Early Years Foundation Stage, 'Positive Relationships' is one of the four themes on which good practice is based. For you, this refers to your relationship as an early years practitioner with both adults and children. Being able to meet the communication and language needs, wishes and preferences of the individual you work with is crucial if you are to form positive, effective relationships with them.

In this section you will find out how you can support communication and language needs that could take a range of forms, as shown in Figure 3 below.

Key term

Bilingual: speaking two languages

Multilingual: speaking more than two languages

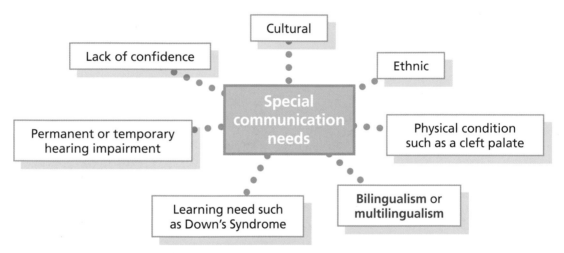

Figure 3: A range of different communication and language needs

Individual needs, wishes and preferences

Link

See information on language development in TDA 2.1 for more about children's pattern of speech.

When you are working with young children, it is important that you do all you can to find out each individual's communication and language needs, wishes and preferences. You will be aware that a child's communication skills develop in sequence. However, do keep in mind the fact that children develop at different rates: if a child does not have the pattern of speech described, it should not necessarily be seen as a concern.

There are ways of finding out if an adult or child has communication and language needs, wishes or preferences.

When children enter your setting you will need to:

- talk to their parents to find out if there are any needs their child has
- seek support and advice from other professionals such as speech and language specialists

Over to You

Your area will have a Children's Trust that aims to ensure that:

- communications with all children and young adults are supported
- professionals work together to improve the outcomes for children.

Find out about Children's Trusts, including your local one, at www.dcsf.gov.uk/everychildmatters

- talk to your SENCO (Special Educational Needs Coordinator) if you need advice as to where to gain information for a child with learning needs
- observe the children
- find out from your line manager if there are any reports on record about a child's communication needs.

Functional Skills English: Reading

Completing this task and using the information on the website in 'Over to You' on this page is a good way to develop your reading skills. Maybe you could discuss your findings with a tutor to show what you have understood.

Finding out how an adult may need to be communicated with might be a little more difficult. Here are some examples.

- If an adult has a need such as a hearing impairment, you may be able to ask them how you need to communicate with them, for example by signing or always ensuring that you are facing them when talking so that they can read your lips.
- If an adult has English as an additional language, you will need to find out if they need somebody to translate for them.
- A parent who works and does not pick their child up from school may appreciate emails, phone calls or notes in the communication book.
- Some adults may not recognise the written word.

Meeting an individual's needs, wishes and preferences

Talking is not the only way of communicating with adults and children in your setting. It may be useful to think of different ways that you communicate during the day, such as:

- telephone
- email
- video conferencing
- letters
- memos
- sign language
- interpreting.

You will want to choose a way of communicating that suits the situation. Look at Table 3, which gives examples of the methods of communication you could use in different situations.

Table 3: Methods of communication in different situations

Method of communication	Reasons for communication	Thinking about the individual	
Verbal	• Giving information, perhaps about a child or incident • Discussion at a meeting either with a parent or a colleague • Giving feedback to a parent, colleague, etc. • Receiving information about your setting from a colleague or about a child from a parent	• Where you communicate • If an adult needs someone else with them if they have English as an additional language • If an adult needs support such as signing	
Written	• Letters about trips, activities in setting, etc. • Notices perhaps about changes to staffing, routine, etc. • Newsletters keeping everyone up to date with events in your setting • Reports about incidents, children's progress, etc. • Notices giving information to a parent, child or colleague • Agendas, minutes, records of meetings with parents or colleagues, such as weekly team meetings	• Consider if the written language needs translation • Be sensitive to adults who may find reading a challenge • Be sensitive to parents or colleagues who may be dyslexic • Make sure that written information is available where all parents can access it such as email, home school communication books, etc.	
Computer/ internet	• Emails, either as a personal response to a communication or more general, to remind adults about events, etc. • General information on website for parents and colleagues, such as forthcoming events	• Ensure that each adult has access to the internet • Make sure you address adults in emails with their preferred name • Ensure you are confidential • Consider parents who may need computer information to be translated into their home language	
Telephone	• Relaying information about a child to his/her parent • Receiving information • Arranging a meeting • Ordering resources • Arranging a visit	• Consider another form of communication if perhaps an adult is hearing impaired or has English as an additional language • Consider whether the adult you are communicating with can receive a phone call at that time. For example, a mum with a small baby may be feeding or a parent at work may have to ring back if they are in a meeting	

Table 3: Methods of communication in different situations (contd.)

Method of communication	Reasons for communication	Thinking about the individual
Video	• Conferences • Training • Records of children's learning	• Consider whether every individual involved in a conference has access to video facilities • Some adults may not want their child's learning to be recorded by video
Sign language	• Communicating face to face with adults, parents or children	• Be aware of what type of sign language a child uses: for example, British Sign Language (BSL), Makaton or one from their own country • If you do not sign, there are people who will sign for you; the adult may know someone
Interpreting	• Giving written or verbal information, perhaps about a child or incident • Discussion at a meeting either with a parent or a colleague • Giving feedback to a parent, colleague, etc. • Receiving information about your setting from a colleague or about a child from a parent	• Ensure that the person interpreting is qualified to do so • Ensure that the adult is confident with the person interpreting • It is sometimes better to find out if the adult knows an interpreter • Ensure that the interpreter is interpreting in the right dialect, as regions in countries can have different uses of language • Be sensitive as to where you communicate using an interpreter. Ensure that you have privacy

Functional Skills Maths: Interpreting

You could create a tally chart of the different ways you communicate in a week. At the end of the week you could use your tally chart to create a graph or work out what percentage of your week is spent communicating in each different way.

It is also worth noting that a professional colleague outside of your setting might be asked to support communication methods with parents. For example, a speech and language therapist might be able to help a parent understand that their child needs support. This is called advocacy.

Skills builder

Talk to your line manager and ask if you can design a communication note for parents of children who you are looking after in your setting. It could be placed in your home/setting link book if you have one. You will be doing this to inform them about what has been happening in one aspect of the curriculum in your setting, such as:

• interests you have been following with their children, such as pirates or mini-beasts

• a special visit perhaps from a local vet or policeman

• a new piece of equipment, such as a tunnel in the garden.

Keep the information to one page of A4. Use simple language. Consider adding photos and children's artwork.

You could talk to your line manager about whether the information should be sent by email, goes into the children's bags at home time or is placed on a noticeboard in your setting. This will depend on the individual communication needs of parents in your setting.

Older children and young people could even get involved in creating the information.

Functional Skills ICT: Developing, presenting and communicating information

You could design and produce your newsletter on the computer and practise using a range of different editing techniques. Refer to line manager if this can be done. You could add images, clipart and text to your leaflet to make it look attractive.

Link

In MU 2.9 you will find out more about the professionals and services that are available to support you in working with children and young adults who may have specific communication needs.

How and when to seek advice about communication

In your role it is important that you feel able to seek advice when you are not sure how to communicate, or when you need to know more, perhaps a child with a hearing impairment or an adult who has English as an additional language.

There are many people who can support you, and agencies are in place to give advice to you, so that you can communicate effectively with everyone during your working day.

Where to look for support

- You should always talk first to your line manager, who may be able to advise you or work with you to seek support.

- Your line manager will then advise you about where you can find support, and will probably be the person to find appropriate support if it is external.

- If you work in a children's centre you are likely to have support services to help both children and adults develop their communication skills.

Case study:
Getting support

Danny is a trainee in an extended school facility at Hillside Primary School, working with a group of seven- to ten-year-old children after school. He is finding it difficult to persuade Santiago, who is eight years old, to listen and follow instructions. Santiago's behaviour is often inappropriate and is beginning to influence other children. Danny talks to his line manager Zita, who invites Sandra, the Extended Schools Manager, to attend a team meeting. Zita suggests that Danny talks to Santiago's teacher and finds out about his behaviour in class. She also suggests that they have a meeting with Santiago's mum, who collects him each day. Danny finds out that Santiago has support from BEST (Behavioural Support Service) and that his teacher has been shown ways of managing Danny's behaviour. Danny and his manager, Zita, are able talk to the teacher and Santiago's mum to try some of the suggested strategies. The result is that Santiago's behaviour continues to improve in the following few weeks.

- How do you think Santiago's behaviour improves because of Danny's actions?

- How important do you think it is that Danny works with his line manager, Zita, to seek support about Santiago's behaviour?

When to look for support

Look at Figure 4, which shows when you should seek advice about communication with an adult or child.

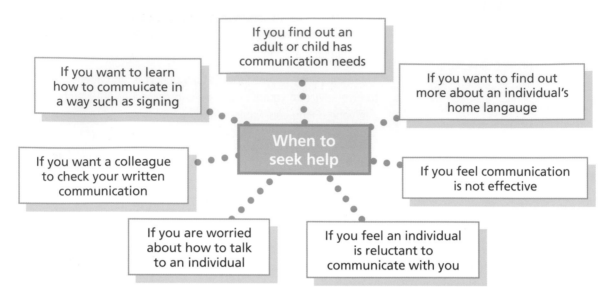

Figure 4: When to seek advice about communication with an adult or child

Key term

Barrier to communication: something that means that communication cannot be effective

Be able to reduce barriers to communication

If you can learn to summarise what some of the reasons may be for ineffective communication you will be more likely to find ways to communicate effectively. These can often happen however much you work hard to communicate with others.

Barriers to effective communication

There are a range of events and situations that can stop communication working. It is important that you learn to find out what stops people in your work setting communicating effectively so that you can learn to change the way you communicate in different situations. These **barriers** may be physical, organisational, attitudinal, personal, to do with language and culture or to do with the presentation of information.

Physical

- Poor lighting or background noise, which can affect people's concentration and the way they communicate

- Staff absences or shortages, meaning that meetings have to be cancelled or you may be in a hurry

- Outdated equipment, such as computers or old photocopiers

- Communicating from different locations or sites

Organisational

- Unclear structure so adults do not know who to communicate with
- Inefficient information systems, such as email
- Lack of clarification of what each person's role is in communication within the setting

Attitudinal

- Personality conflicts between adults
- Lack of consultation
- Lack of motivation or positive attitude to work
- Insufficient support in communicating
- Adults who do not like change
- Different views about practice

Personal

- Adults with personal problems or worries, such as health or relationships
- Adults with depression or other psychological conditions
- Adults with eyesight or hearing needs
- Close friendships among colleagues

Language and culture

- Adults with English as an additional language, so communication is not clearly understood
- Different cultures having different expectations of communication
- Inappropriate or complicated language, which can sometimes stop people from understanding a message
- Poor explanations or misunderstanding, resulting in confusion

Presentation of information

- Written information that is poorly presented with mistakes, such as incorrect dates for events, which can cause confusion

Ways to reduce barriers to effective communication

Working out why communication is not working is perhaps easier than working out how you can communicate in a better way! Once you have found out why communication has broken down, there is no harm in practising your communication skills with colleagues at work or perhaps with fellow trainees. It is also worth talking to someone you trust before you apply a new method of communication, so that you can gain another viewpoint.

Functional Skills English: Speaking, listening and communication

Working in pairs you could practise different forms of communication. Try taking on different roles such as the teacher communicating with a parent or an early years practitioner communicating with a teaching assistant. This is a good way to build your confidence and to help you develop your communication skills.

When you are developing your professional communication skills you must feel that you can ask for advice at any time. The first thing that you need to do is seek advice from your line manager. You may then have to:

- set up a meeting to talk to the other adult if there has been a miscommunication or misunderstanding
- seek advice from your setting's SENCO (Special Educational Needs Coordinator) if you need to be put in touch with another agency that may help, such as a speech and language consultant
- find someone to help if an external service is needed, such as translation
- find advice about how to remove a barrier, such as weak written communication
- clarify your role in communicating with parents or colleagues in your setting
- research ways of improving communication if necessary, such as finding more about how another culture communicates.

Functional Skills English: Writing

When completing this task plan your writing through so that your work is organised and structured. Think carefully about your spelling, punctuation and grammar.

Getting ready for assessment

Reflect on a time when communication in your setting did not work for some reason. This may have been:

- a parent who was upset after a meeting
- confusion about dates for a function, such as a parent communication evening
- an email to all parents that some did not understand
- when you did not understand something that you were asked to do
- when you felt that you did not communicate effectively because you had to work extra hours or your mind was on something else.

Write about the situation, making sure that you do not use real names, and identify why you think that communication did not work.

Active listening means more than just hearing the words

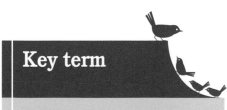

Key term

Active listening: showing that you understand through eye contact, body language and verbal responses

How to ensure that communication has been understood

There are various ways that you can find out if your communication has been successful. If you can do this, it can help to solve any issues that arise and stop barriers from developing.

Active listening is important when you are finding out if people understand your communication. Active listening means more than just hearing the words that someone else is speaking; it means that you show you are listening through making eye contact, your body language and the verbal responses you give, which show that you understand.

To help make sure that the content of your message is understood, you need to:

- send your message using the method preferred by the person you are communicating with, as they will be more likely to understand it

- listen carefully and actively

- give feedback immediately where possible, summarising what has been said. For example: 'So, Judy, are you clear that you will need to come to work half an hour earlier tomorrow?'

Read the following best practice checklist to make sure that you can find out if your communication is successful.

Active listening helps you to make sure you are getting the message

Sources of information and support or services for more effective communication

You have already read that there are services available to you to help you communicate effectively in your setting. Your line manager should be able to contact these services if you think that they will be helpful. Some contact details for a range of support services are given in Table 4.

Functional Skills ICT: Finding and selecting information

You could use a search engine to search for these websites and then explore the information they have available to you on their site. It is important when using information from a website that you take account of any restrictions such as copyright.

Table 4: Support services and how they can help

Support services	How they can help
Royal National Institute for the Deaf (RNID) www.RNID.org.uk	Agencies in different areas will give support to people with hearing and sight loss
Association of Sign Language Interpreters www.asli.org.uk/default.aspx	Qualified in sign language, professionals help people who are hard of hearing to communicate
Royal National Institute for the Blind (RNIB) www.RNIB.org.uk	Agencies in different areas give visually impaired people support in communicating
Teaching Development Agency (TDA) www.tda.gov.uk	Have courses to support teaching assistants working with children in schools
CAF Common Assessment Framework	Gives practitioners a right to seek support in communicating with parents and children who have specific needs
Department of Education www.education.gov.uk	The government website or your local authority website gives information about local agencies that will help to communicate with families from a variety of cultures and religions

Be able to apply principles and practices relating to confidentiality at work

You will come across the term '**confidentiality**' frequently in this book. In the following sections you will find more about how you should manage confidential information and maintain confidentiality appropriately in the work setting.

Over to You

Your setting should have a confidentiality policy about the sharing of information. If you have not seen this, ask your line manager if you can have a copy. After you have read the policy, consider how you are encouraged to use it in your work setting.

What is confidentiality?

Confidentiality means that, as a practitioner, you have a duty to:

- keep certain information confined to agreed people
- respect this confidentiality
- respect each individual's privacy.

Getting ready for assessment

Every Child Matters also protects children's right to confidentiality:

'It is crucial to build trust with the child or young person and their family from the outset by clarifying issues and procedures surrounding confidentiality, consent and information sharing.'

To show that you understand the importance of working in a confidential way as outlined in *Every Child Matters*, you could write five points about how your workplace has clear procedures for maintaining a child and his/her family's right to confidentiality.

Confidentiality in day-to-day communication

Your setting will have a Statement of Intent at the beginning of their policy of confidentiality, and you should follow this in your day-to-day communication as it is important that you follow the agreed approach of your setting. To ensure you understand the importance of agreeing an approach to maintaining confidentiality you may be asked to sign a confidentiality agreement.

Consider the case study below of how Rashid follows his centre's Statement of Intent in his everyday practice.

Case study:
Considering confidentiality

Rashid follows Merton Road Children's Centre's Statement of Intent, which is written at the beginning of their confidentiality policy. Rashid has recently reviewed his setting's confidentiality policy in a team meeting. This is the Statement of Intent at the beginning of the policy:

> 'It is our intention to respect the privacy of children and their parents and carers, while ensuring that they access high-quality early years care and education in our setting.'

After considering this, Rashid and his team decide that they need to ensure that children's portfolios, which are currently accessible to all parents, are kept in a cupboard, and that parents have to ask for them (some parents were looking at other children's portfolios!).

1. How are Rashid and his team considering the importance of confidentiality?
2. How do you think that a parent looking at another child's portfolio could affect the child and his or her family?

Listed below are ways in which your confidentiality should be maintained in everyday situations in your setting:

- keeping observations of children using first name or initials only
- keeping developmental records stored away from general view
- keeping all personal records in locked cabinets
- ensuring any information on the computer has limited access
- ensuring parents only have access to their own child's records
- ensuring staff only have access to their own records
- having a key person who is the only one to pass information on to the child's parents
- making sure conversations take place in appropriate places
- only sharing information with appropriate people.

Situations where confidential information might need to be passed on

There are situations when confidential information has to be shared. If it is in connection with a child, parental consent should be given unless a child's safety is at risk. Here are some situations where confidential information may have to be passed on:

- if a child needs additional support from other professionals
- if a child is suspected to be in a situation that risks their safety
- if an adult has disclosed information that may raise concerns over their ability to carry out daily duties in your setting
- if an outside body such as Ofsted requests to see an adult's or child's records.

Before someone gives you information they say is confidential, you may feel you may not be in a position to keep such information to yourself, so always tell the person that you may have to share the information. The other person can then decide whether he or she wants to tell you.

How and when to seek advice about confidentiality

If you are ever in doubt about an issue that is confidential, always seek the advice of your line manager. This is particularly relevant if someone has asked you to keep a confidence in the workplace and you are worried about the information you have been given. Always do this in an area where nobody else can overhear what you are saying. It is better to seek advice verbally rather than using communication such as email, which other adults could access.

Over to You

Under the Data Protection Act, written information about children and adults should be kept securely. How do you ensure this in your setting?

At times, privacy is essential to maintain confidentiality

Check your knowledge

1. Give three reasons why people might communicate.
2. What is an open-ended question?
3. Which EYFS theme refers to your relationship as an early years practitioner with both adults and children?
4. Who would you seek advice from about communicating with another colleague?
   A) your best friend   B) a parent   C) your line manager
5. Describe three barriers to effective personal communication.
6. What does RNID stand for?
7. In which country do people stand closely to each other when talking?
   A) The Middle East   B) Germany   C) Korea
8. Which Act protects an adult's right to confidentiality?

SHC 23

Introduction to equality & inclusion

This unit focuses on principles concerning equality and inclusion which must underpin all of your work with children and families to ensure that each child has fair chances in life.

Learning outcomes

By the end of this unit you will:

1. understand the importance of equality and inclusion

2. be able to work in an inclusive way

3. know how to access information, advice and support about diversity, equality and inclusion.

Understand the importance of equality and inclusion

As a practitioner in children's settings, your work brings you into contact with:

- children of both genders
- children of a range of ethnicities
- children from a variety of cultural, social and family backgrounds
- children with disabilities.

Each child has a unique combination of such characteristics.

It is every child's right to have fair chances in life; each child should have opportunities to develop and learn that will lay the foundations for their health and well-being, and their chances to achieve.

If you are to play your part in supporting these rights and helping to include all children in early years settings, you need to understand how and why some children may face discrimination. This will enable you to contribute to equality of opportunity for each child, ensuring their inclusion.

Learning about this aspect of practice requires you to think carefully about your assumptions about children and families.

What is equality?

Children all have the right to have access to chances that will support their present and future life. We cannot make all children equal or the same — they are different from one another. However, we can aim to offer each Unique Child **equality of opportunity** suited to their individual needs and requirements.

Practitioners need to understand and value the individuality of each child, taking into account each child's characteristics and the ways they differ from others. This is the first step to being able to offer equality of opportunity to each child.

What is inclusion?

For each child to have equal opportunities, settings must ensure that they and their families are fully included in the setting, taking into account the **diversity** of the children and families who come to the setting. **Inclusion** is the process of making this happen. Working towards inclusion involves striving to remove barriers to children and their families:

- being able to take full advantage of what a setting has to offer (participate)
- feeling that they are truly welcomed and valued in the setting.

Each child is a unique child

Key terms

Diversity: differences between individuals and groups of people

Equality of opportunity: having opportunities to achieve and flourish which are as good as the opportunities available to others

Inclusion: the process of identifying, understanding and breaking down barriers to participation and belonging

It is important to respect difference and not make assumptions

It involves:

- finding out if there are barriers that may be preventing children and families feeling that they can belong to the setting and participate in it
- taking action to overcome those barriers.

What is discrimination?

Even very young children can experience **discrimination** as the result of:

- the colour of their skin and other aspects of their ethnicity (such as their facial features or hair)
- the traditions and way of life of their family, arising from culture and religion
- their disability
- their gender
- their social background — the class or socio-economic group of their family
- the structure or composition of their family (for example, single parent or same-gender parents).

Discrimination hampers children's opportunities by denying them the advantages that other children have. They and their families may see themselves as excluded from certain settings and roles in life. This may prevent them progressing and experiencing success in their lives.

Prejudice

One of the main sources of discrimination is **prejudice**. Prejudice is shown in many ways — in the way people talk about one another, and in the way they treat one another. It arises from a judgement or opinion, often negative, of a person or group, made without careful consideration of accurate, relevant information. When people are worried or unsettled by diversity, the result may be prejudice.

You may have encountered prejudiced thinking at first hand, or read about the way some people express prejudiced ideas. For example, you may have found that some people think that black people whose ethnic origins relate to Africa are less capable and intelligent than white European or Asian people, and are only able to succeed in the fields of sport or music. Some people still think that males are automatically more important than females, simply because of their gender. Disabled people often find themselves treated as of less value and seen as less capable of leading independent lives than non-disabled people. Other people experience such prejudiced thinking because of their sexuality or their appearance.

Prejudice also shows itself when assumptions are made that one culture, religion or social group is superior to another, representing the 'right' way to live. This sort of thinking was common in the days of the British Empire: for example, when the religions, languages and other aspects of the culture of India were seen as inferior to Christianity, the English language and the art and architecture of Europe. In Britain today, you may hear negative remarks about the way certain cultural groups dress, the food they eat, the music they enjoy, or the way they celebrate important life events like weddings and funerals. Such remarks often give the impression that the 'British way' is better.

Families in modern Britain come in many different forms. Single-parent families and families in which there are step-parents, step-children and half-siblings are common. In some families, grandparents, aunts and uncles play key roles alongside parents; these are extended families. In some families, parents are of the same sex, or of different ethnic groups. To assume that only a two-parent nuclear family, with parents of different genders and the same ethnicity, is 'normal' shows prejudiced assumptions.

Prejudice has harmful effects. When children experience prejudiced attitudes that suggest that they or their families are not as valuable as other people, there is a danger of damage to their self-image, self-esteem and self-confidence.

Children are interested in learning about the ways people are different from one another, and you can encourage them to respect and enjoy the differences reflected in our diverse society. This will help them avoid the suspicion and hostility some people develop towards others who are different from themselves which so often leads to discrimination.

Prejudice can damage self-esteem

Discrimination in early years settings

People who work with children generally want to do their best to ensure that children's rights are protected, and to be welcoming and inclusive in their settings. They are unlikely to discriminate against children and families deliberately. However, sometimes discrimination occurs because settings and practitioners are not aware that their attitudes and actions get in the way of children's opportunities to develop and learn.

Case study:
Advertising vacancies

The Little Folk nursery has always relied on 'word of mouth' to pass on information about vacancies. This means that the only families who get to know that their child can have a place there are white, middle-class families similar to those already attending the setting. Families of other ethnic, cultural and socio-economic groups are not aware of the services available at the nursery and the opportunities it could offer children.

When Sara is appointed as the new play leader, she is concerned that this represents a form of discrimination. She begins to put up advertising materials in community facilities used by families from a wider range of cultural groups, including the local mosque and temple, and also in shops and clinics in the areas where there is social housing. This opens up the pre-school to a more diverse range of families.

1. In your opinion, was the pre-school's attitude towards advertising vacancies *unintended* or *intended* discrimination? How far does this make a difference?

2. How does your setting ensure that a wide range of families knows about it?

Visual environment

Another way in which a setting might unintentionally discriminate against some families is by creating a visual environment that suggests that the setting is intended for only a limited range of people. For example, if a black child comes to your setting and sees only pictures of white people, they might get the message that black children are not welcome — that your setting does not welcome them and their families.

Skills builder

Take a good look at the resources in your setting such as:

- pictures, posters and photographs
- books
- puzzles
- dolls, puppets and 'small world' play people
- role-play materials
- DVDs and video tapes, computer games

and consider their visual impact.

Will children find visual images of:

- people of a range of ethnic origins?
- people dressed in a variety of ways associated with various cultures, such as a sari or hijab?
- disabled people using equipment like a wheelchair, hearing aid or walking frame?
- families of various groupings – lone parent, same-gender parents, extended family, parents of mixed ethnicity?

Does the role-play area include cooking utensils (for example, a wok) and eating utensils (for example, chopsticks) associated with various cultures? Do the dressing-up clothes include saris and shalwar kameez, skull caps and turbans, perhaps wrappas (long robes worn by Muslim women in Africa) and dashikis (colourful shirts worn by African men)?

How could your setting's resources be made more welcoming to a wider range of children?

What is in your role-play area?

Functional Skills ICT: Developing, presenting and communicating information

You could produce an information leaflet for new or visiting staff to your setting that shows how your setting promotes anti-discrimination. You could include text and images to make your leaflet look attractive.

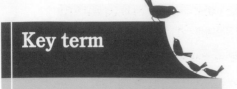

Key term

Stereotypes: assumptions made about a person

Stereotypes

Perhaps the most common cause of practitioners' unintended discrimination is to fall into the trap of thinking in **stereotypes**. This sort of thinking leads to generalisations and assumptions (usually inaccurate) that, because the person is part of a particular group, they:

● will have certain characteristics

● will have the same needs as all other members of that group

● will (or should) behave in a particular way.

Stereotypes may be associated with a child's gender, ethnicity or culture, social or family background or disability. They are often 'below the radar' of our thinking, so we are not aware that we are thinking in that way at all. We have to reflect in honest ways about stereotypical attitudes we may have developed.

Case study:
Stereotypical assumptions

Kamini and her colleagues discussed the stereotypical assumptions that they had observed other people making about a child or family, or they had found themselves making. They listed a number of examples:

● boys are always boisterous and physical in their play but girls are quieter and settle down and concentrate

● African-Caribbean children are good at sport and music, but don't succeed at academic subjects

● Muslim and Orthodox Jewish parents do not want their girls to mix with boys

● physically disabled children and those with sensory (sight and hearing) impairments cannot join in physical play involving climbing

● children from a notorious council estate would be badly behaved and their parents would not want to be involved in the setting.

1. What stereotypes like this have you encountered?

2. Why do you think people make assumptions like this?

If we think about children in stereotyped ways, we focus on only one aspect of who they are instead of seeing them as unique individuals. This can lead us into making assumptions about what an individual child can achieve, and limit the expectations and aspirations which we — and they — have for:

● their abilities

● how it is appropriate for them to behave

● their future achievements.

If we have limited expectations like these, we may be led into discriminating against certain children by:

- failing to offer them challenging and stretching opportunities for learning
- not encouraging them to have ambitious aims for their future.

Case study:
Limited expectations

Kamini and her colleagues continue their discussions by thinking of examples of assumptions about the limitations to roles that will be open to adults according to their gender. They have several examples of ways in which there are still assumptions about what men and women can and ought to do in society, at work and in the home, jobs that are not 'suitable' for women, and how much men can and should contribute to housework and childcare.

They talk about assumptions they have encountered about the jobs or activities like sport and music associated with people of various ethnic groups. They also share experiences of expectations about what disabled people, including people with sensory impairments, will and will not be able to do and achieve.

Kamini and her colleagues try to think of examples of people they know of (personally or those in public life) who have broken stereotypical barriers.

1. What examples can you think of about the assumptions concerning what women and men can and ought to do in life that still limit the roles open to them in society?

2. Do you know people or are you aware of people in public life who have exceeded stereotypical expectations – for women, for people from certain ethnic backgrounds, and for disabled people?

The key to reducing the effect of stereotypes is to see each child as a unique individual. This will help you to offer each child opportunities in their play and learning that steer them away from stereotypes. You will be more able to support the child to develop according to their abilities and their interests, rather than trying to fit them in to the mould of stereotypes for their gender, ethnicity or culture, social or family background or disability.

Seeing each child as individual and unique and avoiding stereotypical thinking is the basis of avoiding discrimination.

Support children to steer away from stereotypes in their play

How practices that support equality and inclusion can reduce discrimination

If settings and practitioners work in ways that promote equality and are inclusive, the negative effects of discrimination will be avoided, and all children will have fair chances.

Reducing discrimination through promoting equality

Offering children equality of opportunity to develop and learn prevents discrimination. This does not mean treating them all the same; we have to acknowledge their diversity and treat children as individuals, with '**equal concern**', a phrase that first appeared in the guidance to the Children Act 1989.

This may require you to treat children differently from one another, according to their stage of development or some other aspect of their individuality. You may have to adapt the way you work with a child according to their individual needs and characteristics, so you ensure they have access to the opportunities that will help them to get the most out of life. For example, you could use foam shapes to provide support for a child with cerebral palsy so they can reach play equipment as well as other children can.

One way of overcoming stereotypical expectations about children's potential and possible future roles and promoting equality of opportunity is by providing **positive images**.

You can provide positive images of a diverse range of people, showing that, for example, black people, female people and disabled people can take on responsible, active and prominent roles in society, and male people

Key terms

Equal concern: taking as much care to promote the opportunities and progress of one child as you do for any other child

Positive images: images showing people who are sometimes discriminated against doing things and taking on roles that go against stereotypes

Functional Skills English: Writing

You could write an account of a time when you have adapted an activity to suit the needs of the children you have worked with. Think carefully about your spelling, punctuation and grammar.

can take on creative, caring and domestic roles. This helps children to develop strong expectations about their own future and what they will be able to achieve in life. They will have positive ideas about the positions of influence and responsibility they will be able to take in society, whatever their ethnicity, gender, cultural or social background or disability.

Skills builder

Carry out a thorough review of the resources and activities provided for children in your setting, looking at:

- pictures, posters and photographs
- books
- puzzles
- DVDs, video tapes and computer games.

Do they include positive images, showing:

- girls and women as strong and independent?
- boys and men as emotional, creative and caring?
- disabled children and adults playing active roles: for example, as the 'hero' of a story?
- black people, women and disabled people taking responsible, challenging and influential roles?

What would you like to add to extend the range of positive images in the setting?

Functional Skills ICT: Finding and selecting information

Once you have looked at all the resources that your setting has you could use the internet to search for further resources that you feel would help to create positive images in your setting. You could also make a list of the websites you feel are particularly good for resources of this nature.

Provide positive images

Reducing discrimination through promoting inclusion

When inclusion is achieved successfully, children and families are not discriminated against. Instead:

- a diverse range of children and families has an opportunity to participate in a setting
- each child is given opportunities to achieve and flourish that are as good as the opportunities experienced by other children.

To include all children and families in a setting and ensure that each child has an equal opportunity to benefit from their time there, you may need to make adjustments to the environment, resources and routines of the setting and your practice. The checklist below highlights some ways to make aspects of your practice more inclusive.

Boys' games can be seen as creative and imaginative, not just noisy and disruptive

Best practice checklist: Inclusive practice

✓ Learn a few words of greeting in the languages used by the families who come to your setting so they feel welcomed

✓ Value the play activities of both genders – for example, seeing boys' fantasy games involving 'super-heroes' as creative and imaginative, not just noisy, disruptive and mostly about fighting

✓ Keep thoroughfares clear of objects that may get in the way of children who use a wheelchair or walking aid

✓ Provide paints in a range of skin tones so all children can depict themselves, their families and their friends accurately

✓ Provide access to frequent snacks for a child with diabetes

✓ Support children whose religious background requires them to keep their bodies modestly covered to engage in physical play

Be able to work in an inclusive way

Laws, codes of practice, policies and procedures

Your setting should have policies that guide the way you and your colleagues ensure that equality and inclusion are promoted. These policies should have been developed in the context of legislation – the law of the land. Legislation regulates the way we interact with one another in society by establishing a framework of what is considered to be appropriate or inappropriate behaviour.

Over to You

Ask your manager to help you identify how the laws listed here apply to your setting, and how they are reflected in your setting's policies and your day-to-day work with children.

Functional Skills English: Speaking, listening and communication

This discussion with your manager is a good way of developing your speaking, listening and communication skills. You could prepare some questions before your discussion so that you are able to respond in appropriate ways.

Here are some of the laws that apply to your setting:

- Race Relations Act 1976, together with Public Order Act of 1986 and Racial and Religious Hatred Act 2006
- Children Act 1989 and 2004 and Care Standards Act 2000
- Education Act 1981, together with Education Acts 1993 and 1996, Special Educational Needs and Disability Act 2001, and Disability Discrimination Acts 1995 and 2005
- Equality Act 2006.

Laws alone cannot change prejudiced attitudes and assumptions or influence the way people think, but they are important in reducing practical aspects of discrimination.

The 'letter of the law' often needs interpretation to make it usable in real situations. Examples of this are:

- the Code of Practice for Children with Special Educational Needs (SEN Code of Practice), which gives guidance on meeting the learning needs of children with special educational needs
- The Early Years Foundation Stage (EYFS) guidance, which explains how to put the EYFS into action.

Good inclusive practice that promotes equality goes beyond what the law commands.

Over to You

Find out how the SEN Code of Practice applies to your setting and work.

Over to You

The Statutory Framework of the EYFS indicates the legal responsibility of settings to 'promote equality of opportunity' and 'ensure that every child is included'.

Discuss with colleagues some of the ways you discharge this legal responsibility in your setting.

Interaction that shows respect

To make children and families welcome and feel included in your setting, it is important that you show that you value and respect them, however different they are from you and your family. You need to show this by the way you communicate, with the children and their parents. Showing respect involves you making it clear that you see each person as an individual, valuable in their own right, and that you do not think that the way you lead your life is superior or better to the values and preferences of other people's culture and faiths.

There are many ways to show respect in your interactions

Case study:
Valuing and respecting

Vicky and her colleagues in the children's centre take a critical look at this aspect of their practice and identify ways they need to improve.

- None of the staff speak any of the languages spoken in the local community.

- Admission forms ask for a child's 'Christian name', and families from other religions or none feel this means they are not welcomed in the setting.

They think about how names are an important part of our identity and individuality. This leads them to work harder to ensure they address people correctly.

They make more effort to check how to pronounce and spell names that they are not familiar with, especially those from languages other than their own. They stop Anglicising names (creating English versions of them), realising that it is lacking in respect to use another name just because it seems easier to pronounce.

They also acknowledge that they need to find out more about the systems used for names and titles in various ethnic and social groups, so they can use given names and family names appropriately, and also address family members in ways seen as courteous in the culture to which they belong.

1. Are there aspects of practice in your setting that might make families feel that they are not respected and valued?

2. How can you improve your practice in interacting with families in your setting?

Language

Part of being respectful towards other people is being sensitive to the language you use to refer to them. Some people will dismiss attempts to use words carefully as 'just being PC' (politically correct), but do not let this distract you from being thoughtful about how language can cause offence. We no longer use terms like 'cripple' or 'imbecile' to talk about disabled people, but some practitioners still refer to 'a special needs child'. This is labelling the child in an unhelpful way, which can stop us looking at the child as an individual who consists of far more than their impairment.

The words we use to express ourselves can affect the concepts, values and attitudes we develop; they mould the way we think and may lead us to distorted or limited opinions. If we talk about someone as 'a wheelchair user' we see the person in control of their own life, making use of a piece of equipment that gives them independence. 'Wheelchair bound' suggests someone who is confined and dependent.

Language both reflects and influences how we think about ourselves and others. It can reinforce the development of stereotyped and prejudiced ideas, or it can help us to think more constructively and treat others respectfully. Talking about 'a child with Down's syndrome' rather than 'a Down's child' puts the child first and their disability second, and helps us to focus on the child as a person, not just on their learning difficulties.

Not a Down's child but a child with Down's syndrome – child first and foremost

Children copy the way adults talk and behave, so it is important that practitioners provide a good role model. You should talk about differences in a positive way, showing that you think differences are interesting and enriching to all our lives.

Skills builder

Over the next few weeks, think about the way you interact with other people. Note down examples of how you show your positive and respectful attitudes towards:

- people from ethnic, cultural and social groups different from your own
- people who live in families different from your own
- disabled people
- people who look or sound different from you.

Talking about differences

You can also show your respect for other people by being prepared to discuss differences openly with children and to answer their questions. Young children are very observant and notice differences between people from a surprisingly young age. Some practitioners feel uncomfortable dealing with children's natural curiosity about people who are different from themselves and talking about variations in skin tone, hair texture, shape of features, physical abilities and impairments. If you respond readily to children's questions and comments about differences in gender, ethnicity, culture and family and physical appearance, you will help them to see these differences in a positive light, and to enjoy the diversity of our society.

Over to You

The EYFS recommends that you 'encourage children to recognise their own unique qualities and the characteristics they share with other children.'

Talk with a group of children about the ways they are different from one another. Who is tall, who has freckles, who has the darkest hair or the brownest skin? What colour eyes do we all have? How does our hair grow? What sort of clothes do we and our families wear? What language(s) can each of us speak? Do we say words the same way, or do some of us have different accents? What are we each good at? Guide the conversation so the differences are brought out as interesting and enjoyable, not something to laugh at or be wary of.

Talking about the differences between us

Celebrations

Another way of showing you respect the faiths and cultures of the families who come to your setting is to find out from the children's families about the festivals they celebrate and think about how you can contribute to the children's celebration. You can show the child and family that you are interested in their special occasion and welcome opportunities to be involved in some appropriate way.

However, a word of warning is needed here. 'Celebrating' the festivals of a culture that is not your own, especially if it is one based in a religious faith, needs to be approached with great care and sensitivity. A festival may have great sacred significance, and it could be very disrespectful to claim to be celebrating a festival that has no personal meaning for anyone in the setting. If you have a religious faith of your own, you may have strong feelings about non-believers celebrating one of your religion's festivals and copying its sacred elements.

You can share celebration foods

Best practice checklist

✓ If your setting is joining in celebrations of a festival, make sure you do so as thoughtfully and authentically as possible

✓ You can share celebration foods with the children and their families, or tell traditional stories and sing songs associated with the festival

✓ It is not respectful to use a festival simply as a theme for craft activities. Making a Hanukkah card has no meaning unless some of the symbolism is explained, and is lacking in respect for the significance of such a festival for Jews

✓ Think carefully about whether the children in your setting are really ready to explore the complex ideas of symbolism and belief that make up religion

✓ Consider whether you could achieve aims of widening cultural awareness and respect better by focusing on the everyday aspects of cultural diversity, rather than on festivals

Challenging discrimination and encouraging change

In your working life you may encounter discrimination. You may observe or hear a child or an adult saying or doing something that reveals their prejudice against others. You should never ignore or excuse such discriminatory behaviour, any more than you would ignore or excuse someone if they inflicted physical pain on someone else. Don't feel that you will make things worse by drawing attention to what has been said or done. If you do not respond and just let the incident pass, you are contributing to the person feeling that it is acceptable to speak or behave in that way.

Children

Children are influenced by the adult world around them — at home, in their local community and in the media — and can acquire stereotyped and prejudiced views at a surprisingly young age. Even the under-fives sometimes behave in discriminatory ways, making hurtful remarks or excluding others from play because of some aspect of their individuality — gender, ethnicity, family background, disability or appearance. Practitioners must intervene when this occurs, following the checklist below.

Best practice checklist: Countering discrimination

✓ Intervene immediately, pointing out to the child who has behaved in a bullying or discriminatory way that what was said or done is hurtful and that the behaviour cannot be accepted (using words like 'unfair' or 'cruel'), but don't suggest that they will be punished

✓ If necessary, point out anything that is untrue and give correct information and new vocabulary

✓ Help the child to learn from the situation, to see the consequences of their actions, and to understand why their behaviour is regarded as inappropriate (ask 'how would *you* feel?')

✓ Don't leave the child with the feeling that you dislike them personally for what they have said or done — make it clear that what you won't tolerate is what they have said or how they have behaved

✓ Support the child who is the object of the discrimination, reassuring them and helping to maintain their self-esteem

Don't think of name calling such as 'fatty' or 'four eyes' as a minor or unimportant matter, and dismiss it as merely teasing. When it is repeated and done with intent to hurt, it becomes bullying or harassment. Some adults play down what they see as 'just toughening children up for the real world' and don't intervene. However, a child should not be expected to endure comments that undermine their self-image and self-esteem; be ready to support them if they have been discriminated against.

Skills builder

Think how you would respond in situations like these.

- A three-year-old white girl says she won't hold hands with an African-Caribbean boy. She says his hands are dirty and he should wash them properly.

- A four-year-old girl is playing with the dolls, cuddling them and putting them to bed. But she won't let the boys anywhere near 'because boys don't play with dolls'.

- Some of the children seize the patka of a Sikh boy and throw it around the room, chanting 'J wears a hankie on his head'.

Always intervene to stop discriminatory behaviour

Adults

It isn't easy to respond to children's expressions of prejudice or discriminatory behaviour; it takes patience and a consistent approach. Responding to the comments and behaviour of adults can be very daunting, and requires strength and, at times, even courage. If it becomes necessary to challenge adults — whether parents or colleagues — use a similar approach as with children and follow the checklist below.

Best practice checklist: Challenging adults

✓ Challenge the remark, politely but firmly

✓ Choose your time and place – you may not want to speak strongly in front of children, but you should act as soon as you can

✓ Remain as calm as you can but make it clear that you find the remark or behaviour offensive or inappropriate

✓ Offer support to the person who has been the object of the remark or excluding behaviour

✓ Offer accurate information if the person's comments or actions seem to arise from being unaware of the implications of what they are saying or doing

Be prepared to challenge the prejudices of adults

Functional Skills English: Speaking, listening and communication

These short scenarios are good discussion starters. You could discuss how you would handle these situations; you need to make sure that you present your views in a clear and concise way.

Skills builder

Think how you would respond in situations like these.

You overhear a parent referring to the disabled children in your setting as 'the spazzes' and 'the crips'.

One of your colleagues becomes agitated in a staff meeting about two children who are being fostered by a gay couple who hope to adopt them, saying how disgraceful it is. The worker uses some aggressive and quite unpleasant language, talking about gay men as if they were all promiscuous and paedophiles, saying that it will ruin the children's future and it was irresponsible of social services to place them with the couple.

Know how to access information, advice and support about diversity, equality and inclusion

The part of your work practice concerned with diversity, equality and inclusion is crucial. It is your professional duty to play a part in protecting children's rights and offering them fair chances in life. However, it is not always easy to put the ideas we have looked at in this unit into practice, and sometimes you will need some help and support. It is also important that you go on extending your knowledge and developing your practice. To do this you need to know where to turn for new information, for advice on good practice, and for support when you encounter uncertainties and difficulties.

Sources of information, advice and support

Professional practice requires you to be open to new ideas and ready to think about ways of developing and improving the way you work. To achieve this for any aspect of your work practice, you will turn to a variety of sources for information, advice and support.

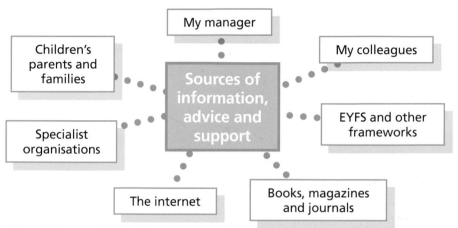

Figure 1: Sources of information

Your manager

It is part of the role of a manager to develop the knowledge and skills of members of their team, and you should have regular opportunities to discuss with your manager any aspects of your work that you are finding demanding or where you have become aware of gaps in your knowledge. This will enable you to benefit from the experience of an established practitioner.

Your colleagues

In your team, some of your colleagues may also have experiences that will make their advice and support valuable, and some may have special responsibilities for aspects of equality and inclusion. For example, all settings must have a Special Educational Needs Co-ordinator (SENCO), to whom you can turn when you need information, advice or support in your work with a child with a disability or one with special educational needs.

Over to You

Find out who the SENCO is in your setting. Ask them to find some time to talk with you about the sort of help they might offer you in working with particular children.

Functional Skills ICT: Developing, presenting and communicating information

You could create an information chart for your setting that shows who is who and what their responsibilities are. This may help you as you continue your course as you will then know who to turn to if you need some information.

Over to You

Take a look at the guidance given on EYFS Principles into Practice cards:

- 1.2 Inclusive practice
- 2.1 Parents as partners.

How can you put this guidance into practice in your setting?

Getting ready for assessment

Spend a little time looking at some websites, though beware of spending hours at your computer – you will probably just confuse yourself!

Try searching for 'Diwali' to see if you can find out about the legends associated with the festival, and what city in the UK is known for its major Diwali celebrations. Keep a record of your findings, as these may be useful as evidence for you later.

Functional Skills ICT: Finding and selecting information

Completing this task will help you to develop your ICT skills. Try using a range of different search engines to broaden your search.

Frameworks

A framework consists of broad guidance for your work, and describes principles which you should keep in mind to help you deal with individual circumstances. It may also include statutory requirements – regulations that must be complied with by law. This can be a useful starting point in considering what to do in a specific situation. If you work in England, the framework which your setting must comply with is the Early Years Foundation Stage (EYFS). There are different frameworks in other UK countries.

Books, magazines, and journals

You or your setting may subscribe to magazines like 'Nursery World' or 'Professional Pre-school' which have regular articles on many aspects of diversity, equality and inclusion. You could keep copies filed in folders for future reference when a relevant matter arises. There are several books which can provide detailed guidance and help you to think through situations. You can find out about these by looking on websites like Amazon.

The internet

The internet is a huge source of information, although it cannot offer advice or support. However, a word of caution: not all information on the internet is reliable. The websites of government departments and public sector organisations like the BBC, early years organisations, major charities and voluntary organisations can provide valuable up-to-date information, but 'help' websites can be written by anyone, and the writer may or may not have experience and in-depth knowledge. The entries in Wikipedia can be useful, but are of variable quality and accuracy.

Specialist organisations

The internet will lead you to many organisations that specialise in a particular aspect of equality and inclusion issues. In particular, there are many websites that can give you detailed information about a variety of impairments and conditions that may affect children.

Getting ready for assessment

- Look at the website of the Sickle Cell Society and find out which ethnic groups are mainly affected by the condition.
- Use a search engine to help you find out how learning about Makaton might help you in your work.

Parents and families

In any aspect of your work with children, remember that normally parents are the most knowledgeable people about their own child — they live with them day in, day out, and are often the best source of information. A website or magazine article can only give you general information about an impairment or condition; parents can tell you precisely how it affects their individual child and how you can best help and support that child. Families can explain about the dietary requirements of their faith or principles, or tell you about the skin and hair care their child needs. They can tell you exactly how to pronounce a child's name and share some words of their home language with you. They can also explain how their particular family celebrates a special festival — not all families participate in the same way.

Normally, parents know the most about their own child

How and when to seek information, advice and support

It is a sign of professionalism to recognise when you need additional information, advice and support. Struggling on alone is not good practice. No-one knows all there is to know, and it is a sign of maturity and good sense to seek help.

Equality and inclusion are aspects of practice that are complex and can raise sensitivities. You may encounter situations that you find challenging and even distressing. It is essential that you seek support and use the experience as a professional development and learning point.

Skills builder

Identify what sources of information, advice and support might help you if you found yourself in the following situations. You might turn to more than one source for each situation.

- You have discovered that a Sikh family who come to your setting celebrate Vaisakhi and you want to contribute to their celebrations.

- A child with epilepsy comes to your setting.

- You want to know how to look after the skin and hair of an African-Caribbean child.

- A child whose first language is Urdu is joining your setting.

- You are asked to help plan meals for a vegetarian child.

- You are being given responsibility for working with a child with learning difficulties.

Case study:
Asking for support

Jamie is helping to welcome new parents. His manager, Tracey, outlines the inclusion and equality policy, including the nursery's intent to give girls and boys equal opportunities to participate in the full range of activities. She explains that girls are encouraged in physical play, construction and using technology, and boys are encouraged in creative and imaginative activities and to try out domestic roles in home-play.

One of the fathers says to Jamie: 'I don't want my son to play with dolls. As a bloke, you'll be able to make sure he plays football and with the cars, like a proper boy.'

Jamie is not sure how to respond, so he calls Tracey over. She talks to the father about taking a wider view of gender roles in society today and how they may change even further by the time the child had grown up. She carefully explains the pre-school's position, trying to show respect for the family's traditional views.

Later Tracey praises Jamie for seeking her help and not trying to deal with a situation he felt unsure about. Jamie says he would be more confident about responding to a similar situation in future.

1. What situations have you encountered where you needed support and advice concerning equality and inclusion?

2. Who would you turn to in your setting for support over these sort of issues?

Check your knowledge

1. What do we mean by 'diversity'?

2. What do we mean by 'equality of opportunity'?

3. What do we mean by 'inclusion'?

4. What do we mean by 'discrimination'?

5. How can prejudice and discrimination harm children?

6. What might be the consequences if we think about children in stereotypical ways?

7. How can positive images help children?

8. Which law brought together regulations making it unlawful to discriminate on grounds of age, disability, gender, race, religion or belief, sexual orientation and transgender status?

9. Why should you respond to incidents of discrimination?

10. Name four sources of information you might use when seeking information, advice and support about equality and inclusion.

Introduction to personal development

In this unit you will be looking at how you can use the process of reflection to identify the strengths and weaknesses of your own practice and seek ways in which you can continually improve your skills and knowledge. Continuing your professional development is essential in ensuring you are working in accordance with regulatory requirements, with the requirements of the setting and, most importantly, in the best interests of the children in your care.

Learning outcomes
By the end of this unit you will:

1. understand what is required for competence in own work role

2. be able to reflect on own work activities

3. be able to agree a personal development plan

4. be able to develop own knowledge, skills and understanding.

Understand what is required for competence in own work role

To take part in personal development you must first understand the requirements of your work role. In doing so you can identify areas of your practice that need developing and would benefit from further training and experience. This learning outcome requires you to think about your work role and to consider what is required of you, from your place of work and from regulatory bodies.

Your duties and responsibilities

When starting any new job or training placement it is important that you know what is expected of you. When you applied for the job you may have had an insight into the roles and responsibilities before even completing the job application. This is because many posts are advertised along with a **job description**, particularly those advertised on the internet. Many employers will send a job description and sometimes a **person specification** with the application form.

If you are in a job role as a student on placement, the setting should issue you with a student job description or guidelines for student placements. Having this information from the start will mean you can be sure of what you are expected to do while you are there.

Key terms

Job description: a description of the tasks you are required to do in a job

Person specification: an outline of the skills and attributes needed by an individual for a job

Over to You

Do you have a job description or student placement guidelines? If not, ask your supervisor or manager for a copy.

Now look at the duties and responsibilities that it details. Next to each one, can you write down an example of how you fulfil your duties and responsibilities?

Functional Skills ICT: Developing, presenting and communicating information

This task is a great way of focusing yourself to set targets for your own development. You could create a table on the computer with three columns: What my job role says, What I do to fulfil this and then What I need to do to fulfil this. If you save this document you can come back to it over time to see how you achieve what you need to.

Duties and responsibilities will vary from setting to setting. For example, if you are working or intending to work in a full-day care setting you may be required to work with very young babies and have some skills in baby care; alternatively you may be working in a community pre-school where you will be required to have skills in providing activities for children aged 3–5 years.

Managers and supervisors will recognise that some applicants do not possess all the skills required for the post. However, if they think you are the most suitable candidate for the position and you show a willingness to learn new skills, then you may be successful at interview.

At an interview you will be expected to convince people that you are the person for the job – or that, with training, you could be

Continuing your personal development is key to ensuring you continually fulfill your duties and responsibilities at work. Later in this unit you will find out about how you can do this.

A special set of skills

You will find that working with children requires a range of skills far beyond what can be thought of traditionally as 'playing with toys'! Figure 1 outlines some of the knowledge and skills that may be expected of you if you were to apply for an assistant's job in a day nursery working with babies aged 0–2 years.

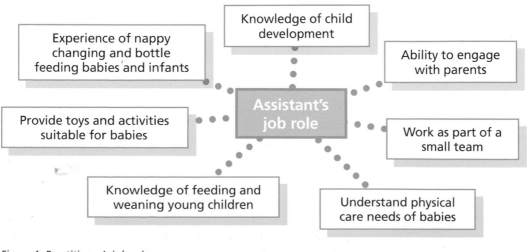

Knowledge of child development

Experience of nappy changing and bottle feeding babies and infants

Ability to engage with parents

Provide toys and activities suitable for babies

Assistant's job role

Work as part of a small team

Knowledge of feeding and weaning young children

Understand physical care needs of babies

Figure 1: Practitioner's job role

Over to You

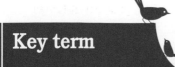

Take time to write down what you have done during the course of one day at work or in your placement. You are sure to see the wide range of skills you use to ensure the needs of the children are met. Playmate, cleaner, cook, dishwasher, toilet attendant, secretary, receptionist … do these skills sound familiar to you?

A job working with children often means being on the go all day, and it is fair to say that no two days will be the same. Working with children is a rewarding job: where else can you see a child take their first steps or say their first words and feel proud? Children bring us much pleasure in what they say and do, and you can guarantee that you will have some wonderful memories of the children you have worked with, which will stay with you forever. That said, working with children can be hard work and extremely demanding. You are required to consider the ever-changing needs of the children in your care from the moment you arrive at work to the moment you leave.

As a part of an effective team, your job will require you to employ a range of skills and complete a multitude of tasks. All these will play their part in meeting the needs of the children and providing a safe and stimulating environment — and that is something everybody should actively contribute towards.

Take time to write down what you have done during one day

Key term

Induction: an introduction to the workplace, other staff, policies and so on for a new member of a team or company

Starting a new job

When starting a new job or placement it is important that you are informed of what is required of you and that you are supported to ensure you can do what is expected of you. Your manager or supervisor should ensure that you get a thorough **induction** at the start of your employment. This will be valuable in helping you to find your way around the setting, understand the routine of the setting, gather information on the policies and procedures of the setting and get to

Skills builder

It is always a good idea to have a personal notepad to hand in which you can write down anything that you think about: questions you need to ask, points you need to clarify or instructions you need to remember for specific tasks. If it is written down you are less likely to forget what it is you needed to know!

know the team you will be working with. You may have had an insight into this if you have had a working interview or been able to visit the setting before starting.

Your first week will no doubt be an education as you find your way in your new position. Don't be afraid to ask questions if something hasn't been shown to you or explained properly: it is much more professional to ask and find out than to assume and get something wrong.

Standards that influence your role

All early years settings are regulated and have to meet a required standard to ensure the health, safety and well-being of children, parents, staff and visitors. It is from these that settings start to build their own policies and procedures, which will influence the way in which you work. It is very important that you take these requirements seriously as they are designed for the well-being of both children and adults, and not for the sake of creating more paperwork. Once you have read about the standards identified below you will understand why you there are so many files in your setting's office.

Standards that influence your role are:

- codes of practice, such as internal policies and procedures of setting
- regulations, such as the Health and Safety at Work Act, Children Act 2004
- National Minimum Standards, such as EYFS welfare requirements
- National Occupational Standards, such as Sector Standards used to develop qualifications and courses.

Internal policies and procedures

Every setting should have robust policies and procedures for safe and effective practice. On joining the setting, regardless of whether you are an employee or a student, you should be given access to these and have the opportunity to discuss their content with your supervisor or manager.

Some policies and procedures can be lengthy and difficult to digest. Most settings recognise this and will provide you with relevant information for your role in your job induction or student placement pack. Policies and procedures are often visited in staff meetings, so this provides you with the opportunity to gain a greater understanding of what they mean in terms of how they apply to your own practice.

Health and Safety at Work Act

Under this Act, settings have a legal obligation to provide a safe and healthy working environment for all their employees; at the same time, you as an employee have a legal responsibility to act in accordance with the principles of the setting and not put yourself at unnecessary risk. Much of this is common sense, but a gentle reminder is good for everyone. Your setting will have a written health and safety policy that will detail safe working practices.

It is important that you understand your setting's policies and procedures

Children Act 2004

This has been updated from the Children Act of 1989 (implemented 1991) and places a legal duty on local authorities to improve the well-being of children and young people. Safeguarding children, young people and vulnerable adults is a key priority for the government and partnership working with Local Safeguarding Children's Boards is a requirement for all local authorities. You may already be familiar with the following aims for children: be healthy, stay safe, enjoy and achieve, make a positive contribution and achieve economic well-being. No matter what your work role is within the early years profession, everyone has a responsibility to make this happen.

Welfare requirements

Since September 2007 settings have been required to adhere to the guidelines set out in the Statutory Framework of the Early Years Foundation Stage. Within this there are five welfare requirements that must be met in all early years settings:

- safeguarding and promoting children's welfare
- suitable people
- suitable premises
- environment and equipment
- organisation and documentation.

National Occupational Standards

The National Occupational Standards have been developed to raise performance in the early years sector and identify the skills, knowledge and understanding required by practitioners. Awarding bodies, colleges and training providers will use these to develop qualifications, courses and workshops to improve practice in the early years sector.

Over to You

Broaden your own knowledge by finding out a little bit about the following: Child Care Act 2006; Protection of Children (Scotland) Act 2003; Getting it right for every child (Scotland).

Functional Skills English: Reading

Reading around these areas listed above is a good way of developing your reading skills. To show your understanding of these documents you could discuss specific areas further with your tutor.

All employees have a responsibility in ensuring they are working in accordance with required standards. As discussed earlier, a thorough induction will help you to understand what you should do and how you should be going about it. However, support to enable you to do this should be available beyond the initial induction period, continuing throughout your employment or your placement time at the setting.

Your manager or supervisor will keep you updated on current requirements of practice in different ways including one-to-ones, staff meetings, in-house training and short courses. Later on in this unit you will explore the benefits of these in greater detail. While your manager or supervisor has a duty to provide such information, you also have a duty to take this on board and apply it in practice.

Keeping your personal views and your work separate

Our own **attitudes** and **beliefs** shape us as individuals and make us 'unique'. Our attitudes and beliefs stem from a variety of sources including our own childhood, our prior experiences and the attitudes of those close to us.

Everyone is entitled to an opinion shaped by their beliefs, but it is important that the opinions of others shaped by their beliefs are not dismissed or challenged negatively. It is also important to ensure that your own opinions and attitudes do not have an undesired impact on your work.

Attitudes and opinions can also change over time. Again, our life experiences will have a big impact on this. For example, you will often hear people say they would always comment on the way other people managed their children's behaviour — that is, until they have children of their own! Often there is no right or wrong way, just different ways.

Key terms

Attitude: a feeling about someone or something

Belief: opinion firmly held

Case study:
Attitudes

Sophia is a practitioner at preschool. One of her tasks is to supervise the children at snack time. She insists that they sit quietly until their snack is served, and asks that they do not start until everyone has been served.

- What do you think Sophia's own experience of mealtimes has been like?

- Do you think this has a positive or negative impact on her practice?

Differences in opinion need to be managed carefully

You need to ensure your own attitudes and beliefs do not obstruct the quality of your work. The checklist below gives you some ideas on how you can do this.

Best practice checklist:

✓ **Be an effective contributor**. Discussions with colleagues give you the opportunity to present your thoughts and ideas and enable you to listen to their contributions. While you may hold the same opinions as others, you will understand the viewpoints of others that differ from your own if you have taken the time to listen to what they have to say.

✓ **Keep an open mind.** Be receptive to the way other people do things. Just because it's not your way, it doesn't mean it's an unacceptable way of doing things.

✓ **Take a step back**. If someone else is carrying out a task, stand back and let them do so even if their method is different to yours. You will find the outcome is the same.

✓ **Listen to other people's points of view**. This will help you to see things from another angle and can often give you an alternative solution to a problem.

✓ **Don't be confrontational.** Challenging other people's opinions negatively will not only create discord in the setting but can also make them feel worthless, which can have devastating consequences for effective teamworking.

Over to You

Reflect on a situation where your own values and beliefs affected your practice. Having read the information above, how do you think you could have approached the situation differently to ensure that this did not obstruct your work?

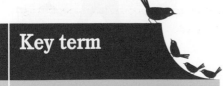

Key term

Reflection: giving due thought and consideration to something you have said or done

Be able to reflect on own work activities

Reflective practice is an essential skill in helping you to identify if something works well, if it needs changing and what you can do about it. Think about it as like looking in the mirror at what you are doing. What do you see? This learning outcome requires you to consider how you can reflect on what you have done and the importance of doing so.

Reflection for personal development

Reflection is important if you are to develop your knowledge, skills and practice. Reflection is a way of helping you to think about what you have done and how you might do things in the future.

Even the most experienced practitioners will consider the effectiveness of their practice and how they can change or adapt things to meet the ever-changing needs of the sector. Time does not stand still and neither does early years practice. Children and family needs are constantly changing, and so must your practice to support this. As well as changing to meet people's needs, you will be influenced by changes in the standards that influence our practice.

Figure 2: Areas to reflect on

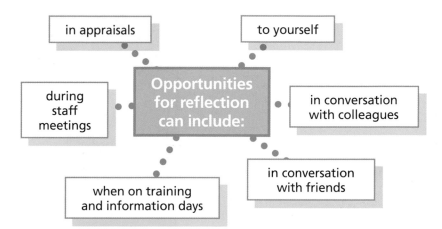

Figure 3: Opportunities for reflection

To yourself

You can often be absorbed in your own thoughts and think about what you have done and why you have done it. You can work out in your own head the processes you went through and what you would do if you were faced with the situation again.

In conversation with colleagues

There are many formal and informal opportunities with colleagues when you can think about your practice. At the end of an activity you may discuss how it went, how the children responded and whether it was a success. You may also have more informal opportunities where you seek their professional advice.

In conversation with friends

You may talk to your close friends and seek their opinion on what you have done and why you have done it. Remember that your friends know you very well — they know how you think and how you work — and you will value what they have to say.

On training and information days

You will often find that listening to others' reflection on practice during these opportunities gives you time to consider your own responses. Their ideas and opinions can get you thinking about what you do, even in areas that you had never considered before.

During staff meetings

Staff meetings give you the opportunity to see things from your colleagues' perspectives and help you to consider the way in which they reflect on their own practice.

Staff meetings can give you valuable food for thought

In appraisals

One-to-ones with your manager or team leader can help you to consider your ways of working and your responses to particular situations. They also help you to think about how these can be developed and how you can gain a greater understanding of the processes of reflective practice.

Networking

Liaising with others can help you to compare and contrast what you say and do with other early years practitioners. Networking can also help you to identify best practice benchmarks and reconsider your own practice in light of what others have done or said.

Professional development opportunities

Going out of the setting on courses and information days provides you with the opportunity to gather new information and skills but also enables you to take time to reflect on your own practice. Such events will help you to think about how you can move your practice on by looking at where you are and where you need to go.

The Early Years Foundation Stage in England puts great emphasis on reflection and asks practitioners to think about their practice and how they can drive forward and continually seek to improve what they do. Working as a team and having a common shared approach to the process of reflection can prove to be helpful to all involved as it is the responsibility of all practitioners to analyse the effectiveness of the provision and experiences on offer.

Do you meet the standard?

The process of reflection will help you to think about how far your own knowledge, skills and understanding meet the standards expected, and recognise where gaps exist. Now that you have taken time to look at the guidance of the EYFS, you may be able to see where you need further guidance and support and, indeed, areas of your practice that are strong.

There are many tools available to help individuals assess how well their own knowledge skills and understanding meet standards. One that all practitioners need to become familiar with is OFSTED's self-evaluation form, or SEF for short. Many people think that it is the role of the settings manager or supervisor to complete this with little or no input from the team. It is important to stress that *all* team members should be involved in the self-evaluation process and be able to share their views and opinions.

Staff meetings can provide the ideal opportunity for self-evaluation activities to take place. By doing this you can identify and record:

- evidence of good practice
- what has yet to be achieved
- how it is going to be done
- the roles of those in the setting in making this happen.

Appraisals

Appraisals provide you with a good opportunity to assess whether you meet required standards. Before any appraisal, your manager or supervisor should provide you with a pre-appraisal form, on which you can record your own reflections on practice and think about your own strengths and weaknesses. While this can be a difficult task, it is extremely useful in enabling you to take a good, long look at where you are at in terms of your knowledge, skills and understanding. Some appraisal forms will pose specific questions, asking you to consider how confident you are with an element of your work or how much you understand about a particular policy of the setting. This is your opportunity to openly and honestly state how much you know and understand. From this form, your manager or supervisor can conduct an appraisal that is genuinely worthwhile and effective. They can discuss with you specific aspects of your knowledge, skills and understanding that you both think will benefit from further development, be it from formal training or another method, such as information gathering or a thorough induction in the setting.

Later in this unit you will look at how you can use feedback from others to develop your own knowledge, skills and understanding.

How to reflect on your work

An effective practitioner is one who can stand back and question what they did and if they achieved their objective.

This skill comes more naturally to some people than to others. As a rule, it is very hard to look at yourself and think about what you did well and what you could have done better, as you like to think you give your best all the time. However, reflection does not imply that you haven't given your best; rather it will help you think about whether doing something a different way would have had greater benefits. For example, you may have had a messy play activity out for a group of toddlers. While none of your colleagues would question the fact that you gave your best throughout the activity, it may be that the activity was unsuitable for them and reflection would help you to think of more appropriate alternatives.

Reflection can help you choose better activities!

Your role may include the observation and assessment of children's development (this will depend on the level of responsibility you are given at work and the systems in place for allocating key person responsibility). Observations, both incidental and planned, can help you to take a look at many elements of your own practice as well as assessing the development and learning needs of the children in your care.

Getting ready for assessment

Think about an activity you have done with the children in your care recently, then answer the following questions.

- Did all the children have access to the activity?
- Did many children choose to join in the activity?
- Did the children enjoy the activity provided?
- What did you do during the activity?
- What went well?
- What didn't go so well?
- How would you change the activity?
- What would *you* do differently next time?

Functional Skills English: Writing

You could record your reflection in the form of a report. Use the questions in the 'Getting ready for assessment' section to help you to organise and plan your work out. This is something that you may share with your manager or tutor so focus on your spellings, grammar and punctuation.

Recording your reflections can help you to build a picture of your effectiveness in the workplace. It will also help you to identify where and how you may need to consider changes to what you do, where you need to seek advice and where you can develop your knowledge, skills and understanding further.

Think about how effective you are at work

Case study:
Activity evaluation

Seema is working in the toddler room with children aged 2–3 years. She is asked to supervise and support play at the sand tray. Through the session children freely choose access and come and go, indulging in play, digging, scooping and building with the wet sand. At the end of the session Seema's supervisor asks her how the activity went. She replies 'Ok. I think the children enjoyed themselves.'

- What other information could Seema give to her manager?
- If asked to support this activity again, how could Seema develop it?

As you will have discovered throughout this unit, the process of reflection is ongoing. It is designed to help you think how you can move forward and develop your ideas, activities and approaches. When analysing and reflecting on your work activities you will find that every situation will end with you learning something and wanting to consider things further, even when you have judged that your work activity is a success.

Peer observations are also a good way to develop your practice. This is when you and your colleagues have the opportunity to observe and learn from each other.

Be able to agree a personal development plan

For this learning outcome you will need to show your input into a personal development plan. A personal development plan may have a different name, but it will be a document in which you record information such as:

- agreed objectives for your development
- proposed activities to meet those objectives
- timescales for achieving your objectives
- times for reviewing your progress.

Having such a plan can prove valuable in helping you think about specific areas of development needed in your own skills and knowledge.

Sources of support

Learning and development is never-ending, and needs good support. During your career you will find that opportunities for getting support for your learning and development are provided from many different sources, both in your place of work and beyond.

Sources of support include:

- formal support
- informal support
- supervision
- appraisal
- support within the organisation
- support beyond the organisation.

Formal support

Training courses and information days studying particular topics of relevance offer more formal opportunities to broaden your knowledge base and develop your skills. How formal this is will depend on the

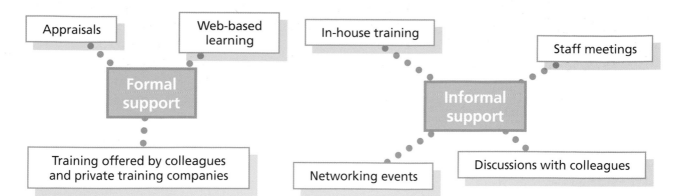

Figure 4: Formal support for learning and development

Figure 5: Informal support for learning and development

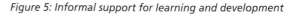

type of learning activity you are undertaking. For example, studying for a nationally recognised qualification will be more time-consuming and detailed in content than attending an information day about current issues in early years.

Formal support will be offered by your training provider, which could be:

- your local college
- a private training company
- web-based learning.

Which of these you access will depend on what learning activity you are undertaking and your commitment to this need.

Before taking on any formal study or development there are some issues you need to consider.

- **Access** Will you be able to get to the training venue easily? If you need to attend a centre of study regularly, you will need to think about how accessible this is to you, particularly if you live in a rural community and have little or no access to private transport.

- **Will the training programme meet my objectives?** Find out as much as you can, from the training provider, the web and others who have had the same training.

- **Cost** Is the training going to be cost-effective? Can you or the setting afford to fund the training? Are there any additional costs you will need to consider before committing? Your manager can help you find any local funding or may have a training budget.

- **Time** Will you be required to take time out of work to attend training? Or to train in your own time? Is the timescale realistic and achievable? You must think about how you can manage your time effectively so you can study and still meet all your other commitments.

It is important to discuss these questions with your manager before agreeing to sign up to any courses.

In-house training

If your manager is providing training in the setting this can be done during working hours, after your shift has ended or during staff meetings. Doing this can make good use of everyone's time, and avoid any problems about accessibility. In-house training can be beneficial to settings as they can make sure that all members of the team attend and receive the same information.

Staff meetings

These provide a vital communication link between teams of people that may not come together on a regular basis, perhaps due to the working patterns of individuals and the distribution of people around the setting. Such meetings provide opportunities for you to discuss practice and gain information from those around you, as well as seeking ways forward in working practices. Many managers will use staff meetings to look at the setting's policies and procedures, to discuss matters that have come up during the working day and to share information on current issues in early years. Staff meetings also provide opportunities for colleagues to '**cascade**' information from training and learning activities they have been involved in.

Discussions with colleagues

Inevitably your working day will involve many informal discussions and conversations with colleagues. Your colleagues will be able to share their own knowledge and skills to benefit your practice. As outsiders looking in when you are doing things, they can offer constructive advice and support. Having a good working relationship with your colleagues is essential in helping to build a culture with a two-way flow of information. Having open communications will help you when you need to ask their advice or need a question answering.

Agreeing your personal development plan

Personal development plans should not be the sole responsibility of the person who the plan is designed for. This is because other individuals have an interest in what you are doing. The people involved will depend on the setting you are working in and the level of support that you need. The individuals that could be involved in building your development plan include:

- you
- carers
- advocates
- your supervisor, line manager or employer.

You should be given time and support to draw up your personal development plan. How and when this is done will depend on whether you are a student in placement or an employee in a setting.

If you are a student, it would generally be the role of your training provider to help you to devise a personal development plan. This would be done on a one-to-one basis, when you would discuss together exactly what should go in the plan.

Key term

Cascade: send information or messages down through the layers of an organisation

Functional Skills English: Speaking, listening and communication.

Reviewing your own skills and practice often leads to a number of different discussions with people. It is important that you listen carefully to what is said during these discussions so that you can use the information in a positive way and respond appropriately.

As an employee in a setting, your manager should set aside some time specifically for you so that you can do this together. Part of your plan should be a list of the things that you want to focus on in the coming year. These are often called 'performance targets'. While most managers or supervisors of settings will look at your development plan during your appraisal, this should not be the only opportunity they use to look at it with you. As most appraisals happen on a yearly basis it would not be good practice to only pull your development plan out then. Throughout the year your plan should be reviewed and updated and both parties should be responsible for making this happen.

These opportunities can be presented in a variety of ways including:

- updating your training and development plan when training has been completed

- having time for one-to-one sessions with your manager or supervisor so they can discuss any aspects of your practice, training and development with you

- being involved in the SEF (Self Evaluation Form) of the setting, when you and your manager can highlight training undertaken and consider how this has benefited your practice and the setting.

Your manager plays a key role in your personal development

Contributing to your personal development plan

Writing up a personal development plan will help you to see clearly what activities you are intending to do and the reasons for doing them. When drawing up your plan try using the SMART approach as detailed in Table 1. Using SMART will mean that you can really be sure that the learning and development activities you are going to undertake will be of benefit to you.

Development plans can only be of benefit to the individual if they set out clear and specific objectives. To ensure that the training and development plan is specific to your needs, ask yourself the following questions:

- What skills and knowledge do I need to develop?
- What are my areas of weakness?
- How do I learn best?
- How much time do I have to give?
- What do I want to achieve?

Table 1: SMART objectives

Specific	Be clear about what it is you want to achieve	I want to complete my Level 2 Certificate in Children's and Young People's Workforce
Measurable	You should be able to track progress and achievement	I have support from my assessor who informs me of my progress every time he visits
Achievable	Ask yourself *'Am I in the right job role for this and do I have the necessary time and support?'*	My manager thinks I am more than capable and is really supportive
Relevant	Consider if the training or development you are going to do will benefit you and/or your role	This will help me to gain more knowledge about the development of young children and give me more confidence at work
Time-limited	Setting realistic time limits will help you to keep focussed	I can do this in a year as I have a lot of support. Just think this time next year I will have finished!

Functional Skills ICT: Using ICT

You could use a computer to create your personal development plan, and then you could save it with an appropriate name in a folder on your computer. It is often very useful to have electronic copies of documents such as this because once you have achieved a target you can edit your plan appropriately.

Best practice checklist: Your personal development plan

Ensure you have a copy of your personal development plan and consider these questions.

- ✓ Does it detail personal development undertaken?
- ✓ Have you recorded dates of personal development you have completed?
- ✓ Does it show future personal development activities?
- ✓ Does it show how these activities are going to benefit knowledge and skills?
- ✓ Do you have evidence of personal development activities undertaken?

Training and Development Plan

Use the template below to build your own training and development plan. Ensure you use the information gathered from your own reflections and the feedback of your manager to inform the plan. Complete all sections of the plan to enable effective evidence gathering.

Personal Objective	Specific Target	Costs and Location	Duration of training/ development	Review date	Completion date

Figure 6: Example of a personal development plan

Be able to develop own knowledge, skills and understanding

Throughout this unit you have looked at ways of understanding your own work role, the process of reflection and agreeing a personal development plan. This learning outcome asks you to consider how you develop knowledge skills and understanding. What you have learnt about reflection will really help you identify how personal development has improved your practice.

What have you learnt?

Learning activities can hugely improve your knowledge, skills and understanding. As you will have discovered in this unit, you have already undertaken many learning activities and training opportunities that have benefited your practice, and will be planning to undertake more in the future.

The results of this will become apparent in your daily working life in your approach and your attitude to your work. Many practitioners find that they gain increased confidence from attending training and development opportunities, which in itself has a positive impact on their practice.

You always learn something

It is always useful to know that any training or development opportunity has not been a waste of time. You are the only one who can judge this and consider how it has helped you. To walk away from any learning activity and say 'That didn't teach me anything I didn't already know' would only serve to prove that an individual has to develop the skill of reflecting on their practice!

Perhaps you have been on some training where the group talked about everything you already do in practice – but even this is a useful exercise, as it affirms your ability to meet best practice benchmarks. This in itself is a vital learning tool. In addition, any learning activity gives you the opportunity to network and liaise with other practitioners whose ideas can generate new ways of thinking for your own practice; you in turn can share good practice with them, providing a win-win situation.

Attending training and development opportunities will enable you not only to gather new information, but also to get the resources, tools and templates you need to move forward with your new-found knowledge on return to the setting. There is no point in reinventing the wheel and if there is an easier solution to a problem then it is in your best interest to use it. It is also important that you share any new knowledge with your colleagues, to help them develop their practice too.

Getting ready for assessment

Think about the paperwork you currently use in your setting. Is there anything you have recently brought back from a training course that you have used in practice? If so, how has this helped you?

Skills builder

Take a look at your training and development plan and answer the following questions.

- What was the most recent training event you attended?
- Why did you agree to do this?
- Did you get what you expected from the training?
- How have you applied these new skills and/or knowledge to your practice?

Every training opportunity holds something useful for you

Functional Skills English: Writing

You could produce an information leaflet containing information on a day or particular college session that you have attended recently. You could pass this leaflet on to other members of your team at placement as a way of sharing the information that you have gained. Think carefully about your audience and the fact that you are writing to inform someone.

The rewards of reflection

By reflecting on a situation, you can improve your knowledge, skills and understanding for the future benefit of all. There are many situations in which you reflect on your actions. It would be easy to assume you only reflect on the activities and experiences that you provide for the children in your care, but in actual fact you will reflect on many situations throughout your working day.

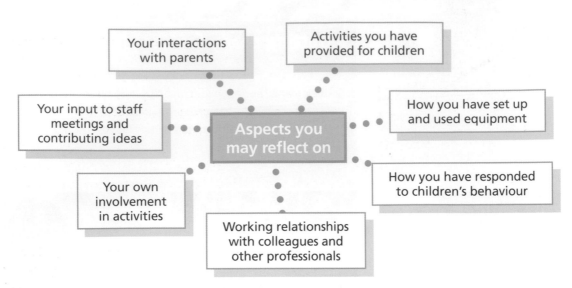

Figure 7: Situations you might reflect on

Activities you have provided

Planning activities and experiences for children is a major part of the role of an early years practitioner. In accordance with the requirements of the EYFS it is necessary to plan for individual children and the group as a whole. To know how effective the opportunities you provide for children are it is important to evaluate their effectiveness. In the 'Getting ready for assessment' feature on page 59 there were some key questions that you should ask yourself as part of the evaluation and reflection process. By doing this you will be able to see whether the activities met their desired intentions and the needs of the children in your care.

Setting up and using the play environment

Being able to reflect on how you provide a stimulating and encouraging play environment can help you to see any changes you need to make to the layout of activities and equipment. Watching the children at play and then thinking about how they used the environment will help you establish if you used this to best effect. By doing this you will develop your own understanding of the children's play needs and choices. In the EYFS framework, the practice of watching children play and then, as a result, providing what they are interested in to stimulate their learning is referred to as 'following the child'.

Functional Skills Maths: Interpreting

You could do a scale drawing of the classroom that you work in and show on your plan how you set it up for the activity that you were doing. You could then write on your plan any changes that you would have made to the layout of the room and why.

Case study:
Creating the right play environment

Emma has been watching the children in the pre-school room as they use the room for freely chosen play. The book corner is situated by the door to the room and has low level shelves for children to choose their own books. During the morning Emma notices that the children are not using the book corner at all. She talks to her manager about this who asks her to reflect on why the children may not be using the book corner.

1. What information do you think Emma might record about the children not using the book corner?

2. What do you think Emma should do to encourage the use of the book corner?

Over to You

Next time you are talking to a parent ask yourself these questions.

- Were my communications polite and courteous?

- Did I give them all the information they needed?

- What could I do to improve my communications with families?

Responding to children's behaviour

When responding to unwanted behaviour you will often be required to think on your feet —something often referred to as 'reflection *in* action'. This is because you do not have the luxury of time to stand back and think about what to do (known as 'reflection *on* action'), particularly if a child is in danger of harming themselves or others. In these situations, it is often after the event that you reflect, think over how you handled the situation, and consider what you might do differently if faced with it again. Equipped with this new thought, strategy or process you can be better prepared when faced with behaviour management issues in the future.

Your interactions with parents

It is important in your work that you are sure of your roles and responsibilities in relation to communicating and sharing information with children and families. A key aspect of relationships with parents is to gather information to help care for their child and provide feedback on their child's day. This process will of course require you to think about what has happened throughout the day and ensure an accurate exchange of information. Your communications with parents should always be courteous and respectful, with their needs and wishes taken into account and given due consideration. To enable you to have effective relationships with families it is important that you reflect on your interactions with them to make sure you are acting in a professional manner.

Make sure all your interactions with parents are courteous and respectful

Your own involvement in activities

When supporting children's learning and development you play many roles, including:

- passive – standing back and letting play occur freely and uninterrupted
- facilitative – providing children with the resources and equipment they need and being on hand to do so
- interactive – engaging in children's play alongside them and seeking ways to help develop and move their play on.

Understanding how children wish to use adults can help you identify your own effectiveness in supporting them.

Different areas of the play and learning environment and the activities provided for children will require different levels of support and engagement from the adults. Reflecting on your role will help you to see where and when children need you to help move their play on, and where they need little or no intervention from you. This can really help when you sit down with colleagues to plan future experiences and opportunities for the children in your care, as you will be able to identify the role of the adult and know how to go about it.

Staff meetings and contributing ideas

Attending staff meetings provides an ideal opportunity to reflect on your work activities and discuss these with your colleagues. You have already identified how these meetings can be a source of support for your own learning and development. However, they can also help you to reflect on your whole working day, taking into account the needs of the setting and others within it. You can then think about what happens next, who is involved and what the desired outcomes should be.

Working relationships with colleagues and other professionals

You will have established by now the importance of teamwork and how to build effective working relationships with colleagues and other professionals. Communication is vital for the smooth running of any early years setting, and it is important for all practitioners to reflect on the effectiveness of their communications with others. Reflecting on your communications and interactions with colleagues and other professionals will help you identify whether you are getting the best from relationships with others.

Information exchanges take place in many forms, so it is important for you to reflect on these and ask if the best methods are being applied at all times. If there is a breakdown in communication at work, or if information is not getting through to the relevant people, then you will need to stand back and ask how this can be improved and what needs changing.

Getting ready for assessment

On a piece of paper write down the subheadings listed above. Under each give an example of how you have improved your own practice through reflection and changes you may have made. Share this with your assessor and discuss why you think your thoughts and actions have improved your practice.

How feedback helps you develop

Feedback from others can come from both formal and informal sources.

Opportunities to get feedback from others include:

- appraisals
- mentoring
- peer observations
- parent questionnaires.

An appraisal with a supervisor or manager can provide you with important feedback on your performance. People often worry about appraisals as they think it is about being told what to do better, when in reality it is primarily to 'praise' you for what you do well.

Appraisals are not the only form of formal feedback you can receive. Mentoring can be very effective in providing individuals with the necessary support to develop their practice from having good practice modelled to them. A mentor should be a guide who can look constructively at practice and advise how it can be improved, as well as boosting confidence through praise of the individual they are supporting for what they do well.

Peer observations are a tool for feedback used by many settings now. These do not have to be carried out by the manager or supervisor of the setting, but can be carried out by colleagues who can explain what they see from observing you. While this can be a daunting experience initially for all concerned, if done well it can be very beneficial.

Parent and child questionnaires are crucial in meeting parents' needs and wishes for their children. Their perspective will differ from your own and will give you information and feedback you may not have considered. Feedback from children is important too, as their view really does count and helps you see the world through the eyes of a child.

Recording your personal progress

Recording your progress not only provides evidence that you have undertaken personal development but is also a great way for you to see your own achievements, which can help build your confidence and self-esteem. Being able to say 'Look what I have done' is a real morale boost to anyone!

Figure 8 shows some of the different ways you can record your progress.

Figure 8: Ways to record progress

CV

Your CV is vital in giving prospective employers an insight into your knowledge base. On your CV, you should record in detail your high school education, further education and professional development. If you have access to a computer, make sure you have an electronic copy of your CV available so that you can update it whenever you have undertaken a learning activity. Updating your CV regularly is much easier than waiting until you apply for a job you like the look of. If you wait until the last moment, you may find yourself frantically trying to remember all the courses you have been on.

Over to You

Have a look at your CV. When did you last update it? Take some time to ensure it is current and valid, showing the most recent training and learning opportunities you have been on.

Functional Skills ICT: Developing, presenting and communicating information

Your CV is a professional document that you are going to use again and again in the future. You could produce your CV in a word processing package such as Word so that you can alter it easily. Think carefully about the layout of this document and make sure that it looks neat and tidy.

Portfolio of achievement

Keeping your original certificates of all training and information events you have attended is a great way of showing how you have continued your development. This is extremely morale-boosting for you and useful for prospective employers, who will be able to see what you have achieved.

Certificates offer clear proof of what you have achieved

Staff training folder

Your manager or supervisor will hold a file detailing all staff training completed and being undertaken. This can then be used to show how training and development opportunities benefit individuals and the setting as a whole. Both you and your manager should have regular access to your personal plan, so that you can update and revise it to include all new training and development undertaken, as and when the need arises.

Early Years Workforce Qualifications Audit Tool

The Early Years Workforce Qualifications Audit Tool is an online database to help early years settings maintain information about their setting and staff. You may work in an authority that sets this out as a requirement. While you will not be able to access the database yourself, it is important for you to know of its existence because information about you will be held on it. This information is not available to the general public or to other early years settings, but it is available to local authorities and to the Children's Workforce Development Council (CWDC).

The owner, manager or other senior practitioner will be the individual in your setting nominated to be able to access the database and upload information relating to your qualifications. They will do this for everyone who works in your setting. The database will not hold your personal details, so do not be alarmed. The toolkit will benefit the setting and the local authority you work in as it can help in identifying and planning the training and development needs of all early years practitioners.

Best practice checklist: Evidence of achievement

This is a short exercise to help you organise your evidence.

✓ Do you have your original certificates of all training and development undertaken?

✓ Has your employer got copies of those relevant to your work?

✓ Do you know how to replace certificates that have been lost?

If you haven't done so already, it would be useful to build your own portfolio of achievement to show prospective placements and future employers.

Check your knowledge

1. Describe the key responsibilities of your job role.
2. Explain the factors that determine your roles and responsibilities.
3. What is reflection?
4. Why is it important to reflect on your own practice?
5. Who is available for support in the workplace and beyond?
6. List the key benefits of an appraisal system.
7. What should your personal development plan contain?
8. Explain why ongoing training and development is important.
9. How and when should you review your personal development plan?

Child & young person development

In this unit, you will learn about what most children and young people can do at different points in their lives and also what things can affect them.

Learning outcomes
By the end of this unit you will:

1. know the main stages of child and young person development

2. understand the kinds of influences that affect children's and young people's development

3. understand the potential effects of transitions on children's and young people's development.

Know the main stages of child and young person development

In order to plan for children's play and learning, it is essential that you know what they are likely to be able to do. This of course changes according to their age and stage of development. The term 'development' is quite large. For this unit, it covers not only what children and young people can actually do — for example, kick a football or know their colours — but also some aspects of their growth.

While lots of things come together in order that children can do things such as do a jigsaw, as we will see later, this development is often looked at in separate areas. For this unit, they have been split into three main parts.

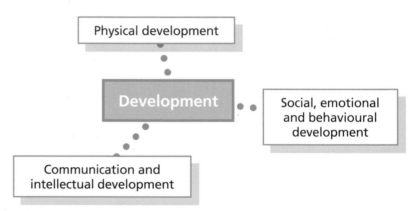

Figure 1: The three aspects of development

Physical development

This is mainly about physical skills. Children need to master a lot of different types of movements as they grow, including:

- large movements — being able to control their head, arms and legs — known as **gross motor movements**

- moving around and balancing — being able to walk, jump and move around — known as **locomotive movements**

- Fine movements — being able to control their hands and make their hands and eyes work together — known as **fine motor movements**.

Communication and intellectual development

This is about the way that children learn to talk and understand others as well as the way in which they learn to think and work things out.

Social, emotional and behavioural development

This is about the way that children learn to play and be with others. It is also about the way that they learn to express their feelings and learn to control their behaviour.

Expected patterns

From birth to 19 years of age, children and young people tend to follow a broad developmental pattern.

While all children and young people are different, the way in which they grow and develop is often quite similar. This means that we can work out a pattern for development and from this we can pinpoint particular skills or milestones that most children can do at different ages. For example, most children are walking by 18 months and most children can talk by the age of four. Milestones have been drawn up by researchers looking at children's development and working out what an 'average' might be. As children get older, the variations between individuals can be larger. This is especially true when it comes to learning skills such as reading and mathematics, but is also true in terms of their emotional maturity. This makes it harder to draw up a pattern of development.

Babies at birth

Most babies are born around the 40th week of pregnancy. Only 3% of babies arrive exactly on time. Some are a week early; others are a week late. Babies who are born more than 37 weeks early are known as premature. Premature babies are likely to need a little more time to reach the same levels of development as babies who are born at around 40 weeks. Many people think that babies are helpless, but in reality they are already born being able to do quite a few things. They can recognise their mother's voice and smell. They are able to cry to let everyone know when they need help. They are also actively learning about their new world through their senses particularly touch, taste and sound.

What you might observe in a newborn

Physical development
Reflexes

Babies are born with many reflexes, which are actions that they do without thinking. Many reflexes are linked to survival. Here are some examples of these reflexes.

Swallowing and sucking reflexes

These ensure that the baby can feed and swallow milk.

Rooting reflex

The baby will move its head to look for a nipple or teat.

Grasp reflex

The baby will automatically put her fingers around an object that has touched the palm of her hand.

Startle reflex

When babies hear a sudden sound or bright light, they will react by moving their arms outwards and clenching their fists.

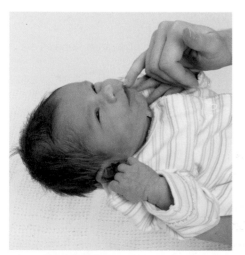

The rooting reflex

The startle reflex

The walking and standing reflex

Walking and standing reflex

When babies are held upright with their feet on a firm surface, they usually make stepping movements.

Falling reflex

This is known as the Moro reflex. Babies will stretch out their arms suddenly and then clasp inwards in any situations in which they feel that they are falling.

Communication and intellectual development

Babies at birth cry in order to communicate their needs. They also start to look around and react to sounds.

Social, emotional and behavioural development

Babies and their primary carers, usually their mothers, begin to develop a strong, close bond from very early on. You might see that the baby at times stares at the mother and the mother is very aware of her baby.

Babies at one month

In a short month, babies have changed already. They might appear less curled up and more relaxed. Babies at one month have usually started to settle into a pattern. They sleep quite a lot of the time, but will gradually start to spend longer times awake. They cry to communicate their needs and their parents may be starting to understand the different types of cries. Babies too are learning about their parents or carers. They may stop crying when they hear their soothing voices. They also try hard to focus on the face of whoever is holding them.

What you might observe in a baby at one month

Physical development

Some reflexes are not as strong at birth.

Communication and intellectual development

Times when the baby stops crying because he hears a familiar voice

Social, emotional and behavioural development

Babies who stop crying as they are picked up, but start crying when they are put down

Babies who are starting to relax at bath time or when their nappies are changed

Fleeting smiles when asleep (smiles of contentment begin from five or six weeks)

Coos when content (from around five or six weeks)

Babies at three months

Babies at three months have grown in height and weight. They are wearing new sets of clothes and have changed in many ways. Some babies have learned the difference between day and night and are able to sleep through the night, which is a great help for parents. Babies are also crying less and most parents are getting better at knowing what their cries mean. Babies are starting to sleep a little less and are far more alert. They may smile quite often and show that they know the sound of their parents' voices and movements. Babies' bodies are also developing. They are able to lift their heads up and look about when they are put on their tummies.

What you might observe in a baby at three months

Physical development
Babies who lift and turn their heads

Interest in playing with fingers

Communication and intellectual development
Excitement when it is time to be fed

Babies who are starting to notice mobiles and objects around them

Social, emotional and behavioural development
Enjoyment of bath time

Babies who smile back when they see a smiling face

Babies at six months

Babies at six months have learnt many skills. They are very alert and turn their heads to see what is happening. They enjoy playing and show it by smiling and squealing with delight. They can now reach out and grab a toy and move it from one hand to another. They are able to focus on an object and explore it if it seems interesting. Babies also start to show us that they understand a little of what we are saying and try to communicate with us.

They usually enjoy their food and are beginning to try to feed themselves by grabbing a spoon, although this can be quite messy for everyone! Many babies will also be getting their first teeth through, which can be quite painful for them.

Babies at this age are also getting stronger. They are pushing themselves up with their hands if they lie on their fronts and can hold this position for a little while. They also sometimes look as if they are parachuting as they lift both their hands and feet up in the air and balance on their fronts. These movements help them to get ready for crawling later on. Babies at six months have usually settled into a routine, having periods in the day when they nap and others when they are keen to play and to be held.

What you might observe in a baby at six months

Physical development
Exploring toys and objects in the mouth as well as with fingers

Sitting up with support

Rolling over from back to front

Communication and intellectual development
Enjoyment when simple games such as pat-a-cake are repeated

Curiosity as babies look to see what is happening around them

Babbling, laughing and squealing

Social, emotional and behavioural development

Smiles of delight when they are playing with their primary carers

Arms lifting up to show a parent that they want to be picked up

Babies at nine months

Finding ways of being mobile

Babies' physical development is now very noticeable. Many babies will be crawling or finding ways of being mobile. They are also able to sit up without any support. These new movements mean that babies can explore more and also spend a little time sitting and playing. When they are mobile they can move quite fast, so this is a period in which adults really need to think about safety. As well as large movements, babies are also picking up objects and handling them, and becoming more skilled at touching things. Things still get popped into the mouth so, again, adults need to be aware of what is around. Babies' language is also coming along. Babbling has become more tuneful and longer strings of sounds are put together. Babies are also learning what some key words mean. They may start to get excited when they hear words such as drink or dinner. Babies are also starting to show us who they enjoy being with. From around eight months, babies start to cry when they are left with a stranger and actively try to be with their parents or main carers.

What you might observe in a baby of nine months

Physical development

Crawling or rolling

Sitting up without any support

Using fingers to feed

Communication and intellectual development

Tuneful strings of babbling

Exploring objects using hands and also mouth

Social, emotional and behavioural development

Trying to stay nearby their parent or carer

Babies at one year

The first birthday of a child is for many families a special event and a cause of celebration. This in part dates back to times when not all babies survived their first year. The baby has come a long way, is now mobile and may be on the verge of walking. They may try to stand up by holding onto furniture, and some babies are already walking by holding onto things. Good adult supervision is essential. Babies are able to crawl very quickly and have eyesight that is just as developed as adults. This means that, if they spot something that they want, they will quickly make a move to get it. As well as gaining mobility, babies are also becoming quite skilled at using their hands. Objects are touched, moved and organised. Babies enjoy putting things in and out of containers, or dropping things and looking to see what happens to them. A strong feature of their play is the way in which they enjoy doing something over and over again. They may keep taking their hat off or pulling off their socks.

Babies enjoy doing something over and over again

At one year, babies are now able to sit up and feed themselves using their fingers. Most one-year-olds know what they do and don't like. Food that they enjoy gets eaten, while food that they are not hungry for may be thrown onto the floor.

Babies also know who are their parents and main carers. They are keen to stay near their parents and carers and will stop playing to see what they are doing. Babies are also able to understand more of what is happening around them. They not only notice what other people are doing, but also understand more and more of what is being said. Long strings of babbling are still the way in which babies try to communicate, but hidden in the babbling are the beginning of babies' first words. Parents and carers usually notice these from around 13 months.

What you might observe in a baby of one year

Physical development
Standing up and holding onto furniture

Small objects being picked up and handled

Communication and intellectual development
Waving bye-bye

Fingers pointing at objects to draw an adult's attention to them

Tuneful babbling that sounds like talking

Social, emotional and behavioural development
Repetitive play as the baby enjoys doing something over and over again

Crying if they cannot see their parent or carer

Children at 18 months

The term 'toddlers' is used about children who have begun to walk. It is a delightful term as the child literally does walk with a side-to-side movement. At 18 months children have literally begun to find their feet. They start to move quickly and enjoy the freedom that being able to move easily will give them. They may even encourage adults to chase them! At 18 months, children are also keen to play with adults and are often fascinated with other children. They notice what older brothers and sisters are doing, as well as noticing children of their own age. As well as their growing physical confidence, we also notice that at around this age toddlers want to be independent. They have learnt that they are separate from their parents and start to become their own people. At around this age, children start to cry and protest if they want something and do not get it. They can be quite persistent and this can be a cause of accidents. For example, a child who wants to hold a cup of tea will notice where it has been put and may even try to climb up to reach it.

Children's language skills are also still developing. Most children will have several words that they use and will be able to understand a lot of what adults are saying. However, this does not mean that they can understand the need to share, wait and be co-operative! This means that many parents say that, at this age, their children really start to develop minds of their own.

Toddlers can also be quite restless and change moods quickly. This can be tiring for parents and carers. Toddlers also become distressed when they are left with unfamiliar people; if they are not with their parents or carers, they need a familiar adult.

What you might observe in a child of 18 months

Physical development
Walking up and down stairs with adult help

Sitting and pushing off with legs on sit-and-ride toys

Able to feed self with spoon

Playing on sit-and-ride toys

Signs of temper and frustration

Communication and intellectual development
Less babbling and more recognisable words

Social, emotional and behavioural development
Signs of temper and frustration

Eagerness for independence — trying to feed themselves with a spoon

Interest in other children

Distress if not with people that they know well

Children at two years old

By two years old, children are very much showing their individuality. They know what they want to do, touch and hold. They can now move confidently and are enjoying walking, being able to pick up things and playing with them. They enjoy doing things for themselves and are keen to do more — and get frustrated when they are not able to. Sometimes this is because adults realise that what they want is dangerous, while at other times it is because their level of skill is not yet matching what they want to do. Their frustration can lead to temper tantrums and emotional outbursts. This is often a toddler's way of communicating how they are feeling and is why this period is sometimes known as the 'terrible twos'. While toddlers do get frustrated and angry, they are also emotional in other ways. They smile, laugh and squeal with enjoyment.

They notice other children and enjoy being near them, even though they may not actively play together. They love exploring, picking up objects and seeing what they can do. Favourite toys and games are played over and over again. Children are also starting to enjoy pretend play. They may take an empty cup and pretend to drink from it or give a teddy a hug. Two-year-olds are often starting to chat aloud. They are likely to have around two hundred words, pointing out objects and naming them.

Some two-year-olds are starting to be ready to move out of nappies, although this varies with some children not being physically ready until they are three years old.

What you might observe in a child of two years

Physical development
Playing on sit-and-ride toys

Running and climbing

Building bricks, doing simple jigsaw puzzles

Communication and intellectual development
Points to pictures of familiar objects and names them

Social, emotional and behavioural development
Anger and frustration if they cannot do what they want to do

Delight and happiness when they are enjoying something

Keen to show things to adults

Pedalling a tricycle

Children at two years and six months

Children at two and a half years are still keen to be independent. They may still find it hard to wait and to understand why they cannot always have what they see or do want they want. However, their language is really starting to develop. Some children are starting to use sentences, while others are putting two words together to express their ideas. Good supervision is still needed as children's developing physical skills combined with their determination can mean that may go to extremes to get hold of an object. Moving chairs to climb up on or standing on tables to reach up high is fairly common!

Children are also starting to play more with other children of their own age, although some of their time will be spent simply playing alongside others. Pretend play and play with small-world toys becomes popular, along with tricycles, slides and climbing frames. They are still keen to have plenty of adult attention and will enjoy snuggling up for a cuddle as well as spending time helping an adult. Separating from parents remains difficult unless children really know who they are staying with. This is often the period in which toilet training starts in earnest; if children are ready, they can be out of nappies within a few days.

What you might observe in a child aged two and a half years

Physical development

Pedalling a tricycle or pushing it along with feet

Turning pages in books and pointing out objects

Communication and intellectual development

Phrases such as 'daddygone' or 'drinkno' where two words are used

Social, emotional and behavioural development

Playing alongside other children and copying their actions

Temper tantrums if they are frustrated

Children at three years old

Most children at three years old make a huge developmental leap. This is linked to their use of language, as suddenly instead of showing us they are not happy, they can tell us. Being able to express their frustration, needs and thoughts is a real breakthrough. Temper tantrums start to decrease and children seem to become more settled.

Their breakthrough in language also means that they can start to understand more about what is happening and begin to understand the needs of others. From this point onwards most children start to be able to play with other children, whereas before sharing toys and equipment was very difficult for them. This is exciting as, suddenly, other children start to become important in children's lives. They start to enjoy going to pre-school or nursery and actively play with other children. Children are also happier at being separated from their parents, as they can now understand that their parents will return and are more able to talk to the staff who are looking after them.

Interest in other children and some cooperative play

What you might observe in a child aged three years

Physical development

Able to walk up stairs on alternate feet

Able to use the toilet

Communication and intellectual development

Speech that adults unfamiliar with the child can understand

Interested in mark-making, painting and books

Enjoyment of sand and water play

Social, emotional and behavioural development

Interest in other children and some co-operative play

Enjoys dressing up and playing with small world toys

Keen to help and copy adults

Children at four years old

By four years old, most children have made huge steps forward in their development. Most children will be fairly fluent in their speech, and adults who do not know them should be able to understand them easily. There will still be the odd grammatical mistake and interesting pronunciations of words, but by and large they will have mastered the spoken language. Most children's behaviour will be co-operative, but this depends on them getting plenty of praise and recognition from adults. Most four-year-olds also enjoy playing with other children and will be starting to plan their play together. Most four-year-olds are also learning to be independent. They can dress and feed themselves and can organise their play if they are given the opportunity. They also enjoy being with responsive adults, especially when they are being given responsibility and encouraged.

Most children will be attending some pre-school provision such as a playgroup, nursery or crèche. This is important for them as most children enjoy the company of others and are beginning to learn about friendships. They will also be learning, often without realising it, as activities will be planned for them. Depending on where they live, many children during this year will be starting off at school. For some children, this is a difficult transition, as they have to adapt to being part of a much larger group.

What you might observe in a child aged four years

Physical development

Children riding on tricycles, climbing and enjoying simple ball games

Skilful use of the hands to do activities such as threading, pouring and using scissors

Communication and intellectual development

Children asking questions and enjoying talking

Pretend play that models adult life

Speech and pretend play that models adult life

Concentration when an activity has caught their interest

Drawings that have meaning for the child and are recognisable

Social, emotional and behavioural development

Children who are settled into the routine of the setting and are able to separate from their parents easily (if they have been in the setting for a few months)

Co-operative play between children along with the odd squabble and argument

Children responding well to adult praise and recognition

Skills builder

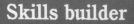

Talk to three parents who have children under five years old about their child's development.

Find out what their child can currently do. How does this relate to the pattern of development given for their age group?

Functional Skills English: Speaking, listening and communication

It is important that you prepare some questions before your discussion with different parents so that you can contribute to the discussion and share your ideas and thoughts. Try to be flexible in your discussion so if someone asks you a different question you can respond in an appropriate way.

Children at five to six years

In these years, the rapid changes in physical development come to an end. Instead children gain in confidence and co-ordination. This is also true for other skills such as their spoken language and social skills. A good example of this is the way that, at around this time, children begin to enjoy hearing and even making jokes. At around five years, most children have begun in formal education. This can be a difficult transition period for some children, especially if they are not interested in learning to read and write. For children who are ready, learning to read and write can prove exciting and they may enjoy the intellectual challenge of a classroom. As well as school, some children will also be doing activities such as swimming, dance or music. They may also attend afterschool clubs, where they can play and meet other children. Ways in which children play is also starting to change. Children in this period are keen to work out rules of situations and enjoy playing games with rules.

Friends are also important to children of this age. Many children will have started to establish friendships and preferences. Staying for tea or even overnight is quite common and helps children to learn about other families. This having been said, children still rely on their parents to meet many of their emotional needs.

What you might observe in a child aged five to six years

Physical development
Ability to kick and control a ball

More legible handwriting and increased fine manipulative movements

Communication and intellectual development
Enjoyment of jokes

Beginning to decode some familiar words

Enjoyment of jokes

Social, emotional and behavioural development
Keen to understand and use rules

Some friendship preferences

Children from seven to nine years

Children's development in this period continues but is more gradual. While children continue to grow in height, the main changes are in the way they think and reason. This can be seen in the way that children play. Their games and play become more organised and they make up rules as well as follow rules. The way in which children think and reason also shows itself as children start to be able to solve simple problems and also enjoy practical situations in which they have to work things out for themselves. Most children are also co-operative and enjoy being given responsibility. They respond well when adults give clear explanations for rules and when their behaviour is acknowledged and praised.

In these years, reading and writing becomes easier, although there will be variations in the speed at which children become competent and confident.

Children are also becoming more physically skilled. This results in children being able to do things more quickly, confidently and accurately. For example, putting on a coat is now an easy task, as is cutting out with scissors or drawing a simple picture. Friendships are becoming increasingly important for children. Many children will have groups of close friends with some girls having 'best friends'. The lack or temporary absence of a friend starts to become an issue. Children may only want to attend a club if they know a friend is also likely to be there.

As most children are at school, life in the classroom and playground is a major influence on them. This is also a period in which children really start to compare themselves with others. In some ways this is part of the thinking process as they carry on the process of working out what they are like. They may notice which children are the fastest runners, best readers or quickest at finishing tasks. This can start to affect their confidence and even enthusiasm.

What you might observe in a child aged seven to nine years

Physical development

Skilful, precise and confident hand movements

Good at balancing, running and throwing

Communication and intellectual development

Children telling jokes and enjoying chatting

Enjoyment of playing and making up games with rules

Verbal arguments, persuasion and negotiation

Children beginning to read books silently

Children writing short stories and text with less adult help required

Social, emotional and behavioural development

Clear differences in play activities that interest boys and girls

Co-operative play with children having stable friendships

Play that involves turn-taking

Children who understand rules and consequences

Children who tell others the rules and are keen to point out when rules have been broken

Cooperative play

Children at nine to eleven years

In some ways this period in most children's lives can be summed up as the 'calm before the storm'. Most children are fairly confident and have mastered many skills, although they will often have decided what they are good at. They can now read, write, draw and use some logic. They are often skilled communicators and enjoy having friends. This is a time when many children feel quite settled, although early puberty in girls is not uncommon.

What you might observe in a child aged nine to eleven years

Physical development

Skilled at drawing, colouring and manipulating small objects

Skilled at throwing, kicking and using whole-body movements

Communication and intellectual development

Detailed and representational pictures where children enjoy drawing

Stories and writing that shows imagination as well as being legible and reasonably grammatical

Problem solving, e.g. how to play co-operatively, how to use materials fairly

Social, emotional and behavioural development

Enthusiasm when given areas of responsibility

Greater co-ordination and speed when carrying out both fine and large movements

Stable friendships that are usually same-sex

Awareness of consequences of behaviour and increased thoughtfulness

Drawing detailed and representational pictures

Young people at 11–13 years

This period in children's lives marks the start of their growing independence. While parents remain important, children begin to show signs of wanting to grow up. For example, they may now ask to walk home or get buses home by themselves. Some children also begin to question rules at home and may try to push the boundaries. Young people's relationships with others of the same age become increasingly important. This can put a lot of pressure on children as their friends may have very different ideas to their parents! This period also holds other pressures for them. They are likely to be changing to another school for the next stage in their education. Quite often the new school will be larger and the curriculum more formal. They may have a series of teachers during the day, rather than just one or two.

This period also marks physical changes for young people as their bodies begin to prepare for adulthood. Girls' puberty usually begins at around eleven years, while boys' may not start until they are 13 or 14 years old. The physical changes can cause embarrassment and anxiety, and so create further pressure.

Relationships with others of the same age become increasingly important

What you might observe in a young person aged 11–13 years

Physical development

Changes in body shape

Increased strength and stamina

Communication and intellectual development

Able to read and write fluently

Beginning to manage own time and take responsibility

Social, emotional and behavioural development

Enjoyment when with their friends

More confidence around the home and in familiar situations

Arguments with parents as young people start to become independent

Times when young people enjoy 'childish' activities, e.g. sitting on a swing, watching cartoons, playing games

Young people aged 13–16 years

In this period, young people inch closer to adulthood. Physically, by around the age of 15 or 16, girls will have finished becoming women. For most boys, puberty will start from around 14 years and is likely to take around three years to complete.

Pressure in school is likely to increase as most young people are preparing for exams and may be starting to think about their futures. At around 16 years, young people will need to decide whether to leave school and education and take a job. Some children in this period will have developed skills that are on a par with adults, such as the ability to use computers or draw. Being with friends is likely to be more important than being with family members. Young people who do not have a group of friends are likely to feel that they are missing out and may become anxious. This is a time when young people are also trying to explore their own identity. They may have tastes in music, clothes and prefer activities that are different to their parents. This may sometimes cause clashes as young people are trying to develop their own personality and space.

In this period, young people also want to be independent and may test the boundaries at home and even at school. As the transition to adulthood is not complete, young people will also at times revert to 'child-like' comments, activities and games.

While for some young people this period can be one of anxiety and conflict, for others it can be an enjoyable period as they spend time with friends and are able to dream a little about the future!

What you might observe in a young person aged 13–16 years

Physical development
Changes to body shape as a result of puberty

Increase in strength and stamina

Communication and intellectual development
High level of skills in some subjects

Uncertainty about how to talk to unfamiliar adults

Social, emotional and behavioural development
Confidence and enjoyment when with friends

Thoughts and ideas that may be different to their parents'

Young people 16–19 years

While girls will have finished going through puberty, boys will still be developing physically. Boys and girls are likely to be interested in

Confidence and enjoyment when with friends

developing intimate relationships with others and this can be a source of both pleasure and distress. Young people also have to focus on their future as their school days end. They will make decisions about taking further qualifications or starting out in employment. This can therefore be a stressful time, particularly if parents and young people do not agree about decisions taken. Some young people may move out from their homes either to avoid conflict with their parents or in order to study away from home. In this period, young people's friendships may change. They may make new friends if they go on to college or into employment. Friendship groups may also become smaller. Some young people find the transition from school to a more independent form of study or employment fairly easy; others find it more difficult.

What you might observe in a young person aged 16–19 years

Physical development

Girls now fully developed

Boys likely to be still growing until they reach 18 years or so

Boys with higher levels of stamina and strength

Communication and intellectual development

Increasing levels of intellectual maturity, allowing young people to make more informed decisions

Growing confidence in communicating with older adults

Social, emotional and behavioural development

Good levels of confidence in young people who have identified their future goals

These young people have decided to study at their local college

Low levels of self-esteem for some young people if relationships with their peers or parents are not strong

Many young people exploring their sexuality

Young people now responsible for their own behaviour, some beginning to question their families' attitudes and beliefs

Functional Skills ICT: Developing, presenting and communicating information

You could take one area of development and produce a chart on the computer showing how this one area, for example physical development, changes from birth to 19 years. You could also insert relevant images to support your chart.

How different aspects of development can affect one another

While we have looked at the different areas of development, they actually tend to work together. For many skills that children need to develop, more than one area of development is involved. For example, being able to play a game of snap requires that a child can hold their

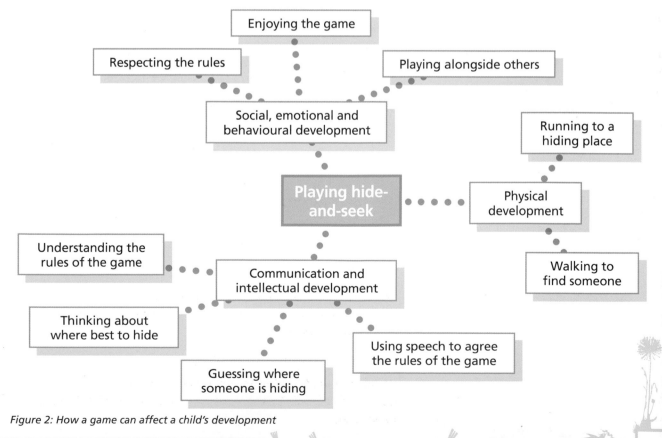

Figure 2: How a game can affect a child's development

cards, take turns and also understand how to play the game. Figure 2 shows how being able to play hide-and-seek requires all of the areas of development. If a child has a developmental delay in one area, this can affect the others too: for example, a child whose language is delayed will find it hard to play in the home corner where other children are talking as they are playing.

Understand the kinds of influences that affect children's and young people's development

What makes children so different even when they are the same age? This is an important question and one that has not yet been fully answered. However, we do know that children's development is shaped both by what they are born with and by the experiences that they have. For this learning outcome, you will need to show that you understand some of the main influences that affect children's development, and that you also know the importance of recognising and responding to concerns about children's development.

Different kinds of influence

While some of children's development seems to be determined by their genetic code, what happens to them after they are born is also important. The factors that might affect children's and young people's development can be grouped into three broad areas.

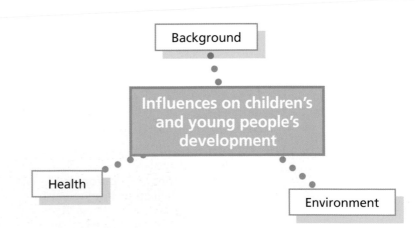

Figure 3: Influences on development

Background

Families and parents play a huge part in children's and young people's development. There are many factors linked to a child's background that can affect their development.

Family dynamics

Families are important in children's lives. Most children do grow up in families, but there are some who grow up either in foster families or in the care of the local authority. The perfect family does not exist. Some families seem to be closer than others and this can help children's development, but all families will have times of stress. Children who have good relationships with their parents, brothers and sisters can gain confidence and they also seem to do better at school. When families split up or are often arguing, children's and young people's emotional and social development can be affected. They may feel left out or uncared for. As children become more independent, some will avoid spending time with their families and may, for example, hang around with friends on the street or stay out late. This can make them more vulnerable to the attention of undesirable adults or to straying into anti-social behaviour.

Parenting styles

Most parents want to do their best for their children. Some parents find it harder than others to know quite what they should do with their children. This means that some parents can be too strict, while others

Parents play an important part in children's development

may be too relaxed. Others may find they go from one extreme to another. Some parents may find it hard to show their love and approval, so their relationships with their children are more strained. Parents can also find it hard to know what they should do as their children grow up and become teenagers. Parenting style seems to be important in helping children to learn about behaviour and also about taking responsibility. It also seems to make a difference in terms of helping children to feel settled emotionally.

Poverty

How much money a family has to live on seems to have an impact on development. There are many reasons for this. Firstly, parents who are struggling to make ends meet may be very stressed. This can affect their parenting style. Then lack of money can also mean that families cannot afford to eat properly or to live in nice areas. It also means that families cannot always afford to do things that help children's learning such as buy a computer or take their children out on visits.

Culture/religion

Every family is slightly different. Each family will have its own traditions, values and beliefs. One family will believe that sitting down for a meal together is important, while another family will not care about this. Some traditions in families are linked to their religion or culture. Some children who grow up in families that have a strong culture or religious beliefs can benefit because it gives them a strong identity. Other children may find it difficult because their family is different to their friends' or because they feel restricted by what their parents or family want them to do.

Health

Health is a complex issue. Quite often our health is a mixture between our genetic make-up and factors such as where we live, what we eat and our stress levels.

In some cases children are born with a condition that will automatically affect them: for example, they may have diabetes or a blood condition. Other children may have a **predisposition** towards certain diseases. This means that they do not automatically develop them, but certain circumstances will trigger them. A good example of this is asthma. Asthma is a condition that affects children's breathing and is currently on the increase. Children who live in areas where the air quality is poor, live in damp conditions or whose parents smoke are more likely to develop it.

Where children are unwell or have an ongoing medical condition, this may affect their development. They may not feel like playing or their condition may restrict what they can do. Health can affect many aspects of children's development. Children may find it harder to make friends because they are not well enough to attend regularly or they cannot physically join in the play. Being unwell can also affect children's

Key term

Predisposition: a natural tendency

emotional development as it can make them feel that they are not 'normal' and are different to the others. Finally, being unwell can affect children's cognitive development. They may not be able to concentrate because they feel poorly or because drowsiness is a side-effect of the medication that they are taking. Children may also miss out on learning because they are not able to attend regularly.

Sleep

As well as medical conditions, sleep can also have an influence on children's development.

Sufficient sleep is essential for children's cognitive development. When children are tired, they find it hard to remember new information and to concentrate. Some parents are not aware of just how much sleep children and young people need. It is thought that children under five should be having at least 12 hours sleep, while teenagers need nine or ten hours. Being tired also affects children's social and emotional development. Children who are tired find it hard to control their anger, frustration and other emotions. This means that they may find it hard to play with other children without falling out.

Diet

Children's growth, behaviour and development can be affected by their diet. A balanced diet will help children to remain healthy as well as to grow. The awareness of children's diets is growing. This is because numbers of children who are overweight or obese have been steadily rising. Being overweight or obese as a child can have many effects. Children may not develop the strength in their bodies needed to develop high levels of physical skill. They may also be prone to ill health. Their social and emotional development may also be affected. They may lose confidence and not want to try out new activities or play games with other children.

Environment

Where children grow up and what they do is often linked to their background. It can also have quite an effect on their development.

Opportunities for education and learning

Some children are lucky because they have plenty of different opportunities for education and learning. They may go to a good childminder, pre-school or nursery. As they get older, they may be able to go to a school that has good facilities and teachers. Children may be in an environment where talent can be nurtured: for example, a child who has a natural talent for singing may be noticed and encouraged to play an instrument or join a choir.

Play and stimulation

We know that young children need plenty of opportunities to play in order to help their development. Some children are lucky because their environment has plenty of different resources in it and there is the space to play. Other children are less fortunate. They may be in environments

This child is lucky. He is learning through playing with an interesting material

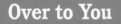

Over to You

Find out more about the importance of challenging play areas in keeping children safe by visiting www.rospa.org.uk.

Link
Look at MU 2.2 for more on your role in supporting the assessment of children's and young people's development.

that are small or have limited resources. They may not be able to play with a wide range of different materials or are with people who do not understand the value of play. This can affect their cognitive development because they are not doing new things or having a wide range of experiences.

Language and interaction

As well as play, children need plenty of opportunities to talk with adults. This helps children to develop language, which in turn helps them to learn and think. Some children are lucky because their parents take time to talk and they spend time in good-quality early years settings, where adults show them things and encourage their speech.

Opportunities to be active

We now know that children benefit from being physically active. It helps them to take exercise while having fun, but also allows them to learn. Some children are in environments that are perfect for this. They may live near fields, parks or by leisure centres. Being active gives children confidence and also helps their physical development. It seems to help their cognitive development, as activity can be stimulating for the brain.

Safety

Children need to be kept safe, but still need the chance to explore. Good environments are safe ones for children, but are still ones that are challenging. Children who are in areas where there are no exciting playgrounds or areas to play may do things that are unsafe, such as playing by canals or on building sites. This can mean that they have accidents leading to long-term injuries or medical conditions.

Recognising and responding to concerns about development

As you have seen, there are many reasons why some children may have advantages and also disadvantages when it comes to development. While differences will also exist, some children and young people will need extra support. This is why professionals working with children and young people will always keep an eye out for those whose pattern of development is not typical.

Getting support quickly can make a lot of difference to children. Sometimes this will mean supporting parents by giving them advice or practical help so that they know what to do with their children. At other times this will mean that the child needs the specialist support of a speech and language therapist or a counsellor. Many interventions are very short-term. A child may need additional help for just a few weeks or an operation to help their hearing. For other children — for example, those with learning difficulties — support may be required for much longer. When a child, and sometimes their parents, gets the support that they need quickly, they are more likely to do better and in some cases the child can even catch up with children of a similar age.

Functional Skills Maths: Representing

How many children are identified as needing support? What is this as a percentage of the whole setting or of your whole class?

Case study:
Concerns about development

Harry is four years old. He has just started the reception class. The teacher notices that Harry's speech is not quite clear; he does try to talk but only when he is by himself with an adult. Over a couple of weeks, she observes Harry closely and spots that other children do not always understand him and he is finding it hard to make friends. He also seems to be a little unsure of himself. She talks to his parents and they agree to refer him to the speech and language service. A few weeks later, Harry is seen by a speech and language therapist. The family are given some tips and also some exercises. Over the next few months, Harry's speech becomes clearer. His teacher notices that he talks more in class and that he seems confident. She is also pleased to see that he plays with the other children and has made two very good friends.

1. How was Harry's speech difficulty affecting his development?
2. Why was it important that his teacher recognised his difficulty?
3. Why did Harry benefit from being helped?

Understand the potential effects of transitions on children's and young people's development

There are several points during children's and young people's lives when things will change for them. The term '**transitions**' is used to describe these changes. While some changes will be positive for children, others may be quite difficult and so can affect children's development. For this learning outcome, you will need to know what type of changes can take place for children and how these might affect them. The information that you have gained from this learning outcome will help you in unit 5.

Key term

Transition: any significant stage or experience in the life of a child or young person that can affect their behaviour or development

Transitions that most experience

Changes are part and parcel of growing up in a child's life. Change starts early on when a child at first has to spend time with someone who is not their parent or when they stop wearing nappies and go on to using the toilet. While these are small transitions, they are important for children. Learning to cope with changes gives children confidence, and many changes will have positive outcomes for children: for example, playing with other children in a nursery. Table 1 shows some common transitions that are experienced by most children and young people.

Table 1: Transitions that most children and young people experience

Transition	Age	Reason
Being cared for by someone other than a parent	0–2	Many children will be left by parents with relatives and friends for short periods of time. Some babies and toddlers may also go to a childminder or day nursery as their parents work
Joining a nursery or pre-school	2–3	Many children's first experience of being in group care is at around two years as they start in a pre-school or nursery
Going into a reception class	4–5	Most children will attend a reception class between the ages of 4–5
Moving from one class to another	4–11	At the end of each school year, most children will change teacher as they change class
Attending breakfast club, afterschool provision and holiday playschemes	4+	Some children once they are at school will have an extended day, perhaps going to a breakfast club before going on to school and after school going to a childminder or an afterschool club; in addition, many children will attend holiday playschemes
Starting secondary school	11	Most children at 11 will transfer to a secondary school, which is often much larger than their primary school; they may also be taught by a range of different teachers for the first time
Going through puberty	11+	At around 11 for girls and 13 years for boys, children develop into adults – a process known as puberty; during this time, the young people have to adapt to the changes in size and shape of their body
Starting a new college or employment	16+	Most young people will move into the sixth form, start at a college or begin employment, so they need to make new friendships and adapt to new expectations

Some transitions are common to all children

Transitions that only some experience

While many children and young people will have fairly straightforward childhoods, other children may have to cope with some difficult periods in their lives. Understanding the range of difficult transitions that some children need to cope with is important as it can affect their development.

Table 2: Transitions that only some children and young people experience

Transition	Age	Reason
Moving area/ country	Any	Changing area or country may mean learning a new accent or language. There are many reasons why children may move area or country. • Some families may change area because they cannot afford to live in the same home. Others may change area because they can afford a different lifestyle • Some children will move area or country because their parents have separated • Sometimes families move because of a parent's job e.g. army families • Some families change country because they are refugees or are trying to escape war or poverty
Change in family structure	Any	Significant changes to a family's structure can be difficult for children to deal with. • Some parents will separate and children will have to adapt to being in a single parent family • Some families change when parents separate and meet a new partner. A new family may be formed with step-brothers or -sisters and a parent may go on to have a baby with the new partner • Some children may be moved into foster care because of difficulties in the family, while other children who are in foster care may be adopted
Bereavement	Any	Some children have to deal with a death of a close relative such as a parent or sibling. This changes the family structure as well as creating an emotional loss
Abuse	Any	Some children and young people experience abuse, which can sometimes happen within a family or be carried out by someone trusted by the child or young person
Bullying	From 5+	Serious bullying can disrupt a child or young person's education and also their sense of confidence. Bullying can become particularly serious after the age of 11 years
Significant illness or disability	Any	Some children and young people have to cope with a significant illness such as diabetes or a disability. Illness and some types of disability may mean time spent in hospital or undergoing treatment. Adjusting to a change in health or learning to live with a disability is a significant transition for both the child and the child's parents

Over to You

Find out about how children who have been bereaved or who are facing bereavement can be helped by visiting www.winstonswish.org.uk

Functional Skills ICT: Finding and selecting information

Using the website in the 'Over to You' on this page to search for further information on supporting children who have been bereaved will help you to develop your ICT skills. Can you find any other useful information on the internet that will help you to support children going through transitions?

How transitions may affect behaviour and development

Most transitions have some effects on children's behaviour and development. Fortunately these effects are usually short-term ones; however some may have a longer-term impact.

Short-term effects

A common effect in terms of development is regression. Regression means that a child takes a step or two back in terms of their behaviour and their development. For example, a child who is normally potty-trained may start to wet themselves, or a child who can normally speak quite clearly starts use babyish language. Recognising that a child is affected by a transition is important as, when children are given support, the effects of the transitions can be reduced. Figure 4 shows some of the ways in which a child or young person might be affected.

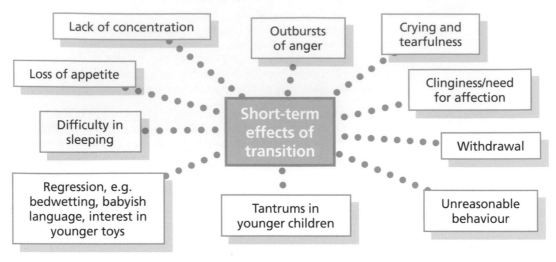

Figure 4: Short-term effects of transition

Longer-term effects

Any change or transition that unsettles children or makes them seriously unhappy can affect their behaviour or development over a longer term. For example, children tend to learn best when they are happy and relaxed, so a child who is worried is likely to find concentration quite difficult. This in turn can affect a child's intellectual development, as you need to concentrate in order to learn new information. Happy and settled children also tend to behave fairly well, so a child who is upset because his father has left may start to be quite aggressive with other children. Recognising the signs that a child is being affected by a transition is essential so that support can be offered. Table 3 shows the possible long-term effects on children's and young people's development and behaviour if a transition is particularly traumatic or lengthy.

Table 3: Possible long-term effects of transition on children's and young people's development and behaviour

Physical development	Growth may be affected if children are not sleeping or eating properly Some children and young people may turn to food for comfort and gain weight Some children and young people may restrict their food intake as it is one way in which they can take control of what is happening to them Some young people may self-harm or abuse alcohol or drugs
Communication and intellectual development	Some children may withdraw and avoid social contact Children's and young people's learning may be affected because they cannot concentrate or are not interested by schoolwork
Social, emotional and behavioural development	Some children may find it hard to make or keep friends as they feel 'different' Some children and young people may find relationships with their parents are strained Some children's and young people's self-confidence and self-esteem are affected by what has happened or is happening to them Some children and young people may lose trust in adults as a result of what is happening or has happened to them Some children and young people try to gain attention by showing unwanted behaviour

Case study:
Understanding transitions

Charlie is four years old. Recently, staff at his nursery have noticed some changes in him. He has started to wet himself and seems very withdrawn. He seems very reluctant to try out new activities. He has also started to cry when he comes into the nursery and it has been hard for his mother to leave. His key person has decided to talk to his mother about his change in behaviour. She tells the key person that she has split up with Charlie's father and that he moved out last week. She says that Charlie has been crying each night and that he keeps asking for his dad.

1. Why is this a big change for Charlie?

2. Why is it important for the nursery to understand what has happened?

3. How might Charlie be affected by this change?

Functional Skills ICT: Developing, presenting and communicating information

By creating the leaflet in this 'Getting ready for assessment' you will be able to develop your ICT skills. Try and use a range of different editing techniques and include text, images and different colours to make your leaflet look attractive to its audience.

Getting ready for assessment

Create a leaflet that will provide information about the types of transition that children in the age group that you work with might face. Your leaflet should:

- identify the types of transitions that children might face

- explain the short-term and long-term effects on their development and behaviour.

Check your knowledge

1. Identify three skills that most babies at nine months can show.

2. Identify three skills that most two-year-olds can show.

3. Identify three skills that most four-year-olds can show.

4. Explain how the areas of development link to each other.

5. Describe how a child's background might influence their development.

6. Explain how living in poverty can affect a child's development.

7. Why is it important that children whose development is not following the expected pattern are recognised?

8. Give an example of a transition that most four-year-olds will have experienced.

9. Identify three short-term effects of transition on children.

10. Identify two long-term effects of a traumatic transition on children.

My Story

Carl, assistant in a pre-school

When I was at college, I didn't really enjoy or see the point of the development units. All I wanted to do was work with children, not worry about at what age they could do this or that. It was only after I started work here that I started to realise just how important it was to know about children's development. A couple of times, I had planned activities that just didn't work at all. I was gutted because I had put a lot of work into getting them ready. When I talked it through with my supervisor, I blamed the children at first – for not trying – but then I came to the conclusion that it was down to me for not understanding their level. Nowadays, my planned activities work because I am more in tune with the children. I observe them carefully before planning activities.

Viewpoint: Bed times

It is now recognised that many children are not sleeping for long enough. This is affecting their development, as tiredness affects their concentration and also their health. Many parents tell nursery staff that they must not allow their children to have a nap. As sleep is a basic need for humans, what should nursery staff do? Follow parents' wishes or meet the needs of the child? In a recent inspection, a nursery was told that they had to meet children's needs rather than the parents' when the inspector found out that they were waking children up. Perhaps, parents need more information about how many hours sleep young children need and maybe we need a return to a 6 pm or 7 pm bedtime.

Ask the expert

Q If every child is meant to be different, what is the point of milestones?

A Yes, every child's development is slightly different, but overall children do develop in similar ways and at similar times. Having milestones helps us to work out whether a child is showing very unusual development, as quite often such children will need additional support.

Q We have a parent who won't believe that her child's speech is delayed.

A There are many reasons why parents will not accept that their child needs help. Sometimes it is because it has not been explained well and they do not realise how much difference it might make to their child. Some parents are also concerned that their child will be labelled or bullied later on. Other parents are simply not ready to accept that their 'perfect' child is in any way different to other children. There is no 'trick' to working with parents, other than by trying to listen and understand their fears and concerns.

MU 2.2

Contribute to the support of child & young person development

In this unit, you will be looking at how to support children's and young people's development by observing them, helping them to meet their needs and encouraging positive behaviour. You will also be looking at the importance of reflecting on your practice.

Learning outcomes
By the end of this unit you will:

1. be able to contribute to assessments of the development needs of children and young people

2. be able to support the development of children and young people

3. know how to support children and young people experiencing transitions

4. be able to support children's and young people's positive behaviour

5. be able to use reflective practice to improve own contribution to child and young person development.

Be able to contribute to assessments of the development needs of children and young people

One of the most important things that professionals do when working with children is to think about their needs and interests. This is done by observing them, coming to some conclusions and then deciding on a plan. For this learning outcome, you will need to show that you can be part of this process in your workplace.

Observe and record aspects of the development of a child or young person

All early years settings observe children routinely. There are many different ways as we will see later. Knowing what to look at is important. Most settings will observe children's development to see how they are doing in the following areas:

Physical

As we saw in TDA 2.1, children's physical development is about the way that they use their hands, move and balance and also manage skills such as kicking a ball. Most play involves physical development, so that you may be able to observe a child's physical development as they are playing e.g. a child pushing a teddy in a pushchair or a child rolling out some dough.

Communication

Children's speech and language is important to their overall development. Most children will talk as they play if they are using speech. Babies and toddlers might use gestures or body language to communicate with us. A good way of looking at speech is to carry out recordings.

Intellectual/cognitive

Intellectual/cognitive development is about the way that children think, problem-solve and also remember things. It is also about concepts that children learn such as colours, sense of time and space. To observe children's intellectual development, we might think about creating a play opportunity and see what the child does or says. We may also sometimes put out something that means that a child has to problem-solve such as a jigsaw puzzle or tell children that teddy's bucket is leaking and seeing if they can find a way of fixing it.

Intellectual development is about thinking and problem solving

Social, emotional and behavioural

Being with others is important for children. Even very young babies make eye contact and show pleasure at being with others. Observing children's social and emotional development means looking at whether they enjoy being with others and whether they have strong relationships with people that they spend a lot of time with. Observing behaviour is about looking to see whether children can show behaviour that is expected for their age or stage of development e.g. can a three-year-old wait a moment for their turn. Quite a lot of information can be gained about these aspects of development while children are playing.

The checklist below shows a few things that are useful to look out for when observing children.

Best practice checklist: Observing children

✓ Does the child seem relaxed and happy?

✓ Does the child make eye contact or smile at anyone?

✓ How interested is the child in the play or activity?

✓ Does the child seem tired or in any pain?

✓ Does the child enjoy playing with other children?

✓ Does the child approach any adults?

✓ How does the child react when an adult approaches?

✓ How much speech or communication does the child show?

✓ Does the child have a favourite friend?

Over to You

Observations do not have to be written down. You can simply watch children. This is a good way at first to learn about observing children. Ask your supervisor for permission to observe a child. Stand a little way back and use the checklist as a starting point. What can you find out about the child?

Observation is key to working professionally with children

Using different observation methods

There is not a single perfect method of recording children: different methods are appropriate for different situations. The way in which you observe and assess children will also vary according to where you work. It is useful, however, to have an understanding of the range of different recording methods and also their limitations.

Figure 1 shows the different types of methods that you need to know about for this unit.

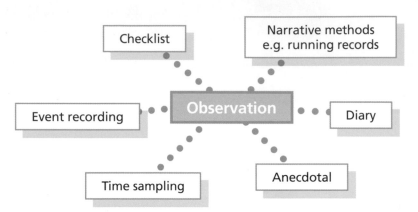

Figure 1: Different observation methods

Observing children in different situations

Children can change according to who they are with and whether they know that they are being watched. This means that you will need to observe children in a range of different situations e.g. with other children, playing by themselves and when they are with an adult. It is also important to see what children can do when they do not know that an adult is watching them. This is sometimes known as naturalistic observation as in theory we are watching children being 'natural'.

Narrative methods including running records

Narrative methods are ones where you write at the time what children are doing. Popular variations are running records, when you keep writing over a period of time, and snapshot observations, when you just catch a little of what the child is doing.

How it works

The observer either notices something that is interesting and starts to write it down, or has already decided what skill or area of development to look for. The observer simply writes down what he or she can see as it is happening.

It can be useful after a few recordings to read through what you have written to check that it makes sense while it is still fresh in your mind, especially if your handwriting is hard to read. Always include the start and finish time of each burst of recording.

Brightlands Day Nursery
107 St. Georges Road
Cheltenham
Gloucestershire
GL50 3ED

Brightlands

Ravi is standing up in front of Michaela, who is sitting on a chair. Ravi seems to be looking down at Michaela. She is saying 'Shall we dress up?' Michaela nods and smiles, Ravi smiles too and they both walk over to the dressing-up corner.

Ravi takes a pink dress, grasping it in her right hand, and places it on the floor. She pulls the back of the dress open with both hands. She steps into the dress using her right foot first and pulls up the dress gradually to a standing position, placing her right arm into the dress and then her left.

Ravi walks over to the nursery nurse and looks up. She asks 'Can you do my buttons up?' and turns around.

A running record

Table 1: Advantages and disadvantages of narrative methods

Advantages	Disadvantages
• No preparation is needed • You can record anything that is of interest • It can provide a rounded picture of a child • You can use this method to record any area of development	• Different observers pick up on different things • It is hard to write down exactly what a child is doing while also watching the child • You need to be able to write quickly • It can be hard to find the right language to describe what you are seeing • Observations are not continuous, as the observer usually has to have breaks in order to keep writing

Diary

In some settings a daily record is kept of what children have done. This is often shared with parents and is useful for children and young people who do not have speech i.e. a baby or a young person with learning difficulties.

Functional Skills English: Writing and Reading

You could produce an information booklet on observations. Once you have read all the different types of observation along with the advantages and disadvantages you could write a short summary for each different type. This task provides you with the opportunity to write for a different purpose and develop your reading skills.

You can keep a daily diary of what a child does

How it works

The adults or parents working with the children write down things that they think are important. With babies for example, it might be the times of feeds while with toddlers it might be about what they have enjoyed doing. Photographs can also be added into diaries.

Table 2: Advantages and disadvantages of a diary

Advantages	Disadvantages
• It can help others to know what a child has been doing • It provides a long-term record	• Different observers pick up on different things • If done every day, observers must have enough time to fill it in properly

Anecdotal

Anecdotal observations are ones that you have not actually seen, but are points that others such as parents might tell you about. Parents may for example have seen their baby walk for the first time or a staff member might at break time have noticed that a pupil is not joining in with the others.

How it works

After something that seems important or interesting, the person who saw or heard it tells the observer about it. The observer can then write it down in a diary, event recording or just add it into the child's or young person's records.

Table 3: Advantages and disadvantages of observation

Advantages	Disadvantages
• It can help others to know what a child has been doing • It may help us find out about a child in a different situation	• It is not possible for the observer to 'see' what has happened • Anecdotal information might be inaccurate or exaggerated

Time sampling

Time sampling allows you to look at what a child does over a period of time, such as a morning or part of an afternoon. This means that you gain a more complete picture of the child.

Time	Activity	Social group	Comments
11.00	Snack time	Whole group	Anna is sitting with her legs swinging on a chair. She is eating an apple. She is holding it in her left hand and she is smiling. She puts up her hand when a staff member asks who wants a biscuit.
11.15	Outdoor play Climbing frame	Anna and Ben	Anna is on the top bar of the climbing frame. She is smiling at Ben. She is calling 'Come on up here!'
11.30	Taking coats off	Anna, Ben and Manjit	Anna unzips the coat and pulls out one arm. She swings around and the coat moves around. She laughs and looks at Manjit

Figure 2: An example of a time sample

How it works

This type of observation needs some planning, as the observer needs to be free to keep an eye on the children. A sheet is prepared with the times marked out. At each of the times on the sheet, the observer watches what the child is doing and records it on the sheet. This provides a snapshot view of what the child is doing. It is possible to record the activity of more than one child.

Table 4: Advantages and disadvantages of time samples

Advantages	Disadvantages
• They can provide a lot of information about a child. • They are interesting observations to carry out. • You can use time samples to look out for particular skills or to focus on areas of development • More than one child can be observed	• A piece of significant behaviour may not be recorded if it falls outside of the time slot • The observer may find it hard to do anything else but record

Event sample

This observation method is used to look at how often and in what circumstances a child shows a particular behaviour. Some settings use this method to look at unwanted behaviour such as biting. It can also be used to find out about how often a child talks or plays with other children.

Event	Time	Situation	Social group	Dialogue
1	9.16 am	Curren is hovering near the painting	Susan + 2 children table	A–C 'Do you want to come and paint a picture too?' C–A nods head
2	9.27 am	Curren is finishing painting	Susan + 2 children	A–C 'Have you finished?' C smiles 'It's a lovely picture. Tell me a little bit about it.' C–A 'It's my mum. Can't take my apron off.' A–C 'Wait still, I'll do it.' Curren hands apron to Susan and runs over to sand area
3	10.12 am	Curren is waiting for his drink snack time	Curren is sitting next to Ahmed. Jo is handing out drinks	A–C 'Milk or squash, Curren?' C–A 'Milk.' A–C 'Can you remember the magic word?' C–A 'Thank you.' A–C 'Good boy.'
4	10.19 am	Curren is putting on his coat in the cloakroom area	Jo + 5 children	C–A 'Can't put coat on.' A–C 'Keep still. There you are. You can go out now.'
5	10.36 am	Curren is waiting for his turn by the slide	Jo + 2 children	A–C 'Good boy. It's your go now.' C smiles C–A 'I go fast down now.'

Figure 3: This event sample was drawn up to look at how often and when a child played co-operatively with others

How it works

A prepared sheet is drawn up in advance after considering carefully the type of information that needs to be collected. A column is put down for each piece of information. When the behaviour is seen, the person who has seen it should fill in the sheet.

Table 5: Advantages and disadvantages of event samples

Advantages	Disadvantages
• They can help you to understand the reasons behind a child's behaviour • They can be repeated to see if a certain behaviour is increasing or disappearing • They can be used to record other aspects of children's development	• An adult may not always be present at the time of the behaviour • An adult may forget to fill in the event sample or may not know that he or she should be looking out for a particular behaviour

Checklist

Checklists are popular, especially where people are working with large groups of children. Many checklists are commercially produced, but it is also possible to design your own.

How it works

Checklists are easy to use because they focus the observer on particular aspects of child development. The observer either watches as the child is playing or asks the child to do something such as hop on one foot. The observer then notices whether or not the child is able to show the skill.

Child's name .... Date ....

Date of Birth .... Observer ....

Developmental checklist

By 12 months	Yes	No	Sometimes
Pick objects up with finger and thumb?			
Transfer items from one hand to the other?			
Look for an object hidden under a beaker?			
Look at a person who is speaking to him or her?			
Make tuneful babbling sounds such as Da-da			
Respond to different sounds e.g. drum, bell			
Imitate gestures such as pat cake and bye bye			
Hold beaker using two hands?			
Use fingers to eat finger foods such as squares of bread?			
Pick up dropped toys?			
React to the word 'No'?			
React to own name?			

Figure 4: This checklist has been designed to look at young children's physical skills

Table 6: Advantages and disadvantages of checklists

Advantages	Disadvantages
• They are quick and easy to use • You might be able to use them with more than one child at a time • You can repeat the assessment and see the differences	• You have to be a very accurate observer • Different observers might produce different results • The recording sheets usually focus the observer on skills that the child is showing, not on how happy or confident the child is • Children might feel that they have failed if they cannot do a task • The checklist sheets have to be relevant and appropriate

Supporting assessments of development needs

Once children have been observed, the next step is to think about what you have learnt about the child's development, interests or needs. This is done so that settings can plan activities, resources or think about how best to work with the child or children. For this leaning outcome, you will need to show that you can be part of the assessment process of children or young people. Although every setting will have their own way of assessing children that you will need to use, there are some common points to bear in mind as the spider diagram shows.

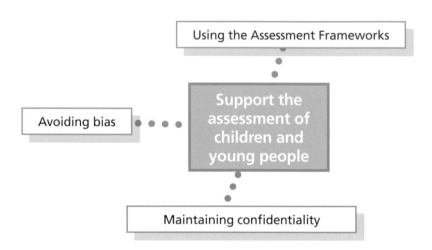

Figure 5: Points to bear in mind when assessing children

Over to You

Find if your setting uses an Assessment Framework.

Using the Assessment Framework(s)

In many settings, children and young people need to be assessed against the curriculum requirements or frameworks. If you work in England, you will for example need to think about what a child is doing in relation to the Early Years Foundation Stage, while if you are working in a school, you may think about curriculum requirements.

Confidentiality

We learn a lot about children and young people as a result of carrying out observations. This information is confidential and however tempting, you must not gossip about it. You must also make sure that anything that you have written down cannot be seen by people who are not working directly with the child or do not have a reason to see it. This means that if you do something for your tutor or course, you should not put the child's real name on anything. The case study shows what happens if confidentiality is broken.

Case study:
Breach of confidentiality

Tara is a trainee at a nursery. One of the children in her group, Sam, is the nephew of her next-door neighbour. After work one day, the next-door neighbour asks her about him. Tara tells her that the nursery are starting to worry about his speech and also that he doesn't seem to be playing with the other children. The next day the manager calls Tara into the office. She is not pleased at all. Sam's mother has been on the phone to complain that she has heard that Sam is being bullied and that he can't talk properly. Tara is shocked. She explains to the manager what she said. The manager tells Tara that she is never again to say anything about a child outside of the setting. She also tells Tara that if anything ever happens again, she will be sacked.

1. How did Tara breach confidentiality?
2. Why was Sam's mother angry?

Respect for a child's feelings is crucial

Avoiding bias

When we observe children it is important that we stay as objective as possible. This means just for a moment forgetting what we already know about them and really focusing on what they are doing at the time that we are watching them. If we cannot do this, the danger is that we can miss things about children and only notice what we are expecting to see.

Children's wishes, views and feelings

As children learn to communicate, we can encourage them to talk about their feelings and also what they have been doing. A child might say that the drawing that he has done is not very good or a young person may say that they would prefer that we did not assess them. When writing or talking about children we should always think about what we are saying and whether it is hurtful, even if they are not there. Showing respect at all times is, as we have already seen in this book, very important.

Information from parent, carers, children and young people, other professionals and colleagues

Children and young people behave in different ways according to who they are with and what they are doing. A child in our outdoor area may be keen on the tricycle, but when they are in the park with their parents, they may choose to use the climbing frame. A child who is quiet in a setting, may be a chatterbox with a childminder or with their parents. This means that when drawing conclusions about a child, it is essential that we use a range of sources.

How to meet identified development needs

After observing and then assessing children, the next thing that we need to do is to work out what the child's next steps are. Learning to do this can take time and experience. It is also important that you refer to the expected developmental norms for the child's age group. This will help you work out what is appropriate. Once you have worked out a child's needs, the next step is to think about how you might meet them e.g. if a child needs support with their hand—eye co-ordination, you might help think of toys, games and activities that will help them to practise them.

Reflect children's interests and views

Activities or ideas to support children's development do not work if children do not like them or are not interested. This is why it is important to base our ideas around what we have seen children doing and enjoying. Parents and others can also tell us about what the child enjoys doing. Once children can talk, we can also ask them what they would like to do. For children and young people who may have learning difficulties, we can use photographs and pictures so that they can point out what they would like to do.

Skills builder

Look at the following children's needs. For each child, think about how you might meet their needs.

- Leo is four years old. He loves playing with dinosaurs and dressing up. He needs to play more with the other children.

- Rosie is three years old. She loves helping adults. She needs work on her hand-eye co-ordination.

- Petra is eight years old. She enjoys making up games. She needs to work on her writing skills.

Functional Skills ICT: Finding and selecting information

You could use the internet to search for different activities that are suitable to develop the needs of the children listed above. You could print them off and show them to your tutor. When using the internet to find information, make sure that you consider any copyright restraints.

Through play for children in early years

Play is an important way of helping children to develop. As children love playing, it means that they can practise and develop skills without realising it. For children to enjoy their play, it has to be interesting for them and this is why it is important to understand their interests.

Play is an important way of meeting developmental children's needs

Providing challenge

Children do not like to be bored. This means that any ideas for activities or play opportunities must be exciting and be interesting for the child. They must also be challenging so that the child is doing something that will help them to make progress. Things that are too easy for children can also sometimes be boring for them.

This activity is helping these children's fine motor skills. These children are finding it exciting and challenging

Planning to be flexible

While we can draw up plans for activities and play opportunities, it does not mean that we have to stick with them rigidly as the case study shows. Children may come in not feeling like playing or may have other ideas about what they would like to do. The weather may change and it might be useful to do something outdoors or a child's interest might change. This is why it is important for planning to be flexible.

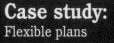

Case study:
Flexible plans

Jamie is working as a childminder. One of the children he works with is keen to ride a bicycle. Jamie watches her on the tricycle and can see that she is ready, so he plans to take the children to the park. He packs for an outing, including the bikes, helmets and a picnic. The little girl arrives late, wearing a plaster cast as she has broken her arm, very disappointed that she cannot go cycling. Jamie realises that he needs to change plan quickly. He decides to go to the park, but asks the children if they would like to build a field hospital with some tarpaulin and rugs. The children have a wonderful time. Some pretend to be bicycle 'ambulances', while the little girl in their makeshift hospital is the star patient. They have a picnic inside their hospital.

1. Why can't Jamie carry on with his original plan?

2. How does he change the plan to keep all the children happy?

Be able to support the development of children and young people

While it is useful to observe and plan for children's interests and needs, it is also important to work in ways that will support their development. This means carrying out activities that are tailored to meet their needs. It also means thinking about how well the activities work.

Activities to support holistic development

Most play opportunities and activities are supporting more than one area of development at once. The term for looking at all areas of development at once is 'holistic development'.

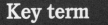

Key term

Holistic development: looking at all aspects of a child's development

It is important to consider children's emotional needs when carrying out activities

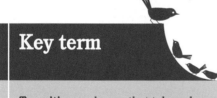

Record observations of the child's or young person's participation in the activities

It is always useful to observe children or young people as they take part in an activity. You need to think about whether the activity is enjoyable and whether the child is learning from it. This will help to plan other activities. When you can see that a child is interested and is gaining from an activity, it would be sensible to try to either repeat it or do something very similar another time.

Contributing to the evaluation of activities

It is important that we think about how the activities or play opportunities have helped a child or young person and also whether they were suitable. In some cases, we may realise that while the activity was useful, the child did not enjoy it. We may also realise that an activity or play opportunity could be repeated or adapted as a child seemed very interested and it worked well.

Know how to support children and young people experiencing transitions

There are times during children's and young people's lives when there will be changes. Some changes will be quite positive ones such as moving to a larger home, while others might be more difficult such as leaving a carer after a number of years. In this learning outcome, you will need to show that you understand the different type of changes that might take place and also that you know how adults can support children.

Different types of transition

Throughout childhood there are many different points when children have to cope with changes. Many of these are about growing up such as the change from being a child to becoming an adult or starting at a secondary school. Some changes are difficult for children such as when parents separate or when someone close to them dies. As a result of changes, some children's development can be affected. They become afraid, tearful or on the other hand angry and frustrated. Knowing what type of **transitions** children might face can help us to support them. The table over the page shows some of the more common transitions.

Table 7: Types of transition

Emotional	
Change in family circumstances	Parents may separate New people might join the family, e.g. step-brothers Siblings might be born Someone close to the child might become ill or die Families may become short of money or become wealthier Parents might start working away from home or longer hours Parents might lose their jobs or work from home
Changes in friendships	A friend might move away Friendships might change
Changes in carer/practitioner	Children might change nanny, au pair or move from one childminder to another
Physical	
Change in location	Families might move area or country Families might move home
Physiological	
Changes in health and body	Children may become ill or develop a chronic medical condition that requires treatment Older children will go through puberty
Intellectual	
Changes in setting (Each setting will have its own rules/style and expectations)	Children may move from one pre-school or nursery to another Children may move from one class into another Children may move from a small school where they are taught by just one teacher to a larger school where there are several teachers Children may start going to a breakfast club or an afterschool club
Other	
Daily transitions	As part of the routine — moving from one setting to another or going to a club or lesson
Between carers	Going between parents and practitioners Being with several practitioners e.g. going from one class to another or from one adult to another

Giving adult support

How to support children through transitions depends on:

- the age of the child/young person
- how difficult the change is likely to be
- the suddenness of the change.

Taking in new information

All of us find it hard to take in new information especially if it is life changing. This means that children and young people sometimes need time to think about what they have been told and may need to ask questions or seek reassurance later on.

Being honest

It is important to be as honest as possible so that children learn that they can trust adults. Telling children that they will love their new school is to be avoided as while it is important to be positive, what happens if they are unhappy to start with?

Timing

Knowing when to tell children/young people about changes can be tricky. With very young children, it is not always helpful to say things far ahead of time as they have little notion of 'after the summer' or 'next year'. It can though be helpful to introduce them to the concept of things ahead of time e.g. showing a child a new baby or reading a book about starting school.

Table 8 shows some specific ways of supporting children during transitions.

Table 8: Specific ways of supporting children during transitions

Emotional	
Change in family circumstances	Work closely with parents and share information about the child's needs Be ready to give children time so that they can talk about what is happening if they wish to Allow children to express their feelings Reassure the child Look out for more information from specialist organisations such as www.winstonswish.org.uk for helping a child to cope with bereavement.
Changes in friendships	Encourage children to express their feelings Help children to make new friends
Changes in carer/ practitioner	Work closely with other practitioners so that you can learn more about the child or they can Visit the practitioners so that the child can either get to know you or get to know them
Physical	
Change in location	Work closely with parents If a child is new, encourage them to talk about where they used to be/go Allow the child time to settle in Spend time with the child doing 1:1 activities so that they can get to know you Find out more about where the child is going
Physiological	
Changes in health and body	Work closely with parents and other professionals involved Look out for more information from specialist organisations Allow time for children to ask questions Be ready to reassure
Intellectual	
Changes in setting (Each setting will have its own rules/style and expectations)	Practitioners will need to work closely with each other to share information about children's needs, strengths and interests Children need to meet the person who will be with them Children need to see where they will be going Children need to be involved e.g. buying a uniform, planning a leaving party
Other	
Daily transitions	Work closely with parents/other settings When arriving, allow children sufficient time to settle in and adjust When leaving, give children plenty of warning and avoid rushing them
Between carers	Work closely with parents/other practitioners Aim to be consistent Consider using a diary that can travel with the child between different carers so that everyone knows what the child has done

This child is going to school for the first time. How can adults who work with this child help to make this a smooth transition?

Be able to support children's and young people's positive behaviour

It takes time and maturity for children and young people to work out how to behave in any given situation. It takes adults as well to act as guide. For this learning outcome, you will need to show that you can support the positive behaviour of children in your work setting.

Explain how a work setting can encourage children's and young people's positive behaviour

There are many ways in which we can help children/young people to learn about positive behaviour.

Developing positive relationships

We are all born to crave attention. Babies smile, make eye contact and enjoy being picked up very early on. Positive relationships play a key part in behaviour because children and young people need support and attention from us. If our relationships are not good, they cannot get positive attention easily and so are more likely to show unwanted behaviours to get our negative attention. Taking time to talk and have fun with children is therefore important.

Listening to children and valuing their opinions

Children need to express their feelings and opinions. Sometimes children may need help to do this, but it is important as otherwise they can become frustrated. Listening to what children want to do, the reasons why they are showing unwanted behaviour and ideas that they have are all ways of helping children to develop confidence.

Providing a stimulating and challenging environment

Children and young people enjoy having fun and learning, provided that the environment is stimulating. This means thinking about the type of equipment, resources and layout that is on offer. It is sometimes worth remembering that many children have the same toys at home and so bringing in unusual resources and activities can provide children with a challenge.

Planning experiences well

A key factor in unwanted behaviour is often boredom. Children and young people will find things to do that are not always desirable if nothing is available or if what has been planned is too easy or not of interest. Planning experiences is linked to understanding children's development, but also the individual needs and interests of the child.

Giving children choices

It can be very frustrating being a child as you do not have much control over where you go or who you see. Giving children choices allows children to learn about having some responsibility. It also means that they can be less frustrated. Choices need to be appropriate for the age and stage of development and also must be genuine. There is no point in asking a child if he would like to go outdoors, if there really isn't any choice.

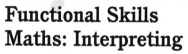

Functional Skills Maths: Interpreting

You could carry out a short survey with the children that you work with. You could give the children a choice of 4 or 5 different activities and ask them which their favourite is. You could record your answers on a tally chart and then put your answers in to a graph. You could set up the children's favourite activities for them and explain to your supervisor why you have chosen these activities.

Choices let children have responsibility

Meeting individual needs

For children to show positive behaviour, their basic needs must be met. These include food, love, attention as well as stimulation. Children also need to have sufficient sleep.

In addition, there is a link between children's behaviour, their language skills and stage of development. This means that young children tend to need more support and guidance, but as children develop language, they usually find it easier to control their behaviour. This means that, when working with children, we have to think about their stage of development.

Being inclusive

Children are individuals. And some children need more attention than others. Some will need more support or need reminding more often. Thinking about children as individuals and thinking about what they need is at the heart of inclusive practice. So too is thinking about our relationships with children and thinking about whether each child feels valued and cared for. When settings are showing inclusive practice, children tend to show positive behaviour.

Acting as role models

Children notice what adults do. It is one way in which they learn positive and sometimes unwanted behaviours such as swearing. This means that adults working with children have to show positive behaviours such as kindness, taking turns and gentleness.

Setting clear boundaries

Children are not born knowing the rules. It takes a while for them to know what is expected. This means that it is important for adults to set fair boundaries that are right for their age. As children become older, they should be involved in boundary setting. Boundaries must be appropriate for age and also explained to children e.g. 'we walk indoors to prevent accidents'.

Reinforcing positive behaviour

Everyone needs a little encouragement. So too do children. One of the ways that we can help children show positive behaviour is by giving them praise, encouragement and rewards. For this to be the most effective, it is important that children understand why we are pleased with them. It is also useful if there is not too much time between the praise and the event.

Encouraging children to resolve conflict

Once children are over three years old, they begin to play cooperatively. This means that by the age of four or so, many children can begin to resolve conflicts. Adults are needed though to help children learn how to do this. As children get older, adults need to take a step back and see if children can resolve conflict by themselves. When this happens, it is important to praise children and listen to how they managed it. Where children are finding this difficult, it is useful to act as a guide rather than to tell them exactly what they should do.

Help children understand why you are pleased with them

Looking for reasons for inappropriate behaviour

If they are happy, most children show positive behaviour for their age, unless they are tired, hungry or poorly. When children are often showing unexpected behaviour, it is important that practitioners work out the reasons why. This may mean talking to parents along with observing the child more closely. Event recordings are quite useful when looking at a child's behaviour as they can tell us how often a child is showing a certain behaviour and also when and where.

Following behaviour policy

Most settings have a behaviour policy. This is compulsory in settings that use the EYFS. A behaviour policy sets out how a setting intends to manage children's behaviour. It also has clear procedures that practitioners must follow to encourage positive behaviour and also to manage unwanted behaviour.

Following plans for individual behaviour

Some children and young people will need additional support so that they can learn to show positive behaviour. They may for example have a learning difficulty or their home circumstances may have changed. To support these children, it is usual for a plan to be drawn up. The plan will show what strategies adults need to use in certain situations. Sometimes these plans may be drawn up with the help of an educational psychologist. It is usual for parents also to be involved so that there is some consistency.

Encouraging engagement in positive behaviour

For this learning outcome, you will need to show that you can follow your work setting's behaviour policy and use some of the above strategies.

Over to You

Find out about your setting's behaviour policy.

Link

You can read more about supporting children's positive behaviour in TDA 2.9.

Functional Skills English: Writing

Writing the reflective account in the 'Getting ready for assessment' task is a good way to develop your writing skills. Organise your account into paragraphs and think carefully about your punctuation, spelling and grammar.

Getting ready for assessment

Look at the previous text and think about which strategies are used in your work setting. For each strategy explain why it is used in your setting. Write a reflective account about how you have used one or more of the strategies to promote a child's positive behaviour.

Reflecting on your own role

It is important for you to understand and think about your role in promoting positive behaviour. This means asking for feedback from colleagues, learning by watching how experienced adults work with children and also observing children's reactions. A good measure of whether you have handled a situation well is to consider the outcome at the time and how things played out afterwards as the case study below shows.

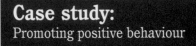

Case study:
Promoting positive behaviour

Dan works in an afterschool club. He notices that a new boy, Aran, is being excluded from a game of football being played by a group. Dan asks the group if he can join in. They agree. He tells the group that it is always nice when a group is friendly and allows others to join in. Soon, one of the boys shouts over to Aran to come and join them. Later, Dan goes up to the boy who shouted to Aran and quietly praises him. Dan is pleased to see that the group is still playing together later and that Aran has settled into it. Dan thinks about why his intervention has worked. He comes to the conclusion that sometimes it is better to help children show positive behaviour rather than just tell them what they should do.

1. Which strategies does Dan use to help children's positive behaviour?

2. Why is it important that Dan does not reprimand the group for playing without Aran?

Be able to use reflective practice to improve own contribution to child and young person development

No one working with children and young people gets it right all the time. There is a lot to learn and it is important that we keep thinking about how to improve. For the learning outcome, you will need to show that you can think about the way in which you work and how effectively it is helping children.

How effective is your contribution to assessments?

Observing children and thinking about their needs is as we have seen very important. While you are working with children, you need to be able to feedback to others about what you have seen. You may also be required to observe children using one of the methods that we looked at earlier. Learning to observe children is a skill and some methods take quite a lot of practice. It also takes a while to accurately work out what the observations mean and for a while you may need to check out how accurate you are.

How effective is your role?

The way that we work with children can have an impact on their development. You will need to show that you can think about how well you are able to work with children. There are many ways in which you can do this. You might like, for example, to ask your supervisor, tutor or a colleague to watch you work and then give you some feedback. You could also film or record yourself. Getting feedback can feel uncomfortable, but it is important as it can be very hard to be objective. As well as focusing on areas that you can improve, think also about what you are doing well. As well as asking for feedback, you could also observe how children and young people are reacting to you and the activity that you are doing. Think about whether they seem interested and also how well they concentrate. You could also consider how enthusiastic they seem and also whether they are enjoying being with you.

Changing your practice

There is no point in spending time on reflecting on your work, unless you are ready to have a go at doing things differently. You might agree what you need to do differently with your supervisor or tutor. Sometimes quite small changes make big differences e.g. bending right down to work with a child or giving a child enough time to answer a question.

Skills builder

Carry out an observation using a method that you have not used before. (You may need to ask your supervisor for permission and for advice first.) Afterwards think about what you have learnt about this child. Think also about what you have learnt from doing this observation. How could you improve for another time?

Functional Skills English: Speaking, listening and communication

Once you have completed this skills builder this opens up a good opportunity to have a discussion with your tutor about how you are developing your skills. Remember to present your ideas clearly and concisely.

Putting yourself at a child's level can make a big difference

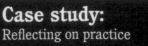

Case study:
Reflecting on practice

Trainee Anji has just started work in the daycare nursery toddler room. She plans a painting activity for two children but they are not interested and paint goes everywhere. Anji spends some time reflecting on what has happened. She realises that she does not know enough about the children's stage of development, and has not handled the situation well. After talking to her supervisor, she does some observations on the two children and also watches another member of staff working with them. She learns that toddlers need to do things in their own time and like to explore rather than follow instructions. She also sees the way in which the staff member makes eye contact and encourages the children rather than telling them what to do. The next week, Anji plans a new activity. She is more prepared and the activity is more appropriate for the children's stage of development.

1. What does Anji learn from reflecting on her practice?

2. Why is it helpful that she talks her ideas over with her supervisor?

Check your knowledge

1. Identify three different types of observation method.

2. Explain why it is important to record children in a range of situations.

3. What is meant by the term 'transition'?

4. Give three examples of transitions that are common in childhood.

5. Explain how you might support a child through transition.

6. Identify how reflective practice can help you to work better with children.

My Story

Vicki, nursery officer

I work in the baby room and we have to observe the babies all day. I carry out observations on my key children each day. We also fill in a little diary so that parents know what their child has done throughout the day. I find that parents like to see photographs of their children and so we try to put these into the diary as well. Recently, we have been experimenting with sending parents emails at work. It is proving very popular, although I am still getting to grips with the technology. It's not just about showing parents pictures though. I also use observations to check on development and to work out what the next steps are for 'my' babies. At first, I was not sure what to write down or what to observe, but now it is almost second nature. My tip for anyone new to this work is to look first of all at the milestones for the age group you are observing. This helps you to know what you should be looking out for.

Viewpoint: Reading

Many parents want their child to learn to read early. In most parts of the United Kingdom, children are being taught to read at around four or five years. In other countries, children do not begin until they are six or seven years. Many experts believe that our early start does not actually help children, as some children are not interested or ready. Interestingly, in international tests, our early start does not seem to make any difference. So at what age should we teach reading?

Ask the expert

Q What should you do if a child wants to leave an activity before it is over?

A Unless there is a safety issue, it is worth letting them go. Children do not learn and concentrate unless they are interested. But you should also be asking why they did not want to stay. Is it because the activity was not enjoyable or interesting? Is it because they were not with their friends? Could it be that there was not enough for them to do? Thinking this through will be the key to getting it right next time.

Q Why are young children not 'taught' more? I am on placement and everything seems to be about play.

A The starting point is to understand that, when young children are playing, they are actually learning. Formal teaching does not work well for young children as it usually involves a lot of sitting and listening. As children's language and thinking skills are still developing, they cannot process much information in this way. You may find that, after these type of activities, children have forgotten much of what was said. Play on the other hand is far more active and, if carefully planned, can provide heaps of learning.

Safeguarding the welfare of children & young people

Helping to keep children and young people safe is one of the basic jobs of anyone working with them. To do this you need to know what to look out for and what to do if you are concerned about the well-being of any child in your care.

Learning outcomes
By the end of this unit you will:

1. know about the legislation, guidelines, policies and procedures for safeguarding the welfare of children and young people including e-safety

2. know what to do when children or young people are ill or injured, including emergency procedures

3. know how to respond to evidence or concerns that a child or young person has been abused, harmed or bullied.

Know about the legislation, guidelines, policies and procedures for safeguarding the welfare of children and young people including e-safety

The news tells us of far too many cases of children or young people dying as a result of abuse or neglect. In many cases, the deaths could have been prevented if all the agencies working with children worked well together and responded to the clear signs that a child was at risk. Behind the headlines are many children who are leading unhappy lives and having their development affected by abuse, neglect or bullying. You can make a difference right from the start of your working life in your setting.

Getting ready for assessment

A clear understanding of the policies and procedures related to safeguarding, and the legislation behind them, is very important for anyone working in a setting for children or young people. To show that you are developing this understanding, think about these suggestions as you work through this unit.

- You could start a folder that you use to gather all such polices and procedures from your setting.

- You could make notes on any incident that affects the safeguarding of the children: for example, a security incident, fire alarm or child at risk.

- You could look out for items on the news about safeguarding issues – such as the Baby P case – or reports of serious case reviews.

- You could find newspaper cuttings or copy items from a news website (e.g. www.bbc.co.uk) and try to identify how the alarm was raised, if everyone followed procedures and any other useful information from the article.

Functional Skills English: Reading

By preparing for your assessment in this way you will be using and developing your English reading skills as you search for information to be included in your folder.

Key terms

Safeguarding: promoting children's welfare and putting measures in place to improve children's safety and prevent abuse

Child protection: action taken to protect a child when there is a reasonable belief that they are at risk of significant harm

Child abuse: harm or the likelihood of harm from physical, emotional or sexual abuse, neglect and failure to thrive not based on illness, or bullying and harassment

Over to You

Have a look at the relevant website below for your home country. Look at the others and see how legislation and policy vary between the UK nations.

- England: www.cpinfo.org.uk
- Northern Ireland: www.ci-ni.org.uk
- Wales: www.childreninwales.org.uk
- Scotland: www.childpolicyinfo. childreninscotland.org.uk

The Department for Education website on *Every Child Matters* (www.dfe.gov.uk/ everychildmatters/ safeguardingandsocialcare/) has a number of links to very useful additional information on safeguarding requirements.

Current legislation, guidelines, policies and procedures

Legislation and guidelines

Polices and procedures for **safeguarding** and **child protection** in settings for children and young people in England and Wales are the result of legislation passed in Parliament, including:

- in England and Wales, The Children Act 1989 and the Children Act 2004
- in Northern Ireland, Children (Northern Ireland) Order 1995.

The Children Act 1989 (England and Wales)/Children (Northern Ireland) Order 1995

These Acts were brought in with the aim of simplifying the laws that protect children and young people. They tell people what their duties are and how they should work together when **child abuse** is suspected.

Working Together to Safeguard Children (1999)

This provides guidelines for professionals in England and Wales to help them work with children who are at risk of harm.

Children Act 2004

The death of Victoria Climbié at the hands of her carers resulted in an independent inquiry, lead by Lord Laming, into her death in 2003. The Laming Report led to the Green Paper *Every Child Matters*, which in turn led to the Children Act 2004 in England and similar bills and Acts in all four countries in the UK.

The Act includes:

- the introduction of local authority's Children's Directors with responsibility for education and children's social services
- councillors for children's services with responsibility for local child welfare
- Local Safeguarding Children's Boards (LSCB) with powers to make sure that social services, the NHS, education services, the police and other services work together to protect vulnerable children
- a Common Assessment Framework to help agencies to identify needs of children
- revised arrangements for different agencies to share information.

Working Together to Safeguard Children 2006

This updates safeguarding and how agencies should work individually and together to safeguard and promote the welfare of children.

The Vetting and Barring Scheme

Anyone who wants to work with children, young people or vulnerable adults must register with the Independent Safeguarding Authority (ISA). The ISA checks every person who applies by looking at their CRB (Criminal Records Bureau) check, any relevant criminal convictions, cautions, police intelligence and other appropriate sources before registering them.

Over to You

Look out for the recommendations from the Munro Review, the final report from which is due in April 2011.

Over to You

Get a copy of your setting's safeguarding policy and find out answers to the following questions.

- Where is it kept?
- Is it available to parents and carers?
- Is everyone's role clear?
- Do you know who the named person for safeguarding is in your setting?

Functional Skills ICT: Finding and selecting information

The internet is a vast resource of information and useful resources to support your role. Searching these websites is a good way of developing your ICT skills.

Policies and procedures

All settings working with children and young people must have the following:

- a policy for the protection of children under the age of 18 that states responsibilities and is reviewed annually

- arrangements to work with the Local Safeguarding Children Board

- a duty to inform the Independent Safeguarding Authority of any individual (paid employee, volunteer or other) who is a threat to children

- up-to-date training on safeguarding for all staff, governors and volunteers

- a named senior member of staff in charge of safeguarding arrangements

- effective risk assessment of the provision to check that the safeguarding policy and plans work

- arrangements for CRB checks on all adults who have regular, unsupervised access to children up to the age of 18

- a single, central record of all checks on provider staff and, where appropriate, governors and volunteers

- contact details of a parent or carer for all children under the age of 18.

Functional Skills English: Reading

This task will help you to develop your reading skills as you use the information contained in your policy to answer these questions.

E-safety

Many children and young people have access to the internet and the use of a mobile phone.

The internet, mobile phones and video games all have benefits, but they also hold a number of risks to children and young people.

The Byron Review (2008) reported on the risks to children from exposure to potentially harmful or inappropriate material on the internet and in video games, and issued guidance on how they should be protected.

Figure 1: Risks from technology

Over to You

- Have a look at the guidance given by the Plymouth Safeguarding board on Cybersafety:
- www.plymouth.gov.uk/safeguarding_children_in_cyber_world.pdf
- Find out if your setting has a policy about e-safety. If so, did it come from the Local Safeguarding Children's Board?

Reducing the risk

No one can make the internet completely safe, and people are constantly thinking of new ways to abuse children through it. However, it is possible to reduce the risk to children and help them to use it safely, through measures including:

- blocking access to unsuitable sites and content
- limiting time spent on the computer
- making children aware of the dangers
- helping children to know how to recognise danger
- helping children to develop skills to deal with situations they are not happy with
- educating parents and carers about the risks and controls.

Skills builder

You can help children to develop the skills they need to recognise dangers when using technology. Design a poster to explain to children the dangers of mobile phones and the internet and what they should do if they are worried.

Functional Skills ICT: Developing, presenting and communicating information

By completing this poster on the computer you could practise using your editing techniques by adding images, colour and text to your poster. You could ask your manager if you could display your poster in your setting.

Key term

ChildLine: a 24-hour free phone service for children to contact if they are in danger or risk of harm from anyone

The roles of different agencies involved in safeguarding

When a child or young person has been abused or harmed, the first response will be at the point of the discovery. This might be at school, in a medical setting or by a child contacting a helpline, such as **ChildLine** (0800 1111).

All children are known to a number of different organisations. Joint working between all those involved is an important part of effective safeguarding. Here are the main organisations, services and professionals that would normally be involved in safeguarding a child or young person.

- Any **setting** a child attends, including a childminder, nursery, school, afterschool or holiday scheme, will have a role to play in safeguarding the child.

- **Social services** have a legal responsibility to support vulnerable children and families in need. Most social workers are employed by social services.

- **Health visitors** have responsibility for the health of babies and young children under five. They provide support and guidance to the parents of young children and carry out assessments of a child's development.

- **General Practitioners** (GPs) work in the community. They are often the first people to identify possible abuse when a child attends surgery.

- **Local hospital services,** such as accident and emergency units or minor injury units, may see a child who has received an injury.

- **Probation services** support people convicted of some offences to be rehabilitated into the community. They monitor people convicted of offences against children to make sure they do not pose a threat to local children.

- **Police** are involved in the criminal proceedings that may result from safeguarding issues.

- **Child psychology services** will often be needed to support children who have experienced abuse or harm.

Case study:
The health visitor's role

Jane is a health visitor based in a health centre. She carries out checks to ensure babies are safe and developing. Jane also runs child health clinics, which are often the first place families go to if they are concerned about their child. Jane also works with school nurses, the local children's centre, social services, housing services, the police and local doctors.

How do you think Jane might find out if a child is at risk?

Know what to do when children or young people are ill or injured, including emergency procedures

It is important to know what to do if a child or young person in your care is ill or injured. It is too easy to panic when faced with this situation. Make sure you are familiar with the signs and symptoms of common injuries and illnesses, what to do and most importantly when to get expert help.

Signs and symptoms of common childhood illnesses

Most children will become ill in their setting at some time. In most cases this will be with a minor illness, showing as one or more of the following:

- raised temperature
- feeling or being sick

Key term

Incubation period: the time before someone shows signs of an illness after catching it

- diarrhoea
- tiredness
- loss of energy
- loss of appetite.

Table 1 shows some of the common signs and symptoms, treatment needed and the **incubation period** (the time before the child shows signs of the illness after catching it).

Table 1: Signs, symptoms and treatment for common illnesses

Illness	Signs and symptoms	Treatment	Incubation period
Common cold	Sneezing, sore throat, runny nose, headache, temperature	Treat symptoms with rest, plenty of fluids Encourage child to blow nose	1–3 days
Gastroenteritis	Vomiting, diarrhoea, dehydration	Replace fluids (encourage child to drink water), seek medical help	1–36 hours
Tonsillitis	Very sore throat, fever, headache, aches and pains	Rest, fluids, medical attention as antibiotics may be needed	Varies
Scarlet fever	Fever, loss of appetite, sore throat, pale around the mouth, 'strawberry tongue', bright pinpoint rash over face and body	Rest, fluids and observe for complications	2–4 days
Dysentery	Vomiting, diarrhoea with blood and mucus, abdominal pain, fever and headache	Medical attention, rest, fluids Strict hygiene measures, e.g. careful hand washing	1–7 days
Chicken pox	Fever, very itchy rash with blister-type appearance	Tepid bath with sodium bicarbonate, and calamine applied to skin to stop itching Try to stop child scratching to avoid scarring	10–14 days
Measles	At first high fever, runny nose and eyes; later cough, white spots in mouth, blotchy red rash on body and face	Rest, fluids, tepid sponging Medical attention to check for complications	7–15 days
Mumps	Pain and swelling of jaw, painful swallowing, fever May be swollen testes in boys	Fluids (may need a straw to drink), warmth to swelling, pain relief	14–21 days
Rubella (German measles)	Slight cold, sore throat, swollen glands behind ears, slight pink rash	Rest, treat symptoms Avoid contact with pregnant women	7–21 days
Pertussis (whooping cough)	Snuffly cold, spasmodic cough with whooping sound and vomiting	Medical attention Rest, fluids, feed after a coughing attack	7–21 days
Meningitis	Fever, headache, drowsiness, confusion, dislike of light, very stiff neck May be red rash that does not disappear with pressure	Immediate urgent medical attention Take child to hospital	2–10 days

What to do when someone is ill or injured

Just think how you feel when you don't feel well. When you have a heavy cold or upset stomach, what do you want?

Probably the answer includes:

- going to bed
- being made a fuss of
- someone to look after you
- being told you will be okay.

Children who are ill need exactly the same. They need comforting and reassuring until a parent or carer can come and collect them. This should be in a quiet area away from the main area of the setting. As a student or junior worker, tell your supervisor if a child is ill and they will make the decision about contacting parents and the medical services.

In nearly all cases a child is infectious to others before he or she has any symptoms. Many illnesses have a cold or fever as their first signs; it would not be possible to exclude all children with these symptoms from nursery, nor would it have much effect on the spread of a disease. Different settings have different rules about excluding children with common illnesses, ranging from excluding all children with symptoms, to exclusion only while the child feels unwell.

You should always make sure that you follow the routines that help to protect children from illness, such as careful hand washing and cleanliness of toilet areas.

Supporting a child who is unwell

Best practice checklist: Supporting a sick child

✓ Take the child to a quiet area of the setting

✓ Sit quietly with them, possibly read a story

✓ Inform parents or carers about the child's condition

✓ Check if the child has any medicines they should be taking

✓ Reassure other children who were with the child

✓ Make sure an incident/illness form is completed

Over to You

- Ask your supervisor for the policy about children being ill in your placement. What does the policy tell you? What is the exclusion policy for illnesses?

- Find out what sort of advice is given to parents by staff when their children are ill.

Medicines

After an illness a child may need to take medicine while at nursery or school. Your setting will have a policy that parents must give written consent for their child to have medicines administered by the nursery nurse or teacher. Childcare workers are not allowed to give medicines to children without this written permission under any circumstances.

Recognising the need for urgent medical attention

Sometimes a child may need urgent medical attention because of an illness or injury. Time can be very important in preventing the child's condition getting worse.

It is important to ensure that a child is seen by a doctor as soon as possible if they have any of the following:

- continuing high temperature
- severe headache
- persistent or strange crying
- breathlessness
- very pale and lifeless appearance
- rash that does not disappear when pressed with a glass
- persistent vomiting
- persistent diarrhoea.

If necessary, phone 999 for an ambulance — do not wait for the child's parent or carer to arrive.

Link See PEFAP 001 and MPII002 for more detail on helping children or young people who may need urgent medical attention.

Responding to emergency situations

Emergency procedures

As part of the Health and Safety at Work Act 1974 and its regulations, your setting will have a safety policy if it employs five or more staff. The policy will cover emergency procedures in the event of a fire, accident or other emergency. There are many different types of emergency and it is important to know what the different procedures are, especially for fires, a security incident or if a child goes missing.

What is an emergency?

Emergencies can be caused by:

- illnesses
- accidents
- fire
- missing children
- security incidents
- other serious threats.

Arrangements for emergency situations

All settings should have clear arrangements for emergency situations including emergency contact numbers, clear instructions and evacuation procedures.

Emergency contact numbers

Every child should have a record card with the emergency contact numbers of parents, grandparents or other relatives. They should be people who are usually easy to contact, and who in turn can contact the parents if necessary.

The person in charge must get in touch with the emergency contact as soon as possible and tell that person about the incident, and where the child is being taken. If the child has to go to hospital before the parents arrive, someone the child knows well should go to the hospital with them.

Clear instructions

Your setting should issue and display instructions that make it clear:

- where emergency exits are
- where to meet if the building has to be evacuated
- who is responsible for what
- what to do if a child goes missing
- what to do if there is a fire
- what to do if there is a threat to the security of the children.

Evacuation procedures

A building may need to be evacuated in the event of a fire, gas leak or bomb scare. In most settings, identified members of staff are responsible for the procedures and they will make sure that all staff know what to do.

Evacuation practices should be held every three months and notices must be displayed telling people what to do.

Fires

Make sure that you know where the fire exits are in your setting. Never put anything in the way of a fire exit. Here is what you should do – and not do – in the event of a fire in your setting.

- Close doors and windows and try to get the children out of the premises by the normal routes.
- Do not leave the children unattended.
- Do not stop to put out the fire (unless very small).
- Call the fire brigade by telephone as soon as possible as follows:
  - lift the receiver and dial 999
  - give the operator your telephone number and ask for FIRE
  - when the fire brigade replies, give the information clearly: for example, fire at the Tall Trees Nursery, 223 Southfield Rd, Anytown, XY5 3ZA, situated between the police station and the Indian restaurant
  - do not replace the receiver until the address has been repeated by the fire operator.

Over to You

Think about how practice evacuations happen in your setting by looking at these questions.

- When did your placement have a practice evacuation?
- What happened during the practice?
- How are children reassured during the practice?
- Are the children praised and thanked for their help in carrying out the evacuation?
- Is an activity, such as reading a story or playing a game, provided afterwards to help the children settle down quickly after the practice?

Security incidents

All settings must have measures to stop unauthorised people having access to the children or young people. Many settings have an audible alarm that sounds when any doors to the outside are opened. Staff should know what to do if anyone tries to gain access to the setting. This should include:

- checking the identity of the person
- making sure they sign the visitor book
- making sure they are not left alone with children unless they are authorised to do so
- refusing entrance to anyone they are unsure of
- calling the police if it is felt anyone is a serious danger to children.

Missing children

If all precautions are taken and policies followed, no child should go missing! However, most people can give an example of a child they know going missing — even if only for a few seconds in a supermarket.

Check all areas of the setting and, if the child is not around, inform the senior person in charge.

If you suspect a child is missing, raise the alarm immediately!

Next actions will depend on where the child is missing from, but they are likely to include:

- making sure all other children are safe and occupied
- checking where and when the child was last seen
- phoning the police and the child's parents
- starting an organised search
- keeping someone at the last point the child was seen if outside.

Know how to respond to evidence or concerns that a child or young person has been abused, harmed or bullied

All settings that have contact with children and young people must have clear polices and procedures to follow in all cases of abuse. Staff must have training in these and there should be a clear line of responsibility within the organisation for dealing with the situation.

Disclosure of abuse by a child can occur at any time, and can be shocking to hear. The way a disclosure is responded to can be very important in the outcome to a child, even many years later. There have been many examples in the past of children not being believed at the time they told someone, often resulting in serious problems later in life. The checklist below shows some of the things you should do if a child tells you that he or she has been abused.

> ## Best practice checklist: Disclosure of abuse
>
> ✓ Listen carefully to what the child says
> ✓ Try not to display shock or disbelief
> ✓ Do not ask direct or leading questions
> ✓ Let the child talk without pressure
> ✓ Accept what is being said
> ✓ Stress that it is right to tell
> ✓ Reassure and support the child
> ✓ Never promise to keep a child's disclosure a secret
> ✓ Do not criticise the abuser – the child may well still love him or her
> ✓ Promptly follow the procedures for your setting

Characteristics of different types of child abuse

The presence of the signs of abuse (see Figure 2) does not necessarily mean that a child has been abused; however, they can help responsible adults to recognise that something is wrong. However, not every sign means a child is being abused. Have you cared for children who always appear a bit grubby and maybe smell a little, but are happy and loved by parents? Some physical signs such as darkened areas can be birthmarks and not bruising: for example, some infants of Asian or African heritage can have a dark bluish area on their lower back and/or buttocks. This is sometimes known as a Mongolian Blue Spot.

Physical abuse

Physical abuse is when a child is physically hurt or injured. Hitting, kicking, beating with objects, throwing and shaking are all physical abuse. They can cause pain, cuts and bruising, broken bones and sometimes even death.

Signs and symptoms of physical abuse include:

- unexplained recurrent injuries or burns
- unexplained bruises
- wearing clothes to cover injuries, even in hot weather
- refusal to undress for games
- bald patches of hair
- repeated running away

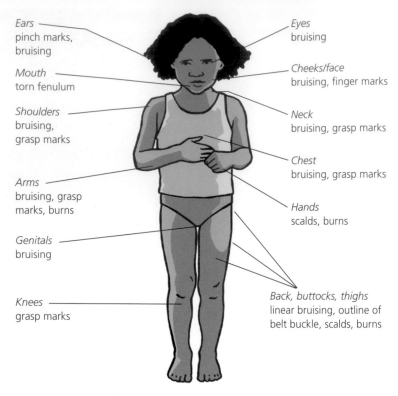

Ears
pinch marks,
bruising

Mouth
torn fenulum

Shoulders
bruising,
grasp marks

Arms
bruising, grasp
marks, burns

Genitals
bruising

Knees
grasp marks

Eyes
bruising

Cheeks/face
bruising, finger marks

Neck
bruising, grasp marks

Chest
bruising, grasp marks

Hands
scalds, burns

Back, buttocks, thighs
linear bruising, outline of
belt buckle, scalds, burns

Figure 2: Indicators of possible physical abuse

- fear of medical examination

- aggression towards self and others

- fear of physical contact – shrinking back if approached or touched.

Many signs of physical abuse can be confused with genuine accidental injuries. However, they are often not in the places or distribution you would expect, or the explanation does not fit, or you may see the outline of a belt buckle or cigarette burn. Your suspicion should be aroused if the parents have not sought medical advice soon after the injury occurs.

Case study:
Suspicious bruising

Jade, aged five, has been away from school for two days due to 'being unwell' in the note from her mother. You are helping her to change for PE in the hall and she jumps when you are pulling her jumper off. The back of her upper arms and back are covered in deep purple bruising. When you gently ask how they happened, she shrugs and says she fell off her bunk bed.

1. What should you do now?

2. What should you not do?

3. Whom should you talk to about this?

Emotional abuse

Emotional abuse is when a child is not given love, approval or acceptance. A child may be constantly criticised, blamed, sworn and shouted at, told that other people are better than he or she is and rejected by those the child looks to for affection. Seeing someone else — especially a child's parent or sibling — being abused is emotional abuse. Think about how domestic violence could affect a child.

Signs and symptoms of emotional abuse include:

- delayed development

- sudden speech problems, such as stammering

- low self-esteem, such as saying 'I'm stupid/ugly/worthless'

- fear of any new situation

- neurotic behaviour, such as rocking, hair twisting or self-mutilation

- extremes of withdrawal or aggression.

Neglect

Neglect, which can result in failure to thrive, is when parents or others looking after a child do not provide the child with proper food, warmth, shelter, clothing, care and protection.

Signs and symptoms can include:

- constant hunger
- poor personal hygiene
- constant tiredness
- poor state of clothing
- unusual thinness
- untreated medical problems
- poor social relationships
- stealing food
- destructive tendencies.

Case study:
Possible neglect

Toby is six years old and has an older sister, Sam, who is 11. Their parents both have drinking problems. Sometimes there is nothing to eat in the house. Sam is often left alone to look after her younger brother. The school they both go to has noticed that they are always tired and appear very thin. Their clothes are often dirty and Toby is often in the same clothes for a few days. One day, when Sam comes to collect Toby from the classroom to go home, he bursts into tears and says he does not want to go home.

1. What do you think Toby's teacher should do?

2. What do you think should have already happened?

Sexual abuse

Sexual abuse occurs when a child is forced or persuaded into sexual acts or situations by others. Children might be encouraged to look at pornography, be harassed by sexual suggestions or comments, be touched sexually or forced to have sex.

Signs and symptoms include:

- sexual knowledge or behaviour that is inappropriate to the child's age
- medical problems such as chronic itching, pain in the genitals or venereal diseases
- depression, self-mutilation, suicide attempts, running away, overdoses or anorexia
- personality changes such as becoming insecure or clinging
- regressing to earlier behaviour patterns such as thumb-sucking or bringing out discarded cuddly toys
- sudden loss of appetite or compulsive eating
- being isolated or withdrawn
- an inability to concentrate
- lack of trust or fear of someone they know well, such as not wanting to be alone with a babysitter or childminder
- starting to wet or soil again, day or night
- becoming worried about clothing being removed
- suddenly drawing sexually explicit pictures
- trying to be 'ultra-good' or perfect and overreacting to criticism.

Bullying and harassment

This is also a form of abuse that affects older children particularly. It can continue for a long time and can include one or more of the following:

- emotional bullying including not speaking and excluding ('being sent to Coventry'), tormenting, ridicule and humiliation

Over to You

Did you know that an estimated 77,000 under-16s run away from home each year, putting themselves in considerable danger of physical or sexual assault? Some 80 per cent of runaways say it is due to family problems. More than 20,000 of the runaways are under 11 years old. Runaways under 11 are more likely to have experienced physical abuse at home.

- physical bullying including pushing, kicking, hitting, pinching and other forms of violence
- verbal bullying including name-calling, threats, sarcasm, spreading rumours and persistent teasing
- racist bullying involving racial taunts, writing graffiti and gestures
- sexual bullying involving unwanted physical contact or abusive comments
- homophobic bullying including hostile or offensive action against lesbians, gay males or bisexuals, or those thought to be lesbian, gay or bisexual.

Bullying can be carried out by one person against another, or by groups of people 'ganging up' on a person. Bullying is not always a personal, face-to-face attack, but can also be through technology such as mobile phones and the internet. This is known as cyberbullying.

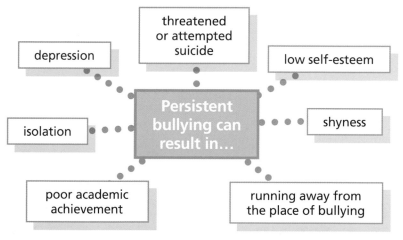

Figure 3: Effects of persistent bullying

Over to You

If you want more information, the websites for the NSPCC, ChildLine or Kidscape have good sections:

- ChildLine www.childline.org.uk provides telephone support and guidance to children being abused (a good source of information for child professionals)
- Kidscape www.kidscape.org.uk a registered charity committed to keeping children safe from harm and abuse
- Bullying Online www.bullying.co.uk offers advice on bullying.

Case study:
Supporting a child who has been bullied

Aysha, aged 13, rings ChildLine because she is being bullied at school. She often has things stolen from her, especially new school bags or trainers. The two girls who are bullying her started at primary school by calling her names and following her home. Now they have started to push her over if she walks past them. Aysha has started to miss going to school to avoid meeting the bullies. The telephone counsellor encourages Aysha to ask a friend to go with her to talk to the head of her year.

1. Why do you think it has taken so long for Aysha to tell someone?
2. How do you think this has made Aysha feel about herself?
3. What do you think you could have done if you were working with Aysha?

Over to You

Use the weblinks below to look through these two documents:

- the Byron report – both the summary for professionals and parents and the report for children (www.dcsf.gov.uk/byronreview/)

- guidance by the Plymouth Safeguarding Children Board on cybersafety (www.plymouth.gov.uk/safeguarding_children_in_cyber_world.pdf).

Can you think of ways you could use some of the recommendations at work? Find out if your Local Safeguarding Children's Board (LSCB) has produced any guidance.

Functional Skills English: Reading

This task requires you to read a number of different articles. This is a good way of developing your reading skills.

The risks involved with new technologies

'By 2012 every household in Britain should have access to Broadband.'

Gordon Brown, January 2009

An admirable ambition with huge benefits for everyone – especially in relation to research and learning. However, it is also fraught with dangers, as the internet and mobile network also offer possibilities for the abuse of children and young people. Most children and young people have access to the internet and the use of a mobile phone. Both offer benefits to children but equally can expose them to threats to their safety and well-being.

The risks that the internet, mobile phones and video games pose to children and young people include cyberbullying, access to unsuitable sites, exposure to commercial sites and danger from adults seeking to exploit children. The independent Byron Review (2008) reported on the risks to children from exposure to potentially harmful or inappropriate material on the internet and in video games, and issued guidance on how they should be protected.

Supporting a child using technology

Reducing the risk

Short of banning all access to the internet and mobile phones, it is not possible to eliminate the risks to children and young people. No one can make the internet completely safe, and people are constantly inventing new ways of misusing it. However it is possible to build children's resilience to the material to which they may be exposed so that they have the confidence and skills to use the internet more safely.

The Byron Report identified three key objectives to protect children:

● reduce availability

● restrict access

● increase resilience to harmful and inappropriate material online.

There are a number of measures available that start to meet some of these objectives, including:

● parental controls that allow internet sites with unsuitable material to be limited

● blocks on use, such as blocking out sites through content controls

● improving the knowledge, skills and understanding around e-safety of children, parents and other responsible adults.

The last point is one that schools and other educational settings can be involved in.

Ways in which you can help to improve children's knowledge and skills include:

● making them aware of the dangers

● helping them to develop the skills to recognise danger

● supporting them in dealing with situations they are not happy with.

Combined with a sensible approach — making sure that children do not spend time on the computer unsupervised or for too long a time — these tools can make using the internet a useful and enjoyable experience.

Educating parents and carers is also important. Many parents and carers are less skilled at using the internet than their children are, and they may not be aware of the dangers or know how to control access to certain material.

Functional Skills ICT: Developing, presenting and communicating information

You could do a short presentation on how to stay safe on the computer and deliver this presentation to other people on your course. You could link this back to how your setting promotes internet safety; this is a good way to share good practice.

Functional Skills English: Writing

This skills builder exercise provides you with a good opportunity to practise writing for a different purpose.

Skills builder

You can help with educating parents. Using the information from the Byron Report — especially the report for children — design a booklet or poster aimed at informing parents of:

● the dangers of mobile phones and the internet

● the actions they need to take to protect their children when using the internet.

Responding to concerns about a colleague

If you are worried that a colleague may not be correctly applying safeguarding procedures or harming a child or young person you have a responsibility to the child.

Key term

Whistle blowing: passing on information about the behaviour of colleagues or managers in your setting

Confidentiality: making sure that personal information is available only to those authorised to have access

Named person: a senior member of staff with responsibility for safeguarding including contacting social services if there is concern about the welfare of a child

In either of these situations you need to 'blow the whistle'. The children at risk are the most important people. You should immediately speak to the designated person for safeguarding in your setting. If that person is the one you are concerned about, go to the senior person in the setting. If neither is available or you cannot tell them for any reason, you have two options:

- contact your local social services emergency desk – look the number up in your local telephone directory

OR

- contact your country's inspectorate, which has a legal responsibility for complaints about providers.

Ofsted is able to take action when there are concerns about:

- child protection concerns about a specific child/children or
- concerns/allegations about wider or systemic failure in safeguarding practice in a local authority or in a care or educational setting.

You can reach Ofsted for England on 0300 1233155 (their dedicated whistle-blowing hotline) or try emailing them at whistleblowing@ofsted. gov.uk. For more information, visit the Ofsted website at www.ofsted. gov.uk/Ofsted-home/About-us/Contact-us/Safeguarding-children-Ofsted-s-whistleblower-hotline.

Remember – you have a responsibility to the children and young people you work with to report incidents that put children at risk – even if people much more senior than you are involved! Failing to do so is a breach of that responsibility.

Confidentiality and when to share information

Link You will have read about confidentiality in SHC 21. You may wish to reread the section there before reading on.

As a practitioner, you need to have a clear understanding of the principles and boundaries of **confidentiality** – and also when you do need to share information.

How many times has someone asked if you can keep a secret? Some things like what your friend is buying someone as a gift can be kept secret. A child telling you they have found something exciting in the play area can be kept secret. However, a child asking if you can keep something secret that they are upset about needs treating with care.

Anything a child tells you that could affect their safety or well-being cannot be kept to yourself – it needs sharing through the bounds of professional confidentiality. This means that colleagues who need to know must be told. The first person you should tell anything to do with safeguarding is your setting's **named person**. This person will then take the burden of information from you. You should not share the information with others unless asked to by the named person.

If you find yourself in this situation, tell the child that you might not be able to keep the information secret. It is not fair to say that you will and then break their trust.

Information about or from children should be confidential. This means it should only be shared with those who need to know. This includes the child's parents and other staff or professionals who need to know the results (for example, psychologists or speech therapists). All records about a child should be kept in the child's file. The Data Protection Act and Freedom of Information legislation give parents access to information written about their children. You should never put anything on paper or file that is untrue or not based on evidence.

If you feel a child is at risk, you should share that information with the designated safeguarding person or your supervisor.

Functional Skills English: Speaking, listening and communication

This case study is a good discussion starter. You could hold this discussion with other people on your course to see how they would have dealt with this situation. Listen carefully to what they say so that you can respond in an appropriate way.

Case study:
Maintaining confidentiality

Jason is finishing an activity with Dylan, a four-year-old boy. He notices some strange marks on Dylan's arms that look like cigarette burns and Dylan is being unusually quiet, although he is talking about mummy's new friend. On the bus on the way home, Jason tells his friend about Dylan and what he has noticed.

1. What is Jason doing wrong?

2. Who should Jason tell?

Check your knowledge

1. Identify three requirements of the Children Act 2008.

2. Name three different agencies that might be involved in the safeguarding of children and young people.

3. When might a child need urgent medical attention?

4. What does the term 'incubation period' mean?

5. What are the main signs and symptoms of meningitis?

6. List three indicators of physical abuse.

7. List three indicators of emotional abuse.

8. List three indicators of sexual abuse.

9. What should you do if you suspect a child has been harmed or abused?

10. What does 'confidentiality' mean in a work setting?

My Story

Sonya, Support worker in Seaview Children's Centre

For the last two years I have been working at a children's centre, providing play and educational activities. The centre has children from babies to children aged 11 years in the breakfast club and the afterschool club. I'm working in the toddler room at the moment but have spent time with all the age groups. I recognise the importance of following safeguarding procedures and making sure the setting is a safe place for children. We work with families who live in a very deprived area of the town and many who are under a lot of stress.

Viewpoint

The Laming Report was very critical about the way different agencies work together to protect children, and you may often read stories of social workers not realising how neglected a child was, or not passing messages to other agencies.

What key points about safeguarding have you learned that would help you in the role of a support worker in a children's centre?

Ask the expert

Q Have you had any cases of children who you were concerned about? If so, how did you deal with them?

A We have a number of children at the centre who have been at risk or we have been concerned about. We work closely with parents to help them develop better skills to look after their children. One young mum was not coping very well and told her social worker that her boyfriend was abusing her. At our team meeting, we discussed the risk to her son Cain who was three at the time. I was working with him when I noticed he was very quiet and withdrawn- he is usually quite noisy! I told Jean, our named person, about my worries and she contacted the social worker. It turned out that Cain had seen his mum's boyfriend hitting her and being verbally abusive. Social workers helped her to find a safe place to live and worked with the family.

Contribute to children's and young people's health & safety

Anyone who works with children should know how to identify and minimise risks to the safety and well-being of children and young people. It is also important to know what to do if an accident or incident happens.

Learning outcomes

By the end of this unit you will:

1. know the health and safety policies and procedures of the work setting

2. be able to recognise risks and hazards in the work setting and during off-site visits

3. know what to do in the event of a non-medical incident or emergency

4. know what to do in the event of a child or young person becoming ill or injured

5. be able to follow the work setting procedures for reporting and recording accidents, incidents, emergencies and illnesses

6. be able to follow infection control procedures

7. know the work setting's procedures for receiving, storing and administering medicines.

Know the health and safety policies and procedures of the work setting

Childhood is all about learning from experiences. However, children and young people often do not think about the risks or dangers of their actions. When a toddler reaches to try to get hold of that exciting curly wire, they cannot know that it leads to a kettle full of very hot water; when they see those brightly coloured sweets, they cannot know that they are actually drugs. A four-year-old who can't wait to get into the sandpit does not know about the dangers of dog faeces.

Every year over 300 children under 15 years of age die in the UK from an accidental injury. Accidents are the greatest cause of death and a major cause of disability and ill health. Over 100,000 children are admitted to hospital and over two million visit accident and emergency departments each year.

Health and safety policies and procedures of the work setting

There are a number of legal and regulatory requirements that help to protect children and adults in any setting.

Since 2008, all early years settings in the UK have to comply with the Statutory Framework for the Early Years Foundation Stage. This covers every aspect of the welfare of children in all early years settings, including:

- safeguarding
- suitable people
- suitable premises and equipment
- organisation
- documentation.

England, Scotland, Northern Ireland and Wales each have a slightly different version of the framework. The Inspectorates for each country check that settings follow the framework. These are:

- Ofsted in England
- HMIe in Scotland
- ESTYN in Wales
- The ETI in Northern Ireland.

In addition to the Early Years Framework, health and safety legislation sets out legal requirements to keep everyone safe in different situations in each of the countries in the United Kingdom. Table 1 gives details of the main pieces of legislation you need to be aware of.

Over to You

Find out what the EYFS requirements are in your country.

Table 1: Health and safety legislation

Legislation	What it applies to	Extra information
Health and Safety at Work Act 1974	Safety of anyone in a work or public place	Responsibility of employers for buildings, equipment and policies Everyone has responsibility to apply it
Kitemarking CE product safety marking	Safety of all products — paid for by manufacturer Legal standards for products including toys	 Product safety markings
Motor Vehicles (Wearing of Seat Belts) (Amendment) Regulations 2006	Wearing of seats belts in vehicles	Children under 12 years of age should not use an adult seat belt in the front seat
Control of Substances Hazardous to Health (COSHH) Regulations 2002	Clear labelling of dangerous substances, e.g. cleaning materials	The labelling of hazardous substances
Reporting of Injuries, Diseases and Dangerous Occurrences Regulations (RIDDOR) 1995	Reporting of accidents or incidents at work or in public places	
Childcare Act 2006 Regulation of Care (Scotland) Act 2001 and the appropriate National Care Standards	Standards for care settings, including ratios of staff to children	
Smoking ban — UK-wide in indoor public places from July 1st 2007	Smoking in public places or places of employment	EYFS also states no smoking in childcare environments
Food hygiene legislation 2006 (European directives)	Safe storage and preparation of food	Anyone involved in handling food to have a food hygiene qualification
Manual Handling Operations Regulations 1992	Safe lifting and moving of people and equipment	

The Health and Safety Executive website has more detail about these and other health and safety issues, at www.hse.gov.uk/

Health and Safety at Work Act 1974

All places of work are covered by the Health and Safety at Work Act 1974 for Great Britain. Your employer has responsibility for the health and safety of the children, staff and visitors. However, everyone who works for them also has a responsibility for the health and safety of anyone who is there.

The Act states that:

- buildings should be well maintained and be planned and designed with safety of users in mind
- the general environment should be clean and safe
- equipment must be used and stored safely
- working practices must promote the health and safety of children.

The Act helps to protect you as an employee, stating that:

- the workplace should be safe and not be a risk to your health
- safe systems of working should be in place
- articles and substances should be stored and used safely
- adequate welfare facilities should be available
- appropriate information, training and supervision should be made for the health and safety of employees
- any protective clothing needed should be provided free of charge
- certain injuries, diseases and occurrences should be reported to the Health and Safety Executive
- first aid facilities should be provided
- a safety representative should be consulted about issues affecting health and safety in the workplace.

As an employee you should:

- know about the safety policy in your setting
- take care of your own health and safety and that of others affected by their actions
- co-operate with your employer on health and safety.

Over to You

Have a look at your setting's health and safety policy.

- When was it last reviewed, and by whom?
- Where is the policy displayed?
- What is covered by the policy?

Functional Skills English: Reading and Writing

Reading the health and safety policy of your setting will help you to develop your reading skills. You could answer the questions and then write a short paragraph at the end to say how you comply with the health and safety policy whilst you are at the setting.

Manual Handling Operations Regulations 1992

It is important that you are trained in how to lift properly and how to use any equipment for lifting. Caring for children and young people naturally involves lifting and carrying babies, children and equipment. Incorrect lifting techniques can result in serious back injuries as well as the risk of fractures and sprains to limbs. Injuries due to poor lifting cause a quarter of all injuries reported each year. The checklist opposite gives you some advice on how to lift a child or an object safely.

Best practice checklist: Lifting

✓ Stand in front of the child or object with your feet at shoulder-width apart

✓ Always bend your knees, not your back and keep your back straight

✓ Assess the weight of the child or object

✓ Make sure you are holding the child or object firmly

✓ Test that you can safely lift before actually lifting

✓ Avoid twisting or bending as you lift

Lifting a child properly is important for the child's safety and yours

Functional Skills ICT: Developing, presenting and communicating information

It is really important that we do lift heavy items safely. You could use the information in the best practice checklist to create a poster that could be displayed in each room of your setting or college that shows how you should lift heavy items safely. You could include text, different colours and images to make your poster look attractive.

Policies and procedures in your setting

All settings must have a health and safety policy covering all these pieces of legislation, and clear procedures for staff to follow. Your setting will also have policies and procedures on health and safety that are not directly linked to a law but that give guidance: for example, procedures for avoiding accidents, or on the cleanliness of the setting.

Procedures tell you how to work correctly to make sure that you, other staff and visitors and the children are all in a safe environment.

Over to You

Check out what sort of information is available on the internet. The Child Accident Prevention Trust is dedicated to child safety. Take a look at their website at www.capt.org.uk/links/default.htm.

Functional Skills ICT: Finding and selecting information

Once you have had a look at the Child Accident Prevention site then you could search the internet for further information. Try using a number of different search engines when looking for further information.

Responsibility and reporting

Your setting's health and safety policy will have the names of those responsible for health and safety. Have a look for a poster that has the following sort of information on:

HEALTH AND SAFETY RESPONSIBILITIES

Overall and final responsibility for health and safety is that of;

Jane Smith   Owner of Happy Tots Nursery, Southdown Rd, Eastby

Day-to-day responsibility for ensuring this policy is put into practice is delegated to

Simon Jones   Manager

To ensure health and safety standards are maintained/improved, the following people have responsibility in the following areas

Name	Responsibility
Rob	Head of baby room
Leanna	Head of toddler room
Nathan	Head of preschool
Aisha	Head of afterschool club

All employees have to:

- Co-operate with supervisors and managers on health and safety matters
- Not interfere with anything provided to safeguard their health and safety
- So far as is reasonably practicable safeguard the safety and welfare of these persons who they are supervising
- Take reasonable care of their own health and safety
- Report all health and safety concerns to an appropriate person

Figure 1: Health and safety notices are no good unless you read them!

Everyone is responsible for health and safety in any setting. The manager or head teacher has the ultimate responsibility, with heads of department or rooms responsible for their area. Any accident, incident or near miss must be reported to your supervisor.

Rooms, outdoor areas and equipment should be checked at the start and end of every session. You should also be aware of any faults or broken equipment during activities. If you find anything that is faulty or broken, then it must not be used. Faults should be reported to the appropriate person. Find out who that is.

Risk assessment

What is risk assessment?

It would be impossible to prevent every single minor bump and graze — but it is possible to eliminate most risks and protect children. Risk assessments have to be carried out in all public places, places of employment, care settings and similar to make sure that people are not injured unnecessarily. All day-to-day activities and places at your setting will be risk-assessed. Any new activity has to have a risk assessment before children are involved.

Risk assessments take into consideration:

- a large number of everyday things that may appear harmless or go unnoticed but could be dangerous
- a range of areas from the condition of toys and equipment to hygiene and cleanliness to access to children by members of the public.

Risk assessments are not expected to be perfect but they must be suitable, sufficient and reasonably practical.

Managers must be able to show that:

- a proper check was made
- they asked who might be affected
- they dealt with all the significant hazards, taking into account the number of people who could be involved
- the precautions are reasonable and the remaining risk is low
- they involve staff, children and parents where applicable in the process.

Managers and staff in a setting must think about:

- who is responsible for carrying out risk assessments
- who has responsibility for safety in the different areas
- how risk assessments will be displayed
- how they will be implemented
- how they will be monitored and reviewed
- how they will link to health and safety policies, training and induction sessions.

Be able to recognise risks and hazards in the work setting and during off-site visits

Most accidents can be prevented. Thinking ahead about what you are planning to do, who with and what risks and hazards there might be can help to reduce accidents to those in your care.

Creating a safe but challenging environment

Children learn by trying out new experiences and making choices. However they do not have the skills and judgement to always make safe choices. Carers have the responsibility not only to identify potential hazards in any situation, but also to judge when it is safe to allow a child to undertake an activity or make a choice.

It is important to make sure children are safe, but it is also very important to give them the chance to explore and experiment. Children learn their limits through experimenting and pushing their level of skill, and you have to help to support them to do that safely. There are many myths around health and safety that suggest children cannot do anything that is slightly dangerous. Risk itself won't damage children, but ill-managed and overprotective actions could!

You can't wrap children in cotton wool – nor should you!

Skills builder

As a practitioner, you need to create activities with children to make them aware of how they can look after themselves – but these can be fun and interesting. Have a look at the activity page on the Child Accident Prevention Trust website (www.capt.org.uk/activity/default.htm) for activities and quizzes you can do with children on safety. There are some for you as well!

Key term

Likelihood: the probability of any harm from the hazard actually happening

A balanced approach to risk management

Any activity a child does has some risk attached, even something as simple as painting. If the activity is planned and organised well, with thought given to possible risks, the **likelihood** of an accident or injury should be minimal. The secret is to balance the risk of an activity against the benefit to and safety of the child.

Understanding the stage of development a child is at and their individual needs can help you to provide the right amount of risk in activities. For example, children under the age of eight cannot safely judge the speed or distance of a car on the road – so a child under eight should never be allowed to cross the road alone.

Risk and challenge are important to a child or young person's development. Avoiding them would result in a very timid adult lacking in many everyday skills and abilities. It would be easy to respond to all the risks to which children are exposed by not allowing them to explore or experiment. However, just think about how that would affect their development. Children need to explore their environment – it is one of the ways in which they learn – but it needs to be a 'safe' environment where adults control the risk. It is important that children are given the freedom to develop their skills, with adult support but not too much intervention.

Some children need this freedom to explore risk even more than others. For example, a child who has epilepsy may be restricted in play at home because of parental concern that the child may have a fit. In a well-controlled setting the child can be encouraged to explore and try out new skills.

Case study:
Encouraging safe play

Tahira is seven years old and has epilepsy. Her parents are worried that if she goes on the climbing frame she will fall if she has a fit. Tahira gets very upset that she cannot join in with her friends.

- What could be done to let Tahira enjoy climbing and at the same time make sure she is safe and her parents do not worry too much?

Tahira on the climbing frame

Key terms

Hazard: something that has the potential to cause harm

Risk: the outcome or likely impact of the hazard associated with the activity

Risk or hazard?

When someone carries out a risk assessment, the person has to think about the **hazard** and the **risk**. For example, a childcare setting being on a main road could be a major risk; the hazard is the road and the traffic. However, although the risk is serious, it is unlikely to cause harm as the entrance on to the road is secure and carefully controlled, and a child could not get out into the road.

A risk assessment identifies potential hazards. It is a legal requirement, as the person responsible needs to be able to show that they are aware of any risks and that plans are in place to control and minimise these risks.

Identifying potential hazards

Any setting or activity carries a level of risk. By identifying and reducing hazards and risks in advance, you can make full use of the setting or activity to maximise the value to and enjoyment by the children in your charge. Figure 2 shows the different types of hazard you need to be aware of.

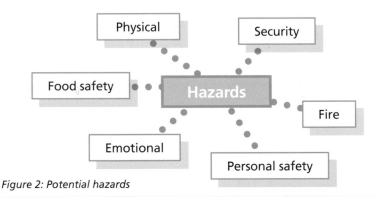

Figure 2: Potential hazards

Every person working with children is responsible for their safety. It is important that the environment children are working in is regularly checked, before and during activities. Some of the things to think about are set out on the checklist below.

Best practice checklist: Checking your environment

✓ Does any of the equipment have broken parts or sharp edges?

✓ Are large pieces of equipment and toys arranged to allow safe use by all children?

✓ Are the outside play areas free of broken glass, syringes and other dangerous litter?

✓ Are the toilet and washing facilities clean and supplied with toilet paper and soap?

✓ Are all locks, catches and so on that stop children leaving the building alone working?

✓ Are any dangerous items or substances (e.g. knives or bleach and other chemicals) out of the reach of children?

✓ Are procedures for dealing with spillages of urine, faeces, blood and vomit clear, and are the facilities available to deal with them?

✓ Are the procedures for dealing with visitors to the setting clear?

✓ Do the alarms work and are visitor books and badges in place?

✓ Are all areas for the preparation of food and drink clean, and is suitable equipment present?

How many hazards can you spot in this picture?

Over to You

Have a look at the picture. Can you list the hazards in the room?

Functional Skills English: Speaking, listening and communication

Once the children have gone home or before they arrive, you could take a picture of the room where you spend a lot of time working. You could then hold a discussion with your supervisor and tutor explaining how you set the room up in a safe way or what controls are in place in the room to ensure that health and safety requirements are met.

Contributing to health and safety risk assessments

As a practitioner, you will need to play your role in risk assessments, both in your work setting and for off-site visits. Here are the four main steps to assessing the risks in a childcare setting.

Step 1: Identify the hazards
You need to walk round your setting and look at what could reasonably be expected to cause harm. Are there trailing electrical wires? Are toys left around to form trip hazards?

Step 2: Decide who might be harmed and how
For each hazard, be clear about who might be harmed. How might they be harmed and what type of injury may result? For example, if a child pulls the kettle that is attached to the trailing wire, they will be scalded.

Step 3: Evaluate the risks and decide on any control measures
Once you have identified the hazards ask yourself these questions: Can I get rid of this hazard altogether? if not, how can I control the risks so that harm is unlikely?

Step 4: Record your findings and implement them
Write down your results, keeping it simple: for example, name of hazard identified; what you have done about it; who has been informed; who is going to act on it and how often.

The checklist below shows things you should consider before embarking on an activity with children.

Key terms

Control measure: any activity or measures put in place to control or minimise identified risks

Activity: what will be happening

Best practice checklist: Safety

✓ Is there a suitable space for this **activity**?

✓ Is there enough room?

✓ Is the surface safe for, for example, water or sand play?

✓ Is all the appropriate safety equipment in position, such as mats under large play equipment and guards on the cooker?

✓ Are all materials used safe, especially for very young children, such as paint or dough?

✓ Are there too many children?

✓ Is another activity going on that will clash with it?

✓ Are there enough adults to ensure adequate supervision?

✓ Is help available if a child is harmed by the activity?

Off-site visits

Visits or outings present different hazards to indoor activities in a controlled environment. Staff have a responsibility to ensure that outings are properly planned and carried out. If a proper risk assessment is carried out and suitable control measures put in place, off-site visits are enjoyable activities for children and staff. The best way to assess risk for an outing is to make a provisional visit yourself.

Deaths on educational visits are very rare — about three or four each year among an estimated 7–10 million school visits. Even these very low numbers are too high and it is important that you pay attention to recommendations by the Health and Safety Executive to make off-site trips safe and enjoyable.

If you are involved in any way with an educational visit, you'll want to know the most important questions to ask. The following ten questions cover the main arrangements that should be in place for a visit. These questions are important for everyone, whether parent, child, helper, leader, head teacher or governor. They are equally relevant to visits run by youth organisations.

Special care needs to be taken on any off-site visit

Best practice checklist: Off-site visits

✓ What are the main objectives of the visit?

✓ What is 'Plan B' if the main objectives can't be achieved?

✓ What could go wrong? Does the risk assessment cover:

- the main activity?
- 'Plan B'?
- travel arrangements?
- emergency procedures?
- staff numbers, gender and skill mixes?
- generic and site-specific hazards and risks (including for Plan B)?
- variable hazards (including environmental and participants' personal abilities and the 'cut off' points)?

✓ What information will be provided for parents?

✓ What consents will be sought?

✓ What opportunities will parents have to ask questions (including any arrangements for a parents' meeting)?

✓ What assurances are there of the leaders' competencies?

✓ What are the communication arrangements?

✓ What are the arrangements for supervision, both during activities and 'free time'? Is there a code of conduct?

✓ What are the arrangements for monitoring and reviewing the visit?

(Source: www.hse.gov.uk/schooltrips/tenquestions.htm)

Case study: Risks in outdoor activities

Jason is planning an outing to the local wood with a small group of children from his childcare setting. Jason hopes that he can include some nature work, physical skill development and artwork with the children. They are planning to take a group of eight seven- and eight-year-olds from the afterschool group.

1. List the possible hazards.

2. What are the risks?

3. What control measures should be put in place?

4. How much freedom will the children be able to have when they are in the wood?

Over to You

In your setting ask to have a look at examples of risk assessments for off-site visits.

Skills builder

Think about these two common and popular activities: junk modelling and a walk in the local park. How can you reduce the risk of accidents for each of these? Table 2 presents a sample risk assessment with some hazards, risks and control measures identified. Can you complete the risks and control measures?

Table 2: Examples of risk assessment for two common activities for younger children

Activity	Hazard	Risk	Control measures
Junk modelling			
Use of scissors	Sharp points and blades	Injury to child	Control use by very young children Make sure children are familiar with safe use, especially Lia who has poor fine motor skills
Containers and other materials being used	Rough or sharp edges	Cuts to child	
Cleaning up after the activity	Wet surfaces and floors	Risk of slipping	
Outing to the park			
Walk to the park	Traffic dangers		
	Child wandering off and getting lost		
Use of play equipment	Broken or damaged equipment		
	Equipment not suitable for age of child (e.g. very high slide)		
Recent rain	Lack of waterproof clothing (wet, cold children)		
	Effect on play equipment		

Over to You

Can you think what other factors might change the risks of an activity?

Did you think about the weather for an outdoor activity, time of day, what the children had been doing before? Why would these factors matter?

A good risk assessment is only valid at the time you carried it out. Although the setting, outing or activity may be one you have used many times, one very important factor will change — the children taking part. Effective risk assessments take account of each child taking part and the number of children in any group.

Once you have started the activity you have risk-assessed, it is important that you monitor the risks you identified. If anything changes, review and change your plan if necessary.

Know what to do in the event of a non-medical incident or emergency

Non-medical incidents and emergencies do happen in any setting. Make sure you are familiar with the procedures in your setting for dealing with them.

Non-medical incidents and emergencies

Most days in your setting will pass with children safe from harm. This is because staff are aware of possible threats to safety and take the right action to prevent them – in other words, an effective risk assessment has been done and control measures have been put in place.

However, sometimes incidents and emergencies do happen. You need to know how to identify when the children or young people in your setting are at risk from an incident or emergency.

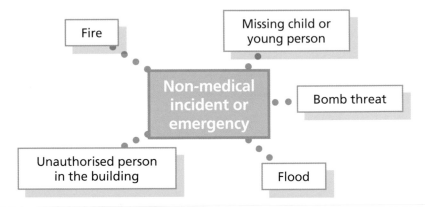

Figure 3: Non-medical incidents and emergencies

If you think an incident or emergency has happened you *must* immediately raise the alarm. In all these examples, early action is vital.

Actions to take in response to fires, security incidents and emergency incidents

Evacuation procedures

There are many reasons why a building may need to be evacuated (for example, in the event of a fire, a gas leak or a bomb scare). All adults need to know what to do. In most settings, one member of staff is responsible for these procedures and will need to make sure that all staff are aware of the evacuation procedures. Practices need to be held regularly and signs and notices must be kept in place. Drills and practices should always be taken seriously so that any difficulties can be reviewed.

Over to You

Find out what the emergency procedure is at your setting.

- How is the alarm raised?
- Who contacts the emergency services?
- Who takes out the registers and checks them?
- What are the safest exit points?
- Where is the assembly point?
- How often is there an emergency practice?
- How are visitors to the setting made aware of evacuation procedures?
- How are children reassured during evacuation practices?
- Are there regulations and notices on view?

Fire

If there is a fire in your setting, here are the steps you should follow.

- Close doors and windows and try to get the children out of the premises by normal routes.
- Do not leave the children unattended.
- Do not stop to put out the fire (unless it is very small).
- Call the fire brigade by telephone as soon as possible as follows:
  - lift the receiver and dial '999'
  - give the operator your telephone number and ask for 'Fire'; when the brigade replies give the information clearly (for example, 'Fire at the First Start Nursery, 126 Beach Drive, Blackpool AB2 6PY, situated between the clock tower and the promenade'
  - do not replace the receiver until the address has been repeated by the fire operator.

Best practice checklist: Fire practice

- ✓ Have a fire drill every three months.
- ✓ If there are problems with the procedures, repeat the drill or seek advice from a fire officer.
- ✓ Reassure children during a practice by staying calm and explaining what is happening.
- ✓ Praise children and thank them for their help in carrying out the evacuation.
- ✓ Provide an absorbing activity, such as reading a story or playing a game, to help the children settle down quickly.

Fire safety is of paramount importance

Missing children

A child should never go missing from a care or education setting if all procedures are followed. A small child should not be able to open gates or doors, and any adult going through them should follow all precautions to ensure they are properly closed and locked. You should follow strict procedures that only allow the collection of children by parents or authorised carers. On outings, always ensure the right ratio of adults to children.

However, if a child does go missing you should raise the alarm immediately and follow the setting's procedures, including:

- making sure all the other children are safe and with responsible adults
- making sure any external exits are secure
- informing the person in charge
- starting a systematic search, based on where the child was last seen, and with whom, and make sure all areas are covered
- Informing the child's parents
- Informing the local police.

Functional Skills Maths: Representing

What is the correct ratio for the age of children that you are working with? Think about the last time you went out on a trip or carried out a more complicated activity in the classroom. What was the ratio then? How do you think the ratio affected the activity?

Security incidents

There should never be any unauthorised person in a childcare setting. Most settings have an alert system if doors are opened. Anyone who does not work in a setting should sign in a visitor book, have a badge identifying them as a visitor and always be accompanied by a member of staff.

Always ask someone who you do not recognise for their identity badge. If they cannot produce one, you must immediately tell your supervisor or another manager and, if possible, stay with the unauthorised person until you get help.

Know what to do in the event of a child or young person becoming ill or injured

Children and young people have accidents and become unwell. From happily playing or working, a child can rapidly need medical help. When this happens it is important that you:

- can recognise when a child is unwell or injured
- can identify when urgent help is needed
- know your role and responsibilities in these circumstances.

Identifying the signs and symptoms

Most children will let you know when they are not well. You may see obvious **signs** of this, such as the child being pale or vomiting, or a child may tell you their **symptoms**, saying for example that they feel sick or have a pain. Often when a child is unwell they may behave in a different way to usual. Even a mild illness may cause a normally active happy child to lose their energy, not want to play, cry or be very quiet.

When urgent medical attention is needed

You need to be able to identify the circumstances when a child or young person needs urgent medical attention, and to be able to do so swiftly and confidently. Children will arrive at your setting apparently well and happy, and later in the day become unwell or have an accident. In most cases, it will be enough to look after the child until parents or carers can collect them. In some cases, the condition may be life-threatening and needs urgent medical attention if the child is going to survive. It is very important to recognise when a child may be seriously ill so that you can take rapid action.

Key terms

Sign of illness: something you can see that suggests a child is ill or injured

Symptom of illness: an observable change in the body that indicates disease or illness

You should dial 999 for an ambulance for <u>any</u> of the following:

- difficulty in breathing
- asthma attack that does not respond to use of an inhaler
- child is floppy or unresponsive
- significant change in behaviour — much more withdrawn or less alert than usual
- child is unconscious
- child is unable to swallow
- purple, blue or grey skin or lips
- fits
- wounds that will not stop bleeding
- burns or scalds
- any of these symptoms after a head injury: headache, confusion, vomiting, wobbling, problems with seeing
- suspicion that the child may have meningitis: severe stiff neck, fever, headache, purple or red rash that fails the glass test
- severe pain, especially if it gets worse
- dehydration: sunken features, not passing much urine, lethargic
- vomiting blood
- signs of frostbite
- heat exhaustion
- eating or drinking any poison
- raised itchy lumps (hives) accompanied by any swelling of the mouth and/or nose.

You should get urgent medical attention for a child or young person who has:

- severe vomiting or diarrhoea
- a very high temperature, especially if the child appears ill
- a cut that may need stitches
- difficulty in walking or using their arms after a fall
- severe bruising
- any animal bites that break the skin
- bites or stings where the redness and swelling spreads or the child seems ill
- any other condition that gives you serious cause for concern.

A child may have a long-term medical condition such as asthma, serious allergies, or a blood disorder such as sickle cell anaemia. In any such case, the parents or carers will have given the setting information on what to look out for and what to do about it if the child needs medical help.

Meningitis

Meningitis is a potentially life-threatening illness that can become serious very quickly. There are several strains of meningitis and the immunisation programme offers protection from some of them. However, if you suspect a child may have meningitis, you must get medical help immediately.

Both adults and children may have a rash. One sign of **meningococcal septicaemia** is a rash that does not fade under pressure (the 'glass test'). The rash is caused by blood leaking into the tissues under the skin. It starts as tiny pinpricks anywhere on the body, and can spread quickly to look like fresh bruises. The rash is more difficult to see on darker skin; look on the paler areas of the skin and under the eyelids. If someone is ill or obviously getting worse, do not wait for a rash — it may appear late or not at all. A fever with a rash that does not fade under pressure is a medical emergency.

Role and responsibilities for urgent medical attention

A child who is very ill or has been injured will be frightened and upset, as indeed will any other children who are in the area. Your main responsibility as a learner is to tell a qualified member of staff who will:

- know what to do in an emergency
- carry out the required actions calmly and confidently
- help to preserve life and to prevent the effects of the illness or injury becoming any worse than necessary.

While you are training you should never be left alone with a group of children. If you do find a child who seems to be in need of urgent medical attention, tell someone immediately and be ready to do what they ask you to do, such as:

- ringing for an ambulance
- fetching the first aid kit
- contacting other people
- reassuring other children in the area.

If a child is seriously ill or injured and you do find yourself in a situation with no one else around, take a deep breath, try to stay calm and follow the immediate actions in the checklist below.

Best practice checklist: Immediate actions

✓ Survey the scene: check you will be safe, see what has happened and who is involved

✓ If anyone is around, call out for help

✓ Check the child is breathing and take action if not (see PEFAP001)

✓ Make sure any other children in the area are looked after

✓ Find out what is wrong with the child, to see if an ambulance is necessary and what immediate care is needed

✓ Provide the immediate first aid care

✓ Call for an ambulance

✓ Notify parents or carers

✓ Talk to the child and any other children involved as soon as possible after the incident

Ambulances

When dialling 999, always have ready the details of the accident or illness, the age of the child and of course where the injured child is. Stay on the phone until the person in the control room tells you to hang up — they may need more information from you.

First aid kits

All children's settings should have a well-equipped first aid kit that is easily to hand in the case of an accident. All staff should know where it is. Always make sure you know where the first aid box is kept, and what is in it.

A named person should be responsible for checking the kit and replacing missing items, although anyone using an item from the kit has a responsibility to report this to the named person.

After the event

When all the action has settled down you may need to:

● write down what happened in the accident or incident book

● fill in an accident form

● talk to your supervisor about what happened and what you learned from the situation.

Over to You

Find out where the first aid kit is.

● Is it easy to find?

● Who is responsible for ensuring the kit is full and in a good state?

● Do the contents match those in the photograph? Is anything missing?

● Are there any extra items and, if so, what are they for?

Case study:
Accident outdoors

You are in the outdoor play area with a small group of four-year-olds. There are two qualified staff with other children. Jamil runs over to you to tell you that one of the children, Anna, has fallen and bumped her head. You go over to the slide where Anna was playing and see that she is crying, is very pale and has a very large bump on her forehead. Jamil and the other children are all gathering round to see what has happened.

1. What do you do immediately?

2. What do you do with the other children?

3. What else should happen?

Be able to follow the work setting procedures for reporting and recording accidents, incidents, emergencies and illnesses

When a child or young person has been injured or become ill, or there is an incident, very often this must be recorded and possibly reported to the authorities. Keeping accurate records is important so that any patterns of incidents are noted and action is taken to prevent them happening again.

Reporting procedures

All settings must have a clear procedure for recording and reporting any incident, accident, emergency or illness.

Reporting accidents or illness

Some accidents must be reported to the Health and Safety Executive, particularly if the child is seriously injured. Examples of this would include:

- a major injury (e.g. fractured limbs, electric shock, unconsciousness)

- if the child is absent due to the injury for more than three days.

More information is available on the HSE website for education settings (www.hse.gov.uk/services/education/index.htm).

Settings must:

- keep a signed record of all accidents to children

- notify Ofsted (HMIe in Scotland) of any serious accident, illness, injury or death of any child or adult on the premises

- tell local child protection agencies about any serious accident, injury to, or death of a child in the setting and act on any advice given.

Notification must be made as soon as is reasonably possible but in any event within 14 days of the incident occurring.

Ofsted (or HMIe) inspectors may look at records of significant accidents and incidents. All need to be signed by the parent/carer. For confidentiality there should only be one page per child, per accident or incident.

Reporting incidents

All incidents should be recorded in detail. The setting's management will have decided what incidents should be recorded. These should always include bullying and fighting and any security incidents. Records should include:

- the child's name

- the time and location of the incident

- what triggered the incident

- the nature of the incident

- others involved

- witnesses

- how the situation was handled

- if any restraint was used and any consequences.

Your responsibility

For any of these the manager of the setting cannot complete their responsibility if they do not have the correct information.

Your responsibility after any accident, incident, emergency or illness you were involved in, is to make a note of:

- what you saw – including just before the incident as well as during it

- what you did

- who else was involved

- what they did

and then pass this on to the person recording and reporting.

Completing workplace documentation

Your setting will have particular documentation for recording accidents, incidents, emergencies and illnesses. All settings should make sure they have parental permission to get emergency medical advice or treatment and that:

Over to You

Find the procedure at your setting for reporting accidents, incidents, emergencies and illnesses. Read it and make sure you know what you should do in any such event.

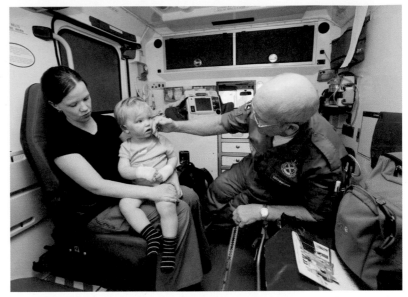

Your role in passing on information to the emergency services could be crucial

- staff know about parents'/carers' wishes, such as cultural and religious beliefs
- parents/carers know about the setting's emergency arrangements.

Accident records should contain details of:

- any existing injuries that a child arrives at the setting with
- the time, date and nature of any accident
- details of the children affected
- the type and location of any injury
- the action taken at the time, any action taken later and by whom
- the circumstances of the accident, names of any adults and children involved and any witnesses (including the contact details of the witnesses)
- the signature of the staff member who dealt with the incident, and of any witnesses
- a countersignature by the parent when the child is collected.

Be able to follow infection control procedures

Infection only passes between people if the conditions are right for the bacteria or virus. Putting a barrier in the path of the infection can be fairly easy, and is a simple way of preventing other children, young people or adults becoming ill.

Accident Report Form – Lower Farm Nursery and Afterschool Club
Tick the boxes as appropriate

Name of Injured Person Jane Brown	Date of Birth 12 March 2007	Female	
☐ Employee ☐ Child	☐ Visitor ☐ Contractor	☐ Trainee	☐ Other

About the incident / accident

2. ☐ Accident			☐ Near Miss
Location Home corner	Date 3/6/2010	Time 2.15 pm	Date reported 3/6/2010

What actually happened?
Jane tripped over a toy on the floor and fell, banging her head on the wall

What was the outcome e.g. injury or property damage?
Bump to forehead resulting in approx 3 cm lump. Jane started to vomit and complained her head hurt

State what, if any, medical action was taken
Mother contacted, came to nursery to take Jane to Accident and Emergency department for check up

What, in brief, was the cause of the accident/incident? **If the injury is as a result of a violent incident, please complete a separate violent incident form**
Toy car left on floor in home corner
If any equipment was involved give details

Name & type of equipment	None	

3. Lessons learned and recommendations to prevent similar incident in the future
Staff to check toys cleared from floor

Details of witnesses

4. Name and address of any Witnesses	Nursery assistant Jamie Smith

6. Signature of person completing the report	Date

Figure 4: A completed accident form

Key term

Infection control: rules and advice for practice aimed at preventing the spread of disease

Coughs and sneezes spread diseases

Procedures in your setting

Your setting will have a policy and detailed procedures for **infection control** based on this advice from the Health Protection Agency.

Good hygiene practice

Hand washing is one of the most important ways of controlling the spread of infections, especially those that cause diarrhoea and vomiting, and respiratory disease. The recommended method is the use of liquid soap, warm water and paper towels. Always wash hands after using the toilet, before eating or handling food, and after handling animals. Cover all cuts and abrasions with waterproof dressings.

Coughing and sneezing easily spread infections. Children and adults should be encouraged to cover their mouth and nose with a tissue. Wash hands after using or disposing of tissues. Spitting should be discouraged.

Personal protective equipment (PPE) Disposable non-powdered vinyl or latex-free CE-marked gloves and disposable plastic aprons must be worn where there is a risk of splashing or contamination with blood/body fluids (for example, nappy or pad changing). Goggles should also be available for use if there is a risk of splashing to the face. Correct PPE should be used when handling cleaning chemicals.

Cleaning of the environment, including toys and equipment, should be frequent, thorough and follow national guidance. For example, use colour-coded equipment, COSHH and correct decontamination of cleaning equipment. Monitor cleaning contracts and ensure cleaners are appropriately trained with access to PPE.

Cleaning of blood and body fluid spillages All spillages of blood, faeces, saliva, vomit, nasal and eye discharges should be cleaned up immediately (always wear PPE). When spillages occur, clean using a product that combines both a detergent and a disinfectant. Use as per manufacturer's instructions and ensure it is effective against bacteria and viruses and suitable for use on the affected surface. Never use mops for cleaning up blood and body fluid spillages — use disposable paper towels and discard clinical waste as described below. A spillage kit should be available for blood spills.

Laundry should be dealt with in a separate dedicated facility. Soiled linen should be washed separately at the hottest wash the fabric will tolerate. Wear PPE when handling soiled linen. Children's soiled clothing should be bagged to go home, never rinsed by hand.

Clinical waste Always segregate domestic and clinical waste, in accordance with local policy. Used nappies/pads, gloves, aprons and soiled dressings should be stored in correct clinical waste bags in foot-operated bins. All clinical waste must be removed by a registered waste contractor. All clinical waste bags should be less than two-thirds full and stored in a dedicated, secure area while awaiting collection.

Sharps should be discarded straight into a sharps bin conforming to BS 7320 and UN 3291 standards. Sharps bins must be kept off the floor (preferably wall-mounted) and out of reach of children.

Sharps injuries and bites If skin is broken, encourage the wound to bleed/wash thoroughly using soap and water. Contact GP or occupational health or go to A&E immediately. Ensure local policy is in place for staff to follow. Contact your local HPU for advice, if unsure.

Animals

Animals may carry infections so wash hands after handling animals. Health and Safety Executive (HSE) guidelines for protecting the health and safety of children should be followed.

Animals in school (permanent or visiting)

Ensure animals' living quarters are kept clean and away from food areas. Waste should be disposed of regularly, and litter boxes not accessible to children. Children should not play with animals unsupervised. Veterinary advice should be sought on animal welfare and animal health issues and the suitability of the animal as a pet. Reptiles are not suitable as pets in schools and nurseries, as all species carry salmonella.

Visits to farms Please contact your local environmental health department who will provide you with help and advice when you are planning a visit to a farm or similar establishment. For more information see www.hse.gov.uk/pubns/ais23.pdf.

Vulnerable children Some medical conditions make children vulnerable to infections that would rarely be serious in most children. These include those being treated for leukaemia or other cancers, on high doses of steroids and with conditions that seriously reduce immunity. Schools and nurseries and childminders will normally have been made aware of such children. These children are particularly vulnerable to chickenpox or measles and, if exposed to either of these, the parent/carer should be informed promptly and further medical advice sought. It may be advisable for these children to have additional immunisations, for example.

Source: Guidance on Infection Control in Schools and other Child Care Settings, *Health Protection Agency, April 2010*

Over to You

Find and read your setting's infection control procedures. Is everything in the HPA guidance included?

Think about some activities you could do with the children you work with to help them to understand the importance of good hygiene practices.

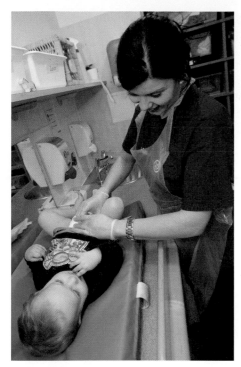

Make sure you wear the correct PPE

Personal protective clothing

Your setting will provide the personal protective clothing and equipment you need to protect yourself and others from the risk of infection and to prevent infection spreading. Personal protective clothing includes:

- disposable non-powdered vinyl or latex-free CE-marked gloves
- disposable plastic aprons
- goggles for use if there is a risk of splashing to the face.

How to use personal protective clothing

Personal protective clothing must be used when:

- changing nappies
- taking children to the toilet
- dealing with a child who is bleeding or vomiting
- clearing spillages of bodily fluids
- washing soiled items.

Best practice checklist: Using protective clothing

✓ Use a fresh set of apron and gloves for each situation

✓ Wash your hands before you put on the apron and gloves

✓ Remove the protection as soon as you have finished the activity it was needed for

✓ Correctly dispose of the apron and gloves

✓ Wash your hands again after you have taken it off

How to wash and dry your hands

Washing and drying your hands properly is the very best thing anyone can do to avoid the spread of infection. Children should wash their hands before or after such activities as:

- toileting
- snacks
- outside play
- messy play
- sand/compost play.

Staff members should wash their hands before and after activities including:

- toileting, including emptying potties
- before and after preparing snacks
- before and after wearing gloves, for food preparation or nappy changing
- after changing nappies
- messy play
- outside play.

There is a skill to washing your hands properly. If it is not done properly germs will still be left on your hands.

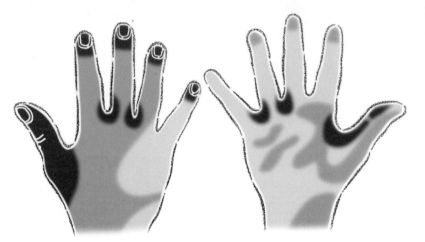

Areas often missed during hand washing

Effective hand washing

You already know that children learn by example, and learning about hygiene is no different. How you behave in terms of hand washing and other hygiene activities is very important. You will need to tell the children about the importance of hand washing, show them how to do it and think about when this might be needed.

Children should have easy access to sinks, soap and towels to wash their hands, and should be encouraged to do so. Provide lots of praise when they do. You could even have a competition with stars recording regular appropriate hand washing.

Case study:
Teaching children about hand washing

Jed works in a pre-school group and wants the children to learn the importance of washing their hands as part of their toileting routine. During a group time, Jed tells the children all about unfriendly bacteria. He then tells them about the importance of washing their hands using soap and water and how they must use paper towels to dry them.

He shows them some colourful notices he has made on the computer to remind them what to do. After the group time, he puts the notices up in the toilets at the children's height. Two children help him.

1. Do you think that Jed made the information fun? If so, why is this important?

2. How will the children understand the importance of hand washing from this activity?

Safe disposal of waste

Your setting will have a procedure to dispose of waste that is guided by local health policy. This requires you and everyone else to:

- separate domestic and clinical waste, in accordance with local policy
- put used nappies/pads, gloves, aprons and soiled dressings in correct clinical waste bags in foot-operated bins
- never fill clinical waste bags more than two-thirds full
- store clinical waste bags in a dedicated, secure area while awaiting collection
- have all clinical waste removed by a registered waste contractor.

Know the work setting's procedures for receiving, storing and administering medicines

Often a child will return to a setting after being ill, still taking medicine from their doctor. Some children are on regular medication or need it occasionally: for example, if they have asthma.

Dealing with medicines

Your setting will have clear guidelines about receiving, storing and administering medicines to children and young people. All settings should have:

- an effective policy on the administration of medicines in their setting, including systems to support individual children with medical needs

- written records of all medicines administered to children

- guidelines on informing parents of any medicines given to children

- written permission for each and every medicine from parents before any medication is given.

The policy should cover:

- what prescribed medication, if any, they will administer: they must make sure that parents understand their policy

- procedures for who will administer any medication

- storage of medication

- recording administration of medication

- training of staff if there is a specific medical need

- action to be taken if a child becomes ill or has a long-standing medical condition.

Your setting will have clear guidelines about receiving, storing and administering medicines

Parental permission

Written permission and instructions must be received from parents before any medicine can be given. This must state what the medicine is, how much and how often it is to be given. This applies to each and every medicine a parent wishes a provider to administer. For example, permission will be needed at the start of a course of antibiotics, but will not be needed for every time each dose of the antibiotic is given during the course of treatment. This information should be kept in a safe place for inspection and future reference.

How procedures protect people

Procedures around medicines are there for one important reason: to protect children, young people and practitioners.

Giving medicine to a child is a serious matter. It is too easy to give a small child too much medicine, or give them something they are allergic to. Equally if a child needs medicines, either for a short time because they have been ill or because they have a long-term condition such as asthma, it is important that they are given them regularly and in a safe way. Make sure you know what your setting's policy is and ask to have a look at records that are kept.

Knowing how to give medicines properly not only helps children in your care, but protects you from the risk of harming a child.

Check your knowledge

1. What does COSHH stand for?
2. Name two other regulations that cover health and safety in children's settings.
3. List six routine daily checks you should make of the indoor and outdoor environments in your setting.
4. Identify two ways in which you can make sure children are secure in your setting.
5. List three aspects of welfare covered by the statutory requirements of the EYFS.
6. Give three examples of how you might assess the risk of particular activities, taking the children's ages into account.
7. Why is it important to record accidents and incidents?
8. List six items from a first aid kit.
9. What should you do in the case of an accident before you start to give first aid?
10. List three key signs of meningitis in a baby or young child.

My Story

May, Nursery assistant

When I started working with children I used to worry about meeting all the requirements of the Early Years Foundation Stage – planning how I would help the children I look after to make progress with their development. But even more important than that is making sure they are safe from accidents by thinking through any risk involved in activities I am planning. I never realised how dangerous an everyday place might be for a small child! Now I always have safety in mind with everything I do.

The first aid section in this unit was really good. At least when children do have an accident I know what to do – and in fact I am now doing a more advanced first aid course.

All children are ill sometimes, and I know it can be hard for parents to cope with illness in their children, especially when they are working. But I enjoyed finding out what to look for so that I can spot when a child is starting to be ill.

Viewpoint

You will often see accusations that we are not giving children enough freedom to play out or explore their environment, often written by people who have an idealistic view of the freedom they had as children. Then the same people get upset when a child is injured and start demanding more restrictions and health and safety checks.

What do you feel about how much freedom children should have to physically play and explore their environment? Are we guilty as a country of producing 'cotton wool' children?

Ask the expert

Q Aren't all these risk assessments just form filling? Have you ever really used one?

A I used to feel the same until I was just carrying out a routine check of the outdoor play area. Our nursery unit is in the middle of the country and we hardly ever have any trouble, but one morning I spotted something glinting in the sun and there was a plastic bag with two used syringes and needles in there.

Q OK, but what about trips out? Surely anywhere you can take children must be safe?

A Don't believe it! Next time you go to the park or an adventure centre, have a look at the possible exits. Most places have several gates or doors that a child could wander off through.

TDA 2.9

Support children's and young people's positive behaviour

In this unit, you will learn about the importance of following policies and procedures, what to do to encourage positive behaviour, and what you might do when children and young people show unwanted behaviours.

Learning outcomes

By the end of this unit, you will:

1. know the policies and procedures of the setting for promoting children's and young people's positive behaviour

2. be able to support positive behaviour

3. be able to respond to inappropriate behaviour.

Know the policies and procedures of the setting for promoting children's and young people's positive behaviour

Over to You

In most modern settings practitioners will talk in terms of positive and negative behaviour, rather than good and bad behaviour. Why do you think this is? Note down some thoughts and share with a partner.

We are not born knowing the rules of how to behave. Children and young people learn these over time and with the support of parents and those that work with them.

Children and young people need guidance and also clear boundaries when it comes to behaviour. When several people are working with the same children or young people, it is not fair if the rules and boundaries keep changing. For this learning outcome, you will need to know the policies and procedures in your setting and also why it is important that all staff use the policies and procedures.

Policies and procedures relevant to positive behaviour

There are many ways and strategies in which we can manage children's behaviour and guide them to show positive behaviour. The starting point though is to have a clear direction or vision. Most settings will therefore have a behaviour policy in place. For early years settings in England, for example, it is actually a legal requirement. A behaviour policy is a document that sets out how the staff team intend to manage children's behaviour and the principles behind this. As part of a behaviour policy, there will also be procedures. These are the practical details of what staff should do in any given situation e.g. what to do if a child swears or if a child bullies another. Some specific areas of behaviour, such as bullying, may even have their own separate policies and procedures. The way that policies are written will vary according to the setting that you work in. The following may well be covered.

Codes of conduct

Many settings will have a code of conduct. Ideally, there should be two codes of conduct. One that relates to how the staff should behave and another one outlining the expectations for children and young people.

Staff code of conduct

As we will see later in this unit, the way that adults behave can influence children and young people. An adult who shouts is likely to encourage children and young people to be more aggressive in the way that they deal with situations. The following may be included in a staff code of conduct.

Respect

Staff may be encouraged to show respect to children and young people at all times. Respect can be seen in the way that staff talk and listen and act.

Calm

Staff may be asked to remain calm as becoming angry or agitated can make situations more difficult.

Non-aggression

While staff never have the right to physically reprimand children, shouting or roughly handling children can be just as bad. Being aggressive in any way with children or young people sets a bad example and can also escalate a situation.

Role model

Some settings require in their behaviour policy for staff to set a good example all the time. This may include showing thoughtfulness, sharing and saying please and thank you. School settings may also ask that teachers be on time to their lessons while youth groups may ask that staff do not swear or smoke in the presence of young people. In early years, staff may be asked to wear aprons if they are engaged in messy play so as to encourage children to do the same.

Over to You

If you were responsible for writing the staff code of conduct, what would you highlight as important?

What you do sets a model for children's behaviour

Children's or young person's code of conduct

As children become older, it can be helpful if there are clear codes of conduct for them. These may be negotiated with them but in order for them to work, everyone including the children or young people will need to know what they are. The key elements in most codes of conduct are about safety, playing nicely, respecting others and doing one's best. This may translate to things such as not running indoors, taking turns with equipment and not bullying others.

Rewards and sanctions

Children and young people need to be helped to show positive behaviour. This means that most settings will have ways of rewarding children. These we look at in the next learning outcome. It is important that everyone working in the setting uses rewards appropriately as otherwise children can become confused. In the same way, staff have to know what sanctions can be used. Sanctions in an early years setting may include the removal of a toy or resource if it is being used unsafely or in some situations the removal of the child from a situation. Sanctions have to be applied fairly and so procedures as to when and how to use them are likely to be given in a setting.

Dealing with conflict and inappropriate behaviour

One of the reasons why a behaviour policy is important is so that everyone working with the children knows what is inappropriate behaviour. This is important as people may have different standards e.g. one person may feel that young children should have to tidy carefully, while another might feel that as long as they have made an effort it doesn't matter. As part of the behaviour policy and procedures, you will need to find out how you are meant to deal with conflict and inappropriate behaviour. In early years settings, it is likely that conflict will mean a child that refuses to co-operate in some way, while settings working with older children might also consider conflict between children.

Anti-bullying

Bullying is an issue that particularly affects older children and young people. It can be extremely serious and a child who is being bullied can suffer long-term effects. This means that most settings working with children and young people will have an anti-bullying policy as well as including it in their behaviour policy. As part of the procedures of your setting, you should also find out what you should do if a child insults another or makes racist or other discriminatory remarks. Schools may also be able to sign up to an Anti-bullying Charter to show their commitment to tackling all forms of bullying, and use the principles of the Charter to evaluate their own anti-bullying policies and practices.

Over to You

Read your setting's behaviour policy. Find out what you should do if a child:

- swears
- is uncooperative
- is aggressive towards another child.

Attendance

Schools working with children and young people are likely to have an attendance section in their code of conduct and also behaviour policy. This is because children's education can be affected if they do not attend regularly or are often late for lessons. If you work in an early years setting, this is not likely to be part of a behaviour policy.

Functional Skills English: Reading

Reading your policy to obtain this information is a good way of developing your reading skills.

The importance of consistency and fairness

In your setting, it is crucial that all staff consistently and fairly apply boundaries and rules for children's and young people's behaviour, in accordance with the policies and procedures of the setting.

Children find it much easier to show positive behaviour if they know what is expected of them. Young children in particular need staff working with them to be absolutely consistent. While an eight-year-old can understand that there are some situations in which you can eat standing up, a toddler finds this very difficult. The need for consistency is one reason why staff working with young children will often work closely with parents so that the child does not become confused. With older children and young people, boundaries and sanctions can be drawn up with them. This often helps them to take responsibility for their behaviour and also means that they feel part of the process.

Setting fair boundaries

Boundaries and goals for behaviour have to be drawn up in ways that are appropriate for children's age and stage of development. Behaviour is linked to many things including children's emotional development, but also their intellectual development. This means that the boundaries and goals for the behaviour of a two-year-old is very different from those set for an eight-year-old. A two-year-old does not understand the concept of sharing and possessions and so they will often snatch things from other children. Two-year-olds are also impulsive and find it hard to control their emotions. On the other hand, most eight-year-olds know that taking something from another child is wrong. Most eight-year-olds also understand the need for rules and they are able to think ahead more.

Table 1 shows how what we might expect of children changes according to their development.

Table 1: Expectations and support for behaviour at different ages

Age	Stage of development	Goals for behaviour	Role of adult
1–2 years	Actively explores environment Imitates adults in simple tasks Repeats actions that gain attention Alternates between clinging and independence Has understanding that toys and other objects may belong to others	To play alongside other children (parallel play) To carry out simple instructions such as 'Please find your coat'	**Good supervision**, as children of this age do not understand the dangers around them **Distraction**, to stop unwanted behaviour, as children often forget what they were doing: for example, if a child wants another child's toy, offer him or her a different toy instead **Praise**, so that children understand how to get an adult's attention in positive ways and to help develop self-esteem **Calm and patience**, as children of this age are often persistent and may, for example, keep going back to something that is potentially dangerous **A good role model**, as children are learning behaviour by imitating those around them
2–3 years	Wants to be independent but does not always have the skills Becomes frustrated easily and has tantrums Is jealous of attention shown to other children Has no understanding of the need to wait Finds sharing difficult Is active and restless	To wait for needs to be met: for example, at mealtimes To share toy or food with one other child, with adult help To play alongside other children To sit and share a story for five minutes To say 'please' and 'thank you' if reminded To follow simple instructions, with help, such as 'Wash your hands'	**Good supervision and anticipation** — the keys to working with this age range Children are trying to be independent, but lack some of the physical and cognitive skills they need. This can make them frustrated and angry. Adults need to anticipate possible sources of frustration and support children, either by offering help or by distracting them. For example, a child who is trying to put on a coat may need an adult to make a game of it so that the child does not become frustrated. Where possible, adults should try to provide as many opportunities as possible for children to be independent. **Calm and patience**, as children who are frustrated can trigger negative feelings in adults This has the potential to inflame a situation. It is a good idea to allow plenty of time for children to complete day-to-day tasks. Children of this age often forget and need reminding about boundaries and goals. **Praise and encouragement**, to enable children to learn what behaviour adults are expecting of them Some unwanted behaviour that is not dangerous should be ignored so that children do not repeat it in the hope of gaining adult attention. Adults should also provide plenty of love and attention if children have had a tantrum, as some children can be frightened by the force of their own emotions. **Consistency**, as children are trying to work out the limits on their behaviour **A good role model**, as children model their behaviour on others This is especially important at this age as they act out their experiences through play.

Table 1: Expectations and support for behaviour at different ages (contd.)

Age	Stage of development	Goals for behaviour	Role of adult
3–4 years	Follows simple rules by imitating other children: for example, collects apron before painting Is able to communicate wishes Enjoys activities such as painting Enjoys being with other children Can play co-operatively Enjoys helping adults	To follow rules in games (e.g. lotto) when helped by adult To say 'please' and 'thank you', often without reminder To take turns and share equipment To follow instructions of adults (e.g. 'Let Simon have a turn') most of the time To help tidy away	**Praise and encouragement**, to build children's confidence and make them more likely to show desirable behaviour **Explanation** of rules, as children are now more likely to remember and understand them **Patience**, as children will still need reminders about the boundaries and goals for behaviour **Good supervision**, as, although children are able to do many things for themselves, they are still unaware of the dangers around them Most of the time children will be able to play well together, but squabbles will break out. **A good role model**, to help children learn the social skills they will need to resolve arguments and express their feelings
4–5 years	Plays with other children without help from adults Is able to communicate feelings and wishes Understands the needs for rules Can wait for needs to be met	To consider other people's feelings To comfort playmates in distress To say 'please' and 'thank you' without reminder To ask playmates for permission to use their toys To tidy up after activities	**Providing activities and tasks** that are stimulating and allow children to develop confidence Children of this age are keen to help adults and enjoy being busy. Tasks such as setting the table or fetching things allow children to feel independent. **Praise and encouragement**, so that children feel good about themselves This is important because children are often starting school at this time. They need to feel that they are able to be 'good'. **Explanation**, to help children to remember and understand the need for rules or decisions **A positive role model,** to help children to learn social skills, as they are copying what they see
5–8 years	Is developing strong friendships Will argue and question decisions Copies behaviour of older children (e.g. swearing and spitting) Understands the needs for rules and plays games that have rules Understands the difference between right and wrong Has many self-help skills such as getting dressed, wiping up spills	To apologise to others To listen to others To follow instructions **From six years onwards** To work independently and quietly in school settings To be helpful and thoughtful To take responsibility for actions	**Praise and encouragement**, as children become more aware of others and compare themselves critically Praise also prevents children from looking for other ways of gaining attention. **Explanation**, so that children can understand the reasons for rules and decisions Children should also be made to consider the effects of their actions on others. **Setting and enforcing clear boundaries**, to counter children's tendency to argue back as they become older **Still being a good role model,** as children are trying to understand more about the adults they are with Speech and actions are modelled increasingly on adults whom children admire. **Encouraging children to take responsibility for their actions** by asking them what the boundaries or limits on their behaviour should be **Providing activities and responsibilities** to help children to 'mature' as they learn more about their capabilities Small responsibilities help children to become independent and give them confidence (e.g. they may be asked to tidy areas of a setting or pour out drinks for other children).

Applying boundaries and rules

There are many ways in which we can help children to show positive behaviour. Many settings will remind children of the expectations by either telling them or putting up messages. In early years settings, it is important to guide children little by little rather than give them too much information. This means that adults will often tell children at the time what they need to do, rather than expect that they can always remember: for example, 'Now you've finished with those cars, you need to put them away.'

Over to You

Think about the way in which staff in your setting help children to apply the boundaries and rules.

Functional Skills English: Speaking, listening and communciation

This task could be completed in the form of a discussion with your friends on your course. Discussing how all the different settings apply rules and boundaries is a lovely way of sharing good practice.

Case study:
Behaviour and boundaries

Jenny is a student in a day nursery, working with two-year-olds. She is finding it very hard because the children do not seem very well behaved. She tells her supervisor that one of the toddlers has just taken a toy away from another. Her supervisor tells her not to make a fuss, but instead to use distraction. She reminds Jenny of the behaviour policy and procedures, and explains that very young children do not have the language to understand what is right and wrong, so staff have to work in quite different ways than with older children. When Jenny says that she doesn't think that the toddlers have any rules, the supervisor says that there are boundaries, but only ones appropriate to the age group. The supervisor takes Jenny to see the older groups of children and explains that, once children are talking well, then more is expected of them.

1. Why is it important that staff work in similar ways with children?

2. Why is it important that new staff understand how behaviour is managed in the setting?

3. Why is it important that boundaries are appropriate to the age and stage of children?

Be able to support positive behaviour

The way that you behave when you are at home or with your friends is not likely to be the way that you behave when you are in a waiting room or in the supermarket. This is because, as you grow up, you learn to adapt your behaviour according to the social situation that you are in. Children and young people are not born being able to do this; it is something that they learn.

When they do this, they are showing positive behaviour. It is a skill that takes a number of years. It is also, as you have seen, dependent on children's development particularly speech and intellectual development. Figure 1 shows some of the skills that children over time have to learn. Notice how most of the skills are about thinking of others.

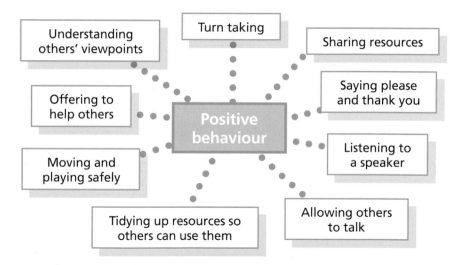

Figure 1: Positive behaviour that children have to learn

Benefits of encouraging and rewarding positive behaviour

When it comes to behaviour, it can be easy to focus on what we need to stop children from doing. The problem with this approach is that it does not help children to know what they should be doing. This means that nowadays there is much more emphasis on encouraging positive behaviour.

A good starting point is to think about the positive behaviour or goals that you should be encouraging in children. This may be outlined in your setting's policy or you may need to observe what other staff seem to encourage. If you are working in a setting that has several ages of children, notice the way in which there are different expectations according to the age of the children.

Over to You

Make a list of the positive behaviour that is encouraged in your setting.

Functional Skills ICT: Developing, presenting and communicating information

You could write your list on the computer in a table and then insert a new column that says 'I encourage this behaviour by...' and link in how you encourage this positive behaviour in your setting. You could then insert another column with the heading ' I will try to do this by...' and in this column you could set yourself a target to try and encourage this area of behaviour more.

Why encouraging and rewarding positive behaviour works

There are many reasons why encouraging positive behaviour works well in settings.

1. It helps children to learn what they need to do

In settings that encourage positive behaviour, they may say things such as 'You need to walk' rather than 'Stop running!' The focus is on what children should do. This is particularly important for young children who may not work out what they need to do. By telling them clearly, children can change their behaviour.

Encouraging positive behaviour can be more effective than saying 'No!'

Over to You

Do you remember as a child being in a situation where the adults were constantly sounding angry or annoyed? How did it make you feel?

2. It creates a calmer environment and stronger relationships

When adults are constantly saying 'no' or telling children off, the atmosphere in a setting can be stressful for everyone. On the other hand, if adults encourage children, the environment is often better. This often allows children to relax and improves their learning. Encouraging and rewarding children also creates better relationships between adults and children. This is important as children are more likely to show wanted behaviour for adults whom they like.

3. Children respond well

While some adults feel that by telling children off they will learn, the evidence suggests that the effects of this approach are quite short-lived. Children will often just wait until an adult is out of sight before carrying on with what they were doing before. By encouraging and praising children, they are more likely to choose to show positive behaviour because they enjoy it.

4. Children learn from adults

When we manage children's behaviour, children are also learning from us. If adults are constantly negative or angry, children will behave this way towards others. Interestingly, we can often see and hear this when children are playing together. A four-year-old may speak in the same tone of voice that they have heard to a two-year-old or in their pretend play.

Skills and techniques for positive behaviour

There are many skills and techniques to support children's positive behaviour. The most common technique is based around rewarding children for positive behaviour. It is based on the idea that, if you have had a positive experience, you are likely to repeat the same action: for example, if someone thanks you for being kind, you are more likely to help them again in the future.

Types of reward

There are many types of rewards that work well with children. It is important though to follow the reward system that is used in your setting.

Attention

Making eye contact, smiling or showing that you have noticed a child is a very effective reward. It helps the child to know that you have seen what they have done. Children need plenty of attention and sometimes, when they do not get enough, they show unwanted behaviour. Attention is one of the best ways of reinforcing positive behaviour.

Praise

Saying to a child 'well done' or 'good' helps them to know that they have shown positive behaviour. If you praise a child, it is helpful to explain why you are pleased: for example, 'Well done for taking your turn.' This means that the child knows what they have to do in order to gain praise. Praise is an extremely effective way of reinforcing positive behaviour.

This child is helping to tidy up because he is being praised and he is getting adult attention

Being given responsibility

In many settings, young children who have shown positive behaviour are given some extra responsibility, such as being allowed to hold the door open for the others.

Publicly acknowledged

In some settings, children will be publicly acknowledged by adults in front of their peers. They may be asked to stand up in assembly or be given a round of applause at the end of the session. Children may also be taken to another member of staff so that their achievement can be shared. This type of acknowledgement is again linked to attention, but can give the child a sense of pride.

Stickers

In some settings, children are given stickers if they have shown positive behaviour. The stickers act as a reward, but also as a reminder as the child can see the sticker for the rest of the session. Not all settings use stickers: unless they are carefully monitored, they can cause resentment between children, especially if it is thought that some children get more than others.

Treats

Some settings will give children small treats if they show positive behaviour. In settings working with older children, treats are often given if positive behaviour has been shown over a number of days. While many parents give children food treats such as sweets, this is not thought to be a good idea for settings working with children for many reasons. Settings are meant to be encouraging children to be eating healthily and also some children learn that food is about being good.

Star charts

Star charts work well with children from six years or so and for young people. With a star chart, a child collects stars or stickers when they are showing positive behaviour; when they have collected a certain number, they are then able to have a treat. The key to successful star charts is that the child should understand what they need to do in order to gain the stars. Just saying to a child 'be good' will not help them, so it is better that a specific goal is given such as 'tidying five items away' or 'sitting down at lunch table for five minutes'. It is also important that the child can complete the star chart fairly easily. If the number of stars, points or stickers to be collected is too many, the child may give up. The need to collect a number of stars or points and therefore the need to wait a while before getting the rewards means that it is not so effective with young children. (Some people do not agree with this as a reward system as children may only behave appropriately if they receive a reward!)

A simple star chart can work wonders on behaviour

Over to You

Look to see how your setting rewards positive behaviour.

Using a reward technique effectively

If you are using a reward technique, there are ways to make it effective. Below are some ways of using rewards with young children, although they can also be applied to older children and young people.

Timing

Children often remember a positive reward (which includes praise and attention) if it is given during or very shortly after the wanted behaviour. This helps children to associate what they have done with the positive experience. Waiting a few hours has much less effect on the child.

Explanation

A short explanation alongside the reward is helpful as then children know exactly what it is that they are being rewarded for. Avoid phrases such as 'because you were a good girl', as this does not help the child to know what they have done. Instead use phrases such as 'because you waited your turn.'

Reminding children

It can be helpful to remind children about what they need to do: for example, 'Last time, I was pleased with you because you tidied up.' This helps children to remember that they may gain attention or praise.

Realistic expectations

It is important that we make it easy for children to be acknowledged for their positive behaviour by having realistic expectations. Realistic expectations means thinking about what individual children can achieve given their stage of development, as the case study shows.

Case study:
Realistic expectations

Jasmine is on placement in a nursery attached to a school. She is asked to spend time with four-year-old Carl. Carl has a speech level similar to that of a two-year-old, so he is often aggressive with the other children and has tantrums. The nursery is trying to help him with his language and his behaviour. Jasmine is told that she must praise Carl when he is being co-operative and join him when he is playing with other children. At first Jasmine feels that this is giving in to him, but over time sees how giving him attention and praise is working. She changes her ideas about children's behaviour, as before she thought that you should treat all the children the same.

1. Why does Carl need different goals from the other children?

2. Why is it important that he is encouraged to show positive behaviour?

3. Why is it important to look at the individual needs of children when supporting them?

Best practice checklist: Promoting positive behaviour

✓ Give positive reinforcement when children show desired behaviour (e.g. praise when they are sharing equipment, being thoughtful)

✓ Praise or give some other form of positive reinforcement while the children are showing the behaviour, or immediately afterwards, so that they associate a reward with their behaviour

✓ Make sure children understand why they are being rewarded (e.g. 'Here is a special sticker because I saw how kind you were being to James')

✓ Praise children frequently as it helps children to keep on showing wanted behaviour

✓ Choose rewards carefully so that children do not simply show behaviour to gain a large reward (it would be inappropriate to give a child a whole chocolate bar because he or she said 'thank you')

Other techniques and strategies to promote positive behaviour

While rewarding children is one strategy, there are others as well. Most settings will use a combination of strategies rather than just one.

Reminding children of the expectations

To help children show positive behaviour, we can remind them of what they need to do. Young children will need to be told at the time rather than a long time beforehand.

Showing children what they need to do

Young children often find it easier to 'see' what they need to do. This means that adults will often show them what needs to be done and also act as role models (see also SHC 21). In practice this might mean sitting with children at mealtimes or tidying up alongside them. Joining in with children is a key way in which you can shape their behaviour.

Giving children responsibility

It is helpful if children are given some responsibility. This needs to be done according to their age. Toddlers might be asked if they can find their shoes, while three-year-olds might be encouraged to pour their own drinks. By being given some responsibility, children can feel good about themselves. This can give them confidence and prevent them from feeling frustrated.

This child is learning about taking on responsibility. It should make her feel good.

Giving children sufficient time and warning

Young children, especially toddlers, do not like to be rushed. It is helpful if adults take time to let them know what is happening and to give them sufficient time beforehand. In many early years settings, children will be told that it will soon be time for lunch or to get ready to go home. This helps children to be more co-operative as they have time to finish their play or adjust to the new situation. Some children with learning difficulties also benefit from being able to see what will happen during a session and so some settings put a series of photographs or drawings out so that the child can work out what is about to happen next.

A visual timetable can help promote positive behaviour

Preventing inappropriate behaviour

As part of the focus on helping children show positive behaviour, it is important for adults to think about how they may prevent inappropriate behaviour.

Recognising children's unmet needs

When children have needs that are not being met, they often show inappropriate behaviour. To support positive behaviour means adults being aware of what children need. Figure 2 shows some of children's basic needs.

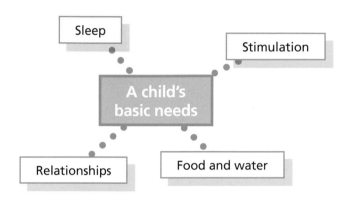

Figure 2: Children's basic needs

Food and water

Children who are hungry or thirsty are more likely to show unwanted behaviour. They may find it harder to concentrate and they may become irritable. Breakfast is particularly important. To promote positive behaviour, adults need to keep an eye out that young children do not become hungry.

Stimulation

Children and young people are more likely to show unwanted behaviour when they are bored or when the activity is not suitable for them. This means that adults working with young children need to plan stimulating activities and play opportunities. It is also important to introduce new materials and resources so that children do not become bored.

Relationships

Children need strong relationships with the adults who work with them. They need to feel that they are valued and understood. In addition, once children reach three years old, they are likely to be developing friendships. Friends can also be important if children are to show wanted behaviour. This means that adults need to encourage children's friendships and also to notice if children have fallen out or that their friend is absent.

Sleep

Children and young people who are tired find it much harder to control their behaviour. They are more likely to become irritable and uncooperative. In toddlers, tiredness leads to tantrums. For adults working with young children, this means checking that they do not need to sleep or rest.

This child is tired. How might this affect her ability to concentrate and show positive behaviour?

Realistic, consistent and supportive responses

Children react very much to the person that they are with. Overall children try hard to show positive behaviour for adults that they respect and like. They also need to feel that you notice when they have made an effort. In particular, they need you to be consistent in your approach with them. Young children in particular cannot cope if one day you seem to be relaxed and encouraging, and another day you seem to be always cross with them. In the same way, if one day you insist that children need to wear an apron before painting, yet on another you say that it does not matter, children will not be sure what to do. Add to this other staff members who also seem to change their minds and you can imagine that it becomes very hard for a young child to know what the boundaries are. This means that staff have to work well as a team and be consistent in their approach. For this assessment criterion, you will need to show that you are positive, but consistent with all of the children that you work with. You will also need to show that you encourage children, while also taking into consideration their age and stage of development.

Skills builder

Make a list of the children that you work with. Think about their individual stage of development. What are their needs? What might their goals for behaviour be?

Providing an effective role model

The way you behave in your setting will act as a role model for the standards of behaviour expected of children, young people and adults within the setting.

A key way in which children learn about positive behaviour is by watching others. Children can also learn about unwanted behaviour this way. This has been carefully researched over time. This means that behaviours such as being thoughtful, sharing or saying 'thank you' can be helped along if children see you doing them. In the same way, children also seem to pick up unwanted behaviours such as swearing, shouting or being selfish from adults. Knowing that children can copy both adults and also older children is important when supporting children. It means that you may sometimes be able to work out why a child is doing something such as hitting another child. In view of the importance of being a good role model, many settings will have a code of conduct for staff and will discipline staff who are not acting as a good role model.

Combining role modelling and praise

When children try and copy thoughtful behaviour, it is important to praise them. This may mean smiling at a toddler who is wrapping their teddy in a blanket to keep it warm or saying 'well done' to a child who has said 'thank you' when you have handed them something.

Skills builder

Children learn by watching us. Try doing something such as tidying up in the book corner or rolling dough into long sausages when children are around. Observe which children copy your action or come and join you.

Case study:
Being a role model

Ben is working in a pre-school. Helping with the children who stay for lunch, he stands up to eat his sandwich, talks loudly and reaches across the table to grab the last piece of cake. One boy gets up and walks around with a sandwich. The noise level is also higher than usual and the supervisor notices that some children leave the table without asking. Afterwards she has a quiet word with Ben. The next day, Ben sits down at the table with the children, puts his sandwich on a plate and asks if anyone would like water before serving himself. He makes sure that he says 'please' and 'thank you'. He notices that many of the children are sitting and eating nicely.

1. How did Ben's behaviour on the first day affect the children?

2. Why did the children's behaviour change on the second day?

3. Why is it important that adults act in ways that will help children to learn positive behaviour?

Getting ready for assessment

Write a reflective account that explains how you act as a positive role model in your setting. Your reflective account should include:

- examples of how in your day-to-day practice you act as a role model
- how your practice might help children to show positive behaviour.

Functional Skills English: Writing

You need to plan your writing first so that you can organise it into paragraphs. Use clear and appropriate language and think about your spelling, punctuation and grammar throughout the reflective account.

What positive behaviour is this child learning by watching this adult?

Be able to respond to inappropriate behaviour

There will be times when all children and young people will show behaviour that is not appropriate. There will be many reasons for this. Sometimes a young child is simply exploring the boundaries or an older child is just being silly. For this learning outcome, you will need to show that you can manage inappropriate behaviour and that you recognise when the child needs to be referred to others.

Selecting and applying agreed strategies

There are many ways in which we can work with children when they show unwanted behaviour. For this assessment criterion, you will need to show that you can choose the correct strategy and that it is appropriate for your setting's approach to managing behaviour. Below are some strategies that are commonly used in early years settings, but can also be used for other age groups. If you use any of these strategies, do not forget to praise and give children plenty of attention when they are showing positive behaviour at other times, especially after children are no longer showing inappropriate behaviour.

Ignoring the behaviour

This may seem odd, but it can work especially with very young children and also with children who are showing attention seeking behaviours. The idea behind this is that if children are not getting any response from the adult, they will then change what they are doing. Once children stop whatever they are doing, the adult must then give them plenty of positive attention.

Explaining the consequences of actions

Explaining the consequences of actions helps children to understand why they must not carry on with their behaviour and what will happen if they do. For example, children who are throwing balls at a window must be told that the window might break and if they carry on the balls will be taken away from them. It is important that if a sanction has been threatened it is carried out. Do not impose sanctions that you cannot justify or carry out.

Facial expression

In some situations, adults can use their facial expression and eye contact to make a child realise that what they are doing is not acceptable. This works well if children have a strong relationship with you as, when you change your expression, they really do care. As with ignoring the child, it is often better for the adults not to say very much, but to just to stare at the child. (You may remember adults doing this when you were a child.)

Saying 'no'

If 'no' is said in a quiet but firm voice, many young children will stop what they are doing. This only works if 'no' is rarely used, so that children do take notice of it.

Removal of equipment

In some situations, it is important to remove equipment as a strategy. This can send out a powerful message to the child that what they are doing is not safe or acceptable. With children who have good language, it is worth warning children first that you will remove the equipment or resources if they carry on. For toddlers, equipment should be removed if there is a likelihood of the child having an accident. Warnings will not necessarily work with toddlers because they do not have the language or the control to resist temptation.

Case study:
Applying a strategy

Akim and George are four years old and are playing with the sand. George starts tipping it over the side and onto the floor. Akim starts to copy him, but also throws it in the air. The adult walks over to them and asks them to stop it, explaining that sand can get in eyes and be painful. A moment later the children start throwing the sand again.

1. Why is it important for the adult to intervene again?

2. How should the adult intervene this time?

3. What should the adult do once the children begin to play nicely later on?

Distraction

With young children, especially toddlers, distraction can really make a difference. The advantages of using distraction are that children do not get any attention for their inappropriate behaviour and it avoids conflict. To use distraction, you need to show the child something different or to get out a toy or resource that they can turn their attention to.

Case study:
Using a technique

Tom is two years old. He is with his mother at a parent and toddler session. Anna is on placement at the group. She notices that Tom is trying to pull a toy telephone out of the hands of another toddler. She goes over and without saying anything shows Tom a finger puppet. Tom is so entranced by the puppet that he forgets about the toy telephone. Afterwards Tom's mother comes over and thanks Anna for helping him.

1. What technique did Anna use?

2. Explain why this technique worked.

3. Why was this the best technique to use with a child of this age?

Time out

This is often used with older children and young people who are not coping with a situation. The idea is that children are given some time to calm down before returning to the situation. This technique can work quite well, although it should not be used as a punishment — once children feel they are 'naughty' and excluded, they are less likely to show appropriate behaviour.

On occasions time out gives a child the chance to reflect

Best practice checklist: Dealing with inappropriate behaviour

✓ Stay calm

✓ Think about the reasons why children are showing unwanted behaviour: e.g. are they tired, hungry, bored or is it typical for their age?

✓ Try to sort out the behaviour without creating a new conflict

✓ Use distraction for younger children

✓ Only use sanctions that are agreed in your setting

✓ Praise children afterwards when they are showing appropriate behaviour

✓ Remember that it is normal for children to experiment, explore and have times when they are not co-operative

Specific types of unwanted behaviour

There are some specific types of behaviour that early years practitioners may need to deal with if you work in an early years setting.

Table 2: Types of unwanted behaviour

Behaviour	What a child does	How to deal with it
Attention seeking	Many children show attention-seeking behaviour at times. It can be a sign of insecurity or in some cases mean that children have become used to having a lot of adult attention. There are many ways in which children show this type of behaviour, including answering back, making noises and challenging instructions	• It is often best to ignore attention-seeking behaviour unless it is dangerous, as by challenging it you may be teaching children that they can get attention this way • Plenty of praise when children are showing appropriate behaviour can teach them the right way to get your attention
Biting	Many toddlers bite especially if they are in group care. Biting is often linked to frustration and can become a habit	• Act immediately • Give the victim your attention first • Once a child has bitten, it is likely that another bite will follow • Supervise the child who has bitten for the rest of the session • Keep the child busy at all times until the end of the session
Destructive	Some children may show aggressive behaviour towards their surroundings and towards others. This can be a sign of frustration or unhappiness, but it is important that children are not allowed to become out of control as this is very frightening for them and teaches them that there are no limits on their behaviour	• You should stay calm when dealing with children who are aggressive. It is important that they can see that you are in control of the situation • Talk quietly but firmly to the child. It is often best to take the child to a quiet place where they can calm down. (If you are in a large setting you may need to ask another member of staff for help) • Once the child has calmed down, it is important to find out what has upset them and to make sure that they understand that their behaviour is unacceptable
Name calling, swearing and other offensive remarks	Children who call names and make offensive remarks are often repeating comments that they have heard. Remarks such as 'fatty' or 'stupid' need to be challenged, but in such a way that children are not blamed for what they have said	• You should ask children where they have heard the remark • Explain that what they have said is hurtful and why • Tell children that these comments are not to be made in the setting

To refer or not to refer?

Some children's behaviour may be a sign that they need additional support. This means that we need to recognise when children need to be referred to another colleague or a professional.

As you have seen, the starting point for responding to inappropriate behaviour is to consider whether the behaviour is linked to the child's development. This is important as, while you do not want to encourage this behaviour, you must not make a fuss over it either as it is likely to be temporary. When working with children under three, it is likely, for example, that there will be some instances of snatching and also biting. This type of behaviour needs managing, but is not likely to need a referral as most children with support will grow out of it. On the other hand, if a child of four years is still biting, this will need referring. Opposite are some types of behaviour that might need referral.

Biting

Most children stop biting by three years. Biting is common in toddlers and is linked to frustration, as they are not yet talking. If older children are biting, there needs to be some investigation.

Aggression

While most children will squabble and toddlers will hit out, older children should be more controlled. Aggressive acts such as hitting another child for no reason would need referral.

Change of behaviour

Children whose behaviour changes on certain days or who were fine before may need additional support. There are many reasons why children's behaviour may change suddenly including abuse, family separation or bereavement. Sometimes a change in children's behaviour is a sign that they need help.

Attention seeking

While all children need attention, most children as they get older find appropriate ways of getting this attention. Attention-seeking behaviours such as shouting, tipping things on the floor or deliberately being unco-operative may be a sign of an underlying difficulty.

Self-harming

Self-harming is anything that a child or young person does to harm themselves. It includes pulling out hair and head banging as well as cutting with a razor. There are a number of reasons why children and young people may self-harm. While self-harming behaviours are quite rare in young children, they become more common in young people.

Bullying

There are many reasons why children and young people may bully. It is important for both the victim and the bully that their behaviour is stopped quickly. While bullying is not such an issue with children under five years, it can be a problem with older children and young people and should be taken seriously.

What to do if you have a concern

If you have a concern about a child's behaviour, your first port of call is your supervisor, manager or teacher. You should explain what you have seen and you may be asked to do further observations. From this point, parents may be asked to come in so that more information can be gained.

It is usual for most settings to try a few strategies first before referring to other professionals. Sometimes unwanted behaviour is a result of a medical condition or learning difficulty while others might be linked to an emotional difficulty that the child has. Table 3 shows some of the professionals who may support the child and their family.

Table 3: Professionals who may support a child showing unwanted behaviour

Professional	Role
GP/family doctor	This is often the first port of call as the family doctor will be able to refer onto other specialists
Health visitor	A health visitor may visit the family at home and give some advice. They may refer on if necessary
Educational psychologist	The educational psychologist will look at the children's learning and behaviour. They may give some strategies as to how to support the child
Child psychiatrist	A child psychiatrist will help children and young people who may have mental health issues
Family counsellor	Some behavioural issues are a result of difficulties within the family. A family counsellor may work with the child and the whole family
Play therapist	Children who have had some trauma may see a play therapist so that they can work out and move on from what has happened to them

Check your knowledge

1. What is a behaviour policy?

2. Give two examples of issues that might be covered by a behaviour policy.

3. Why is it important that staff follow the setting's behaviour policy?

4. Explain why expectations of children may vary according to their stage of development.

5. Why is it important to focus on supporting children to show positive behaviour?

6. Give two examples of ways in which adults might reward positive behaviour.

7. Describe why it is important for adults to be consistent with children and young people.

8. Explain the importance of adults being good role models.

9. Identify two strategies that could be used with children aged two to five years.

10. Identify two professionals who may support a child or young person showing unwanted behaviour.

My Story

Molly, nursery officer

I have been working in a Children's Centre for three years. When I first arrived, I had very set ideas about behaviour and discipline. This meant that I spent a lot of my time nagging children or saying 'no' to them. My manager had a quiet word with me and told me to watch some of the other staff. I learned from them that a quiet word is often enough and that it is better to make things into a game with the very little ones. Now I have more experience, I am much more relaxed and find it easy to sort out behaviour. I have also learned that sometimes the best strategy is to ignore children who are playing you up as they quite often just want your attention. My tip for anyone starting is to get to know what is 'normal' for children's behaviour and not to overreact to it.

Viewpoint: Saying sorry

Whether children should always have to say 'sorry' is a hot topic. While many people feel that children should say 'sorry' to learn that they have upset or hurt someone, many experts feel that there is little point if a child is too young to know. There is also the danger that some children can get into the habit of saying 'sorry' while not really feeling it. A further problem is that many children tend to say 'sorry' to the adult who has caught them, rather than to the child they have hurt or upset. This begs the question – at what age is saying sorry useful?

Ask the expert

Q We have a three-year-old boy who is always attention seeking. What should we do?

A Attention-seeking behaviours are usually a sign that the child is not feeling secure and needs more adult attention. The trick is to ignore the child at the time, if it is safe to do so, but give the child a lot more attention at other times: for example, read the child a story or join the child in play.

Q We have a two-year-old child who cries every morning. Does she do this for attention?

A No, she is not doing this to get your attention; she is missing her parent. The best thing that you can do is to find ways of getting her comfortable with one person in the setting so that, when she comes in, she does not feel so alone. This may take some time as when children have had many mornings of being unhappy, they find it hard to trust. You might like to try using a puppet to help the child settle.

Contribute to the support of positive environments for children & young people

The environment that children and young people spend time in is essential to their learning and development. In this unit you will find out how to support an environment that is safe, reassuring, challenging and enabling.

You will also find out that any environment should encourage children and young people to take control of their own learning.

Learning outcomes
By the end of this unit you will:

1. know the regulatory requirements for a positive environment for children and young people

2. be able to support a positive environment that meets the individual needs of children and young people

3. be able to support the personal care needs of children and young people within a positive environment

4. understand how to support the nutritional and dietary needs of children and young people.

Before you start this unit remember that the environment should be welcoming for children, staff and parents, safe and secure, with well-organised space to promote children's learning and development.

Know the regulatory requirements for a positive environment for children and young people

All registered early years provisions should ensure that children are learning and developing in a safe and secure environment. You should remember that 'environment' does not just refer to the physical space that is provided but also to the adults, children and activities that they engage in.

The Childcare Act 2006 has simplified early years regulation and inspection arrangements, and provides a new, integrated education and care quality framework of inspection that will make sure that all environments are right for the children concerned.

There are two compulsory registers for childcare providers working with children under the age of five years. They have to follow the EYFS Framework.

- The Child Early Years Register (EYR) is compulsory for most childcare providers working with, or caring for, young children from birth until the August following their fifth birthdays. Unless they are exempt, these providers must offer care and early learning to meet the Early Years Foundation Stage (EYFS). EYFS is the framework that sets standards for learning, development and care; for children from birth to the age of five.

- The General Childcare Register (GCR) is compulsory for providers of childcare for children from 1 September following their fifth birthday (for example, the end of the Foundation Stage) up to the age of eight, and where at least one individual child attends for a total of more than two hours in any one day.

Functional Skills English: Reading

As you use the information on the website to create your factsheet in the activity opposite, you will have the opportunity to develop your reading skills.

Getting ready for assessment

Find out more about the two compulsory registers on the Ofsted website. To show that you understand them, you could create your own factsheet, perhaps with six main points, and use it as evidence for assessment.

In England, many providers and authorities use the Early Childhood Environment Rating Scales to help teams look at their environment and make it positive. The standards are simple yet rigorous, and help you meet the requirements of Ofsted and the EYFS.

When you have rated your environment against the scales you will find out:

- the strengths of your setting
- what needs to be developed.

Your management can use the scales to help fill in the self-evaluation form (SEF) required by Ofsted, which helps you to improve continually.

All legislative requirements for children under five years can be found in EYFS statutory guidance on the Department of Education website (www. education.org.uk). All settings with children under 16 for more than two hours each day will be regulated by Ofsted. When they inspect the settings, they will want to see a **positive environment** in which children's individual needs are being met.

What is a positive environment?

Whatever age group or setting you are working with, you must plan an environment that encourages the development of the whole child. In this unit you will study in more depth the different ways in which your role in the environment can affect a child's development.

First of all, think about the different settings that children and young people aged 0–16 years may experience. These settings have both indoor and outdoor physical spaces that need to be considered.

Key term

Positive environment: an environment that supports every child and young person's learning and development in a challenging but achievable way

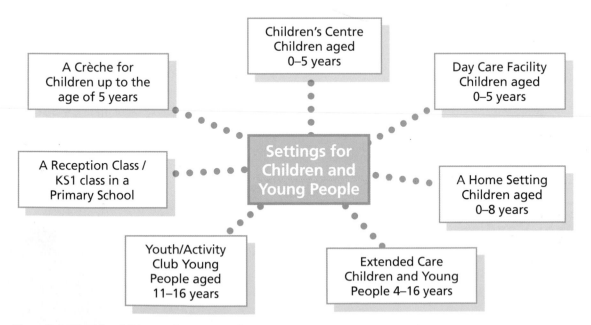

Figure 1: Settings for children and young people

You may be lucky enough to work in a purpose-built setting, but not all settings are like this. For example, many groups use a hall that is shared, and have to set up and clear away at the end of each session.

The layout of the physical environment is your team's responsibility and contributes to giving each child positive outcomes in their learning and development. The available space will influence the way the furniture and equipment is set out. While it is important to create an attractive environment, everything should be safe, secure and have a purpose that supports each area of the children's development.

Best practice checklist: Creating a positive environment

✓ Divide the setting into areas so that children can experience a variety of activities (often called 'continuous provision')
✓ Provide space between activities for children and adults to move freely
✓ Carefully place activities to promote development
✓ Ensure access areas are clear
✓ Try to ensure that the environment encourages children to solve problems and think creatively
✓ Encourage independence and choice
✓ Ensure surfaces are safe and washable
✓ Celebrate diversity
✓ Ensure areas for display are visible and accessible to all children
✓ Provide opportunities for a link between home and the setting, e.g a role-play area
✓ Ensure the outdoor environment is an extension of the indoors, e.g. painting, stories, etc. can be conducted outside
✓ Ensure outdoor surfaces are safe and varied
✓ Provide safe paths for bikes, etc. as well as visible areas for children to play quietly

Functional Skills ICT: Developing, presenting and communicating information

You could design a leaflet for new parents to your setting that explains how their child would be working in a positive environment. You may want to include some photographs in your leaflet that show what you are saying.

Functional Skills English: Speaking, listening and communication

Completing this 'Over to you' activity is a good way of developing your discussion skills. Planning your discussion first will help you to present your information clearly. It is important to listen carefully to what others say so that you can respond in an appropriate way.

With this information in mind look at the two layouts in Figure 2.

Over to You

Using the layouts in Figure 2, make notes for discussion with your tutor or study group about whether the children could:

• play a game quietly in pairs
• choose resources to do their own activity
• move freely between activities, indoors and outdoors
• move easily in a wheelchair
• play safely on bikes outside
• listen to a story in a small group.

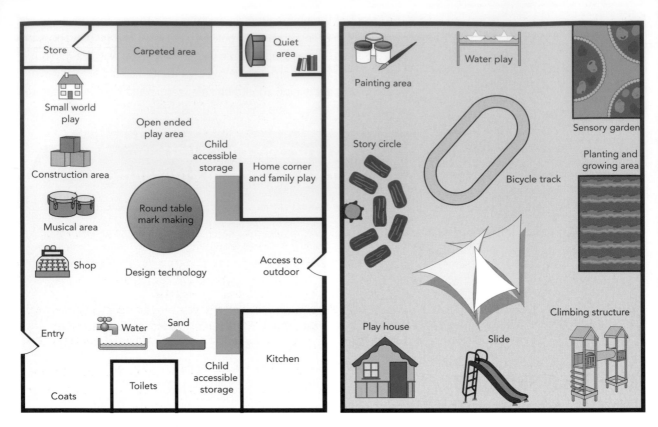

Figure 2: Layouts of an indoor and outdoor play area at a purpose-built day nursery

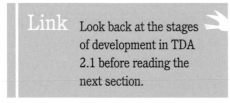

Link Look back at the stages of development in TDA 2.1 before reading the next section.

By providing the right environment for the children in your care you will be able to promote their physical, intellectual, emotional, social and linguistic development. Table 1 shows ways in which a positive physical environment can meet the needs of the child you are working with.

Table 1: How a positive environment can support children's development

Aspect of development	Type of skill the environment should support	Ways to make the environment suitable for specific needs
Physical development	• Large and fine motor skills • Fine manipulative skills • Spatial awareness • Balance • Sensory awareness	• Clear spaces • Appropriate-sized furniture • Tactile objects and surfaces • Outdoor spaces and varied equipment • Appropriate resources and equipment
Social and emotional development	• A sense of identity • Confidence • Socialising with other children and adults • Independence, creating and choosing own activities • Positive behaviour	• Positive images in visual displays • Appropriate play and group time areas • Accessible resources • Appropriately sized furniture • Secure and comfortable areas • Clear behavioural expectations shown in displays/notices

Table 1: How a positive environment can support children's development (contd.)

Aspect of development	Type of skill the environment should support	Ways to make the environment suitable for specific needs
Intellectual development	• Exploratory play • Imitative play • An understanding of causes and consequences • Imaginary play • An understanding of time • Developing mathematical concepts • Use of language • Concentration • Curiosity	• Provision of age-appropriate resources • Provision of wide range of appropriate activities and experiences • Space to explore through play • Informative displays and labelling • Accessible book area • Displays and activities that invite exploration and discussion
Language development	• Communication between adults and children • Communication between children • One-to-one communication • Understanding of instructions • Listening and taking part in musical activities • Development of verbal and written communication • Participating in story activities and exploring books • Expression of feelings and wishes	• Provision of comfortable areas to have adult/child communication • Appropriate posters, notices and pictures • A wide range of appropriate experiences, activities and resources • Extensive and attractively presented reading resources • Imaginative play opportunities • Provision of co-operative play opportunities

A positive environment also depends on the relationships between the adults and children and how the children are respected. The adults can ensure that the environment is positive for each child by:

- respecting each person and young child as an individual and ensuring that the curriculum follows the needs and interests of each child

- for under threes, having a key person who can make a strong link with home for each child, as there is great emphasis on the relationship between the adult and the child

- ensuring adult-led activities are planned but achievable and child-led activities are enabled with a variety of resources for children to choose from

- working in partnership with other settings or agencies for the benefit of the child.

Link You can read more about working in partnership with other settings, agencies and individuals in MU 2.9.

Ensure child-led activities are enabled with a variety of resources

Case study:
Ensuring the environment follows each child

Following an Ofsted inspection, the team at The Maltings, a 20-place daycare nursery, discusses how they can ensure that they as adults follow each child's interest more, as outlined in the EYFS framework.

Jim, the manager, holds a team meeting to discuss how the environment can be developed. The Ofsted inspector has observed that the children's drawers are difficult for them to reach, and that resources such as building bricks are only labelled with words. She has also observed that the children have a story while the staff clear away activities and set the tables for lunch. At lunchtime staff serve the children and clear their dishes for them.

1. How can the adults encourage the children to use their drawers throughout the day?

2. How can Jim and his team encourage children to help with set up and clear away activities?

Regulatory requirements underpinning a positive environment

A positive environment for children and young people must be a safe place to work in, so a number of legal **health and safety requirements** are in place. Whatever the setting, policies and procedures guide the working practice of the staff and ensure the requirements are carried out.

All settings that have under-16-year-olds on site for more than two hours a day are likely to be inspected by Ofsted and will have to meet certain requirements. These are detailed in Ofsted's National Standards. Here are the requirements to make your setting safe and healthy.

Key term

Health and safety requirements: the laws governing safety in your country

Heating
- Temperature at 15–18°C, or 20–22°C for babies
- Fireguards in front of fire
- Radiators and pipes covered
- Smoke alarms and emergency equipment available

Lighting and electricity
- All areas well lit for full visibility
- Current breakers for all electrical equipment
- Plugs covered

Functional Skills Maths: Interpreting

What is the temperature in the room that you work in? Is this in line with Ofsted's National Standards for heating? Is the temperature throughout your building consistent? You could take the temperature in each class and then calculate the mean and range of temperatures in your building.

Ventilation

- Window opens when necessary to circulate air so that there are no draughts
- The space used must meet basic requirements
- Locks and toughened glass on windows

Doors and gates

- All the external gates and doors locked and coded as appropriate
- Handles and locks out of reach of children
- Safety gates to BSI standard
- Toughened glass where necessary

Outdoor and indoor surfaces

- Stable
- Non-slippery
- Soft under climbing equipment
- Easily cleanable

Access points

These must be kept clear, unlocked and made known to all children and adults, including visitors, in the case of an emergency evacuation.

Best practice checklist: Environment policies and procedures

- ✓ Welcoming
- ✓ Clean and well-maintained
- ✓ Sole use of premises during session
- ✓ Clear telephone communication with emergency numbers, etc. available
- ✓ Appropriate temperature
- ✓ Adequate space and storage
- ✓ Appropriate rest areas
- ✓ Safe and appropriate toy and play equipment
- ✓ Appropriate outdoor space with suitable equipment
- ✓ Appropriate toilet facilities
- ✓ Appropriate kitchen and laundry facilities
- ✓ Safe and adequate supply of hot, cold and drinking water
- ✓ Safe supply of gas and electricity
- ✓ Adequate security
- ✓ Appropriate supervision
- ✓ Awareness of fire safety
- ✓ Safe outings and use of transport
- ✓ Adequate insurance
- ✓ Appropriate plants

Outdoor areas should be checked each time they are used. The RoSPA (The Royal Society for the Prevention of Accidents) guidelines are a source of useful advice with regards to the security of boundaries.

Functional Skills ICT: Developing, presenting and communicating information

Producing the checklist that you need to carry out the audit in the 'Over to you' could be done on the computer. This would be a good opportunity to practise your editing, formatting and layout techniques.

Over to You

Ask your supervisor if you can carry out an audit of your setting to check if doors and gates comply with safety regulations and that access points meet required standards. You could produce a simple checklist.

Ofsted requires settings working with children to meet certain standards in order to ensure that children can play in an environment that is appropriately heated and ventilated. Any appliances, such as heaters, must be regularly checked and maintained.

Remember it is your responsibility as a working member of your setting to help to ensure that policies covering temperature and ventilation are followed correctly for the sake of the children in your care.

Your manager will also have to ensure that all fittings conform to safety requirements and that all work and regular inspections of equipment are carried out by qualified people. They will also need to retain and display installation and servicing certificates.

When working with young children your setting will also be required to provide enough adults to work with children so that they can be safely supervised in the environment and access all the activities and resources provided with appropriate supervision.

Skills builder

In your work setting you will have risk-assessment procedures for regular checks.

Ask if you can see a risk assessment form and identify what relates to heating and ventilation.

Ask if you can help to complete a risk assessment form when you next plan a trip outside your setting.

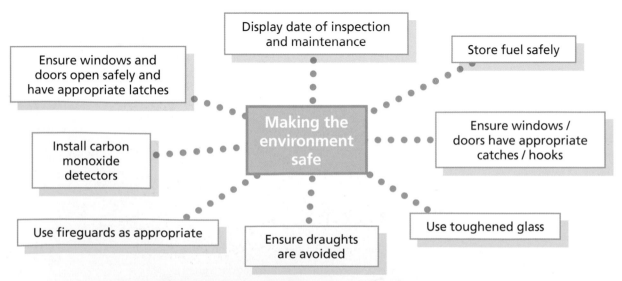

Figure 3: Making the environment safe and meeting requirements

Link

The Common Assessment Framework is a statutory framework that ensures that children and young people who have specific needs or are vulnerable can be fairly assessed, protected and supported. You can read more about this in SHC 21.

The legal requirements for registered settings are:

- under 2: 1 adult to 3 children
- under 3: 1 adult to 4 children
- in school reception classes when the day is between the hours of 8 am and 4 pm: 1 adult to 13 children
- in daycare: 1 adult to 8 children.

If you want to find out more about the legal requirement of the qualifications of adults working with young children you can visit the website of the Department for Education National strategies (see www.education.org.uk).

To protect children in your environment you should have a safeguarding children policy.

Be able to support a positive environment that meets the individual needs of children and young people

Over to You

In the EYFS Framework one of the four themes is 'A Unique Child'. Visit the Department of Education website (www. education. org.uk) and look at 'Themes and commitments to supporting a Unique Child' in more detail.

Following children and young people and meeting each of their needs will involve you working closely with:

- parents
- your team
- colleagues from other agencies
- the child.

You will learn that one of the best ways to support the needs of each child and young person is to observe them and use these observations to help you support their individual needs.

Use observations to help support individual needs

Meeting and greeting

Some people believe that the first few minutes of a child entering a setting can affect the rest of their day, so it is important that they feel welcome. You can support this by:

- ensuring that you talk to the child's parent and exchange information
- finding out how the child is
- including the child in the conversation
- giving the child time to settle in and say goodbye to their parent
- taking the child to a favourite place, such as the sand area, spending time with them if needed
- if a child has a specific communication need, finding ways to make them feel welcome
- if they have English as an additional language, perhaps learning a few words of greeting in their home language
- if they have a hearing impairment, perhaps learning to sign your greeting in the language they use
- if they are reluctant to talk, using a puppet to talk to them.

Many settings will have settling-in plans for young children. These may consider the needs of the child as discussed with their parents, and clarify how the adults are going to support the child's transition into the setting from home. This may include:

- information about the child's likes and dislikes
- information about routines at home
- plans for visiting with the parent
- plans for the parent to gradually spend time out of the room
- ways that the child will be greeted when they enter the setting.

Reviewing the plans

In early years settings, the key worker plays an important role in meeting and greeting young children and their parents. They are the familiar face for the parents and child, and will know enough about the child to greet them appropriately. This is especially important for children under three, where the whole curriculum is based on the relationship between the adult and the child.

Meeting and greeting can also be a way of encouraging young people who may find communication awkward. They can develop their skills coming into a setting and feel encouraged to respond to a positive greeting such as 'Good morning. How are you?' and make eye contact. However, the professional should always take the lead and offer some words of greeting first. A positive way is to know the young person so that you can ask something about a programme they will have watched or a football match they might have played in! This builds a relationship and the young person feels valued.

Link Find out more about the role of the key person in SHC 21.

Functional Skills English: Speaking, listening and communication

Meeting and greeting is a great role play theme. You could work in small groups of 3, one taking the role of the EYP, one the parent and one the child. Practising how to meet and greet a family and making them feel welcome is a good way of developing your speaking, listening and communication skills and your own professional development. You could share your role play with your tutor and listen carefully to any feedback that they give you.

Giving children a choice

When considering approaches to encourage children and young people to engage in activities of their choice, you must communicate at a level appropriate to their stage of development. You should ensure that they do have choices and are involved in any decision-making by giving them as much responsibility as they are ready for. If you encourage participation, children may become involved in preparing for an activity, such as by mixing paint or setting out a tabletop game. You should also find out if any of the children in your setting have additional or special needs.

You may need to vary an activity to encourage participation: for example, rolling a ball instead of throwing it as a child may not be ready to catch and throw. Perhaps you can remember the time when the ball fell through your fingers no matter how hard you tried to catch it!

Decision-making and **active involvement** are an important part of children's social and emotional development. If a child feels confident making choices, he or she will grow into an independent adult who will take the initiative.

Wherever possible, make sure that children have an element of choice in activities and experiences that you provide. This could include deciding where to plant some sunflower seeds, or where to listen to a story outside.

Link Read TDA 2.1 to remind yourself of the developmental needs of the children you are working with.

Key term

Active involvement: children having a say in what happens in their environment by saying what they want and by helping to make things happen (where this can be done safely)

Encourage children's participation in activities

Best practice checklist: Encouraging children to participate

✓ Tell the children about the activities to be offered: for example, a group session before activity time could be an opportunity to explain the planned activities

✓ Start to do the activity: for example, tapping a tin with a spoon may encourage a 9-month-old baby to imitate the activity

✓ Explain to the children how to carry out the activity: a group of eight-year-olds cooking bread in an afterschool club will need clear guidance and encouragement to succeed.

✓ Consider asking children to plan activities with you: a holiday club council is a good way to find out what sort of activities children want

✓ Ensure you are at the child's eye level: children can be intimidated by an adult standing over them

✓ Make sure the activity is attractively laid out: for example, a set of small-world play toys can be set up as a town or farm

✓ So that children and young people can choose their own activities ensure that they have access to clearly and appropriately labelled resources

Ensure children have choices and are involved in decision making

Table 2 shows ways in which different age groups can be involved in making decisions about their environment.

Table 2: How children can be involved

Age group	How children can be involved
0–3 years	• choosing play materials • deciding where to play • helping to put toys out, e.g. putting soft toys in an area of their choice • selecting crayons to use
4–7 years	• selecting activities • helping to plan a display • helping to decide agreements for the environment, such as turning off taps • choosing helpers • choosing books for the book area from the library • selecting paper, etc. to use • designing a play area such as a wild garden
8–12 years	• setting up activities • helping to decide upon the curriculum • designing areas such as a sensory area • making agreements about the use of the environment, e.g. as a poster or display • making a display • creating healthy menus for drinks and snacks
13–16 years	• selecting and setting up activities • designing different areas in the setting, such as a 'chill-out room' • making behavioural agreements • making displays • painting or cleaning areas, e.g. painting a mural on a wall

One of the most important ways of giving children and young people the opportunity to engage in activities is to know their interests. In the EYFS, practitioners are encouraged to plan their curriculum following the interests of the children.

Over to You

Observe how the children or young people in your setting are encouraged to make decisions about their environment. Are there any more decisions that they could be involved in?

Functional Skills English: Writing

You could complete this 'Over to you' in the form of a short report. You could use the information in the chart to help you write your report. Take care with your spelling, punctuation and grammar throughout your writing.

Link

Look at SHC 22 for more detail on how to provide a range of activities to meet children's and young people's needs and stages of development.

Case study:
Involving children in decisions

Trevor is leading an afterschool club and has a group of ten-year-old boys who seem uninterested in any of the activities. Their behaviour is becoming quite disruptive. Sharma, the extended schools adviser, suggests that Trevor get the boys together and finds out exactly what they are interested in and would like to do. She also advises that they are encouraged to organise the activity themselves.

1. Why do you think the boys are showing disruptive behaviour?
2. How do you think Trevor can find out about their interests?
3. How do you think that planning their own activity will help them to be more involved?

Providing activities and resources that meet children's needs

To provide the right resources for the children and young people you are working with and to achieve the appropriate outcomes in their learning, you need to take time to observe and share the results of these observations with your team.

Always ensure that:

- the activities are appropriate
- you have the appropriate tools and resources
- the experiences are appropriate.

Observing the child or young person will help you to know what you need to provide for them.

Look at Table 3 for examples of activities provided after an observation by an adult.

Table 3: Examples of activities provided

Observation	Activity
A four-year-old beginning to write recognisable letters in the mark making area	Ensure that the child has the opportunity to write his own name on his pictures and is encouraged to make lists and label items
An 18-month-old is transporting bricks in the pushchair around the setting	Provide more pushing resources indoors and outdoors such as wheelbarrows and trucks
A group of seven-year-olds is spending a lot of time in the playground helping and watching the school gardener	Involve them in creating their own growing area and taking responsibility for this
A 14-year-old is bored in the youth club and is always doodling on bits of paper	Encourage her to start a doodle wall for people to add to or ask her if she would help create some doodle canvases for the club's walls

Over to You

Observe a child playing in your setting and provide an activity the next day that extends what they are doing. This could be as simple as supporting a child in the water tray who is beginning to tip water into different-sized containers by encouraging them to use the language 'more' or 'less'. You could even encourage them to extend their own thinking by asking them a question starting with 'What if?'

Be aware of the age and stage of the child you are providing activities for and any curriculum that is being followed. This could include:

- the Early Years Foundation Stage (EYFS)
- the English National Curriculum
- the International Baccalaureate (IB)
- Primary Years Curriculum PYP.

You will have read about the EYFS Framework for children from birth to five years already in this unit. Take time to reflect on the areas of development that practitioners should consider when planning activities for children following the EYFS:

- personal, social and emotional development
- communication, language and literacy
- problem solving, reasoning and numeracy
- knowledge and understanding of the world
- physical development
- creative development.

Case study:
An activity encouraging communication

Sanita, a trainee in a daycare setting, is planning an activity that ensures that Billy and Evie, both aged two, are encouraged to enjoy and achieve through learning by listening and responding.

Sanita has noticed that they love taking items out of baskets and shaking them! She collects a basket of objects that make different sounds for them to play with. Billy takes a shaker tin and makes noises that imitate the beans in the tin. Sanita gives Evie a bottle with coloured water in and takes one herself. Billy laughs when Sanita makes a 'whooshing' sound and joins in. Sanita, Evie and Billy spend a happy ten minutes listening and responding to the sounds of the objects in the basket.

1. Why do you think it is important for children to enjoy their learning to achieve? How did Billy and Evie do this?

2. How are Billy and Evie encouraged to listen to the sounds of the objects? Why is listening an important part of communication?

Each area of learning is linked to the five outcomes of the *Every Child Matters* framework and key early learning goals.

- The development stages outlined are broad and intended to show the different ways that children can achieve the early learning goals.

- The framework is intended to be holistic and centred on the needs of the individual child, to enable children to progress through the areas of learning and development.

- The guidance can help you provide appropriate activities and resources for children of this age.

Functional Skills ICT: Finding and selecting information

If you choose to download a copy of the EYFS you could bookmark the internet page and add it to your favourites. This way you will have access to the information again should you need to use it again in the future.

Over to You

Get a copy of the EYFS framework and find out how the children's developmental stages are presented. You can order a copy on 0845 602 2260 (ref. 00013-2007BKT-EN) or download it from http://nationalstrategies.standards.dcsf.gov.uk/node/151379

The boxes below give pointers to good practice when supporting the older child within the EYFS. It is important to remember that activities provided should be holistic and consider a number of areas of development.

Personal, social and emotional development

- Encourage sharing and taking turns.
- Give the children clear guidelines and ensure all staff interpret them in the same way.
- Set a good example in the way you talk to and treat others in the setting.
- Stress the child's positive aspects.
- Learn about other cultures and religions.
- Use positive language, e.g. say 'Please walk' not 'Don't run'.
- Always give the child a chance to avoid confrontation.
- Encourage children to sort out their own problems, e.g. sharing the bicycles.
- If the children cannot sort out their own problems, offer strategies, e.g. 'Have one more turn then let someone else have a turn'.

Problem solving, reasoning and numeracy

- Talk to the children about age, buttons, pairs of gloves/socks, house numbers, car registration numbers (numeracy).
- Count the children at group time.
- Get the children to set places at the lunch table — 1:1 cutlery items.
- Offer children milk and a snack — 1:1 correspondence, e.g. child to milk.
- Line up the children in height order — relative size, ordering by size.
- Group the children by various criteria — sorting.
- Discuss whether there are more boys than girls, etc.
- Observe shapes in the environment.
- Conduct weighing activities, e.g. a see-saw is a simple weighing machine.

Knowledge and understanding of the world

- Provide well-planned activities in sand and water.
- Provide more structured activities, e.g. magnets, magnifiers, reflection, etc.
- Talk about healthy food at mealtimes and brushing teeth.
- Discuss personal hygiene, e.g. hand washing.
- Discuss the need for and carry out physical sense.
- Discuss the weather and the natural environment.
- Take walks around the area and talk about buildings, jobs and other features.
- Talk to the children about your own life and culture, providing examples of your home life, culture and language if appropriate.
- Talk about the sequence of the day or the week.
- Discuss events in the lives of the children.

Physical development

- Provide activities to develop manipulative skills, e.g. threading, cutting, small construction.
- Offer help with threading, cutting, pencil grip, dressing/undressing.
- Encourage children to perform physical activities in the appropriate place.
- Inside activities could include large construction, dancing, action songs or role play — but these need to be in a safe, large area.
- Play games, e.g. football, throwing and catching, rolling hoops.
- Help children to ride bicycles and tricycles.
- In PE, teach the children how to find a space that is safe to work in, e.g. unable to touch nearest child with arms outstretched.
- Stress the importance of fitness.
- Talk about the children's interests, e.g. football, ballet, swimming.

Communication, language and literacy

- Talk to children at a level appropriate to their understanding.
- Extend the child's vocabulary.
- Listen to children and add to the conversation.
- Provide activities to promote language development, e.g. role play, stories, Lotto.
- Work on phonics, letter recognition and names.
- Ask the children to carry verbal messages and follow and issue instructions.
- Read to children and stress that print carries the meaning.
- Run a finger under the words as you read so that children can see the relationship between the word and the sound.
- Look for words and letters that match.
- Provide children with a variety of writing media e.g. pens, pencils, chalk.
- Provide sand, tea, rice, etc., so that children can experiment with it in their writing.
- Help with pencil control, e.g. correct size of pencil, correct pencil grip, and provide finger grips if necessary.

Creative development

- Encourage role play in the role-play area and outside.
- Provide a variety of dressing-up clothes and role-play equipment.
- Provide a wide range of artistic media.
- Provide a balance of activities which do/do not involve paint.
- Observe sound in the environment.
- Display finished work attractively, using work by all the children.
- Do not take work from children if they do not want you to have it: ask them to do two — one for you and one for them.
- Play music — use instruments from a variety of cultures.
- Sing songs from different cultures, in different languages and with or without accompaniment.
- Ensure there are opportunities for free expression, interpretation of moods, interpretation of action words, e.g. bang, crackle, float.

To prepare for any activity consider the checklist.

Best practice checklist: Preparing for an activity

- ✓ Prepare everything you need to
- ✓ Be aware that children will have their own ideas so things may change!
- ✓ Consider issues that may arise
- ✓ Always try new things out, such as a recipe
- ✓ Allow enough time so that the activity is purposeful
- ✓ Ensure you have a variety of materials
- ✓ Ensure the activity is in the right place

- ✓ Ensure the activity meets the children's needs and stages of development
- ✓ Consider the learning opportunities that arise in routines, such as hand washing
- ✓ Make observation notes if possible
- ✓ Allow for the children to make choices and be engaged
- ✓ Ensure your team knows what you are doing

Activities that promote use of the senses

From birth, children learn through the five senses:

- touch
- taste
- sight
- hearing
- smell.

They use their senses to develop an understanding of their world.

There is another type of sense called the **inner sense,** which is something we sense from within our own bodies, and which varies from person to person. These senses are:

- **the tactile sense,** which is what we feel when our skin comes into contact with something. Some babies and young children are very sensitive about what they feel. Even as an adult there are some textures that you don't want to have next to your skin!

- **the vestibular sense,** which comes from inside our ear or 'inner ear'. It sorts out information about movement, gravity and balance

- **the proprioceptive sense,** which processes information about body parts and body position. This is important as babies start to move.

The activities and resources you provide play an important part in children's sensory development.

Case study:
Making a tactile display

Tam is working in the baby room of Willows Children's Centre. To encourage the children to develop their sense of touch, he is asked to provide some resources that the babies can explore. He is told they have to be safe and secure. The setting's resources are limited.

1. List some objects from home that Tam could use.

2. How can Tam ensure that the objects are safe for the babies to touch?

There are many more ways that the you can encourage children and young people to engage in sensory activities, using a variety of:

- colours
- textures
- sounds
- smells.

Visual and tactile displays
For younger children these could involve mobiles and texture boards. Young people could be encouraged to design and create their own multi-sensory displays

A variety of colours in displays and resources
Research into the effect of some colours in children's learning says, for example, that soft pastels can have a calming effect while bold colours can cause restlessness

A range of textures to experience
For young children this can be in activities using materials such as paint, sand and water. For older children and young people, consider the surfaces they walk on and the furniture you provide, such as cushions with different textures

Sensory gardens that the children can sit in, help to create and grow
Different ages can have different levels of involvement. Scented plants like lavender are known to have a calming effect

Music and sounds by having open access to instruments
Give children and young people opportunities to learn instruments as they develop, and to listen and record natural sounds, such as running water or trees rustling in the wind

Cooking activities
These are a good way to develop children's sense of smell and taste and can be planned according to the age and interest of the children and young people involved

Functional Skills ICT: Finding and selecting information

You could use a variety of search engines to expand your search across the internet. It is important to type in key words to ensure that your results are accurate.

Functional Skills Maths: Interpreting

You could draw your room to scale and then use different shapes to show what equipment you would put in it.

Key terms

Self-esteem: feeling worthwhile and respected as an individual

Confidence: feeling self-reliant enough to be able to carry out a task or activity

Resilience: being able to cope with a variety of situations

Getting ready for assessment

A multi-sensory room is space that has a range of resources to stimulate children through their senses. Such a room may be used to calm children with behavioural issues or support children with sensory needs such as visual impairment.

Use the web to find out more about multi-sensory rooms or see if there is one that you can visit in your area.

Now design a room for children in your setting, listing the equipment that you would use.

Praising and encouraging achievement

Everyone needs praise in order to feel confident, and a child is no different. To develop into a confident adult, children and young people need to be praised when they have achieved something. You can do this by:

- praising and acknowledging the achievements of each child and young person

- encouraging children and young people to recognise their own achievements.

You have an important role to play in creating a positive emotional environment for children and young people in your care and developing their **self-esteem**, **confidence** and **resilience** through praise and encouragement. When they are praised and encouraged their self-esteem rises, they take more responsibility for themselves and their environment, and they relate better to other children and adults.

Best practice checklist: Showing praise and encouragement

✓ Display children's work in a celebratory way, taking care to mount work carefully and label it appropriately. Do not be tempted to cut into the work to suit your display! Show respect and display it all.

✓ Draw attention to these displays in group times and share them with parents. Children might even like to talk about their work to others.

✓ Give children stickers or badges for effort. This will be recognised by other adults and children as a sign of a positive achievement.

✓ Praise children appropriately without attaching any conditions. Do not say, for example, 'Well done, Sam, you have washed your hands. Now make sure you always do that.' This will make Sam feel that some of the praise has been taken away. His self-esteem could be affected or he may feel it is not worth washing his hands properly again.

✓ Praise children for attempting a task even if they do not fully succeed. Children who try to pour their own drink but spill a little are more likely to develop the skill of pouring if they are praised for their effort and the spillage is ignored.

✓ Give positive feedback by starting your comments with words such as 'I really liked what you did today…' A child will immediately know that they are being encouraged

✓ A smile or a nod can be a very positive signal to a child

These two examples show how you can ensure that children and young people are resilient in a variety of situations.

A group of ten-year-olds from a holiday activity club are told they cannot have a football match as the visiting team's minibus has broken down. They have always been encouraged by their youth worker to plan their own matches and have been given the skills to do so. They are continually supported and encouraged to lead their own activities. As a result, they arrange a five-a-side match among themselves instead.

A supply teacher is working in a Foundation Stage class alongside two regular staff members. The children are welcoming and happy because the teacher has warned them about the change. The teacher encourages them to welcome visitors to their nursery and has told them how proud she is of the way they make visitors feel welcome.

Note that the way the children cope with change is because of the way they have been praised and encouraged.

Be able to support the personal care needs of children and young people within a positive environment

Children's personal care needs cover hair, teeth, and personal hygiene, so that they can be healthy and develop appropriately. You will play a part in supporting these needs and ensuring that they are an important aspect of your setting. For younger children, hygiene and care are seen as an important part of the curriculum.

The EYFS Framework goes further, saying: 'Self care is about how children gain a sense of self respect and concern for their own personal hygiene and care and how they develop independence' (EYFS *Principles into Practice*, 2007).

Effective care for skin, hair and teeth

You will need to make sure that children's skin, hair and teeth are appropriately cared for. Babies have different needs to older children and young people. As children grow up they become more independent in their skin and haircare routines. You must work with parents to find out about a child's skincare and haircare routines. Every family has different routines, needs and traditions. The parents will also be able to advise on the best products to use if their child has an allergy or irritation.

Skincare

Skincare helps to stop infection to the rest of the body. If a child has dirty skin or an infection, he or she will feel uncomfortable. Encourage the habit of washing hands.

Best practice checklist: Skincare

✓ Change nappies carefully to avoid infection

✓ Wash sweat off bodies regularly to avoid sore areas and inflammation

✓ Moisturise skin as appropriate

✓ If working in a child's home, find out if the family prefers showering to baths

✓ Ensure water is not too hot – 63°C is a recommended temperature

✓ Encourage older children to wash themselves

✓ Show young children how to wash hands and praise them well

✓ When washing a younger child's face ensure any flannels are only used once and are thoroughly washed

✓ Use soap carefully as it can dry skin

✓ Never leave young children alone by water

✓ Use recommended products if children have allergies or skin conditions such as eczema

✓ Ensure feet are washed and dried properly and that footwear fits to avoid blisters and sores

Haircare

- Find out about children's needs by talking to them or their parents.

- African-Caribbean children often have oil rubbed in hair, wear braids and need less frequent hair washing.

- Allergies will require specific products.

- Head lice are common. Treatment varies and can include special combs and lotions.

African-Caribbean children's hair needs different care from Caucasian children's hair

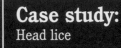

Case study:
Head lice

One morning, 13-year-old Beth storms into the club and says she has caught head lice off Maria. Some of her friends tease Maria, who asks to go home, although her hair has been treated. Two of the teenagers tell her she is dirty because she has lice.

In a group council session, Jim, the manager of the scheme, informs the young people about head lice. He tells them that head lice are often attracted to clean hair and that anybody can catch them. He emphasises that it is important to treat people with sensitivity and not name or blame them. He gives them informative leaflets about head lice. A discussion follows and the council agree on how they would support another outbreak. Beth apologises to Maria.

1. Why do you think Beth was angry?

2. Do you think Maria should have been upset?

Suncare

Skincare in the sun is essential. While you will have to do more for young children, you will have to ensure that older children understand why they must protect their skin from harmful rays. Exposure to the sun can cause skin cancer (melanoma), which causes many deaths each year. Children have delicate skin and you need to observe the following guidelines during strong sunlight.

- Always keep babies under six months out of direct sunlight.

- Keep children out of the sun between 11 am and 3 pm.

- Cover up children using sun hats, T-shirts, etc.

- Use a high-factor sun cream with not less than 15SPF.

- Ensure faces are protected.

- Ensure older children understand the importance of protecting themselves against the sun.

Over to You

Find out the policies and procedures in your setting for protecting children against the sun. Does your setting have any information for parents and children?

Toothcare

The way teeth are cared for is important to ensure healthy adult teeth. Look at the diagram of the jaw in Figure 4 to find out how teeth usually develop.

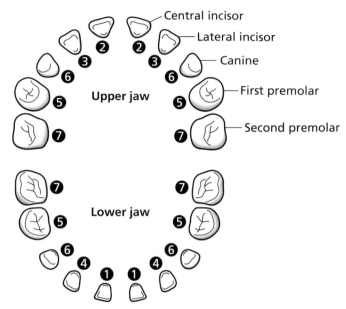

Figure 4: How a child's teeth usually develop

Teeth facts

- Babies are born with teeth growing inside their gums.
- The average age when teeth start to appear is six months.
- There are 20 teeth in the first set of teeth, called 'milk teeth'.
- All milk teeth appear by the age of 2–3 years.
- From the age of five, milk teeth begin to fall out.
- Permanent teeth start to come through when children are about six years old.
- Milk teeth are replaced by teeth that are larger.
- The 12 extra molars make a set of 32 teeth.
- The first permanent teeth to come through are molars and incisors.
- Sometimes permanent teeth are crooked and teenagers may need braces to correct this.
- Chewing is good for the teeth, but sweet and sticky foods can cause decay.

Encouraging children to clean their teeth after every meal is important. You can make this fun, perhaps by putting a sequence of actions to music or making an attractive poster. By the time children are older, thorough teeth cleaning should be an accepted part of their routine.

In areas where water supplies do not have enough fluoride, children should be given fluoride drops.

Functional Skills English: Writing

You could design a leaflet for children all about how to care for their skin, hair and teeth. This leaflet will need to include appropriate language for the age of the child that you have chosen. It must be colourful and contain words and pictures.

Skills builder

To build strong and healthy teeth, the children in your care will need:

- calcium
- fluoride
- Vitamin A
- Vitamin C
- Vitamin D.

Plan an activity for the children in your care to promote healthy teeth.

Supporting personal care routines

Routines are the regular things that occur throughout a child's or young person's day. This can range from nappy changing to mealtimes.

When carrying out routines you should:

- keep children informed in a way that is appropriate to their age and stage of development so they know what is happening
- always inform new children and parents of routines or any changes
- ensure that children who have English as an additional language are supported
- ensure that children understand expected behaviour, such as during an emergency evacuation practice
- involve children in routine tasks, such as handing out drinks
- allow children to make mistakes
- help children to carry out routines, for example by including footprints to the cloakroom
- turn routines into learning opportunities as they are part of the curriculum.

> ## Over to You
>
> Make a list of the routines for children that take place in your setting. What do you think would happen if some of the activities in a routine were neglected, such as washing hands before lunch? How do you think that the children might be affected?

> ### Case study:
> Teaching children about routines
>
> Frank works in a pre-school group and wants the children to learn the importance of washing their hands as part of their toileting routine. During a group time, Frank tells the children all about unfriendly bacteria. He tells them about the importance of washing their hands using soap and water, and how they must use paper towels to dry them. He shows them some colourful notices he has made to remind them what to do. He puts the notices up in the toilets at the children's height. Two children help him.
>
> 1. Do you think that Frank made the information fun? If so, why is this important?
>
> 2. How will the children understand the importance of hand washing from this activity?

How a positive environment and routine meets emotional needs of children and their families

The wishes of the child's parents must be taken into consideration, as must the routine of the setting. You can get to understand the family's needs by building up a relationship with them through daily communication and, in the case of young children, a settling-in plan.

A positive environment and routine will be flexible enough to meet the individual needs of children.

- If parents are working they may want their child to rest in the setting so they can have more time with them in the evening.
- In some cultures children go to bed at the same time as their parents, and this may result in more rest during the day.
- A child living in accommodation with shared bathroom facilities may have to get up earlier than usual to wash and may need rest during the day to compensate.
- A child who is unwell may need more rest during the day.

It is good practice to allow children who do not want to sleep to undertake quiet activities that will not disturb other children, such as reading, drawing or listening to story tapes or gentle music.

Balancing rest and play for physical and mental well-being

Physical activity encourages children and young people to develop all their physical skills and to practise the skills that they already have. Your role in supporting a child's physical development will be to ensure that the child has a wide variety of experiences in a safe environment.

Any setting should offer a wide range of equipment that can be used both indoors and outdoors.

It is considered important that children are given opportunities to develop their gross motor skills indoors as well as outdoors. Such opportunities may be provided by designated areas such as a soft play area or by activities such as drama.

Some settings may be lucky enough to have designated areas for physical play or have the opportunity to use other facilities. These could include:

- a soft play area
- a swimming pool
- a sensory room
- a games pitch (for example, for football, netball or tennis)
- a cycle path or course
- a climbing area
- an obstacle course or exploring area using things such as tractor tyres.

Children with additional or special needs may have limited play opportunities. It is your role to ensure that they can do as many activities as possible, for example, by adapting equipment.

Best practice checklist: Adapting equipment

✓ Place fluorescent strips on the steps of a slide for a child with a visual impairment

✓ Make sure that a child in a wheelchair has enough space to turn the chair in a game of catch.

For children with special needs

✓ Discuss their requirements with their parents, colleagues, SENCO and the child

✓ Encourage children to support and learn about their peers with special needs

✓ Have a positive attitude towards exercise

✓ Refer to role models such as stars in the Paralympics.

Rest and quiet time is also essential when children and young people are spending lengths of time in a setting. They will be more likely to enjoy and benefit from physical activities as they will be rested. Rest and quiet times will vary according to the age of the children and their need.

Table 4: Opportunities for rest

Sleep time for under fives	Some still need sleep during the day
Quiet activities for young children	If children do not sleep they may be able to read and listen to music in a calm environment
One to one with an adult for children and young people	Calm interaction or playing a game can be very restful
Relaxation exercises for children and young people	Techniques can help children and young people relax
Individual or small group drink or snack for children and young people	This can be an opportunity to socialise quietly or enjoy some time alone

Understand how to support the nutritional and dietary needs of children and young people

There has never been a more important time to develop the dietary needs of children and young people. Current research shows the importance of a healthy and balanced diet for the best possible learning and development outcomes of children and young people, starting from birth.

A healthy and balanced diet is important for learning and development outcomes

Basic nutritional requirements for children and young people

A balanced, nutritious diet that meets government guidance is now high on the list of priorities for schools. In England the School Food Trust has been formed to ensure that schools adopt the:

- 14 nutrition-based standards, and

- 5 food-based standards.

The School Food Trust 2010 says: 'Our remit is to transform food and food skills, promote the education and health of children and young people and the quality of food in schools.'

Children need to be given a balance of certain foods to grow and function properly. Figure 5 will help you understand the functions of food and drink.

Over to You

Find out more about the work of the School Food Trust on their website – www.schoolfoodtrust.org.uk.

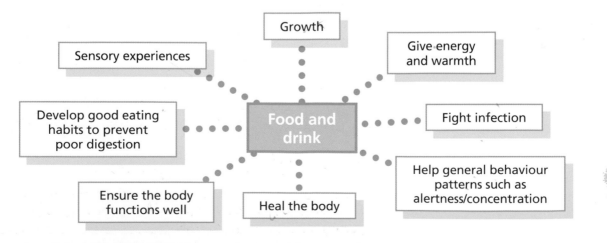

Figure 5: Functions of food and drink

- Growth
- Give energy and warmth
- Sensory experiences
- Fight infection
- Develop good eating habits to prevent poor digestion
- **Food and drink**
- Ensure the body functions well
- Heal the body
- Help general behaviour patterns such as alertness/concentration

The seven nutrients

All food is made up of one or more of the following seven nutrients.

Proteins: build the body, are good for the brain, blood, skin and other tissues. **Carbohydrates:** give energy, are present in foods such as pulses, bread, oats. **Fats:** give energy, stored as body fat if too much is eaten. **Minerals:** build bones and teeth, come from the earth, include calcium, iron, and fluoride, are present in most foods. **Vitamins:** help to maintain a healthy body. **Fibre:** maintains a healthy bowel, adds bulk to foods, is known as roughage, cannot be digested, is made of plant material, is present in foods such as bread, pulses, oats. **Water:** makes up two-thirds of the body's weight, is essential for children to drink

A variety of these foods needs to be eaten to maintain a healthy lifestyle. Water is continuously lost through sweating, breathing and urinating, so it needs to be replaced through food and drink.

The five food groups

A balanced diet for any child requires a recommended portion from five different food groups, to make sure the body gets all the nutrients it needs in the right amounts. Table 5 shows what children need to eat each day, with each representing one group of foods.

Table 5: The right foods for a balanced diet

Food group		For children
Potatoes and cereals (group 5) • Include high-energy foods: bread, pasta, rice, breakfast cereals and potatoes • Provide 'bulk' of the diet and energy, as well as some protein, vitamins, minerals and fibre • Fibre content can be raised with whole-grain pastas, rice or chapattis, wholemeal breads and potatoes in skins • Fibre provides bulk, helps digestion, prevents constipation, and encourages chewing and healthy gums		Children need five portions per day – a portion included in each meal of the day One portion: one slice of bread, one small potato, one small bowl of cereal, two tablespoons of rice or pasta, a slice of pizza
Fruit and vegetables (group 4) • Provide rich sources of vitamins and minerals as well as fibre • Fibre helps digestion and prevents bowel problems such as constipation • Citrus fruits and potatoes have high Vitamin C content for healing and healthy skin and blood formation • Green vegetables contain iron • Orange-coloured fruits tend to contain more vitamin A (for healthy skin and good vision).		Children need five portions per day, at least one rich in Vitamin C • One portion: one glass of fruit juice, one piece of fruit, two tablespoons of cooked vegetables, one piece of salad such as slices of cucumber, or a tablespoon of dried fruit • If children will not eat vegetables then give fruit, salad or fruit juice instead

Table 5: The right foods for a balanced diet (contd.)

Food group	For children

• Tinned, frozen or dried fruit and vegetables still provide required nutrients if stored and cooked correctly. Many vitamins are destroyed by poor storage and in cooking.
• To keep vitamin content high:
   ○ eat food as fresh as possible as sunlight destroys vitamins
   ○ eat whole raw fruit and vegetables where possible, or peel and chop immediately before eating
   ○ use cooking water for gravy or sauce as it contains any vitamins which have dissolved into the water	

Milk and dairy products (group 3) • Foods include milk, yogurt, hard and soft cheeses • Contain protein, Vitamins A and B (for the healthy working of the nervous system) • Rich source of calcium for forming healthy bones and teeth 	Children need three portions per day One portion: one glass of milk, or one yogurt or fromage frais, or a tablespoon of grated cheese Because of lower energy and smaller fat-soluble vitamin content, reduced-fat dairy products should not be given to children under five years of age One pint of milk or equivalent each day will give a child enough calcium; if milk is not taken more of other foods from this group must be taken instead
High-protein foods (group 2) • Foods include meat, fish, poultry, eggs, tofu, Quorn, pulses (beans, lentils, ground nuts and seeds, etc.) • With dairy foods, provide main source of protein in diet (essential for growth and repair in the body) • Meat, eggs and pulses contain iron for healthy blood formation and many B vitamins • Oily fish and liver contain Vitamin A • The pulses provide an alternative source of protein for vegetarians 	Children need two portions per day One portion dependent on age for this group. For example, one portion of meat or fish fingers varies from two slices/fingers for a young child to three or four for an older child
Oils and fats (group 1) • Concentrated source of energy, but too many saturated fats (animal fats) may cause heart disease in later life • Processed foods contain hidden saturated fats, as in sausages, cheese, chips, crisps, pies, biscuits	• Use unsaturated fats where possible • Grill or use oven rather than frying • Take care to ensure children do not eat main diet from these foods. • Children do need some fats so that fat-soluble vitamins are taken. • Children under two years need a diet with more fat and less fibre than older children. Fat provides extra energy needed at this stage; too much fibre will fill young children up and other more important foods may be left out

Other aspects of nutrition

Sugary foods

Sugary foods, including sweets and chocolate, are not essential for a balanced diet, so are not included in the food groups. They are a source of rapid, short-lived energy and have little or no other nutritional value, so should not replace foods from the other groups. Too many sugary foods may cause a child to become overweight or suffer tooth decay. Naturally occurring sugars, such as those found in fruit, are the only ones necessary for health.

Salt

Salt occurs naturally in many foods, so a well-balanced diet should contain all that is necessary, without adding extra. Too much salt can cause ill health in later life for children; and can cause kidney problems for babies and young children.

Liquids

Liquids are just as important as foods in a healthy diet. Many squashes and fizzy drinks have high sugar content and no other value. Water is far better, or natural fruit juices. However, a mixture of different drinks may be more realistic, including milk. Do not add sugar to drinks as this will encourage a 'sweet tooth'.

Additives

Additives are substances added to food to preserve it or to improve its look or taste. All manufactured foods are required by law to list any additives in the food – these are all coded with recognisable 'E' numbers. Offer fresh or frozen vegetables, or fresh fruit, as much as possible.

Snacks

Children often require snacks at mid-morning and mid-afternoon to maintain their energy. This is an ideal time to introduce new tastes and unfamiliar foods. Snacks should include a portion from the appropriate food group, such as:

- raw vegetables, such as carrots, celery, white cabbage, cucumber
- pieces of fresh fruit, e.g. apple, orange, mango, kiwi, banana, grapes
- dried fruit, e.g. apricots, sultanas, raisins, figs and apple rings
- natural yogurt with fresh fruit
- different sorts of bread and rolls, including wholegrain, with a healthy topping such as tuna, cheese, or hummus

---

Functional Skills Maths: Representing

You could focus on what you eat in a day. You could categorise the different food into the 5 food groups and then work out what percentage of each food group you eat in a day. Is your diet healthy? Are you eating too much of one type of food?

Establishing children's dietary requirements

You will encounter children with different dietary needs and it is important that you understand what can affect a child's dietary requirements.

Medical conditions

The following medical conditions can affect a child's diet.

- **Diabetes** means that the pancreas cannot regulate the body's sugar levels. Children need to avoid sugar but should have regular meals and snacks. Each child's needs will be different, and you will have to work closely with your supervisor and parents to support a diabetic child.

- **Coeliac disease** means that children cannot absorb their food normally. Coeliac children need to avoid gluten, which is found in cereals such as wheat and barley. Coeliac disease is usually detected after a child has been weaned from breast milk.

Religious or cultural beliefs

It is important to respect the diets of a variety of different religions. Look at Table 6, but remember that this may apply to only some members of each religion.

Table 6: Religious groups' ideas about food

Muslims	• Eat halal meat, fish and shellfish, which is slaughtered and prepared in a certain way • Do not eat pork or dairy products that contain rennet • Fast during Ramadan
Jews	• Eat kosher lamb, beef and chicken, which is slaughtered and prepared in a certain way • Dairy products are not eaten with meat • Eggs must not have blood spots • Fish should have fins, scales and backbones • Fast during Yom Kippur
Sikhs	• Rarely eat pork • Do not eat beef as the cow is a sacred animal • Some Sikhs eat chicken, cheese, fish and shellfish
Hindus	• Usually vegetarian • Do not eat beef as the cow is seen as a sacred animal • Do not eat dairy products that contain rennet • Eat fish with fins and scales
Rastafarians	• Some Rastafarians do eat lamb, beef and chicken, but do not eat shellfish

Food preferences

Vegetarians do not eat meat or fish. Vegans do not eat meat, fish or any other products that come from animals, such as milk, eggs and cheese.

Allergies

Some children may have food allergies. This means they cannot tolerate certain foods and may become very ill if they eat them. Common food intolerances are:

- lactose – found in milk and dairy products

- histamine – found in strawberries and ripe tomatoes

- tartrazine – found in yellow food colouring and some drinks and sweets.

Link See PEFAP 001 on how to give first aid for anaphylactic shock.

Over to You

Find out if your setting has a nut allergy statement, stating that nuts or related products may not be brought onto the premises.

You will need to be aware that some children can go into anaphylactic shock if they eat certain foods. You will learn how to deal with this on your basic first aid course.

Children who have nut allergies must not eat any food that contains nuts or has come into contact with nut products. Some children cannot even tolerate nut-free food that has been prepared in the same factory as a nut product. Manufacturers must declare any traces of nuts, so you can help by carefully reading the ingredients on food labels.

You must work closely with parents when a child has specific dietary needs. However, as children get older they will know their own requirements and will be able to make suggestions about their diet.

Basic food safety

All children in your care must be able to eat and drink safely so that food poisoning or related illnesses are avoided. Bacteria can grow quickly on food and your role in handling food and drink appropriately is essential. You need to understand how to store, prepare and serve food.

It is a legal requirement that all people working with children undergo a basic food-handling course, usually for one day. Ofsted inspectors will check that every member of staff has been on a course by looking at their certificates.

Understand 'use-by' and 'sell-by' dates on food

Storing food

- Regularly check 'use by' and 'sell by' dates and throw away anything out of date.
- Use a fridge thermometer to make sure that a fridge temperature is kept between 0°C and 5°C.
- Ensure the freezer is working and the temperature is below 18°C.
- Cool hot food quickly before placing it in the fridge.
- Do not leave food out at room temperature; store food as soon as you can.
- Store raw meat and fish separately.
- Store raw foods at the bottom of the fridge to avoid juices dropping onto other foods.
- Never refreeze food that has begun to thaw.
- Date food you put in the fridge so that other members of staff can discard it if you are not there.

Preparing food

- Wash hands thoroughly before preparing food.
- Remove watches, bracelets, rings and jewellery.
- Tie back hair and wear an apron.
- Cover cuts and wounds with a coloured, waterproof dressing.
- Do not touch your nose or mouth, or cough and sneeze over food.
- Never smoke in a room where food is being prepared.
- Clean the floor, surfaces, sink, utensils, cloths and bins regularly.
- Cover waste bins.
- Disinfect work surfaces before preparing food.
- Wash tops of cans before opening.
- Wash equipment in hot, soapy water before preparing raw food.
- Keep a separate cutting board and knife solely for poultry and wash them thoroughly after use.
- Use a separate cutting board for bread.
- Cook foods thoroughly according to instructions.
- Only reheat food once, ensuring it is heated all the way through.
- Ensure that whites and yolks of eggs are cooked thoroughly and are firm.

Serving food

- Only use clean crockery and utensils that are not cracked or chipped.
- Provide all children with their own cups and utensils.
- Ensure all children and adults wash their hands before serving and eating.

- Ensure children sit down and are able to reach their food safely.

- Do not give younger children sharp knives for cutting their food.

- Always supervise children when eating.

- Do not allow pets in the eating area or allow children to touch pets during mealtimes.

- Ensure meals and drinks are not too hot and never heat plates for young children.

Check your knowledge

1. Which Act simplifies early years regulation?

2. What does the following paragraph describe?
   One that supports every child and young person's learning and development in a challenging and achievable way.
   It is the place, setting or service where you work with children and young people.

3. Name three physical skills that your environment should support.

4. Which regulatory body will inspect sites that have 16-year-olds on for more than two hours?

   A) HMI

   B) Ofsted

   C) Local authority

5. What should you do with access points?

6. How can you greet a child who has a hearing impairment?

7. Describe active involvement.

8. Which sense is the one that we feel when we come into contact with something such as a fabric?

   A) Tactile

   B) Vestibular

   C) Proprioceptive

9. When do milk teeth appear?

   A) 9 months

   B) 4 years

   C) 2 to 3 years

10. How many food-based standards should there be in England?

    A) 5

    B) 14

    C) 7

My name is Ruth and I work in a reception class of a primary school in a busy city centre. I absolutely love my job and am made to feel very much part of the team by Lucas, who is the teacher with QTS in our class. I am a key person to one child, Xiao Sun, who speaks mainly Mandarin and was really worried that I was not welcoming to him and his mum in the morning. We sat and chatted as a team and I decided to find out from one of the parents what good morning is in Mandarin! It has made such a difference to the child and his mum when they come in each morning when I say "Zao shang hao"! The rest of the team now say good morning in Mandarin and Lucas says this to Xiao Sun when he takes the register. I think it has really made a difference to him and his mum as they feel valued because we have taken the time to learn a phrase in their home language.

Viewpoint

There has been much controversy following the famous chef Jamie Oliver's series of television programmes about the quality of school lunches. The School Food Trust has been set up to ensure that schools provide nutritionally balanced meals for children. Many people welcome this new legislation and focus on healthy eating as more children are being classed as obese. Schools are also being encouraged to provide healthy snacks at snack times and in school shops. Parents are also being encouraged to be involved with the Change4Life campaign. However, some parents feel that this is a "nanny state" approach and have protested against this campaign.

Ask the expert

Q I have a child in my nursery whose parents don't like him to sleep for long as they feel he is not sleeping at night. What can we do while the other children are sleeping?

A My advice is to ensure that he has a quiet time, which he probably needs. It can be in an area where the lights are lower than normal and where you have quiet activities such as sharing a book or drawing. You could even play some calming music. If you have enough staff you could sit in the shade outside with him and share these activities.

Understand partnership working in services for children & young people

There are many people who work with children and young people in different ways. This unit will help you to find out who these people are and how everyone working with children and young adults can work much more effectively if they work together.

Learning outcomes
By the end of this unit you will be able to:

1. understand partnership working within the context of services for children and young people

2. understand the importance of effective communication and information sharing in services for children and young people

3. understand the importance of partnership working with carers.

Understand partnership working within the context of services for children and young people

Partnerships involve a wide range of individuals, agencies and organisations, and you will be **working in partnership** with many people during your working life.

You may already have come into contact with adults other than your fellow early years professionals who have come to visit your setting or even work in the same building as you. These might include people such as advisers who help you to develop your practice or health visitors who support the well-being of young children and their families in the community.

You may also already know about some of the different agencies that have been set up in your area to encourage professionals to work together for the benefit of the child and young person. The adults here could range from a speech and language therapist to somebody working in a voluntary organisation.

It is important that you think about your own work setting and find out about the people who you may be involved in working in partnership with, including the parents and carers of the children.

This section aims to help you to find out about the different adults who will work together with you, with the shared aims of making sure that each child has the best possible start to their life and that their families are supported.

The government framework *Every Child Matters* (ECM) places great importance on partnership working. The five outcomes make it clear that all adults working with children and young people should be working in partnership. This approach is called **holistic**, where all areas of a child's needs are considered to be important.

The five outcomes for ECM are:

- Be healthy
- Stay safe
- Enjoy and achieve
- Make a positive contribution
- Achieve economic well-being.

It is very important that everyone working together with children and young people finds out about the five outcomes and bases their working practice on them.

Key terms

Working in partnership: different services and individuals working together to meet the needs of children and young people

Holistic: dealing with the whole person, rather than just one aspect of them

Over to You

Go to the government website www.dcsf.gov.uk/everychildmatters to find out more about the five outcomes and how they encourage adults working with children and young people to work together.

The services for children and young people are many and varied, and can refer to several different groups, such as those shown in Figure 1.

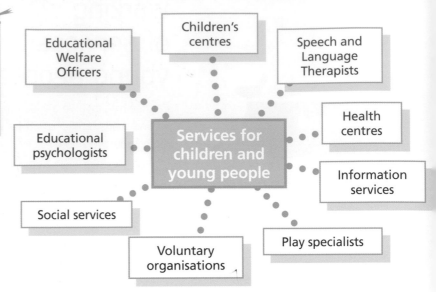

Figure 1: Services for children and young people are many and varied

Why working in partnership is important

When people working with children and young people work together, it can be very positive for the children and young people concerned. The adults could be:

- parents
- professionals
- carers
- multi-disciplinary teams
- colleagues.

They need to:

- communicate
- share their knowledge and expertise
- exchange information
- understand each other's roles.

This partnership working can be called either **multi-agency working** or **integrated working**.

If you work well as a team in your setting, then you will enjoy your work more and work more effectively — and the children will benefit. If this applies to everyone, then it can have a positive impact on children's and young people's:

- health
- development
- learning
- relationships.

The Early Years Foundation Stage (EYFS) makes it very clear that, if different agencies work together, it will improve the outcomes for the children in their learning and development. It also shows the importance of creating effective relationships with the people you work with and respecting their expertise. You will also be encouraged to develop the skills of understanding when it is important to seek the help of other professionals. While you may not be responsible for making contact with another professional, you will hopefully have the opportunity to observe a colleague making contact with other professionals. As the EYFS says: 'Knowing when and how to call in specialist help is one important element of inclusive practice' (Source: EYFS Principles Inclusive Practice 1:2 card).

The partnerships you experience could range from a speech and language therapist to sharing an observation with a reception teacher and the child's parents, to a full assessment of a child including a meeting of all the adults involved in working with the child. This could involve you at some point in your career.

When done well, working in partnership:

- gives children and young people the best possible start
- ensures that everyone working together communicates about the child
- means that specialist advice can be given to support everyday practice
- will encourage all those suporting children and young people to think about the whole child
- will give support and improve communication with the whole family.

Over to You

Look at Table 1, which shows the different types of partnership. Do any of them match your current experience?

Partners in your own work setting

If you work in a Children's Centre or a school you may already know the other adults in your setting who provide support for young children. You may also have met other professionals who have visited your setting such as an adviser, health visitor or a colleague from another setting. By providing a range of services in one setting agencies can work more closely together for the sake of each child.

Table 1: Different types of service in children's settings

Early years setting	Services	Comments
Children's centre	- Health visitor - Speech and language therapist - Jobcentre plus - Information services - Day care - Parenting support - Nurseries - Outreach workers	- Set up by Sure Start to provide a range of services to young children and their families in local communities
Nursery school	- Early education - Extended care	- Run by the local authority - Sometimes part of Children's Centres but often offering extended care to support working parents
School	- Early education - Extended care - Counselling services - Behavioural support services	- Schools run by the local authority often offer breakfast and afterschool facilities to support working families - Sometimes support services can be located in schools

Here are some of the professionals and adults in your setting or authority who may work together for children in your care:

- Mentors such as those supporting you in training
- Monitoring groups such as Ofsted
- Parents/carers
- Health visitors
- Health workers such as speech and language therapists
- Educational psychologists
- Colleagues from other settings
- Advisers
- Social workers
- Play specialists
- Parents

These adults may come from:

- the private sector
- the voluntary sector
- the state sector
- the independent sector
- Primary Care Trusts (PCTs).

Children's Centres are places where children under five years old and their families are supported by a range of services. Every community should be able to access a Sure Start Children's Centre:

'The Government's vision, set out most recently in the Children's Plan, is that every child and young person should have the opportunity to fulfill their potential. Sure Start is at the forefront of transforming the way services are delivered for young children and their families.' (Source: *Every Child Matters* website www.everychildmatters.gov.uk)

There is a partnership of private sector and public sector organisations, called Together for Children (TFC). It has been set up to support people from different professions working together for children in Sure Start Children's Centres.

The services offered vary according to each centre and the needs of the community, but will consider:

- information about services
- improve outcomes for children
- health screening/health support
- specialist services
- affordable, flexible childcare
- part of each local authority's Children's Plan
- parenting advice.

Functional Skills ICT: Developing, presenting and communicating information

You could design an information leaflet for the staff in your setting. Your leaflet could contain a list of the people that your setting works with and the contact details for each of them. You could also send this leaflet as an attachment to an e-mail to ensure that people have an electronic version that they could edit if they needed to.

Over to You

Visit the Together for Children website to find out more about resources, good practice, case studies and discussion forums.

Functional Skills ICT: Finding and selecting information

You could use a search engine to search for the Together for Children website. Read the website carefully to find the information that you require. There may be a search tool within the website to help you find the information that you need.

Getting ready for assessment

Children's Centres are part of your local authority's Children's Plan and part of the good practice being promoted to encourage people to work together for children. Find out about your local Children's Centre as evidence for assessment. To find your information you could:

- visit the website for the centre
- visit the centre and find out more about the services
- collect information about the services at the centre.

You could present a simple information leaflet about the services that are provided in the centre.

Functional Skills English: Writing

Completing this 'Getting ready for assessment' task will help you to develop your English writing skills. Think carefully about your audience for your leaflet so that you can make sure the language that you use is appropriate.

What makes partnership working effective?

There are ways to work together as professionals from different settings working with children. Outcomes are more likely to be positive if practitioners can share the way they:

- observe children and young people
- assess children and young people's needs
- plan support
- implement action plans.

For the children to be supported, it is important to work in partnership with the parents of the child, so that everyone can have a shared approach. Everyone concerned also needs to understand:

- what information can be shared, and
- the importance of confidentiality.

Look at Figure 2, which outlines the core values that should be followed when working together in partnerships.

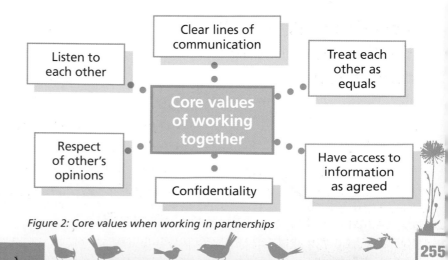

Figure 2: Core values when working in partnerships

Parents are essential to any partnership working. Just as you are encouraged to acknowledge the parents' knowledge of their child, other professionals need to do this too because little can be achieved without the knowledge and skills that parents bring.

- Parents need to be equal in any decision-making. This is called being 'empowering'.

- Joint planning with parents can be done through Early Support Family Service Plans, part of the Early Support Family Service that aims to support young children and their families.

- Any practitioners involved should be competent enough to provide the right support and acknowledge that they are unable to do much without the knowledge of the parents.

- All partners will work effectively if they can agree aims and goals through negotiation with everyone concerned including the parents.

One initiative of the Early Support Family Service is the use of **family files**. These help parents to write down everything they would like someone meeting them for the first time to know about their child and family. Family files also give them the opportunity to add information over time to keep track of what was said and agreed, including contracts and agreements. A family file is seen as a great source of information to effective partnerships.

The template for the introduction includes sections that consider:
- how families like to be communicated with, and

- when they are available for appointments.

Here are some of the headings in a family file.
- Some of the important people in my child's life

- Other things we would like you to know about our family

- The things we would like you to know about our child so we don't have to repeat it every time we meet someone new

Barriers to partnership working

Anyone who works in a team knows that it can be a challenge at times.

Take a few minutes to think about a time when you found working in your team difficult. It could have been for a variety of reasons ranging from different opinions to a misunderstanding or poor communication skills. Exactly the same issues can arise when working in partnerships that might take place in:
- a Children's Centre

- a school

- a community centre

- a health centre

- different centres, communicating or working together for specific cases or situations.

Key term

Family file: a file of information that parents compile and update about their children and the family as a whole

Over to You

You can find out more about the family file on the *Every Child Matters* website in the section 'Early Support – helping every child succeed'.

Key term

Barriers: issues or practical matters that are stopping people from working together effectively

Read Table 2 find out what some of the common **barriers** could be.

Table 2: Potential barriers to effective partnership working

Could be managed by person with a different set of skills: e.g. in a Children's Centre where the manager may oversee all the professionals
People with different skill bases may have different priorities and manage risks differently
May not be used to sharing knowledge
Each profession may use their own language often called 'jargon'
May resent having to work with others outside their chosen profession

It is important that each profession is respected and the knowledge that they have is valued. In such situations the adults will need to:

• find ways to share practice and learn to work together

• find ways to let people know about their skills and expertise by shadowing each other or giving information workshops

• be very clear about their roles when working together.

Case study:
A barrier to communication

Stoneway Children's Centre is managed by a lead person called Pam, who was originally a health professional. Her role is to ensure that the different aspects of the centre run smoothly and work together for the community. The nursery, for children aged 3 to 5 years, is led by Davina, who is a qualified and experienced teacher. She is unsure about being line-managed by Pam because she is used to being managed by a Head Teacher. However she gradually realises that Pam is there to organise the centre services and to ensure that the children and their families she has in her class have effective support. Davina has a child whose mother is having issues with bringing up her large family and is delighted to have Pam's support in arranging for the health visitor on site to contact the mum. Pam also leads regular meetings for all the professionals in the centre and, on a monthly basis, asks them to lead a workshop to talk about their particular professions.

1. What is the barrier to communication for Davina?

2. What is Pam's title?

3. How does Pam try to break down the barriers of communication in Stoneway Children's Centre?

Best practice checklist: Breaking down barriers

✓ Employ a lead person

✓ If different professions are sharing an office, make sure each has their own desk, telephone and computer

✓ Make sure a space is available to hold meetings

✓ Have a confidential space available for work with children and parents

✓ In integrated settings such as a Children's Centre, different professionals should have dedicated phone lines on which they can be contacted by parents, etc.

Understand the importance of effective communication and information sharing in services for children and young people

Link Reread the sections in SHC 21 on the importance of effective communications, to remind yourself of the skills that you need to communicate with your colleagues.

You have already learned how to communicate effectively with both children and adults in your work setting. When working in partnerships, effective communication is particularly important. When communication is made and information shared, you must remember that you may be dealing with sensitive information.

You may work with a number of different groups of professionals

The groups you may work with may be:

- home visitors
- outreach workers
- health and social care professionals
- from educational services.

To communicate effectively, the two things you need to do are:

- listen carefully to everyone involved
- put the needs of the children first.

Skills builder

Create a simple guide on how other professionals can be welcomed into your setting to ensure that everyone communicates well for the children. You could call this guide 'Welcoming other professionals into our setting'.

The first two points could be:

- Make sure the visitor is welcomed and introduced to everyone
- Make sure that all the team knows the visitor is coming and what their role is.

When you have created this leaflet on the computer, share it with your line manager or mentor. You could then use this knowledge to get ready for assessment, to show that you understand the importance of effective communication between partners.

Functional Skills ICT: Developing, presenting and communicating information

This 'Skills builder' activity is a good way of developing your use of different layouts and editing techniques.

Why clear, effective communication is needed

Effective communication is needed when working with different partners to ensure that everyone can:

- work towards the same aim
- achieve the best outcomes for the child and his/her family.

There are many different reasons why effective communication is needed. Consider these examples.

- A child or young person attends more than one setting, such as a school and the extended facility.
- A child receives support from an educational psychologist and is attending a daycare facility in a nursery.
- A child is looked after by a childminder and is attending a speech and language centre.
- A child who is autistic, who is in a mainstream KS1 class, has a dedicated learning support assistant and support from an adviser.

Best practice checklist: Communicating well

✓ Negotiate to ensure everyone's views are valued

✓ Consult so that each person's view is considered

✓ Show knowledge of the child so that the best support can be given

✓ Listen to everyone to show **respect**

✓ Build a rapport so that trust between everyone is developed

✓ Summarise and explain so that everyone understands and choices can be made

Key term

Respect: showing that you value other adults' and children's opinions and views

Many children or young people attend more than one setting. If they are moving from one setting to another, it is important that the key people involved with the child communicate by:

- sharing information about the child's learning and development
- planning together for the child's learning and developmental needs
- sharing information about the child's interests so that these can be built on shared observations
- ensuring that experiences are not repeated, such as an outing or even a meal.

The EYFS guidance states: 'It is vital to ensure that everyone is working together to meet the emotional, health and educational needs of children in all settings that they attend and across all services provided.'

When communication works well, it is because the child and his/her family are at the centre of any meeting, discussion or written communication. The checklist on the left shows some points that all the adults concerned should consider.

Policies and procedures for information sharing

Whatever the setting you are working in, you need to be aware of the policies and procedures that are in place concerning sharing information. Policies and procedures give clear messages to staff about their roles and responsibilities and set the boundaries within which they are expected to work.

It is important to remember policies and procedures are there to make sure that the best possible practice is maintained and developed, to provide the best care and learning environment for the children or young people. This is an effective way of communicating requirements to all the adults involved with the children and young people.

To encourage effective communication, each setting should have policies to consider:

- transition from one setting to another
- continuity of care between settings and carers
- multi-agency working for the different adults who may work with the children or young people.

These policies can be shared with the groups of people in Figure 3.

You may feel uncertain about whether or not you can share information and what you are able to do legally. This is often true in the early stages of a situation, when information sharing may not be as clear as where a child or young person's safety is at risk.

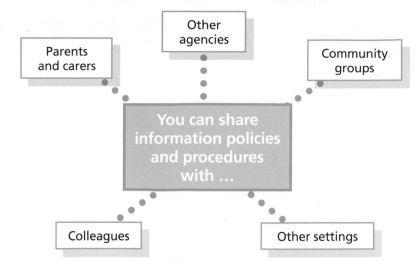

Figure 3: Information sharing policies and procedures

You may feel uncertain about sharing information

There is statutory guidance from which your setting will have developed an information sharing policy, including:

- the Data Protection Act of 1998, which provides a framework to make sure that information is shared appropriately

- the Children Act 2004, which sets out clear expectations for information sharing

- the Children's Plan 2007, which includes information-sharing exceptions throughout

- *Every Child Matters*

- the Early Years Foundation Stage Framework.

Best practice checklist: What a policy for information sharing should do

✓ Outline the roles of everyone in the decision-making process

✓ Stress confidentiality

✓ Consider where information is shared

✓ Clarify how information can be shared

✓ Ensure information is shared across children's services with parents'/carers' consent

There is usually a confidential register of children with additional needs used to share information across agencies.

Translating policies and procedures for information sharing should be considered if English is a second language. This allows parents and carers to have equal access to the procedures for consent, to enable information sharing for all.

The Common Assessment Framework

The Common Assessment Framework (CAF) aids effective communication between various agencies involved with children and young people who have additional needs. CAF offers very clear procedures for sharing information.

Conflicts or dilemmas over sharing information

If you are being asked to share information with partners but also to maintain confidentiality, conflicts or dilemmas may well arise. One of the most difficult decisions that you may have to face as a practitioner is when you feel you want to share information that you may have been asked not to disclose. This can often relate to a matter of safeguarding the children or young people in your care.

As a rule you should always talk to your line manager if you are placed in such a situation, however guilty you may feel at breaking a confidence. Avoid discussing this with other colleagues, however much you may trust them.

If a parent or carer withdraws consent for information, your line manager or the lead professional can seek a second opinion or take action through the **Child Concern Model**, which means that information can be shared without permission to safeguard the child.

Over to You

Find out from your line manager what your setting's policy is with regard to verbal information exchange and emergency information exchange. Take time to read this as it is a useful guide for your everyday practice.

Key term

Child Concern Model: a model setting out shared definitions, guidelines on assessment and referral, etc. for professionals working together with vulnerable children

Getting ready for assessment

Find out about the Child Concern Model in your area. You will be able to go onto your local authority website to find out how this model protects vulnerable children and young people in your area and what procedures it outlines for how confidential information is shared. You could highlight the points that give you guidance on how to manage sharing information that is confidential and download this so as to prepare for your assessment. You will be gaining knowledge about the dilemmas involved sharing sensitive information.

If you share information, you must do it using the right process with children and young people in mind. To minimise any conflict when disclosing information, follow the points in the checklist below.

Best practice checklist: Disclosing information

✓ Only share information with relevant people

✓ If a child is in any kind of danger, information must be shared

✓ Information shared may protect a child who is at risk from an adult

✓ Adults have a duty to protect a child's health and development

✓ Children must always come first and be communicated with where possible

✓ Record all information and actions

✓ Always consult with your line manager

Over to You

Your setting will have a child protection person whose role it is to ensure that you have the information you need to safeguard the children or young people you are working with. Talk to your child protection person and find out how the setting approaches the disclosure of sensitive information without consent from parents or children.

Functional Skills English: Speaking, listening and communication

You could prepare some interview questions before you meet with the child protection person in your setting. Being prepared for the discussion will help you to hold a detailed discussion where you can gather information to support you in your role. Listen carefully to what they have to say so that you can respond appropriately and gather the correct information.

Recording information clearly, accurately and concisely

As a practitioner, you must play your part in making sure that information is recorded clearly, accurately and concisely, and in a way that meets any legal requirements you or your setting are under. Your setting should have very clear procedures for how you record any information, ensuring that you meet the requirements of the law and of statutory bodies such as Ofsted.

Your setting will have required ways to record information. These may include:

- observations
- assessments
- incidents
- injury
- medical information
- concerns about a child
- risk assessment
- records of meetings
- records of conversations.

If you have to write a report as a record of something that has happened, you should be aware that there are different sorts of report. The one that you are most likely to be involved in is a **factual report**. A factual report is one that gives information, such as an accident report. It should be written only stating what has happened, without descriptive language such as 'sadly' or 'terrible'!

If you have to record information, ensure that you:

- seek support from your line manager if you need guidance
- make notes at any meetings so that you can use them to help you write a record
- write legibly and free of errors — ask for help if needed to check spellings, etc.
- use required formats
- keep wording brief and to the point
- if using the computer, use the required format and store confidentially if you are interrupted when writing
- maintain confidentiality by avoiding using children's full names, photos, etc.
- record information within an agreed timeframe.

Key term

Factual report: a report that gives information, such as an accident report

Functional Skills English: Writing

This checklist of points outlines the importance of having good writing skills when working with children and young people.

There are times when you will need to record in an agreed format. For example, earlier on in this unit you read about the Common Assessment Framework (CAF), which has clear guidance for recording information and templates for practitioners to use when a child is being referred for initial assessment for support.

You will also be required to record information in a required format in your setting.

Three Corners Nursery
Medicine Administration Record

Name of child: Sophie Gee   DoB: 18.07.2006

Name of Parent: Johan Gee

Name of Staff Member: Tac Browne

Date permission given: 12.09.10

Period of permission: 12.09.10 until 16.09.10

Details of medication

Amoxicillin liquid antibiotic following an ear infection

Instructions for administration

Give to Sophie after lunch.

Give 1 5ml spoonful

Store in fridge with name on

Give to parent at end of day

Initial when given

Only to be given by Tac, her key person

Administration details

Date: 12.09.10

Remarks: 1 5ml teaspoon given

Given by: Tac Browne

Signature: T Browne

Date: 13.09.10

Remarks:

Given by:

Signature:

Figure 4: Example of a medicine administration record

Your setting will probably be registered with Ofsted and will have legal requirements for recording some information as outlined in the Statutory Framework for the Early Years Foundation Stage (EYFS). The example in Figure 4 of one of these requirements is with regards to the way you keep records of giving medicine to children, with clear permission from parents. Ofsted says that you must 'keep written records of all medicine you give to children, and tell parents about these records' (Source: Ofsted website www.ofsted.gov.uk).

Communicating and storing records securely

There are a number of ways that communications and records can be made and you will find that you have to do this during your time at work.

You may do this through:

- electronic means
- memos
- a communication book
- a required format, such as an incident form.

Always share any information that you have recorded with your line manager or the designated person. Take a look at Figure 5 below on storing information.

The Data Protection Act of 1998

The Data Protection Act of 1998 is concerned with the storing and accessibility of personal information. Data stored about an adult and child, such as a reference for an employee, must not be shared without the person's permission or kept longer than is necessary. You should be aware that everyone has a right to see information stored about them, including you!

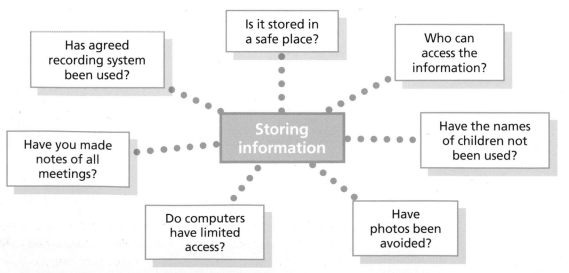

Figure 5: Storing information

Functional Skills ICT: Using ICT

Any confidential files stored on a computer should be password protected. You need to create passwords that are secure and that only the relevant people have access to. A secure password is one that contains a mixture of numbers and upper and lower case letters.

When information is stored it should be secure, so be careful not to mislay any portable devices that you use to store confidential information, such as USB sticks.

When information is stored it should be secure

Case study:
Storing information insecurely

Ruth, an early years professional, is asked by the reception class teacher to check the emergency contact number for a child in her class. The school admissions administrator goes to the file and finds the information. Ruth notices that the filing cabinet with the child's personal information and records in is not locked – the key is still in the lock – and is in an unsupervised area, which both parents and teachers enter during the day.

1. Why do you think that Ruth is concerned about the storing of children's information?

2. How do you think this storage could be improved?

Key term

Referral: when details are sent, with permission, to another setting, multi-agency panel or professional to help support the child or young person's needs

Making referrals to different agencies

Sometimes a child or young person in a setting such as a nursery or school may need extra support from another setting. There are many reasons why this may happen and it is important that you know how these **referrals** are made.

A child may be referred for:

- a medical condition, such as a hearing impairment

- a learning need, such as dyslexia

- an emotional need, such as bereavement or personal loss

- a physical condition, such as brittle bones.

Multi-agency panels have been set up to support referrals in between settings. Usually they:

- are made up of different professionals

- are organised by local authorities

- ensure children's needs are quickly identified

- make sure children are referred to the right setting

- monitor the provision between settings

- ensure that there is a close partnership between settings

- include parents in the process.

Early intervention teams have been set up in local areas to ensure that referral processes go smoothly for children from birth to five years. This follows the *Every Child Matters* framework, which states that all children are entitled to the best start in life.

Earlier in this unit you read about the Common Assessment Framework. This has three main steps to follow in the referral process for children, which all practitioners working with children and young people can use.

- **Step 1** Find out if the child has additional needs by using the CAF checklist.

- **Step 2** Discuss the child's needs using the CAF checklist.

- **Step 3** A decision is made to seek support.

Using the CAF checklist

Completing a CAF checklist can help you to find out if a referral and an assessment should take place. A CAF checklist includes:

- details of child

- record of child's or young person's:
  - health
  - learning
  - development
  - safety

- impact on others such as family members

- impact of poverty on child

- a recommendation as to whether a CAF assessment should take place

You can complete a CAF checklist online.

Over to You

To see a sample of the official CAF checklist, visit www.everychildmatters.co.uk.

Understand the importance of partnership working with carers

If you want to support the needs of each child you are working with, your relationship with their parents or carers is very important. You will have read much about the importance of working in partnership with parents and carers. You can now consider how important this part of your work is.

As stated in the Early Years Foundation Stage framework (EYFS), **positive relationships** are a key to a successful setting. Showing that you value the parents and carers will create the basis of a good relationship. The EYFS says:

> 'Parents are the children's first and most enduring educators. When parents and practitioners work together in early years settings, the results have a positive impact on children's development and learning.' (Source: EYFS Principles into Practice)

Positive relationships that reflect effective communication between key adults in a child's life are a way of ensuring that he/she will get the best possible start.

Key term

Positive relationships: relationships that benefit children and young people and their ability to participate in and benefit from a setting

Your relationship with a child's parents or carers is very important

Why partnership with carers is important

We work in partnership with parents and carers because it is one of the best ways that we can find out information about the child at first hand!

- Parents know their child better than anyone else.

- They are aware of the child's interests, strengths and needs.

- They usually know how to best support their child.

- They usually have strategies to support their behaviour.

There are also many situations where parents may need support in their parenting, and working in partnership is the most effective way to support this.

Other reasons to work in partnership with parents and carers include:

- to support children during their development by working together and sharing knowledge of the child
- to develop a relationship that is relaxed enough to cope with children with additional needs
- to enable the key people in children's lives to work together and share information so that professionals can support adults who may need support in their parenting
- to support parents who may be experiencing emotional or social problems
- to give parents confidence in their parenting
- to improve a parent's understanding of children's need for stimulation
- to provide extra support in settings.

There are many projects that encourage working in partnership with carers in the early years. One you may have heard of is Sure Start, which aims to give young children and their families the best start in life by offering a variety of services for children under five.

Here are some other successful projects that encourage working in partnership with parents and carers.

- **Early Years Support Programme** – funded by the Department for Education to design support services for young disabled children and their families (www.dcsf.gov.uk/everychildmatters/healthandwellbeing/ahdc/earlysupport/home)
- **Effective Partnership with Parents** EPP – creating projects to help develop schools working with parents (www.mosaic-ed.com)
- **Early Bird** – the National Autistic Society Programme to support home families at home with autistic children (www.nas.org.uk)
- **Peers Early Educational Partnership** PEEP aims to support parents and carers to support children's learning (www.peep.org.uk)
- **Portage** – recognises that working with parents can develop every child's full potential (www.portage.co.uk)

Over to You

You have read that Early Intervention Teams have been set up across England to work with children from additional needs from birth to five years. They encourage parents and multi-agencies to work together. Find out more about your local Early Intervention Team on your local authority website.

Functional Skills English: Reading and Writing

You could write a short summary of the information that you have found from the website and how this will support you in your role. You could share your report with your tutor to show how you are developing your knowledge and skills.

Developing and sustaining partnerships with carers

In many of your settings you will work closely with parents and carers of the children that you look after. There are many ways of developing and sustaining these partnerships to ensure that children get the best possible care.

One of the main ways of doing this is through the key person system. Ofsted says: 'All of these settings have key workers (a specially named person for the children and parents) who spend time talking with families to learn all they can about their children before they start'(Ofsted Annual Report Focus on Early Years 2008/09).

A key person will:

- communicate with parents of key children on a daily basis
- support any transition or attachment issues.

The key worker is especially important with children under three, where the curriculum is based on relationships that the child experiences. Most settings should have a settling-in policy, which will guide parents and practitioners through the best ways to settle a child into a setting.

Skills builder

In your setting, the key person may have to write a settling-in plan for young children. This is always done in partnership with parents and should include:

- the child's name and date of birth
- information about family members
- key facts such as a child's likes/dislikes, sleep habits, food preferences, sleep times, special comforters, etc.
- parental preferences, such as preferred methods of communication
- planned visits by parent and child and notes of how these initial visits went.

Talk to your line manager about the settling-in plan that your setting operates and ask if you can be involved in creating one with the parent.

Another way to develop and sustain partnerships with parents and carers is to share as much information as possible with them. If you keep them informed about their child then communication will become more effective, as you discovered earlier in this unit. There are many ways of doing this, but you should consider the checklist overleaf carefully to find out the main ways of sharing information with parents and carers.

Best practice checklist: Sharing information

✓ Invite parents/carers to a meeting before their child's admission to share policies and procedures and to complete the required contact forms

✓ Ask parents/carers for information about their children, individual needs and requirements

✓ Display daily routines and details of the setting on noticeboards

✓ Give information about the curriculum via regular newsletters/posters/website

✓ Give information about outings by newsletters/letters/home–school link books

✓ Ensure parental/carer permission is given for outings, with information given about the purpose of the visit

✓ Welcome parents/carers in to discuss their child with the key worker

✓ Encourage parents/carers to share any relevant information about changes to their child's normal family life or routine

✓ Give any changes about a child's situation to the appropriate person in charge of records so that these can be updated, where appropriate

Effective communication is the key to developing relationships with parents and carers. Take time to read the second section of this unit to review your understanding of effective communication.

One of the most important things you can do is to encourage parents and carers to feel that they can ask questions about their child or the setting. To do this they will need:

● to be listened to, for you to encourage conversation

● time to communicate with you

● respect and value for their opinions

● different opportunities for asking questions, such as one-to-one communication, website or group meetings.

Parents will also sometimes need to gain information to support their parenting. They can be guided by the setting in a variety of ways. If this is encouraged, parents and carers will develop trust that your setting is keen to support them. Find out how by looking at Figure 6.

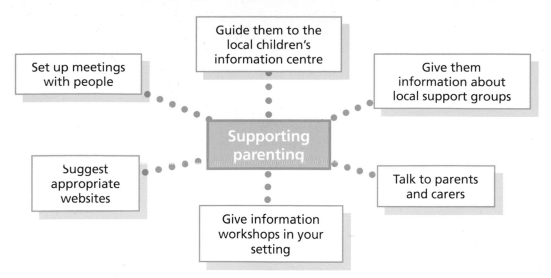

Figure 6: Ways in which your setting can support parenting

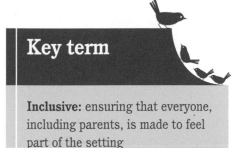

Key term

Inclusive: ensuring that everyone, including parents, is made to feel part of the setting

Your setting might have a number of group functions. All too often these events are attended by the same group of people. Your setting will have to work hard to be **inclusive**.

These functions might include:

- parent/teacher communication sessions
- curriculum meetings
- information sessions
- parenting workshops
- open governance meetings
- social occasions
- fundraising groups
- focus groups.

There may be many reasons why someone is reluctant to attend a group meeting. It could be a lack of confidence, lack of English speaking or accessibility because they live a long way from your setting. To make sure people are made to feel they will be welcome consider:

- providing a translator or translated information
- asking parents or carers to meetings personally
- trying to have a link person, such as an outreach worker, who might accompany the adult or carer to your setting
- putting a record of meetings on your website
- giving reluctant attendees a task, such as making refreshments, to make them feel involved.

Parents will come to your setting with a range of skills and knowledge, and this is often the best way to develop a relationship. Perhaps they

Functional Skills ICT: Developing, presenting and communicating information

You could design a poster for the next function that your setting is holding. Your poster should be designed in a way that encourages more people to attend and makes them feel part of your setting.

can come and lead an activity such as cooking, or give their expertise in, for example, translating for other parents. This not only supports your setting but also ensures a close relationship that can only benefit the child.

Case study:
Developing a relationship with parents/carers

Ron knows that two of the parents in the daycare nursery are not happy that Rakesh is their children's key person. In the mornings they wait to talk to Ron as she is the lead person in the room. Ron talks to her line manager about this. She suggests that their local early years adviser comes to talk to the parents and carers about how the key worker system operates. This takes place and the parents come and have lots of time to ask questions.

1. How has Ron attempted to develop her relationship with the two parents?

2. How do you think the workshop will help their relationship with the setting?

One of the best ways to develop relationships with parents in your setting is to involve existing parents in welcoming new parents, by:

- encouraging parents to welcome new parents

- asking new parents to hold coffee mornings for new parents

- 'buddying' parents, so that new parents have a link

- asking existing parents to email new parents before they move into the area

- making contact with new parents to inform them about events.

When partnerships may be difficult

There is a range of reasons why partnerships with parents and carers may be difficult to sustain in a setting. Dealing with such situations requires sensitive and appropriate support from managers or external agencies.

Some potentially difficult situations are listed below. Take a few minutes to consider each of these. You may have experienced some of these situations; even if you haven't, it is important to be aware that these can happen.

- There is a breakdown in communication due to disagreement with regard to care of child, such as lack of boundaries

- The home language or culture may make communication very difficult to sustain: for example, in a culture where women do not leave the family home

Key term

CAF: the Common Assessment Framework, which provides an agreed strategy for assessing children's needs and working with the family where possible

- A child is exposed to inappropriate caring and has to be placed on a child protection or Children in Need plan
- Consent is refused for a child to be assessed through the **CAF** framework and the adult's opinion is overridden
- The family has a chaotic lifestyle due to drug or other substance abuse
- The parents have their own learning needs
- A parent actively avoids contact with professionals perhaps because of a family situation caused by poverty or abuse
- The home situation involves separation, divorce, etc.
- The parents are vulnerable
- The parents lack parenting skills
- Working parents do not communicate with the setting

There is a range of reasons why partnerships with parents and carers may be difficult to sustain

Check your knowledge

1. Name three groups of services for children and young people.
2. What is multi-agency working?
3. Who set up Children's Centres?
   A) Sure Thing
   B) Sure Start
   C) Early Childhood Committees
4. Name two characteristics of effective partnership working.
5. What is a family file?
6. What is the CAF?
7. What is a factual report?
8. Which Act allows us to access information about ourselves and is concerned with the storing and accessibility of personal information?
   A) The Data Protection Act of 1998
   B) 1998 The Children Act
9. What does PEEP stand for?
10. What does the term 'inclusive' mean?

My Story

Hi, my name is Jenni and I am a key person for Ralph in the Keyway Children's Centre. I have a level 2 qualification in Early Years and am currently working with one- to two-year-olds. Ralph is two years old and his mother was very keen to leave him in our daycare setting and go to work. When they first visited Ralph was very upset and clung to her. She was very sweet with him but was clear that she did not want to stay. The leader in my room, Lydia, was great and talked to Ralph's mum and myself, introducing a 'settling-in' plan. This gave Ralph's mum time to talk about Ralph and for us to plan some times when she could bring Ralph and gradually leave him. She eventually understood that Ralph would benefit from a settling-in plan. This was the first time that I had used one of these with a parent and I think it is a great idea as it shows how important it is for the key people in a child's life to communicate.

Viewpoint

A range of extended care is now available to working families with children and young people. In fact, most schools will have an extended schools manager. Children can have breakfast and do their homework at these facilities. There are people who believe that this type of provision puts a strain on children and young people, and that they should be at home before and after a normal school day. Perhaps you could discuss this with your working team or friends studying with you.

Ask the expert

Q I have a child in my school reception class whose mother speaks Urdu. It is very difficult to communicate with her as she is very shy. Also I am not sure if the family understands the notes that we send home. They are a lovely family. What can I do?

A Try to find out if she has a friend or older child who can translate. If not then ask for help from your Children's Information Centre, who can find a translator. You could also consider translating the messages that go home. Perhaps you could also find out if she can come into school and share an activity from her culture with the children, such as cooking.

Paediatric emergency first aid

This unit looks at how to deal with potentially life-threatening situations and safely assess what might be happening in an emergency situation. The unit provides you with the knowledge to develop the first aid skills you need to practise under qualified supervision.

Learning outcomes

By the end of this unit, you will:

1. understand the role of the paediatric first aider

2. be able to assess an emergency situation and act safely and effectively

3. be able to provide first aid for an infant and a child who is unresponsive and breathing normally

4. be able to provide first aid for an infant and a child who is unresponsive and not breathing normally

5. be able to provide first aid for an infant and a child who has a foreign body airway obstruction

6. be able to provide first aid to an infant and a child who is wounded and bleeding

7. know how to provide first aid to an infant and a child who is suffering from shock.

It must be emphasised that while this unit provides you with the underpinning knowledge and theory of emergency first aid, it cannot take the place of a valid, recognised first aid qualification. Until you have been on a first aid course, you should be very careful about any actions you take in an emergency, because the wrong action could cause more harm to the casualty. If in doubt, you should summon help first.

Understand the role of the paediatric first aider

First aid is the immediate response to someone with an injury or illness. First aid can prevent the injury or effects of the illness worsening.

Children and young people have accidents and may suddenly become ill and need help. You will not work in a children's or young people's setting for long before you are in a situation requiring someone with first aid knowledge and skills. Everyone who works with children and young people should have a paediatric first aid qualification.

The responsibilities of a paediatric first aider

Your responsibilities as a paediatric first aider are simple. They are to:

- assess any situation in which a child appears to be ill or injured to:
  - ensure your own safety, and protect yourself from any danger
  - prevent further injury to the child
  - prevent injury to other children
- provide care to a child who has suddenly become ill or injured until either
  - medical help or an ambulance arrives or
  - the child's parent or legal guardian arrives
- prevent the condition of the child becoming worse, if possible
- provide reassurance to the injured or ill child and other children who may be involved in the area
- pass on information about the event or circumstances to the professional help or parents.

Minimising the risk of infection

It is important that you know how to minimise the risk of infection, to yourself and to others. Bacteria and viruses can cause infection and are easily spread in:

- the air on droplets of moisture — for example through sneezing (airborne)
- food — both cooked and uncooked
- water that is contaminated
- body fluids such as blood

You should be aware of preventing infection in all your work with children and babies.

Over to You

Ofsted has certain requirements of anyone working in an early years setting, as regards their first aid skills. Visit the Ofsted website and see what you can find out about their requirements and any first aid training you might need to get.

Over to You

Reading about first aid is one way of preparing to help children who are injured or ill. Seeing examples in action is another way. Have a look at the Red Cross website (http://childrenfirstaid.redcross.org.uk/) for video clips and other useful information.

Make sure you prevent the spread of infection when dealing with injured or ill children by following the simple rules in this checklist.

Best practice checklist: Minimising infection risk

✓ Wear gloves whenever possible to protect yourself

✓ Wash your hands immediately after any contact with blood or other body fluids

✓ Make sure any cuts or grazes on your own hands are covered with a plaster

✓ When a child has an open wound, if possible rinse well with soap and running water to get rid of dirt and any other contamination, but control any bleeding first

✓ Put all dirty materials into a plastic bag and dispose of correctly

Link Go back to MU 2.4 and check the section on infection control procedures.

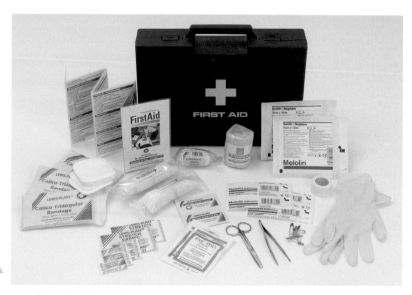

A well-stocked first aid kit

Over to You

Find out where the first aid kits are kept in your setting.

- How many are there?
- What is in them?
- Who checks the contents to ensure they are complete and still in date, and how often?
- Do your kits contain all the items in Table 1?

First aid equipment

First aid equipment, including personal protection, such as gloves and aprons, is only useful if you can identify it and use it appropriately. Wherever there are children or young people, there should always be a well-equipped first aid kit, kept in place where anyone needing it will quickly find it. A first aid kit should always be taken on outings away from your setting; in addition to the main kit in the setting, an easy to carry kit should be available for such occasions.

Table 1: Items in a first aid kit

First aid item	Purpose
Disposable vinyl or latex-free gloves	Protecting first aider's hands from blood and other fluids
Scissors	Cutting dressings and possibly clothing
Sterile gauze pads	Covering small bleeding wounds
Adhesive tape	Securing gauze pads
Large combined dressings (large gauze pad and bandage)	Covering larger wounds
Stretch bandage	Holding dressings in place on body or limbs
Crepe bandage	Supporting sprains to leg or ankle
Triangular bandage or sling	Supporting arm or shoulder injury
Safety pins	Fastening slings
Eye dressing	Covering eye to protect it after injury or foreign body entry
Plasters	Covering small cuts or grazes
Plastic bags	Disposing of soiled waste
Notepad and pen	Making notes about the incident
List of items in the first aid kit	Checking the contents

Best practice checklist: Using first aid kits

✓ Check contents weekly

✓ Keep kit on display in an easy to access place

✓ Only use for first aid incidents

✓ After use, replace all used items

Personal protective equipment is important to stop you coming into contact with blood, vomit, urine or faeces when dealing with a sick or injured child. Bacteria and viruses are carried in blood, saliva and other bodily fluids and can be passed through open wounds and saliva. Also it is not pleasant to handle fluids – gloves make it easier! Aprons protect your clothing.

Personal protective equipment includes:

● plastic aprons

● plastic gloves

● personal responsibility to keep any open cuts on your hands covered.

They should always be used when dealing with a first aid incident where a child is bleeding or vomiting.

Recording accidents

Any accident at work should be recorded and all accidents involving children should be reported to the child's parent or carer. Some accidents need reporting to the Health and Safety Executive (see MU 2.4). It is important that you know what you need to record and how to do it.

Information should be recorded in an accident book that is available for inspectors to view. Managers should use the book to monitor accidents happening in the setting. This can help them identify any patterns that suggest a problem with safety.

Information recorded should include:

- date, time and place of accident
- name and group or class of the child
- details of the injury or illness and what first aid was given
- details of the incident or accident
- what happened after first aid was given (did the child go to hospital/ get taken home by parents/go back to class or group?)
- name and signature of the person (or people) dealing with the incident.

Infant or child?

For the purposes of first aid treatment, an infant is a child of 12 months or less and will be held in your arms while giving many forms of first aid. Calling for help involves carrying the infant with you. A baby has a much larger body surface in comparison to body volume; dehydration through losing body fluids can set in quickly. Babies can lose consciousness much more quickly than children and their entire system is immature. A seemingly mild injury or illness can quickly get much worse and become life-threatening.

A child is defined as one over 12 months of age for first aid purposes. As a child grows in size, you will need to carry out first aid at the scene of the incident and get help to you.

As you work through this unit you will read about different ways of giving first aid to babies and children.

Getting ready for Assessment

First aid incidents cannot be planned. All you can do to prepare for supporting a child when they need emergency help is read this unit (and the next) and practise your skills on models.

When accidents or incidents do happen at your setting, make sure you get the information on them even if you were not directly involved. Fill out a mock accident form and keep a record of them all, including incidents you observe as well as those you are involved in.

You could also carry out a mock risk assessment to identify what could be done to prevent such an incident happening again.

Link The 'Getting ready for assessment' feature in this unit will also help with your assessment for MU 2.4.

Be able to assess an emergency situation and act safely and effectively

How to conduct a scene survey

The very first thing you should do when you see an accident happen or when you find a child who has been injured is to stop and think — even if only for a few seconds. Rushing to help without that slight pause before helping the child can:

● put you in danger

● put other children in danger

● stop you doing the best for the injured child.

If you are helping a child who has, for example, fallen, as you are approaching them to help just look around and make sure that you are not going to trip over the same hazard the child has fallen over!

A scene survey takes no more than 30 seconds and helps you to assess what has happened and what you need to do. It is important to check that you are not going to be in danger, or that any other children are not at risk of injury. You simply need to stand still briefly and look at the scene. That very short pause will also help you to act calmly and not panic.

Stop and think about …

Safety — is it safe for you to help and are other children safe?

● Your first instinct is to go and help an injured child, but there are a number of possible dangers that could result in you or other children being injured. Look for hazards such as:

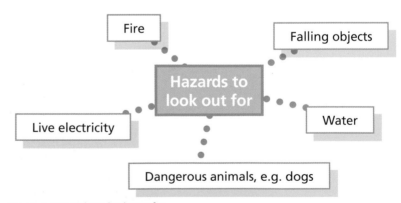

Figure 1: Hazards to look out for

If the scene is not safe, you should try to make it safe: for example, by switching off any electrical supply or removing the child from the scene. If this is not possible, do not try to provide first aid until you have got help and the scene has been made safe.

Functional Skills ICT: Developing, presenting and communicating information

Functional Skills English: Reading and Writing

You could produce a booklet of information 'what to do in an emergency' outlining the key things that you have read about in this section. You could aim your booklet at other students who go into your setting. Think carefully about the language that you use and the information included must be factual. You could produce your booklet on the computer and develop your editing and formatting skills.

Scene — what has happened?

What has happened? Try to assess what the incident is: a fall from a piece of equipment or a trip? Is the child choking? Have two children bumped into each other?

Situation — who is involved?

How many children? How old are they? If more than one child is injured, you will need more help if it is available. Someone will need to check that all the children who should be there, are there, and remove other children from the scene, supervise and possibly comfort them. Sometimes, adults who are at an incident may not know what to do — the best thing is to ask them to look after any children who are not injured, or go and call for help.

Help — is anyone else around to help you?

If other adults or older responsible children are in the area, use them to help. They can help by:

- looking after other children
- fetching the first aid kit
- getting other adults involved
- calling for an ambulance if needed.

Case study:
Scene surveys

Jade, a nursery assistant, is supervising children in the outdoor area. Lily aged four years runs after her friend and trips, falls and bangs her head on the climbing frame. Lily is crying loudly, but so is her friend. It is difficult to see who is hurt. Other children are gathering round.

Scene 1

Jade stops as she approaches the scene. She can see that Lily has blood running down her face, the other children are not in danger, and Alisha, one of the students, is nearby.

Jade calmly asks Alisha to take the other children indoors and ask one of the other staff to bring the first aid kit out to her. She then goes over to Lily to see what action is needed.

Scene 2

Jade rushes over to the scene calling Lily's name. It is difficult to see what is wrong with Lily because the other children are crowding round. Several of the children are crying. Jade does not have anything with her to clean the blood from Lily's head. She tries to get one of the children to go and find someone to help her and shouts out for help.

Which scene was the best action? Why?

How to conduct a primary survey on an infant and a child

When you have carried out your scene survey, you then need to find out what is wrong with the child so you know what first aid is needed. The first survey — as soon as you have carried out the scene survey — is a 'primary survey'.

Hands-off ABC

A hands-off ABC survey gives you an immediate idea of how seriously ill or injured the child is. It tells you if breathing and circulation is working; if they are not, the child may die unless they receive immediate help. You will see this within seconds of approaching the child. The ABC you are looking at are Airway, Breathing and Circulation — and you will be checking the response of the casualty.

- **Response** Look for signs of a child who is very still, does not respond to your voice, and does not look normal. Call for an ambulance immediately. This is a possible life-threatening situation.

- **Airway** If a child is on his back, the tongue falls back and blocks the airway. You need to open the airway. Place one hand on the forehead and gently tilt the head back to bring the tongue away from the back of the throat.

- **Breathing** Look for a child who is obviously finding breathing difficult. Call for an ambulance immediately.

- **Circulation** Look for obvious difference to the child's usual skin colour — extreme paleness, bluish tinge, very blotchy or very pink — which are all signs of problems with circulation. Call for an ambulance immediately.

Link Carrying out observations for MU 2.2 will link in with this 'Skills builder' feature.

Skills builder

Practise looking at children and babies with ABC in mind. You should be familiar with the normal appearance of children you work with so that you quickly know when they are ill or injured.

When and how to call for help

If in doubt, always call for help — if you are at work or in a placement, this should be a qualified member of staff. You might be in a situation when a child is taken ill or is injured without qualified support around — again, if in doubt, call for an ambulance by dialling 999. Urgent help is needed for any baby or child in any of these situations.

- difficulty in breathing

- asthma attack that does not respond to use of an inhaler

- floppy or unresponsive baby or child

- significant change in behaviour — much more withdrawn or alert than usual

- unconscious baby or child

- unable to swallow

- purple, blue or grey skin or lips

- fits or convulsions

- wounds that will not stop bleeding

- burns or scalds

- headache, confusion, vomiting, wobbling, problems with seeing — all after a head injury

- suspicion that the child may have meningitis: severe stiff neck, fever, headache, purple or red rash that fails the glass test (see MPII 002)

- severe pain especially if it gets worse

- dehydration: sunken features, not passing much urine, lethargic

- vomiting blood

- signs of frostbite

- heat exhaustion

- eating or drinking any poison

- raised itchy lumps (hives) accompanied by any swelling of the mouth and/or nose.

When to get urgent medical attention

- Severe vomiting or diarrhoea

- Very high temperature especially if the child appears ill

- A cut that may need stitches

- Difficulty in walking or using arms after a fall

- Severe bruising

- Any animal bites that break the skin

- Bites or stings where the redness and swelling spreads or the child seems ill

- Any other condition that gives serious cause for concern.

Calling for an ambulance

Everyone in a setting must know how to call for an ambulance. Clear, simple information should be by the telephone as a reminder.

- Dial 999 and be ready to give details of:
  - the injuries
  - where you are
  - the age of the child.

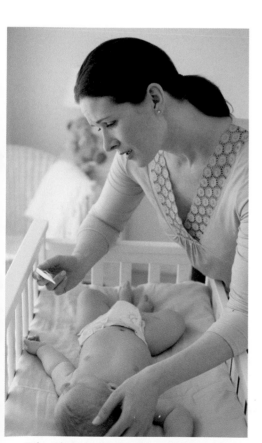

Take a baby or small toddler with you when you call for an ambulance for them

- Stay on the phone and respond to all instructions you are given.

- Do not hang up until the person at ambulance control tells you to do so.

- Make sure you can see and monitor the child while you are making the call.

If you are alone with a child — for example, babysitting — and need to call for an ambulance, if the injured or ill child is a baby or small toddler, take them with you to the telephone and continue to give first aid.

Be able to provide first aid for an infant and a child who is unresponsive and breathing normally

If a baby or child is not responding to you but they are breathing normally, you have three important things to do:

- keep their airway open, to keep them breathing

- put them into a safe position to maintain breathing

- call for an ambulance.

If someone else is around, ask them to call for an ambulance and tell the operator who answers that a child is unconscious but breathing. Always carry on monitoring the child until the ambulance arrives.

The appropriate recovery position

You may be familiar with putting someone into the recovery position. However, the appropriate position varies according to the age of the child or young person.

Maintaining an open airway

Opening and maintaining an open airway is the single most important first aid action for anyone who is unconscious, whether it is an adult or child. It is a simple action that can and does save lives.

The body needs oxygen for survival. Oxygen comes from the air and enters the body through breathing. If air cannot get into the lungs so that the circulation can transport oxygen round the body, death will occur. If a baby or child (or adult) has a blocked airway — something, for example the tongue, blood or vomit, will be blocking the throat — this means they cannot breathe.

If someone is unconscious, it is important to make sure that their airway is kept open so air can enter the lungs.

- Place your hand on the forehead and tilt the head back slightly.

- Place the fingers of your other hand under the chin and lift gently.

- Look, listen and feel for breathing.
- Look for any obvious obstructions, such as blood or vomit, in the mouth and remove.
- Call for help.

Recovery position

An unconscious baby or child who is breathing and has no other life-threatening conditions should be placed in the recovery position.

Children

- Turn the child onto his or her side.
- Pull the knees forward to act as a balance.
- Lift the chin forward in open airway position and adjust the hand under the cheek as necessary.
- Make sure the airway is open.
- Check the child's breathing and pulse continuously.

If a neck or back injury is suspected

- Place your hands on either side of the child's face.
- With your fingertips, gently lift the jaw to open the airway.
- Take care not to tilt the child's neck.
- Stay with the child.

Babies

- Hold a baby under 12 months in your arms.
- Make sure the head is tilted downwards to prevent the baby from choking on the tongue or inhaling vomit.
- Keep checking for breathing and call for help.
- Take the baby with you if you need to go into another room for the telephone.

Over to You

So that you have some skill ready to use in case of need, practise on a friend:

- opening the airway
- putting them into the recovery position.

Let them practise on you too, so that you know how it feels.

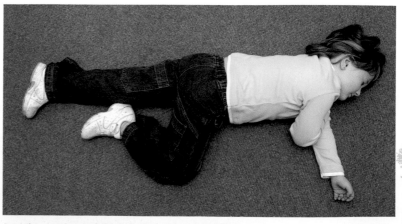

Practise putting a child into the recovery position

Continual assessment and monitoring

If you are providing first aid for a baby or child you must keep checking on their condition until medical help or an ambulance arrives. This is quite simple. Keep checking using the ABC: Airway, Breathing, Circulation. Keep asking how they are and give lots of reassurance that help — and mummy or daddy — are on the way.

Be able to provide first aid for an infant and a child who is unresponsive and not breathing normally

A child who is not responding to you and not breathing normally is in a life-threatening situation. Without your help, they could die. A child who is not breathing needs immediate help in the form of 'rescue breaths'.

Rescue breaths

If your ABC check shows a child is not breathing, you must try to help them to start breathing again.

Before starting rescue breathing, make sure it is needed by gently tapping on the child or baby's body and shouting 'Are you OK?'. Call for help and ask someone to call 999 for an ambulance. If you are alone, carry out one minute of rescue breathing then call 999. Take a baby or small child with you to the phone and start rescue breathing as you call.

1. Open the airway.
2. Look, listen and feel for breathing — watch the chest, put your ear close — for ten seconds.
3. Tilt the head back and blow into the child's mouth for one second, until the chest rises — this shows air is going into the body:
    a. for a baby, seal your mouth over the nose and mouth
    b. for an older child, pinch the nose and seal the mouth with yours.
4. Breathe into the child in this way five times. If the child is not breathing after five attempts, stop and begin chest compressions or CPR.

Practising administering rescue breathing

You will need to practise rescue breathing on a baby and child manikin or model. Ask your supervisor if your setting has one, or your tutor if you attend a college or training centre.

When and how to administer cardiopulmonary resuscitation (CPR)

If after giving five rescue breaths the child is still not breathing, the heart may have stopped. If this is the case, any oxygen you are putting into the child is not being pumped round the body and you need to start CPR.

CPR procedure

CPR on a child or baby requires 30 chest compressions and two rescue breaths. This continues for 1 minute. To give a chest compression:

- find the lower end of the flat bone running down the centre of the chest (this is the sternum)

- compress the chest to about one third of the depth of the chest
  - for a baby, use your first two fingers to do the compressions.
  - for an older child, use the heel of one hand.

Giving rescue breaths and chest compressions – demonstrated on an adult

How to deal with a seizure

A seizure or fit may be due to many causes. The most common for a baby or child are:

- fever

- epilepsy.

Seizures can be very mild and involve a few moments of staring into space — you may hear people talking about 'petit-mal seizures'. More serious seizures may include convulsions, shown by:

- shaking or jerking movements
- rolling eyes
- drooling
- loss of consciousness
- loss of bladder or bowel control (only obvious in an older child).

If a child is having a **convulsive seizure**:

- make sure they are in a safe area
- put the child on their side
- slide your hand or a folded towel or blanket under the head
- loosen tight clothing
- do not put anything in the mouth
- move toys and furniture out of the way
- make a note of what is happening.

An ambulance should be called for any unconscious child or baby and for any child who has not had a seizure before.

Be able to provide first aid for an infant and a child who has a foreign body airway obstruction

Choking on a simple small object can lead to a child's death. Children put all types of objects in their mouths as well as food! Too big a lump of food can cause choking, or simple laughing whilst eating can make a small piece of food 'go down the wrong way'. As well as helping to prevent a child swallowing small objects they could choke on, make sure you know how to deal with a child who is choking.

Mild or severe?

The first thing you need to do when dealing with a foreign body airway obstruction is to decide whether the obstruction is mild or severe.

A child with a mild airway obstruction will still be getting air into their lungs. They will still be breathing and able to cry and speak. To get rid of the blockage they will be coughing – the body's natural reaction to something in the airway.

A severe airway obstruction will result in a child who cannot breathe, cough or make a noise. They may well be holding their neck as they try to breathe – this is the 'universal distress signal'. A complete blockage needs immediate care and emergency help from an ambulance.

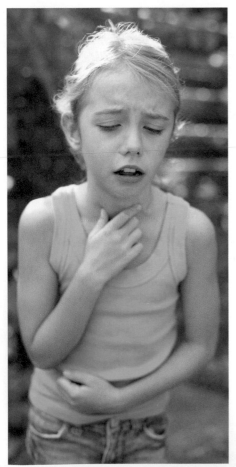

Holding the neck – the universal distress signal

Treating an infant or child who is choking

If a child starts to choke and cannot clear it themselves by coughing make sure you:

- get someone to call for an ambulance — if you are alone try treatment for one minute, then dial 999

- lean an older child forward or put a baby over your knee, face downwards, and give five back slaps between the shoulders

- remove any obvious obstruction from the mouth

- next, give five chest thrusts: stand behind the child, make a fist against the lower breast bone, grasp the fist with the other hand and press it sharply into the chest

- for a baby, press two fingertips on the lower half of the breast bone.

After administering treatment

After administering the treatment, there is still important work for you to do.

If you do remove the obstruction through your emergency treatment, you will need to carry out a check on the child or baby. Check that breathing is normal and that the child is behaving normally. If in doubt about the condition of the child or baby, call for medical help.

If you cannot remove the obstruction and the child or baby is becoming unconscious, you will need to start CPR — rescue breathing and if needed chest compressions — until the ambulance arrives.

Be able to provide first aid to an infant and a child who is wounded and bleeding

Bleeding from a wound can be very distressing to a child. Even very small wounds on some parts of the body, for example the head, can bleed a lot. Heavy blood loss from a major wound can cause a child to go into shock.

Common types of wound

Accidents can cause a number of different types of wound. Wounds can be open or closed.

Minor wounds

- abrasions — top layer of skin removed but little blood loss

- lacerations or cuts — a cut to the skin with a gap between the edges

- puncture wounds — can be deep or shallow and may contain the item that has caused the puncture

Severe wounds

- large or deep incisions — caused by sharp instruments, such as knives or glass
- avulsion wounds — where a piece of skin has been torn loose, common when a ring on a finger has caught and dragged
- amputations — involve the cutting or tearing off of a body part.

Types, severity and effect of bleeding

Cuts to the skin usually also involve cuts to blood vessels. Three main factors affect how serious the bleeding will be:

- the size of the cut
- how deep it is
- the size of blood vessels that are cut.

Minor bleeding

Capillaries are tiny little blood vessels throughout the body that stop bleeding quite easily with gentle pressure. Most minor wounds will have capillary bleeding.

Severe bleeding

Severe bleeding — bleeding that does not stop quickly with pressure or that is 'spurting' from an artery can quickly cause a child to go into shock; if not treated, they may die.

Serious bleeding may occur from:

- arteries, which are deep blood vessels that carry blood away from the heart and, if cut, can lose large amounts of blood in a very short time
- veins, which are nearer the surface and carry blood to the heart. Bleeding from veins can be heavy, but will usually stop with firm pressure
- cuts to parts of the body with lots of blood vessels, such as the head, will bleed a lot more than, say, a cut to the foot, which has fewer vessels
- internal bleeding: a serious type of bleeding that is not always obvious. This usually occurs in the chest or abdomen as the result of a blow to the body.

Controlling minor and major external bleeding

Pressure on the cut or around it is the best way of stopping bleeding.

- **Direct pressure** on a wound with a clean pad is usually effective for bleeding from a vein.
- **Indirect pressure** around a wound but not directly on it may be needed where there is a foreign body in the wound, such as a piece of glass. The object should be left for medical attention and pads pressed around the wound to stop the bleeding. Do not try to remove the object as this may make the wound worse.

Here are other things you should do.

- Elevate the wound.

- Reassure the child.

- Do not move the child unnecessarily.

- Treat for shock, reassure the child and keep him or her warm.

- Lay the child down, lower the head, raise the feet and loosen tight clothing.

With any sort of bleeding if it does not stop quickly, or if you are worried, call for help.

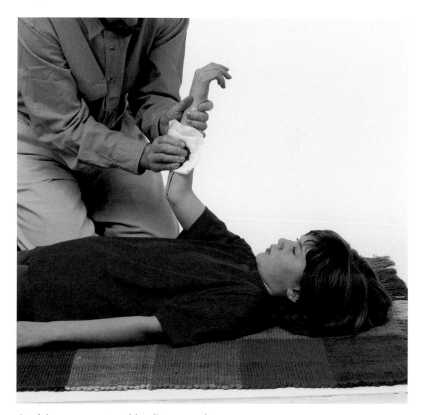

Applying pressure to a bleeding wound

First aid for minor injuries

Minor cuts and bruises are easily treated by:

- making sure the injured part is clean

- checking for more serious bleeding

- applying a dressing

- comforting the child

- making sure you fill out an accident form and notify the parents at the end of the day.

Know how to provide first aid to an infant and a child who is suffering from shock

Shock can be caused by a number of events, but usually by blood loss in children. Shock can also occur as a reaction to other situations such as falling into very cold water. Shock can be dangerous and threaten a child's life

Circulatory shock is the result of the heart failing to pump blood around the circulation system in the body, often resulting in a heart attack. It also occurs when the blood vessels have all opened up (dilated) or if the blood supply to the vital organs has fallen due to blood loss. If the body does not have a good blood supply, it will have a poor oxygen supply as well. When it occurs, blood loss is the usual cause of shock in children and babies.

Recognising and managing shock

Always be alert for a child showing signs of shock if they have had an accident, especially if they are bleeding.

Signs of shock

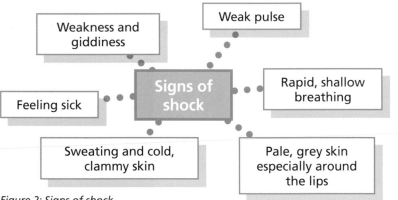

Figure 2: Signs of shock

In the later stages of shock, as the oxygen supply to the brain falls, the following symptoms may occur:

- restlessness
- yawning and 'gulping' for air
- unconsciousness.

Managing shock

- Find the cause — usually blood loss — and if possible stop the bleeding.
- Lay child down and keep the head low.
- Raise child's legs to improve blood supply to the brain; for a baby, hold in arms with the head lower than the legs.
- Loosen clothing but keep warm with a blanket.
- Check ABC and be ready to use CPR.
- Call for an ambulance.

Recognising and managing anaphylactic shock

Anaphylactic shock is a severe allergic reaction by the body to an **allergen**. It is a life-threatening situation. Common triggers include peanuts, pollen and cats, but any allergens can cause anaphylactic shock. The trigger does not have to be something that you know the child is allergic to.

Look out for:

- red blotchy skin that starts to swell

- swelling of face and neck

- puffiness round the eyes

- problems with breathing

- anxiousness.

Anaphylactic shock is an extreme emergency and can kill a child.

- Dial 999 for an ambulance.

- Check if the child has an adrenaline pen — if so, use it.

- Put the child into a comfortable position — often this is sitting up to help breathing.

- Monitor the airway, breathing and pulse.

- If the child becomes unconscious, put in the recovery position.

Being able to use an adrenaline pen can save a child's life

Key terms

Anaphylactic shock: a severe allergic reaction by the body to an allergen

Allergen or trigger: a substance that causes an allergic reaction

Over to You

Look on the internet to see if you can find out more about peanut allergy in young children. A good starting point is the Eat Well site of the Food Standards Agency http://www.eatwell.gov.uk/healthissues/foodintolerance/foodintolerancetypes/peanutallergy/

Check your knowledge

1. Identify the main responsibilities of first aid.

2. What does ABC stand for?

3. When should you call for an ambulance?

4. Why is it important to keep the airway open, and how would you open it?

5. When would you start rescue breaths?

6. How would you know when a child has a severe airway obstruction?

7. List three types of bleeding. Which is the most severe? Why?

8. How would you control bleeding in a wound with a foreign body?

9. List four signs of shock.

10. Why is it so important to deal with shock as soon as possible?

Managing paediatric illness & injury

Correct management of an illness or injury by the carers in a setting can make all the difference to how a child feels. In this unit, you will learn how to recognise and treat the most common illnesses affecting children and young people, and how to manage the most common injuries.

Learning outcomes
By the end of this unit, you will:

1. be able to provide first aid to an infant and a child with a suspected fracture and a dislocation

2. be able to provide first aid to an infant and a child with a head, a neck and a back injury

3. know how to provide first aid to an infant and a child with conditions affecting the eyes, ears and nose

4. know how to provide first aid to an infant and a child with a chronic medical condition or sudden illness

5. know how to provide first aid to an infant and a child who is experiencing the effects of extreme heat and cold

6. know how to provide first aid to an infant and a child who has sustained an electric shock

7. know how to provide first aid to an infant and a child with burns or scalds

8. know how to provide first aid to an infant and a child who has been poisoned

9. know how to provide first aid to an infant and a child who has been bitten or stung.

It must be emphasised that while this unit provides you with the underpinning knowledge and theory of emergency first aid, it cannot take the place of a valid, recognised first aid qualification. Until you have been on a first aid course, you should be very careful about any actions you take in an emergency, because the wrong action could cause more harm to the casualty. If in doubt, you should summon help first.

Functional skills
English: Writing

Writing and recording accidents and injuries is a very important job. You must ensure that you only record facts and that the writing is very clear so that other people can understand exactly what happened. If you were able to get a blank copy of the accident form that your setting uses it is often a good idea to do a practice one based on a made up accident.

Link

The information you gather in a log for this Getting ready for assessment will be valuable evidence for your assessment for TDA 2.2 and MU 2.4 on safeguarding and health and safety, as well as this one.

Getting ready for assessment

During your training you will probably see a number of first aid incidents, and may be involved in the management of them. Whenever you do have any accidents or sudden illnesses at work make notes after each event under these headings.

- What caused the accident or illness?
- What were the signs or symptoms shown by the child?
- How was the incident handled?
- What first aid was given?
- What happened after that?
- Could the incident have been prevented? If so how?
- What are they interested in?

Gather any other information that is relevant. If you can get a copy (with names blacked out), even better. See example of an incident report form on p.178, Unit MU 2.4.

There are very few, if any, children who reach adulthood without experiencing an injury or illness. Many of these incidents are not life-threatening but do cause the child pain and distress. Keeping calm and level-headed while providing the correct first aid treatment and calling for expert help if needed are all very important roles for you in your work.

Always be aware of the limits of your role. First aid is not about heroics, but about preventing any worsening of a child's condition, protecting them and other children from further harm and providing immediate care and reassurance.

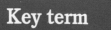

Key term

Fracture: a break in a bone

Dislocation: the separation of a bone from a joint

Be able to provide first aid to an infant and a child with a suspected fracture and a dislocation

Fractures and dislocations are common for children. An active child running around and playing may fall over or off things in the course of their development and injure themselves, resulting in a bone or soft tissue injury.

The common types of fracture

A fracture is simply a broken bone. When a bone breaks, the blood vessels, muscles and nerves around the site of the break will also be damaged.

Closed and open fractures

Fractures can be one of two main types: closed or open.

- **Closed fracture** This is where the skin does not break at the site of the fracture, and is the most common type of fracture.

- **Open fracture** If an open wound occurs at the site of the fracture, that is an open fracture. Sometimes the fractured bone sticks out of the wound; this creates a big risk of infection in the bone.

Young children's bones are more flexible than adults', and often a fracture may not break the full bone. This sort of fracture is sometimes referred to as a **greenstick fracture**.

Dislocation

The separation of a bone from a joint can occur easily in children. Never tug or pull on a child's arm or hand, and never pick up young children by their hands or arms.

How to manage a fracture or dislocation

When managing a fracture or dislocation, recognise that the child has an injury and call for an ambulance or get the child to hospital. First aid does not involve treating the injury.

It is usually easy to tell if a child has a fracture or dislocation. A child who is older is likely to tell you that their arm or leg hurts. Alternatively, look for:

- deformity — is the injured part in an unnatural position?
- open wounds or breaks in the skin
- tenderness
- swelling around the injured area
- loss of power/ability to move
- unnatural position.

Ask the child, "can you move it?"

Your role as a first aider is to maintain the injured part in the most comfortable position while waiting for the ambulance. A child will usually keep an injured arm or leg very still and will hold an arm close to their body, forming a natural splint.

Key terms

Closed fracture: a fracture where the skin does not break

Open fracture: a fracture where there is an open wound

Greenstick fracture: a fracture that does not break the full bone

Applying a support sling or an elevation sling

In the case of an injured arm, a sling may help to give support until medical help arrives. Never insist on putting a sling on a child if they do not want you to do so — you may cause more damage. The only way to learn how to apply a sling is to be shown and then practise on someone who does not have an injury.

The child with an injury will 'show' you which type of sling is needed. Look at how they are holding their arm.

- If their arm is across their front at an angle of about 90 degrees, they need an arm sling.

- If their arm is up across their chest, they need an elevation sling.

An elevation sling supports the forearm and hand in a raised position, with the fingertips touching the casualty's shoulder.

Whatever position their arm is in, maintain it in this position.

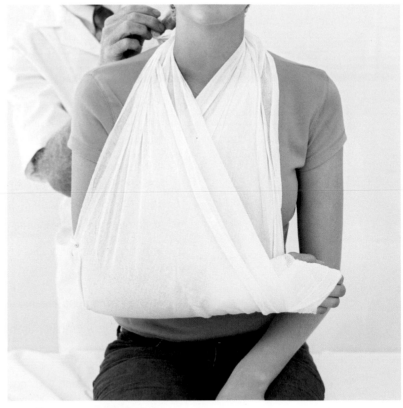

Arm sling on an adult

Be able to provide first aid to an infant and a child with a head, a neck and a back injury

Head, neck and back injuries are common among children and young people They need careful attention to prevent them leading to more serious injuries to the brain or spine, or to more lasting problems.

Recognising and managing head injuries

It is important that you know what symptoms to look out for and what actions to take for head injuries including concussion, skull fracture and cerebral compression.

What is a head injury?

The brain is a delicate organ wrapped in three layers of tissues and then well protected by the skull, which is basically a bone box. If the skull receives a hard blow, the brain is shaken around in the box and blood vessels supplying the protective tissues can be torn and start to bleed. Because the skull is a hard box, the bleeding builds up and causes pressure on the brain.

A head injury can result in:

- concussion — dizziness and nausea, with or without a spell of unconsciousness.

- skull fracture — a break in the skull

- cerebral compression — pressure on the brain due to bleeding

The most common way a head injury presents is that a child will complain or show signs of concussion.

Signs of a head injury include:

- a bump

- bruising

- swelling

- severe headache

- nausea (feeling sick)

- vomiting (more than once)

- being pale and sweaty

- blurred vision

- pupils of the eyes uneven in size

- severe drowsiness (difficult to wake up)

- irritability and aggression

- fits
- difficulty in walking or talking
- loss of consciousness, which may only be for a few seconds
- clear or blood-stained fluid from the ears or nose
- bleeding from any part of the head
- changes in behaviour
- swollen fontanelles (or soft spots) on a baby's skull
- change in the type of cry of a baby.

What should you do?

Continued bleeding inside the brain can cause serious disability or death. Bleeding can happen immediately after the injury or a few days later, or blood may build up slowly. If any of the symptoms above occur, you should call for an ambulance and call the child's parents immediately. While waiting:

- control any external bleeding by applying pressure with a pad
- lay the casualty down
- if the child is unconscious, act as if there is also an injury to the neck
- make a note of the symptoms: vomiting, pupil size, how long the child has been or was unconscious, etc.

Often after a bang to the head a child may just seem a bit dazed and have a bump and not need to go to hospital. It is still really important to monitor the child closely for about six hours after the accident, and then be alert for any changes for a few days. You must inform parents after any bang to the head and give them clear instructions about what to look for and encouragement to seek medical help if they are worried at all.

External bleeding from the scalp

The scalp is full of small blood vessels, so even a small cut can produce a lot of blood. Treat by providing gentle but firm pressure with a pad. If the bleeding does not stop, call for an ambulance.

How to manage a suspected spinal injury

Injuries to the spine can involve one or more parts of the back and/or the neck. The spine is made up of 33 bones (called vertebrae) with a hole through the middle. The spinal cord, which is made up of all the nerves that take messages to the body, runs through the hole from the brain. A fracture or dislocation of any of the vertebrae can damage the spinal cord and can cause serious damage, including paralysis. Spinal injuries are unusual in young children but can occur after falls from a height: for example, from a slide or if knocked down by a car.

Functional Skills English: Writing

Your setting will probably have a letter that they send home with any child that has had a bump to the head. You could write a letter to the parent of a made up child telling them that their child has had an accident at school involving their head. You need to include the relevant details and any signs and symptoms of serious injury that the parents need to be aware of. Think carefully about the layout of your letter and organise your work so that the information is presented clearly and concisely.

Treatment is simple.

- Do not move or attempt to move the child.
- Steady and support the neck and head.
- Dial 999 for an ambulance.

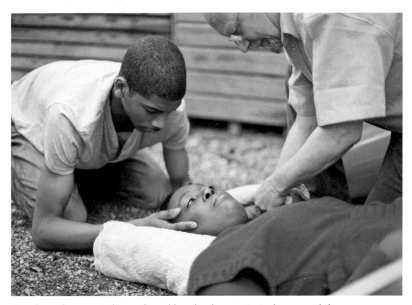

Steady and support the neck and head – demonstrated on an adult

Know how to provide first aid to an infant and a child with conditions affecting the eyes, ears and nose

Conditions that affect children's eyes, ears and noses are common. Many need only routine treatment, but you will need to be aware of some basic precautions to prevent further complications with these delicate areas.

Foreign bodies in the eyes, ears or nose

Young children with small objects in their nose or ears are common sights in **minor injuries units** or **walk-in centres**. Small beads fit into ears and noses very well, and once there can become stuck. Attempts to remove them usually have one result — they simply get more firmly stuck.

Take the child to the nearest NHS walk-in centre or minor injuries unit.

Key terms

Minor injuries unit: units, usually attached to a hospital which treat straightforward injures such as cuts, foreign bodies in noses, eyes and ears, simple fractures

Walk-in centres: NHS centres providing 24-hour access to a doctor for illnesses and other health problems

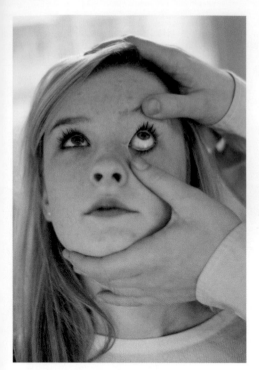

Pull down the lower eyelid

Many children get foreign bodies in their eyes, such as dust, sand or paint. Even a tiny speck can feel very big and irritating. Most of these can be easily removed by following these steps.

- Put on disposable gloves.
- Sit the child down.
- Gently pull down the lower eyelid and gently remove any speck with a clean, wet handkerchief or piece of gauze swab.
- If that does not work, pull the upper eyelid over the lower to try to flush out with tears.
- If the object is still there wash the eye with water by:
  - positioning the head over a sink or bowl with the eye open and facing down
  - using a clean plastic cup pour water on the eye from the nose side outwards.

If none of these works or the eye is still red and painful, you should take the child to the nearest point of medical help.

Eye injuries

If the delicate covering or interior of the eye is damaged or penetrated this can cause injury to the eye. Such injuries can be caused by:

- chemicals
- sports injuries
- toys
- finger nails
- any sharp object, such as a tree branch.

Look out for:

- problems with vision, such as loss of or double vision
- sensitivity to light
- pain when moving the eye
- blood in the eye
- redness or swelling
- numbness
- being unable to open the eye.

Urgent treatment is important to stop further damage and treat the injury, so get immediate medical help.

Know how to provide first aid to an infant and a child with a chronic medical condition or sudden illness

Where a child has a **chronic** medical condition, you need to be as prepared as possible. Often, the parents of children with chronic health conditions and older children themselves are very knowledgeable about the management of the condition. For sudden illness, you need to make sure that you can spot the signs of potentially life-threatening conditions and understand when to get expert help.

Recognising and managing chronic medical conditions

Any setting caring for a child should know if they have any chronic medical conditions. Staff should be clear about when the child may need help and have easy access to any medicines needed to help. It is important to listen to the child.

Key term

Chronic: persisting for a long time or constantly recurring

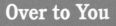

Over to You

Find out if any of the children in your setting have a **chronic** medical condition. If they have- find out more about it, and in particular how would you know if they needed help and what would you do

There are many different chronic health conditions, but the most common ones that you may come into contact with are asthma, sickle cell anaemia and diabetes.

Asthma

Asthma is caused by the airways in the lungs closing up. This makes it difficult for the child to get rid of the air in their lungs and to take in air with oxygen. You can usually hear this as the child wheezes and breathing in/out is more difficult. Asthma attacks can be brought on by:

- exercise
- very cold air
- pollen or dust
- stress.

Managing an asthma attack

Children with asthma usually use one or more inhalers to control their asthma. Often they need to use these before exercise. They should always have their inhaler available to help them deal with an attack. If left untreated, a child can die from an asthma attack.

- Make the child comfortable. The child should be seated in the position most comfortable for them, away from other children in a quiet area.
- Help the child use their inhaler if he or she has one — usually a blue reliever.
- Encourage the child to breathe slowly.
- If the attack does not subside, call for medical help.

Over to You

Find out your setting's policy about asthma inhalers. Where are they kept? Which children in your setting have asthma and what can cause their attacks?

Functional Skills Maths: Representing

Can you calculate what percentage of the children in your setting is asthmatic?

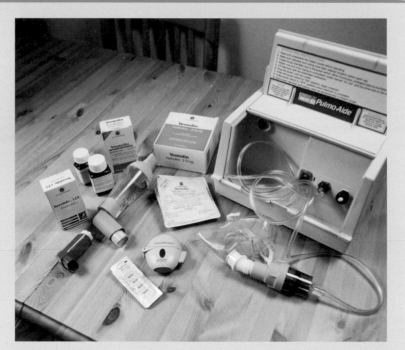

Asthma inhalers

Sickle cell anaemia

Sickle cell anaemia is caused by unusually shaped red blood cells. It is a genetically inherited condition, especially common in children of an African–Caribbean heritage.

Children with sickle cell disease can have a sickle cell crisis. This is a result of the misshapen blood cells gathering in clumps and getting stuck in joints in the body. This causes extreme pain and distress to the child. Your setting should have instructions from the child's parents about the care of their child.

Key terms

Hypoglycaemia: when the body has too much insulin and not enough sugar

Hyperglycaemia: when the body has too much sugar and not enough insulin

First aid treatment

- Reassure and comfort the child.
- Take to medical help or call an ambulance.

Diabetes

Diabetes is a lifelong medical condition. With diabetes, the body does not produce insulin to control the sugars in the body. Most children with diabetes need insulin injections at different times of the day. If they have too little or too much insulin, they are at risk of one of two serious conditions: **hypoglycaemia** and **hyperglycaemia**.

Dealing with a hypoglycaemia or 'hypo' attack

A child going into a 'hypo' may be:

- drowsy
- confused
- irritable
- pale
- trembling
- sweating.

The child needs sugar in their system to balance the insulin. This can be by sugar directly in the mouth or a drink of orange juice. Usually the child will respond rapidly to easily absorbed sugar and will not need any more treatment. It is important to make sure that a child with diabetes eats when they should do and that you know what to give them if they start to show signs of not having enough food.

Dealing with a hyperglycaemia or 'hyper' attack

A child going into a 'hyper' attack may show the following signs:

- very thirsty
- passing urine very often
- drowsy
- have a fruity-smelling breath
- vomiting
- eventually become unconscious.

As a 'hyper' attack is caused by a lack of insulin, medical help is needed, so call for an ambulance.

Best practice checklist: Managing chronic illness

✓ Work with and listen to the parents and child to have clear guidelines for care and support

✓ Make sure all staff in the setting know about the condition and what to look out for and any special diet, management, etc. for the child

✓ Follow parents' guidelines in the case of any related health incident

✓ Make sure any medication is available when it is needed

✓ Contact the parents or inform them when an incident related to the illness has occurred

Serious sudden illnesses

Children in any setting may become ill during the course of a day. In most cases the development of a high temperature, vomiting and a rash are just part of a mild illness. However, in a few cases they can be the start of a life-threatening or serious illness. If you are in any doubt about the seriousness of symptoms, you need to seek medical help. Babies and young children can deteriorate rapidly.

Meningitis

This is a condition in which the linings that surround the brain and the spinal cord become inflamed. There are different types of meningitis; some of them can quickly develop into a life-threatening illness. If a child is showing signs of meningitis, they need urgent medical help.

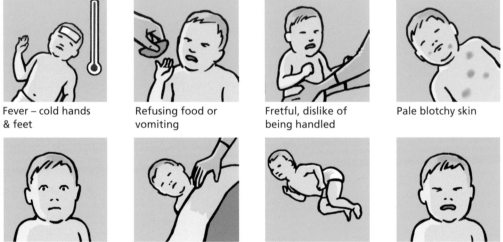

| Fever – cold hands & feet | Refusing food or vomiting | Fretful, dislike of being handled | Pale blotchy skin |
| Blank, staring | Drowsy | Stiff neck | High-pitched crying |

Figure 1: The signs of meningitis and meningococcal septicaemia in babies and very young children (Source: Meningitis Trust)

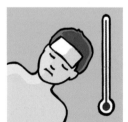
Fever – cold hands & feet

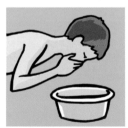
Vomiting

Headache

Stiff neck

Dislike of bright lights

Joint/muscle pain

Drowsy, difficult to wake

Confusion

Figure 2: The signs of meningitis and meningococcal septicaemia in older children (and adults) (Source: Meningitis Trust)

Make sure you are aware of the common signs and symptoms of meningitis, which are:

- headache

- stiff neck

- reaction to light

- high temperature

- irritability

- bulging fontanelles in a baby.

Both adults and children may have a rash. One sign of meningococcal septicaemia is a rash that does not fade under pressure (the 'glass test'). The rash is caused by blood leaking into the tissues under the skin. It starts as tiny pinpricks anywhere on the body. It can spread quickly to look like fresh bruises. The rash is more difficult to see on darker skin; look on the paler areas of the skin and under the eyelids. If someone is ill or obviously getting worse, do not wait for a rash, as it may appear late or not at all. A fever with a rash that does not fade under pressure is a medical emergency.

The glass test: a rash that does not fade under pressure will still be visible when the side of a clear glass is pressed firmly against the skin

Febrile convulsions

Convulsions in a baby or young child are frequently caused by the body being unable to cope with a rapid rise in body temperature. They usually only last for a very short time and a child who has had one febrile convulsion may have others. You may see:

- loss of consciousness

- a short spell of not breathing

- body rigid and shaking
- neck and back arching
- eyes rolling
- heavy dribbling.

First aid should prevent the child choking or injuring themselves, so:

- put the child on their side making sure the airway is open
- protect the child from injury – clear surrounding objects
- if the child is hot, help to cool the child by removing clothing, opening a window or putting a fan on in the room
- sponge the child with tepid water
- place the child in the recovery position
- dial 999 for an ambulance if this is the first convulsion, if it does not stop after three minutes, or if you are concerned.

Even if the child's condition has improved, you may still want to consult your GP or NHS Direct for advice.

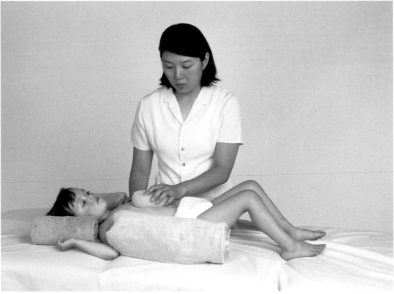

Dealing with febrile convulsions

Over to You

If you work with babies or young children, find out if any of them do have febrile convulsions. If so, check the process for dealing with them.

Know how to provide first aid to an infant and a child who is experiencing the effects of extreme heat and cold

A baby or young child cannot tell you when they are too hot or too cold, yet they react more to extremes of temperature. To test whether a baby or young child is too hot or too cold, take their temperature. Normal body temperature is 37°C (98.6°F).

Recognising and treating the effects of extreme cold

A cold, windy day will feel much colder than a day of the same temperature that is still. Body temperature reduces faster in the wind, as heat is carried away. Wet adds an extra factor: falling into cold water rapidly reduces the body temperature.

If body temperature drops below 35°, hypothermia will cause a slowdown in the working of the body and can lead to tissue damage and death.

Look for:

- low body temperature
- being sluggish or unconscious.

How to treat

- Bring the child into a warm room or close to a warm body.
- Take off wet clothes and replace with dry.
- Wrap in a blanket or coat.
- Encourage drinking warm drinks.
- Call for an ambulance.

Keep the child warm

Recognising and treating the effects of extreme heat

Overheating a baby or young child is life-threatening. Overheating is also one contributory factor to babies dying from **sudden infant death syndrome**. Heatstroke occurs when the body temperature is over 40°C and can result in brain damage and death. Heat exhaustion is more common in children, especially if they have been playing out in hot weather.

It is easy to recognise when children are too hot. Look for:

- heavy sweating (although in very hot environments or in the case of heatstroke the child may not sweat)
- red, flushed face
- tiredness
- signs of feeling sick and generally ill
- rapid breathing
- high temperature
- febrile convulsions in babies and small children.

Key term

Sudden infant death syndrome: the death of a seemingly healthy baby in its sleep

How to treat

- Move out of the heat.
- Remove excess clothing.
- Cool by applying cool water or cool cloths.
- Give plenty of water to drink.
- If there is no improvement, or you suspect heat stroke, call an ambulance.

See http://fsid.org.uk/Document.Doc?id=25

Know how to provide first aid to an infant and a child who has sustained an electric shock

Electricity enters the body and then finds the easiest way out. If the entry has been the fingers, the easiest way out is through the body and out of a foot, which can cause damage all the way along the body.

Electric sockets are tempting for children to poke things into. All sockets should have protective covers to protect young children.

Safely managing an incident involving electricity

If you do have an incident where a child has been in contact with electricity, the priority is to isolate the source. Rushing in to get hold of the child will result in you also being injured, so protect yourself. If possible, switch the power off at the mains or master switch. If this is not possible, get a wooden broom or chair and push the child well way from the electric source. Alternatively you can use a thick towel looped round the legs to pull someone away.

First aid for electric shock incidents

Exposure to electricity can stop the heart. If this is the case, start ABC (see also p.284):

- **A**irway
- **B**reathing
- **C**irculation.

Call for an ambulance immediately.

The entry and exit sites of the electricity may have burns that require the first aid treatment of lots of cool water. But only after the power source has been switched off, or the child removed from it. Then call an ambulance or seek medical help.

Case study
Electric shock incident

Josh, age seven, is playing happily in his bedroom. Joanne is looking after him while his parents are out. All of a sudden there is a loud bang and all the lights go out. Joanne runs upstairs to find Josh looking very dazed, holding an electric plug in his hands. He has been trying out an experiment they did at school about electricity, linking a small torch bulb to a battery with wire to light it up. Josh has reasoned it would be even better with a plug and some wire and has wrapped some wire round a plug and connected it to the mains.

1. What effect would the electricity have on Josh?
2. What should Joanne look for on Josh?
3. What should she do to check he is alright?

Know how to provide first aid to an infant and a child with burns or scalds

Burns and scalds can cause long-term scarring and disfigurement. They can also cause death from loss of fluid from the body if the burn or scald covers a large area of the body. For these reasons, your ability to provide first aid can be crucial.

Assessing burns and scalds

Scalds are caused by liquids — usually water or hot drinks. Burns can be caused by:

- fire
- chemicals
- electricity
- very hot materials, such as metals
- the sun.

Three factors affect the severity of a burn or scald: size, depth and location.

- **Size** Burns are usually described as the percentage of the body skin area that is affected. The palm of the hand is about 1%. Another way to describe size is to compare with a common object of a set size, such as a credit card or a 50p piece.
- **Depth** Burns and scalds can be:
  o superficial, affecting the top layer of skin cells and causing redness
  o partial thickness, causing blisters
  o full thickness, causing charring or ash whiteness.
- **Location** Burns to the face, hands, feet or genitals are more serious.

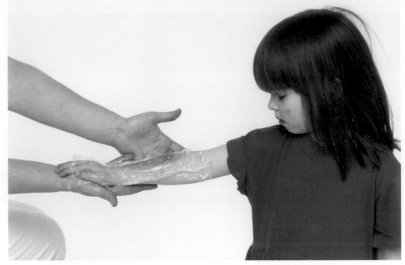

Once cooled, you can use cling film to cover a burn to keep the air out of the burn

Seek urgent medical attention for any child with a burn that is:

- deep or blistering
- no larger than a postage stamp
- on the face or hands
- a chemical or electrical burn
- accompanied by inhaling smoke or fumes
- causing serious pain.

How to treat burns and scalds

Burns and scalds need urgent action, so act immediately.

- Cool the burn with cold water – preferably under gently running water – for at least ten minutes.
- Remove any clothing that is not stuck to the burn.
- Cover the burn with a sterile or clean dressing, or even a clean plastic bag.
- For any burn or scald on a baby or very young child, call an ambulance or take the child to hospital.
- For older children, assess as above.

Know how to provide first aid to an infant and a child who has been poisoned

There is a range of common substances and plants that can cause a child to be poisoned. By being aware of these, you can help stop an accident before it happens.

How poisons enter the body

Poisons can:

- be swallowed: for example, cleaning fluids, tablets, berries

- be breathed in: for example, fumes, dust

- enter the body through the skin: for example, fluids, powders.

Each poisonous substance will have a different effect on a child's body, so expert help is needed.

Common poisonous substances, including plants

Although poisonous substances vary greatly, you will need to be able to recognise and treat the effects of more common ones.

Many substances can be poisonous if they are swallowed by mistake. Table 1 shows some common examples.

Table 1: Common items that can be poisonous

Common items	Danger if found and taken by children
Sleeping tablets from unattended handbag	Unconsciousness, possible death
Cleaning fluids in unlocked cupboard	Burns to mouth and digestive system
Berries on bushes or trees, e.g. laburnum	May cause death due to reaction in the body
Poison ivy plants	Severe irritation and blistering to skin
Carbon monoxide from faulty gas heater or boiler	Stops the blood functioning properly and can lead to death

A child who has been in contact with a poison will have a range of signs and symptoms depending on what the poison is and how it has entered the body. Look out for evidence such as:

- open drug containers

- open chemical containers

- unusual smells, such as gas fumes

- unusual smell on child's breath.

A child may be showing signs of:

- vomiting

- pain

- burns around the mouth

- drowsiness or unconsciousness

- severe rash or itching of the skin

- blisters or swelling.

If possible, find out what the child has ingested

How to treat

- Dial 999 for an ambulance or take the child to the nearest accident and emergency unit.
- Try to find out what the child has taken, how much and when or what they have been in contact with and give the evidence to medical help.
- If the child is unconscious, check the airway and put the child in the recovery position.
- If poisonous plants are involved, rinse the skin under running water.

Know how to provide first aid to an infant and a child who has been bitten or stung

Although the UK has very few poisonous snakes or spiders, we do have lots of dogs that can bite and insects that sting — usually in response to sudden movements by small children. And of course, small children may use their mouths to bite other small children in frustration!

Some children are very allergic to wasp or bee stings, and bites can easily transmit infection. In addition, stings and bites are painful and unpleasant.

Assessing bites and stings

Most bites and stings are quite minor and just require cleaning or stings removing and reassurance. It is important that you can recognise when medical intervention is needed and make sure that the child gets it.

Luckily, rabies is not a problem in the UK, but it is in parts of Europe. In any case, any animal bite is likely to become infected and may carry the risk of disease. It is a good idea to get animal bites checked at a walk-in centre or by the child's doctor.

The most dangerous reaction to a sting or bite is if the child is allergic to the bite or sting. Allergic reactions usually develop quickly, as you read in PEFAP 001.

To remind you look for:

- severe swelling at the site

- redness and a raised rash

- difficulty in breathing

- swelling of the face.

In case of this type of a reaction, call an ambulance immediately.

A child who has previously had a severe reaction to a sting or bite may well have an autoinjector of epinephrine. Be ready to use it if needed.

Recognising and treating bites and stings

Bites

Bites are usually easy to recognise.

- Teeth marks are often present or puncture wounds.

- Bites usually have bruising with them so the area will be red and may be slightly swollen.

- Any cuts will usually be jagged.

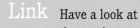
Link Have a look at the section on anaphylactic shock in PEFAP 001.

Over to You

Make sure you know if any children at your setting have an autoinjector. If so, are there guidelines for staff on how to use it?

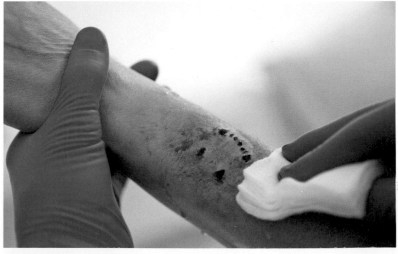
An animal bite

How to treat

If the bite is bleeding badly or the child is seriously injured, control the bleeding and call an ambulance. For less serious bites:

- wash the area thoroughly with soap and water.

- apply a dressing if there are breaks in the skin

- apply a cold pack to the area to ease the swelling.

Make sure the child is seen by a doctor if the skin is broken, to assess for infection risk.

Snake bites

Snake bites are rare in the UK: the only poisonous snake is the adder, and Ireland does not have any snakes at all. Adder bites usually only occur in the summer in long grass or sand dunes, so they may be a hazard on summer outings.

Look for:

- one or two small puncture marks

- severe burning sensation at the site

- rapid swelling

- blood-filled blisters or discoloration

- some children may react badly with signs of shock – nausea, vomiting and weakness.

How to treat

- Remove the child from the snake. Do not attempt to move the snake.

- Keep the child still and quiet to slow the spread of the venom. If an arm or leg has been bitten, keep it lower than the heart.

- Call for an ambulance.

Applying a cold pack

Stings

Insect stings usually only cause symptoms for a day or so. These include:

- redness
- pain
- itching
- mild swelling.

How to treat

- Move the child away from any risk of further stings.
- Check the sting area and remove any stinging or other insect body parts by scraping away from the area with a fingernail or credit card.
- Wash well with soap and water.
- Apply a cold pack to the area to reduce any swelling and ease the pain.

Check your knowledge

1. Explain the different types of fracture.
2. What is the first aid treatment for a fracture of the lower leg?
3. What should you *not* do if you suspect a child has injured his neck?
4. Describe how you would help a child who has had dust in her eyes.
5. What are the main signs of meningitis in a baby?
6. How would you know a child was at risk of heatstroke?
7. How should you approach a child who has been electrocuted?
8. What is the general aim when treating burns or scalds?
9. What should you always keep when you think a child has been poisoned?
10. What would give you serious cause for concern if a child had been stung by a bee?

Functional Skills English: Reading

Answering these questions will allow you to practise your reading skills. When reading a text to find answers try to highlight key words in the question so that you can skim the text for these words.

Maintain & support relationships with children & young people

This unit will help you to develop the skills you need for an essential part of your role: to maintain and support relationships with children and young people – and to support their relationships with others – in your work setting, through effective communication and respect.

Learning outcomes

By the end of this unit you will:

1. be able to communicate with children and young people

2. be able to develop and maintain relationships with children and young people

3. be able to support relationships between children and young people and others in the setting.

Be able to communicate with children and young people

You will read in a number of places in this book how important it is to communicate effectively with children and young people in your care. Communication can come in many forms and this section aims to raise your awareness of the range of skills you may need.

Communicating in ways appropriate to the individual

Communication can take a variety of forms, using both conventional language and body language. The communication may be formal, which is a situation you may have created such as an adult-led activity, or informal, such as playtime or social situations.

In order to communicate in the right way with any child or young person, it is important that you know that children's communication skills develop in a sequence. However, not all children's speech will develop at the same rate. Look at Table 1 below, bearing in mind that, just because a child in your care is not at the pattern of speech described, this does not necessarily indicate a delay or concern.

Key term

Pre-linguistic stage: the stage of communication before recognisable words appear

Table 1: Stages of communication in children and young people

Stage of communication	Adult response
Pre-linguistic stage **3–6 months** • Cries when hungry, upset or tired • Coos and gurgles when happy • Differentiates tones of voice • By 3 months, reacts positively to main carer's voice • Begins to smile at people	Comfort child with close contact and reassuring voice Ensure that you talk to child so that they hear voice and use different tones Respond to a smile by smiling too!
3–6 months • Cries but can be comforted • Adds babbles to sounds • Makes sounds such as 'da da' • Chuckles, laughs and sometimes squeals with pleasure	Continue to comfort child with close contact and reassuring voice Respond to babbling Talk to child even though you think that they may not understand!
6–12 months • Babbles much more • Begins to use vowels and consonants, e.g. dadadadadada! • By 9 months uses sounds needed for language • By 10 months understands about 18 words • Begins to gesticulate, e.g. to point • Begins to love games such as 'round and round the garden'	Continue to talk clearly Repeat simple words and phrases Sing and use rhymes Play games

Table 1: Stages of communication in children and young people (contd.)

Stage of communication	Adult response
Linguistic stage (when first recognisable words appear) **12–18 months** • Main carers recognise first words • Words can be used to mean a number of things • At 15 months main carers will recognise about 10 words	Repeat words and phrases Continue to talk to child ensuring clear eye contact Talk clearly
18 months–2 years • Strings together two words, e.g. bye-bye car • Uses phrases, e.g. Mummy gone • Learns at least 10 words per month • At 2 years may have 200 words	
2–3 years • Still acquires new words quickly • Begins to recognise more than one, e.g. cat(s) • Makes some mistakes, e.g. 'sitted down' • Starts to question, e.g. Where Mummy? • Begins to use negatives, e.g. no doggy	Continue to talk to child and introduce new words Try not to correct child but ensure that you use the right phrases such as 'sitting down' so that they can learn from example!
3–4 years • Begins to copy adult speech • Uses more than four words in sentences • Vocabulary includes body parts, animals, etc. • Makes errors in past tense • Understands nursery rhymes • Asks questions • Speech understood by strangers	Give children lots of opportunities to use their language through singing, rhymes, talking, communicating with other adults and children Continue to use correct language rather than copy their errors!
4–8 years • Begins to define language • Uses language to recount and socialise • At 5 years vocabulary is about 5,000 words • Uses more complex sentences • Tells and hears jokes • At 8 years is more fluent as a speaker, reader and writer	Create opportunities for children to communicate and develop in a variety of ways both formally and informally Informal situations could be social opportunities such as play times and more formal opportunities could be curriculum learning such as giving a brief talk or reading something they have written!
8–16 years • Language is fully developing • Uses complex sentence structure • Able to use language to negotiate, etc. • Able to converse in large groups	It is very important to continue to communicate fully with children as they develop and give them opportunities to express their own opinions Facilitate a variety of formal and informal situations in small and large groups

Key term

Linguistic stage: the stage of communication after recognisable words appear

Over to You

Take time to observe two children in your setting of the same age. Are they using the same words? Do they have the same level of communication? If you find that there are differences it is probably because they are developing at an individual pace.

Functional Skills
English: Writing

It is important when writing an observation that you only record what you see. Writing an observation is a good way of developing your skills and practising writing in a different style.

Link For more information about verbal and non-verbal communications, see SHC 21.

Over to You

Turn off the sound on your television and see if you can guess what the person is talking about without hearing the words. Your favourite soap opera will probably be a good choice of programme for this activity!

When you communicate with the children or young people in your setting, you will use three different skills:

- body language
- facial expressions and gestures
- speech.

Body language

Children will know you are listening to them before you speak.

Best practice checklist: Using appropriate body language

✓ Make eye contact

✓ Make sure that you are at the children's level

✓ Try not to move too closely towards a child so that you 'invade their space'!

✓ Avoid communication barriers such as crossing your arms

✓ Ensure that children who may have issues communicating such as hearing impairment can see your face

It is important to remember that cultures vary with regard to acceptable body language. For example, in some cultures such as South Asian it is considered disrespectful for a child to have eye contact with an adult.

Facial expression and gestures

It is often easy to find out what someone is saying by looking at their facial expression or the way they use their hands (gesticulate).

Children should be given the time and opportunity to understand people's facial expressions and gestures as part of developing their communication skills. Table 1 shows that one of the first facial expressions that a baby responds to is a smile. A variety of activities and resources can help children to explore the use of facial expressions.

There are a number of ways that you can use facial gestures to communicate. You can also encourage children to use them as a form of communication through the games that you play with them. Look at Figure 1 for some ideas.

Speech

When you are talking to children it is important that you use simple language but are not patronising. Children do not need you to use 'baby' language such as 'bicky' for biscuit or 'broom broom' for car. When a child is using this language, it is because they are developing and learning the real words to use! Your role is to model correct language and usage rather than imitate what a child is saying.

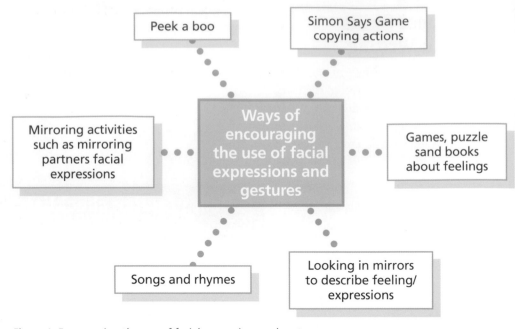

Figure 1: Encouraging the use of facial expressions and gestures

Case study:
Using the right words

Tamara is a childminder looking after Irma in her home. Irma loves to play with the small cars under a tree in Tamara's garden, often making the sound 'brmm brmm' when playing. One day she is upset. When Tamara tries to find out why, Irma says that she has lost the red 'brmm brmm'. Tamara quickly realises that she means car and says 'Shall we find the red car, Irma?' Irma agrees and they look for it.

1. Why do you think that Tamara used the word 'car' instead of 'brmm brmm'?

2. Discuss the way that Tamara modelled language in this situation. Do you think it will have helped Irma to use the word 'car' in future?

When you are listening to children you can show you are giving them your full attention in a variety of ways.

- Give them time to say what they want to even though you may be in a hurry.

- Take advantage of unplanned opportunities to talk to them that might occur during a planned activity or during a routine, such as washing hands.

- Reflect phrases that a child has said to show you are listening: for example, 'So you played with your mum?'

- Avoid interrupting them, however long they take to tell you something.

Key term

Open-ended question: a question that encourages a discussion, usually beginning with how, why, or what

- Encourage them to talk without being patronising by using simple but correct language.
- Ask **open-ended questions** that encourage children to talk and to show that you respect their opinions.
- Do not finish their sentence for them, as this can cause frustration and indicate that you might not be listening or interested.
- Be sensitive to any child who has a barrier to communication, such as a speech disorder.

Your role in developing a child's speech is to ensure that they are given sufficient time to express themselves and that they are not hurried or interrupted. If children are not given these opportunities they might find it difficult to concentrate or reason.

Best practice checklist: Helping children express themselves

- ✓ Help them to use language to predict and anticipate
- ✓ Encourage them to recall events and incidents
- ✓ Give them time to socialise with their peers
- ✓ Provide activities where they have to learn to give instructions
- ✓ Encourage assertiveness so that they will be happy to cope with interruptions
- ✓ Ensure they have time to ask questions
- ✓ Give them plenty of time to talk about things that have happened to them
- ✓ Encourage them to ask for reassurance and help

You may have children who speak English as an additional language in your setting. It may take longer for them to develop their speech patterns, as they have to learn more than one language. However, this does not mean that their language development will be affected. Children respond to the person who is caring for them and will cope with two languages if they are sensitively supported and communicated with appropriately. Often young children are only able to speak their home language with their family, as they associate the home language with that particular environment.

It is important that you show children that you value the fact that they speak more than one language, as it is part of their identity and therefore their self-esteem.

> ## Best practice checklist: Communicating with bilingual or multilingual children
>
> ✓ Involve parents of the children who have English as an additional language in your setting
>
> ✓ Promote an understanding of the appropriate culture
>
> ✓ Learn a few key words to develop communication with both the child and family and make them feel that you value their culture and home language
>
> ✓ Ensure that the setting is labelled with familiar words from the child's home language
>
> ✓ Ensure that the children are included during the day so that they can access the curriculum and are not excluded

Actively listening

How many times have you thought someone is not really listening to you? Perhaps that is because they have not shown some of the signs needed to show that they are really thinking about what you are saying to them. This kind of response is called active listening.

Active listening means showing that you are really listening to a child. It means that you show certain things to the child so that they are confident that you are interested in and are absorbing what they say, experience and feel.

Table 2 shows four important steps in showing a child or young person that you are listening to them.

Active listening means showing a child you are really listening to them

Table 2: Four steps in listening to a child

What to do	How to do it	Why
Stop what you are doing!	Stop whatever you are doing and, if necessary, <u>get down to the child's height</u> to make sure you have eye contact Even if you are unable to stop for long, let the child know that you will talk when you have finished your task	The child will feel that they are important because you have taken time to focus on what they want to communicate
Look at the child	<u>Make eye contact</u> and face the child Look for some <u>non-verbal</u> clues, such as teary eyes or a nervously biting lip, to guide you in the way that you respond to them A <u>smile</u> may well encourage children to talk openly	Appropriate facial expressions will encourage the child to communicate openly
Listen to what the child is saying	Really <u>focus on the words</u> they are using by listening to the tone of their voice Sometimes young children need help to express their feelings and may need you to help them, so listen to what they are saying and what they may be <u>trying</u> to say!	If you have really listened and understood what a child is saying, you will then be able to open up or extend communication
Respond to the child	You can <u>repeat</u> what you think you may have heard by trying to put the child's feeling into words or <u>reflect</u> what they say, such as 'You do seem cross that you cannot play outside today' <u>Ask open questions</u> to find out information, such as 'Can you tell me what upset you?'	These responses acknowledge and help to clarify what a child is trying to communicate and should open up discussion

You will find that many situations can be resolved or prevented when you use active listening in your communication with children and young people. By using the four steps above you should also be able to encourage children to solve their own problems and challenge their own thinking.

Checking your message is understood

In the previous section, you considered how you can check that you understand what a child is communicating to you. It is also essential that you check that children and young people understand what is communicated to them. This will vary according to the age of the child and young person, but could involve formal or informal communication, such as checking that they have:

- understood instructions
- understood rules or boundaries that have been agreed
- understood something that has been taught.

You will need to develop the skills to summarise a child's or young person's understanding in a way that is appropriate for the individual, considering each individual's:

- age and stage of development
- understanding of language of communication — for example, they may have English as an additional language
- personality — for example, a child who is shy may be reluctant to ask if they do not understand.

Functional Skills
English: Writing

You could choose an activity in your room that the children often do, maybe a toy or an action such as washing their hands. You could write the instructions for that activity in a way that the children would understand. Think carefully about your language and you may want to add images to support the instructions you have written.

To check understanding formally is to use a recognised method such as a test; to check understanding informally may be through situations such as everyday conversation. Checking understanding can involve:

- assessing knowledge levels to assess any gaps in understanding, which is often called summative assessment
- checking the understanding of a situation, such as a four-year-old understanding that they have to wear a sunhat to protect their head in the heat.

The way that you check understanding is important. Sometimes questions that can just be answered with a 'yes' or 'no' do not encourage a child to seek clarification.

Earlier on in this unit, you found out about the importance of using open-ended questioning. Using words such as 'why' and 'how' will encourage children and young people to be more open about what they do not understand. Consider the questions below that will encourage children and young people to discuss or ask for clarification about what they do not understand.

- Can you tell me what you remember about the rules we made last week?
- How many bricks do you think we have to add to make ten?
- Can you tell me what we discussed yesterday when we were talking about how we can share our farm animals?
- We have talked a lot about dinosaurs today and this is a lot to remember. Can you tell me what you can remember already?'

Using sensory methods can also be a good way to check understanding, particularly in young children or children who may have barriers to communication, such as hearing impairment or having English as an additional language. You could use:

- drawings
- dolls
- models
- photographs.

Functional Skills ICT: Developing, presenting and communicating information

You could design your visual timetable on the computer. This would be a good way of practising different editing and layout techniques. You could take pictures of your setting so that the images you include in your timetable are relevant to the child.

Skills builder

You will know that it is often an issue for young children to begin to learn what their routine is such as lunchtime, hometime, etc.

Consider the children that you work with. To check that the children understand what happens during their day, you could make a visual timetable, using photographs, of key times while the children are in your setting.

If a child seems unsure about any aspect of their routine you could take them to the visual timetable and show them the photographs as a way of checking and reinforcing their understanding.

You could discuss with your assessor if you can use this as evidence for your portfolio for assessment.

Here are some key things to remember to help ensure that children or young people understand what has been communicated.

- Use the child's age as a starting point to estimate their level of understanding.

- Offer children the information they need in a way appropriate to their level of understanding.

- Constantly check children's understanding. Ask them if they can tell you, or show you, something they have heard.

Functional Skills
Maths: Representing

Can you calculate the ratio for the number of children to adults in your setting? Is this ratio the same throughout the setting or does it change in different classes?

Link You can find out more about the role of the key person in MU 2.9.

Over to You

Consider how you would treat a new child you were welcoming into the setting. List ways you might make them feel welcome.

Functional Skills
English: Speaking, listening and communication

You could discuss in small groups how you make children feel welcome in your own settings. This discussion would be a good way of sharing ideas and good practice. Listen carefully to what others have to say so that you can respond in an appropriate way.

Be able to develop and maintain relationships with children and young people

Relationships with children and young people are key to the way that they develop. In early years, this relationship is recognised through the importance of the key person system. In the Early Years Foundation Stage (EYFS) theme of 'positive relationships', it is a key person who is encouraged to help young children feel secure in a setting: 'A key person meets the needs of each child in their care and responds sensitively to their feelings, ideas and behaviour' (EYFS Positive Relationships 2.4 Key Person, 2005).

Establishing rapport and respectful, trusting relationships

Whether you are working with adults or children, it is important that you show sensitivity and respect. While your language may be more developed with adults you still need to be caring, respectful and clear.

Caring for children and young people is shown by the way you treat them. This includes smiling, saying please and thank you, and generally making them feel supported and welcome.

It is also important to build a rapport — a way of communicating and having a special understanding of each other. You can do this by finding out:

- how children like to be greeted

- what a child is interested in

- what makes them laugh — a sense of humour is a great way of sharing rapport

- knowing small details of things that they have experienced and referring to these, such as a holiday or a birthday

- taking time to talk and play with a child

- take time to get to build up a professional relationship with the child's parents/carers.

It is an important part of your role to develop the way that you respect children and young people's opinions. Being respectful is about valuing what adults or children think. If you communicate this respect by listening, acknowledging and thanking children and adults, then relationships will be positive. Even if you don't share a child's or adult's point of view, the way you express your disagreement should not make the other person feel their view is worthless.

Case study:
Respecting opinions

Jude, a youth worker at a group for teenagers, is holding a council meeting about the next club party. Both Tracy and Kelis are keen for the party to be advertised locally to attract more people. Jude tells them that he understands why they want to attract more people, but he is worried that if they admit strangers the party could be difficult to control. Tracy and Kelis offer to sit at the door to screen any suspicious behaviour. Jude thanks them for offering but feels that they would be too vulnerable. He says that, while he does not agree with them, he respects the fact that they have obviously thought of ways to enable more people to attend.

1. What do you think about the way Jude responds to Tracy and Kelis's idea?

2. Do you think they would have felt that their viewpoint was respected?

3. Do you think Tracy and Kelis will feel they can still express their opinions at the next meeting?

Best practice checklist:
Showing respect

✓ Be clear, simple and direct with your communication

✓ Always give reasons and take the time to explain your thoughts or actions

✓ Value the opinions of the adults with whom you work

✓ Make sure that your own personal preferences and prejudices do not get in the way of your work

✓ Try not to show any favouritism to either adult or child

✓ A good relationship with the parents of the child in your setting should build trust and will benefit the child

✓ Remember that the parent is the main carer of the child and that the parent's wishes must be respected

Over to You

Talk to members of your team and find out ways in which they ensure that the parents of children they work with feel that they are listened to.

Make a list of these ways and share them with your study group. Can you add to the list in any way?

Getting ready for assessment

It is essential that you understand the power of the language that you use and how being respectful means using sensitive language. To prepare for assessment in this unit, consider which of the following sentences you think would show that you respect the views and opinions of the children or young people whom you work with.

- Why on earth have you chosen to do that activity? I would never have chosen that!
- You know far more than I do about building this tower, so can we do this together?
- I think that you are wrong about this Mia.
- How do you think we should tell Tom that his car is broken?

If you have not chosen any of the sentences, explain why.

Over to You

Make a list of the opportunities you might have in your setting for children to have an individual conversation with you. These might include:

- in the playground
- lunchtime or snack time
- quiet periods
- story sharing.

If you discuss these opportunities with your study group or assessor, you might come up with ideas you have not considered.

Functional Skills English: Speaking, listening and communication

When holding this discussion it is important that you contribute your thoughts, ideas and opinions. You could consider when other members of staff have opportunities and share them with your group. For example the lunch time supervisor may have the opportunity to speak to the children on the playground.

Giving individual attention

The United Nations Convention on the Rights of the Child (signed by the UK in 1991) states in Article 12 that: 'All Children have the right to be heard.'

In your practice, you need to be able to give attention to individual children and young people in a way that is fair both to them and to the group as a whole. Your role is to ensure that each child or young person is respected as an individual, while making sure that they understand the importance of being part of the larger group.

It is your role as someone who is working with children to make sure that each individual has the opportunity to talk and be listened to, however difficult this can be. Quieter children can often be overlooked, particularly in a group activity. Older children may have to raise their hand if they wish to speak, but this is not so for younger children. You may need to encourage individual children to speak by prompting them or asking appropriate questions. Some children may really need you to give them time to build their confidence in you.

Group activities can also be an opportunity for individual children to be heard and to develop their confidence with other children listening. Figure 2 on the following page will help you find out which group activities will give individual children the opportunity to be heard. You can easily adapt these activities to suit the children you are working with.

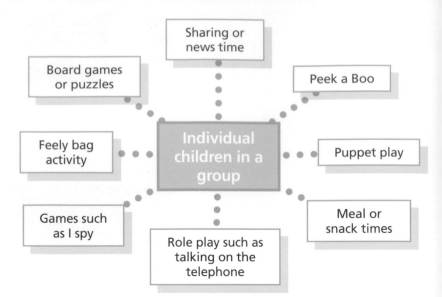

Figure 2: Giving individual children an opportunity to be heard

Giving supportive and realistic responses

Every Child Matters has raised awareness that children and young people's questions, ideas and concerns should be listened to by the adults who work with them. If children are able to have a voice about the world around them, this can have a positive impact on their futures.

Here are some of the laws and policies that encourage consideration of children and young people's views:

● United Nations Convention on the Rights of the Child 1989

● Every Child Matters 2004

● Children's Act 2004.

A framework called *Hear by Right* gives ideas to adults, young people and children on how they can be involved in the services provided for them and have their concerns taken seriously. *Hear by Right* has standards used by both statutory and voluntary sector groups, aiming to improve practice, actively involving children and young people as a way of developing each organisation's activities.

Did you know too that young people in England have a voice through a UK Youth Parliament (UKYP)? Local authorities have Youth Forums, from which a representative attends the National Youth Parliament, ensuring that the voices of their peers are heard.

To ensure that children are heard and responded to, here are some things you could consider doing.

● Consult with them about issues and consider their individual comments. In young children, this may be as simple as listening to where they would like a piece of equipment in the outdoor area, or asking young people to help make rules for their after school club.

Functional Skills ICT: Finding and selecting information

You will need to use the internet to search for information on these websites. It is important to take any copyright restrictions into consideration when using information from the internet.

Functional Skills Maths: Interpreting

You could carry out a simple survey with the children that you work with asking them what activity they would like to be set out on a particular day. You could collect your results in the form of a tally and then transfer these on to a graph. Your results could then determine what activity you provide the children with on a set day.

- Seek children's opinions and use them in a decision-making process, such as finding out what their favourite foods are before creating a lunch menu.
- Give them appropriate information and wait to receive comments, such as telling them that you have a small amount of money to buy some seeds and discussing with them what they would like to buy and plant.

Table 3 shows the benefits of listening to children's views.

Table 3: Benefits of listening to children's views

Gain a deeper understanding of children's and young people's wants and needs
Engage children and young people in their learning as they will feel respected and involved
Help children and young people to develop responsibility
Help children and young people to develop the skills of decision-making, including debate and negotiation, at an early age
Can sometimes create a new perspective

As well as the benefits of listening and gaining children's and young people's views, there are also the challenges. These can include:

- creating enough time to consult effectively
- ensuring that all children or young people involved are listened to
- using the right consultation methods for the group
- ensuring that children or young people are not affected by peer pressure, so that they are confident to express their own opinions in front of their friends
- ensuring that children are safe when they are involved in decision-making, so that any consent is given by parents or photographs are used appropriately.

Case study:
Seeking opinions

The Blackstock Heath Community Centre has a piece of land that they want to develop for the children in the area. Greg, the community leader, visits assemblies in primary schools in the area and collects ideas in a large book. Children are encouraged to send in drawings and notes about what they want. Greg then creates a children's focus group to look at the ideas and come up with a plan that would work which also considers the practicalities as outlined in advice from the local planning consultant. As a result, an outdoor play area is created that is now widely used by the community.

1. How do you think Greg's approach to the development of the play area works?
2. How do you think Greg is realistic about the final plans for the area?

Providing reasons for actions

Children and young people have a right to know why you are taking an action. Sometimes you have to do this because you know it is in the best interest of the children and young people concerned. However, there will be situations when you are unable to inform children, as it will increase the risk of harm to them or another person close to them. You also have to judge when you have to involve other adults in a situation.

One way of providing reasons for actions is to ensure that children have an understanding from the outset, particularly if you are involving them in a decision-making process.

Table 4 offers examples of actions that you may have to give reasons for. You may well be able to add to this from your own experience.

Table 4: Actions and reasons you may give for them

Actions	Reasons
Choosing groups of children to work together	Make it clear why you are doing this – because you think that they will have lots of different views or perhaps are all interested in the same thing
Taking a piece of equipment away, such as a favourite bike that is faulty	Clarify that it is unsafe and that it will be mended as soon as possible
Informing parents about negative or concerning behaviour	Tell children from the outset that this will happen and remind them of this, explaining that you want to work through this together
Referring a child for assessment	Try to explain the process and reassure the child that their opinions will be valued throughout the process

Over to You

The EYFS requires practitioners to follow the child so that they can have choices in their play. Take time to observe a child in your setting playing independently. Note how they make their own choices in their play. Are there ways in which they can safely be given more choice?

Encouraging children to make choices

As adults life is about making choices and feeling confident about the choices we have made. You will need to help the children and young people in your setting to express their needs and make choices so that they can develop this skill.

It is always important to make it clear to children that they can safely make their own choices and to create an environment that encourages this.

Table 5 shows how you can help children and young people to make choices.

Table 5: Helping children and young people to make choices

Allow children to choose who they work with
Give children time to make their own choices: for example, during free play activities
Ensure there is a flexibility in routines, such as children choosing when to have their snack
Respond positively to children's contributions, especially when you are leading an activity
Be prepared to change an aspect of the environment, routine or an activity in response to children's suggestions
Ensure that the children know that they are healthy and safe in the activities that they have chosen
Encourage children to become involved in planning — for young people this may even be the recruitment of staff
Make resources accessible to the children so that they can make choices
Praise the choices that children and young people make

There is a range of activities that can encourage children and young people to make their own choices by being involved in decision-making processes. The activities listed below can be adapted for a variety of ages. Never underestimate the fact that very young children can be involved in making their own choices, even if it is choosing an object from a treasure basket at nine months old!

- **Marble jars** Children and young people vote by placing a marble in a jar.

- **Agree/Disagree** Place four large pieces of paper around the room and write on them 'agree', 'disagree', 'strongly agree' and 'strongly disagree'. Share statements or questions. The children or young people have to stand by the label that they feel best represents their view.

- **Thought bubbles** Children and young people can draw ideas on thought bubbles and share them with others.

- **Postcards** Children and young people write their ideas or draw picture symbols on a postcard and post them on a special board.

- **Graffiti wall** Hang large sheets of paper on a wall and invite the children and young people to draw their ideas on the sheets in the form of graffiti.

- **Send a text!** Give children and young people the chance to vote or express views by text.

- **Video** Set up a video camera in a private space with a chair for children and young people and encourage them to talk about their ideas and suggestions.

Functional Skills Maths: Representing

You could carry out one of these activities for allowing children to make choices. What were your results as a fraction? Could you calculate what they were as a percentage? For example if 15 out of 20 children voted for singing songs at dinner time then you could say that ¾ of the children wanted to sing songs or 75% of the children wanted to sing songs.

Be able to support relationships between children and young people and others in the setting

You have discovered the importance of your relationship with the children or young adults in your setting; however, it is equally important to ensure that children have positive relationships between each other that show understanding and respect.

Supporting effective communication

For adults and children to communicate effectively with others, there are a number of key features to remember and encourage. Much of this can be done through example.

- Always make eye contact with the person you are communicating with.

- Ensure you smile as appropriate, as this can be reassuring.

- Be patient and listen carefully.

Skills builder

Observe a group time in your setting and note the following.

- How were children encouraged to listen to each other?

- If open questions were used, how did the children respond?

- How were the children given time to speak?

- Describe the body language of the practitioner leading the group.

- Do not interrupt or finish sentences, as this shows that you are not listening properly.

- Give the other person time, as they may pause to think or reflect.

- Concentrate on what the other person is saying to you.

- Ensure that questions are open to encourage further communication.

- In a group situation, ensure that everyone is listened to and that their opinions are valued.

Understanding individuality, diversity and differences

Encourage children and young people to understand other people's individuality, diversity and differences when communicating. You can do this through the way you treat people and also through play, the environment and activities. For example, you could:

- ensure that children know about signing and perhaps learn some signing or have someone come and talk to them

- encourage children and young people to find out about Braille and even have a few signs in Braille

- ask young people or parents from different cultures to come and talk about how they communicate

- encourage children to learn simple words, such as greetings in the home languages of their peers.

Helping children to understand and respect others

The Early Years Foundation Stage (EYFS) guidance refers to the importance of children respecting their own needs, but also those of other people: 'a sense of community is how children understand and respect their own needs, views, cultures and beliefs and those of other people' (EYFS Learning and Development PSED 2007).

Best practice checklist: Valuing others' opinions

- ✓ If they disagree, be constructive: for example, 'I respect your point of view. However …'
- ✓ Avoid being personal: for example, 'Why do you always look like that when …'
- ✓ Exchange ideas openly and seek colleagues' views: for example, 'What do you think …'
- ✓ Ask for advice when you need it: for example, 'How do you think I could have …'

Link Reread TDA 2.1 on child development to remind yourself of children's different expected levels of understanding.

You can help younger children to recognise other people's feelings. For example, when a young child does not want to play with another, you can say 'Jo enjoys playing on the bikes with you, but at the moment he would like to play in the sandpit', or you can encourage Jo to say 'Thank you for asking, but I would like to play in the sandpit.'

For a child who is still developing language and understanding, you could explain how another child might feel: for example, 'Can you see that Lila is crying because you made her hand sore when you dropped the brick on it?'

Case study:
Valuing others' feelings and opinions

Christy is concerned that children are not really listening to each other in her Key Stage One class and that a few of the boys are dominating the play outside with football. In a group she encourages the children to help make an agreement about how they play and create areas for choices of play. She carefully listens to the views of all the children and what they want. She places this agreement in the classroom at the children's height so that they can all see. Christy

regularly refers to this in any group sessions and gently reminds the boys of this if they are dominating choices of games in their play.

1. In what way do the boys need support in valuing the other children's views and opinions?

2. How do you think a group agreement encourages the feelings and opinions of the other children to be considered?

To encourage respect of other's opinions and views, the environment should reflect all the children's or young people's families and cultures. This will make sure that children feel positive about themselves and their families, and act as a role model to respect throughout the setting. To do this you can do things such as:

- provide a variety of skin-tone paints and crayons
- make sure various people are presented: for example, an Asian woman doctor, a black teacher
- incorporate other cultures in projects, such as making bread from around the world
- make sure that special needs are represented and that children with varied needs can participate in all aspects of displays
- use more than one language where necessary.

Developing group agreements

One of your main roles is to encourage children and young people to agree about the way they interact with each other. If they have worked this out then they are more likely to follow the rules set and take some ownership. Your role will be to guide them through this process. One of the most effective ways to do this is for the children and young people to agree themselves, as Christy implemented in the case study.

"What shall we draw?"

There are a variety of ways you can encourage group agreements, as you can see in Figure 3.

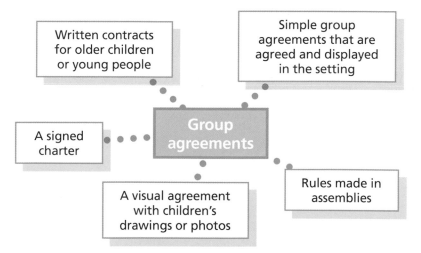

Figure 3: There are a variety of ways of encouraging group agreements

When helping children and young people to make agreements in a group you should:

● encourage sharing and taking turns

● give clear guidelines about what you expect

● stress the positive aspects of the way they interact already

● consider different children's needs

● encourage them to consider coaching language such as 'What if?' and 'How about?'

● encourage them to interact positively to sort out their own issues

● encourage them to avoid confrontation

● give them strategies to negotiate such as 'You can have one more go and then someone else can have a turn.'

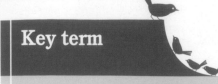

Key term

Conflict: a difference of opinion that does not appear to have a resolution

Dealing with conflict

You can encourage and support children and young people to deal with **conflict** for themselves, and learn how to sort out conflict in a way that makes everybody agree.

You will know that some adults manage conflict aggressively and try to tell other people that their way is the best. Children and young people are constantly exposed to television and media programmes that are full of conflict and aggression. It is therefore even more important for you to model positive ways of dealing with conflict that are calm and measured.

Table 6 shows steps that are useful in helping children to find peaceful ways of solving problems with others. You can adapt the language you use depending on the age of the child.

Table 6: Ways to help children deal with conflict

Help the children to understand that they can find a good solution: 'I know we can work this out together...'
Encourage children to discover how they are feeling and to express their emotions: 'You're looking a little sad, Joe – I'm wondering if you're feeling a bit sad and hurt, that you can't play with the others'
Ask the children to brainstorm different ways that they could solve the problem and to find a range of ways that they could go about it
Encourage children to work out what they really want and ask them what they would like to happen
Ask the children to choose a way that will suit everyone, and ask them to plan how this will happen, giving help if needed
Encourage children to understand the other person's point of view, what they think the other person might be feeling, or how they might feel if they were in the same situation
Read stories or poems that have positive results to conflict

Check your knowledge

1. Name the two main forms of communication.

2. When you communicate with the children or young people in your setting, you will use four different skills. What are they?

3. Does an open-ended question:

    A) encourage children to talk and to show that you respect their opinions?

    B) encourage children to think of their own opinions?

4. What are speech patterns generally known as?

5. Name four sensory methods that could be used to check understanding in young children.

6. Which framework requires practitioners to follow the child so that they can have choices in their play?

    A) ECF

    B) EME

    C) EYFS

7. What is the UKYP?

8. Describe one way you could encourage children and young people to value the opinions of others.

9. What is conflict?

10. Why would you read stories or poems to children that have positive results to conflict?

My Story

My name is Jocasta and I work in a small evening social club for young people in a rural area. Recently a group of our boys has been really aggravating each other and arguing over a number of silly things. However hard we try as a team, there always seems to be some sort of conflict. My team and I decided that we had to put an end to this as it was making many of the kids unhappy and reluctant to come along. We were given a new video camera and decided to show some of the kids how to use it. We then set up a room and suggested that they recorded how they felt about the atmosphere caused by the continuing conflict in the club. It was agreed that we would play the results in a safe way, so that nobody felt threatened. Everyone was encouraged to end their video clip with a suggestion for a solution.

When this was shown the boys were shocked at how people felt. After much discussion, supervised by my team, we decided how to agree to respect each other. It has been a much better place to be since.

Viewpoint

There are a lot of criticisms about the youth culture today and how young people are often unruly and spoiling our society. Something is being done to give young people a voice and a say in how their communities are run. This is called the UK Youth Parliament and representatives from Youth Forums all over the country meet and debate topical issues. Do you think there are other ways of making young people feel valued so that they can contribute positively to our society?

Ask the expert

Q I am not really sure when to use open-ended questioning. Can you advise me?

A Open-ended questions are questions that encourage more than a 'yes' or 'no' answer. They usually begin with words such as 'why?', 'how?' or 'what if?'. If they are used sensitively and children are given time to answer, you will find that this is a great way to open up communication with the children who you work with.

Support children & young people with disabilities & special educational needs

Anyone who works with children will from time to time be in contact with disabled children or children with special educational needs. You need an understanding of the underlying principles involved in working with such children in order to ensure their inclusion in your setting in ways that make sure that they have opportunities to develop and learn alongside other children.

Learning outcomes

By the end of this unit you will:

1. know the rights of disabled children and young people and those with special educational needs

2. understand the disabilities and/or special educational needs of children and young people in own care

3. be able to contribute to the inclusion of children and young people with disabilities and special educational needs

4. be able to support disabled children and young people and those with special educational needs to participate in the full range of activities and experiences.

Know the rights of disabled children and young people and those with special educational needs

Legal entitlements

The basis of disabled people's legal rights is contained in the Disability Discrimination Act 1995 (DDA), which was a landmark in the way our society regards disabled people. It made it unlawful to discriminate against disabled people in the provision of services or to treat a disabled person 'less favourably' than someone else for a reason related to their disability.

This means that a setting providing a service for children must not:

- refuse to provide a service to a disabled child in circumstances where they would offer that service to a non-disabled child

- offer a lower standard service or a service on worse terms than they would to a non-disabled child.

The setting also has a duty to make 'reasonable adjustments' to:

- policies, practices and procedures to accommodate disabled children

- the environment, in order to overcome barriers to access.

The duty to make reasonable adjustments is 'anticipatory': a setting must not wait until they are asked to offer a place to a disabled child, but think ahead about the sort of changes they could make to policies, routines and the environment so they would be able and ready to provide a service for a particular disabled child. However, the word 'reasonable' to describe the adjustments indicates that a setting is not expected to make huge financial outlay beyond their budgetary means on equipment or on major alterations to the building.

Functional Skills English: Reading

Completing this task will help you to develop your reading skills as you will need to read and understand the DDA so that you can link it to your setting and practice.

Getting ready for assessment

Find out more about the DDA from Early Years and the Disability Discrimination Act 1995 (National Children's Bureau, 2003) and www.equalityhumanrights.com.

How does your setting comply with this law in its policy and practice?

Various laws have gradually built up rights concerning the education of disabled children and children with special education needs. The Education Act 1981 was a turning point, introducing the concept of special educational needs (SEN). Its main feature was that local education authorities (LEAs) were given a legal duty towards a child who is thought to have special educational needs. They must:

- assess the child's special educational needs

- issue a 'statement' which sets out the child's specific learning needs

- identify the provision required to meet these needs and what the authority will do.

This is the process of **statementing**.

The Education Acts 1993 and 1996 replaced and improved on this Act, with greater rights for parents and rules about 'statementing' that set time limits for each stage of the process. The Special Educational Needs and Disability Act 2001 (SENDA) strengthened the rights of children with SEN to be educated in mainstream provision, and brought new duties to local authorities to offer parents advice and information.

The Code of Practice for Children with Special Educational Needs (also known as the SEN Code of Practice) plays a key role in promoting the rights of children with special educational needs. In England and Wales, it sets out guidance about the provision that should be made for children with special educational needs. The principles of the Code of Practice include:

- the special educational needs of children will normally be met in mainstream schools or settings.

- children with special educational needs should be offered full access to a broad, balanced and relevant education, including an appropriate curriculum for the Early Years Foundation Stage in England or the Foundation Phase in Wales, and the National Curriculum.

Every setting must have a **SENCO** who plays a key role in implementing the Code of Practice. The SENCO is responsible for:

- ensuring liaison with parents and other professionals concerning children with special educational needs

- advising and supporting other practitioners

- ensuring that appropriate Individual Educational Plans (see later in this unit) are in place

- ensuring that relevant background information about individual children with special educational needs is collected, recorded and updated

- taking the lead in assessing a child's particular strengths and weaknesses

- planning future support for the child

- monitoring and reviewing any action taken

- making sure that appropriate records are kept.

Key term

Statementing: assessing a child's special educational needs and setting them out in a 'statement'

Key term

SENCO: a Special Educational Needs Co-ordinator

SENCOs liaise with parents

Frameworks for assessment and intervention

Assessment

In the early years, the framework in England that enables assessment to be made of the development and progress of all young children is the Early Years Foundation Stage (EYFS), which focuses on six areas of learning:

- personal, social and emotional development

- communication, language and literacy

- problem solving, reasoning and numeracy

- knowledge and understanding of the world

- physical development

- creative development.

About 20 per cent of children are likely at some stage to appear to be not making progress as might usually be expected, either generally or in a specific aspect of learning. Practitioners may become aware of this through regular, ongoing assessment of children's development.

- Careful observation of each child will reveal what they can do in each area of development, and what they are ready to progress to.

- Settings can use the 'Development matters' and 'Look, listen and note' sections of the EYFS Practice Guidance to help reflect on the developmental progress of individual children.

- The EYFS Practice Guidance warns against using these sections as a checklist. Children do not all develop in the same way and at the same pace, so care must be taken not to be rigid in expecting every child to have reached a particular stage of development at any given age. The range of 'normality' is wide.

- If observation and assessment lead to concerns about a child's development, settings should discuss these concerns with the child's parents in the first instance.

- When practitioners and parents work together, strategies can often be planned, with input from the setting's SENCO if necessary, to offer the child activities and experiences which support specific areas of their development.

- Sometimes it is necessary to seek additional information and advice from specialist professionals such as speech and language therapists.

Intervention

If a child has an impairment or assessment reveals a special educational need, they and their family are likely to require additional support of some kind; intervention by the setting and perhaps specialist professionals may be necessary.

Perhaps the most positive development in recent years for young disabled children and their families in England has been Early Support. Early Support is a programme for parents of babies and children under five with additional support needs associated with disability or emerging special educational needs. Early Support aims at early identification of children's impairments and better coordinated, 'family focused' services.

The programme provides parents with information about living with a disabled child and interacting with 'the system'. It explains which professionals they may meet and how health, education and social services can provide support, as well as giving information about sources of financial support and childcare. The most innovative feature is a family file which the family holds and which the professionals involved with the child and family use to record information so it can be shared effectively with the family and with other professionals. This is a great boon to parents who do not have the frustration of having to 'tell their story' from the beginning every time they encounter a different professional or service. It also prevents professionals working in a vacuum — they are aware of the advice and support being provided elsewhere and are able to identify priorities for their contribution as part of a whole strategy for the child, planned jointly with the family.

Early recognition and intervention

There is a growing body of evidence about the importance of identifying children's impairments and requirements for additional support at an early age. Early intervention may overcome an emerging difficulty relating to a particular area of development by getting specialist input, and prompt action may prevent longer-term disadvantage for a child.

Link See MU 2.9 for more information on family files.

Over to You

Find out about Early Support at www.direct.gov.uk/en/CaringFor Someone/CaringForADisabledChild/ DG_10027494

Case study:
Recognising an impairment early

The Rainbow Pre-school practitioners are concerned about three-and-a-half-year-old George. His vocabulary is limited, his speech is indistinct and he does not seem to understand a great deal of what is said to him. This is beginning to affect his social development; when he can't communicate, he gets angry and destructive, and the other children do not want to play with him.

They suggest to George's parents that George may have 'glue ear'. Fluid fills his ear from time to time so he often cannot hear.

The pre-school's SENCO consults a local speech and language specialist who suggests simple strategies like making sure he can see the face and lips of the person talking to him, using signs and pictures to back up speech, and keeping background noise like the television to the minimum.

George's communication skills begin to improve, he is more able to interact with other children and is a happier little boy.

1. What might have happened if the Rainbow staff had not taken action?

2. What long-term effects might his hearing impairment, lack of clear speech and poor social skills have had on his long-term development?

Individual plans

Often a difficulty will be overcome with early intervention. However, if the combined efforts of practitioners and parents are not proving effective after a while, the SEN Code of Practice recommends moving on to another step. The setting's SENCO should put together an Individual Education Plan (IEP), specifically designed for the individual child, to address their difficulties and to help them progress.

An IEP should set out:

● the short-term targets set for the child (focusing on three or four key targets)

● the strategies used and provision to be made for the child.

This plan might outline the provision of different learning materials or special equipment, or training to help practitioners introduce new strategies for the child's learning. For most children, the help given through an IEP will be enough to enable them to progress satisfactorily. However, for about 2 per cent of children, a statutory assessment may be necessary, which can lead to a statement of special educational needs ('statementing').

Principles of inclusive practice

Working effectively with disabled children and children with special educational needs doesn't depend on having a mass of theoretical knowledge about forms of impairment. What is necessary is to understand some basic principles, such as:

- the medical and social models of disability

- the significance of focusing on the child, not on their impairment.

Medical and social models of disability

To ensure that you can promote equality of opportunity for disabled children and ensure they are included in your setting, you need to appreciate the **medical model of disability** and the **social model of disability** as ways of understanding the effect of disability on individuals.

The medical model of disability treats the person as a sick patient and tends to focus on 'How can we make this person more normal?' The problem is seen as the disabled person and their impairment, and the solution is seen as adapting the disabled person to fit the non-disabled world, often through medical intervention. The medical model is a traditional view of disability, that it is something to be 'cured', even though many conditions have no cure.

The social model of disability is a more constructive approach to disability. It recognises that discrimination against disabled people is created by society, not by disabled people's impairments. It focuses our thoughts on 'What do we need to do to enable this person to achieve their potential and have a fulfilling life?'

The social model helps us to see that impairments are a fact of life — many people have impairments. However, the restricting effects of impairment can be reduced when:

- adjustments are made to the environment

- appropriate resources and facilities are provided

- people have positive attitudes and assumptions.

This can enable disabled people to have opportunities to make choices, develop their potential, become independent and play a full part in society.

The social model of disability puts the emphasis on the way in which society needs to change; the medical model expects disabled people to change to fit into society. The strength of the social model is that it identifies problems which can be resolved if the adjustments are made to the environment, resources and attitudes, whereas the medical model dwells on problems which are often insoluble. The social model asserts the rights of disabled people; it involves listening to individual disabled people to see what that person wants and, when there are barriers to their requirements, looking at ways of removing those barriers. The social model has been constructed and promoted by disabled people themselves, so it should be respected.

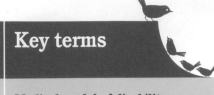

Key terms

Medical model of disability: a traditional view of disability as a sickness, seeing the disabled person as the problem

Social model of disability: a progressive model recognising that discrimination against disabled people is created by society

Focusing on the child, not the impairment

When medical labels are placed on the disabled person in order to define their needs (for example, referring to people with diabetes as 'diabetics'), the individual is seen merely as their impairment. That can prevent us developing a picture of the whole person, including their gender, ethnicity and culture, and social background. It can lead to too much focus on what is 'wrong' with a child and what they cannot do, rather than paying attention to what a child can do and is achieving and to their potential to develop, learn and progress.

The term 'special needs' is often used to refer to disabled children. This is unhelpful because it implies that disabled children have different needs from other children. But their needs are not 'special'; they have the same needs as other children. All children need.

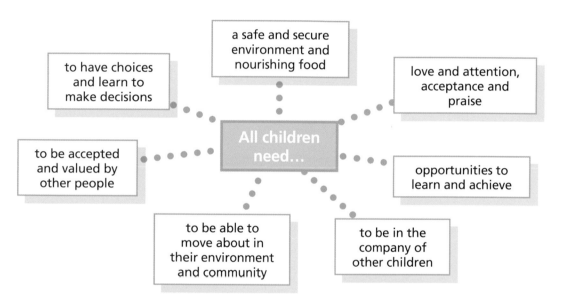

Figure 1: Disabled children's needs are the same as other children's needs

Disabled children's needs are the same as other children's needs — although they may have different requirements about how those needs are met; they require some additional support. Unfortunately, the term 'special educational needs' is embodied in legislation, so we have to live with it at present.

When you work with disabled children, it is important, of course, to take their impairments into account, but they should not be taken as the definition of that child, or the centre of the focus of your work with the child.

Best practice checklist: Focusing on the child

✓ Base the way you work with disabled children or children with special educational needs on your usual practice for working with all children, even if you sometimes need to adjust or extend it.

✓ Try to see the child as a child like all others, who happens to have some additional requirements.

✓ Take into account all aspects of the child – their gender, their ethnicity, their social and family background – not just their impairment.

✓ Use your observation and assessment skills to find out about the needs and requirements of each particular child, in the way you would for all other children.

✓ Beware of talking about 'special needs children'. This could lead you into the mistake of thinking that you cannot use your existing knowledge and skills of working with all children – that you need some alternative approach entirely when you work with disabled children.

✓ Don't let a label placed on a child's disability lead you to overprotect them, or to limit your expectations of their potential achievements and behaviour.

✓ Refer to 'a child with epilepsy', not 'an epileptic'. That will help you to think in ways that put the child first and their impairments second.

Understand the disabilities and/or special educational needs of children and young people in own care

Disability and special educational needs

Impairment and disability

Many people have impairments. Impairment describes a condition that is different from what you would usually expect from a child at a particular age or stage of development or an adult. (Talking about what is 'usually' expected is more helpful than 'normally'. It avoids labelling someone who develops differently from what is considered usual as 'abnormal'.)

An impairment may be:

- an impairment of the senses (sight, hearing)
- a physical impairment
- associated with a medical condition or disease
- a learning difficulty
- a difficulty with emotional or social development.

An impairment may give rise to **disability.**

When children have a 'mental impairment', we normally talk about them as having 'learning difficulties' or 'special educational needs'. However, special educational needs may also arise out of physical impairments.

Special educational needs

Not all children learn in the same way. If a child learns in ways that are different from most children of their age, they are said to have special educational needs. The legal definition of a child with special educational needs is one who has a learning difficulty that requires special educational provision to be made for them. This might be because:

- they have a significantly greater difficulty in learning than the majority of children of the same age – such a child may have language, learning or behaviour difficulties

- the child is disabled and is prevented or hindered from making use of educational facilities provided for children in their area – in other words, they need additional or different provision to enable them to learn.

It may be the child's physical requirements (instead of or in addition to their learning difficulties) that mean that they cannot use local educational facilities. A child must not be seen as having a learning difficulty solely because their home language is different from the one used in educational provision in the area.

Particular disabilities and special educational needs

'Disabled children' include those with a wide range of impairments or conditions including 'hidden' ones. A child's sensory impairment may consist of hearing loss (deafness) or restricted vision (blindness). A physical impairment and/or learning difficulties may be the result of:

- a genetic inheritance such as:
  - cerebral palsy
  - muscular dystrophy
  - sickle cell and thalassaemia
  - haemophilia
  - cystic fibrosis
  - brittle bones

- events before or during birth, such as a mother's excessive drinking during pregnancy resulting in foetal alcohol syndrome, or shortage of oxygen to the baby's brain during birth

- an accident (including a 'medical accident' such as the prescription in the 1960s of the drug thalidomide to pregnant mothers)

- a disease such as polio, meningitis, measles or rheumatic fever.

Medical conditions include:

- asthma
- epilepsy
- diabetes
- coeliac disease.

Some children's disability relates to learning difficulties which may or may not have a specific title, like Down's syndrome. For others, their difficulties are with emotional or social development, communication and interaction, and behaviour, including conditions like autism. No list of disabilities could include every impairment or condition, so you are likely to encounter children with impairments not referred to here, and each child will be affected differently by their impairment or condition.

Some children have more than one of these conditions. Sometimes conditions are linked: for example, diabetes can cause visual impairment; sometimes they are not directly connected: for example, a child may have the unconnected conditions of asthma and autism. Some children have multiple impairments and are often described as having 'complex needs'. The development of medical techniques which keep even very premature babies alive has led to the survival of more children with such complex requirements for their care.

Special provision

An impairment usually brings some restrictions and limitations to a person's life, but there are ways of avoiding or reducing the consequent disability. It may be possible to remove or reduce disability for many people with impairments if special provision is made for them. For example:

- a person with a sight impairment may wear spectacles and/or use a strong light, or read Braille, be supported by a guide dog, and be helped by announcements on public transport and audible signals at traffic lights

- a person with a hearing impairment may use a hearing aid or a loop, or communicate in sign language, or be supported by a hearing dog

- a person who uses a wheelchair can get into and move around in buildings and use public transport when ramps and lifts are provided, when sufficient space is available (for example, wide aisles in shops) and when counters and lift buttons are at a height that can be reached from a wheelchair

- a person who cannot use their hands may use a voice-activated computer to write or communicate by pointing to symbols on a board with a head stick.

Getting ready for assessment

With the help of your manager and/or the SENCO in your setting, identify the children you work with who have impairments or who have special educational needs. Think about how impairments lead to disability for each child, or how their learning is affected.

Adjustments to the environment and provision of resources like these support people with impairments in leading a more independent life and reduce the impact of their impairment.

Your setting must make provision for the disabled children who attend it. This 'special provision' is in addition to or different from what the setting usually provides. Exactly what this special provision consists of will depend on the specific impairments or special educational needs of the individual children, and will need to be changed as they grow and develop.

We have seen that the social model of disability emphasises that the response to impairment should be ready to make adjustments in your setting in order to meet the requirements of disabled children. The special provision in your setting may be observed in:

- the environment
- resources
- routines
- aspects of practitioners' practice.

Environment

Special provision in the environment may consist of those that help a child with a visual impairment to find their way around a setting and identify an area or activity by:

- different scents or smells in certain indoor areas
- different scented plants or plants with interesting textures to touch (bark, 'furry' or smooth leaves, pine cones) and wind chimes in various parts of the outside area
- variations in textures on floor coverings and panels on walls and rough or smooth stones and bricks outdoors
- white strips along the edge of steps.

Avoiding shiny surfaces and having adjustable window blinds can prevent visually impaired children being dazzled, and intense, focused light from small lamps will help them make the best use of their sight in their play and learning activities.

Resources

There are many resources on the market that enable settings to make special provision for disabled children, such as hand-propelled trikes. Some of this equipment is designed to high technical standards and is expensive. However, other simple and inexpensive resources can make a great difference to a child.

Functional Skills ICT: Using ICT

It is important that you know how to adjust the system settings of the computers that you work with so that you could adapt your setting if someone needed it. Could you show your assessor how to...

Alter the height of the computer chair?

Change the angle that the monitor sits at?

Adjust the brightness and size of the writing and images on the screen?

Case study:
Making special provision

Practitioners in the Long Lane Children's Centre worked together to make special provision for Ethan who has cerebral palsy.

Tina found some chunks of foam for sale on the market that could be used to create shapes to help Ethan to sit more upright and securely, so he could join in with the other children to play with equipment such as small world people on a table.

Nick found Velcro and rubber suction mats in a specialist catalogue. These prevented toys like puzzles moving around, and also kept dishes fixed and steady so Ethan could begin to feed himself.

1. What simple resources like this could you use to support disabled children in your setting?

2. What can your colleagues in your setting tell you about suppliers of specialist equipment for disabled children, including the catalogues and websites of relevant companies?

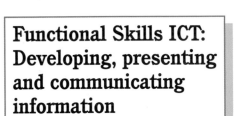

Functional Skills ICT: Developing, presenting and communicating information

You could produce a leaflet which contains information on good websites, catalogues or local suppliers that stock a good range of specialist equipment. You could even email your leaflet to staff in your setting so that they could alter it to suit the needs of the age of children that they work with.

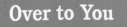

Over to You

Find out more about Portage at the website of the National Portage Association www.portage.org.uk.

Routines

Some disabled children or children with special educational needs may require special routines. For example, some may be working through a specified programme such as

- physiotherapy
- speech and language therapy
- activities suggested by a Portage worker
- specialist programmes such as patterning.

Portage is a system of helping children to learn by breaking down skills into a series of small steps. It is based on home visiting which enables parents and a Portage worker to develop a programme to suit the individual child.

Patterning is an intensive system that involves adults repeatedly moving the limbs of a child with brain damage with the aim of stimulating other parts of the brain to take over physical movement. Patterning is carried out several times a day, sometimes for quite lengthy periods.

Practice

Some children with special educational needs have communication difficulties which mean that special provision for them consists of using a specialised communication system like Makaton. This requires not only specialised equipment but also training and skills development for practitioners.

Over to You

Find out about the Makaton system at www.makaton.org.

Getting ready for assessment

With the help of your manager and/or the SENCO in your setting, identify the special provision made for children in your setting.

Small movement

The Makaton sign and symbol for 'A drink'

Flat hand, palm down, covers top of other fist

The Makaton sign and symbol for 'More'

Link   For more on observation, see MU 2.2.

Functional Skills English: Writing

You could ask your supervisor or manager if you could observe a child in your setting for a short time. Focusing on the questions opposite you could write a short report that you could then share with your colleagues. It is important to remember that this information will be confidential and your setting may ask to read what you have written. Think carefully about your spelling, punctuation and grammar so that the meaning of your report is clear.

Be able to contribute to the inclusion of children and young people with disabilities and special educational needs

Obtaining information

Whatever your role in your setting, to be able to make your contribution to provision for disabled children and those with special educational needs, you need to be well informed about each child. You should develop a picture of what each child needs, what they are capable of, and what especially interests them. You need to know all of this if you are to be able to help each child to learn and develop, offering experiences and activities suitable to help them progress. It will help you to avoid making assumptions about their potential capabilities based on stereotypes; you will develop realistic and accurate expectations for each child's progress and you will not be held back in aspirations for them because of their impairment.

The main ways to gather such information are:

- observation
- talking with the children's parents
- talking with colleagues and other professionals.

Observation

Active observation of a child is perhaps the most important way of developing your understanding of them as an individual.

Active observation means consciously watching and listening to children, really paying attention to them, and asking yourself questions like:

- What are they doing and saying?
- What are they trying to do? What do they almost have the skill to do?
- What can't they manage yet? What do they need help with?
- What are they interested in?

The EYFS sums this up as: 'Observe children to find out about their needs, what they are interested in and what they can do.'

Active observation helps you to know each child as an individual

Parents

Parents of disabled children are often the greatest experts on their child's disability and the specific effects an impairment has on their particular child, which may be different from the way it affects other children. For example:

● parents of a child with sickle cell disease may describe exactly how they know that a crisis is building up for him

● parents of a child with epilepsy may share their knowledge about how to support and help her through an epileptic seizure

● a parent of a child with autism may explain the obsessions and fears he has.

Parents can be a key source of information about their children's impairments

Colleagues and other professionals

Besides the information you gather yourself through your own observations and through listening to what parents can tell you, you will find that:

● colleagues in your setting will also have valuable information about each child from their own observations

● other professionals like physiotherapists, speech and language therapists, and health visitors can add their expertise.

Barriers to participation

The aim of all settings working with children should be to promote **inclusion**.

Once you are familiar with the children you work with, and have gathered information about them, you will be able to identify anything in your setting that is acting as a barrier to each child joining in with all the activities and experiences you offer.

Key term

Inclusion: a process of identifying, understanding and breaking down barriers to participation and belonging

You may find aspects of the environment present physical barriers. The layout of the setting may, for example, prevent wheelchair users getting from one area to another. You may find a lack of appropriate resources is an issue. Policies can also present barriers. For example, some settings have a policy that they will not accept children who still wear nappies; this can have the result of excluding some disabled children with physical impairments or learning difficulties that mean they have to go on wearing nappies longer than most children do.

However, you may also find that the attitudes of staff in the setting are acting as an invisible barrier because they make assumptions about disabled children, perhaps based on stereotypical views. **Stereotypes** about disabled children often have the negative effect of limiting expectations of what those children can achieve, so they are not even offered experiences and activities that could support their development.

It is often the assumptions that are made about what a person with an impairment can and cannot do that lead to restriction or limitation – which makes them disabled. Low expectations of the potential of a disabled child, or being overprotective of them, can limit what they achieve. You should always keep a balance between being realistic about the way a child's impairments result in limitations, and at the same time having high expectations for their progress and achievements.

Key term

Stereotypes: assumptions (usually inaccurate) that, because a person is part of a particular group, that individual will have certain characteristics, have the same needs as all other members of that group, or will behave in a particular way

Getting ready for assessment

With the help of colleagues, identify any barriers – physical or invisible – in your setting that may be preventing disabled children participating fully in activities and all that the setting offers.

What actions could be taken to remove these barriers?

Best practice checklist: Avoiding assumptions

✓ Beware of picking up information like lots of children with Down's syndrome are affectionate, or love music, or have heart problems, or are clumsy, and then assuming that the child with Down's syndrome who has just joined your setting will be affectionate, love music, have heart problems and be clumsy

✓ Avoid this sort of assumption because none of this may apply to that child who is unique, different from all other children with Down's syndrome

✓ Keep an open mind about what a disabled child might try and achieve

Don't have limited expectations of disabled children

Removing barriers

When barriers to participation have been identified, the next step, of course, is to seek ways of removing them and ensuring that your setting offers all children opportunities. In the past, disabled children were often seen as having needs so special that separate provision was necessary for them. In more recent years, the emphasis of policy has become integration, aiming to adjust mainstream settings as far as possible so the requirements of disabled children can be met. This can be achieved for most disabled children and children with special educational needs if barriers to participation and inclusion are removed.

You cannot remove such barriers on your own; it is important to work as part of a team with the colleagues in your setting and other professionals.

Remember too the importance of the knowledge parents have about their individual children, and listen carefully to what they tell you about meeting their children's requirements.

Case study:
Removing a barrier

When Gurdeep joined the Ladybird Nursery, Gina became his key worker. She noticed that he was finding it difficult to hear what was being said to him, despite his hearing aids. She talked to the nursery's SENCO who sought advice from the local team of specialist teachers working with children with hearing impairments. One of their suggestions was to increase the carpeted areas in the nursery so there were fewer hard surfaces in the playroom. This cut back the noises which Gurdeep's hearing aids picked up so he was able to concentrate on voices.

1. Which colleagues would you turn to in your setting for advice about removing barriers to children's inclusion?
2. What professionals does your setting have access to for such help and advice?

Case study:
Listening to parents

Fraser has cystic fibrosis and requires chest physiotherapy a couple of times a day to keep his airways clear of mucus. His parents were able to show the practitioners at the Children's Centre he attended the techniques to use that were effective for Fraser.

1. Why is it important to listen to parents of disabled children?
2. What knowledge do parents have about their children that is different from practitioners' knowledge?

You may also be able to involve the children themselves in this, according to their stage of development, most importantly by listening to them and tuning in to how they see the opportunities available to them.

Case study:
Labelling

It is four-year-old Tyler who gives the staff at the Red Robin Nursery a 'wake-up call' when he overhears Mal and Farah talking about whether he can take part in the Christmas play. 'I NOT 'a Downs', I Tyler! I CAN dance' he shouts.

1. What stereotypical traps have Mal and Farah fallen into?
2. How did the labels put on Tyler's impairments limit their expectations of Tyler?

Supporting inclusion

As we have seen, it is the social model that provides you with a guide in your work with children, and you can help to remove or reduce the disability resulting from impairments by:

- finding ways to adjust the physical environment in your setting

- providing or adapting resources and activities

- organising routines and the way you work in a different way

and, perhaps most important of all:

- not making assumptions about what a child can do, or may be able to achieve.

All of this helps to remove the barriers to children's participation and enables them to be included in settings.

Tackling assumptions — yours and other people's — can be the most difficult to achieve. Don't assume, for example, that a child with physical disabilities will not be able to join in physical play and will just sit on the sidelines and watch. Get to know the child as an individual and find out whether any of this is true of that particular child. Observe their physical strength and confidence and support them to join in.

Much inclusive practice depends on being ready to be flexible and ready to acquire new skills, such as using Makaton or sign language.

Keep an open mind about what disabled children are capable of

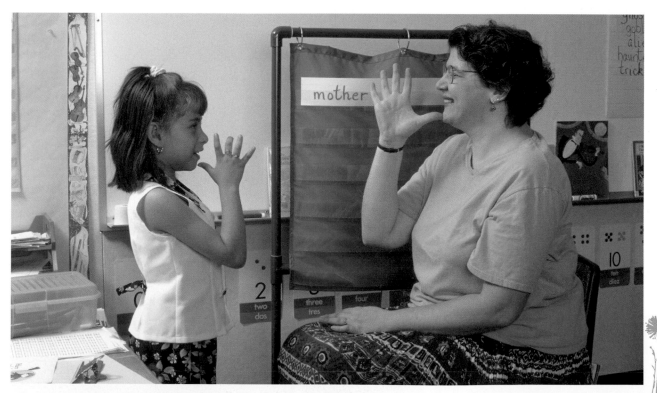

Be prepared to learn new skills like signing

Functional Skills ICT: Developing, presenting and communicating information

You could carry out this 'Getting ready for assessment' task by taking some pictures, displaying them on a short presentation and sharing it with your study group. This way you could see how different settings actively try to remove barriers to children's participation and you could share good practice.

Getting ready for assessment

Think about your own practice in working with disabled children and children with special educational needs. In what ways do you support inclusion by helping to remove barriers to the children's participation in your setting?

Be able to support disabled children and young people and those with special educational needs to participate in the full range of activities and experiences

Inclusive practice enables disabled children and children with special educational needs to participate in a setting, and to take advantage of all the activities and experiences it offers.

Adaptations

The social model of disability helps us to see that inclusive practice is not just about making special provision, but also about adapting the environment, resources, activities and practice to the requirements of each individual child.

Adapting the environment

You cannot plan in advance an environment which will suit the needs of every disabled child — the requirements of a child with visual impairment are different from those of a child who uses a bulky walking frame, and the requirements of two children with the 'same' impairment are unlikely to be identical as their impairment may affect them in different ways or to a different extent. What matters is that the layout of your setting's environment has the potential to be flexible and adaptable — and, perhaps even more importantly, that you and your colleagues are willing and ready to contemplate making changes to that layout so you can remove any barriers to disabled children's inclusion.

Case study:
Adapting the environment

Puddleducks Pre-school reviews their environment and discovers that:

- the layout of furniture is creating narrow pathways which are preventing Daniel, who uses a walking frame, from getting access to several areas of the pre-school so he is excluded from certain sorts of play

- play equipment is often left lying in thoroughfares and this is a hazard to Billy who has a sight impairment

- a lot of the equipment and materials are kept on open shelves so the children can have access to what they want to play with; Qiang, who is unable to walk and gets around by bottom shuffling, often finds that the resources he wants are out of his reach, too high up.

1. How can the Puddleducks staff make sure that Daniel can move about from one part of the setting to another?

2. How can they make sure that toys and equipment are cleared up regularly, and how can they involve the other children in helping Billy by being tidy?

3. How could they re-arrange materials so Qiang can reach those he especially likes, and how can they encourage the other children to understand that Qiang might sometimes need their help to reach things on shelves?

Adapting resources

We have seen that good practice with disabled children should arise out of your usual good practice with all children, and this applies to use of resources too; think about how you can use your usual resources with disabled children. You may find that with some imagination and some simple basic materials you can adapt some resources, or improvise with what is usually at your disposal to be able to use them with children with various impairments.

Case study:
Adapting resources

The practitioners in the Long Lane Children's Centre explore ways of supporting Ethan who has cerebral palsy, Chloe who has visual impairments, and Hassan who uses a wheelchair.

Fatima stitches bells onto some gloves so Ethan can join in music-making sessions. Fran makes a shape and texture lotto game which Chloe can play with other children. She makes pieces of various shapes (circles, squares, triangles) with different textured surfaces, using bubble wrap, fur, foil, and sandpaper.

Laverne brings in some long-handled rollers, used for painting behind radiators, to extend Hasan's reach so he can join in with painting.

None of these solutions requires great financial outlay; it is the practitioners' imagination and creativity that is the key.

1. What ideas can you think of like this to adapt resources in your setting?

2. How much would your ideas cost?

Adapting activities

Some children's impairments may prevent them joining in activities in your setting. Remember that the social model of disability guides us to find ways of adapting to suit the child, not expecting the child to fit in with what usually happens. With a bit of thought and imagination, many activities can be adapted to offer children opportunities to take part in them.

Case study:
Adapting activities

Leila described to her colleagues in the Stepping Stones Nursery some of the ways that a dance class she belonged to included disabled children that she thought could also be used in the nursery:

'We play parachute games with all the children sitting on chairs rather than standing so Kwasi who uses a wheelchair can take part, and he joins in the dancing by wheeling his chair around or using streamers of ribbon to dance with his arms and hands. Aidan, who has a hearing impairment, dances in bare feet and picks up the rhythms and pulsations of the music through the vibrations of the floor.'

1. What adaptations like this can you think of to help disabled children join in activities in your setting?

2. How will disabled children benefit from being able to participate alongside other children?

Adapting working practices

An example of an aspect of practice that it may help to focus on is routines. Routines can become set and unquestioned, but they need to be flexible so they can be adjusted to take into account the individual needs of children. For example, physiotherapy sessions may have to be incorporated into the daily pattern for some children, or a child with diabetes may need frequent small snacks, not just food at the usual mealtimes; other children may require medication to be administered at certain times of day.

Case study:
Changing the routine

In the Paintbox Nursery, the usual routine is to put out a different activity at the beginning of each session – puzzles one day, painting another and so on, to offer the children variety and keep them interested. But when Connor joined the nursery, he found it bewildering. He has autism and he gets agitated and angry when things change – he likes a very set routine and without it, he feels insecure and frightened.

The nursery staff thought about changing the practice of having varied activities each day, but they felt that would have a negative effect for the other children.

Then Penny came up with the idea of making Connor his own chart with a picture for the activity starting each day. As each session starts, she gets out his chart so he can check which activity is available today. He has slowly adjusted to the feeling of a weekly routine and is much more settled.

1. What changes to routines could benefit some disabled children in your setting?

2. Who would need to be involved in decisions to change routines?

Specialist aids and equipment

Some children can only participate fully in the activities in a setting if they make use of specialist aids or equipment. These might include:

- spectacles or a reading light

- a hearing aid or hearing loop

- a Makaton board or electronic communication aid, perhaps with a head stick or mouth stick, or a voice-activated computer

- a wheelchair, crutches or a walking frame or roller

- a prosthetic limb or a caliper

- a feeding tube or a catheter.

You may have to learn how to maintain the equipment, or keep it clean, and be able to use it safely and effectively in ways best suited to the individual child. Even if you become accustomed to using an aid with one child, you may find you have to adjust your practice with another child who needs to use it in a slightly different way because their impairment affects them in a different way.

You cannot be expected to have detailed knowledge of every sort of equipment. What matters is that you are prepared to learn how to use such aids if necessary when working with a particular child, listening to advice from the child's parents and other professionals like occupational therapists.

You also have a role to play in helping non-disabled children understand the importance of such equipment to disabled children and how to treat it with respect.

Case study:
Understanding special equipment

Jack describes what happened when Leroy who uses crutches and Luke who uses a wheelchair joined the Children's Centre:

'The other children were fascinated and several of them wanted to 'try out' the wheelchair and the crutches. We had a discussion about how these items of equipment are not toys. We said it was up to Leroy and Luke to decide if someone could share their aid briefly, but they were to be returned as soon as Leroy or Luke asked for them back.'

1. Why did the children want to 'have a go' with the crutches and wheelchair?

2. Why is it so important that Leroy and Luke get their equipment back as soon as they ask for it?

Supporting participation and equality of access

Current policy towards disabled children and children with special educational needs is to include them as far as possible in mainstream settings, giving them access to opportunities to develop and learn alongside other children.

When children are included in mainstream provision, they have access to opportunities alongside other children

Review and improvement

All professional practitioners should spend time reviewing the way they work and looking for ways to improve all aspects of their practice. This is often referred to as being a 'reflective practitioner'. A reflective practitioner is someone who takes a questioning approach to their work, taking time to:

- think critically about what they do in their work, how they do it and why they do it that way

- assess the effectiveness of what they are doing and how they can become more effective.

Link See SHC 22 for more on reflective practice.

Getting ready for assessment

Spend time thinking about your work with disabled children and children with special educational needs. What improvements could you make to the activities and experiences you help to offer them?

Functional Skills English: Writing

You could look back at the last activity that you carried out with the children. You could write a short evaluation of how the activity went and what you would change or adapt if you had a child with a special educational need completing the activity.

Reflection or self-assessment is not something you do once: it's not taking a snapshot of yourself on one day or one week in your working life. It needs to become something you do regularly and throughout your professional life. It is worthwhile to put in the time and effort this requires because you will reach higher standards in your work and provide a better service to children and families. Reflective practice is not something someone else can do to you or for you — you have to take responsibility for your own professional development.

The feedback you receive from your manager or supervisor and other colleagues, as well as from parents and the children themselves should help you to identify:

● your good practice — your strengths

● gaps in your knowledge and skills — your weaknesses or areas for development.

Check your knowledge

1. What does the Disability Discrimination Act require early years settings to do?

2. Local authorities have a legal duty of 'statementing'. What does this consist of?

3. What are the key principles of the SEN Code of Practice?

4. What do the initials SENCO stand for, and what is the role of this person?

5. What is the difference between the medical and social models of disability?

6. What is an impairment?

7. What is meant by the term 'disability'?

8. What are the main ways of gathering information about a child?

9. What is meant by the term 'inclusion'?

10. Name three examples of specialist aids or equipment a disabled child might need to use.

Support children's & young people's play & leisure

Play and leisure are a large part of the lives of children and young people. In this unit you will gather more information about the role this has in their development and learning.

Learning outcomes
By the end of this unit you will:

1. understand the nature and importance of play and leisure

2. be able to support children's and young people's play and leisure

3. be able to support children and young people in balancing risk and challenge

4. be able to reflect on and improve your own practice.

Play: engage in games or other activities for enjoyment rather than for a serious or practical purpose

Leisure: time spent in or free for relaxation or enjoyment

Understand the nature and importance of play and leisure

To understand the importance of **play** and **leisure** to children and young people you must first be able to identify what play and leisure are and the many forms they come in. From this you will see the many benefits children gain and the impact this can have on their holistic development, social skills, self-esteem and interest in the world around them.

Why play and leisure are important

From the moment they are born, babies find out about and discover the world around them through play. They explore with their bodies and through their senses. Throughout childhood, children continue to learn and develop through a vast range of play experiences. As they reach adolescence, they often categorise their play as 'leisure', where it takes on a more mature and structured meaning, with activities focused around particular interests and peer groups.

As early years pioneer Susan Isaacs said, 'Play is indeed the child's work', as children seek to make sense of what they see and experience and gain a greater understanding of the world in which they live.

To children, play has no end product or defined purpose; it is just what they do. Allowing children to play freely enables them to find their own direction, seek answers to their own enquiries and gain a great sense of satisfaction from being absorbed in the enjoyment of what they have chosen to do.

Play can involve others but doesn't necessarily have to. Practitioners should respect the wishes of children as they watch the process of play unfold.

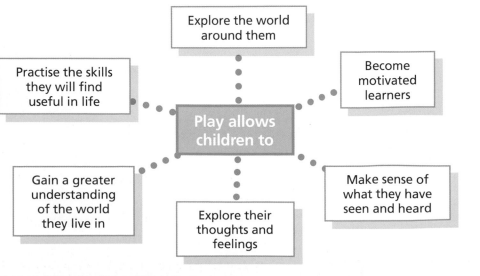

Figure 1: What play allows children to do

Mildred Parten (1933) looked at stages of children's play and identified how children begin their play experiences. Table 1 explains in detail her stages of play. However, Mildred Parten also recognised that children may go back to solitary play at any given time, showing that throughout childhood children need time on their own to play, as well as being in the company of others.

Table 1: Mildred Parten's stages of play

Stage of play	Description of play
Unoccupied play	A child is an observer and not indulged in actual play
Solitary play	A child is playing alone and happy to indulge in activities, often unaware or uninterested in others at play around them
Onlooker play	A child looks in on others at play; they may try to talk about the play that is happening without actually joining in
Parallel play	As the name suggests, a child will play alongside another, often at the same activity, but not with other children
Associative play	A child is involved in activities alongside others and begins the process of turn taking, sharing and indulging in conversation about an activity
Cooperative play	A child is involved in activities with others where play often has a focus, with roles and rules to play

Skills builder

Using Table 1 as your guide, take time to watch the children you work with when they are playing, at a particular activity or playing outdoors.

- Can you see children at various stages in play?

- Are all the children involved in the same stage of play?

Play comes in many forms

Over to You

Observe children in your care 'at play'. Now write down five words to describe the children while they are playing.

Did you write any of the following: happy, content, talkative, concentrating, inquisitive, imaginative, sociable?

What were they doing or saying to make you write down the words you did?

Do you think play is important to children? Why?

Functional Skills
English: Writing

This 'Over to you' is a good topic to discuss and share ideas about. You could write your opinion and thoughts in a short report and share it with your assessor. You would need to ensure that you organised your work so as to cover all the questions.

Play comes in many forms and can happen both with and without props. A play environment such as preschool will provide children with many resources to engage their interest, and allow their imaginations to run wild. Even children who do not have access to a wide range of toys enjoy the freedom of play, be it with a cardboard box, a secret den, or simply their own imagination.

As children get older and enter adolescence their play can evolve into leisure pursuits. This can be:

- more structured, where they are involved in clubs and groups such as Scouts, Guides or athletics
- more unstructured, where they spend time just 'hanging out' together at each other's houses or the local park.

While older children may not see this type of activity as play, it still has the same purpose: — spending time in the company of others they like. Listening to music sitting in a friend's lounge may have no end product, but it is simply enjoyable and fun for the individuals involved.

How play and leisure contribute to development

With the introduction of the Early Years Foundation Stage (EYFS), practitioners are increasingly aware of the benefits of play for children's learning and development. They can see the holistic nature of development through their regular observations of children at play, experiencing a range of activities and opportunities.

While many may still argue that there is no need for formal assessment of young children, the process of observing and assessing has increased practitioners' knowledge and awareness of the many benefits play brings. From this they can see how they can support and encourage children's play to progress development and learning, at a pace suited to each child.

It is impossible to define or categorise children's play clearly due to its broad, holistic and integrated nature. While many practitioners focus on specific aspects of the EYFS under the six areas of learning when observing play, it is important that they do not see this in isolation and consider the benefits gained for all aspects of children's learning and development.

Figure 2 shows a few examples of the types of play children choose when they are provided with an appropriate environment both indoors and outdoors to choose freely.

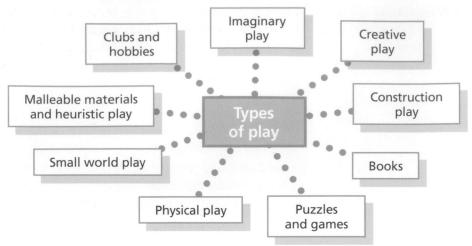

Figure 2: Types of play

So how do these experiences benefit children's development and learning?

Imaginary play

Children learn to make sense of the world around them by imitating adults and children's actions around them. From an early age, babies will involve themselves in imaginary play by copying adults' language (for babies this will be babbling) and responding to facial expressions, building their communication skills. As babies reach toddlerhood, they will play out roles using their developing imagination, which they build on and rehearse well into childhood. They will take on roles of people they know and will dress up to act out their ideas. Role play or 'pretend play' can provide social opportunities among peers as they indulge in cooperative play and between them ascertain the roles of individuals as the play unfolds. Turn taking and sharing are also skills acquired through such play.

Creative play

Link To find out more about creative play, see the section in OP 2.17.

This involves the use of many media, and includes art activities and messy play. These experiences allow children to express themselves freely in a creative way. From an early age, children can become involved in creative activities such as hand and foot painting. As babies become toddlers they become aware of their ability to control materials — such as paintbrushes, glue spreaders and scissors — for creative play, enabling them to understand their personal responsibility for safe use of equipment. Pre-school children begin to make representations in their creative work and will often tell you what their painting or junk box model is going to be long before it is finished. They enjoy indulging in creative play and being freely expressive, but will be equally pleased with their finished product, which gives them a great sense of achievement.

Construction play

We are all familiar with play items such as plastic building bricks, which are also known as construction toys. A baby's experience of construction begins when they have developed the dexterity and hand—eye

Construction toys challenge children's skills of connecting pieces, problem solving and physical ability

coordination to place two or three blocks on top of one another. Construction toys test and challenge children's skills of connecting pieces, problem solving and physical ability as they manipulate the objects of choice.

Books

From the moment of birth, babies can and should be exposed to the delights of books and stories. Older babies will begin to handle books and enjoy learning to turn the pages. Toddlers will begin to understand the purpose of books and attempt to 'read' them (if only upside down at first!) Pre-school children will continue to gain much pleasure from listening to stories, looking at books and telling stories of their own, using the book as a prop. With books, imagination flows, communication skills are practised and self-esteem is escalated.

Puzzles and games

Babies enjoy pop-up toys and shape sorters as they discover cause and effect: 'What will happen if I press that button?' Toddlers enjoy inset puzzles requiring them to use their growing problem-solving skills and 'trial and error' to fit pieces in the appropriate place. Pre-school children enjoy simple jigsaws, and older children begin to enjoy the complexities of puzzles with little pieces. There is a wide variety of games with simple rules for children, toddlers and pre-school children alike to enjoy. These encourage them to work together, share and take turns. Older children will enjoy more complex games with a series of rules, and will continue to develop the ability to take turns and understand that there are winners and losers.

Physical play

This lets children develop large bodily movements (gross motor skills) and smaller body movements (fine motor skills). Running around out of doors is an ideal way for children to indulge in physical play and gain fresh air and exercise. Although equipment is not always necessary, it has many benefits for the developing child. Activity gyms, which babies can kick and hit, help develop physical skills, then push-along trucks aid their ability to walk. Toddlers enjoy slides, tricycles and rocking toys, which develop muscle tone and spacial awareness. Riding a bike, skateboard or scooter becomes a keen outdoor activity for older children. Using equipment enables children to balance challenge and risk in play as they seek to understand the limitations of their own capabilities. Physical play is not just for the out of doors; appropriate activities can be provided indoors too.

Small-world play

There are many commercially available resources for small-world play, from play people with sets for hospitals and houses to animal sets including farms, zoos and dinosaurs. Young children take great delight in setting up such play, and can be happy doing this alone or with others. You will often see children taking on roles of characters and animals as they play. While children are happy to use the props and resources available to them, it is also important to let their imaginations flow. There is nothing more detrimental to small-world play than hearing an adult say 'Keep the zoo on the carpet, please.' Such comments can stifle and limit the play experience for children. While it is important for practitioners to be in sight and sound of the children and to be mindful of the needs of other children, what is wrong with them going off for a mini-adventure around the room?

Malleable materials and heuristic play

This includes sand and water, play dough and clay. With close supervision, babies can experience malleable materials from an early age. Developing their senses through touch, these materials also enable children to gain an understanding of scientific and mathematical concepts: for example, how many little containers of water will it take to fill this big one, or what will happen if I add water to this dry sand. **Heuristic play** can be provided by devising 'treasure baskets' full of natural materials found in the setting, including a wooden spoon, a fresh lemon, small containers and cardboard tubes. These items help children to explore in a relaxed way, choosing objects of interest to feel, taste, smell, hear and see. Adults should sit close by and observe, but not direct play with words or actions. Elinor Goldschmied (1996) recognised children's fascination with objects such as wooden spoons and saucepans and was concerned that such materials were not given to children, but were readily replaced by commercial toys and equipment. She believed that natural materials help children develop their senses – and so came the 'treasure basket'. Many early years settings now use heuristic play as part of the continuous provision for babies and young children.

Key term

Heuristic play: a form of exploratory or discovery play using natural materials

A treasure basket

Over to You

Look around your setting and identify some experiences you provide for children that we have not already mentioned.

- How do the children use the activity or experience?
- What do they learn from this?
- How does this aid their development?

Functional Skills ICT: Developing, presenting and communicating information

You could produce a reference booklet that explains what each type of play is and what activities in your setting cover this type of play. You could share your booklet with other members of staff at the setting and maybe other students.

Clubs and hobbies

As children get older their play can become centred on specific interests and activities, sometimes of a sporting nature or craft-orientated. They are driven by interests that engage them and give them pleasure and a sense of achievement. Clubs such as Scouts or Guides give them a wider experience of the community and enable them to engage in meaningful social interactions in their leisure activity. They can also give them a sense of belonging and an understanding of the needs of others, while still being something they want to do.

Getting ready for assessment

You will need to show you know and understand how play contributes to the development of the children you work with. Take time to consider the evidence that you can present to demonstrate this. This can include the following:

- observations and evaluations of children in your care
- contributing to planning and the learning intentions
- reflecting on an activity you have done with the children
- discussion with your assessor about the resources provided for play and why.

The UN Convention on the Rights of the Child on relaxation and play

The UN Convention on the Rights of the Child is a treaty set out by world leaders in 1989 to protect and uphold the rights of children and young people. Countries have signed up to this treaty in a bid to ensure children are treated fairly and not exploited in any way. By doing so, national governments become accountable for ensuring the protection of children and in turn declare this commitment to the international community. While there are fifty-four articles in this important piece of legislation, the key commitments are shown in Figure 3.

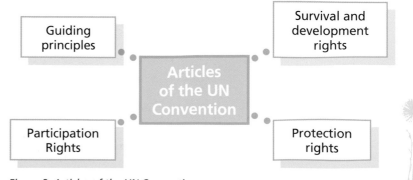

Figure 3: Articles of the UN Convention

Functional Skills English: Reading

Finding out more about the UN convention on the rights of the child is a good way of developing your reading skills. You could make a note of how your setting provides experiences in line with the UN Convention.

Under the heading of survival and development rights sits Article 31 (Leisure, play and culture), which states: 'Children have the right to relax and play, and to join in a wide range of cultural, artistic and other recreational activities.'

What is freely chosen, self-directed play and leisure?

Play has many characteristics. While these will vary from activity to activity, Figure 4 shows some characteristics that are common to all types of play.

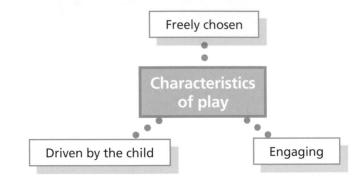

Figure 4: Characteristics of play

Freely chosen

Sounds simple enough, doesn't it? But just how free is freely chosen play? Freely chosen isn't free if you tell a child they can play with anything they want from those six boxes in the cupboard; nor is it free if you tell them they can 'go off and play', but only on the carpeted area. 'Freely chosen' means being able to choose their play with few limitations and having a sense of being in control of what happens. Access to a spacious, well-equipped environment both indoors and outdoors provides children with the foundations to build their play on. Many settings aim to provide an environment where children have free access to the indoors and outdoors, allowing them to make choices about where and when their play can occur. This is not the case for all settings as there may be restrictions on buildings and access to outdoor areas.

Engaging

Children need to feel engaged in their play. It needs to motivate them and interest them. Children who are engaged in play can spend long periods engrossed in an experience, either on their own or with others. Capturing their imagination and their interest is what helps drive their play and take it in any direction they want. You can often see this when watching children role-playing: for example, pretending to be dinosaurs taking over the world and then having a dinosaur tea party!

Driven by the child

Play should be driven by the child and not by practitioners. Why? As you have already seen, children are more motivated and engaged when it is something of their choosing, something they like to do. They do not need adults telling them what they should do next. Have you ever watched children playing perhaps in the role-play corner and decided to go and join them? Often you will be greeted by a willing child ready to give you a drink and plenty of snacks too! However, sometimes you will be greeted by a stony silence and a dispersal of four-year-olds. Why? Because that is not the direction they wanted their play to go in, and they didn't invite you to join in.

Being able to understand the characteristics of freely chosen play helps practitioners in ascertaining the role they have in supporting children's play.

Tina Bruce (1996) identified the twelve features of play. She said that, if adults observe seven or more of these, then quality play would be taking place.

Children pretend when playing

The twelve features of play

1. Quality play comes from children using previous first-hand experiences of people, objects and materials.
2. When children play they make up their own rules, and so keep control of their play.
3. Children make play props.
4. Children choose to play. They cannot be made to play.
5. Children rehearse the future in their role play. They pretend to be other people and take on adult roles.
6. Children pretend when playing.
7. Children play alone sometimes.
8. Children play in pairs, in parallel or in groups with other children.

9. Each child has their own play ideas, often called a play agenda. The adult's play ideas are not more important than the child's play ideas.

10. Children will be deeply involved in their play. Children at play wallow in their feelings, relationships and ideas.

11. Children try out what they have been learning. They show their skills and competencies.

12. Play helps children to coordinate what they learn, bringing together all the different aspects of their development.

Be able to support children's and young people's play and leisure

Understanding your role in children's play will help you to identify when support is needed. Your role will vary considerably from activity to activity and day to day. Knowing what your role is at any given time will ensure that you do not obstruct play or alter its natural course. There will be times when adults get it wrong but this then provides an ideal opportunity to reflect on practice and consider changes to benefit children and their play.

What is your role?

Figure 5: The role of adults in children's play

Many practitioners believe they should guide children's play at all times, but this is not true. Children can and do like to play independently. Playing a supervisory or passive role whereby you maintain a watchful eye on play but have no need to intervene in the course of play or become involved in what they are doing will be all that is required of you. It is always very tempting to engage with children but, before you do, stand back and see if this will really be of benefit, or if their play is already providing them with wonderful experiences.

Children need practitioners to facilitate play, to provide them with the resources and materials they may need. While you should make them readily available to children, it is important that you do not insist on their use; the children should think things through themselves and draw their own conclusions about what props and resources they may need.

While independence in play should be encouraged, there are many opportunities for practitioners to engage fully and interact in play with children. This can be when being invited into the role play for a cup of tea, or responding to a child's request to play a game with them. As children get older, they enjoy games with rules and often benefit from the input of an adult to ensure fair play for all. That is not to say that children cannot negotiate and manage the rules of play for themselves; rather, they actively enjoy the adult's involvement in the game and obviously winning against them!

There are many opportunities for practitioners to engage in play with children

The course of play does not always run smoothly, and a practitioner can sometimes be needed to be a negotiator or boundary setter. Play can get out of hand when the dynamics of the group do not work; there may be a clash of personalities, where individuals seek to dominate play rather than work in harmony with their peers. It is important that practitioners acknowledge conflict in play and work out a successful resolution.

Practitioners must also intervene when play becomes dangerous, and again must seek to negotiate with those involved so they are aware of their own safety and the boundaries for behaviour in play. Consider the checklist when supporting children's play and leisure.

Best practice checklist: Your role in play and leisure

✓ Recognise when to stand back

✓ Be available to offer support and guidance

✓ Know when you may be needed to intervene

✓ Remember that supervising children can be done from a distance

✓ Balance the needs of the children

✓ Actively engage in play when requested to by the children

Giving attention while being sensitive to your own impact

When supporting children at play, you can give your attention in many different ways, from being the passive observer to being fully engaged in play. To understand what play is to children you must look to them, observe what they are doing and watch their play unfold.

Most practitioners would like to think that they allow children to decide the content and course of play all the time; however, in reality practitioners often have in their minds what they anticipate children will get from a play activity or opportunity.

Nobody is saying that this is not acceptable; there are many benefits in practitioners thinking about their role and how the environment can be resourced. However, practitioners must be careful not to assume the direction of play – or, indeed, alter the course of play – to suit their own preconceived ideas. It is therefore extremely important that practitioners do not always seek to find a purpose to children's play or insist on the use of resources in a particular way, because this very process can alter the course of play and take it to where the adult wants to go, rather than where the child wants to.

Functional Skills Maths: Representing

What is the ratio of boys to girls in your setting? Do they often play together nicely? Are there any games in your setting that attract one gender over the other? You could carry out some research to support what you are saying. Maybe a graph to show which gender plays with certain activities more than others.

Case study:
Stereotyping play

John is supervising the children from the out-of-school club on a trip to the park. As the children run around John asks the boys to look after the girls and not be too boisterous.

1. Why do you think John said this?
2. Do you think this is 'stereotyping'?
3. What could John do differently?

Our own value and belief systems can often impact on how we interpret things, as can our own experiences. You must be careful about these because they can result in assumptions and judgements about play and stereotypes too.

Routine safety checks on play and leisure areas

Link See PEFAP 001 and MPII002 for more on health and safety.

All practitioners have a duty to ensure the environment in which children are being cared for is safe. Your setting will have its own health and safety policies and procedures and they should make you fully aware of these and your roles and responsibilities.

It is good practice to conduct both written and visual checks of the play environment. Written checks show that an individual has taken time to consider specific aspects of the play environment and prove it has been carried out. Many settings conduct written safety checks of the environment at the beginning and end of the working day, and remind practitioners to conduct visual checks throughout the working day.

Written risk assessments are a legal requirement of the EYFS for all registered settings. The specific legal requirements of suitable premises, environment and equipment states:

> 'The provider must conduct a risk assessment and review it regularly – at least once a year or more frequently when the need arises. The risk assessment must identify aspects of the environment that need to be checked on a regular basis: providers must maintain a record of these particular aspects and when and by whom they have been checked. Providers must determine the regularity of these checks according to their assessment of the significance of individual risks.'

Some settings go so far as to have a written risk assessment clearly displayed in areas of play as a constant reminder to practitioners of the hazards they need to be aware of.

When thinking about the health and safety of the play environment, it is extremely important to consider all environments that the children have access to.

Figure 6: Play environments

The safety checks carried out will vary depending on the area or environment you are in and the activities that the children have available to them.

Over to You

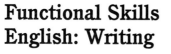

Find out about your setting's systems for checking the environment. Ask how often checks are done and who is responsible for doing them.

Functional Skills English: Writing

You could develop your writing skills by having a go at writing a risk assessment for an activity that you have carried out. You could share this with your supervisor; do they agree you have covered all the risks for your setting and that activity?

Best practice checklist: Safety checks

✓ Is the equipment age-appropriate?

✓ Is anything damaged or broken?

✓ Is the equipment clean?

✓ Have safety measures been considered, such as crash mats around climbing frame?

✓ Are activities set up appropriately: for example, sand and water play where it can be easily swept or mopped up?

✓ Is the play area secure?

Supervising play and leisure

It is essential that practitioners maintain overall supervision of children while they are playing, and that this is done without overprotecting them and undermining their own capabilities. Children's skills, understanding and capabilities can vary immensely. Practitioners must also be aware of the support that children with special needs should be given. Children with identified needs should have access to a rich play environment alongside their peers, but you may need to consider adaptations to activities and equipment so that they can participate. Just as important is the level of support and supervision they may need from practitioners to feel secure and included.

With all activities there is an element of risk, but knowing the children you work with and their own capabilities and stage of development will help you to ascertain how much support they will need from you.

One of the main aspects of ensuring their safety is to consider the environment. Knowing about risk assessments and health and safety checks, you will be well equipped to ensure the environment is safe, reducing the likelihood of accidents and incidents.

Carrying out risk assessments and health and safety checks is crucial, but remember that even then children will not be totally free from hazards, as the very nature of play can result in unforeseen incidents.

Best practice checklist: Playing safe

✓ Ensure risk assessments have been carried out

✓ Complete health and safety checks regularly

✓ Use any safety equipment given

✓ Consider the individual abilities of children

✓ Ensure children are supervised at all times

✓ Inform them of their responsibilities and the boundaries set for play

How you interact during play

Interaction that shows you are interested

The way in which practitioners act and speak to young children says a lot about their ability to relate to children in a positive way — to show that they are interested in what the children say, experience and feel.

When children are talking and sharing their experiences it is important that the adult demonstrates that they are listening and value what the child has to say. Figure 7 shows many ways this can be done.

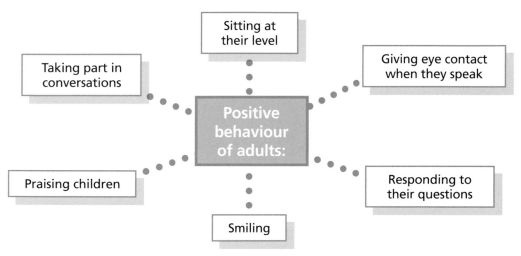

Figure 7: Positive behaviour of adults

Children will disengage from communications and will be reluctant to share their experiences if they feel that the adult is not interested in what they have to say. They may then not share their feelings and experiences with other adults, as their self-esteem can be lowered and they can have little self-worth.

Taking an active interest in children's conversation about what they are doing has many benefits to children, including:

- building self-esteem
- making them feel important
- making them feel valued in the setting
- helping build relationships with others
- building their skills of communication
- helping to acknowledge and identify own feelings
- helping them to find positive outlets for expression.

Case study:
Taking an interest or not?

Jane is working in an out-of-school club. It is nearly closing time so she decides to start sweeping the playroom floor. Jody is eight years old and waiting to be collected by her mum, She sits at the table doing a jigsaw while she waits. Jody starts a conversation with Jane about her weekend and what a lovely time she had at the zoo with her family. Although Jane acknowledges Jody with a nod of the head, she continues to sweep the floor and asks Jody if she could stop what she is doing and move the chairs for her. Jody stops talking about her weekend and responds to Jane's request without any further exchange of words.

1. Do you think this is good practice from Jane?
2. What could she do to show she is interested in what Jody has to say?
3. How do you think Jody is feeling?

Interaction that shows respect

Adults need to understand children's need for privacy, and to respect their freedom to make choices for themselves. Even younger children seek the quiet and privacy of the book corner when they want to be alone. Children seek privacy in different ways; in play this can be seen as acting out roles and indulging in conversations with other children without being overlooked by adults. Adults should respect children's desire for privacy in these situations and allow them the space for this to happen. Older children will often want to have private spaces away from adults. In an environment where practitioners are responsible for the overall care of older children they will need to discuss with them what they think is acceptable in terms of having their own privacy. Children should be able to hold conversations and write notes to one another without the threat of being listened in on. The only exception to this rule is when you think the child is in imminent risk and your duty to protect their rights comes before their right to privacy. Adults also need to respect children's choices in play and avoid saying 'Why don't you…?' when they are quite happily absorbed in what they are doing.

Case study:
Rights to privacy

Lesley is a play leader at a village summer play scheme. A ten-year-old sits with her friend on the bench outdoors texting on her phone. As the phone bleeps the two girls squeal with delight and respond to the text they have received. Lesley is watching from a distance. After a snack, Lesley notices the phone has been discarded on the table as the girls go out to play. The phone bleeps again. Lesley picks up the phone and reads the text before taking the phone out to the girls.

1. Should Lesley have read the text?
2. How can this affect the relationship between the children and the adult?
3. What should Lesley have done?

Interaction that gives praise and encouragement

Children and adults alike enjoy receiving praise from others as it gives individuals a sense of self-worth, increases their confidence in their abilities and boosts their self-esteem. Encouragement is the process of supporting an individual to take on a challenge or task and actively highlighting their ability along the way. In early years settings, praise and encouragement often go hand in hand as by praising a child's abilities and efforts practitioners are encouraging them along. As children get older, they still benefit from praise and encouragement from family members and childcare professionals — or even more so, as children doubt their own skills and abilities, comparing themselves to their peers and their siblings.

Best practice checklist:
Praising and encouraging children

✓ Be at the child's level and give eye contact when praising so they feel they have your focused attention

✓ Be specific about the words or actions you are giving praise to: this helps the praise carry more meaning

✓ Ensure the method you use to praise is appropriate to the age of the child; claps and cheers may be appropriate for a baby, but may not be well received by a teenager

✓ Praise and encourage little achievements and successes: the steps to achievement are just as important as the end point

✓ Recognise the individual achievements of children and acknowledge that there are similarities and differences in what they can do

✓ Avoid offering praise on the back of another child's achievement as this can be seen as comparing their abilities

Praise and encourage little achievements and successes

Be able to support children and young people in balancing risk and challenge

In a society where we have become risk-averse due to the potential legal outcomes from exposure to **risk**, it is easy for practitioners to openly avoid situations where there is an element of risk in play. Here you will look at the practitioner's role in supporting children to take safe risks in play, to provide them with the **challenges** they need to develop and learn about the world around them.

The value of risk and challenge

With any challenging situation there comes an element of risk. Rather than avoid risk altogether, which can restrict children's development and learning, it is important to allow safe risks and consider how these challenge children and help them develop. To be able to identify challenge and risk in play you must first be able to understand what these risks are.

The types of risk children take in play are detailed in Table 2.

Table 2: Risks and challenges in play

Physical	• learning to crawl, walk, run and climb • managing tools and equipment, such as scissors and knives • managing environments including uneven pathways, slippery surfaces
Intellectual	• taking on a challenging experience • trying out new activities • developing use of logic and common sense
Social and moral	• peer pressure as children get older, venturing out beyond parental boundaries, e.g. coming in late, going into town • social pressures, e.g. resisting persistence of others to try drugs and/or alcohol • developing an understanding of boundaries and rules

Allowing children challenge and risk in play will help them understand how they are personally responsible for their behaviour. For example, with adult support and clear explanations, children can learn how to hold and use a pair of scissors safely, and that running with scissors in their hand can result in injury.

While children should be encouraged to try new activities and experiences that present them with challenges and potentially put them out of their comfort zone, it is important to acknowledge when they feel unsafe. Children often experience physical symptoms, such as a

Over to You

Can you identify some of the feelings children experience when they are faced with a challenge or risky situation?

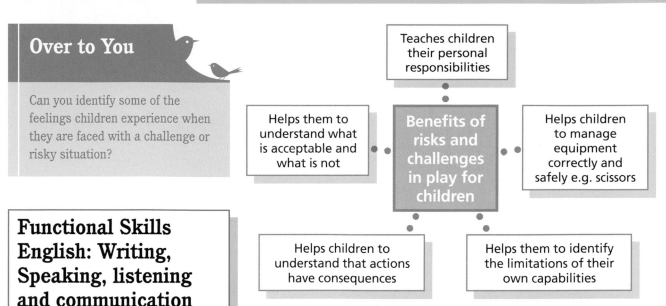

Figure 8: Benefits of risks and challenges in play for children

Benefits of risks and challenges in play for children

- Teaches children their personal responsibilities
- Helps children to manage equipment correctly and safely e.g. scissors
- Helps them to identify the limitations of their own capabilities
- Helps children to understand that actions have consequences
- Helps them to understand what is acceptable and what is not

Functional Skills English: Writing, Speaking, listening and communication

Before you carry out this 'Over to you' you may want to think about yourself and how you have felt in a risky situation. When was the last time you experienced a risky situation? How did you feel at the time and again after? You could share your thoughts either written or verbally with your tutor.

funny feeling in their tummy, feeling sick or their heart beating faster. Practitioners need to talk to the child about how they feel to help them understand their feelings and identify if these feelings are linked to nervous energy or sheer terror. Some children will adopt the approach of 'feel the fear and do it anyway', while others will recognise this as a warning sign. Either way, this provides children with valuable knowledge about the limitations of their own capabilities.

When is a risk or challenge unacceptable?

It is important that any practitioner can recognise when a risk or challenge in children and young people's play and leisure goes beyond the limits of acceptability.

Key term

Zone of proximal development (ZPD): the difference between what a child can do with help and what he or she can do without help

Over to You

Look at the statements below and identify if you think they are acceptable or unacceptable challenges and risks.

1. A three-year-old in a nursery is sitting with friends using scissors to cut up junk box models; an adult is also sat at the table.

2. A six-year-old who goes to a childminder after school climbs a tree in the garden while the childminder cooks tea.

3. A ten-year-old makes some cakes while their parent is in another room.

4. A 9-month-old baby crawls on the kitchen floor

5. A two-year-old plays in a garden containing a pond.

Functional Skills English: Speaking, listening and communication

These statements are good discussion starters. You may feel different about these situations from someone else in your study group. Listen carefully to what others say so that you can respond in an appropriate way.

When something is beyond their capabilities

We all accept that children need challenges in play to help them progress and develop. However, as Vygotsky pointed out, these need to be within their **zone of proximal development (ZPD)**. It would be inappropriate to expect a child who had just mastered the art of riding a tricycle to ride a two-wheeled bike without the aid of stabilisers first. Mastering one skill at a time enables a child to make steps to achieving a bigger goal.

When something is beyond their understanding

Children need information about danger to be repeated and reinforced constantly to help them consider the consequences of inappropriate actions. Babies rely totally on the adult to remove them from danger; their inquisitive nature will draw them to danger such as open fires, plug sockets and anything small enough to put into their mouths. Adult intervention is required until they reach an age where they have learned about the dangers around them.

When there is no supervision and support

It is unacceptable for any practitioner to leave children unsupervised at activities and experiences. Even if children have gained an understanding of how to manage risks safely, adults should still be on hand for unforeseeable events. While accidents can still happen in the presence of adults, with adequate support and supervision these can be kept to a minimum, without exposure to unnecessary risks.

When there are no guidelines

To help children manage risks and take personal responsibility for their safety and that of others around them, adults must be clear in their expectations. This does not mean calling out a series of orders to children, but discussing with them how to use the equipment they have been given, or how to manage themselves as they challenge their skills. Open and honest discussions with older children and young people about the dangers of drugs, alcohol and smoking will help them understand that these are unacceptable risks, as well as the possible consequences.

When health and safety are not taken into account

When there are lapses in health and safety procedures, children can be exposed to unnecessary risks. The role of risk assessment is to eliminate hazards or reduce them to an acceptable level. As you read earlier in this unit, it is a legal requirement of the EYFS that settings undertake procedures to adequately risk-assess the environments in which children are cared for. Further to the specific legal requirement outlined earlier, providers should give due regard to the statutory guidance, which states: 'The risk assessment should cover anything with which a child may come into contact'.

Practitioners should consider allowing risks so children can learn to manage them safely

Getting ready for assessment

Write a reflective practice account detailing how you have supported a child in your care to manage their own risks and challenges in play. Explain why it was important to do this.

The importance of children managing risk and challenge for themselves

'Exposure to well managed risks helps children learn important life skills, including how to manage risks for themselves ... children in particular need to learn how to manage risks, and adventure activities such as rock climbing, sailing and canoeing are an ideal way of doing this' (RSA Risk Commission Conference, 31 October 2007).

The early years foundation stage (EYFS) emphasises the important role that the outdoor environment plays in children's learning and development. With this come additional challenges and risks for children.

Rather than avoiding situations where children come into contact with challenges and risks, practitioners should consider the importance of allowing risks so they can learn how to manage them safely.

Children do not learn by simply being told: they need to experience things at first hand. In this way they are more likely to understand the risk to which they are exposed. It can also help them to learn about the consequences that their actions have, making them more responsible individuals. Managing risks can also increase their skills of independence and resilience, which have a significant impact on children's confidence and self-esteem.

It is tempting to limit exposure to risk but, when adults overdo this, it can stifle children's development and learning. It can also have dire consequences when they are older, when having no concept of risk can put them in a very dangerous situation.

How children can manage risk and challenge

Leading by example can encourage children to try challenging activities for themselves. For example, if a practitioner is sitting at a table using scissors to cut up egg boxes, this shows children what to do and how to manage the tools that have been provided for them. As children get older they will be exposed to other equipment that needs clear guidelines and demonstrations from adults, such as woodworking equipment, using a cooker or kettle when cooking and making a campfire.

Holding discussions with children will help them to understand the whys, whats and hows of managing risks safely. It is important to be honest with children so that they have clear answers as to the consequences of their actions. Without adequate information, some children may find their own answers to their questions, putting them in unnecessary danger.

Praise and encouragement is important in building children's self-esteem and self-confidence. Be on hand to provide the necessary support to children as they try out new experiences and challenges in play, so that they know you are close by if they get in physical or emotional difficulty. A reluctant child climbing the slide in the garden on their own for the first time will look for reassurance from an adult close by, as they climb each step one by one. With praise and encouragement they can reach the top in next to no time and feel a great sense of achievement.

'I can do it by myself' is a phrase practitioners often hear as children assert their ability in managing risks and challenges. You should not undermine children by saying 'No you can't': this can have a negative impact on their self-confidence, and may result in them becoming risk-averse or developing a reluctance to try out new challenges.

Criticism will not make for good relationships between adults and children as children will feel undervalued and have little self-worth. A child will already feel a sense of failure or disappointment when things have gone wrong for them, and may be physically hurt or upset. Jumping from a tree may have resulted in a cut knee. Fun skidding on a patch of ice could have ended with a bumped head. Whatever the situation, children benefit far more from comfort and sensitive discussion about why that happened than an adult saying 'See, I told you that would happen'. Rather than dwelling on the mistakes, practitioners should guide children through these, helping them to understand what went wrong and how to avoid such occurrences in the future.

Be able to reflect on and improve your own practice

Being a reflective practitioner is a skill that comes with practice. The ability to stand back and analyse events develops over time as you gain experience in your role and seek to question why, what, when and how. By looking back at how things went you can see a way forward in ascertaining how you would respond in the future which helps to develop your own knowledge and skills.

Reflecting on your own practice in play and leisure

There are many ways in which you can reflect on your own practice to help you see how effective you have been in supporting children's play and leisure. These include:

- observing children's responses in play
- evaluating the effectiveness of play and play environments
- asking the children for their feedback
- asking colleagues to give you feedback
- asking yourself some key questions.

Reflection on practice is a valuable tool for planning for the future play and leisure needs of children, as you can identify aspects of your practice that you should repeat — or avoid — in the future. Writing your reflections down can help you to hold onto the valuable information you have gathered, so you can refer to it at a later date. This will also help you to identify the strengths of your own practice and where you might need further development, training and advice.

Best practice checklist: Reflecting on practice

Asking yourself the following questions can aid the process of reflective practice in supporting children's and young people's play and leisure.

✓ Did the children enjoy what they were doing?

✓ Did I give appropriate support when needed?

✓ Did I allow them to decide the course of play?

✓ Was it child led?

✓ Did I initiate any aspects of play or leisure activities?

✓ What went well?

✓ What didn't go well?

✓ What would I change?

Although these may seem like broad questions, applying them to specific play and leisure activities will give you valuable information about your role.

Functional Skills English: Writing

Using the key points in the 'Best practice checklist' you could write a reflective account on the last time you were in your setting. Choose a section of the day to write about. Take care with your spelling, punctuation and grammar.

Identifying your strengths and improvement points

Reflection should not be solely about what you could have done better or what went wrong; it should also be about acknowledging the strengths of your practice. It is after all these strengths that make us effective and help boost our confidence in what we do. Nobody can be good at everything and it is the varying strengths and abilities of individuals that create an effective team, where everyone plays a part. Also each individual's strengths can be modelled in the workplace to improve the practice of others.

Getting ready for assessment

On a piece of A4 make two columns headed 'strengths' and 'weaknesses'. Now think about this with particular reference to supporting children's play and leisure and write down your strengths and weaknesses.

Talk through these with your assessor. Highlight your strengths and look at what you need to develop. Perhaps you and your manager or assessor can then decide how you can go about improving your practice.

Case study:
Improving practice

Seema is working in a day nursery with preschool-aged children. There is a high proportion of boys in the room who love to run around and be superheroes. Seema spends a lot of time running around after the caped crusaders, making sure play does not become too rough and reminding them not to run indoors. She finds this exhausting and would rather they didn't play at being superheroes. Seema has been approached about a course on superhero play, which her manager thinks will be useful to her practice.

1. Do you think Seema is supporting the children's play?
2. What benefits do you think the course may have for Seema?

How has your practice improved?

It is important that the reflection process does not begin and end with the acknowledgement of what has been said, seen and done. It should go further, to establish specific areas for improvement and future ways of working and supporting children at play.

Learners who attend college to undertake training and development are often asked to keep journals about their practice, detailing what has happened during the day. This builds a learning journey for the individual and can show how practice has improved, how confidence in ability has increased and how responses to situations have changed when they are equipped with increased knowledge and skills. Whether you are a student on placement or an employed member of staff, there should still be opportunities for you to reflect on your practice, with your training provider or through activities in your work environment.

Reflection doesn't necessarily give you all the answers, but it will certainly raise the questions that need answering. It is ongoing professional development both in the workplace and beyond that will help to improve your practice.

Over to You

Ask your supervisor if you can help evaluate the planning of the setting. This will help build skills of reflection and help identify ways to move forward and improve practice.

Functional Skills English: Speaking, listening and communication

This diary could be the basis of a discussion with your tutor where you could discuss your targets. Being prepared for your discussion will help you to present your information clearly.

Skills builder

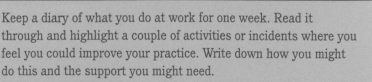

Keep a diary of what you do at work for one week. Read it through and highlight a couple of activities or incidents where you feel you could improve your practice. Write down how you might do this and the support you might need.

Revisit your diary after a couple of months. Do you think your practice has improved since then? If so why and how?

Check your knowledge

1. Why is play and leisure important to children and young people?

2. How does play and leisure benefit children's development?

3. Give three features of freely chosen play.

4. Explain one role an adult may have in supporting children's play.

5. How would you show you are interested in what children say and experience?

6. How can you respect children's privacy?

7. What types of physical risks do children take in play?

8. How do risk and challenge in play help children learn?

9. What would be an unacceptable risk for children in play?

10. Why is reflecting on your own practice important?

Support children & young people at meal or snack times

As a practitioner you are expected to know what healthy food is and the long-term benefits for children. Settings are required to ensure that the food they provide for children and young people meets a set of required standards. In this unit you will find out how to provide appropriate meals and snacks for the children or young people who you work with.

Learning outcomes

By the end of this unit you will:

1. know the principles of healthy eating for children and young people

2. know the benefits of healthy eating for children and young people

3. know how to encourage children and young people to make healthier food choices

4. be able to support hygiene during meal or snack times

5. be able to support the code of conduct and policies for meal and snack times.

Link

MU 2.8 gives detailed information on the nutritional and dietary needs of children and young people. You will be referred back to MU 2.8 several times in this unit.

Know the principles of healthy eating for children and young people

You will have read much in the press about the importance of a healthy and balanced diet for children and young people. To provide snacks and meals that are healthy for the children and young people in your care, you first need to know what makes up a healthy and balanced diet. You will find that the principles are simple to follow, and that snacks and meals can be created from everyday ingredients that you see in your local shops and markets.

Key term

Nutrition: food or nourishment that all children and young people need to grow and be healthy

Functional Skills English: Reading and Speaking, listening and communication

You could look at your local media and collect all the articles that you think link to young children and healthy eating. Finding these articles will not only help to develop your reading skills but you could then discus them in your study groups.

Link

Before reading on, reread the section of MU 2.8 that outlines what is needed to make up a diet that meets all the basic requirements for children and young people in your care.

Nutritional requirements of a healthy diet

You will read about the School Food Trust, created in 2005 to make sure that schools use the 14 nutrition-based standards. Table 1 lists the **nutrition**-based standards as outlined by the School Food Trust.

Table 1: The 14 nutrient-based standards (Source: based on information from the School Food Trust Standards www.schoolfoodtrust.org.uk)

Standard	Why it is important	Advice on this standard
1 Energy	Enables children to concentrate, learn and play at school	• Encourage pupils to eat to their appetite and stop when they feel full • Hungry pupils should be encouraged to choose starchy carbohydrates listed below instead of food high in fat and sugar, such as cakes and crisps
2 Carbohydrate	Starchy carbohydrates should provide the main source of energy in the diet	**Sources of carbohydrate** Bread of all types, rice, pasta, noodles, potatoes, yam, oats, cassava, couscous, breakfast cereals, wheat grains like bulgar wheat, lentils, red kidney beans and black eye beans **Good practice** Wholegrain varieties of bread and cereals are best as they are good sources of fibre

Table 1: The 14 nutrient-based standards (contd.)

Standard	Why it is important	Advice on this standard
3 Non-milk extrinsic (NME) sugars	A diet low in NME sugars will help to prevent tooth decay	**Sources of NME sugars** Table sugar, jam, honey, sweetened drinks, cakes, pastries, ice cream, sweets, biscuits, confectionery and chocolate **Good practice** Use less sugar in your recipes Serve fruit-based or dairy-based desserts instead of cakes and biscuits which often contain lots of added sugar Restrict access to sugar to be added to hot drinks. When choosing prepared products, check the label and choose those products lower in sugar
4 Fat	Lower fat intake can prevent weight gain	**Sources of high fat** Butter, lard, margarine, fat spreads, oils or dressings such as mayonnaise, chips and other deep-fried food, potato waffles, garlic bread, pastries, cakes, biscuits, creamy puddings, meat or meat products such as pasties **Good practice** • Grill and bake food instead of frying • When making sandwiches, try not using any butter or spread if the filling is moist enough; if using fat spread, choose a reduced-fat variety and spread thinly • When choosing prepared products, check the label and choose those products lower in fat
5 Saturated fat	A diet low in saturated fat can prevent high cholesterol and decrease the risk of coronary heart disease, diabetes and some cancers	**Sources of saturated fat** Butter, lard, some margarine, cream, coconut oil or cream, palm oil, mayonnaise, salad cream, meat products (e.g. pies, burgers or sausages), hard cheeses (e.g. cheddar), cakes or biscuits **Good practice** • Choose lower fat dairy products — skimmed or semi-skimmed milk, low fat yogurt and reduced fat cheese • Choose lean cuts of red meat and remove the skin from chicken • For cooking, use an unsaturated vegetable oil such as rapeseed oil or olive oil • Avoid adding butter or oil to food (e.g. vegetables) after cooking • When choosing prepared products, check the label and choose those products lower in saturated fat: FSA guidance on labelling states that 5 g or more saturated fat per 100 g is 'high' and 1.5 g or less saturated fat per 100 g is 'low'
6 Protein	Protein is important for the growth and repair of body tissues like muscles Pupils are growing fast so protein is particularly important for them	**Sources of protein** Meat, fish, milk, cheese, eggs, yogurt, nuts* and seeds, red kidney beans, lentils, meat alternatives (e.g. tofu, chickpeas and cereals) These food items can be incorporated into dishes, e.g. chicken and vegetable jambalaya, chickpea and cauliflower curry, salmon sandwiches, cauliflower cheese, nut roast*, chicken casserole, omelette with ham and cheese **Good practice** • Including plant protein as well as animal protein on your menu will ensure that pupils are eating protein from a variety of sources • Vegetarian pupils should have adequate protein intake if they eat cereals, beans and lentils, soya products, eggs, milk and dairy products • For vegan or lactose intolerant pupils, soya, oat or rice drinks provide an alternative to milk *** Be aware of nut allergies. You can find out more about this in the next section of this unit**

Table 1: The 14 nutrient-based standards (contd.)

Standard	Why it is important	Advice on this standard
7 Dietary fibre	Fibre assists bowel function and prevents problems like constipation	**Sources of fibre** Brown rice, oats, wholegrain cereals, muesli, potatoes with skins, wholemeal pasta, wholemeal bread, bulgar wheat, lentils, chickpeas, red kidney beans, fruit and vegetables These food items can be incorporated into dishes, e.g. vegetable and lentil bake, chilli con carne served with brown rice, jacket potato with beans and fruit salad **Good practice** • Choose wholegrain, wholemeal or brown varieties where possible • If children reject wholemeal varieties, use combinations of wholemeal and white varieties to encourage consumption • Leave the skins on potatoes • Add pulses and vegetables to stews and pies to add fibre
8 Sodium	Low salt can decrease the onset of high blood pressure, which may lead to conditions such as stroke, heart disease and kidney problems	Sodium is a component of salt. Salt is needed to maintain fluid balance in the body and for nerve and muscle function. Most salt consumed is contained within processed food **Sources of sodium** Ready-made soups and sauces, gravy, processed food, some breakfast cereals, salty snacks (e.g. crisps and salted nuts), bacon, ham, sausages, pizza, cheese and condiments **Good practice** • Limit the amount of salt added during cooking and instead flavour with herbs and spices • Cook meals from raw ingredients rather than using manufactured products high in salt • When choosing prepared products, check the label and choose those products lower in salt: FSA guidance on labelling states that 1.5 g or more salt (0.6 g sodium) per 100 g is 'high' and 0.3 g or less of salt (0.1 g sodium) per 100 g is 'low'
9 Vitamin A	Vitamin A is important for growth and tissue repair, good eyesight and the immune system	**Sources of Vitamin A** Oily fish, eggs, liver, cheese, butter, milk, yellow, orange and red coloured fruits and vegetables (such as carrots, peppers, apricots, oranges, papaya, mango, butternut squash, sweet potato, tomatoes) and dark green leafy vegetables **Good practice** • Serve a variety of fruit and vegetables • These food items can be incorporated into dishes, e.g. salmon fish cakes, baked sweet potato wedges, red pepper and tomato omelette, carrot and coriander soup and fruit salad • Yellow, orange and red coloured fruits and vegetables contain the most Vitamin A
10 Vitamin C	Vitamin C is an antioxidant which may help to protect the body from infections and other illnesses Vitamin C is needed for wound healing and the structure of blood vessels and skin Vitamin C enhances iron absorption	**Sources of Vitamin C** Fruits, especially citrus fruits (oranges, lemons, limes, and grapefruit), berries and kiwi fruits; vegetables (including frozen), especially broccoli, green and red peppers, sweet potatoes and potatoes These food items can be incorporated into dishes, e.g. jacket potato with salad, lemon chicken, berry smoothie, fruit salad, mixed vegetable hotpot and casserole **Good practice** • Raw fruit and vegetables contain the most Vitamin C • Vitamin C may be lost during preparation and cooking, so pepare and cook food as close to lunchtime as possible • Steam vegetables to minimise vitamin losses or cook them in a minimum volume of water

Table 1: The 14 nutrient-based standards (contd.)

Standard	Why it is important	Advice on this standard
11 Folate	Folate is essential for blood cells and the nervous system, and helps prevent anaemia	**Sources of folate** Liver, yeast extract, orange juice, green leafy vegetables (e.g. spinach), green beans, beetroot, chickpeas, black-eye beans, broccoli, peas and brown rice Breakfast cereals are often fortified with folate These food items can be incorporated into dishes, e.g. pea and ham soup and spinach and potato curry **Good practice** • Folate may be lost during the cooking process so prepare and cook food as close to lunchtime as possible • Steam vegetables to minimise vitamin losses or cook them in a minimum volume of water
12 Calcium	Calcium is essential for strong teeth and bones, and important for muscle and nerve function, as well as blood clotting A diet containing enough calcium will decrease the risk of developing osteoporosis or brittle bones in later life	**Sources of calcium** Dairy products such as milk, cheese, yogurt, canned fish with bones (e.g. salmon and pilchards), broccoli, cabbage, dried fruits, tofu, red kidney beans, chickpeas and soya beans White and brown bread are fortified with calcium These food items can be incorporated into dishes, e.g. cheese and potato pie, salmon quiche, rice pudding and custard made with milk **Good practice** • For people who do not drink milk, choose soya, oat or rice drinks enriched with calcium • Use lower fat dairy products; they contain as much calcium as their full fat equivalents
13 Iron	Iron is needed for production of red blood cells, which carry oxygen around the body Iron also plays an important role in maintaining a healthy immune system Iron is especially important for teenage girls	Iron deficiency in pupils may be linked with slower intellectual development and poor behaviour in the longer term. **Sources of iron** Red meat, offal (especially liver and kidney), canned fish, eggs, dark green leafy vegetables, peas, wholegrain (e.g. brown rice), nuts and seeds, red kidney beans, black-eye beans, lentils, chickpeas, dried apricots and raisins These food items can be incorporated into dishes, e.g. lamb casserole, houmous, spaghetti bolognaise, shepherd's pie, mixed bean wrap and dried fruit compote Breakfast cereals are often fortified with iron **Good practice** • Iron from animal sources is more easily absorbed by the body than iron from plant sources, but plant sources are important because they provide most of the iron in the diet • Consuming food high in Vitamin C at the same time as food containing iron enhances iron absorption • Vegetarian dishes should regularly include a variety of lentils and peas, eggs, dark green leafy vegetables
14 Zinc	Zinc is used by the body for growth and tissue repair, wound healing and the immune system	**Sources of zinc** Red meat, offal (especially liver and kidney), eggs, fish, milk and other dairy products, cereals, red kidney beans, soya products, lentils, chickpeas and nuts These food items can be incorporated into dishes, e.g. cottage pie, roast pork or beef, lentil bake; brown rice and vegetarian bolognaise using soya mince **Good practice** Vegetarian dishes should regularly include whole grain cereals, kidney beans, milk and eggs

Functional Skills Maths: Representing

You could collect some labels of the foods that you have in either your home or your setting. Are these foods high or low in fats? What percentage of their nutritional value is fat? You could write a short conclusion to your findings.

Functional Skills ICT: Developing, presenting and communicating information

Designing your poster will help to develop your ICT skills. You can experiment with different layouts and editing techniques to make sure that your poster is suitable for the audience.

Getting ready for assessment

The Food Standards Authority (FSA) guidance on labelling states that for products containing fat 20 g or more per 100 g is 'high' and 3 g or less fat per 100 g is 'low'.

Visit your local supermarket and make a record of some of the fat content of some of the following products. You will find this on labels on the products as this is required by the FSA.

- Butter
- Lard
- Margarine
- Fat spreads
- Oils or dressings such as mayonnaise
- Chips and other deep-fried food
- potato waffles
- Garlic bread
- Pastries
- Cakes
- Biscuits
- Creamy puddings
- Meat
- Meat products, such as pasties

You could then make a poster of these products and their fat content and post it on your parents' information board.

You could discuss with your assessor how to use this research as evidence for your assessment.

Water

It is also important to remember that water is an essential part of a diet and should be readily available to children and young people.

- It makes up two-thirds of the body's weight
- It is essential for children to drink water as it is continuously lost through sweating, breathing and urinating, and needs to be replaced through food and drink.

When you next have a day when your brain does not seem to be working properly, then you should try drinking a glass of water. This is because the brain depends on the water flowing around your body to work efficiently, and your brain cells are part of this. So ensuring that the children and young people you work with have sufficient amounts of water is a simple thing to do to help their learning and development.

Over to You

Review how you provide water for children or young people in your setting. If you do not think it is available enough, consider how you could make it more available. You could also think about ways that you could encourage children or young people to drink more water!

Functional Skills English: Writing

You could design a short information booklet for children on the benefits of water. Your booklet would need to contain images and be attractive to children. Think carefully about the level of language that you use in your booklet.

Healthy meals and snacks

Once you have learnt about the basic nutritional requirements for children and young people then you can begin to consider the types of meals and snacks you can provide that are healthy but still attractive to them — not always an easy task in a world of fast-food restaurants in most towns!

Every day, children should eat:

- five portions of fruit and vegetables
- milk, yogurt or cheese
- lean meat, fish, poultry, eggs, nuts or legumes
- cereal, rice, pasta, porridge or noodles.

Functional Skills ICT: Developing, presenting and communicating information

This 'Skills builder' activity is a good way of developing your ICT skills. You could use a software package on the computer that helps you to design a booklet, leaflet or fact sheet. The layout of your information is very important and it is important to remember that you are trying to encourage them to drink milk.

Skills builder

Children under two should really drink full-cream milk to support their calcium intake. However, from two years onwards they can drink semi-skimmed milk. Children should not drink purely skimmed milk until they are at least five years old.

Not all children enjoy drinking milk. See if you can create a list of ideas for parents showing how they could encourage their children to drink milk. You might even include a recipe!

Before finding out what sort of healthy recipes can be provided for children and young people consider the following points.

- Snacks and drinks should not have added sugar and can be replaced with items such as fresh fruit or dried fruit and seeds. Commercial cereal bars, often seen as a healthy alternative, can sometimes have a large amount of fat, salt and sugar in them.
- A variety of fruit and vegetables should be available to help to contribute to the '5 a day' expectations.
- If breakfast is offered, it should be a healthy alternative to ensure that children feel fuller for longer and to prevent snacking before the next meal.
- Portions should be controlled according to the age of the children. For example, a four-year-old might eat two servings of milk, yogurt or cheese a day, whereas a 12-year-old may need three servings.
- Fat content should be controlled by avoiding starchy foods fried in fat and deep-fried foods.

Here are some ideas for a variety of snacks and meals that you might offer in your setting:

Ideas for healthy breakfasts

- Scrambled eggs, baked tomatoes and wholemeal toast; cheese, ham, smoked salmon or chives could be added
- Boiled egg with wholemeal toast 'soldiers'
- Ham and poached eggs with tomatoes/mushrooms and wholemeal toast
- Baked beans, grilled bacon and tomato on wholemeal toast
- Fruit, yogurt and honey; any fresh fruit can be used, and seeds could be sprinkled on top
- Homemade muesli with seeds, fresh apple, honey, toasted oats and yogurt
- Porridge with fruit and honey
- Muffins made with wholemeal flour and served with fruit
- Wholewheat pancakes with fresh fruit and honey
- Fruit smoothies made with yogurt and fruit, using milk and add honey if wanted

Ideas for healthy snacks

Since September 2007, schools have to meet new food-based standards for food and snacks. Cakes and biscuits are not advised for snacks. The list below gives some suggestions for other items that can be provided as snacks at times other than lunch.

You may well give snacks as part of your provision. These can easily be nutritious and enjoyable. You can even encourage young people and children to be involved in preparation.

- Children's trail mix with dried fruit, seeds and cereal flakes
- Homemade ice lollies made with fruit juice, pieces of real fruit, yogurt, milk, etc.
- Cone of fruit – a paper cone full of chopped fresh fruit
- Oatcakes with cubes of cheeses and grapes
- Fruit smoothies
- Popcorn
- Vegetable sticks/wholemeal pitta bread/wholemeal breadsticks, such as carrots and celery with homemade dips such as hummus
- Cubes of cheddar cheese and slices of apple
- Mini muffins made with wholewheat flour using a variety of flavours such as apricot, blueberry, banana, raisins
- Bananas, strawberries, pineapple, etc. on sticks

Ideas for healthy lunches or other main meals

Your setting will most probably provide lunches, or children will bring their own packed lunch. You can also use these ideas if you have to provide any other meals as part of your provision for children and young people.

Here are just a few suggestions. The list could be endless!

Lunches

- Stir fries using vegetables, chicken or tofu
- Healthy fish and chips – white fish in a light, breaded covering, baked in oven with baked potato wedges and peas
- Fried brown rice with eggs, chicken and diced vegetables, using a small amount of healthy oil
- Homemade beefburgers using lean mince with salad
- A variety of homemade soups with wholewheat pitta bread, croutons, etc.
- Chicken tacos or beef fajitas with salad
- Bolognese with lean mince or soy mince and brown rice
- Baked potatoes with a variety of fillings and salad – tuna and sweetcorn, cheese and homemade pickle, vegetable chilli, baked beans, etc.
- Tuna pasta bake with wholewheat pasta
- Homemade pizza with a range of toppings and salad
- Vegetable, fish or chicken skewers with brown rice and homemade sauce
- Shepherd's pie with lean or soya mince
- Homemade fish fingers, lightly breaded, baked with vegetables or baked beans

Puddings

There is nothing wrong with puddings if they are made from fresh, healthy ingredients. Here are just some ideas; there are many more.

- Natural yogurt, honey and fresh fruit with granola sprinkled on top
- Fresh fruit crumble with a topping made from granola, oats and wholewheat flour
- Jelly with fresh/tinned fruit chopped in and natural yogurt
- Fruit pies made with wholewheat flour — apple, rhubarb, plum, etc.
- Fresh fruit skewers
- Baked apples with muesli and natural yogurt
- Wholewheat pancakes/crepes with a fresh fruit filling
- Homemade rice pudding with fresh fruit

Packed lunches

Encourage parents to send packed lunches to school in an insulated bag. Drinks can be frozen to act as ice packs and to keep contents cool, providing an icy drink at lunchtime.

- A variety of sandwiches made with:
  - bread — wholewheat pitta, baguette, wraps or homemade rolls
  - filling — chicken salad; turkey and tomato; tuna and mayonnaise; cream cheese and cucumber; lean ham and salad; egg and cress; sardine and tomato with cream cheese; hummus and cucumber
- Cold barbecued chicken wings
- Vegetable sticks — carrots, celery, cucumber, pepper, etc. — and homemade dips
- Homemade salads such as pasta salad, nicoise salad (tuna, potato, lettuce, egg, etc.), coleslaw
- Homemade soup in insulated containers
- Homemade granola or flapjack bars
- Mini wholewheat muffins
- Natural yogurt and chopped fruit
- A mix of dried fruit — raisins, blueberries, cranberries, pineapple, papaya, etc.
- A variety of fresh fruit
- Jelly with fresh, chopped fruit inside

Culture, religion and health conditions

In MU 2.8, you will have read about some of the ways in which culture, religion and health conditions impact on people's food choices.

- Muslims eat halal meat, fish and shellfish, which is slaughtered and prepared in a specific way. They do not eat pork or dairy products that contain rennet.

- Jewish people eat kosher lamb, beef and chicken, which is slaughtered and prepared in a certain way; dairy products are not eaten with meat; eggs must not have blood spots; fish should have fins, scales and backbones.

- Sikhs rarely eat pork and do not eat beef; some Sikhs eat chicken, eggs, cheese, fish and shellfish.

- Hindus are usually vegetarian, do not eat beef and do not eat dairy products that contain rennet.

- Rastafarians do not eat shellfish but some do eat lamb, beef, and chicken.

- Vegetarians do not eat meat or fish.

- Vegans do not eat meat, fish or any other products that come from animals, such as milk, eggs and cheese.

> **Link** In MU 2.8 you have learned about different dietary needs that are influenced by:
> - culture
> - religion
> - health conditions.
>
> Review this section of the unit before you continue.

Functional Skills ICT: Developing, presenting and communicating information

You could design a poster that shows the culture, religion and health conditions which impact on people's food choices. Your poster could be displayed in the kitchen area and used as a point of reference for the catering staff in your setting.

You will have read about health conditions that impact on food choices, such as diabetes and coeliac disease. You will probably come across a variety of conditions during your work with children and young people, and will have to ensure that you work closely with appropriate health professionals and parents to provide an appropriate diet. As children get older, it is important that they can take more responsibility for their diet if they have certain needs, such as diabetes.

Case study:
Supporting a child with coeliac disease

Fran is an early years professional in a reception class and is key person to Cassie, who has coeliac disease. Fran works very closely with Cassie's mum and knows that Cassie has a list of foods containing gluten that she will be very ill if she eats. At lunchtime Cassie receives specially cooked meals that are appropriate for someone with coeliac disease. The cook tries to ensure that they are as much like the other children's food as possible. Problems do arise when children sometimes bring in cakes to celebrate their birthdays. Fran always warns Cassie's mum about this and she provides a special cake that Cassie can eat.

1. How do you think Fran's role as key person can support Cassie and her mum in managing her coeliac disease?
2. Is there any way that you can think of celebrating birthdays in class so that Cassie does not have to have anything different to the other children?

Know the benefits of healthy eating for children and young people

It is always important that you understand the reason for initiatives such as current campaigns to encourage healthy eating. You will have already discovered that eating healthily is based on years of scientific research and evidence, showing that, if a child or young person eats healthily, this will have a positive influence on all aspects of their learning.

The benefits of healthy eating

As adults, we are all probably well aware that, if we eat healthily, we will be fitter, have less risk of heart disease and related illnesses, such as diabetes, and stay physically fit. It is essential that you see these benefits as just as important for young children, so that they can progress into healthy adulthood. At a time when childhood **obesity** is increasing, it is even more important to emphasise the benefits of

Key term

Obesity: the state of being seriously overweight, to a degree that can have serious effects on health

healthy eating to children, young people and their parents. Obesity in childhood is linked to many health complications and tends to indicate the child will be obese as an adult.

Table 2 shows the benefits for children and young people eating a healthy diet each day.

Table 2: Benefits of a healthy diet

Benefit	Why
Keeping active	Boosts energy levels; improves bodily functions; boosts the immune system to increase resistance to illnesses and infection; increases life expectancy
Getting daily nutritional needs	Reduces risk of minor and more serious illnesses such as cancer and diabetes; healthy teeth, hair, skin and bones
Enjoying learning and life	Can make them feel more positive and learn more effectively; reduces stress levels
Sleeping well	Will be able to sleep more easily and feel more rested
Losing weight without a diet	Healthy eating is more likely to promote a steady weight loss and to be maintained

The consequences of an unhealthy diet

One of the most common causes of an unhealthy diet is being overweight. It is thought that at least 27 per cent of children in the UK are overweight due to a diet too rich in sugar and fats and not high enough in fibre and carbohydrates. This is often combined with a lack of exercise.

Obesity and diabetes are two of the most common consequences of an unhealthy diet. Of course, there are sometimes other medical reasons for these illnesses.

Obesity can cause:

- problems with joints
- headaches
- drowsiness
- snoring
- gall bladder disease
- high blood pressure
- high cholesterol
- low self-esteem
- risk of Type 2 diabetes later in life, although children can contract this disease.

Skills builder

Plan an activity for the children or young people in your care that will tell them about the effects of eating unhealthily. You will need to consider the following when planning your activity:

- the age and understanding of the children and young people concerned
- the number of children you will effectively want to work with
- the message that you want to get across
- different activities you could use such as a Smartboard, designing posters and presentations and making video clips.

Functional Skills

Completing this 'Skills builder' exercise will give you the opportunity to develop a number of your Functional Skills as you design resources, make things, write instructions and explain rules.

Recognising and dealing with allergic reactions

You may already work with children or young people who have food allergies. They are common in younger children and fortunately many children grow out of allergies. However, there are some children who retain allergies or develop them at any time during their childhood. It is important for you to know how to recognise and deal with allergic reactions to food. Figure 1 shows some common food allergies.

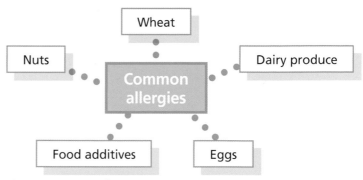

Figure 1: Common allergies

Symptoms of food allergies can develop quite quickly, and can include:

- difficulty breathing
- itchy skin
- rashes
- vomiting
- diarrhoea
- nausea
- stomach pain
- swelling around the mouth or in the throat.

Anaphylaxis

Anaphylaxis is a severe reaction to a food, which can involve difficulty breathing, swelling in the mouth or throat, lowering of blood pressure, shock and even death if not treated immediately. If you have to manage an allergic reaction, you should have received training in your paediatrics first aid course. If you have children or young people who have auto-injectors to administer because of likely allergic reactions, you will have received training from that child's health professional.

Best practice checklist: Managing food allergies

- ✓ If a child has had an allergic reaction to a food, make a note of any advice about when to introduce the food to see if the allergy remains
- ✓ Ensure that everyone you work with is aware of the allergy and how to manage it
- ✓ Educate children about their allergy, so that they can learn to avoid foods that they are allergic to

- ✓ If a child has a severe allergic reaction or anaphylaxis, he/she should wear a medical alert bracelet to let everyone know about the allergy, and should carry an auto-injector to treat the allergic reaction quickly
- ✓ Read food labels, look for ingredients that children and young people in your setting may be allergic to and practise strict avoidance of those foods

Nut allergies

Nuts and related products can be very dangerous for any child or adult. Your setting must have a 'nut free' policy, which should ensure that:

● all parents know that your school is a nut-free zone

● food brought into school, such as packed lunches, is nut free

● everyone, including all parents, is aware of the seriousness of this policy

● any child or adult with a nut allergy carries an auto-injector, which is stored with their photo in a place known to all adults in the setting

● everyone working with the child or young person has auto-injector training.

Getting advice on dietary concerns

If you need dietary advice to support children and young people in your setting, your manager may be able to seek advice from a health visitor on how to ensure that children have effective diets. In *Every Child Matters*, one of the outcomes is specifically devoted to 'being healthy'. This has resulted in a focus on supporting the healthy development of children and young people. More advice and guidance is available with regard to children and young people's dietary needs.

Sure Start, which aims to give young children the best start in life, actively encourages parents, carers and healthcare professionals to work together to ensure that children have healthy diets. Sure Start Children's Centres may well have advisers and literature about healthy diets available in the setting.

Table 3 lists some organisations that give dietary advice or list it on their websites.

Table 3: Where to get dietary advice

Organisation	Advice
British Nutrition Foundation www.nutrition.org.uk	Advice on diet during pregnancy
Food Standards Agency www.eatwell.gov.uk	• Advice on diets for pregnant women and breastfeeding • Weaning advice • Nutritional advice for children
NHS www.healthystart.nhs.uk	'5 a day' programme
The Schools Food Trust www.schoolfoodtrust.org.uk	Dietary advice for school-age children
BBC www.bbc.co.uk/health/treatments/healthy_living/nutrition	Advice on diet and nutrition
Caroline Walker Trust www.cwt.org.uk	Charitable trust dedicated to improving public health through good food; produces guidelines for parents, carers and practitioners concerning babies and young children in early years settings
Healthy Schools www.healthyschools.gov.uk	Information on diets in schools
National Children's Bureau www.ncb.org.uk	Information on promoting healthy lifestyles among children and young people

Know how to encourage children and young people to make healthier food choices

You will have already found out how important it is to ensure that children, however young, begin to take responsibility for their own learning. This is just as important when it comes to choosing healthy food.

Your setting's food policy

Since new food standards have been introduced into England's schools, settings have been encouraged to meet these standards by having an effective food policy. Where there is a governing body, this will have responsibility for putting food at the core of a healthy approach to the curriculum.

Ofsted will inspect any setting providing services for children and young people to make sure that they are meeting the *Every Child Matters* outcome 'being healthy'. A whole-setting policy on food will show how the setting intends to implement healthy eating.

A school policy will include:

- **background** outlining the setting's aims in developing healthy eating and drinking activities

- **aims and objectives** with reference to the different provision of food and snacks as outlined by the British Nutrition Foundation, as regards:
  - o providing nourishing food
  - o connection between a balanced diet and effective learning
  - o how water is to be provided and accessible
  - o involvement of the whole school community
  - o a positive eating environment
  - o religious, ethnic, vegetarian, medical and allergenic needs of children and young people
  - o training of staff in diet, nutrition, food safety and hygiene
  - o breaktime, encouraging children to bring healthy snacks or the setting to provide healthy snacks (a commitment to any snacks bought in should also be evident)
  - o how the nutritional guidelines are to be met through lunch provision by on-site or external caterers (there should be detailed referencing to the required food groupings as outlined earlier in this unit)
  - o packed lunch requirements brought in by children

- **menus** – details of how these will be compiled and shared with children, young people and parents

- **environment** – how the setting will provide a suitable environment for children and young people to eat in

- **celebrations and festivals** — how the setting will celebrate these through food provision

- **curriculum** — how healthy eating will be promoted in the curriculum, including growing of food

- **partnership with parents** — how a healthy food provision is going to be shared with the whole community

- **monitoring and evaluation** — how the food provision of the setting will be regularly reviewed and when the policy will also be reviewed

- **communicating the policy** — how this will be done to probably include website, prospectus, school foyer, display boards, staff and parent meetings.

Ways to encourage healthy eating

Making changes to eating habits

To make children and young people begin to understand what foods are healthy and to change eating habits, you could do a variety of activities that could be adapted to any age group, such as:

- making collages of healthy foods

- creating recipes together from healthy foods

- healthy cooking activities

- planning and making snacks together

- planting, growing and harvesting healthy foods, such as salads and tomatoes

- making healthy eating posters

- making healthy eating videos of cooking activities or interviews about favourite healthy foods.

Creating recipes together

The checklist below offers a variety of ways you can encourage children to make healthy eating choices and thus change their eating habits.

Best practice checklist: Encouraging healthy food choices

✓ Try to set an example with your own eating habits
✓ Provide a choice of healthy meals and snacks
✓ Involve children and young people in choice of snacks and meals
✓ Encourage children to eat when their tummy is empty
✓ Offer alternatives to high fat and sugary snacks and meals
✓ Don't make fast food a reward but try activities like strawberry picking instead
✓ Encourage children and young people to eat slowly and enjoy their food
✓ Involve children and young people in the preparation of meals and snacks
✓ Try not to label foods as 'good' and 'bad' as often a little in moderation is absolutely fine!

Eating the food provided

It is important that children do eat the food that you provide. However, if they are involved with those choices, they are more likely to eat what is provided!

You also need to be aware that food can have an emotional significance. Make sure that you don't use food to comfort your child or reward them, as they might then use food in this way rather than eat what is normally provided.

Case study:
Eating the lunch provided

Matthew works as a chef in a primary school and notices that many of the children are not always eating the food offered to them. Matthew and his team talk about this and decide to involve the children in choosing the menu, giving them healthy choices and finding out what the foods are that they especially enjoy. They do this and begin to include the children's choices, such as fish pie, healthy pizza, baked potatoes and fruit crumble! After this, the children are much more inclined to eat the food provided at lunchtimes.

1. Why do you think that Matthew involved the children in choosing the menus for their own lunch?

2. What sort of guidelines do you think Matthew would give the children when making their choices for the menu?

Look at Figure 2 to find out how to encourage children and young people to eat the food provided for them.

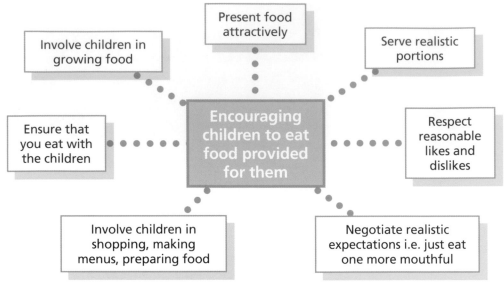

Figure 2: Encouraging children to eat the food provided

Be able to support hygiene during meal or snack times

As part of healthy eating, it is important that you promote hygiene, for both your preparation and serving of food and for the children and young people themselves.

The importance of personal hygiene

You will need to guide the children or young people in your setting by clearly explaining the importance of personal hygiene at meal and snack times. Often this should be done by example.

- They should wash their hands thoroughly before eating, to reduce the risk of infection.

- Anti-bacterial soap and disposable towels should be provided.

- Children should be discouraged from eating snacks sitting on the floor, as germs could be spread by the soles of their shoes.

- Encourage hair to be tied back, as germs can be carried in unclean hair or stray hairs can fall into food.

- Also ensure that children do not touch other people's food or put food back, such as pieces of fruit, if they do not want it or have taken a bite!

- Ensure that any cutlery dropped on the floor is replaced with a clean item, to avoid infections.

- Children should also not openly sneeze or cough around food, so as not to contaminate food with germs.

Showing good hygiene practice

As a practitioner, you will need to show good hygiene practice in relation to food handling and waste disposal. You will most likely have your food safety certificate if you are working with children or young people, as it is a requirement of Ofsted that you have this if you are handling or serving food.

Even if you have this qualification, read the checklists below to remind yourself of best practice when handling food and waste.

Best practice checklist: Handling food

✓ Wash hands thoroughly before preparing food

✓ Take off watches, bracelets, rings and jewellery

✓ Tie back hair and wear an apron

✓ Cover cuts and wounds with a coloured waterproof dressing

✓ Do not touch your nose or mouth, or cough and sneeze over food

✓ Do not smoke in a room where food is being prepared

✓ Thoroughly clean the floor, surfaces, sinks, utensils, cloths and bins regularly

✓ Always cover waste bins to avoid bacteria

✓ Always disinfect work surfaces before preparing food to eliminate bacteria

✓ Wash tops of cans before opening as they may be dusty

✓ Always wash equipment in hot, soapy water before preparing raw food to eliminate bacteria

✓ Keep a separate cutting board and knife for poultry to avoid any cross contamination, and wash these thoroughly after use

✓ Use a dedicated cutting board for bread to avoid any cross contamination

✓ Cook foods following instructions

✓ Reheat food once, ensuring it is heated all the way through and evenly

✓ Ensure that whites and yolks of eggs are cooked thoroughly and are firm

Best practice checklist: Serving food

✓ Only use clean crockery

✓ Use utensils that are not cracked or chipped

✓ Give children their own cups and utensils

✓ Make sure children and adults wash their hands thoroughly before serving and eating

✓ Ensure that children sit down and can reach their food safely

✓ Give age-appropriate utensils

✓ Ensure children are supervised

✓ Ensure meals and drinks are not too hot

✓ Do not heat plates for young children

Ensure that waste is disposed of according to the guidelines of your setting. Food in store cupboards should be regularly checked to ensure that it is in date. If it is out of date, it should be disposed of safely.

Encouraging personal hygiene at meal and snack times

You can explain personal hygiene according to the age of the children or young people. For younger children you could place visual reminders above sinks, with photographs of the hand-washing process, whereas young people could create posters, listen to talks on personal hygiene or even make a promotional video for their peers.

Be able to support the code of conduct and policies for meal and snack times

In this unit you have read about what a setting's food policy should contain. This section considers how you can implement the policy with regard to positive behaviour at meal and snack times.

Your setting's code of conduct and policies

Figure 3 gives you some ideas on what your setting's section on behaviour at mealtimes might contain.

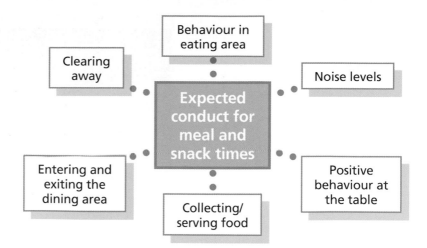

Figure 3: Expected conduct for mealtimes

Skills and techniques to promote positive behaviour

Your role will involve supporting and encouraging children's and young people's positive behaviour in the dining area, including good table manners. One of the most important ways of supporting and encouraging positive behaviour in children or young people of any age is by example. The best way that you can do this is to sit and eat with them, and make meal and snack times a very social and calm occasion. In this way you can encourage them to:

- socialise
- pass food to each other
- pour water for each other
- serve each other
- eat with their mouths closed

- use utensils appropriately
- clear up any mess made
- eat appropriate-sized mouthfuls
- take time to digest food.

Snack times can be when children are hungry, so choose when to have the snack. Even when there are just two children snacking at a time, you can encourage self-help skills and awareness of others' needs through socialising, sharing food and perhaps even pouring drinks for themselves or each other!

Positive behaviour can also be encouraged by making agreed codes of conduct and displaying them in the dining area as a visual reminder for children.

Case study:
Observing mealtimes

At the Growyourown Nursery, Bina and her team are concerned about the general behaviour of the three- to four-year-old children during mealtimes. They each observe lunchtime over a week. As a result they decide to place the tables in a square instead of an oblong, so that the children can face each other. Food is placed in bowls on tables and children help themselves instead of adults helping them. They also decide that the adults will sit and eat with the children instead of serving them and supervising them standing back from the tables.

1. Do you think that these changes will encourage more positive behaviour during lunchtimes?

2. How do you think that the adults sitting with the children will make a difference to their behaviour?

Dealing with inappropriate behaviour in the dining area

How you manage inappropriate behaviour will depend on the situation and on the age of the children and young people.

Here are some reminders of the basic skills you will need to manage any inappropriate behaviour.

- Encourage and reinforce a child's positive behaviour.

- Find the reason for any inappropriate behaviour before responding, such as tiredness, hunger or provocation from another child!

- Set agreed boundaries.

- Set achievable individual targets or actions, such as talking to parents, behaviour charts, etc.

- Acknowledge when inappropriate behaviour stops!

Link Look at the section called 'Support positive behaviour' in MU 2.8 to remind you of the skills and techniques that you will need.

Check your knowledge

1. What is nutrition?

2. Which vitamin is important for growth and tissue repair, good eyesight and the immune system?

   A) Vitamin A

   B) Vitamin B

   C) Vitamin D

3. How much of your body weight is made up of water?

4. What are the three things that diets are influenced by?

5. What is anaphylaxis?

6. Which organisation gives dietary advice for school-age children?

7. List three things that are important when maintaining personal hygiene at snack and mealtimes.

8. What is the certificate that you should have if handling food in your setting?

Contribute to the support of children's communication, language & literacy

In our day-to-day lives, we might not realise just how much we depend on our communication skills. For children, these skills have to be learnt from scratch. This unit looks at ways in which you might support children's communication skills which include language and literacy.

Learning outcomes
By the end of this unit you will:

1. understand the importance of communication, language and literacy for children's learning and development

2. be able to contribute to children's learning in communication, language and literacy

3. be able to evaluate own contribution to children's learning in communication, language and literacy.

Understand the importance of communication, language and literacy for children's learning and development

It is amazing that babies come into the world and cannot say a word, but by the age of four years they are able to talk quite fluently. They are also able to understand most of what is being said to them. Being able to talk and understand others opens a whole host of opportunities for them. It is also the first step in the process of learning to read and write. This learning outcome looks at the importance of these skills for children's learning and development

Describe why communication, language and literacy are important to children's learning

A good starting point for this assessment criterion is to understand what the terms communication, language and literacy really mean in this unit.

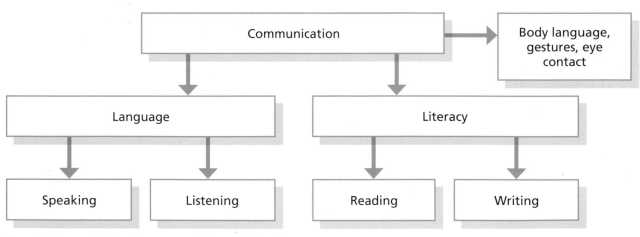

Figure 1: Communication, language and literacy interaction

- Communication is an overall term that includes eye contact and body language, as well the skills of speaking, listening, reading and writing.

- Language is about speaking and listening. Babies learn to listen and understand what words mean before they can say them. (Some deaf children will also learn to use sign language. This is a language.)

- Literacy is about the way that we write language down. To be literate children need to read and write. Most children will crack this by the age of eleven, although some will find it difficult.

Why communication skills are important for children's development

The first thing that babies learn to do is to communicate with the adults who are with them by using body language. They will quickly learn to make eye contact and smile. They will also pick up the signs that an adult is unhappy, stressed or uninterested. These skills will come in handy for the rest of their lives as to communicate well we need to work out what someone else is feeling or thinking. For children, these early communication skills will be used to make friends with other children and to join in play. They also help them to understand adults' reactions: for example, taking something that an adult says seriously.

Why language is important for children's development

Being able to understand what others are saying and also being able to talk are essential. The starting point for this is for babies to learn what individual words mean, such as 'look' or 'mummy'. From around 12 months, babies begin to use the odd word. Progress is very slow and it is not until children are two years old that they can start to put words together. At four years, most children are talking quite well. Not being able to talk is very frustrating for children. This means that unwanted behaviour such as biting, snatching or hitting out tend to be linked to a child's language level — so a four-year-old who has few words is more likely to show these behaviours.

Language and thinking

Language is not just about saying what you want. It is also about being able to think and use words to express your ideas. This means that, once children are able to talk well, they can start to use their language for reasoning and problem solving. Of course it is not only children who use language in this way. Next time you have something to organise or are trying to get somewhere on time, see if you can 'hear' yourself talk in your head.

Language and play

Alongside being able to use language to think, children also use language in their play. Look out for three-year-olds who are now using their language to play pretend games in the role play corner. Being able to play in this way allows children to enjoy being with each other and gives them quite a few social skills.

Language and social skills

Language helps you to express yourself, but also to understand what others are saying. From three years onwards, most children who have some language start to be more cooperative and less impulsive.

Language and literacy

Before children can learn to read, it is useful if they can speak fluently. This means that they have some knowledge about words and the sounds in words. Children who go into the school and are not speaking well are likely to find learning to read quite difficult.

Over to You

Look at the way that a young baby takes time to stare at people's faces before reacting.

Over to You

It is normal for young children to spend time talking to themselves or to 'blurt' out what is on their mind. Observe children aged 3–5 years playing by themselves. Listen out to see if they are talking to themselves.

These children can enjoy playing together because they can communicate

Why literacy is so important

Reading and writing are key skills in modern life that we can easily take for granted. Think about when you go shopping. The chances are that you are constantly reading labels or the prices of items. Learning to read and write takes quite a few years and most children will be on their way by the age of seven or so. Children who have good language skills and who are motivated to learn to read and write are likely to make good progress. In the early years, it is important that adults read books to children as this helps to extend their vocabulary. Children also learn other skills, such as turning the pages of the book and seeing that print runs from left to right in English.

Link with other areas of learning and development

Communication, language and literacy are so important that they are part of the early years frameworks in each of the countries. For this assessment criterion, you will need to look at the early years framework that your setting uses.

- England — Early Years Foundation Stage
  - Communication, language and literacy

- Wales — Foundation Phase
  - Language, Literacy and Communication Skills
  - (Children are likely to be learning Welsh and English)

- Scotland — Curriculum for Excellence
  - Languages
  - (Literacy is not a separate area as such. Practitioners are meant to be looking for opportunities to put it into different types of activities)

- Northern Ireland
  - Language and literacy (for children in schools)
  - (No formal framework for pre-school education at present)

How communication, language and literacy link in

Within each of the early years frameworks there are other areas or outcomes that practitioners have to plan for. Table 1, based on the EYFS, shows how communication, language and literacy has links with the others areas. If you do not work with the EYFS, the brief explanation of each area of development will help you to work out the equivalent area for your framework.

Table 1: Links to communication, language and literacy

Area of learning	Outline	Links to communication, language and literacy
Personal, social and emotional development	This area is about children developing social and emotional skills including behaviour, confidence and concentration	• Children will talk about their feelings and emotions • They will also find it easier to socialise and show positive behaviour when they have language • Children will also gain in confidence as they make their early marks
Problem solving, reasoning and numeracy	This area is about children's problem-solving and mathematical skills including number, shape, space and measures	• Children need language in order to understand and remember concepts
Knowledge and understanding of the world	This is a broad area. It covers early science, design and technology, as well as helping children to learn about past and present, where they live, and looks at sense of community	• Children need language in order to talk about what they are seeing, doing and learning • Children also need language in order to co-operate with each other
Physical development	This area looks at children's gross and fine motor skills as well as their movements. It also looks at helping children to learn about being healthy	• From making movements, children will gain some of the skills that they will need for their later handwriting. Children will also need speech in order to talk and understand about being healthy
Creative development	This area is about children expressing themselves through a range of media including dance, role play, music and art	• Children benefit from talking about what they have been doing. Early mark making is also about self expression. Making music, especially responding to the beat is also useful if promoting children's early sound awareness

Be able to contribute to children's learning in communication, language and literacy

In this learning outcome, you will need to show that you can work with children to support their communication, language and literacy. It is quite a wide area of learning as you will see.

Identify the types of equipment and activities that are used to support children's communication, language and literacy

Communication, language and literacy is quite a broad area. In the EYFS, it is divided into six further components. We will use these as a basis for looking at the type of equipment and activities that are likely to be used. The type of equipment and activities used will also vary according to the age or stage of children's development.

Language for communication and language for thinking

In the EYFS, this covers two separate aspects, but it is essentially about helping children to learn to use speech to communicate with others and to support their reasoning and logic. With babies and toddlers, the main requirement is that adults spend time talking and communicating with them. This is more important than the type of equipment or toys that are put out. As children become more fluent in their speech, it is useful for adults to give them chances to use their language for explaining and reasoning.

Table 2: Equipment and activities to support communication and language

Age	Activities	Toys and equipment
Babies 0–18 months	• Any opportunity for adults to talk to babies and engage with them • Traditional games such as peek a boo • Outings and opportunities to see different things so as to stimulate interest in communication	• Musical instruments • Objects that babies can explore by touching and mouthing, e.g. large sponge, wooden spoon
Toddlers (18 months – 3 years)	• Opportunities to chat to adults, e.g. at mealtimes • Times when adults play alongside toddlers e.g. during sensory play • Songs and rhymes • Opportunities for outings to learn about local area e.g. going to the shops	• Sound recorders • Pretend telephones
Children (3–5 years)	• Games such as 'What's in my bag?', picture lotto • Storytelling • Opportunities for role play and small-world play • Opportunities to do things alongside adults who will talk to them, e.g. cooking, tidying up • Songs and rhymes • Opportunities for outings to see different things, e.g. farm, library	• Puppets • Small-world toys • Dressing-up clothes • Role-play areas, e.g. shops, home corner

Functional Skills Maths: Analysing

Can you work out how much of your day is spent promoting children's language skills? What resources does your setting have to support children in this area? How often are these resources used?

Puppets can encourage children to talk

Linking sounds with letters

One of the skills that children need in order to read is to be able to hear sounds and rhymes in words: for example, being able to hear that 'pat' and 'picture' start with the same letter or that 'cat' and 'hat' rhyme. This means that adults working with children of all ages need to say and sing different types of rhymes. As children get older, you can play games that help them to pick out individual sounds: for example, in teddy's suitcase we are only putting in objects that begin with the sound 'c'.

Table 3: Equipment and activities to support linking sounds with letters

Age	Activities	Equipment
Babies 0–18 months	• Finger-rhyme play • Nursery rhymes	Rattles and shakers
Toddlers (18 months – 3 years)	• Nursery rhymes • Action rhymes • Musical games	Musical instruments
Children (3–5 years)	• Nursery rhymes • Action rhymes • Poems • Musical games • Pointing out letter shapes and sounds in children's names • Playing sound games, such as finding objects that begin or end with the same sound • Going on sound walks	• Musical instruments • Magnetic letters • Sound records

Reading

No one is expecting babies to read, but we do know that babies who share books with adults go on to develop an interest in reading. Learning to read requires that children learn that, in English, print goes from left to right and pages turn from front to back. As children become older, you can help them recognise words such as their names.

Table 4: Equipment and activities to support reading

Age	Activities	Equipment
Babies 0–18 months Toddlers (18 months – 3 years)	• Share books with babies and toddlers • Encourage babies and toddlers to hold books and turn pages	• Simple picture books • Homemade books with photographs of children inside
Children (3–5 years)	• Share books with children • Make books with children • Show children how print moves from left to right • Encourage children to find their names • Play games such as picture lotto, snap	• A good range of books including factual and picture books • Story DVDs • Labels • Name cards

Writing and handwriting

It is not until children begin to read that they will write in ways that adults can understand. However, children can enjoy mark making, which is the first step towards writing. Mark making is about children exploring how to make marks. With babies this may mean smearing jelly on a tray, but with older children this will mean 'pretend writing' in the role-play corner. As well as mark making, we also help children to develop the movements in their hands needed for handwriting. This is partly through mark-making activities, but also about activities that will help fine motor skills.

Table 5: Equipment and activities to support writing and handwriting

Age	Activities	Equipment
Babies 0–18 months	• Sensory materials, e.g. jelly • Pop-up toys	• Safe sensory materials for babies to smear, touch and taste
Toddlers (18 months – 3 years)	• Painting • Sensory materials, e.g. gloop, shaving foam	• Paint, large brushes, large crayons, felt tips • Dough • Toys that help hand movements, e.g. bricks, hammer and pegs
Children (3–5 years)	• Mark-making activities in all areas, e.g. pads in the role-play corner • Opportunities to use sensory materials for marking • Opportunities to develop hand movements e.g. using tools, cooking, collage	• Pens, markers, jotters, pads, paints, brushes • Sensory materials, e.g. sand, dry coloured rice • Tools, e.g. scissors, graters

Early writing does not have to involve pens and paper!

Engaging children's interest and attention

You can support children's communication, language and literacy in a variety of ways. While the obvious ways are through taking time to chat, comment and point things out to children, there are also some specific activities that can be helpful. Figure 2 shows some of the methods that are often used.

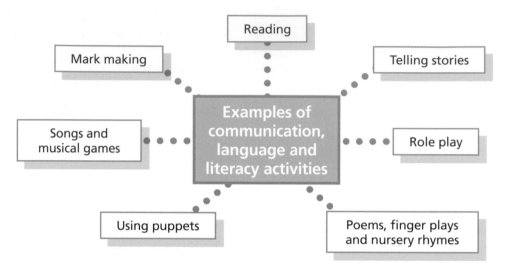

Figure 2: Examples of communication, language and literacy activities

Reading

Books provide wonderful opportunities for children to develop language, but also a love of reading. It is never too early to start, so books need to be shared with babies as well as with toddlers and older children. Here are five tips worth following to gain children's interest and attention.

1. **Choose the right book**

   For books to be enjoyable, children have to understand them. This means matching the book to the child's language stage. With babies, try simple picture books rather than story books; for toddlers, choose books that have a simple story with plenty of repetition; with children whose language is developed, choose books that are slightly longer.

2. **Think about the size of group**

   Children will get more from sharing a book if they can touch it, spend time on certain pages and enjoy being with you. This means that it is always better to share a book with just one or two children at a time.

3. **Choose the right time**

   Children do not get much out of an activity if they are tired or wanting to do something else. This means it is important to choose the right time to share books with children. It is important also to choose the right length of book if a child is tired.

4. Let children set the pace

Always remember that you are reading books for the benefit of children. This means that, if they want to spend longer on a particular page or go back and look again, there is no problem. This also means that sometimes you may need to read a page or even a book over and over again. You may also find that sometimes a child will lose interest, so you will need to stop and do something else.

5. Read with energy

For children to be interested in a book, the adult has to sound interested too. If you are not sure about a book, read it quietly to yourself first. This preparation will help you to read it with more energy.

For children to be interested in a book, the adult has to sound interested too

Telling stories

Storytelling has been a traditional way by which children have heard stories and also learned language. Telling stories can begin with babies as you can tell them what you are seeing, what you have done and what you might do in the future: for example, 'Look at that cat! He's gone up the tree now.' While that may not seem much of a story, it is the starting point.

How to tell a story

Telling a story is easier than it seems. With toddlers, tell simple stories about what a child has been doing, but aim to use traditional lines, such as: 'Once upon a time, Sammy played hide-and-seek in the house. He hid and he hid, but in the end we found him.' These short stories can be told when children are having a snack or while you are helping them on with a coat.

Once children have more language, you can tell slightly longer stories. Look out for story bags, which have a story inside them as well as props. You can also make up your own stories with children. The checklist shows some of the skills that you should use.

Best practice checklist: Reading

✓ Do storytelling with very small groups of children

✓ Involve children with props or actions

✓ Use traditional story lines, such as 'Once upon a time' and '… lived happily ever after'

✓ Repeat phrases so that children can join in: for example, 'He ran and he ran and he ran'

✓ Be ready to shorten or adapt a story if you see that children are losing interest

Songs and musical games

Children can learn some language from hearing and joining in with songs, and playing musical games. Singing to babies is the starting point for this. The good news is that babies and young children do not care what you sound like! It can be a good idea to choose a nursery song that you know well and look for a time to start singing it. With a baby, it is also good to make eye contact and perhaps also to hold, rock or gently swing the baby to the rhythm. With toddlers and older children you can also include musical instruments, so that they can shake and rattle along while singing.

Musical games

There are quite a lot of musical games that older children will enjoy playing in small groups. Try out games such as pass the parcel, find the keys or musical statues. If you are not sure, look out for a traditional party game book for ideas.

Poems, finger plays and nursery rhymes

Poems, finger plays and nursery rhymes are all good ways for children to join in and develop a love of language. They also help children to develop a knowledge of sounds in words, sometimes known as **phonemic awareness**.

Poems

Poems work well for children whose speech is quite good. There are many poetry books around, so choose ones that you think the children will understand and enjoy. Children often enjoy funny poems that rhyme.

Finger plays

Finger plays are little rhymes that are often played with babies and toddlers. Popular ones include 'Two little dicky birds sitting on the wall' and 'Round and round the garden, like a teddy bear'. Finger plays need to be done often so that babies and toddlers become familiar with them

Key term

Phonemic awareness: recognising different sounds in words and start to be able to recognise or join in with them. It is also important to put a baby on the lap or to sit up close to a toddler, which means that finger plays are usually carried out just with one child at a time.

Nursery rhymes

Traditional nursery rhymes are important for children's speech as they help children to recognise, but also practise, some of the sounds in language. Many nursery rhymes have strong end rhymes and also some **alliteration** such as 'How many **p**eas in a **p**ea **p**od **p**ressed?' As some traditional nursery rhymes are racist or sexist in tone, it is important to choose them with some care. Fortunately, there are many nursery rhyme books to use.

You can begin using nursery rhymes with very young babies as they can be rocked gently to them. Interestingly, many toddlers will start to join in with rhymes from two years onwards if they hear them several times. Once children know some rhymes, it is important to keep adding to their repertoire. Think about looking for action rhymes as well as counting rhymes. It is also useful when using counting rhymes to put out some props so that children can see objects disappear or appear.

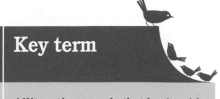

Key term

Alliteration: words that begin with the same sound

Functional Skills ICT: Developing, presenting and communicating information

You could use your research into these different rhymes to produce a song book. You could do this for your class and include the children's favourite songs in the book. This could be your class song book and you could use it every song time with the children.

Skills builder

How many of these nursery rhymes do you know?

- Little Jack Horner
- Diddle diddle dumpling, my son John
- Mary, Mary, quite contrary
- Sing a song of sixpence, a pocketful of rye
- There was an old lady who lived in a shoe
- Five little ducks went swimming one day

Do some research, using books, recordings and the internet, to familiarise yourself with these and find new rhymes you can use.

Using puppets

Puppets hold a real fascination for children if they are used well. Puppets can help children to forget to be shy and really act as a stimulus for talk. It is important though to choose and use puppets in the right way. Here are five tips that should really help you.

1. Choose a puppet that you really like

Puppets work best when you enjoy using them. Children can sense this and become more relaxed and enthusiastic.

2. Choose a puppet that fits your hand

Puppets come in different sizes. Choosing one that fits your hand is important as it means that you can manipulate it well. Think also about choosing one with a mouth so that it looks as if it is talking.

3. Make sure that your puppet seems real

For children to believe that your puppet is real, you should bring it out of a bag or box with your hand already inside it. It is harder for children if they see you put your hand in the puppet. In the same way, you should put your puppet away so that their last view of it is 'alive'. You can tell children that it is going to sleep.

4. Make eye contact with your puppet

One of the best ways of making a puppet seem real is by making eye contact with it. Smile at it and stroke or touch it as if it is really alive.

5. Avoid going crazy

Some people become very loud and make sudden movements with their puppets. This tends to frighten children and so is to be avoided! Interestingly, small repetitive movements such as a dog wagging its tail or a rabbit looking slowly from left to right are more lifelike.

Role play

Pretend play or role play is a key way in which children can practise and extend their language. Children tend to enjoy playing in this way once their language is established, which means it usually works best with children from around three years. When children are involved in role play, they are learning how to play with other children and also trying out being someone else. In most settings, adults will also at times join in with children as they role play so that children can learn what to do with the props, but also to learn the language that is used in a situation such as buying a train ticket or at a library. Using language in this way is known as modelling language. The idea is that, after hearing it, children can copy it.

Maintaining children's interest

The great thing about role play is that you can vary situations for children so that they do not become bored. Having said this, it is always worth keeping a role-play corner in place at the same time because children do enjoy it. It also acts as a base for them to, for example, 'go shopping'. You can also maintain children's interest and enjoyment by using as many real props as possible: for example, real saucepans in the play kitchen and real vegetables in the shop. Table 6 gives some ideas for role-play areas which can be done both in and out of doors.

Functional Skills English: Speaking, listening and communication

Role play is a good way of demonstrating good language skills to children. This is why your functional skills are so important. Make sure you always think carefully about your audience and remember that you are the child's role model.

Table 6: Role-play areas

Indoors	Outdoors
Optician	Garden centre
Fruit and vegetable shop	Petrol station
Pet shop	At the train station
Shoe shop	Getting on the bus
Supermarket	On the train
At the doctor's	At the market

Case study:
Extending children's language

Kiera works in a pre-school with four-year-olds. She and her colleagues realise that not many children have visited a library. They arrange a visit with the children and afterwards Kiera decides to turn the story area into a library. She moves the bookcases to create an entrance, puts up a sign and then creates some cards with the children's names. When the children come in the next day, they are excited to see a pretend library. Before the children start to play, Kiera gives each of the children a 'library' card with their name on. The children enjoy choosing books and then giving their card to Kiera, who acts the role of the librarian. Kiera models the language used in libraries by reminding the children of the date that the books are 'due' back. She also asks the children if they want their books 'renewed'. The following session, Kiera plays the part of someone taking out books and two other children play the part of the librarians. She is pleased to see that the children start to use the words and phrases that she used.

1. How does this experience help extend the children's language?

2. Why is it useful for adults to be involved in role play?

Mark making

Children's early writing is often known as mark making. Mark making can start very early on with babies being interested in using their whole hands to smear yogurt on a tray or to touch paint between their fingers. From two years onwards, toddlers tend to enjoy using large felt tips, but also making marks using brushes and water outdoors. As children's awareness of words and letters takes off, so they make shapes that look like letters.

Figure 3: See how children's mark making changes as they learn more about words and letters

Supporting children's early mark making

Children need to enjoy mark making. To do this, they need adults to give them encouragement and not to be critical. The term 'scribbling' is therefore not used in most settings, as it does not sound very positive. Children will often want to write more when they can see that adults are also joining in. This means that, if you join in, they are likely to spend longer painting. In the same way, if you pick up a pen and pad to do an observation, they may wish to do the same.

Mark making and sensory materials

Children enjoy the feel of making their mark. You can encourage this by putting out sensory materials that really do 'feel' good. These include large brushes and buckets of water outdoors, paint, shaving foam, damp sand and sticks.

Mark making and role play

Opportunities for mark making are usually created in many different areas within a setting. This means that many settings have a whiteboard or chalkboard outdoors. They may also put out paper, pens and other materials within the role play area, such as a pad next to a play telephone.

These boys enjoy writing as part of their play outdoors

Getting ready for assessment

Write a reflective account about how you have used three different methods to support children's communication, language and literacy. In your reflective account write about:

- the age of the children that you worked with
- why you chose the methods
- how you worked with the children
- what you feel the children gained from the activities
- what you feel that you learned.

Functional Skills English: Writing

When writing your account it is important that you plan it through first to ensure that you have covered everything that you have been asked to cover. Think carefully about your spelling, punctuation and grammar as this can sometimes have an effect on the meaning of a piece of writing.

Using clear language

The way that you talk to children is very important when supporting their communication and language, and this assessment criterion requires that you can use clear language to support children when engaged in activities. Clear language is more than just the way that you say words. It is also about other skills. Figure 4 below shows the range of skills that allow your language to be clear for children.

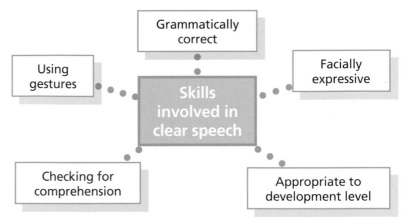

Figure 4: Skills involved in clear speech

Grammatically correct

Wherever possible, you should try to be grammatically correct in your speech with children. This allows young children to learn to construct phrases accurately.

Appropriate to developmental level

Your speech needs to be right for each child's stage of development. This means getting to know what a child can understand and also say. With babies and toddlers, this means repeating key words and keeping sentences fairly short.

Facially expressive

The way you look can help children to understand what you are saying. This means that having positive facial expressions is important. This is particularly important if you are working with babies and toddlers as they will try to work out what you are saying partly from your facial expression.

Using gestures

Babies and young children need you to use gestures so that they can understand what you are talking about. You may point to an object as you are talking about it or wave to a teddy to indicate that you are about to hide him.

Checking for comprehension

You must find ways of checking that children have understood you. You might do this by looking at their expression or, with older children, you might ask a question or make a comment.

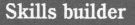

Skills builder

Look at experienced colleagues as they are working with babies or young children. See how they use strong facial expressions and gestures to facilitate communication.

Functional Skills English: Speaking, listening and communication

Role play within your study group is a good way of developing your confidence in this area. You can learn a lot from watching your peers and seeing how they use their communication skills.

Using encouragement and praise

Most of children's learning about communication, language and literacy comes from the adults that they are with. So the way that you work with children is vital, and this is one reason why you will be assessed on it. Key to supporting children is to use encouragement and praise, although this takes different forms according to the age and stage of children.

There are many ways that you can encourage and praise children in their communication, language and literacy.

Acknowledgement

One of the most important ways in which you can encourage children's speech is to acknowledge any attempts at vocalisation or speech promptly. This means smiling and picking up a baby that is babbling or bending down when a toddler is trying to talk to us. Acknowledging children promptly helps the child to understand that you are interested in what they have to say or communicate. Ignoring children can mean that they soon learn not to bother trying to tell us anything. With babies and toddlers, you may also find that it can be hard to work out what they are trying to communicate. This does not matter providing that you are showing them your interest, although with toddlers it can be worth asking them to point out or show what it is they want.

This baby enjoys communicating with this practitioner

Tone of voice

Your tone of voice needs to be warm and interested as children are quick to pick up if you are bored, frustrated or irritated. A warm tone of voice helps children to feel comfortable with you and this in turn will mean that they will feel more like trying to communicate or confident enough to try to read.

Allowing sufficient time for children to respond

A key way in which you can encourage children is to allow them sufficient time to think about what they would like to say and to respond.

This is important as many adults forget that babies, toddlers and young children need a little time to process their thoughts. Interrupting a child or not giving them sufficient time can put children off trying to talk.

Recasting

As children are learning to speak, but also to read, they will often make mistakes. This is normal and part of the process. The way that you correct children can make a difference to their confidence. In both speech and in reading, you should not make it obvious that you are correcting the children, but instead you should 'recast' back the sentence in correct form. This way the child is able to hear it correctly, but does not realise that they have been corrected, as the case study shows.

Expanding

You can encourage children's speech by acknowledging what they have said, but in a way that makes a sentence more complex. This shows the child that you have been listening, but also helps babies or toddlers to learn to talk. Again, you can see how this is done in the case study.

Praise

Everyone responds to praise. Praise is particularly important when children are learning to read or write as it does take time and practice. Knowing how to praise children is important. It is often helpful to just put in an odd 'well done' while a child is attempting something, rather than waiting until afterwards and making a big thing out of it. Praise can raise children's confidence, but it has to be used carefully so that children do not worry that there is a right or wrong way to speak or to do early mark making.

Key terms

Recasting: repeating back to a child something that they have said or read in a more accurate form

Expanding: acknowledging what a child has said, but saying it in a more complex way

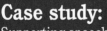

Case study:
Supporting speech

Harry is nearly three years old and goes to Lorna, his childminder, three days a week. Lorna has been working with Harry since he was born and so knows him well. It is just after lunch and Harry is looking for the toy cars.

Harry: Cars, me want the cars. (Is looking around the living room)

Lorna: Did you want me to help you find the cars, Harry? (Bending down next to him)

Harry: (Nods forlornly)

Lorna: We'll need to think about where you last played with them. (Putting her arm around him) What about the garden? Did you take them outdoors?

Harry: Me tooked them there. (Harry points to the garden)

Lorna: Yes, I think you did take them out in the garden. Well done for remembering. That's very clever. We'll get our shoes on and have a look.

Harry: My shoes there! (Points at shoes)

Lorna: And so they are. Your smart blue shoes.

1. Why was it important that Lorna acknowledged what Harry was trying to do?

2. What skills did Lorna use to support Harry's speech?

Be able to evaluate own contribution to children's learning in communication, language and literacy

It takes time and experience to become skilled at promoting children's communication, language and literacy. For this learning outcome, you will need to think about how your practice is coming along.

Reviewing your own working practice

For this assessment criterion, you will need to find ways of reviewing your working practice to work out how it helps children's learning in communication, language and literacy. There are many ways of doing this. You could ask someone to observe you and let you know how you are doing, but perhaps the most effective way is to ask someone to film you working with children or to record your speech using something such as an MP3 player. In this way you can actually see or hear yourself while you are with children. This does require quite a bit of courage, but can really help you to improve your practice. It is useful to watch or hear yourself alongside a more experienced practitioner who can point out things that you are doing well, but also give you some tips as to how you might improve. For you to show that you have contributed to children's learning, use the checklist on the following page to consider the way your practice worked.

Functional Skills ICT: Using ICT

Recording your voice is a great way of reflecting on your own practice. You could share your voice recording with your assessor to demonstrate your ability at communicating with children.

Best practice checklist: Reflecting on communication

✓ Encourage children to communicate in these ways with you: smiling, pointing, babbling, chatting and showing

✓ See that children are relaxed with you and keen to be with you

✓ Show genuine interest in the children's communication and follow their interests

✓ Use the communication skills that you looked at earlier in this chapter, such as expanding

✓ Use vocabulary or ask questions that might develop older children's language for thinking

You might also consider your practice in a range of situations relating to sharing books, mark making and using poems and rhymes. To consider how well you are working in these areas, look back at best practice checklists and tips for these and use them as a starting point for reviewing your work.

Being recorded is one way in which you can review your practice

Adapting to meet individual children's needs

Once you have thought about your own working practice, you will need to think about how to use your skills so that you can meet each child's individual needs. This is important: children do have different personalities, but they are also likely to be at different stages of development. Working with a baby, for example, requires higher levels of facial expression and repetitive language than working with a fluent four-year-old. Changing your style is therefore key to meeting a child's individual needs.

For some children, particular support may be required as they may stammer or have a hearing difficulty. If you are working with children that have additional needs, it will be important for you to find out exactly how best to support the child from the child's key person or your manager. This may mean slowing down your speech and not finishing off a sentence for a child who is stuttering, or checking that a child who has a hearing difficulty is aware that you are trying to communicate with them before talking.

Over to You

Make a list of the children that you currently work with. For each child:

- consider their level of language, their personality and also their interests
- record yourself working with them.

How well are you changing your tone, vocabulary and style to meet their needs?

Check your knowledge

1. Explain the links between language and behaviour.
2. Identify two other ways that language is important to children's overall development.
3. Give two examples of activities that might encourage a child's language.
4. What is meant by the term 'mark making'?
5. Identify two ways in which mark-making opportunities might be provided.
6. Describe how to share books with children.
7. Why is it important for adults to model clear and accurate language?
8. Why is it important for adults to allow sufficient time for children to respond?
9. Explain why recording may be useful in reviewing your practice.
10. Why is it important for practitioners to adapt their practice?

Contribute to the support of children's creative development

In this unit you will find out how you can contribute to a child's creative development. You will learn that creative development is not just about children expressing themselves through activities such as music and painting, but is about the way that you challenge children to think for themselves.

Learning outcomes
By the end of this unit you will:

1. understand the importance of children's creative development

2. be able to contribute towards children's creative development

3. be able to evaluate your own contribution to children's creative development.

Understand the importance of children's creative development

With the introduction of the Early Years Foundation Stage framework (EYFS) and years of extensive research, increasing importance is now placed on the creative development of children. The emphasis is not just on creative activities, such as painting or drawing, but also on the way children solve problems in their learning and think about things. It is recognised that children are curious and should be encouraged to explore in their play. The success of a child's creative development depends on the way that we nurture children's curiosity through a variety of interesting and challenging activities in their play.

Creativity and the way children learn creatively make up a child's creative development. Creativity means:

- the way children explore objects and materials
- the way they try to solve problems, challenge their thinking and make connections in their learning
- how children think imaginatively.

A child can learn creatively through:

- painting and drawing activities
- malleable activities, such as clay and play dough
- sand and water play
- role play and imaginative play, such as small-world play
- music
- dance
- designing, often called design technology.

In the EYFS, Creative Development is one of the six areas of development that practitioners have to consider when planning the curriculum for children under five. Creative Development is divided into four sections:

- Being creative – responding to experiences, expressing and communicating ideas
- Exploring media and materials
- Developing imagination and imaginative play
- Creating music and dance.

Creative development and children's learning

Creative development is important to children's learning because it encourages children to make connections in their thinking and explore their world. It also gives children the opportunity to express their own ideas.

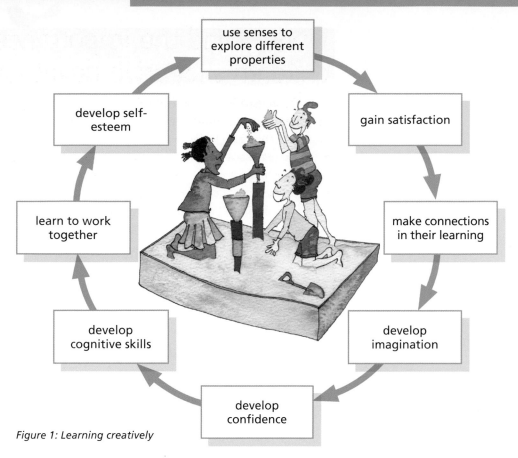

Figure 1: Learning creatively

Children's learning through creative development is important at any age but how they learn will depend upon the stage they are in their play, as you can see from Table 1.

Table 1: Importance of creative development

Stage of play	Importance of creative development
Exploratory play Young babies observe their surroundings, make movements, grasp fingers or rattles	Encourages children to start thinking about how things work as they develop the skills needed to develop cognitively and explore objects
Solitary play **Up to 15 months** Babies or children will play alone	Developing their thinking skills and making connections in their learning when playing through schemas such as pushing the doll's pushchair to transport bricks
Parallel play **Around two years** Children play separately with minimal interaction	Still developing their thinking skills and trying creative activities, still very sensory-based
Association play **From one to two and a half years** Children begin to interact in the same activity. They often still play alone	Starting to involve others in their thinking but still exploring their environment on their own
Taking turns and sharing in play **Two and a half to three years** Playing together more, with some understanding of simple rules	Beginning to play creatively together and develop imaginations through simple role play or other activities
Cooperative play **Three years upwards** Children can play together. They can take on a role within the group, considering others' thoughts and actions	Can work together to challenge each other and increasingly use language to develop ideas and explore creative activities

Case study:
Making connections

In a Berkeley pre-school two four-year-old girls are busy playing with their teddy in a car in the outdoors area. They ask Jerry, their key person, how they can give their teddy a ride across a bridge to go to the seaside. Jerry suggests the block play area. The girls decide to use a plank as the bridge. To make the bridge stable Jerry observes them working out how to support the plank! They have a number of attempts before finding the blocks they need. They then get a teddy and push him across the bridge in a toy car.

1. What aspect of creativity are the girls developing to solve this problem?

2. How do you think Jerry supports the girls' creative development?

How creative development links within your setting

Creative development will link to many other areas of learning and development within the framework of your own work setting. The EYFS framework has six interlinked areas of learning and development. One of these relates directly to creative development:

- Personal, Social and Emotional Development (PSED)

- Communication, Language and Literacy (CLL)

- Problem Solving, Reasoning and Numeracy (PSRN)

- Knowledge and Understanding of the World (KUS)

- Physical Development (PD)

- Creative Development (CD).

Each area of learning is linked to the five outcomes of the *Every Child Matters* framework and the key early learning goals — a statement of what most children should achieve in each area of learning by the end of the EYFS. The development stages outlined are broad and intended to show the different ways that children can achieve the early learning goals. The framework is intended to be holistic and centred on the needs of the individual child, to enable children to progress through the areas of learning and development.

Making connections is essential for children's creative development, so it is important not to consider creativity on its own. Instead you should encourage children to link all areas of their learning so that you can observe, plan and assess children holistically.

You also need to plan for the fact that children will often use resources in a different way to the way you intended. This could well be

Over to You

You can visit the Department of Education website and view the Creative Developmental Learning goals for the EYFS by visiting www.education.gov.uk.

Functional Skills English: Reading

You could develop your reading skills by using the information you find on this website to make links to what you do in your setting.

developing their creative thinking, such as using an oven in the role-play corner as the controls of a spaceship! The focus in all activities should be on experimentation and fun. As the EYFS says: 'When children have opportunities to play with ideas in different situations, with a variety of resources they discover new ways of doing things.' (EYFS Creativity and Critical thinking 2007).

Consider the following two scenarios of activities that involve creative development and link to other areas of learning of the EYFS.

Activity	Links to all areas of learning
A group of five-year-old children is building a den out of blankets on to the climbing frame • **CD** encouraging them to work to explore materials, solve problems, express their ideas and develop their imaginations	This could link to: • **CLL** communicating skillfully and developing speaking and listening skills by interacting together • **PSED** taking turns, expressing ideas and feelings • **PSRN** calculating, space, measure • **PD** using equipment and materials, movement and space • **KUS** designing and making, exploring and investigating
An 11-month-old child is exploring a treasure basket full of everyday kitchen resources, sitting near to his mum. • **CD** exploring materials, responding to experiences	• **PSED** dispositions and attitudes, as children become excited and motivated in their learning • **CLL** language for communication through non-verbal communication; experiencing a warm relationship; responding to different sounds engaging all the senses • **PSRN** making connections • **KUS** exploring and investigating • **PD** using equipment and materials

Holistic learning means developing all areas through a variety of activities. This reflects the fact that it is important that areas of learning relate to each other and make experiences for children more meaningful.

The National Curriculum Key Stage currently has a framework that encourages a holistic approach to learning, thus developing children's creative thinking as they have opportunities to problem-solve, extend and challenge their thinking individually and in groups. Teachers follow a more creative curriculum, planning themes that consider the learning outcomes from different subject areas.

Be able to contribute towards children's creative development

One of your main roles as an early years practitioner is to provide the right equipment and range of activities to be able to support the children's learning in your setting. You will be encouraged to observe and assess children in order to support them. Remember that it is important that children in a play-based setting experience a balance of adult-led and child-initiated activities. This is important for their creative development, so that they can lead their own learning but sometimes be extended by an adult.

Getting ready for assessment

Plan an activity for a group of children in your setting that is a creative activity, such as play dough or painting. Make sure that you refer to other areas of development that might be covered. Evaluate the activity to show how the activity did promote other areas of learning and encouraged links to other areas of learning. Discuss with your tutor how you can use this as evidence for your assessment in this unit.

Functional Skills English: Writing

It is important when working with children that we evaluate often in order to see where we need to improve our practice. Writing your evaluation is a good way of developing your English skills as the spelling, punctuation and grammar is very important. You need to plan your evaluation first to make sure that your work is organised and only contains the facts.

Equipment and activities for creative development

Earlier in this unit you read about different aspects of creative development. You should always give children opportunities to challenge their own thinking and solve problems through adult-led activities and providing resources for more open-ended play. A wide range of creative materials can be made available for children. Once you have studied the range, and probably added your own ideas to the list, you will be able to consider how these materials can be used in activities to encourage different stages.

First consider the range of activities that can support children's creative development. When planning a musical activity in your setting, you will need to agree the type and time of the activity with your supervisor and colleagues. You will need to consider:

- the age of the children

- the time and length of the activity

- the size of the group

- how the activity relates to a theme or project, if relevant

- the resources required
- what children will learn from the activity
- where the activity will take place.

Table 2 will help you understand the importance of choosing songs and musical activities to support children's creative development.

Table 2: Choosing musical acitivites to support creative development

Songs and activities could be:	
familiar	These could include nursery rhymes and lullabies. Children will be encouraged to explore sounds and rhythms
new	These will encourage children to develop listening, rhythm and communication. To develop confidence, familiar and new songs should be mixed in the same session. The stage of development of the children will determine the length of the activity
cross-cultural	Songs and instruments from other countries will encourage knowledge and understanding of a wider environment and encourage children to explore the music and respond to what they hear through dance, using instruments or singing
action-based	Musical actions also give children a chance to respond to what they hear through: • clapping • singing • body actions • using and exploring commercial and home-made instruments

When children are singing or playing musical instruments it will encourage:

- expression
- enjoyment
- exploration through finding ways to make sounds with instruments or voices.

Unplanned and spontaneous music is an important part of any child's day. Children may sing while doing another activity, or ask an adult to join them if musical instruments are available during free play. These opportunities can be as important as any planned activity and should be evaluated as such as part of a child's creative development.

Imaginative play

This can start at a very early age and it plays an important part in any child's creative development. You are going to consider:

- how children use their imagination to make one thing stand for another
- how children can play out different roles
- How children can extend their learning and solve problems through **imaginative play**.

In role play, children pretend to be other people. They will act out situations for enjoyment or to make sense of their own world and challenge their thinking. You will notice that children often lead in their own role play. They may, for example, use wrapped-up towels as dogs and climbing frames as space rockets.

There will be times when you will provide equipment to support role play, but you should always ensure it is safe for imaginative play. You should also ensure that:

- role play fits in with curriculum plan/theme of work setting

- the area is appropriate and has safe access

- enough materials are provided for the children to develop their role play imaginatively and with spontaneity

- activities are appropriate for the age group.

Role play is an excellent way of developing children's skills in many ways. Children as young as two years old will use role play to develop their imaginations. They will also develop their language, communication and literacy skills through role play. Children from 18 months upwards will respond to role play that is set up in a suitable area.

First of all, let us consider role play that links in with the interest that your children display.

Ideas for role play

There are many ideas for imaginative play areas to encourage role play. Figure 2 shows a few examples.

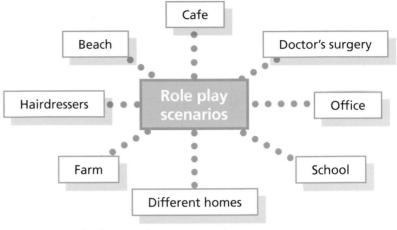

Figure 2: Role play scenarios

Case study:
Using hats

Anika looks after four-year-old twins, Holly and Ben, in their home. They have their cousins, Kate, who is five, and Philippe, who is three, over to play. Anika has collected together a large number of hats for the children. The hats are freely accessible and kept in a large basket in the playroom. The children set up some chairs to represent a bus. Holly finds a flowery hat to put on and becomes one of the passengers. The other children are soon rummaging in the hat basket and sitting on the chairs imagining themselves as passengers on the bus. Kate finds herself a flat cap and decides she is the driver. A great deal of time is spent travelling to the seaside! Holly suddenly gets off the bus and swaps her flowery hat for a large net veil. Soon a wedding is taking place, very much like a family wedding they had all attended last month.

1. How did the hats help to develop the children's creative thinking?

2. What particular creative ability or skill did the hats encourage?

3. Why is it important to recognise that children will play out roles they see in the world around them?

In fact, most ideas can be adapted for a role-play area and children will respond. Through their (usually vivid) imaginations, children will be able to understand and experience the theme that is being explored.

Child-led role play can occur in a theme-led role-play area or spontaneously in everyday play. Role play can be totally unplanned. One child may be playing under a climbing frame using it as a jungle and very soon two or three other children may be joining in this imaginary play.

Remember that role play does not occur only when children are dressing up. You may observe some interesting role play in the following activities:

- small world play, such as Duplo/Lego or Playmobil scenes
- puppets/dolls
- books and stories
- painting and drawing
- play dough.

Hats can be one of the most important visible elements in role play. By providing a box of different hats, early years practitioners can enable children to role play many different characters.

The role-play corner provides a great opportunity for children to explore their environment. Ideally the role-play corner should be separate to an imaginative play area. Consider the shopping list for a role-play corner below so that the children can choose their own type of props to extend their thinking and play imaginatively.

- Multicultural and gender dolls
- Hats
- Clothes
- Bed
- Washing-up facilities
- Cooking facilities
- Telephone
- Cleaning materials
- Washing machine, etc.
- Iron and board/pegs
- Pots and utensils
- Shoes and bags
- Computer

Functional Skills Maths: Interpreting

You could give the children a choice of theme for the role-play area. You could collect your results on a tally chart and then transfer this information on to a graph. From your graph you could write a short conclusion about what you are going to turn your role-play area into and why you have chosen that particular theme.

Best practice checklist: Supporting creative play

✓ Never stress the end product – children often enjoy the process rather than the end product

✓ Ensure there is no competition

✓ Praise children for their efforts

✓ Value the results, but do not compare

✓ Remember that children, unlike adults, will not always visualise an end product

Your role is to provide the right materials for the creative activity and not over-direct the end result.

Sand and alternative materials

If you are working in a nursery or school setting you will probably have a sand tray. However, sand can also be provided in a baby's bath, a washing bowl or a sandpit in the garden. Special play (silver) sand is available which is soft and does not stain hands. Sand can be used in a wet or dry form and can be used by children to create an imaginary environment for diggers, animals and other toys. With simple containers, sand can be dug, raked, scooped, patted and moulded. A sand tray is also an area where children can learn to play creatively together, sharing their imaginative experience.

In addition, sand can be used as part of a collage picture or to provide an interesting sound in a shaker made from a clear plastic bottle. Sawdust, beans or peat can also be used in collage activities.

Water

From an early age, water plays an important part in creative play – starting in the bath! It is an inexpensive material and can encourage creativity in endless ways. Children will play at a water tray, washing bowl, paddling pool or bath for a long time – simply enjoying playing with water. Water can be transformed in creative play by adding ice, colouring, bubbles and even a variety of smells, such as lavender or lemon. Children can be given a range of equipment to stimulate their imaginations, from buckets and bottles to sophisticated water wheels. If your funds are limited, children will display as much creativity from different-sized yogurt pots and an empty washing-up liquid bottle.

Creative play does not have to result in an end product. Sand and water play are excellent examples of this. The children can simply enjoy using their imaginations to play creatively.

Painting and drawing materials

A wide variety of drawing materials is available including:

- pencils
- coloured crayons
- felt-tipped pens
- wax crayons
- chalks.

They can be used as a medium on their own or mixed together. Drawing can be 'free' or topic-related. Drawing materials such as wax crayons can be used to explore and to do rubbings on a variety of textures, such as bark and walls. The medium provided to draw on will also encourage children to explore their imaginations. Papers can range from thin tissue to thick paper they may have made themselves.

Painting can be done with a variety of brushes, depending on the manipulative stage of the child involved. Household brushes can be

Over to You

Look at the resources in your work setting and discuss ideas with your colleagues. See how long you can make the list of paint ideas. It will probably be very long!

Pulling the modelling clay!

Functional Skills Maths: Analysing

You could find the recipe for play dough on the internet and copy it out so you could do it with the children. Using the recipe that you have found you could calculate how much of each ingredient you would need to make enough play dough for every child in the room.

used on large areas. Paint can be applied in many other ways including the following:

- potato printing
- scrubbing pads and nail brush painting
- blowing paint with straws
- painting with rags or scrunched up newspaper
- painting with a roller that is commercially made or made from a kitchen roll
- sponge painting
- drawing with wax and painting over with coloured paint
- roller painting using an old deodorant bottle
- finger painting.

Paint can be bought ready-mixed or in a powder form. The type of paint you provide for a creative activity will depend on the consistency of paint required. You can make your own inexpensive thick paint from powdered glue and powdered paint. Other materials, such as glitter and sand, can be mixed with paint to give it a different texture. Glues, such as PVA, will give a shiny finish.

Malleable materials

Malleable materials can be bought ready-made in forms such as clay whereas materials such as play dough can be made at home or in the work setting.

Dough or clay can be used in a raw form or cooked to make it more permanent, and then glazed or painted and varnished. Dough used in cooking is also creative and children can create their own shapes or use commercial cutters. Children will enjoy rolling, shaping, moulding and cutting dough or clay.

Papier mâché can also be provided, either as strips of paper dipped in glue or soaked pulp that can be moulded and dried out ready for painting.

Cornflour and 'gloop' activities can be provided in shallow trays. Very young children enjoy using this medium, holding their hands in the air and observing it fall slowly from their fingers. Children can help to prepare all these materials.

Collage

Collage can be an imaginative and creative experience for children from a very young age. Your role as the facilitator is to provide the children with a variety of materials, such as:

- different textured and patterned papers and cards
- a variety of ribbons, wool and textured thread
- pasta and beans.

You should note that there is some controversy about using food for creative activities, as some people are concerned that food is being 'wasted' in this way. Be sensitive to such views.

Remember to make sure that you provide strong glue as there is nothing more frustrating for a child than watching all the pieces fall off a collage picture on the way home!

Construction

This is often referred to as modelling from recycled materials and can be an excellent form of creative play if a variety of materials are provided. Your modelling collection could include:

- kitchen roll centres (avoid toilet rolls as they can contain bacteria)
- cereal and food boxes
- circular cheese boxes (good for wheels!)
- large and small cardboard boxes such as egg boxes
- a variety of packaging waste such as cellophane, tissue, etc.

Many manufacturers will provide off-cuts of materials to schools, nurseries and playgroups at no charge.

Case study:
Supporting a construction activity

Catherine, aged four, has decided to make a police car. She is inspired by a visit to the nursery from a policeman the day before. Sophie, her key worker, discusses the visit and encourages Catherine to describe the police car she sat in. Catherine picks up a tissue box and then proceeds to look for some wheels. Sophie sees that she is having difficulty finding anything she wants in the 'junk' box. She finds some empty circular cheese boxes in the store room and gives them to Catherine; she also finds some large paper fasteners and shows Catherine how she could fix them onto the tissue box so that the wheels move around. Catherine then paints the car in white and blue. She places a piece of red cellophane on the top of the car to represent the light. Sophie praises Catherine, who proudly shows the car to her father when he collects her from nursery.

1. How does Sophie stimulate Catherine's imagination?

2. How are the materials chosen?

3. How does Sophie support Catherine without dominating the activity?

The lists below give a number of creative activities that are suitable for certain ages. You can easily add to these lists yourself.

0–3 years

Creative activities and experiences linked to a child's development.

A child learns through senses and movement.

A child can enjoy:

- finger paint
- crayons and non-toxic felt pens
- play dough
- water play (carefully supervised)
- sand.

A child will become easily frustrated if a task is too difficult.

Manipulative skills are developing.

3–5 years

A child can enjoy creative activities using:

- wet and dry sand
- water — to encourage investigation
- a variety of pens and paints for painting activities, cutting and sticking
- construction materials
- clay and dough.

A child will enjoy exploring different materials.

Manipulative skills are developing.

6–7 years

Creative activities will be influenced by Key Stage 1 requirements of the National Curriculum. This starts at the end of the Foundation Stage.

A child will use creativity to learn about other topics.

A child is able to learn specific creative skills and follow instructions.

A child's concentration span and manipulative skills are developed.

Best practice checklist: Encouraging creative development

✓ Encourage role play in the role-play corner and outside

✓ Provide a variety of dressing-up clothes and role-play equipment

✓ Provide a wide range of media

✓ Provide a balance of activities which do/do not involve paint

✓ Observe sound in the environment

✓ Display finished work attractively, using work by all the children

✓ Do not take work from children if they do not want you to have it; ask them to do two – one for you and one for them

✓ Play music – use instruments from a variety of cultures

✓ Sing songs from different cultures, in different languages and with or without accompaniment

Unplanned learning opportunities are essential if you are going to encourage children to extend their own learning and challenge their own thinking. You need to understand how to encourage free-flow imaginative play with minimal intervention.

If you allow children to play freely, they will be building up a strong base for more structured learning at a later stage. Free-flow imaginative play is usually child initiated and sometimes unplanned. For example, a group of children may turn the outside shed into a cake shop and become completely absorbed in their imaginative game.

To encourage free-flow imaginative play you will need to:

● allow time

● allow space

● ensure other children are involved as appropriate

● ensure that the play is calm

● ensure the children can return to their imaginative world at another time

● occasionally intervene if play becomes too boisterous or could be added to in some way.

Child-initiated imaginative play can occur using:

● small-world play such as Lego
● play dough

● dolls/puppets
● dressing-up clothes

● sand and water
● large equipment.

Provide plenty of open-ended objects that will encourage the children's imagination and challenge their thinking, such as large pieces of material and cardboard boxes.

Functional Skills English: Speaking, listening and communication

When holding a discussion it is important that you prepare for it. You need to have planned your ideas and views before the discussion so that you can present your view clearly and keep the discussion going.

Skills builder

It is sometimes challenging and a little daunting just to place materials out for children to use in any way they want. However, this is important in order to support their creative development and independence in their play.

To develop this area in your setting you could observe how the area is used. Make notes and then discuss with your supervisor what is successful and what sort of materials you think are useful to offer to the children for open-ended play.

You could also take photographs of the children engaged in open-ended play and talk to them about what they enjoy using.

There are many different objects that children can safely explore. A child's creative development can be supported through well-displayed objects. You can consider:

- varied textures as backgrounds
- cardboard boxes to create different levels
- children's work labelled with their names
- photographs/pictures
- draped cloths as backgrounds
- ideas for themed displays.

Objects can stimulate:

- an understanding or interest in new topics
- an awareness of the differences, similarities and relationships between objects
- an ability to discuss objects with adults and peers
- the five senses.

Objects can also extend children's understanding.

It is important to involve children in displaying objects. The children's role could be to:

- collect objects
- add to the display
- examine and question the display
- learn to care for the objects.

When you display objects of interest for children it should be done in a way that stimulates the children to explore and question. Consider the examples of displays for the different age groups in Table 3.

Table 3: Using displays to stimulate children

Age group	Display	Stimulation
0–3 years	• Treasure basket using natural objects placed on the floor for a baby to explore sitting up, e.g. wooden spoon, sieve whisk, etc.	• Touch, taste, smell, sight, sound through exploration • Fine manipulative skills
4–7 years	• Seaside items such as shells, seaweed, driftwood, etc. on a low table with printed simple questions and photographs	• Discussion, further interest and research, recall, exploration, questioning
8–12 years	• African clothing on walls with photos and explanations, basket of hats and jewellery to try on	• Discussion, further interest • Geographical awareness, research, understanding of other cultures
13–16 years	• Spanish food displayed on a table with instructions and invitations to try	• Taste, smell, understanding of other cultures, geographical awareness, research, reading, Spanish visit, discussion, debate, understanding language

Functional Skills English: Writing

Look around your room and focus on the displays. You could write a short report that explains how the display stimulates the children to explore and question. You could take some photographs of the display and include it in your explanation.

Using clear language

When encouraging the children's creative development in your setting through play you will need to know how to use:

● open-ended questions

● language to extend learning.

An effective way for you to learn these skills is to observe how your more experienced colleagues use the right language to encourage communication.

The Practical Guidance for the EYFS states that adults should 'provide time and relaxed opportunities for children to develop spoken language through sustained conversations between children and adults' (Practical Guidance for the EYFS, page 40).

Open-ended questions

Open-ended questions encourage children to respond in their own way and develop their own ideas. Open-ended questions start with 'why', 'how', 'which', 'what' and 'when'.

Consider the following questions:

- Do you like that hat?

- Do you have a favourite teddy?

- Are you coming to join us?

You will notice that all the questions can be answered with 'yes' or 'no', which makes it difficult to extend communication further.

Consider how the questions could be asked differently to encourage more conversation:

- Why do you like that hat?

- Tell me about your favourite teddy.

- When do you think you are coming to join us?

When discussing a child's painting with the child, a useful and respectful open-ended question to use is: 'Tell me about your painting'. Sometimes a long and informative dialogue can follow and the child will feel valued that they are being listened to.

Language to extend learning

One of your main roles is to encourage children to explore and investigate in their play and really develop what they are learning. The opportunities you have will be sometimes planned and sometimes spontaneous. New vocabulary is often better used in context. When children absorb new words they will naturally extend the number of words they are able to use.

- When children hear a word in context they are more likely to use it appropriately.

- Children usually learn new words through play experiences rather than formal learning.

- Books are a useful way to introduce new words to children.

- Open-ended questions are a way of extending a child's vocabulary if not too difficult.

- Activities are also a useful way of extending children's language.

- Mathematical language can be extended through play activities.

Children love to question in order to learn. Group times are a great time to encourage children to ask questions, for example:

- talking about a musical instrument

- talking about a new story

- looking at an interesting photograph

- talking to an interesting visitor

- looking at an object, such as a dead wasp's nest.

This is a great painting!

Using encouragement and praise

Everyone needs praise in order to feel confident, and a child is no different. To develop into a confident adult, children need to be praised when they have achieved something. You can support their creative development by:

● praising and acknowledging the achievements of each child

● encouraging children to recognise their own achievements.

You have an important role to play in creating a positive environment for children in your care in order to fulfil their creative potential. When children are praised and encouraged their self-esteem rises, and they take more responsibility for themselves and their environment. They relate better to other children and adults.

Here are some ways you can create a positive creative environment.

● Display children's work in a celebratory way, taking care to mount work carefully and label it appropriately. Do not be tempted to cut into the work to suit your display! To show respect for the work means to display it all.

● Draw attention to these displays in group times and by sharing them with parents. Children might even like to talk about their work to others.

● Give children stickers or badges for effort. This will be recognised by other adults and children as a sign of a positive achievement.

● Praise children appropriately without attaching any conditions. Do not say, for example, 'Well done, Sam, you have washed your hands. Now make sure you always do that.' This will make Sam feel that some of the praise has been taken away. His self-esteem could be affected or he may feel it is not worth washing his hands properly again.

● Praise children for attempting a task even if they do not fully succeed. Children who try to squeeze their own paint but spill a little are more likely to develop the skill if they are praised for their effort and the spillage is ignored.

Be able to evaluate your own contribution to children's creative development

Evaluation of your working practice is evidence that you are keen to develop professionally and are committed to your role in supporting children. There are many different ways to evaluate your practice, both formally and informally.

Link Reread SHC 22 on personal development before reading on.

Professional development:
opportunities to learn more about
your professional role through
training programmes or courses,
seminars, information days,
conferences, exhibitions, study
time, updating through reading, etc.

Over to You

You can find out about these
opportunities through your local
authority website or websites
such as Nursery World at
www.nurseryworld.co.uk.

Functional Skills ICT: Finding and selecting information

You could use search engines on the
internet to search for professional
development opportunities in your
area. You could discuss your findings
with your tutor or supervisor.

Reviewing your own working practice

You need to be able to see how your own practice has contributed to children's creative development. You will already be aware that working with children is a highly responsible profession. You are required to show great sensitivity to the needs of children and their parents or carers. In order to do this, you must be able to be very honest with yourself and to examine what you do and how you do it; you cannot always rely on other people to give you feedback. It is up to you to be able to recognise where you need to improve or develop and to ask for help directly or do something about it yourself.

We all have to accept that occasionally we will get negative as well as positive feedback in our work. In addition, the way we receive feedback may not always be constructive. Positive feedback is, of course, always welcome and it can support you in identifying ways in which you can progress further.

You may identify a particular skill with regards to supporting children's creative development. Perhaps you have creative ideas that you can share; perhaps you have a gift for bringing a story 'alive' or for being patient with children that others find 'difficult' or 'challenging'. These skills can be extended for your **professional development** and for the benefit of the children and your colleagues.

What is important is that you take time to think about the feedback you have been given. As you learn to take more responsibility for your own development, you may identify those areas of supporting children's creative development in which you need to improve.

You should also receive a regular appraisal in your role as an employee. This will give you the opportunity to discuss your strengths and weaknesses in a confidential and supportive atmosphere. It is essential for you and your supervisor to be honest. You will have the chance to set targets and decide how these are going to be monitored. In some settings an appraisal is linked to your salary. Table 4 shows a professional development plan for an early years worker, focusing on creative development.

Table 4: A professional development plan

Objective	Measurement	Delivery date	Self-appraisal	Manager appraisal
Attend EYFS training on encouraging children to make connections	Attendance confirmed by training provider	December this year		
Attend training on developing a challenging outdoor environment	Attendance confirmed by training provider	October this year		
Visit another setting to observe how children are encouraged to initiate their own learning	Write report on visit	December this year		

You could also observe a colleague supporting an area of children's creative development that you are interested in such as:

● open-ended questioning

● leading a creative activity such as music

● mounting a display with children.

Observing a colleague putting up a display with the children

Adapting your practice to individual children

You will need to develop your practice to ensure that decision making and **active involvement** are an important part of each child's social and emotional development, as they will gain confidence in their own skills and abilities to make choices. If an individual child feels confident making choices then their creative development will be effectively supported.

You should, wherever possible, ensure that children have an element of individual choice in most creative activities and experiences that you provide. This could include deciding where they may plant some sunflower seeds or where they may listen to a story in the outside environment.

Table 5 shows ways in which different age groups can be involved in making decisions about their environment.

Key term

Active involvement: when a child has a say in what happens in their environment by saying what they want and by helping to make things happen (where this can be done safely)

Over to You

Observe how individual children in your setting are encouraged to make choices in their learning. Are there any more decisions that they could be involved in?

Table 5: Involving children in decision making

Age group	How children can be involved
0–3 years	• choosing play materials • deciding where to play • helping to put toys out, e.g. such as putting soft toys in an area of their choice • selecting crayons to use • deciding who to play with • asking questions • solving problems
4–7 years	• selecting activities • helping to plan a display • helping to decide agreements for the environment such as where equipment is placed • choosing books for the book area from the library • selecting paper, etc. to use • designing a play area such as a wild garden

It is important to remember that children need guidance when making decisions, and that they should know that it is okay to make mistakes.

A secure and comfortable environment is essential for a child with additional and special needs. You will need to be aware of the additional or special needs of the children in your care in order to help to provide them with appropriate care and education to ensure their creative development. Here are some examples of what you can provide to ensure a child with additional or special needs can be supported safely in their creative development.

Visual impairment

- Space to move safely
- Padded corners
- Stable furniture
- Tactile equipment and activities
- Less frequent change to environment
- Fluorescent tape on steps, etc.
- Positive images of visually-impaired people

Dyslexia

- Areas for quiet work
- More time to complete certain activities
- Support in reading and writing
- Clear but brief instructions
- Praise and reward
- Coloured gels to highlight text sometimes needed to read print
- Activities to promote coordination and spatial awareness
- Positive images of people with dyslexia

Wheelchair use

- Ramps

- Wide entrance and exits

- Tables and surfaces at right height

- Toys and equipment at right level

- Positive images of wheelchair users

Hearing impairment

- Quiet areas to work in pairs

- Special audio equipment

- Appropriate acoustics

- Positive images of hearing-impaired people

You can recognise signs of insecurity and anxiety and provide children with reassurance when they are participating in creative development. Such signs may include:

- unwillingness to eat or drink

- unwillingness to join in activities

- unusually subdued behaviour

- unwillingness to leave one adult

- tearfulness.

When you are reassuring and comforting children remember to:

- remain calm
- show respect
- provide comfort
- provide reassurance
- be sensitive
- be honest.

Functional Skills ICT: Developing, presenting and communicating information

You could design a short information booklet all about creative play for people working with children. You could include a summary of all the information you have learnt about creative play and include some suitable activities for children of different ages. Think carefully about your layout and make sure that your writing is suitable for the audience.

Check your knowledge

1. What makes up children's creative development?

2. What do children do when they are at the stage of solitary play?

3. Which framework is Creative Development part of?

4. Why are hats important in role play?

5. Name two creative activities that a 0- to 3-year-old could enjoy.

6. Children love to question in order to learn. Group times are a great time to encourage children to ask questions. Give an example.

7. What do children need when making decisions?

8. If you are asking a child about the content of their painting, what phrase can you start your sentence with to encourage them to talk?

My name is Josh and I am currently studying for a level 2 childcare qualification. I was a bit nervous at first because I thought that I would have to be artistic to support the children's creative development. I was useless at drawing at school and thought that I would have to draw things for the children! However, I have found that creative development is all about ensuring that the children are encouraged to think about what they are doing and solve problems. I am now learning how to challenge them by asking open-ended questions. I really enjoy it. Of course I have to plan activities using paint or crayons but the children take the lead and I love the end results and displaying their work with them.

Viewpoint

Child-initiated learning in the Early Years Foundation Stage (EYFS) can be seen by some adults as a way of indulging children. Some adults feel that children are too young to know what they want to play. It is also felt that children don't really learn through creative activities such as sand and water play and that their real learning starts when they go to primary school.

Ask the expert

Q I would really like to set up a role-play area that follows the interests of the children and develops their imagination. Can you give some advice as to how I can do this with the equipment that we have.

A While I don't know what you have in your setting, the best thing that you can do is to involve the children. For example, if they are interested in pirates, ask them what they would like to see. You can easily make items from things that you have such as boxes and adult clothes to dress up in. Perhaps you can ask parents for props too.

Glossary

Active involvement: when a child has a say in what happens in their environment by saying what they want and by helping to make things happen (where this can be done safely)

Active listening: showing that you understand through eye contact, body language and verbal responses

Activity: a practical or creative task that the children carry out

Allergen (or trigger): a substance that causes an allergic reaction

Alliteration: words that begin with the same sound

Anaphylactic shock: a severe allergic reaction by the body to an allergen

Appraisal: a process that allows you and your line manager to reflect on your performance and set targets to continue to develop, often as an aspect of 'performance management'

Barriers: issues or practical matters that are stopping people from working together effectively

Barrier to communication: something that means that communication cannot be effective

Belief: an opinion firmly held

Bilingual: able to speak two languages

CAF: the Common Assessment Framework, which provides an agreed strategy for assessing children's needs and working with the family where possible

Challenge: a demanding task or situation

Child abuse: harm or the likelihood of harm from physical, emotional or sexual abuse, neglect and failure to thrive not based on illness, or bullying and harassment

Child Concern Model: a model setting out shared definitions, guidelines on assessment and referral, etc. for professionals working together with vulnerable children

ChildLine: a 24-hour free phone service for children to contact if they are in danger or risk of harm from anyone

Child protection: action taken to protect a child when there is a reasonable belief that they are at risk of significant harm

Chronic: persisting for a long time or constantly recurring

Closed fracture: a fracture where the skin does not break

Communication: a way of exchanging information, either verbally (through speaking), in written form or non-verbally (including body language)

Confidence: feeling self-reliant enough to be able to carry out a task or activity

Confidentiality: making sure that personal information is available only to those authorised to have access

Conflict: a difference of opinion that does not appear to have a resolution

Control measure: any activity or measures put in place to control or minimise identified risks

Convulsive seizure: a seizure involving jerky, violent movements of the limbs or body

D

Disability: 'a physical or mental impairment which has a substantial and long-term adverse effect on a person's ability to perform normal day-to-day activities' (The Disability Discrimination Act 1995)

Disclosure of abuse: when a child tells you or implies to you that he or she has been abused

Discrimination: treating someone less or more favourably than other people, because they or their family are seen as belonging to a particular group in society

Dislocation: the separation of a bone from a joint

Diversity: differences between individuals and groups of people

E

Effective communication: communication in which the right message is both sent and received

Equal concern: taking as much care to promote the opportunities and progress of one child as you do for any other child

Equality of opportunity: having opportunities to achieve and flourish which are as good as the opportunities available to others

Expanding: acknowledging what a child has said, but saying it in a more complex way

F

Factual report: a report that gives information, such as an accident report

Family file: a file of information that parents compile and updates about their children and the family as a whole

Fracture: a break in a bone

G

Greenstick fracture: a fracture that does not break the full bone

H

Hazard: something that has the potential to cause harm

Health and safety requirements: the laws governing safety in your country

Heuristic play: a form of exploratory or discovery play using natural materials

Holistic: dealing with the whole person, rather than just one aspect of them

Holistic development: looking at all aspects of a child's development

Hyperglycaemia: when the body has too much sugar and not enough insulin

Hypoglycaemia: when the body has too much insulin and not enough sugar

I

Imaginative play: pretending or acting, either alone or in a group

Inclusion: the process of identifying, understanding and breaking down barriers to participation and belonging

Incubation period: the time before someone shows signs of an illness after catching it

Induction: an introduction to the workplace, other staff, policies and so on for a new member of a team or company

Infection control: rules and advice for practice aimed at preventing the spread of disease

Integrated working: different services joining together to offer more effective care for children and young people, such as Children's Centres

J

Job description: a description of the tasks you are required to do in a job

L

Leisure: time spent in, or free for, relaxation or enjoyment

Likelihood: the probability of something actually happening e.g. harm from a hazard

Linguistic stage: the stage of communication after recognizable words appear

M

Medical model of disability: a traditional view of disability as a sickness, seeing the disabled person as the problem

Meningococcal septicaemia: a type of blood poisoning that is caused by the same type of bacteria that cause the most common form of bacterial meningitis

Minor injuries unit: units, usually attached to a hospital, which treat straightforward injures such as cuts, foreign bodies in noses, eyes and ears and simple fractures

Multi-agency working: different services working together to meet children's and young people's needs, such as educational psychology services or a behavioural support team

Multilingual: speaking more than two languages

N

Named person: a senior member of staff with responsibility for safeguarding, including contacting social services if there is concern about the welfare of a child

Nutrition: food or nourishment that all children and young people need to grow and be healthy

O

Obesity: the state of being seriously overweight, to a degree that can have serious effects on health

Open-ended question: a question that starts with a word such as 'What', 'How' or 'Why', that encourages dialogue rather than a one-word response

Open fracture: a fracture where there is an open wound

P

Person specification: an outline of the skills and attributes needed by an individual for a job

Phonemic awareness: recognizing different sounds in words

Play: engage in games or other activities for enjoyment rather than for a serious or practical purpose

Positive environment: an environment that supports every child and young person's learning and development in a challenging but achievable way

Positive images: images showing people who are sometimes discriminated against doing things and taking on roles that go against stereotypes

Positive relationships: relationships that benefit children and young people and their ability to participate in and benefit from a setting

Predisposition: a natural tendency

Prejudice: the view that some people are inferior to other human beings, and of less worth and significance

Pre-linguistic stage: the stage of communication before recognizable words appear

Professional development: opportunities to learn more about your professional role through training programmes or courses, seminars, information days, conferences, exhibitions, study time, updating through reading, etc.

R

Rating: a number given to show the seriousness and level of risk; the higher the number, the more significant the risk

Recasting: repeating back to a child something that they have said or read in a more accurate form

Referral: when details are sent, with permission, to another setting, multi-agency panel or professional to help support the child or young person's needs

Reflection: giving due thought and consideration to something you have said or done

Resilience: being able to cope with a variety of situations

Respect: showing that you value other adults' and children's opinions and views

Risk: (1) a situation involving exposure to danger (2) the outcome or likely impact of the hazard associated with an activity

S

Safeguarding: promoting children's welfare and putting measures in place to improve children's safety and prevent abuse

Self-esteem: feeling worthwhile and respected as an individual

SENCO: Special Educational Needs Co-ordinator

Sign of illness: something you can see that suggests a child is ill or injured

Social model of disability: a progressive model recognising that discrimination against disabled people is created by society

Statementing: assessing a child's special educational needs and setting them out in a 'statement'

Stereotypes: assumptions (usually inaccurate) that, because a person is part of a particular group, that individual will have certain characteristics, have the same needs as all other members of that group, or will behave in a particular way

Sudden infant death syndrome: the death of a seemingly healthy baby in its sleep

Symptom: an observable change in the body that indicates disease or illness

T

Transition: a change that takes place in a child's or young person's life

W

Walk-in centres: NHS centres providing 24-hour access to a doctor for illnesses and other health problems

Whistle blowing: passing on information about the behaviour of colleagues or managers in your setting

Working in partnership: different services and individuals working together to meet the needs of children and young people

Z

Zone of proximal development (ZPD): the difference between what a child can do with help and what he or she can do without help

List of Weblinks

SHC 21

www.dcsf.gov.uk/everychildmatters/
www.RNID.org.uk
www.asli.org.uk/default.aspx
www.RNIB.org.uk
www.tda.gov.uk
www.education.gov.uk

TDA 2.1

www.rospa.org.uk
www.winstonswish.org.uk

TDA 2.2

www.bbc.co.uk
www.cpinfo.org.uk
www.ci-ni.org.uk
www.childreninwales.org.uk
www.childpolicyinfo.childreninscotland.org.uk
www.dfe.gov.uk/everychildmatters/
    safeguardingandsocialcare/
www.plymouth.gov.uk/safeguarding_children_in_
    cyber_world.pdf
www.childline.org.uk
www.kidscape.org.uk
www.bullying.co.uk
www.dcsf.gov.uk/byronreview/
www.plymouth.gov.uk/safeguarding_children_in_
    cyber_world.pdf
www.ofsted.gov.uk/Ofsted-home/About-us/Contact-us/
    Safeguarding-children-Ofsted-s-whistleblower-hotline

MU 2.4

www.hse.gov.uk/
www.capt.org.uk/links/default.htm
www.capt.org.uk/activity/default.htm
www.hse.gov.uk/schooltrips/tenquestions.htm
www.hse.gov.uk/services/education/index.htm
www.hse.gov.uk/pubns/ais23.pdf

MU 2.8

www.education.org.uk
http://nationalstrategies.standards.dcsf.gov.uk/
    node/151379
www.schoolfoodtrust.org.uk

MU 2.9

www.dcsf.gov.uk/everychildmatters/
www.dcsf.gov.uk/everychildmatters/
    healthandwellbeing/ahdc/earlysupport/home
www.mosaic-ed.com
www.nas.org.uk
www.peep.org.uk
www.portage.co.uk
http://childrenfirstaid.redcross.org.uk/

PEFAP 001

www.eatwell.gov.uk/healthissues/foodintolerance/
    foodintolerancetypes/peanutallergy/
http://fsid.org.uk/Document.Doc?id=25

MPII002

www.cks.nhs.uk/patient_information_leaflet/poisoning

TDA 2.7

www.nya.org.uk/hearbyright
www.ukyouthparliament.org.uk

TDA 2.15

www.equalityhumanrights.com
www.direct.gov.uk/en/CaringForSomeone/
    CaringForADisabledChild/DG_10027494
www.portage.org.uk
www.makaton.org

TDA 2.16

www.unicef.org

TDA 2.14

www.schoolfoodtrust.org.uk
www.nutrition.org.uk
www.eatwell.gov.uk
www.healthystart.nhs.uk
www.bbc.co.uk/health/treatments/healthy_living/
    nutrition/
www.cwt.org.uk
www.healthyschools.gov.uk
www.ncb.org.uk

OP2.17

www.education.gov.uk
www.nurseryworld.co.uk

Index

DO-WATCH-
LISTEN-SAY

The Autism Institute, under the directorship of Kathleen Ann Quill, provides consultation, professional development, and training to educators serving children with autism. For more information, please contact autism@shore.net.

DO-WATCH-
LISTEN-SAY

Social and Communication Intervention
for Children with Autism

by

Kathleen Ann Quill, Ed.D.

with invited contributions from

Kathleen Norton Bracken
Maria E. Fair
Julie Ann Fiore

The Autism Institute
Essex, Massachusetts

·P A U L·H·
BROOKES
PUBLISHING C<u>O</u>

Baltimore • London • Toronto • Sydney

Paul H. Brookes Publishing Co.
Post Office Box 10624
Baltimore, Maryland 21285-0624

www.brookespublishing.com

Typeset by Barton Matheson Willse & Worthington, Baltimore, Maryland.
Manufactured in the United States of America by
Versa Press, East Peoria, Illinois.

All examples in this book are composites. Any similarity to actual individuals or
circumstances is coincidental, and no implications should be inferred.

Library of Congress Cataloging-in-Publication Data

Quill, Kathleen Ann, 1952–
    Do-watch-listen-say : social and communication intervention for
children with autism / by Kathleen Ann Quill ; with invited contributors.
        p.   cm.
    Includes bibliographical references and index.
    ISBN 1-55766-453-6
    1. Autistic children—Rehabilitation.   2. Autistic children—Education.   I. Title.

RJ506.A9 Q55 2000
618.92'898203—dc21

                                                                99-086525

British Library Cataloguing in Publication data are available from the British Library.

Contents

Preface

Autism is a disorder of social, communicative, and repetitive behaviors. Because impaired social and communication development are the defining symptoms of autism, the assessment and treatment of these skills should be an intervention priority. The purpose of *DO-WATCH-LISTEN-SAY: Social and Communication Intervention for Children with Autism* is to provide intervention guidelines that specifically address social and communication skills. It is an attempt to guide the thinking of educators, clinicians, and parents who are urgently working to bring out the best social and communication skills in their children.

Children with autism display a unique array of behaviors that are perplexing and seem inconsistent with what is understood about child development. It is generally assumed, particularly in education, that all children follow a similar developmental path. Yet, children with autism display patterns of social and communication development that seem to follow a different path. These developmental differences were incorporated into the design of this assessment and intervention guide.

Social and communication skills are complex and dynamic; therefore, intervention to promote these skills must be equally dynamic. The goal of *DO-WATCH-LISTEN-SAY* is to explore creative ways to assess and support the acquisition of these skills while maintaining objectivity and accountability. The book is divided into five major areas: perspectives on autism, assessment of social and communication skills, methodology, curriculum guidelines, and resources.

Chapters 1 and 2 discuss the developmental characteristics of autism. A thorough review of the literature acquaints the reader with relevant findings on the relationships among cognition, communication, and social and ritualistic behavior in autism. Behaviors are described through vignettes that shed light on the children's learning perspectives. This understanding is necessary to effectively use the assessment and intervention guidelines that follow.

Chapter 3 includes the Assessment of Social and Communication Skills for Children with Autism. The purpose of the assessment is to provide a comprehensive profile of a child's functional, social, and communication skills. The assessment is designed as a set of questionnaires and checklists that can be completed through interview, observation, or direct sampling. It is designed to assist in the development of educational goals and objectives. The reader is provided with detailed guidelines for using the assessment, as well as a glossary of terms to assist in its completion and use.

Chapters 4 and 5 describe the continuum of intervention options to build social and communication skills. The reader is given a framework for systematically planning intervention across multiple settings. An eclectic approach is described that combines best practices in contemporary behaviorism and developmental approaches. Emphasis is given to the importance of systematically applying behavioral principles while building skills within the context of typical social experiences and developmental age–appropriate environments. This is followed by a detailed description of various strategies that can enhance the acquisition of social and communication skills. The strategies are classified as organizational supports, social supports, visually cued instruction, and augmentative and alternative communication (AAC) supports.

The final three chapters describe curricular activities to build the skills addressed in the assessment. Each activity sheet corresponds with a subskill listed in the assessment tool's checklists. The chapters list specific behavioral objectives, fun activities, and suggestions to enhance the acquisition and generalization of target skills. Chapter 6 offers detailed and creative suggestions to build nonverbal social interaction, imitation, and organization. Chapter 7 describes activities to enhance solitary play, social play, and group skills. The reader is also given guidelines for planning social intervention in the community. Chapter 8 provides a comprehensive set of suggestions for building functional communication skills, socioemotional skills, and conversational skills. Each of these three chapters includes data collection forms that can be used for purposes of ongoing accountability and program review.

The curriculum is geared toward young children, although the principles and practices can be applied to all children with autism. The assessment and intervention guide is designed for children with a range of communication abilities, including children who use AAC systems. The activities and strategies can be implemented at home and school.

The book concludes with a detailed Resources section. The resource lists are comprehensive but not exhaustive. Included are formal assessments, augmentative and alternative communication devices, children's books, computer software, children's music, toys, distributors, web sites, and recommended readings.

My colleagues and I struggled with the book because the emotional complexity of relationships, including the relationships that we have formed with children with autism over the years, is not adequately revealed within the content. The importance of relationships in optimizing social and communication development must be inferred, and I hope that this cardinal rule is not forgotten. It is important to appreciate the complexity and richness of children with autism.

There have been many times over the past few years when I had serious doubts about the outcome of this book. A social and communication skills guide seems to minimize the complexity and richness of these developmental areas. There is a significant need for intervention guidelines, but I hope that the content of this book will not be applied too rigidly to the children whom it is intended to help.

It is my hope that *DO-WATCH-LISTEN-SAY* expands and refines your approach to intervention and that these ideas interface with other treatment options available for children with autism. It is important that this assessment and curriculum be viewed as a set of guidelines and not a "must-do" dogma. Please use this information flexibly, and let intuition lead your efforts. If this is done for the children, I will feel satisfied with this finished product.

Kathleen Ann Quill

Acknowledgments

I am grateful to many people who offered creative ideas and support during the preparation of this book. *DO-WATCH-LISTEN-SAY* began 3 years ago when a group of dedicated teachers and speech-language pathologists joined me for monthly discussions about curriculum for children with autism. Their enthusiasm and search for intervention guidelines prompted the development of this book. Many of their curricular ideas are embedded within the book. I thank Wanda Ashby, Mary Channell, Sue Constable, Allyson Foster-Poole, Catherine Giles, Gen Gootkind, Cindy Grinnell, Fran Hinchey, Cheryle Lynch, Ann McCarthy, Lynn McCready, Maureen Michaud, Jocelyn Moore, Joy Pencz, Suzanne Rosenberg, and Susan Shea. There were many colleagues who provided feedback in the design of the assessment. Thanks goes to Nancy Dalrymple, Brenda Smith Myles, Abby Stern, and Joanne Weaver for their help. I especially thank Terry Johnson, who allowed us to include Mayer-Johnson Co.'s Picture Communication Symbols in the book. These symbols have been a tremendous help to children with autism. Words cannot express my gratitude to Lisa Benson at Paul H. Brookes Publishing Co. In moments of high stress, a telephone call to Lisa gave me instant relief and a few laughs. I am honored that Brookes Publishing agreed to work with me on this project. Family and friends kept Kathleen, Maria, Julie, and me going through the setbacks, worries, and accomplishments. Thank you Sean, Steve, and Frank. I especially thank Julie for joining the project in its last stages to pick up many pieces. Kathleen, as a speech-language pathologist, Maria, as an early childhood educator, and Julie, as an early intervention specialist, helped significantly with Chapters 3, 6, 7, and 8. Finally, I am most grateful to the children with autism who touch my life every day and teach me so much about love, fear, and the human spirit. If this book makes a difference in the life of one child, then the effort has been worthwhile.

chapter 1

The Complexity of Autism

Kathleen Ann Quill

Autism is characterized by a triad of impairments in the areas of socialization, communication, and ritualistic behavior (American Psychiatric Association, 1994). Within the spectrum of autism disorders, there are different subgroups with various developmental profiles (Bristol et al., 1996; Szatmari, 1992; Wing & Attwood, 1987). Because autism is not a singular disorder, it is unlikely that one intervention approach will benefit all subgroups equally. In order to develop a range of intervention strategies, an understanding of this complex developmental disorder is necessary.

The following cases of children diagnosed with autism highlight the diversity of the disorder. These examples show how socialization, communication, and ritualistic behavior vary significantly among children with autism.

Paul is an anxious 4-year-old child who has many fears and phobias. His language development has followed normal milestones in terms of vocabulary and sentence complexity. Since toddlerhood, he has been fascinated with letters of the alphabet and numbers. He runs to the television for all commercials. He collects and carries toys—always blue—in sets of three. He enjoys solitary play and has always been adept with constructive toys and puzzles. He observes peers playing but rarely interacts with them. Paul's parents report that it is difficult to engage their son in various topics of conversation. He only wants to talk about the alphabet, numbers, and his many fears, and he does so incessantly.

Matty is 4 years old and a very active child. His language is delayed and he currently speaks in one- or two-word phrases, although he can recite segments from his favorite Disney videos. His play consists of lining up cars, trains, and blocks. He enjoys books and computers. He has frequent tantrums, particularly when his activity is interrupted or there is a change in his routine. He shows no interest in peers.

Andrew is 4 years old and very self-absorbed. He is nonverbal, and his only vocalizations are protests and crying. He pulls and pushes adults to make basic re-

quests, or he independently gets what he needs. He occupies his time by playing with ribbons, string, and any object that twirls. He has difficulty sleeping through the night and is a very picky eater. He runs away and covers his ears in the presence of other children.

It is clear that each child displays the social, communication, and ritualistic behaviors associated with autism, although in quite diverse ways. The severity of the social and communicative impairments and ritualistic behaviors varies from mild to severe. For example, Paul has mild social and communication difficulties and severe ritualistic behaviors. Matty displays relatively moderate impairments in social development, communication development, and ritualistic behaviors, while Andrew presents with severe impairments in all three areas. The profiles of these three children also reflect the diversity of the cognitive and language impairments that accompany autism.

Autism commonly occurs in association with other developmental disabilities, including a wide range of related motor, language, and cognitive impairments. Motor impairments range from motor planning difficulties to severe dyspraxia (Hanschu, 1998). Language impairments vary from mutism to atypical language acquisition or language regression (Prizant, 1996). Many children with autism also have some degree of mental retardation (Lord, 1996). Each of these developmental differences contributes to the tremendous variability observed in autism.

THE NATURE OF AUTISM

Research into the origins of the developmental disabilities that accompany autism has shown that the cognitive, language, communication, and social differences interface in complex ways. There is a growing understanding that an inability to process and understand social and affective information in a cohesive manner may lie at the core of autism (Baron-Cohen, 1995; Frith, 1989; Hobson, 1996).

- According to Frith (1989), a cluster of cognitive impairments constrains the child's ability to integrate information in a cohesive and flexible manner. A child with autism is less able to process multiple language, social, and emotional messages simultaneously. This limits the ability to organize the dynamic and unpredictable quality of typical social interaction, fragments understanding of social-communicative experiences, and contributes to rigid, repetitive, and atypical social-communicative interactions.

- According to Baron-Cohen (1995), the core impairment is in processing social information. The capacity to understand the thoughts and feelings of others, termed *theory of mind*, is believed to be profoundly impaired in children with autism. Difficulties with social perspective-taking affect the ability to understand, predict, and respond to the social, communication, and emotional behaviors of others.

- According to Hobson (1996), autism is an inability to perceive and understand emotional expressions. This limits the capacity to share attention and emotion with others. It also explains poor social attention, limited social initiations, and difficulty with social reciprocity.

Although the research views each impairment separately, it is more likely that the inability to interpret emotion, understand social perspectives, and integrate information are interrelated. These impairments underlie the social and communicative deficits in autism. The complexity and relationship of these impairments must be taken into account when developing interventions.

COGNITION IN AUTISM

Attention, information processing, and social-cognition can be impaired in children with autism. In general, difficulties with the integration of information, abstract reasoning, and cognitive flexibility have been reported (Minshew, Goldstein, Muenz, & Payton, 1992). Table 1.1 summarizes the cognitive profile observed in autism. As indicated in the table, differences have been found in attentional processes, processing strategies, and social-cognition. Each cognitive weakness lies on a continuum. The severity can be defined as the degree to which each of these cognitive processes dominates thinking and behavior.

Attention

In order to attend to others, it is necessary to feel comfortable, filter out distractions, and know what is relevant. Research has indicated that the majority of children with autism show hypersensitivities or atypical responses to sensory stimulation (O'Neill & Jones, 1997; Ornitz, 1989). Adults with autism often describe experiences of feeling overwhelmed (Barron & Barron, 1992; Grandin, 1995a; Williams, 1992). Problems with sensory processing cause distractibility, disorganization, and discomfort, and the result is a tendency to hyperfocus or be drawn to the same repetitive stimulus. Repetition is viewed, in part, as a means to create order amid chaos.

Additional research has suggested that children with autism exhibit *overselectivity*, meaning that it is difficult for them to attend to the multiple features inherent in all stimuli (Lovaas, Koegel, & Schreibman, 1979). They also have difficulty determining the most meaningful feature of a given stimulus (Frith & Baron-Cohen, 1987). They focus on fewer features or less relevant cues. As the number of cues in natural contexts increases, responses to those cues decrease (Pierce, Glad, & Schreibman, 1997). Given that learning requires attention to multiple environmental features, attentional difficulties markedly impede development, particularly in the social domain. For example, in order to understand the meaning of someone's message, it is necessary to attend simultaneously to the speaker's words, facial expression, tone of voice, and body gestures as well as the social context. If the child is preoccupied or attending to only one cue, such as someone's gestures, he will be less likely to understand the full meaning of the social message.

Other studies of attentional processes report that children with autism have difficulty shifting attention between visual and auditory stimuli (Ciesielski, Courchesne, & Elmasian, 1990; Courchesne, 1991). This impairs their ability to follow the rapid pace and complex features of social interaction. Children struggle to attend to rapidly occurring sensory, language, and social events.

Information Processing

Cognitive processing is a multilayered system in which information is analyzed, organized, stored, and remembered in complex ways. A person instantly links a new experience to a number of related past experiences. The novel information reshapes and redefines all related knowledge. For instance, a typically developing child sees a new animal. She notices all of its separate attributes through different sensory channels, listens to language information about the animal, and associates certain emotions with the animal. She links all of the separate attributes to similar features in other animals (real and imaginary), assigns

Table 1.1. Cognition in autism

Cognitive trait	Tendency	Weakness[a]
Attention	Overselectivity	Flexibility
	Focused attention	Shift attention
Perception	Visuospatial	Auditory-transient
Information processing	One piece at a time	Integration
	Concrete	Abstract
	Gestalt	Analytical
Memory	Rote	Recall
Social-cognition	Concrete	Theory of mind

[a]Characteristics exist on a continuum of severity.

meaning to her sensory perceptions, combines all of the pieces of language information to her existing body of knowledge about animals, and creates a new and revised concept of animals. In a few moments, she has a new meaning about animals, and the information is stored in an infinite number of ways. This happens unconsciously and effortlessly. Most important, because this animal concept is multilayered and connected to related experiences, there can be an infinite number of ways to recall the new experience.

The way children with autism process information sharply contrasts with the complex and fluid style of a typically developing child. Problems integrating information in meaningful and flexible ways characterize their processing style. First, overselective attention results in a tendency to process information one piece at a time. Thus, a narrow and more restricted understanding of information emerges. Second, information that is fixed in space is more easily processed than rapidly occurring events. Third, material is often stored and remembered as a whole rather than reorganized and integrated in a flexible manner. These processing constraints restrict concept development, generalization, and social-communicative interaction. For example, social interaction requires the simultaneous integration of many sensory, language, social, and affective cues. It demands flexible attention, an understanding of what is relevant, and the ability to disregard what is not pertinent.

For decades, autism has been described as a problem with understanding the meaning of experiences (Wing, 1988). Wing considered the challenges of autism to reflect impairments in one's ability to

- Assign meaning to perceptions in a multitude of ways
- Infer meaning by moving beyond what is seen or heard
- Infer meaning from the social cues of others
- Extract meaning from the emotional cues of others

Children with autism attend to specific, observable information and are less able to look beyond pure perception to assign meaning to their experiences. A propensity toward narrow and restricted conceptual understanding characterizes this learning pattern. Children with autism tend to make illogical concrete associations, especially with regard to social and emotional experiences.

Learning is an active process whereby experiences are assimilated into complex networks of meaning. In the absence of understanding the meaning of an experience, information is merely stored as a whole, unrelated to anything else. For example, when one memorizes the Pledge of Allegiance, it is probably stored in the "American flag file" without really understanding its specific meaning. *Gestalt processing,* when information is processed and remembered as a whole, generally reflects a decreased understanding of the meaning of the parts.

When children with autism are unable to extract meaning from information in a flexible, integrated way, they are left with a series of fragmented experiences that they use in a gestalt manner (Prizant, 1982). Gestalt processing is reflected in specific learning and behavior patterns. *Echolalic speech,* or repeating what others say, and routinized conversations typify gestalt processing.

Research has found that visuospatial information is more easily processed than auditory and transient information in children with autism (Hermelin & O'Connor, 1970). The amount of time the information remains fixed in space influences the child's ability to process. Visuospatial information can be attended to as long as needed for it to make sense, while other inputs, particularly auditory ones, must be encoded instantly. Studies have indicated that children with autism perform best on intelligence test tasks such as matching, block design, object assembly, and pattern analysis (DeMyer, 1975; Harris, Handleman, & Burton, 1990; Lincoln, Courchesne, Kilman, Elmasian, & Allen, 1988; Siegel, Minshew, & Goldstein, 1996), all of which involve stimuli that remain visible at all times. In her personal account of living with autism, Grandin (1995b) termed this *visual thinking,* and she emphasized the need to rely on visual images for understanding.

Successful social and communicative interactions require one to quickly attend to and understand the meaning of fleeting visual and auditory information. The transient nature of language and nonverbal social information is more difficult for children with autism to follow and, therefore, contributes to their social and communicative impairments. They struggle to process the rapidly changing social events that are inherent in social interaction.

Finally, research into the memory capabilities of children with autism has further highlighted information-processing differences (Boucher, 1981; Boucher & Lewis, 1988; Boucher & Warrington, 1976; Prior, 1979; Sigman, Ungerer, Mundy, & Sherman, 1987). Memory is a complex process that reflects how information has been organized and stored for use. Memory tasks vary from short term (e.g., immediate repetition) to long term (e.g., accessing from all previously stored information), and it can require recognition (e.g., multiple choice) or recall (e.g., accessing information without explicit cues). Rote memory and recognition tasks remain intact in individuals with autism (Boucher, 1981; Boucher & Lewis, 1988; Boucher & Warrington, 1976; Prior, 1979; Sigman et al., 1987). Rote memory does not require flexible integration of information, and recognition tasks provide explicit retrieval cues. Because children with autism store information in a more restricted manner, their reliance on these patterns can be expected. Memory tasks that require free recall without explicit retrieval cues are more problematic. These researchers suggest that impaired recall memory contributes to the social-communicative deficit. Individuals with autism are less able to gain access to information that is relevant to the rapidly changing social context. They rely more on concrete retrieval cues to remember language information (Tager-Flusberg & Anderson, 1991) and to initiate spontaneous communication.

Social-Cognition

Typically developing children have a predisposed sensitivity to the feelings of others. An understanding of these feelings results from being able to link emotions and behaviors (Leslie & Frith, 1988). Typically developing infants begin this process of social referencing when they look for a person's reaction to objects and social events (Bruner, 1981). Through social referencing, infants try to understand the socioemotional significance of each experience. Over time, young children develop theory of mind and understand that others have intentions, thoughts, desires, and feelings that differ from their own. This ability to infer the mental states of others allows children to anticipate, comprehend, and predict the social behaviors of others (i.e., "I know what you know"). Most important, this understanding plays a significant role in social-communicative interactions. For instance, in conversation, the child needs to continually monitor what the partner knows and expects in order to make information relevant. Similarly, the child interprets meaning and intent from the verbal and nonverbal behaviors of the partner. Only with this social knowledge can children regulate and adjust their own language and social behavior in social-communicative interactions.

Numerous studies have investigated the degree to which children with autism have difficulty attributing mental states—such as intents, thoughts, and feelings—to themselves and others in order to understand social behavior. Particular deficits in the development of theory of mind have been identified in children with autism. This line of study has prompted additional insights into the core social and communication impairments of autism (see Baron-Cohen, 1995, and Baron-Cohen, Tager-Flusberg, & Cohen, 1993, for a review).

Baron-Cohen, Leslie, and Frith (1985) conducted a seminal study that suggested a specific theory of mind deficit in autism. They tested children's ability to understand different types of social events using a multipicture sequencing task. Three types of sequenced social stories were presented to the children: physical-causal (e.g., a child smiling while swinging on a swing), social-behavioral (e.g., a child crying after someone took his ice cream out of his hand), and mental state (e.g., a child looking confused after someone took his toy when he was not looking). They compared the performance of children with mental retardation and typically developing young children with children of a higher mental age who had autism. The results were striking. In contrast to the children in the control groups, who had no problems with the various social story sequences, the children with autism understood the physical-causal and social-behavioral sequences but had significant difficulty understanding the mental state sequences. Even though all of the stories entailed similar social and emotional content, the children with autism only struggled with social events that required them to take into account what someone else knows or expects in order to predict his or her behavior.

These findings have been replicated—using a variety of tasks, materials, and social events—with similar outcomes (Leslie & Frith, 1988; Perner, Frith, Leslie, & Leekam, 1989). Typically developing 4-year-old children correctly perform tasks that test theory of mind, but most children with autism with a verbal age of 8 years have difficulty with the same tasks. In addition, even when children with autism have been successfully taught theory of mind tasks, they fail to demonstrate an understanding of the concept. They are unable to generalize the concept to new tasks presented in a different format (Ozonoff & Miller, 1995). Furthermore, no measurable effect on the children's ability to develop conversational skills or use mental state terms in their speech has been found (Hadwin, Baron-Cohen, Howlin, & Hill, 1997).

Questions still remain as to whether the theory of mind deficit is a specific impairment of social-cognition. Some research suggests that this phenomenon in autism is actually a social-cognitive delay that correlates with language deficits (Perner et al., 1989) or a result of specific processing demands that impair social problem solving (Pierce et al., 1997).

Perner and colleagues (1989) demonstrated a relationship between language abilities and the acquisition of theory of mind in autism. They found that 17% of the children with autism studied were able to complete theory of mind tasks. Their success with the social-cognitive tasks correlated with higher skills in other areas of verbal cognition. Other studies showed that the children who understood theory of mind tasks demonstrated more flexible conversational skills (Eisenmajer & Prior, 1991) and more social insight (Frith, Happe, & Siddons, 1994).

Pierce, Glad, and Schriebman (1997) found that children with autism were able to answer questions regarding mental states when the task was simplified in terms of processing requirements. They found that the number of social cues influenced the children's ability to interpret social situations. In this study, children were shown videotaped social scenes for which the number of cues leading to the correct understanding of the story varied. Each short scene depicted a social interaction between two children in which an observable action occurred, such as giving a gift. The four types of social cues presented in the scene were verbal (e.g., "I like your toy"), tone of voice (e.g., speaking in an animated voice), nonverbal (e.g., smiling at a person), and nonverbal with an object (e.g., giving someone a present). Children were asked a series of questions to assess their understanding of the social situation. When compared with control groups, children with autism performed equally well on questions relating to stories containing one cue. When stories contained multiple social cues for the correct interpretation of the story, however, the children with autism performed more poorly than those in the control groups. The authors concluded that the complexity of the social environment and the number of social cues that children must simultaneously attend to strongly influence their ability to interpret the meaning of a social situation. When children with autism must simultaneously process multiple social cues within a rapidly changing environment, the attentional and processing demands are too challenging.

Finally, there is a growing recognition of impaired higher order cognitive abilities in autism. The ability to modulate continuous activity, shift problem-solving strategies, and adapt to ongoing information is problematic for children with autism in both social and nonsocial tasks (Ozonoff, 1995; Ozonoff, Pennington, & Rogers, 1991). All of the attentional, processing, and conceptual difficulties reviewed thus far either result in or are influenced by impaired higher order problem solving. Problem-solving flexibility, not IQ score, has been shown to correlate with better social understanding. Similarly, poor social understanding correlates with difficulties in flexible problem solving (Ozonoff, 1995; Russell, 1993). Higher order cognitive strategies allow for integration, inference, analysis, synthesis, creativity, negotiation, assumptions, predictions, anticipation, and clarification of information. It is precisely these skills that are so profoundly affected in the learning, social, and communication behaviors of children with autism.

CORE SKILLS FOR SOCIAL AND COMMUNICATION DEVELOPMENT

The symptoms defining social impairment in autism include "a marked impairment in the use of multiple nonverbal behaviors such as eye gaze, facial expression, and gestures to regulate social interaction"; "a lack of spontaneous seeking to share enjoyment, interests or achievements with other people (e.g., by a lack of showing, bringing, or pointing out objects of interest)"; and a "lack of social and emotional reciprocity" (American Psychiatric Association, 1994, p. 70). These symptoms characterize the nonverbal social-communicative behaviors of children with autism, and they, along with imitation deficits and atypical play behaviors, are the most important diagnostic indices of autism (Baron-Cohen, Allen, & Gillberg, 1992; Osterling & Dawson, 1994). Given that deficits in nonverbal social-communication and imitation are central to autism, an understanding of these core skills is important for planning assessment and intervention. This section describes the development of these two core skills in typically developing children and children with autism. Impairment of these skills varies significantly among children with autism. Table 1.2 summarizes their core skill challenges.

Nonverbal social-communicative and imitation skills develop quickly and naturally in typically developing children during the first 2 years of life and lay the foundation for later social, communication, and emotional development. The emergence of these core skills is influenced by a child's inborn temperament, inherent social motivation, and exploration of his social environment. Comfort level, activity level, and reaction to the physical and social worlds contribute to social motivation and social exploration. The motivation to explore the physical and social environments contributes to a growing understanding of social and communication skills.

Nonverbal Social-Communicative Interaction

During the first year of life, infants acquire the ability to use and respond to eye gaze, gestures, and facial expressions in social interactions. They develop nonverbal social-communicative skills to initiate social interactions, to engage in reciprocal turn-taking, to make basic requests, and to share interests with others. Infants also nonverbally respond

Table 1.2. Core skills in autism

Core skill	Tendency	Weakness[a]
Nonverbal interaction	Respond to others	Initiate interactions
	Eye gaze or gesture	Combine eye gaze and gesture
	Brief turn-taking	Reciprocal interaction
	Regulate others	Share with others
	Perseverative interactions	Flexible interactions
Imitation	Imitate single motor acts	Imitate a sequence of motor acts
	Exact repetition	Modified imitation

[a]Characteristics exist on a continuum of severity.

to the social initiations, requests, and comments of others. The development of nonverbal social-communicative behaviors is marked by the child's increasing capacity for social turn-taking and the ability to coordinate the use of eye gaze with gestures. These early nonverbal social-communicative behaviors are classified as reciprocal social interaction skills, joint attention skills, and behaviors to regulate others (Bruner, 1975).

Reciprocal interaction skills are social-communicative behaviors used to initiate or maintain vocal, nonverbal, or object turn-taking routines. A combination of eye gaze, gestures, facial expressions, and simple play actions is used to engage in reciprocal interactions. *Joint attention* is the coordination of attention among oneself, social partners, and an object. It involves the ability to follow another person's visual line of attention, to coordinate eye gaze and gestures with another person, and to use eye gaze and gestures to direct another person's attention to events or objects. Joint attention behaviors can be used to communicate needs and share interests (e.g., showing or bringing a toy). *Behavioral regulation* is the term used to define the use of eye gaze or gesture to coordinate attention between objects or events and social partners in order to make requests (e.g., pulling a person to or reaching for a desired object). Social turn-taking, joint attention, and behavioral regulation are central to the development of effective social-communicative reciprocity.

Relevance to Autism

The nonverbal social-communicative skills in children with autism are characterized by significant difficulty with nonverbal joint attention skills, some difficulty with social turn-taking skills, and less difficulty with nonverbal behavioral regulation skills (Mundy, Sigman, & Kasari, 1993; Mundy, Sigman, Ungerer, & Sherman, 1986; Wetherby & Prutting, 1984). These fundamental differences define impaired social reciprocity.

Shared attention is affected by the child's level of comfort with social stimulation. Although there is limited empirical research on the responses of children with autism to social stimulation, personal accounts by adults with autism (Grandin, 1995a; Williams, 1992), as well as extensive discussion by Greenspan (1995) and Greenspan and Wieder (1998), have highlighted atypical responses to environmental and social stimuli. Unusual sensitivities to sound, touch, and movement reduce the child's ability to respond to and be comfortable with social interactions.

Lewy and Dawson (1992) found that assessment of joint attention skills discriminates 80%–90% of the young children with autism from young children with other developmental disorders. The precise origin of the joint attention deficit is unclear, although it appears that this nonverbal social-communicative behavior is linked to other features of autism. Difficulty with joint attention skills may mark a child's lack of awareness that others are interested in what he perceives (Baron-Cohen, 1995). Joint attention skills may also be connected to the child's difficulty regulating and understanding the emotional cues of others (Hobson, 1989; Mundy, 1995). Impaired joint attention contributes to the atypical development of reciprocal communication (McEvoy, Rogers, & Pennington, 1993; Mundy & Sigman, 1989b), pretend play (Charman, 1997), and the ability to relate to the emotions of others (Hobson, 1996; Tomasello, 1995).

Curcio (1978) was the first to report a difference in the nonverbal communication of young children with autism. All of the children in this study used various gestures to make requests, but none of them demonstrated joint attention or gestures to share interests. Similarly, Wetherby and Prutting (1984) found that the children studied engaged in turn-taking routines and made requests for objects, actions, and social routines, but they had more difficulty initiating joint attention acts to share an awareness of an object or event with another. A third study by Mundy and colleagues (1986) entailed a more detailed analysis and found significant differences in all areas of nonverbal social-communicative interaction. Eighteen preschool children with autism were compared to control groups. The children with autism engaged in briefer turn-taking sequences than other children, and they responded less frequently to the initiations of others during social interactions. More eye contact and active responding occurred, however, during social routines such as tickling games. In addition, the requesting skills of the children with autism were comparable to those of other children when they combined eye gaze and gesture to obtain or reactivate a toy, but they made less frequent eye contact and pointed less often to objects out of reach than the other groups of children. Furthermore, consistent with previous studies, the most significant impairment identified in the children with autism was in the use of joint attention for indicating and commenting. They alternated eye gaze between an interesting object and others infrequently. Another notable finding was that they rarely showed objects or pointed to objects for the purpose of sharing their interest. Thus, even when the children were able to coordinate eye gaze, gestural communication, and turn-taking, the skills for monitoring and sharing joint interests in an object or event were lacking.

Mundy (1995) reiterated this important qualitative distinction in the social-communicative behaviors of children with autism. It was determined that they are more likely to demonstrate these behaviors when their needs are being met than when the needs of the interactive partner must be considered. For example, eye gaze and gestures may be observed when a child is being tickled, but these behaviors are less likely to be observed when he or she is required to reciprocate by tickling the other person. Studies have also distinguished the capacity of children with autism to initiate joint attention (e.g., showing, pointing) from their capacity to respond to others (e.g., looking in the direction to which another person is pointing). The children generally acquire the ability to respond to others, but self-initiated commenting remains specifically impaired (Mundy & Crowson, 1997; Wetherby, 1986).

All of these studies indicate that children with autism demonstrate nonverbal social-communicative behaviors such as eye gaze and gestures. At the same time, the studies show that the children have a reduced understanding of the various social functions served by these behaviors. Qualitative, not quantitative, measures of eye gaze, gestures, and other nonverbal social-communicative behaviors specify the nature of the impairment.

Imitation

Imitation is an important milestone in the development of cognitive and social skills. It plays a critical role in the development of symbolic thought (Piaget, 1962) and social relationships (Uzgiris, 1981). Imitation is a critical skill for the emergence of symbolic play and is necessary for sustaining social interactions. It provides children with a sense of shared experiences and enhances self-awareness (Vygotsky, 1964).

Piaget (1962) described the role of imitation in the development of symbolism, and Uzgiris (1981) described the link between imitation and social interaction. According to developmental theory, infants first show interest and motor responses when adults imitate them. The motivation to continue an interaction sustains the imitation exchanges. During the first year of life, children progress from repeating motor and vocal actions within their repertoire to imitating novel actions. By 1 year of age, children imitate social acts such as waving "bye-bye" and object use such as drinking from an empty cup. This skill contributes to their growing understanding of the physical world. Imitation also helps children understand the relationship between themselves and others in terms of shared physical, social, and emotional experiences (Ungerer, 1989). By age 2, children can imitate a sequence of novel actions, they can imitate *invisible acts* (i.e., actions that they cannot see themselves do), and they can engage in *deferred imitation* (i.e., repeat actions observed in others at an earlier time).

Relevance to Autism

Research on imitation skills in young children with autism has consistently shown impairments in both verbal and motor imitation relative to other cognitive tasks (Charman & Baron-Cohen, 1994; Dawson & Adams, 1984; Rogers & Pennington, 1991; Sigman & Ungerer, 1984). In a study of preschoolers with autism, Dawson and Adams (1984) found impaired or absent imitative abilities in the majority of children studied. They functioned at a very early stage of imitation, showing an emergent interest when adults imitated their behaviors. The children's imitation delay correlated with restricted levels of social relatedness, play, and language. Additional studies demonstrated that when adults imitate the behavior of a child with autism, an increase in social-communicative attentiveness and responsiveness, as well as exploratory play, occurs (Dawson & Adams, 1984; Dawson & Galpert, 1986; Tiegerman & Primavera, 1984). Imitating the child's toy play provides a clear and predictable response and allows the child to become the initiator of the interaction. Shared imitative play was found to provide a positive experience of shared nonverbal communication for the adults and children studied.

Given the importance that imitation skills play in later development, current treatment emphasizes teaching imitation either discretely (Lovaas, 1977) or developmentally (Dawson & Adams, 1984; Greenspan & Wieder, 1998). Some children are able to apply imitation skills to natural contexts, thus benefiting from peer modeling (Wolfberg & Schuler, 1993). Still, many children with autism show considerable variability in spontaneous imitation and the ability to apply learned imitation skills to novel contexts (Ungerer, 1989).

Libby, Powell, Messer, and Jordan (1998) studied the ability to imitate play actions in children with autism as compared with control groups. Imitation of single actions, unrelated multistep actions, and related multistep actions were studied. The children with autism could imitate single pretend play actions but experienced significant difficulty imitating multistep pretend play actions. Those who were able to imitate multistep actions did equally well with unrelated and related sequences. In contrast, the ability of children in the control groups to imitate multistep pretend actions improved when relative meaning was attached. Thus, the use of meaningful action sequences enhanced the imitation skills in the control groups but did not assist the children with autism. These findings make an important distinction between the ability to copy acts and the ability to imitate with understanding. Although children with autism were able to imitate actions, an apparent inability to understand the meaning of those actions distinguished them from other children of similar developmental levels.

SOCIAL DEVELOPMENT

Social skills represent the ability to accommodate or adapt to ongoing situations and social interactions. Unlike cognitive and language development, which are rule based, social development is constantly changing. Social interactions demand moment-to-moment integration of multiple contextual, language, social, and emotional features. Social interactions require the ability to continually monitor and adjust to the behaviors of others. Cognitive capacities, socioemotional understanding, language abilities, and prior experience all contribute to social flexibility.

Play is the fabric of childhood. It is a learning process, a social process, and an emotional process (Piaget, 1962; Vygotsky, 1964). In addition, it is an avenue for object exploration, social discovery, and self-discovery. Children use play to experiment with their growing knowledge of the world and people. Through play, children explore their bodies, toys, and objects, as well as learn from adults and peers. Play—which can be a reenactment of previous experiences, a means to try newly acquired skills, or a novel approach to both—is creative. It is the full expression of all learning, relationships, and feelings.

During solitary play, children examine the properties and functions of objects. They take on social roles from personal experiences or the world of make-believe. Through social play, children share meaningful experiences and acquire critically important social knowledge and skills. Although inherently pleasurable, play is primarily a means to link the emotions of self and others with various social roles and experiences. It has been said that the social skills of life are learned by kindergarten, and, indeed, most are acquired through play.

Social impairments are the hallmark of autism. In addition to the core social-communicative deficits discussed in the previous section, the diagnostic criteria for autism include a "lack of varied, spontaneous make-believe play or social imitative play appropriate to developmental level" and the "failure to develop peer relationships appropriate to developmental level" (American Psychiatric Association, 1994, p. 70). Children with autism represent a developmentally heterogeneous group whose acquisition of social skills is qualitatively different from other children (VanMeter, Fein, Morris, Waterhouse, & Allen, 1997). A developmental delay or slower acquisition of social skills cannot fully explain the difference between typically developing children and children with autism. Rather, there is uneven development within the social domain. Children with autism acquire some social skills out of sequence, while other social skills are absent. For example, the ability to play simple interactive games is an early developmental skill that is difficult for children with autism, yet playing games with rules is developmentally more advanced but easier for these children to acquire. Other social behaviors observed in autism, such as avoidance of eye gaze or lack of responsiveness to adults, are not observed during any stage of typical development (Wenar, Ruttenberg, Kalish-Weiss, & Wolf, 1986).

Recognizing that social development is multifaceted, this discussion of socialization in autism is limited to two key skills: solitary play and social play. Table 1.3 summarizes the social characteristics of autism. There is significant variation among children regarding the degree to which these skills are impaired.

Solitary Play

Solitary play is intrinsically motivating and exploratory and is marked by an absence of rules. Self-exploration in play is highly individualized. Infants study their body parts, toddlers run and jump, preschoolers dance and do somersaults, and older children engage in private dreams and fantasies (Singer & Singer, 1990).

Play with objects follows a more systematic progression (Garvey, 1977; Westby, 1991). The infant's play is first characterized by exploring and manipulating objects and then develops into an interest in cause-and-effect toys. Play with objects progresses from single, repetitive acts to sets of organized, predictable actions. Toddlers combine toys and objects in multiple ways and explore the relationships among object properties. Gradually, functional play involves using familiar objects in conventional ways (e.g., pushing a car, combing one's hair). By 2 years of age, symbolic play—a critical social milestone—emerges. A child's first use of symbolism in play is self-directed (e.g., feeding oneself with food props); then, there is a shift to other-directed (e.g., giving a person the telephone to talk) and object-directed (e.g., feeding a doll) play. Symbolism is also observed in the children's ability to pretend that an object or situation is something else (Leslie, 1987). Children shift away from realistic props to other means of pretending, such as *object substitution* (e.g., making a block a road), *role taking* (e.g., talking for a doll), creating absent properties (e.g., pretending the stove is hot), and inventing people and objects through language and gestures. In addition, children organize play scripts that are related to personal experiences (e.g., a bedtime routine) and later adopt different roles in their play scripts that move beyond their real-life experience (e.g., acting out roles from books and movies) (Rubin, 1980).

Table 1.3. Social characteristics of autism

Social domain	Tendency	Weakness[a]
Solitary play	Functional	Imaginative
	Perseverative	Flexible
	Contextually driven	Spontaneous
Social play	Passive or awkward	Reciprocal
	Parallel	Cooperative
Socioemotional	Perceive emotions	Infer emotional states
	Sensory sensitivities	
	Anxiety	

[a]Characteristics exist on a continuum of severity.

Relevance to Autism

The play behaviors of children with autism are particularly striking when compared with the richness of typical play development. Despite wide variability in the play behaviors of children with autism, certain qualitative characteristics appear consistently (Roeyers & van Berkalaer-Onnes, 1994; Wolfberg, 1995). The impaired development of imaginative play is a core symptom (American Psychiatric Association, 1994). Thus, the natural flexibility and creativity of play is generally lacking in children with autism. Ritualized and perseverative play routines of various forms and content are commonly observed. Self-stimulatory body rituals and the manipulation of one or more objects in a ritualistic fashion are common as well (Tiegerman & Primavera, 1984). Other object play ranges from simple, repetitive play sequences to elaborate but exact play routines such as reenactments of book, television, or movie segments (Wing & Attwood, 1987). Although these resemble mature forms of pretend play, flexibility and imagination are missing.

There are qualitative differences observed in the symbolic play of children with autism. In free play situations, children with autism display object manipulation and functional acts but minimal or no spontaneous symbolic play (Baron-Cohen, 1987; Libby et al., 1998; Mundy, Sigman, Ungerer, & Sherman, 1987). When symbolic play is present, it is generally limited to object substitution (Jarrold, Boucher, & Smith, 1993). Object substitution can be performed using the perceptual qualities of the object and other contextual cues. In contrast, other forms of symbolism (e.g., imagination) that require a child to generate pretend ideas with no external support are absent. There is some evidence that children with autism understand pretend play acts and can engage in symbolic play when given additional prompts and contextual support (Charman et al., 1997; Jarrold et al., 1993; Jarrold, Smith, Boucher, & Harris, 1994). Nevertheless, they are unable to generalize the skill to novel play contexts (Riguet, Taylor, Benaroya, & Klein, 1981).

Such studies highlight the stereotypic nature of solitary play in children with autism. This play remains repetitive and idiosyncratic and reflects an inability to shift to new play themes (Ozonoff et al., 1991). Children with autism are less able to flexibly create novel play acts and often become "stuck" in using contextually driven play behaviors.

Social Play

At each stage of play (specifically, exploratory, functional, and pretend) children engage in solitary activity prior to social activity. Typical social play development follows a natural progression. First, the child explores the environment and watches others. Functional play schemes develop during solitary play before generalizing to social play, and pretend play occurs alone before with others (Fein, 1981). Next, children engage in parallel play without social exchanges. They then create joint projects with toys but engage in limited social exchanges. Finally, as cooperative play develops, children are able to coordinate both their play activity and social behaviors with others (Howes, 1987). Peer interactions increase in complexity regarding the degree to which they involve shared interests, social behaviors, communication skills, and pretend play skills.

Earliest peer interactions focus on toys and objects. Infants give and exchange toys and intermittently observe each other's play (Vandell & Wilson, 1982). Toddlers play with peers through simple imitation games, shared attention, and exchanges of positive and negative emotions (Eckerman & Stein, 1982; Ross & Ross, 1982). Three general areas dominate peer interactions among young children: shared pretend play, reciprocal communications, and *prosocial behaviors* (verbal or motor acts done to meet the needs of others) (McCune-Nicolich, 1981).

Children use make-believe to take on roles and create imaginary situations. Shared pretend play progresses from parallel activity (e.g., two children pretending to drive a school bus) and evolves into cooperative play (e.g., one child is the bus driver while the other children are the passengers). Integrating social imitation and imaginative play is essential for this level of peer interaction.

Communication with peers is also naturally embedded into their play. Children use verbal and nonverbal means to initiate and maintain interaction as well as to respond to others. Getting their peers' attention is a primary communication skill. This skill is key to communication success in young children (Mueller & Brenner, 1977). Toddlers initiate contact through eye gaze, gestures, and physical proximity. Objects and toys are the focus of shared attention. Preschoolers elicit peer attention by looking at peers, pointing to objects, and showing objects. Although they use verbal means when interacting with adults, preschool children call their peers' names or use other verbal messages to initiate interactions less often. Nonverbal communication is more vital for initiating and sustaining peer interaction among young children (Stone, Ousely, Yoder, Hogan, & Hepburn, 1997).

Prosocial behavior is another important element of peer interactions. Examples of prosocial behavior include expressing positive attention, giving and sharing toys and materials, noting approval through words or emotion, and compromising (Hartup, 1983). Play and prosocial skills that elicit positive responses from peers are rough and tumble play, sharing, providing assistance, and giving affection (Tremblay, Strain, Hendrickson, & Shores, 1981). In addition, good eye contact, emotional response through smiles and laughter, physical proximity, and sharing are key cooperative acts that contribute to successful peer interactions (Hartup, 1983). There is a notable absence of using verbal communication skills as a primary means to receive positive peer response among young children.

Relevance to Autism

Early social behaviors of joint attention, shared object manipulation, and imitation lay the foundation for peer interactions. Unusual eye gaze, difficulty shifting attention, weak imitation skills, and ritualized object use are among the social qualities that characterize autism. As a result, the most basic peer interactions can be problematic for many children with autism. Some of them avoid peer interaction and are nonresponsive to peer overtures. Their solitary play is often accompanied by a strong resistance to others who attempt to participate in or disrupt their play rituals. Other children with autism may be led passively into peer play but do not initiate peer interactions. Still others initiate play interactions with peers but their style is idiosyncratic and awkward (Wing, 1996). Impaired communication and social understanding compound their attempts to coordinate activities with peers. Social-communicative efforts are often misinterpreted by peers, while difficulty understanding the intent of peers results in poor responses (Wolfberg, 1995). McGee, Feldman, and Morrier (1997) compared the naturally occurring social behavior of children with autism and typically developing preschool children. The researchers noted differences in the key social behaviors of proximity to peers, acknowledging the social initiations and responses of peers, and attempts to engage peers.

When a comparison was made between a group of children with autism and a group of children with mental retardation, Hauck, Fein, Waterhouse, and Feinstein (1995) found striking differences regarding the quantity and quality of peer interactions. The children with autism initiated contact one third as often as the children with mental retardation. Interactions that did occur were often routinized. This was consistent with the findings of Stone and Caro-Martinez (1990), who observed that children with autism have low rates of peer interaction and spontaneous communications in unstructured, naturalistic contexts. Both studies found that the language competencies of children with autism, along with their ability to understand emotional cues, determined their level of peer interactions. In addition, the quality of interactions with adults differed significantly from the quality of peer interactions. The researchers concluded that the predictability of an adult's interactions increased communicative effectiveness in children with autism. This contrasts with peers, who are less likely to adapt their communication style. Ferrara and Hill (1980) reported that the social responsiveness of children with autism during peer play was enhanced when they were able to predict the sequence of events. Their social behavior became disorganized when play was not predictable.

Efforts to increase peer relationships have focused on peer-mediated procedures and the use of specific peer supports (Goldstein & Strain, 1988; Roeyers, 1996). Peer mediation has proven successful in promoting increased social-communicative interactions in children who show low rates of initiations and responses to peers (Goldstein & Strain,

1988). Strategies emphasize teaching typically developing peers to understand the communicative attempts of children with autism, to initiate and respond to them, and to maintain interactions with them. Roeyers (1996) had success improving peer interactions by providing peers with general information about autism and engaging them in role-playing sessions. Peers were encouraged to initiate and persist in trying to establish interactions. They were also taught how to react to possible challenging behaviors, but they were not coached during the actual social contexts. The results showed clear improvements in the quantity and quality of the peer interactions of children with autism. Specifically, significant increases were found in responses to peers and continued interactions, but not to initiations on the part of the child with autism. Roeyers concluded, "The first step still has to be made by the nonhandicapped child" (p. 317). Thus, favorable changes are observed when peers are coached in basic means to modify and persist with social-communicative interactions.

The developmental patterns of peer interaction observed in autism appear directly related to the cognitive impairments that characterize the disorder. Nowhere is the need to integrate and generate information flexibly more at stake than during social play. The rapid, transient nature of social interaction places processing demands that pose the greatest challenge for children with autism. Relative impairments in comprehension of social and affective messages, imitation, play, and the ability to understand the perspective of others (Mundy & Sigman, 1989a) all influence interactions with peers. The degree of cognitive flexibility, as well as the presence or absence of core social-communicative skills, determine the degree of social flexibility observed in individual children with autism.

COMMUNICATION DEVELOPMENT

Communication is a reciprocal, dynamic process. It is the instrumental force propelling social knowledge, relationships, and a sense of self. An effective communicator has an inherent motivation to interact, something to express, and a means of communication. Unlike language, which is symbolic and rules based, communication is social and constantly changing. Communicative interactions require moment-to-moment integration of multiple contextual, language, social, and emotional elements as well as an ability to adjust to the behaviors of others. Cognitive capabilities, socioemotional understanding, language abilities, and prior experience all contribute to communicative competence. Active involvement in natural contexts promotes social-communicative interactions.

The quality of social-communicative interactions is remarkably different in autism. In addition to the core social-communicative deficits (joint attention, imitation, use of multiple nonverbal behaviors) and difficulties with play previously discussed, the diagnostic criteria for autism include "marked impairments in the ability to initiate or sustain a conversation with others" and "stereotyped and repetitive use of language or idiosyncratic language" (American Psychiatric Association, 1994, p. 70). The acquisition of communication skills often follows a unique developmental path (Prizant & Wetherby, 1987; Van-Meter et al., 1997) for children who have autism, and problems with reciprocity and atypical ritualized patterns of interaction are observed.

Children with autism struggle to understand the intents, internal states, and meaning behind others' social, communicative, and affective behaviors; therefore, their ability to participate in social-communicative interactions is profoundly impaired (Frith, 1989). This constrained ability to analyze and integrate information in a cohesive manner underlies their patterns of communication, as they are unable to extract meaning from social events in a fluid way. Children with autism are left with a series of fragmented experiences that are manifested as ritualized, context-specific communicative behaviors. They often associate a particular context with a specific communicative behavior and appear less able to see the similarities of related situations necessary to respond flexibly. This creates difficulty generalizing across related contexts. As a result, the dynamic and unpredictable quality of typical social-communicative interaction poses problems for children with autism.

This section examines three related skill areas in greater detail, specifically the process of reciprocal communication, the social functions of communication, and the complexity of conversational discourse. Table 1.4 summarizes the communication characteristics of autism.

Reciprocal Communication

Before the emergence of language, typically developing children are able to initiate social contact, observe others, and maintain reciprocal interaction through vocal or object play. They engage in joint attention, turn-taking, and imitation of simple actions or vocalizations. A variety of nonverbal means are used to call attention to themselves or their actions and to direct another person's behavior. Children direct eye gaze, gesture, or verbalization toward the adult and wait for a response. They initiate communication interaction and respond to the overtures of others.

Adults play an important role in shaping early communicative interactions because they establish predictable interactive routines (Bruner, 1981). They facilitate communicative interactions through predictability, simplicity, redundancy, exaggerated affect, and reference to objects and events in the child's immediate environment. Their style of interaction is modified to enhance reciprocal exchanges (Berko-Gleason, 1985; Snow, 1977). This modified style is based on a desire to be understood and maintain interaction.

From infancy, typically developing children exchange gazes and engage in vocal turn-taking. Social activities such as tickling, playing Peekaboo, and using toys to facilitate joint attention foster reciprocal interaction. An adult's response is contingent on the child's behavior. For example, when the child vocalizes, the adult responds to elicit more vocalizations. Quickly, the child takes a more active role in anticipating the adult's response. The flow of social turn-taking emerges. To maintain interaction, the adult adjusts the amount of support provided to the child (Bruner, 1981). Soon, the child initiates familiar turn-taking sequences and learns to respond to the cues of the adult (Hobson, 1989). This social reciprocity lays the foundation for communication competence.

Relevance to Autism

In autism, communicative reciprocity is not absent but is less spontaneous and flexible. Children with autism are profoundly impaired in their ability to maintain reciprocal interactions. To minimize change and maintain a limited (although somewhat successful) style of interaction, a child often insists on specific routinized interaction patterns.

Children with autism demonstrate greater success responding to communicative partners than initiating social interactions (Layton & Watson, 1995). Nevertheless, the role of the communicative partner accounts, in part, for the success or failure of interactions. Children with autism struggle more when there is a lack of congruence between their communicative style and the demands of the social situation and partners (Greenspan, 1995; Simpson, 1991). In communicative exchanges, the child must know and understand both roles of initiating and responding to information. Yet, adults often anticipate and respond to the needs of children with autism too quickly, without expecting the child to ini-

Table 1.4. Communication characteristics in autism

Communication domain	Tendency	Weakness[a]
Reciprocity	Inconsistent eye gaze	Joint attention
	Respond to others	Initiate
Functions	Requests	Comments
	Echolalia	Generate novel messages
Conversation	Routinized interaction	Reciprocal interaction
	Perserverative topics	Flexible discourse
	Self-directed	Shared conversation

[a]Characteristics exist on a continuum of severity.

tiate interactions. Many children are placed in the role of responding to requests or commands. For example, an adult might ask, "What do you want?" before the child has an opportunity to initiate a request. Questions can often limit the flow of interaction. Strategies that promote communicative initiations and reciprocal interactions are the key ingredients of successful intervention for children with autism (Greenspan & Wieder, 1998; Prizant & Wetherby, 1998).

The Social Functions of Communication

The functional use of language can be interactive (i.e., used with social intent) or noninteractive (i.e., used as a means of self-regulation). The social functions of communication include responding to others and initiating various requests, ideas, and feelings. Noninteractive use of language (i.e., talking to oneself) is a means of regulating thought or behavior.

Before language emerges, children use multiple nonverbal means to express basic needs, interests, and feelings (Bates, 1976). They use eye gaze, physical proximity, facial expression, and gestures—such as giving, showing, manipulating people and objects, reaching, and pointing—to convey a wide range of communicative functions. With the emergence of language, children develop a variety of verbal and nonverbal means to express the full range of communicative functions. They satisfy basic needs, exert control over the environment, establish social relationships, ask for information, share experiences, and express ideas and feelings through language. Studies have found that typically developing children use the full range of communicative functions across structured and unstructured contexts from the prelinguistic to multiword stages of language development (Wetherby & Rodriquez, 1992).

Relevance to Autism

Differences are observed in the functional use of language from the prelinguistic to the verbal stage in children with autism. At the prelinguistic stage, their nonverbal communicative behavior is limited to certain contexts. Eye gaze or gesture is more likely to be used for the purpose of requesting than for sharing. A child may use pointing to request an object out of reach but not to direct another person's attention toward an object of interest. Similarly, eye contact may be used to request but rarely to establish joint attention between an adult and toy. At both the prelinguistic and verbal stages, most communicative efforts serve the functions of requesting or rejecting, not the purposes of sharing information and feelings (Wetherby, 1986; Wetherby & Rodriquez, 1992). Children with autism tend to request objects, toys, food, or adult assistance, but they rarely spontaneously comment on something of interest, express feelings, or use other prosocial statements (e.g., "thank you," "good-bye"). They understand and use communication that has a clear and immediate effect on the environment, but the social means to draw attention to oneself and engage others eludes them. Requests (e.g., "I want juice") or rejections (e.g., "No, I don't want that") are linked to tangible contextual cues (the desired or rejected item) and adult consequences (providing or removing item). Children with autism, however, have difficulty generating or spontaneously sharing information in the absence of explicit cues.

Echolalia refers to the repetition of others' speech, either immediately or at a significantly later time. Echolalia is a common characteristic in many verbal children with autism and is used for a variety of interactive and noninteractive functions (Prizant & Duchan, 1981; Prizant & Rydell, 1993; Rydell & Prizant, 1995). It may be directed toward a social partner to request or reciprocate. Echolalia can be used to initiate communicative acts (e.g., requests, calling, protesting) or maintain communicative exchanges (e.g., turn-taking, providing information). Other forms of echolalia are used by the child as a functional means of self-regulation. Some forms of echolalia may be highly automatic and nonfunctional without any reference to people or objects in the present context.

Clear, contextual cues guide the communicative behaviors of children with autism. Both verbal and nonverbal patterns of communication are contextually driven. It appears that their style of communication stems not from an unwillingness to share information spontaneously but from a difficulty generating novel information without contextual cues (Ozonoff et al., 1991).

Conversational Discourse

The complex dimensions of conversation—such as maintaining appropriate topics, considering another's perspective, and balancing speaker/listener roles—are learned and refined throughout childhood. At the same time, children must use nonverbal features (e.g., vocal quality, eye gaze, physical proximity) in a flexible manner to support participation in a conversation. Refinement of these skills across different social contexts and conversational partners is a lifelong developmental process (Berko-Gleason, 1985).

Conversation skills interface all of the cognitive, social, and communicative dimensions discussed thus far. Conversation requires

- Paying attention to multiple aspects of the speaker's message
- Processing multiple aspects of the speaker's message
- Interpreting the intent and meaning of the speaker's verbal, nonverbal, and affective behaviors
- Processing the speaker's message in relation to the social context
- Understanding the partner's mental state—what the partner knows, understands, and feels—in order to monitor the conversation's relevance for the other person
- Organizing ideas related to the topic of conversation and the partner's needs
- Retrieving information relevant to the topic, partner, and context
- Turn-taking
- Adapting to the ongoing, changing social dynamic, and
- Doing all of these pieces simultaneously

The three main elements of conversation are turn-taking, topic, and perspective-taking. *Turn-taking* requires an ongoing adjustment to the context, partner, and topic. It includes the ability to recognize opportunities to initiate, interrupt, and maintain the flow of conversation. The communicator can take the role of initiator (at onset of a conversation or to maintain the conversation) or responder (by responding to initiations of others and maintaining the conversation). It is also necessary to identify appropriate *topics* to the context and to use a variety of them in conversation. *Perspective-taking* is the ability to continually monitor and adapt content and communicative style to suit the needs of the listener. It also requires skills to seek clarification and accommodate listener needs.

There are multiple features of nonverbal communication in discourse, including proximity, affect, and body language. Proximity is the ability to maintain appropriate distance and orient to the social partner. The use of eye gaze, facial expression, and gesture is an important means to convey affect. Gestures and intonation profoundly influence the meaning of the spoken message. The degree to which these nonverbal features either support or detract from the communicative message is considered an integral part of conversational competence.

Typically developing children quickly gain conversational proficiency with their peers. For example, toddlers engage in intermittent social exchanges with their peers. Preschool children adjust their verbal and nonverbal behavior according to peer feedback. They adapt their language complexity and nonverbal conversational style according to the age, language level, and social level of the listener (Shatz & Gelman, 1973). They persist in their communicative efforts in order to be understood and learn the skills of clarification. By the time children enter elementary school, they have refined verbal and non-verbal communication skills with peers. They become skilled at reading facial expression, tone of voice, and body language. They adapt their verbal information to the needs of their conversational partner. Conversation becomes the focus of social activities with peers. Successful social conversation parallels other important aspects of social play, reciprocity, turn-taking, and responsiveness to others.

Relevance to Autism

The complex, ongoing adjustments and modifications inherent in conversation challenge even the most able children with autism. A stereotypic, routinized style of interaction dominates their discourse skills. Situation-specific language, repetitive or perseverative questions, preoccupation with a narrow range of topics, and routine scripts typify conversation (Capps, Kehres, & Sigman, 1998; Prizant & Schuler, 1987). Conversation requires the ability to shift attention rapidly across a number of social and language elements, to hold in mind one's own thoughts and simultaneously process the partner's message, and to recall topic-relevant information. Impaired attention, processing, and social-cognition all contribute to the discourse difficulties observed in autism. In turn, the inability to initiate novel messages results in children with autism remaining fixed in repetitive discourse patterns. Because of a constrained ability to consider the perspective of others during conversation, they show a limited awareness of speaker/listener roles and have difficulty maintaining topics and repairing conversational breakdowns. This is coupled with a poor understanding of the meaning conveyed by nonverbal cues such as facial expression, body posture, and paralinguistic features.

Tager-Flusberg and Anderson (1991) compared the development of conversational ability in children having autism with control groups. As language increased in the control groups, there was a parallel increase in conversation skills. Children added novel information, introduced new and related topics, and used effective nonverbal strategies. In comparison, as language ability increased in children with autism, the associated conversation skills were not observed. Those children with autism who correctly completed the theory of mind tasks, however, showed better conversational skills and social insights than those children who could not perform the same tasks (Frith et al., 1994).

As expected, verbal children with autism constitute a diverse group. Some children appear only to understand the turn-taking quality of conversation and engage in repetitive questions or statements to maintain a predictable interaction and response from the partner. Other children's propensity for detail results in literal interpretations and responses during conversation. Many children use pedantic speech and can speak perseveratively on a topic of interest to them with no apparent recognition of cues from the listener. Others use metaphoric language, so the intent of the message and the meaning of the message are unclear to the listener. Children with autism make idiosyncratic associations between things that are unrelated resulting in messages that appear out of context. For example, a child sees a friend after many months and opens the conversation by asking, "Was your hair long or short?" The adult who knows the child's intent understands that the question means "When did I last meet with you?"

Furthermore, studies have demonstrated that children with autism have difficulty recognizing and interpreting affect and facial expression in natural social situations (Dawson, Hill, Spencer, Galpert, & Watson, 1990; Ozonoff, Pennington, & Rogers, 1990; Sigman, Kasari, Kwon, Jung-Hye, & Yirmiya, 1992). Although able to identify individual elements of affect in isolation (e.g., emotion, facial expression, gestural meaning, tone of voice), children with autism appear unable to integrate and act on these multiple nonverbal features of conversation that occur simultaneously in natural contexts.

There is significant variation among children in the degree to which communication skills are impaired. In all cases, however, the task of teaching children with autism to become attuned to the multiple dimensions of social-communicative interaction is a formidable responsibility.

RITUALS IN AUTISM

The third characteristic of autism is restricted and repetitive patterns of behavior. Although autism is typically identified by these ritualistic and idiosyncratic patterns of behavior, it remains the least understood characteristic. Rituals in autism are defined as a "preoccupation with one or more stereotyped and restricted patterns of interest that is abnormal in intensity and focus, apparently inflexible adherence to specific, nonfunctional routines or rituals, stereotyped and repetitive motor mannerisms, and persistent preoccupation with parts of objects" (American Psychiatric Association, 1994, p. 71). Rituals are apparent to the observer, have been described in detail through firsthand accounts (Cesaroni & Garber, 1991; Grandin, 1995a; Williams, 1992), and are often painful for both the child and caregivers.

Ritualistic behaviors dominate the social and communication behavior of all children with autism, although they are manifested in divergent ways. Body movements, vocalizations, and verbalizations can be self-stimulatory rituals. Movement rituals include rocking, jumping in place, flapping arms, or staring at fingers in specific positions. Vocal rituals include unusual sounds or nonsense words. Some forms of echolalic language use can be self-stimulatory (Rydell & Prizant, 1995). Play patterns are intensely ritualized. They include single-object rituals such as spinning objects or twirling string. Other play rituals include lining up toys or obsessively watching one small segment of a video repeatedly. Some children engage in more elaborate play rituals such as reenacting segments from a book or video program verbatim. Other children always want to win social games so that the game ends in the same way. Communication patterns are also ritualized. Some children only respond if the cues and prompts are precisely the same or perseverate on the same words or phrases. Other children repeat the same questions incessantly even when they know the answer or engage in the same familiar conversation repeatedly. Many children continually talk or write about a preferred object or activity. Some children become intensely interested in a particular adult or peer and are vigilant in their interactions with that person.

Repetitive activities can be an expression of enjoyment for some children and an expression of fear or anxiety for others. Fears can, in fact, also become ritualized. Children can make negative associations between a fearful event and an unrelated person or object. Their panic reaction can become ritualized. Even self-injurious behavior can begin as a fear response and gradually become a ritualistic behavior.

Virtually every area of learning, socialization, communication, and behavior can have ritualistic elements. There are four general schools of thought regarding the origin of ritualistic behavior:

1. Rituals are a means to regulate sensory stimulation.

2. Rituals are an expression of anxiety.

3. Rituals are a manifestation of impaired cognitive functioning.

4. Rituals are an expression of poor inhibition, a neurological impairment.

The first explanation states that rituals are a means for the child to regulate sensory stimulation (Grandin, 1995a; Williams, 1992). Rituals are used to tune out visual, auditory, tactile, and kinesthetic stimulation that is overwhelming and uncomfortable. The child uses ritualistic patterns to focus attention on one sensory input while avoiding other sensory stimulation. Rituals can also be used to seek more pleasurable sensory stimulation. Behavior that provides visual, auditory, tactile, or kinesthetic enjoyment is repeated.

The second school of thought presents ritualistic behaviors as a means for the child to create order amid chaos. Here, rituals are an expression of anxiety. In a 1998 study by Muris, anxiety disorders were found to be common in the majority of children with autism. Using information gathered through parent interview, the author reported that severe anxiety symptoms were found in 84% of the children. The study concluded that difficulty understanding social information results in children's experiencing the world as chaotic and frightening, thus contributing to anxiety.

The third theory suggests that ritualized patterns of behavior are the by-product of impaired cognitive function (Ozonoff, 1995; Ozonoff et al., 1991). Difficulties in attention, information processing, social understanding, and executive control all contribute to impaired performance. The cognitive inability to shift mental focus and generate novel patterns of behavior results in the child's becoming locked in routinized patterns.

The last explanation is that the routinized behaviors in autism are an expression of poor inhibition and have a neurological basis (Maurer & Damasio, 1982). The similarities between ritualistic behavior in autism and obsessive-compulsive disorder have been well documented (Maurer & Damasio, 1982; McDougle, Price, & Goodman, 1990). Nonetheless, there continues to be a paucity of research on the nature and treatment of these behaviors in autism. One study by McBride and Panksepp (1995) attempted to establish the function of compulsive ritualistic behaviors in adults with autism through caregiver interview. They found the behaviors functioned to reduce anxiety, prevent changes, and maintain interactions or express excitement, but there was significant variability across the individuals studied. Most notably, there was also marked variation in how the individuals responded when their rituals were interrupted. Some had no difficulty, while others became increasingly agitated. More closely examining the degree to which rituals can be redirected may provide some insight into which ritualistic behaviors are neurologically driven. A substantial amount of increased attention is needed in this area of study.

SUMMARY

Although there have been significant gains in understanding the nature of autism, there still is no singular explanation for the disorder. New theories continue to emerge with regard to etiology and treatment. Investigations into the development of shared attention, theory of mind, and socioemotional reciprocity provide insights into autism, but questions still remain about how these aspects of development interface with other characteristics of autism such as ritualistic behaviors, sensory sensitivities, and anxiety. The notion of "a theory" of autism—that is, a singular explanation for the multitude of learning and behavior problems associated with the disorder—is highly unlikely. Rather, it is more likely that each proposed theory is one more piece of the puzzle that contributes to an evolving understanding of the uniqueness of the full spectrum of autism disorders.

Autism must also be viewed within the context of typical development, which presupposes that all areas of development interweave to form a complex tapestry. Cognition, language, socialization, communication, and emotional development interface in intricate ways. In the case of autism, current theories continue to dissect isolated skill impairments without a clear understanding of their interdependence. The challenge of research and treatment is to integrate the understanding of children's perceptions, knowledge, and feelings in order to maximize their whole development. It is necessary to recognize the cognitive, social, communicative, and behavioral uniqueness of autism in order to appreciate the challenges that children with autism face in the social world. Understanding the child's view of the world is necessary to form relationships that foster social growth.

DO-WATCH-
LISTEN-SAY

chapter 2

The Child's Perspective

Kathleen Ann Quill

Children with autism appear to view the world from a perspective that differs from everyone else. They find the social behaviors of others confusing. They struggle to understand the complexity of social relationships. The simplest conversational exchange with others is difficult for them to negotiate. This confusion results in social isolation and frustration. At the same time, the children are intensely preoccupied with small details. They seem to demand order in the physical world as a means to cope with the "social chaos." Their ritualistic behaviors often bring meaning and comfort to them, while at other times they appear to be an expression of uncertainty and anxiety.

Professionals and parents need to understand the thinking patterns, social perspectives, and socioemotional qualities of children with autism in order to help them. This chapter describes various aspects of learning, social skills, and communication in autism through short stories about many different children who have the disorder. Vignettes about the children are used to highlight their unique qualities. The children's perceptions and experiences provide a poignant picture of autism.

It is necessary to respect the children's view of the social world in order to establish realistic expectations for social and communication growth. An understanding of the children's perspective also assists in the development of intervention strategies that take into account both their strengths and their struggles. Through a discussion of autism from the child's perspective, it is hoped that compassion will ultimately dictate intervention.

COGNITIVE PATTERNS

The cognitive patterns of children with autism include a tendency to focus on details, interpret information in a fragmented manner, misperceive the perspectives of others, and become "stuck" in one mode of thinking and behaving. These cognitive patterns have two results. First, children with autism often misinterpret the meaning of experiences (see Figure 2.1). Second, learning and social-communicative behaviors become self-directed and intensely ritualized.

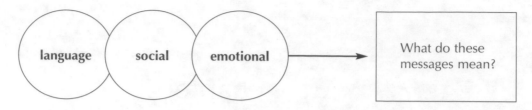

Figure 2.1. The challenge for children with autism.

Selective Attention

An experience must be either interesting or meaningful to maintain some level of attention. Attention to a novel or confusing situation requires a degree of internal motivation or external reinforcement. In the absence of motivation (i.e., internal or external reinforcement) and meaning (i.e., understanding the experience), interest and attention are lost.

Children with autism tend to hyperfocus on sensory experiences that are pleasurable and ignore or avoid multisensory experiences that are uncomfortable or confusing. The following children illustrate this characteristic:

> Two-year-old Sam loves to sit and play in the sandbox for hours. He sifts the sand through his fingers and laughs with glee. Although he enjoys this tactile experience, Sam has a high degree of auditory sensitivity. He is only able to watch television with the sound turned off, and he covers his ears and cries at the sound of the television and the radio.

> Five-year-old Christopher plays well with a wide range of toys at home. In his classroom of 15 children, however, his play is dominated by self-stimulatory twirling of ribbons and string. The discrepancy between skills seen at home and at school appears linked to the amount of stimulation in the classroom environment. When he is overstimulated, Christopher is unable to organize his play, even during familiar activities.

Impaired social interactions are due, in part, to the difficulty children with autism have with shifting attention. The children can sustain attention the same way typically developing children do, but this creates in them a tendency toward perseverative behavior or interest in activities that do not change. The desire for repetition and rituals may be an attempt to have meaningful experiences with objects amidst a socially chaotic world. The children profiled next demonstrate this point:

> Three-year-old Lisa lines up the letters of an alphabet puzzle in order repeatedly. She also lines up her farm animals, toy cars and trucks, stuffed animals, video collection, blocks, and crayons, as well as her mother's shoes and her brother's baseball cards. She can sustain attention while involved in meaningful solitary play but has difficulty in social play that requires her to shift attention back and forth from her own activity to the activities of others.

> Five-year-old Tyler's attention varies during group storytime. He can maintain attention to the story if the teacher reads the book cover to cover without interruption. If the teacher interrupts the story intermittently to ask questions, however, Tyler's attention is lost, and he attempts to leave the classroom. Tyler can attend to the book but has difficulty during discussions that require him to shift attention back and forth from one child to the next.

One aspect of attentional behavior that seems unique to autism is overselective attention to details (Koegel & Koegel, 1995b). Children with autism appear to focus on specific details, often without noticing the most relevant aspect of a situation. This attention to details often translates into misinterpreting the meaning of the situation, as shown in the following examples:

Six-year-old David was having difficulty learning his numbers. He continued to point to the correct answer only 50% of the time. Upon closer examination, it was discovered that David always selected the number card that was in the location of the previously correct answer. He focused on location, not meaning, in his effort to understand the task.

Alex was learning about money in first-grade math. When asked to tell the class what he would do with a nickel, he explained, "A nickel is gray or silver. A nickel is a circle, and a nickel has a man on it with a jacket. The quarter has a man with no jacket." Alex recognized the presidents' attire on U.S. coins, but he had concentrated on details that were not socially relevant and did not appear to understand the purpose of money.

Meaning in the Details

Learning occurs when information is analyzed, organized, stored, and remembered in multiple ways. In a single moment, a person attends to various aspects of a new experience and then links it to an infinite number of related experiences. This novel information reshapes and redefines all related knowledge. In contrast, the processing style observed in autism is characterized by concrete perceptual associations (Peeters, 1997). Children with autism have a tendency to focus on one aspect of a situation. This results in making a more restricted and often singular association between perception and behavior. The outcome, which has been termed *illogical logic* (Michaels, 1998), is seen in the next vignettes:

Seven-year-old Ben learned to ask for a drink in school by bringing a photo of a yellow cup to his teacher. Although he mastered this requesting skill in school, he never used the same communication symbol at home. Ben's mother gradually realized that there was a yellow cup for his drinks in school but not at home. For Ben, the photo of the yellow cup meant "yellow cup," not "drink."

The mother of 8-year-old Mary understands her child's way of thinking. Mary's mother links each outing with a specific object so Mary understands where she is going; for example, a straw bag symbolizes a trip to the market and a heart necklace means a trip to visit Nana. One day, Mary's mother put the heart necklace on Mary and they left for a ride to Nana's house. When they turned left to go to Nana's instead of right to go shopping, Mary began to scream. Her mother was confused by Mary's sudden outburst and immediately stopped the car. In the back seat, she found Mary holding the straw bag.

Eight-year-old Brian went to the mountains for a winter vacation with his family. His mother bought him a new red sweater for the trip. Each day Brian wore the sweater while happily playing in the snow. Three weeks later, his mother dressed him for school in this red sweater, and Brian squealed with excitement. He spent much of the school day anxiously looking out the window. By evening, when his mother removed his sweater for bath time, he had a tantrum. Brian appeared to connect the red sweater with playing in snow, so he became upset when it did not snow on that particular "sweater day."

> *Jennifer is 3 years old and her favorite video is about a baby. She especially likes the part when the mother in the video feeds the baby a bottle and says, "Now, now, not so fast." Every night when Jennifer wants her bedtime bottle she says, "Now, now, not so fast." For Jennifer, the phrase "now, now, not so fast" means bottle.*

Visual Thinking

Just as children with autism have an easier time sustaining attention to events that do not change, it is generally easier for them to process visual information that does not rapidly change. In contrast to fleeting visual auditory information, visuospatial stimuli (e.g., objects, pictures, graphics, written language) are fixed in space and time and, therefore, are often easier for the children to process. As Grandin explained, "I think totally in pictures. Visual thinking is like playing different tapes in a videocassette recorder in my imagination" (1995a, pp. 34–35). The two child profiles that follow exemplify this characteristic:

> *Three-year-old John has mastered most preschool computer software programs. The computer screen displays one piece of visual information at a time, and John can control the sequence and pace of the information. At the same time, he has difficulty following simple directions from his mother. This is because interacting with his mother requires him to process multiple visual and auditory stimuli quickly.*

> *Six-year-old Timmy never follows directions. His teacher tested whether Timmy's lack of following directions is due to poor language and social comprehension or noncompliance. She found that when Timmy is given verbal directions alone or verbal directions with gestures, he does not respond. However, when Timmy is given verbal directions paired with a picture cue, he is consistently compliant. Even fleeting gestural movements occur too rapidly for Timmy to follow. He needs to look at the picture cue for a few seconds in order to understand.*

Another learning quality of children with autism is concrete thinking. When learning is predominantly driven by concrete, physical experiences, the result is an understanding of the world of objects and a greater difficulty with abstract concepts, particularly social meaning. This is commonly observed in the children's literal interpretation of situations, as shown in the following cases:

> *Four-year-old Charlie has a large single-word vocabulary. He can list every character on Sesame Street, every geometric shape, and every automobile make and model. Nonetheless, Charlie is unable to name any attribute or action associated with these things. He does not know how to ask for help or tell his mother when he is sick. His vocabulary is composed exclusively of concrete objects.*

> *Children in a kindergarten class were asked to place their hands in a "feeling bag" and describe how the objects in the bag felt. When it was Amy's turn, the teacher asked, "How does it feel?" Amy answered, "Happy? Mad? Calm? Frustrated?" Although Amy was trying to identify emotions in herself and others, she did not understand that these terms do not apply to inanimate objects.*

> *At 9 years old, Patrick was being taught different safety rules. One of the skills he learned was to telephone 911 for emergencies. His list of emergencies included a stranger in the house when his parents were not home. One evening, Patrick was with a babysitter whose friend stopped by the house for a brief visit. Seeing the babysitter's friend, Patrick ran to the phone, dialed 911, and yelled, "Help—there*

is a stranger in the house and my mom and dad are not home." To the embarrassment of the babysitter, the police quickly arrived.

Gestalt Learning

Another fundamental aspect of the learning patterns of children with autism is that they tend to organize and remember information as a gestalt rather than analyze the interrelated meaning of its parts. In the absence of understanding the integrated meaning of an experience or a concept, information is stored as a whole (Prizant, 1982). The next examples demonstrate how echolalic speech and routinized conversations typify this pattern:

Six-year-old Steven has learned that conversation is an exchange between two people. He is still struggling, however, with the meaning of the words he hears. For example, when his mother says, "Hello, Steven," he replies, "Hello, Steven." If she then states, "No, say 'Hello, Mommy,'" Steven answers, "Say hello Mommy."

Max is 7 years old and enjoys maps. The first time Max meets someone, he asks, "What's your name?" and "Where do you live?" Then he checks his map and describes the route the person takes from his or her home to school. Each time he sees that person—whether it is 1 hour, 1 day, 1 month, or 1 year later—he asks the same two questions, then smiles and details the route. If the person happens to have moved, Max becomes extremely agitated and demands that the person state the old address in order to maintain the whole conversation as he remembers it. Comfort and pleasure are linked to these gestalt, routinized conversational exchanges.

Fragmented Memory

The ability to use what you know is a complex process that reflects how information has been organized and stored. Material that is integrated in flexible, meaningful ways can be accessed and used in the same manner. In contrast, a series of fragmented, concrete associations (i.e., "In situation A, I do this; in situation B, I say this") is manifested as rote and contextually driven (or cue-based) behaviors.

The social and communicative behaviors observed in children with autism are typically more rote and less flexible. Grandin (1995) described her gestalt-driven, visual memory strategies. She stated,

To access spoken information that I have heard in the past, I replay a video of the person talking to me. To retrieve facts, I have to read them off a visualized page of a book or replay the video of some previous event. This method of thinking is slow . . . it takes time to play the videotape in my imagination. (p. 35)

The next profiles further illustrate this concept:

Alan is 8 years old and excels at memorization. In geography class, he made a list of every mountain in the world and its exact height as well as a list of every body of water in the world and its depth. Alan has also memorized the definitions of all the words in his children's dictionary, although he is unable to put any of the words into a sentence or paraphrase their meaning.

Six-year-old Maggie had "mastered" many tasks presented by her classroom teacher. Other therapists at school, however, were unable to get Maggie to complete similar tasks, and Maggie's parents did not observe these skills at home. Upon closer examination, it became clear that Maggie's "mastery" was context specific, limited to specific materials and teacher cues. Lack of generalization reflected lack of meaning.

The learning style in children with autism can be summarized as a series of concrete associations between selective perceptions and their own behavior that are made one situation at a time. They have a tendency to link information in a more restricted and, thus, less typically meaningful way. The fact that fluid analysis and integration of information is compromised for a child with autism influences cognitive, social, and communicative flexibility. Because the child's experiences are learned as a series of single events and are not connected to other related experiences in a broader conceptual sense, the result is rote learning and responding. Cognitive, social, and communication rigidity is manifested by insistence on predictability and routinized interactions.

Social Misunderstanding

Social understanding begins with social interest, shared attention, and social-communicative and emotional reciprocity. These core skills lay the foundation for all social learning. The development of social understanding also requires cognitive flexibility. Social concepts are formed when children compare their perceptions, experiences, thoughts, and feelings with others' during shared social experiences. In children with autism, social concepts are driven by concrete, perceptual information. This limits their development of inferential reasoning, which is required for the development of abstract social concepts and social perspective-taking. The result is limited social understanding and, in turn, self-directed social and communication behaviors that do not take into account the perspective of others.

Figure 2.2 depicts four social messages. The two messages on the left are physical, and their meaning is derived from observable social behaviors. The two on the right, although physical in nature, require an understanding of internal mental states to infer the meaning. Children with autism are more likely to understand the messages shown on the left because the meanings are linked to observable events; they would be challenged by

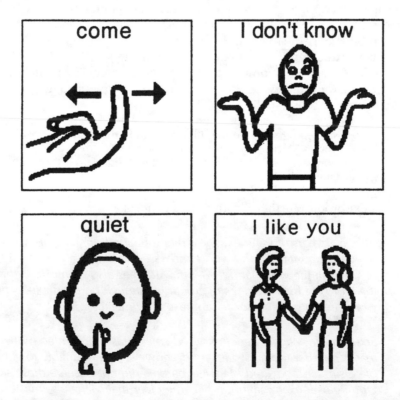

Figure 2.2. Theory of mind display. (The Picture Communication Symbols ©1981–2000 Mayer-Johnson Co. are used with permission.)

those on the right, which require theory of mind for comprehension. The next vignettes demonstrate this distinction:

> Michael was a 9-year-old who was striving to understand the meaning of mental state terms such as "think" or "know." In one instance, he was working with his teacher on story sequencing. They were looking at a picture of a girl holding a pencil near her face and thinking about a drawing that she was preparing to begin. Michael's teacher asked, "What is the little girl doing?" "Thinking," Michael replied. "What is she thinking about?" his teacher asked. "She's thinking at her desk," said Michael. His teacher asked the same question again, this time emphasizing the words "what" and "about." Michael answered, "She's thinking at her desk with a pencil on her head and paper on her desk." Michael did not understand that others have "thoughts" that influence their observable actions and, therefore, struggled to understand the meaning of his teacher's question.

> Nathaniel was participating in a group activity with his kindergarten class. During the lesson, the teacher accidentally tripped over a building block and fell to her knees. The other children expressed concern while Nathaniel laughed. Most of the children cleaned up the materials after the lesson, but Nathaniel arranged the building blocks exactly as they were when his teacher fell. Then he reenacted his teacher's falling over the block three times. The first and second times, Nathaniel laughed. The third time, however, he rubbed his knee because it hurt. He then walked over to his teacher, rubbed her knee, and said, "Okay?" Nathaniel needed to experience the physical pain to understand the situation and express empathy.

> Jared was an 8-year-old who had been learning about his and others' feelings. His teacher was helping Jared to "see" what people are doing when they feel _____, how they look when they feel _____, and what to say when they feel _____. Jared was becoming increasingly able to identify feelings observed in his family and friends and to comment on these feelings. Everyone was very excited about Jared's growing social awareness. Then one day Jared asked his teacher, "Can I look in the mirror to see how I am feeling?" The true meaning behind expressions of feelings continued to elude him.

Without social perspective-taking, children with autism find it difficult to predict the behavior of others and therefore seek social interactions that are predictable. Without an understanding of social concepts such as others' mental states, they find it difficult to monitor, predict, and adjust to ongoing social and communicative interactions

THE PARADOX OF SOCIAL-COMMUNICATIVE INTERACTION

Social interaction is an unpredictable and dynamic activity that requires integrating contextual, language, and social information. The striking polarity between the learning patterns of children with autism and the requirements of social-communicative interaction illuminates the social challenges faced by children with autism. As indicated in Table 2.1, the basic learning patterns of children with autism contrast sharply with social-communicative demands. The following case highlights the discrepancy between the learning style associated with autism and the demands of social-communicative interaction:

> Five-year-old Mark liked numbers. If given the choice, Mark would write numbers during the whole school day. At his school team's initial meeting, Mark's teacher brought a copy of his handwritten number chart (from 1 to 482 in precise columns and rows). She reported that he successfully completed academic worksheets but would not participate in group discussions. He also did not play with the other

Table 2.1.   The paradox for children with autism

Learning style pattern	Requirement of social-communication
Repetitive	Flexible
Organized	Dynamic
Predictable	Random
Visual	Multisensory
Concrete (physical)	Social

children, and the team wondered why. Through a discussion of Mark's activity preferences, they began to understand the paradox between his learning strengths and social struggles and why interaction with peers was hard for him. This understanding helped the team make decisions about appropriate support for Mark.

Mark focused on information that made sense to him and disregarded social activities that did not. His number chart was a predictable, organized, repetitive, visual, and concrete activity that allowed for sustained and focused attention. His interest in that particular item was, in many ways, representative of the learning style of individuals with autism. Numbers, by their very nature, are patterned, sequential, and infinitely orderly. Interest in numbers, letters, books, computers, and videos—as well as manipulative toys and other play activities containing these same elements—is commonly observed in children with autism.

In contrast, typical social and communicative interactions are unpredictable, dynamic, and random; they are multisensory experiences that require flexibility and social understanding. An appreciation of this sharp contrast is useful in understanding the social challenges and instructional adaptations that are necessary for promoting social growth in children with autism.

CORE SOCIAL AND COMMUNICATION CHALLENGES

Two core skills are the foundation for all later social and communication development: nonverbal social-communicative interaction and imitation. Children must be able to engage in shared attention that is mutually meaningful and imitate others to develop social and communicative competence.

Reciprocal Interactions

Nonverbal reciprocal interactions—exchanging eye gaze, gestures, and other messages—lay the foundation for successful social skills and communication. This process is challenging for children with autism due to their restricted learning patterns and difficulty maintaining the natural pace of social interactions. In the absence of understanding the process of reciprocal interactions, they interact in atypical ways or demonstrate shared attention in more limited contexts. As they acquire effective means to interact with others, they are socially motivated to maintain their success. The next two cases illustrate these diverse patterns:

Three-year-old Zachary laughs aloud whenever his parents tickle him or swing him in the air. He looks at them the whole time they play these social games to indicate that he wants to continue playing. Zachary uses eye gaze to sustain many activities that are pleasurable and meaningful. Zachary does not, however, understand that he can also use eye gaze to make other requests or to share interests with his parents.

Ten-year-old Nicholas was taught that the acceptable way to get someone's attention was to tap him or her on the wrist. Consequently, Nicholas awakened his mother one night at 3:00 A.M. by pulling off the bed covers in search of her wrist. Once he found it, he tapped it, then said, "Help." It turned out that he had a high fever. The means he used to initiate social interaction, even when sick, was always done in precisely the same way.

Imitation

The ability to imitate gross motor movements, fine motor movements, and actions with toys and objects is necessary for social learning. Children with autism vary significantly in their ability to imitate what others do. Gross motor, fine motor, and oral-motor planning is challenging for some children (Hanschu, 1998). In addition, there is often a difference between spontaneous imitation in natural contexts and elicited imitation in structured contexts. The children may imitate what others do but not understand what their actions mean.

Kevin, 5 years old, was having no success imitating an adult in the context of an artificially structured activity. After months of face-to-face contact with his teacher and practicing various fine motor movements, Kevin was only passively coopera-tive. Yet, in a different setting, Kevin was following his peers' play on the play-ground equipment, and he imitated the children when they danced to music. His ability to imitate seemed to be driven by motivation and meaning.

Four-year-old Becka was also unsuccessful in structured programs to build fine motor imitation. With toys and objects, however, Becka quickly learned to imitate an adult's simple play actions. Becka, like typically developing children, learned to imitate through simple play. Body awareness emerged later.

SOCIAL CHALLENGES

Social skills encompass virtually every aspect of daily living. For young children, social mastery is usually defined by the quality of solitary play skills, social play with peers, and socioemotional relationships.

Solitary Play

Children's play reflects an understanding of their social experiences. Children explore how to use toys or materials. They reenact personal experiences. The play skills of chil-dren with autism are a window into what they understand. The repetitiveness of their play reflects a more limited understanding of how to use toys in creative ways. This point was demonstrated by an informal survey of the activity preferences of 100 young children with autism. Popular responses included the following: playing physical games, using a computer, watching videos, looking at books, completing puzzles, and using fine motor manipulatives (Quill, 1997). Each of these activities can be done in the same way again and again, or, in the case of videos, the same information can be seen repeatedly in the exact same way. The following vignettes describe this characteristic:

Three-year-old John plays alone with toys for hours. Each time he plays with sand, he sifts it through his fingers. Each time he uses blocks, he lines them up in a pre-cise row. Each time he looks at a book, he counts the page numbers from cover to cover. In every situation, John's play consists of one predictable behavior.

Eric is 5 years old and enjoys playing with cars, but in a way that differs from other children his age. Eric's play can be described as "one toy, one action." Eric focuses on one aspect of cars and repeats the same action. Whereas typically developing children are usually interested in many things that cars can do (e.g., ride, go fast and slow), including in relation to other toys (e.g., carry people, go to a garage), Eric's play consists of spinning the wheels repeatedly.

Six-year-old Polly's solitary play consists of elaborate reenactments of favorite books and videos. Line by line, she replays the stories with toys. The reenactments are precisely the same each time.

Justin, a 4-year-old, was learning to use playdough in a variety of ways. He initially preferred cutting little balls and lining them up in a row. His teacher and preschool friends showed him that other things could be built using animal- and letter-shaped cookie cutters. The first day that his teacher was not directly involved in the activity, she watched Justin using the letter cookie cutters. Within a few minutes, he had spelled out Mighty Joe Young, the title of his favorite movie, in playdough.

Social Play

Social play is complex. Children explore toys and materials, watch and imitate others, and interact verbally and nonverbally with peers. All of these components of play occur simultaneously and flexibly in typically developing young children. Social play also requires social perspective-taking, reciprocity, and creativity. The ability to integrate all of these pieces is a monumental challenge for children with autism, as shown in the following examples:

Frank, a 7-year-old, watches other children during structured activities and plays alone during unstructured activities. His ability to make sense of his peers' activities occurs only when they are all doing the same activity at the same time. When all of the children are doing something different, Frank chooses to play alone.

Tony, a 6-year-old, struggles to understand how to play with his peers at recess. Tony wants to interact with his peers but does so by talking about his favorite movie, The Sound of Music. Every day, he repeatedly asks his classmates questions about The Sound of Music and becomes agitated when they do not know the answers to his questions or ignore him. Tony has difficulty understanding that his interest is not shared by his friends. Furthermore, he finds the social requirements of recess overwhelming.

Eight-year-old Kenny participates in many after-school activities with friends. Kenny and his friends swim, ice skate, ride bikes, and go horseback riding. In addition, they go to the library, children's museums, and the movies. His mother finds that these activities allow Kenny to share experiences with other children without any expectations to cooperate or converse. Any play that requires cooperation or conversation is frustrating for him.

Group Activities

Groups vary in size and predictability. Group activities that are predictable—during which everyone is doing the same thing at the same time—are easier for the children with autism to join. In addition, children with autism are often more successful with group activities that have a predictable sequence of events (e.g., games with rules). The next profiles demonstrate this idea:

Eight-year-old Derek was preparing for a school holiday performance with his class. His teacher placed a blue piece of tape on the stage floor to remind Derek where to stand. She knelt in front of him, touched his shoes, and said, "Derek, toes stay on the blue, okay?" She left the stage and as the children began to sing, Derek stood on the blue tape with his fingers touching his toes, singing joyfully. Derek was following his teacher's gestural directions and did not notice that his behavior differed from that of the other children in the group.

Sally's ability to attend in her first-grade classroom varies according to activity. During reading time, Sally quietly focuses her attention on the pages of the book because the group activity is organized, predictable, and sequential. When discussion begins, Sally becomes distracted and disorganized and starts talking to herself. She is unable to follow the complexity and random flow of group discussion.

Abby is in second grade. She and her mother have made a list of all of the children in her class and decided daily who will be that day's special friend. This special friend is given a red ribbon to wear for the day. Any time that Abby gets confused during group activities, she can look for her special friend wearing the red ribbon to ask for assistance. This helps Abby participate in groups more easily.

Community Outings

The complexities of community activities place great demands on children with autism. They appear more successful in the community when efforts are made to preview upcoming events and help the children feel calm and organized in the setting. This point is demonstrated by the following cases:

Six-year-old Pete was most relaxed during any rhythmic activity, such as listening to books on tape or reciting the alphabet. He was frightened of haircuts, so his teacher made a special storybook about getting a haircut and recorded an accompanying song for him. Pete listened to the story and song as well as practiced getting pretend haircuts at school and the barbershop until the actual haircut day arrived. He had mastered all the steps of getting a haircut except the actual snip. With all of the supports and practice, the barber made his first cut and Pete did fine.

Kathleen, a 6-year-old, went to church with her family. She sat quietly whenever the music was playing but looked for other things to do when the priest was talking. She especially liked running up to people who wore hooded jackets so that she could grab the string to twirl. Once a special church bag containing a Walkman tape player and music along with a rosary (to twirl) was provided, Kathleen was an "angel" at church.

Socioemotional Relationships

Relationships are built on mutually enjoyable, meaningful interactions. The learning patterns observed in children with autism profoundly influence their experience and understanding of interactions. They may only notice extreme expressions of emotion and miss subtle socioemotional messages. They also misinterpret the meaning of others' messages. They make concrete and often incorrect associations between their perceptions and the meaning of others' social and emotional messages. Atypical or unexplained emotional responses can result from these misinterpretations.

The development of relationships is further complicated by the sensory sensitivities, anxiety, and compulsive rituals common in children with autism. Sensitivity to sound or touch can affect their level of comfort interacting with others. Sensory sensitivities can result in atypical ways of seeking comfort from others; attachments to parents and other significant caregivers may be expressed in an atypical manner as well. Anxiety and compulsive rituals also influence the quality of reciprocal interactions. These factors all affect the development of meaningful, pleasurable relationships. As the following vignettes exemplify, this is a challenge for the children's families, teachers, and friends:

Justin is 3 years old and very attached to his mother, who has short blonde hair and wears glasses. At his new school, Justin finds comfort by hugging a teacher who has short blonde hair and wears glasses. He cries with all other adults.

Joshua is a 4-year-old who is very attached to his family. His separation anxiety started with him screaming each time someone in his family left the house. Soon, just the sound of the garage door opening triggered an outburst. Joshua's preschool teacher made a chart called "Who's at School; Who's at Home" for the classroom. The children moved their photos to "school" upon arrival and to "home" upon dismissal. This was successful in calming Joshua at school, so his teacher decided to make a "Who's at Home; Who's Outside" chart for Joshua's family. When Joshua's family left for work the next day, Joshua began to scream. His mother carried him to the chart and moved his father's photo to "outside," and Joshua immediately calmed down. He pointed to "Mommy" and "Joshua" on the chart for reassurance that they were "at home" and remained fine. The entire family continues to use the chart because it helps Joshua understand that they will eventually return any time they leave the house.

Leslie, who is 5 years old, enjoys watching videos. While watching Bambi with her family, Leslie's mother narrates the movie and describes actions and feelings. As Bambi is a sad movie, the name soon became Leslie's definition of "sad." Thus, whenever Leslie is sad, she says, "Leslie's Bambi."

Tom, a 7-year-old whose mother had died 2 years earlier, was nonverbal. With his limited language understanding, his teaching team still felt it was important to explain to Tom the loss of his mother. A book of photos of each family member was developed, with the pictographic symbol for "sad" next to his mother's picture and a symbol for "happy" next to photos of all other living family members. Tom always carried the book in school and at home, and it was shared with him daily. A few weeks later, Tom's father commented that every night Tom went to bed with his photo album and opened it to the picture of his mother.

Ricky liked to complete puzzles with one particular girl in his kindergarten class. His favorite puzzle was of a chicken. Ricky became so excited about playing with his friend that every day he asked her to play the chicken puzzle. Soon he began to approach her dozens of times a day, say, "Chicken, chicken," and laugh. He eventually became uncontrollably excited whenever he saw or heard anything related to chickens. This was how Ricky expressed the joy of his friendship.

COMMUNICATION CHALLENGES

Successful communicative interaction requires that a child quickly attends to and understands the meaning of rapidly changing multisensory, language, social, and affective information. Communicative flexibility poses the biggest challenge for children with autism. Differences are observed in the reasons children with autism communicate, the form of their communication, and the range of topics that they select. A routinized style of communication characterizes the children's efforts. Their communication patterns appear to be the means for creating meaningful interactions amid perceived social chaos.

Initiating Communication

Children with autism often need concrete cues to remember what to say. Without these tangible cues, they often cannot think of something novel to say. This point is demonstrated in the next vignettes:

Lance arrives at preschool every day with a smile. He stops at the doorway, and his teacher says, "Good morning, Lance," to which he replies, "Good morning, Ms. Anne." His teacher then directs him to put his things in his cubby and make a play choice. This exchange is a daily routine. One morning, Anne was out of the classroom when Lance arrived. He stood at the doorway and waited. Becoming increasingly agitated, he stated, "Good morning, Lance; good morning, Lance. Say 'Good morning' Ms. Anne. Good morning, Lance." He stood and rocked at the door, repeating the words that, in his mind, initiated the arrival routine.

Bruce, age 4, used speech to request food and toys but never commented about his activities. Yet, Bruce was interested in a peer's augmentative and alternative communication (AAC) system. One day during snack time, Bruce sat next to his friend and used the voice output system to comment about his snack: "This is good," he said. Bruce also used it to comment on another child's behavior by saying, "Mad, loud." The symbols on the AAC device served as a concrete reminder to Bruce of things he could say.

Nina was 6 years old and screamed when people were too close to her. Many intervention plans were tried to get Nina to replace screams with the phrase "Go away." She was so anxious during the actual situations that she was unable to organize herself to use these words. Because Nina was so motivated by videos, her teachers decided to videotape examples of family members and school friends saying "Go away" when others were too close. There were 10 different episodes on the final tape. Nina was interested in the tape, and soon after she viewed it, she began using the words "go away" with prompting.

Echolalia

Children with autism use echolalia for a variety of reasons. Echolalia typically reflects context-specific learning of whole messages. The generation of novel ideas and messages is more difficult because it is an analytical process that requires flexibility in thinking and planning. *Immediate echolalia,* the partial or exact repetition of a message immediately after it is heard, is common. Many children, unfortunately, have learned to repeat what is said without understanding the meaning of the message. *Delayed echolalia,* the partial or exact repetition of a message at a significantly later time than when originally heard, is also common. It is linked to a specific person or setting and, thus, reflects the child's less effective efforts to link language meaning with events. Echolalia can be manifested in various ways, as shown in these examples:

Six-year-old Danny enjoys listening to books on audiotape. He quickly memorizes a book and then repeats the entire book, including the sound effects that indicate that it is time to turn the page.

Bobby is 4 years old and has been taught to imitate language out of context. A typical exchange between Bobby (B) and his teacher (T) follows:

T: Bobby, what is it?

B: What is it?

T: Say, "It's blue."

B: It's blue.

T: Good boy.

B: Good boy.

T: (presents next item)

B: What is it?

T: Yes, what is it?

B: What is it?

T: Bobby, look; say, "Green."

B: Say green.

Bobby obviously understands that communication is an exchange; however, he does not understand the meaning of the messages shared.

Kim was a 5-year-old girl whose communicative intent was often difficult to determine. She spoke in full sentences, but the purpose of her message was often hard to understand. Kim's favorite activity was watching videos, so she made associations, based on some concrete similarity, between people she met and characters from a video. The first time she met her kindergarten teacher, Kim said, "There's no place like home; there's no place like home." Her teacher was wearing a pair of red shoes, and this reminded Kim of Dorothy's ruby slippers and famous words in The Wizard of Oz. During the entire school year, Kim would say, "Good morning, Ms. Sandy; there's no place like home" each time her teacher wore those shoes to work.

Reciprocal Conversation

The complexity of reciprocal conversation requires combining all of the components of cognitive, language, social, emotional, and communication development. Children with autism do their best to interact with others, applying their own understanding of the situation. Frequently, this entails engaging in routinized conversations:

The process of teaching conversation exchanges to 8-year-old James was an education for his teacher. Just when she thought that James had learned to generalize a particular message, he would remind her of his learning style. For example, James had been practicing asking the question, "Where is _____?" through many games and activities. One game entailed his posing the question, "Where is _____?" Then they would go on a treasure hunt, find the item, and James would say, "I found it." One day, he was looking for a CD-ROM for his computer. His teacher asked, "Do you want the CD? Where is it?" After looking among the CDs for a few minutes, James announced, "I found it." His teacher said, "Where is it? You found it?" James replied, "Where is it?" and the circular conversation continued. James comprehended many pieces of the "say-search-find" activity, but the exact meanings of the words used continued to elude him.

Shana, 9 years old, is striving to understand other people's feelings. Her struggle to comprehend the sentiments of others is demonstrated by the following conversation between Shana (S) and a visitor (V) to her classroom:

S: Were you here before?

V: Yes, I visited your school in October.

S: Was your hair long or short?

V: My hair looked almost the same.

S: I remember it longer. I don't like it now.

V: Oh, I like it.

S: What I said, how do you feel?

V: A little uncomfortable.

S: What I said, and now you're sad?

V: Yes, I'm a little sad. I like compliments. Do you remember learning about giving compliments?

S: Yes. Next time I will say, "I like your hair," and you will be happy.

DRIVEN TO SAMENESS

Ritualistic behaviors dominate the social and communication patterns of children with autism. Rituals seem to express the children's emotional state or understanding and can be an expression of enjoyment, discomfort, fear, or confusion. Rituals can reflect limited skills or be a child's attempt to create order in a confusing social environment. Research is in its infancy regarding the source of many ritualistic behaviors and the relationship between rituals and related anxiety disorders, obsessive-compulsive disorders, and other neurological disorders.

Accounts given by individuals with autism provide some insight into this little understood characteristic. For instance, adults with autism have described their ritualistic behavior as a strong internal drive, a pleasurable experience, or a means to compensate for an overstimulating environment. Alex, a woman who was diagnosed with autism in childhood, explained, "I have pleasurable rituals that help me function and other rituals that are disturbing for me," and "Rituals happen because I have no internal organizational system" (Michaels, 1998). As an adult with autism, Barron described his childhood experiences with rituals: "I loved repetition. Every time I turned on a light I knew what would happen. When I flipped a switch, the light went on. It gave me a wonderful feeling of security because it was exactly the same each time" (Barron & Barron, 1992, p. 143).

The rituals that individuals with autism employ are almost limitless, as illustrated in the next vignettes:

Gary is 3 years old and has learned the names of body parts through the book and song There's a Frog on My Nose. Gary enjoys looking at the book, listening to the song, and touching the body parts named. He also enjoys listening to the song and following directions from a frog puppet used by his mother. Whenever the puppet instructs him to touch a body part that is not a part of the original book, Gary screams. He has generalized the activity to new materials, but the specific body parts that he associates with the frog song have to stay the same.

Matt is 4 years old and insists that objects in his house remain in the same place. One day, Matt's aunt was visiting and having tea with his mother. Matt's mother had tea with milk; his aunt had plain tea. Matt asked his mother for milk. She poured him a glass of milk, and he turned to pour it in his aunt's cup. His mother said, "No." Matt then began to scream, pointed to the teacup, yelled "Milk," and began to cry. When his aunt handed him her teacup, he quickly calmed down, poured some milk into her cup until it looked the same as his mother's, and happily walked away.

Six-year-old Caroline's rituals are marked by her insistence that the daily routine be predictable. Caroline becomes extremely upset when certain events interrupt the routine. Examples include when her teacher is absent, when Friday's normal *school lunch (pizza) is not offered, or when her mother stops on the drive home from school to run an errand.*

Michelle has been collecting and carrying red objects since she was a toddler. On her first day of kindergarten, she arrived at school carrying a large red bag containing 10 pounds of red objects. In addition, her attention was fixated on all red things in the classroom. She would scream when stopped from gaining access to anything red in the room, regardless of location or ownership. It took a year for her to accept the school rule that she could only carry one red item.

Linda, at age 4, never used her left hand for anything other than carrying a blue miniature toy with her at all times. Previous efforts to remove the blue toy resulted in days of panic and refusals to eat and sleep. Only when a lovely blue box that played soft music was placed near her—to hold her blue toy—was Linda gradually able to let go for increasing periods of time. As long as she could see her toy, she was calm. Linda's interest in blue miniatures gradually evolved into a lovely collection of pretty blue boxes that contain beautiful and unusual blue items.

Mia's second-grade teacher has 15 colorful cards hanging in the classroom that define social terms in concrete ways. For example, cope means "try three more times, then ask for help"; change means "I don't know what is next"; and patience means "use the relaxation procedure while waiting." When Mia was asked which of the social rule cards was easy to follow, she looked at her cards for a long time and then replied, "Cope." When Mia was asked which of the social rule cards was difficult to follow, she immediately replied, "Change; I don't like change."

UNKNOWNS

The scientific literature of the past decade has shed light on the complexity of autism. Nevertheless, anyone who has lived with or worked with a child having autism recognizes that the research does not capture the diversity of children with the disorder. The autism continuum is broad and contains many unknowns. The various behaviors of individual children are constantly challenging what specialists think they know about autism. The following vignettes are important to the continued pursuit of understanding autism and humbling to those who dedicate their lives to helping the children:

Bonnie, an 8-year-old who was nonverbal, came to a new school with a history of screaming and vocal outbursts. The behavior gradually worsened over time, even with intensive behavioral intervention. In her new environment, an astute observer noticed that Bonnie had a number of motor rituals that inhibited her movement. For example, she would stop at a doorway if the floor changed appearance and would rock three times before crossing the threshold. Bonnie would also move up and down three times before sitting on or rising from a chair. Whenever these patterns were interrupted by an adult through physical prompting, she would scream or yell. Allowing Bonnie to engage in her movement rituals resulted in the gradual elimination of her screaming.

Marty was a nonspeaking 4-year-old who frequently thrashed his body. At times, his body movements seemed spastic and uncontrollable. There were days when Marty would appear to be in pain and would not eat or sleep. For instance, Marty would be calm while watching a video and then suddenly scream and throw his body to the ground. Neurological testing revealed nothing. Intense behavioral intervention was discontinued after 6 months due to lack of progress and an increas-

ing refusal of food. The focus of Marty's program shifted to helping him feel comfortable. He wore heavy vests, weighted hats, and headphones; used a pacifier; and was silently prompted through all tasks. Another child in Marty's class used a set of elaborate communication boards with about 50 messages on each board. One day, after one of his episodes, Marty took one of the communication boards, grabbed an adult's hand, and spontaneously pointed to the following sequence of pictographs: "help," "mad," "drink." Marty, who originally appeared to have no comprehension of language, spontaneously communicated his pain. After that, his team and family tested him and found better understanding and use of language through AAC systems. In addition, Marty's negative behaviors were significantly reduced after neurologists conducted a more thorough examination and prescribed appropriate medication.

Allysa was a verbal, happy, 8-year-old who stopped talking after a week-long battle with strep throat in January. There was no medical reason for her mutism. A number of interventions were attempted, but she consistently smiled and refused to talk; instead, she used writing to communicate. A few months later, an elaborate story was written for Allysa to explain that her throat was okay and that she could talk after eating a lozenge. Each morning, Allysa's mother would give her a lozenge, reassure her that her throat was okay, and ask her to say something. Allysa continued to smile and to refuse to speak. Family and professionals working with Allysa became increasingly concerned after 6 months of silence. Finally, on Friday, July 11, Allysa took her lozenge and said, "Okay, Mommy." What was the "magical" solution that prompted Allysa to speak? Through careful reflection, the team discovered that Allysa stopped talking on Friday, January 11 (J-11). Why, then, did she not talk on June 11? It was not a Friday, and Allysa apparently connected Friday, J-11 with her speech patterns.

Julian, at age 6, had made significant progress in all areas of development except receptive language. His responses to verbal directions continued to be random even though his hearing was normal. Eventually, Julian's family and team began to notice an unusual pattern. Whenever Julian was sick with a fever, he consistently employed echolalia and responded to verbal information. All other times, he did not respond to verbal language and engaged in self-talk intermittently. Julian continues to follow this pattern.

SUMMARY

Autism is a spectrum of disorders that manifests in diverse ways. This chapter illustrates some learning, social, and communication experiences of children with autism. A complex disorder requires complex solutions. The challenge for educators and families is to respect children's struggles with social and communication challenges while trying to build success in those areas. Assessment and intervention, which are addressed in the following chapters, must take into account each child's unique learning style and social perspective in order to build skills and meaningful relationships.

chapter 3

Assessment of
Social and Communication Skills

Kathleen Ann Quill,
Kathleen Norton Bracken, and Maria E. Fair

Educational assessment of children serves three basic purposes: to provide an estimate of developmental functioning, to describe skills needed for planning intervention, and to document development and progress over time. The two basic kinds of assessment instruments are formal, norm-referenced tests and informal assessments. A *norm-referenced test* is a standardized assessment that is administered in a prescribed way and provides a summary of quantitative scores. These tests are based on typical developmental sequences and describe a child's performance relative to a normative sample. Formal norm-referenced assessments include achievement tests and IQ tests. In contrast, *informal assessments* are not standardized, but their results are directly linked to intervention. Informal procedures are often curriculum driven and are used to determine instruction and to document individual progress. These assessments provide a profile of mastered skills and a list of skills to target for intervention. A child's performance is not compared with others but, rather, is used to design an individual intervention plan. Some informal assessments measure abilities directly, via observation or skill samples. Other informal tools—such as inventories, questionnaires, rating scales, and checklists—measure abilities indirectly by interviewing others familiar with the child.

The purpose of this chapter is to provide a clear and comprehensive curriculum-based assessment of social and communication skills that is specifically designed for children with autism. It begins with a brief summary of the assessments currently available to evaluate social and/or communication skills. These are mostly diagnostic tools or developmentally based curriculum assessments. Next, a summary of typical social and communication milestones that are most relevant to the intervention needs of children with autism is provided as a backdrop to our new assessment instrument.

ASSESSMENT OF SOCIAL AND COMMUNICATION SKILLS

Professionals face specific challenges when assessing children with autism. These include determining which assessments provide useful information and accommodating for children's atypical patterns of development in the assessment process. Although there are many formal assessments that evaluate social and communication development, there are a number of disadvantages with using these instruments to evaluate children with autism. First, a child with autism may demonstrate a particular skill in the natural environment but may not be able to perform the same skill under controlled test situations. As a result, norm-referenced tests may limit the scope of information obtained for planning instruction. Second, the qualities of social and communication behavior in autism are not adequately represented by standardized measures. Development of social and communication skills in children with autism often follows a path that diverges from that of typically developing children. Children with autism may acquire skills in different sequences, use skills in idiosyncratic ways, or demonstrate unusual compensatory skills. Atypical developmental patterns make it difficult to translate standardized assessments into meaningful intervention programs. Third, given that impairments in social and communication development are central to autism, the measurement of these skills needs to be a priority in assessment and intervention.

Table 3.1 summarizes measures that are most commonly used to identify children with autism and/or assess their social and communication development. There is a lim-

Table 3.1. Assessments of social and communication skills

Autism diagnostic scales
  Autism Diagnostic Interview–Revised (ADI-R; Lord, Rutter, & LeCourteur, 1994)
  Autism Diagnostic Observation Schedule (ADOS; Lord, Rutter, DiLavore, & Risi, 1999)
  Childhood Autism Rating Scale (CARS; Schopler, Reichler, & Renner, 1988)

Adaptive behavior scales
  Vineland Adaptive Behavior Scales (Sparrow, Balla, & Cicchetti, 1984)
  Adaptive Behavior Inventory for Children (Mercer & Lewis, 1978)

Autism educational assessments
  Psychoeducational Profile–Revised (PEP-R; Schopler, Reichler, Bashford, Lansing, & Marcus, 1990)
  Autism Screening Instrument for Educational Planning (ASIEP; Krug, Arick, & Almond, 1980)

Curriculum-based developmental assessments
  Brigance Inventory of Early Development (Brigance, 1983)
  Transdisciplinary Play-Based Assessment (TPBA; Linder, 1993)
  The Carolina Curriculum for Preschoolers with Special Needs (Johnson-Martin, Attermeier, & Hacker, 1990)

Play assessments
  Symbolic Play Test (Lowe & Costello, 1976)
  A Scale for Assessing Development of Children's Play (Westby, 2000)
  Wolfberg's informal play assessment for children with autism (Wolfberg, 1995)

Assessments of prelinguistic social-communication
  Communication and Symbolic Behavior Scales (CSBS; Wetherby & Prizant, 1990)
  Checklist for Autism in Toddlers (CHAT; Baron-Cohen, Allen, & Gillberg, 1992)
  Pre-Linguistic Autism Diagnostic Observation Schedule (PL-ADOS; DiLavore, Lord, & Rutter, 1995)

Pragmatic language assessments
  The Rossetti Infant-Toddler Language Scale (Rossetti, 1990)
  Functional Communication Profile (Kleiman, 1994)
  Test of Pragmatic Language (Phelps-Terasaki & Phelps-Gunn, 1992)
  Test of Language Competence–Expanded Edition (TLC-Expanded; Wiig & Secord, 1989)
  Test of Problem Solving (Bowers, Huisingh, Barrett, Orman, & LoGiudice, 1994)

ited selection of assessments available to help educators design and monitor social and communication intervention plans for children with autism. Most tools that address social and communication skills have been designed for diagnostic purposes and are limited in scope. A review of assessment tools commonly used for children with autism follows. More information about these types of assessment tools can be found in the resource section at the end of this book.

Autism diagnostic scales: A few diagnostic tools rate the degree of social, communicative, and behavioral impairment in children with autism. These include interviews, such as the Autism Diagnostic Interview–Revised (ADI-R; Lord, Rutter, & LeCourteur, 1994), and rating instruments, such as the Autism Diagnostic Observation Schedule (ADOS; Lord, Rutter, DiLavore, & Risi, 1999) and the Childhood Autism Rating Scale (CARS; Schopler, Reichler, & Renner, 1988). These tools have been proven reliable in determining whether or not a child has autism. They also provide a structured means to record general diagnostic information.

Adaptive behavior scales: Standardized measures of adaptive skills are commonly used to assess children with various developmental disorders. The Vineland Adaptive Behavior Scales (Sparrow, Balla, & Cicchetti, 1984) and the Adaptive Behavior Inventory for Children (Mercer & Lewis, 1978) use interviews and questionnaires to obtain general social, communication, self-care, motor, and behavioral indices.

Autism educational assessments: A limited number of educational tools have been specifically designed to assess children with autism and to plan intervention. These include the Psychoeducation Profile–Revised (PEP-R; Schopler, Reichler, Bashford, Lansing, & Marcus, 1990) and the Autism Screening Instrument for Educational Planning (ASIEP; Krug, Arick, & Almond, 1980). The PEP-R is an inventory that assesses a range of skills, including imitation, motor performance, and cognition. The ASIEP is a more detailed assessment that samples functional skills. Both can be used for curriculum planning.

Curriculum-based developmental assessments: Criterion-referenced, curriculum-based early childhood developmental scales are generally used to measure children's social skills. These assessments address the full range of developmental domains (i.e., cognitive, language, motor, social). Examples are the Brigance Inventory of Early Development (Brigance, 1983), the Transdisciplinary Play-Based Assessment (TPBA; Linder, 1993), and The Carolina Curriculum for Preschoolers with Special Needs (Johnson-Martin, Attermeier, & Hacker, 1990).

Play assessments: The Symbolic Play Test (Lowe & Costello, 1976) is the most popular formal measure of spontaneous play activities. A Scale for Assessing Development of Children's Play was designed by Westby (2000). Both instruments examine the developmental elements of play. Wolfberg (1995) developed an informal play assessment for children with autism that takes into account the cognitive, communication, and social dimensions of play activities.

Assessments of prelinguistic social-communication: More attention has been given to developing measures that examine prelinguistic social and communicative skills in very young children. The Communication and Symbolic Behavior Scales (CSBS; Wetherby & Prizant, 1990) examine the early social-communicative and symbolic skills of children whose functional communication is between 8 and 24 months of age. The rating scale assesses gestural communication, vocal communicative means, reciprocity, affective signaling, and symbolic behaviors across various communicative contexts. There are two instruments that examine similar skills in young children with autism. The Checklist for Autism in Toddlers (CHAT; Baron-Cohen, Allen, & Gillberg, 1992) was designed to identify autism in 18-month-old children through a simple questionnaire that asks parents about a child's social interest, joint attention, gestural communication, and play. The Pre-Linguistic Autism Diagnostic Observation Schedule (PL-ADOS; DiLavore, Lord, & Rutter, 1995) is a tool that examines these same nonverbal skills in young children whose developmental age is less than 36 months.

Pragmatic language assessments: There is a wide range of commercially available language assessments, but most tools focus on receptive and expressive language abilities and fail to address social-pragmatic skills in detail. Language assessments that do contain some elements of social-communicative development are The Rossetti Infant-Toddler Language Scale (Rossetti, 1990), the Functional Communication Profile (Kleiman, 1994), the Test of Pragmatic Language (Phelps-Terasaki & Phelps-Gunn, 1992), the Test of Language Competence–Expanded Edition (TLC-Expanded; Wiig & Secord, 1989), and the Test of Problem Solving (Bowers, Huisingh, Barrett, Orman, & LoGiudice, 1994).

TYPICAL SOCIAL AND COMMUNICATION DEVELOPMENT

Understanding the critical stages of social and communication development in typically developing children is essential to understanding the intervention needs of children with autism. For more comprehensive information on social and communication development, see Bates (1976), Brazelton (1994), Garvey (1977), Kagan (1994), Rubin (1980), and Wells (1981).

Core Skills

The early developmental growth of infants and toddlers is dominated by social and communication milestones (see Table 3.2). These include the development of skills in the areas of imitation, social regulation, joint attention, and reciprocal interaction. The developmental process during the first 2 years of life begins with the acquisition of nonverbal means to interact with others (e.g., gestures, motor imitation, reciprocal play) and develops into the use of language to interact with others (e.g., verbal imitation, combining gestures and words, reciprocal verbal exchanges). During this stage, children also develop the ability to imitate a growing number of related activities (e.g., imitate a series of related actions or words, engage in a sequence of play acts). These core skills lay the foundation for the development of all other social and communication skills.

In order to understand these early developmental milestones, it is essential to view the child within the context of social interaction. Adult–child interactions are the focus of these first 2 years. Adults focus a tremendous amount of energy adjusting to the behavioral style of the child, and the child exerts a tremendous amount of energy adjusting to the interaction style of his or her caregivers. The child's ability to process the context and meaning of people in the environment contributes to the development of these core skills (Zirpoli, 1995). The following vignette describes the core skills of one typically developing child:

It is Ryan's first birthday party. He sits in his high chair, surrounded by his family, and watches everyone's reactions when the birthday cake appears. Ryan looks at his father, vocalizes to get his father's attention, and then points to the cake. He continuously shifts his focus from the cake and its candles to everyone singing "Happy Birthday." He smiles and rocks his head back and forth to the singing. He then claps when everyone else claps at the end of the song. Ryan watches as everyone pretends to blow out the candles, and he imitates them. Ryan and his mother blow out the candles together. He claps again, raises his arms in the air, and looks at everyone in an effort to get them to do the same thing and to say "hurray." In a few brief moments, Ryan demonstrated all of the core skills that are the foundation of social and communication development.

Social Skills

Social development in early childhood is characterized by three general skill areas: more elaborate and creative solitary play, interactions with peers, and the acquisition of prosocial behaviors. Interactions with peers increase as an avenue for social learning, and there is a gradual decrease in the child's reliance on adults for social and emotional support.

Table 3.2. Early developmental milestones (3–24 months of age)

Core skill	Age (months)
Shares social smiles	3–6
Demonstrates shared attention	
Shows interest in mirror	
Repeats own sounds imitated	
Continues movement imitated	
Establishes joint attention	6–12
Enjoys Peekaboo	
Combines gestures to regulate	
Points to items of interest	
Pulls others to gain attention	
Waves good-bye	
Imitates facial expressions	
Imitates novel actions	
Imitates single-syllable sounds	
Demonstrates interest in cause-and-effect toys	
Shows interest in peers	12–18
Enjoys making others laugh	
Responds to adult praise	
Combines gestures, eye gaze, and words	
Points to and shows things of interest	
Imitates two-syllable words	
Imitates adult actions to solve a problem	
Explores combining toys in novel ways	
Engages in repetitive play sequences with toys	
Shows pleasure in accomplishments	18–24
Comforts others	
Engages in interactive play with adults	
Engages in rough-and-tumble play with peers	
Communicates needs, interests, and feelings	
Engages in parallel play	
Begins to imitate peers	
Begins symbolic toy use	

Sources: Bayley (1993); Johnson-Martin, Jens, Attermeier, & Hacker (1991); Sparrow, Balla, & Cicchetti (1984).

There is an evolution of imagination in solitary play. Children make an important transition from the functional to symbolic use of toys. Pretend play develops out of the ability to assign novel meanings and actions to toys and objects (Fein, 1981). Children use toys and objects in creative ways, and they embed imaginary people and objects into play. They dramatize various roles that derive from personal experiences or characters from favorite books, television, or movies. Children also assign roles to inanimate objects such as dolls or stuffed animals. Their dramatic play themes become increasingly more organized and complex.

The ability to interact with peers is often considered the primary measure of social competence (Odom & Strain, 1984; Strain & Odom, 1986). Children initially show interest in peers through watching, smiling, and touching while engaged in parallel play activities. Gradually, reciprocal peer interactions expand in length, frequency, and complexity. Children offer and exchange toys, share objects, and intermittently imitate each other's play. Quickly, interactions with peers develop into elaborate forms of cooperative play and more sophisticated language use within social play activities.

Table 3.3. Important social developmental milestones (12–60 months of age)

Social skill	Age (months)
Imitates simple adult actions	12+
Shows interest in peer activities	
Plays simple interactive games	
Enjoys listening to simple stories	
Enjoys rough-and-tumble play	
Engages in parallel play	
Attempts to comfort others in distress	24+
Begins symbolic toy use	
Begins to share toys	
Pretends adult roles in play	
Imitates a task previously observed	
Participates in supervised small-group games	
Shows preference for some friends over others	36+
Labels feelings in self	
Assumes different roles in play	
Begins to take turns in play	
Plays group games with supervision	
Has a preferred friend	48+
Plays cooperatively with others	
Develops a logical sequence of events in play	
Follows rules in simple games	
Recognizes another's need for help and gives assistance	
Shares and takes turns without reminders	
Responds positively to the good fortune of others	60+
Has a group of friends	
Follows community rules	
Engages in complex adult role playing	
Plays games requiring skill and decision making	
Plays cooperative group games	

Sources: Johnson-Martin, Attermeier, & Hacker (1990); Sparrow, Balla, & Cicchetti (1984).

Prosocial behaviors are "random acts of kindness" that characterize the socioemotional development of young children. Examples include giving positive attention, providing assistance, and noting approval through words or emotion. Emotional response through smiling and laughing, sharing, and cooperation is a key behavior that contributes to successful social interactions (Hartup, 1983; Tremblay, Strain, Hendrickson, & Shores, 1981). It is important to note that conversational abilities are not considered a primary means to receive positive responses, nor are they necessary to engage in successful social interactions. Table 3.3 summarizes important social developmental milestones for young children. The next two profiles illustrate some of these skills:

Parallel play: *Jake and Billy, both 2 years old, are playing with blocks. If Jake wants a block that Billy is using, Jake takes it. If Billy wants it back, Billy takes it. Each boy occasionally stops his own activity to watch what the other is doing. Their interactions are limited to intermittent observation and brief nonverbal exchanges.*

Cooperative play: *Greg, Doug, and Joey, all age 4, are playing with blocks. The boys proceed to build their own structures with little to no conversing. One at-*

tempt to take a friend's block is handled with a nudge! A second attempt to take someone else's block is handled by the boys nonverbally negotiating a trade. Greg makes sound effects (e.g., shh, pww, brr) that signal that his building is a house on fire and he is a firefighter with a pretend hose. Doug narrates his own activity but does not seek any acknowledgment from his friends. Joey builds his structure in silence and then follows Greg's lead, also pretending to be a firefighter. During the 10-minute activity, the boys say little to each other. Doug asks, "Hey, Greg, how's this?" and Greg says "Wow" a dozen times. Joey calls his friends' names a few times to indicate that he is happy to be a part of the project. Their episode of cooperative play is dominated by imagination, joint focus on a project, and nonverbal interactions.

Communication Skills

As children grow older, their repertoire of communication skills becomes more complex. With the emergence of language, children develop the ability to combine nonverbal and verbal means to express a range of communicative functions and initiate, maintain, and terminate social interactions. They satisfy basic needs, exert control over the environment, establish conversational exchanges, seek information, share experiences, and express their feelings. They converse about past and future events. The complex dimensions of conversation—such as maintaining appropriate topics, considering the listener's perspective, and interpreting the nonverbal behaviors of others—are learned and refined. Children acquire the ability to use nonverbal conversational skills—such as appropriate physical proximity, voice quality, and eye contact—in more flexible ways. Refinement of these conversational skills across different social contexts and with different conversational partners is a lifelong developmental process. Important developmental milestones in the area of communication are summarized in Table 3.4.

Adult–child conversations contrast sharply with peer–peer conversations throughout early childhood. There is a significant difference in the quantity and quality of verbal interactions used by children in their interactions with adults as compared with interactions with peers. When the play of 2-year-old, 4-year-old, and 6-year-old boys was videotaped for analysis, peer interactions were dominated by nonverbal social behaviors and expressions of emotion (Quill & Bracken, 1998). There was a striking paucity of conversation among peers. There was more communication among the 4- and 6-year-old boys, although it typically was either single exchanges (e.g., question and answer, comment or verbal acknowledgment) or parallel talk (e.g., talking about one's ideas and feelings with nonverbal acknowledgment). The same play contexts with adults revealed more elaborate conversational exchanges. The following examples demonstrate this difference:

Two-year-old Christopher, while playing with his mother, said "Look at the dump truck," "No, I don't want to give him a ride," and "I need some dirt." When Christopher later engaged in the same activity with a peer, his language was typically single words, such as "No" and "Mine."

Four-year-old Gary's conversation with an adult during play included, "Wow, we're both using the same color," "I really like this," and "When are we going outside?" In contrast, his verbal interactions during play with peers were much briefer, such as "Hey, look at this," "Thanks," "Wow," and "Don't."

Six-year-old Jimmy's conversation with an adult included, "Do you know what my brother did last night?" "His soccer team won, and he scored two goals . . . it was really cool," and "We all went out for ice cream after the game." Speaking with a peer, Jimmy simply said things such as "Hey, check this out," "Cool," "Use this," and "Cool, man!"

Table 3.4. Important communication developmental milestones (12–60 months of age)

Communication skill	Age (months)
Produces intermittent verbal imitation	12+
Combines gestures for all functions	
Plays simple interactive games	
Combines gestures and words for basic functions	
Indicates preference when given a choice	
Uses nonverbal means to initiate peer interaction	24+
Comments on and describes ongoing events	
Answers simple questions	
Asks simple questions	
Comforts others nonverbally	
Maintains simple conversation exchanges with adults	
Retells a familiar story when looking at pictures	36+
Relates a past experience when asked to do so	
Labels feelings in self	
Conducts intermittent conversational exchanges with peers	
Engages in simple conversational exchanges on the telephone	
Initiates peer interaction verbally	
Uses body language and facial expression with messages	
Expands conversation skills with peers	48+
Retells a popular story, television episode, or movie plot	
Uses social phrases (e.g., "Excuse me," "Sorry")	
Relates events in an organized, logical sequence	
Recognizes how to respond to others' feelings	
Begins to interpret listener's body language	
Communicates about a wide range of topics	60+
Begins to take into account listener's perspective	
Adjusts conversation according to listener's needs	
Uses language to negotiate and compromise	

Sources: Johnson-Martin, Attermeier, & Hacker (1990); Sparrow, Balla, & Cicchetti (1984).

ASSESSMENT OF SOCIAL AND COMMUNICATION SKILLS FOR CHILDREN WITH AUTISM

The Assessment of Social and Communication Skills for Children with Autism (see Appendix A) is a new tool designed to evaluate a wide range of social and communication abilities of children with autism. It is intended to be used by professionals who are responsible for evaluating a child, developing an individual intervention plan for that child, and monitoring the child's progress in the areas of social and communication skills. It consists of a comprehensive set of social and communication skills that are intervention priorities in the treatment of autism. Measures of specific social and communication skills include nonverbal social-communicative skills (Mundy, 1995); imitation (Dawson & Adams, 1984); play (Wolfberg, 1999); communication (Wetherby & Prizant, 1993); and social skills required at home, at school, and in community settings (Schopler & Mesibov, 1988). The Assessment of Social and Communication Skills for Children with Autism can be used along with other formal and informal assessment instruments to obtain a complete evaluation of a child's competencies and to design social and communication intervention.

Purpose

The Assessment of Social and Communication Skills for Children with Autism can be used to

- Obtain a general profile of a child's social and communicative behavior
- Gather a detailed profile of a child's specific social and communicative skills
- Determine how a child functions in his natural environment
- Organize treatment goals and objectives
- Monitor a child's progress

The assessment tool gathers detailed information about a child's social, communicative, and ritualistic behavior, including

- Ritualistic social behaviors
- Ritualistic communication behaviors
- Exploratory behaviors
- Nonverbal social interaction skills
- Imitation skills
- Organizational skills
- Solitary play skills
- Social play skills
- Group skills
- Community social skills
- Basic communicative functions
- Socioemotional skills
- Basic conversational skills

Outline

The Assessment of Social and Communication Skills for Children with Autism is divided into five sections that can be used individually or in any combination.

Section I, the Inventory of Social and Communication Behavior, is a set of questionnaires that can be used to gather general information about a child's social, communicative, and exploratory behaviors as well as motivators and interests. Part A, the social behavior questionnaire, elicits general information about the child's play skills, the conditions under which the child plays with others, and the presence of any social rituals or other social-behavioral challenges. Part B, the communicative behavior questionnaire, determines how the child communicates, with whom the child communicates, why the child communicates, the conditions under which the child communicates most effectively, and the presence of any communication rituals or other communication challenges. Part C, the exploratory behavior questionnaire, gathers basic information about how the child explores his surroundings, the presence of any strong interests or fears, and the conditions under which the child is most focused and calm. Part D ascertains which foods, toys, activities, and interests are motivating for the child and could provide opportunities for social and communication enhancement.

Section II, the Core Skills Checklist, gathers information about the child's 1) nonverbal social interaction skills, 2) imitation skills, and 3) general organizational skills. In Part A, the area of nonverbal social interaction, the checklist includes items that determine the child's ability to attend, maintain reciprocal interaction, interact to make requests, and interact to share interests. These are key skills for children with and without speech. In Part B, the area of imitation, the checklist includes items that determine the child's ability to imitate motor movements and speech in isolation or as a sequence of actions or words. Part C, the organization checklist, is composed of items that determine the child's ability to prepare and complete activities, make choices, attend and wait during activities, make transitions, follow directions, and be comforted by others.

Section III, the Social Skills Checklist, gathers information about a child's 1) play skills, 2) group skills, and 3) social skills in the community. In Part A, the area of play, the checklist includes items that determine the child's solitary play, parallel play, and cooperative play abilities. Part B, the group skills checklist, examines the child's ability to attend, wait, take turns, and follow group directions. In Part C, the area of community social skills, the checklist examines the child's skills in a variety of home, school, and community settings.

Section IV, the Communication Skills Checklist, assesses a child's 1) functional communication, 2) socioemotional skills, and 3) basic conversational skills. Part A, the basic communicative functions checklist, assesses the child's ability to make basic requests, respond to others, comment, and request information. Part B, the socioemotional skills checklist, assesses how the child communicates his feelings and expresses prosocial skills. Part C, the basic conversational skills portion, determines the child's verbal and nonverbal discourse skills.

Section V is the Assessment Summary Sheet. This element of the assessment tool helps the user condense the gathered material and highlight priorities in each of the nine skill areas. This information is then used to generate behavioral objectives for intervention. Chapters 6, 7, and 8 contain intervention curricula that directly correspond to each of the items in the tool.

How to Gather Information

The Assessment of Social and Communication Skills for Children with Autism allows the user to gather information in a variety of ways. Information about a child's social and communication development can be obtained through interview, observation, or direct sampling techniques.

Interview

Interviews are an effective means to gather information, especially when used in conjunction with observation and direct sampling procedures. Interviews provide a historical view of a child and an understanding of the dynamic quality of the child's social and communication skills. In addition, interviews with family members, teachers, therapists, and others who know the child well are invaluable for discovering how the child functions in various social contexts over an extended period of time. The extent and reliability of information increases with the use of multiple informants.

The assessment tool is designed so that each domain can be evaluated using an interview format. The Inventory of Social and Communication Behavior is formatted as a list of questions, and all elements of the core skills, social skills, and communication skills checklists can be phrased as questions. The checklists are organized to answer the following questions about each skill:

- Is the skill ever observed?

- Is the skill generalized? (i.e., Does the child use the skill with both adults and peers, and does the child demonstrate the skill across multiple settings?)

- Is the skill a priority for intervention (i.e., Is it a target instructional objective)?

The format of the community social skills checklist varies slightly to ask 1) are there any challenging behaviors that interfere with the child's functioning in the community and 2) which community settings are intervention priorities? Once specific community settings are selected for intervention, a more detailed assessment and intervention plan can be developed (see Chapter 7).

Observation

The accuracy of the material obtained through interviews should be confirmed through direct observations of the child, which are then recorded on the checklist. For maximum effectiveness, observations should be conducted over several days, in multiple settings, and during various activities. Observations provide vital information about how the child functions in his natural environment. It is important to observe social and communication skills in settings where the child is motivated, relaxed, and focused because ascertaining the conditions under which the child is most interactive is a critical part of the assessment process. It is also important to observe social and communication skills in settings where the child is unmotivated or challenging behaviors occur. Finally, observations should include opportunities for the child to interact with both familiar and unfamiliar adults and peers. This will assist the professional in determining the degree to which the child is able to generalize skills across social settings and social partners. Although these observations are time consuming, the information generated provides a comprehensive profile of the child's functional social and communication skills.

Direct Sampling

Once the interview and observation processes are complete, there may be some unanswered questions that require more direct sampling of specific skills. Skills can be systematically sampled by utilizing

- Structured social opportunities
- Communication temptations (Wetherby & Prizant, 1989)
- Videotaped analysis of adult–child or peer–child social interactions

Structured Social Opportunities

The majority of social skills can be sampled by using toys, materials, and activities commonly found at home or school and by structuring activities that elicit the skill in question. For example, one would set up a group game that requires imitation to assess if a child imitates peers. The sample activities and strategies described in Chapters 6 and 7 provide more detail about eliciting specific social skills.

Communication Temptations

Communication skills can be sampled by creating *communication temptations* (Wetherby & Prizant, 1989). These are natural activities that can be designed to elicit specific communicative behaviors. Samples of this technique include the following:

- Place a preferred item out of reach, and wait for the child to request it.
- Spill something, and wait for the child's response.
- Put on a silly hat, and wait for the child to comment.
- Present a see-through container of interesting toys, and wait for the child to comment on it or request it.
- Look through a picture book, and wait for the child to comment or ask questions.
- Play a preferred game, and wait for the child to request continuation.
- Have a peer give the child a desired object, and wait for the child's response.
- Ask the child to identify an unusual object, and observe how the child indicates that he does not know what it is.

The sample activities and strategies described in Chapter 8 provide more detail about eliciting specific communication skills.

Videotaped Analysis

The most revealing information about the quality of a child's nonverbal and verbal social and communication skills can be obtained through videotaped analyses of various interactions. Structured social activities and communication temptations can be videotaped to sample the child's skills, and then the information gained can be recorded on the assessment checklists. Videotapes reveal the dynamic, reciprocal quality of a child's interactions and are a permanent record of the child's abilities.

Directions for Completing the Assessment

Before beginning the assessment, review the glossary (Appendix B) to clarify the meaning of the terms used in the inventory and checklists. Then, complete the Student Record cover sheet so that it lists the child's name and date of birth as well as the name of the person completing the form. Through the course of assessment, list the names of all individuals interviewed and the interview dates. In addition, list the dates on which observations and direct sampling occurred as well as the settings in which they were conducted. Dates are essential for measuring progress, as this assessment tool is meant to be used for yearly educational planning.

Section I, the Inventory of Social and Communication Behavior, is presented as a series of yes/no questions and allows room for general comments. In addition, there is space to list the child's favorite foods, toys, activities, and interests.

The forms for Sections II, III (with the exception of Part C, community social skills), and IV list general skill areas, which are shaded, and their associated subskills. Beside each specific subskill are multiple columns for clarifying findings. The columns indicate the presence of the specific skill, the functional use of the skill with multiple interactive partners and across multiple settings, and whether the skill will be a target objective. Specific information about the scoring follows.

The first column (Skill) identifies whether a specific skill is present. Circle "Y" for yes or "N" for no. A social skill is considered present if it has been observed at least one time without prompts. For example, in the area of motor imitation, does the child imitate spontaneously or only when elicited with a prompt? A communication skill is considered present when the child spontaneously gestures, speaks, signs, or uses another augmentative and alternative communication (AAC) device as a means of interaction. A communication skill is only coded as present if it has been observed at least one time without prompts. For example, does the child request objects spontaneously or only when prompted?

The second column (Generalized) identifies whether the specific skill is generalized across multiple partners and settings. Circle "Y" if the child has generalized the skill, and circle "N" if the child only demonstrates the skill in specific contexts or with limited partners. For recording purposes, *generalization* is defined as the presence of the skill in five or more settings and with at least one adult and one peer.

The third column (Target three objectives) should be checked if the skill is to become an instructional objective for the next school year. A skill may be targeted for instruction for multiple reasons, specifically, if a skill is absent, needs to be generalized to peers, or requires generalization to multiple contexts.

Once the inventory and checklists have been completed, Section V, the Assessment Summary Sheet, can be completed to develop an individual intervention plan. The purpose of the summary sheet is to establish instructional priorities for the next year. The child's educational team is encouraged to target one to three objectives in each of the nine general skill areas. Priority objectives should be selected in each of the core skill areas (i.e., nonverbal social interaction, imitation, and organization), the social skill areas (i.e., play, group skills, and community social skills), and communication skill areas (i.e., basic communicative functions, socioemotional skills, and basic conversational skills).

Advantages and Limitations

The Assessment of Social and Communication Skills for Children with Autism offers a number of advantages for those seeking a detailed profile of a child's social and communication skills:

- The assessment focuses on the child's functional social and communication skills in his natural environment.

- The assessment is comprehensive in scope.

- The assessment is structured so that information can be obtained directly (from the child through observation and direct sampling) and indirectly (from informants).

- Family members can be involved, via interviews, in the assessment process.

- The assessment can obtain information on any child, regardless of challenging behaviors.

- The assessment promotes recording the child's best skills by gathering information from multiple informants, activities, and settings.

- The assessment is conducive to determining the conditions under which the child is most interactive.

- The assessment results can be linked directly to instructional goals and objectives.

- The assessment examines a wide range of specific social and communication skills, the most critical aspects of development in children with autism.

There are recognized limitations to this assessment tool and other informal measures that lack standardization. First, this tool can supplement standardized assessment measures but cannot be used to document service needs if the child's state or school district mandates standardized assessments for this purpose. Second, the assessment does not incorporate normative data. It is structured to identify discrete skills that are impaired in autism and is not organized in a developmental hierarchy. For example, in the core skills area of nonverbal social interaction, all of the listed skills emerge simultaneously in typically developing infants, but one or more can be lacking in children with autism at various levels of cognitive ability. Similarly, in the communication domain, most of the communicative functions emerge simultaneously in typically developing toddlers, but one or more may be absent in children with autism. The authors of this assessment tool determined, however, that the application of a typical developmental hierarchy of skills would not capture the complexity of social and communication issues for which children with autism require direct instruction. Third, the profile of a child's skills obtained via this tool depends on the reliability of the informants. Inaccuracy is always a concern when information is gathered indirectly. Informants can misinterpret a child's skills, underestimate the child's abilities, or assume that he or she possesses greater skills than those actually demonstrated. Nevertheless, this matter can be easily controlled because the measure advocates the use of multiple informants and the verification of information through observations and direct sampling. Finally, the assessment is limited by the observation skills of the person conducting the evaluation. Observation skills are highly dependent on the examiner's understanding the skills to be observed. This book provides many ways for augmenting observation skills, including the glossary of terminology (Appendix B) found at the end of this chapter and discussions about each of the social and communication skills addressed in Chapters 6, 7, and 8. It is hoped that the assessment will be used as an ongoing diagnostic planning tool to expand the scope of social and communication goals integrated into a child's intervention plan.

SUMMARY

Intervention planning requires systematic measures of a child's skill repertoire. The Assessment of Social and Communication Skills for Children with Autism examines numerous discrete skills in the domains of social and communication functioning. Unfortunately, there is no easy way to assess social and communicative competence except by artificially separating it into various components. It is imperative to recognize, however, that the end product of social and communicative interactions is greater than the sum of its individual parts. Social and communication development is a dynamic event that takes place in a context that, by its nature, transforms the experience into something qualitatively different from the mere sum of its parts. In that way, this particular assessment tool is intended to guide one's understanding of the child, to foster discussion about the core issues challenging children with autism, and to promote educational planning that takes into account the most critical elements of intervention.

Appendix A
**Assessment of
Social and Communication Skills
for Children with Autism**

Assessment of
Social and Communication Skills
for Children with Autism

by

Kathleen Ann Quill, Ed.D.
Kathleen Norton Bracken, M.S.
Maria E. Fair

Student Record

Child's name: _____

Child's date of birth: _____

Person completing form: _____

Team members interviewed: _____

_____

Interview dates: _____

Observation conducted at: _____

Observation dates: _____

Planning for the _____ school year

DO-WATCH-LISTEN-SAY: Social and Communication Intervention for Children with Autism
by Kathleen Ann Quill © 2000 Paul H. Brookes Publishing Co.

I. INVENTORY OF SOCIAL AND COMMUNICATION BEHAVIOR

A. Social behavior	Yes/No	Comments
Does the child play		
1. Alone	Y N	
2. With adults	Y N	
3. With peers	Y N	
Does the child play		
1. Social interactive games	Y N	
2. Appropriately with a variety of toys	Y N	
3. Creatively with toys	Y N	
Does the child play best when others are		
1. Active	Y N	
2. Quiet	Y N	
3. Predictable	Y N	
4. Creative	Y N	
Does the child		
1. Accept changes in routines	Y N	
2. Transition when directed	Y N	
Does the child have any of the following social-behavioral challenges?		
1. Self-stimulatory behaviors	Y N	
2. Perseverative and/or ritualistic play	Y N	
3. Negative reaction to change	Y N	
4. Behavior challenges at home	Y N	
5. Behavior challenges in the community	Y N	

DO-WATCH-LISTEN-SAY: Social and Communication Intervention for Children with Autism
by Kathleen Ann Quill © 2000 Paul H. Brookes Publishing Co.

I. INVENTORY OF SOCIAL AND COMMUNICATION BEHAVIOR *(continued)*

B. Communicative behavior	Yes/No		Comments
Does the child communicate using			
1. Gestures	Y	N	
2. Speech	Y	N	
3. Sign language	Y	N	
4. Other:	Y	N	
Does the child			
1. Request what he/she wants	Y	N	
2. Indicate what he/she doesn't want	Y	N	
3. Comment about what he/she is doing	Y	N	
4. Share how he/she feels	Y	N	
Does the child communicate with			
1. Adults	Y	N	
2. Peers	Y	N	
Does the child communicate best when others use			
1. Simple language	Y	N	
2. Gestures	Y	N	
3. Animation	Y	N	
4. Other:	Y	N	
Does the child have any of the following challenges?			
1. Echolalia (repeats what is said)	Y	N	
2. Talking to himself/herself	Y	N	
3. Perseveration on a topic or question	Y	N	
4. Repeating book or video scripts	Y	N	
5. Inappropriate conversational topics	Y	N	
6. Other:	Y	N	

DO-WATCH-LISTEN-SAY: Social and Communication Intervention for Children with Autism
by Kathleen Ann Quill © 2000 Paul H. Brookes Publishing Co.

I. INVENTORY OF SOCIAL AND COMMUNICATION BEHAVIOR *(continued)*

C. Exploratory behavior	Yes/No		Comments
Does the child appear			
1. Active	Y	N	
2. Passive	Y	N	
3. Curious about his/her environment	Y	N	
Is the child an active learner?			
1. Visual: Does the child enjoy/explore toys/objects with visual effects, books, computers?	Y	N	
2. Auditory: Does the child enjoy/explore toys/objects that make noise, music?	Y	N	
3. Tactile: Does the child enjoy tickling, deep pressure, a variety of textures?	Y	N	
4. Kinesthetic: Does the child enjoy rocking, jumping, running, active play?	Y	N	
Is the child a passive learner?			
1. Visual: Does the child avoid visual exploration or close eyes frequently?	Y	N	
2. Auditory: Does the child avoid certain sounds or cover ears frequently?	Y	N	
3. Tactile: Does the child avoid touching certain textures or dislike head/face touched?	Y	N	
4. Kinesthetic: Does the child avoid movement or prefer quiet play?	Y	N	
Does the child explore new toys/objects			
1. Visually	Y	N	
2. Through sound	Y	N	
3. Through touch	Y	N	
4. Through movement	Y	N	
What intense interests or fears (if any) does the child have?			
What does the child do to calm himself/herself?			

DO-WATCH-LISTEN-SAY: Social and Communication Intervention for Children with Autism
by Kathleen Ann Quill © 2000 Paul H. Brookes Publishing Co.

I. INVENTORY OF SOCIAL AND COMMUNICATION BEHAVIOR *(continued)*

D. Motivators

What are the child's favorite foods?

1.

2.

3.

4.

5.

What are the child's favorite toys?

1.

2.

3.

4.

5.

What are the child's favorite activities?

1.

2.

3.

4.

5.

Does the child have any unique interests?

1.

2.

3.

4.

5.

DO-WATCH-LISTEN-SAY: Social and Communication Intervention for Children with Autism
by Kathleen Ann Quill © 2000 Paul H. Brookes Publishing Co.

II. CORE SKILLS CHECKLIST

A. Nonverbal social interaction	Skill Yes/No	Generalized Yes/No	Target three objectives
Social attention			
1. Stops activity/looks at person in response to name	Y N	Y N	
2. Looks at objects when directed	Y N	Y N	
3. Attends to one-to-one familiar activity for ____ minutes	Y N	Y N	
4. Attends to one-to-one novel activity for ____ minutes	Y N	Y N	
Reciprocal interaction			
1. Uses eye gaze to maintain social interaction	Y N	Y N	
2. Repeats own behavior to maintain interaction	Y N	Y N	
3. Repeats action with toy to maintain social game	Y N	Y N	
Social regulation			
1. Gestures: Pushes/pulls/manipulates person to request	Y N	Y N	
2. Gestures: Gives/manipulates object to request	Y N	Y N	
3. Points to object to request	Y N	Y N	
4. Combines eye gaze and gesture to request	Y N	Y N	
Shared attention			
1. Alternates gaze between toy/object and person	Y N	Y N	
2. Gives toy/object to share interests	Y N	Y N	
3. Points to toy/object to share interests	Y N	Y N	
4. Gains attention prior to sharing interests	Y N	Y N	

DO-WATCH-LISTEN-SAY: Social and Communication Intervention for Children with Autism
by Kathleen Ann Quill © 2000 Paul H. Brookes Publishing Co.

II. CORE SKILLS CHECKLIST *(continued)*

B. Imitation	Skill Yes/No	Generalized Yes/No	Target three objectives
Motor imitation			
1. Imitates an action with a toy	Y N	Y N	
2. Imitates a single body action	Y N	Y N	
3. Imitates a sequence of two actions	Y N	Y N	
4. Imitates a sequence of three or more actions	Y N	Y N	
5. Imitates a novel act during a familiar activity	Y N	Y N	
6. Imitates in novel contexts	Y N	Y N	
7. Imitates actions from a previous play activity (delayed)	Y N	Y N	
Verbal imitation			
1. Imitates mouth movements/vocalizations	Y N	Y N	
2. Imitates word(s):			
a. during songs, fingerplays, stories	Y N	Y N	
b. during social routines	Y N	Y N	
c. during movement activities	Y N	Y N	
d. during all activities	Y N	Y N	
3. Imitates word(s) upon request	Y N	Y N	
4. Repeats words from a song, book, or play activity (delayed)	Y N	Y N	

DO-WATCH-LISTEN-SAY: Social and Communication Intervention for Children with Autism
by Kathleen Ann Quill © 2000 Paul H. Brookes Publishing Co.

II. CORE SKILLS CHECKLIST *(continued)*

C. Organization	Skill Yes/No	Generalized Yes/No	Target three objectives
Space			
1. Prepares for activity by locating area/materials (chair, coat)	Y N	Y N	
2. Keeps toys/materials in designated locations	Y N	Y N	
3. Completes activity by putting away materials	Y N	Y N	
Choices			
1. Makes choices within an activity	Y N	Y N	
2. Makes choice between two objects/activities	Y N	Y N	
3. Makes choice among multiple objects/activities	Y N	Y N	
Time			
1. Attends to activity until completed	Y N	Y N	
2. Waits when directed	Y N	Y N	
Expectations			
1. Independent with familiar activities	Y N	Y N	
2. Follows directions during novel activities	Y N	Y N	
Transitions			
1. Makes transitions to the next activity when directed	Y N	Y N	
2. Accepts when activity is interrupted to make a transition	Y N	Y N	
3. Makes transitions when an unexpected change occurs	Y N	Y N	
Possessions			
1. Recognizes personal belongings (mine)	Y N	Y N	
2. Recognizes belongings of others (yours)	Y N	Y N	
3. Recognizes shared belongings (ours)	Y N	Y N	
Comfort			
1. Can be comforted	Y N	Y N	
2. Can calm self	Y N	Y N	

DO-WATCH-LISTEN-SAY: Social and Communication Intervention for Children with Autism
by Kathleen Ann Quill © 2000 Paul H. Brookes Publishing Co.

III. SOCIAL SKILLS CHECKLIST

A. Play	Skill Yes/No	Generalized Yes/No	Target three objectives
Solitary play			
1. Functional: Uses one action with one toy	Y N	Y N	
2. Functional: Closed-ended activities	Y N	Y N	
3. Functional: Open-ended activities	Y N	Y N	
4. Symbolic: Routine scripts	Y N	Y N	
5. Symbolic: Creative	Y N	Y N	
6. Plays independently for ____ minutes	Y N	Y N	
Social play			
1. Plays parallel with own set of toys/materials	Y N	Y N	
2. Plays parallel with organized toys/materials	Y N	Y N	
3. Participates in choral/unison group activity	Y N	Y N	
4. Turn-taking with one partner with predictable turns	Y N	Y N	
5. Turn-taking in a group game with predictable turns	Y N	Y N	
6. Shares materials	Y N	Y N	
7. Cooperative play with one partner	Y N	Y N	
8. Cooperative play in structured groups	Y N	Y N	
9. Cooperative play in unstructured groups	Y N	Y N	

DO-WATCH-LISTEN-SAY: Social and Communication Intervention for Children with Autism
by Kathleen Ann Quill © 2000 Paul H. Brookes Publishing Co.

III. SOCIAL SKILLS CHECKLIST *(continued)*

B. Group skills	Skill Yes/No	Generalized Yes/No	Target three objectives
Attending			
1. During meals (snack time, lunchtime)	Y N	Y N	
2. During structured projects (art, work)	Y N	Y N	
3. During listening activities (stories, music)	Y N	Y N	
4. During structured games (board games, outdoor games)	Y N	Y N	
5. During play activities (play center, recess)	Y N	Y N	
6. During discussion activities (circle time, meeting)	Y N	Y N	
Waiting			
1. Sits for group activity	Y N	Y N	
2. Raises hand for a turn	Y N	Y N	
3. Stands in line	Y N	Y N	
Turn-taking			
1. During structured activity	Y N	Y N	
2. During unstructured activity	Y N	Y N	
Following group directions			
1. Nonverbal directions (quiet gesture, turn off light)	Y N	Y N	
2. Attention-getting directions ("Everybody _____")	Y N	Y N	
3. Routine verbal directions ("Clean up," "Line up")	Y N	Y N	
4. Verbal directions in familiar contexts	Y N	Y N	
5. Verbal directions in novel contexts	Y N	Y N	

DO-WATCH-LISTEN-SAY: Social and Communication Intervention for Children with Autism
by Kathleen Ann Quill © 2000 Paul H. Brookes Publishing Co.

III. SOCIAL SKILLS CHECKLIST (continued)

C. Community social skills	Skill Yes/No	Challenging behaviors?	Target three objectives
Shopping			
1. Grocery store	Y N	Y N	
2. Toy store	Y N	Y N	
Restaurant			
1. Fast food	Y N	Y N	
2. Sit down	Y N	Y N	
Indoor recreational activities			
1. Movies	Y N	Y N	
2. Swimming pool	Y N	Y N	
Outdoor recreational activities			
1. Organized sports	Y N	Y N	
2. Playground	Y N	Y N	
Visiting			
1. Relatives	Y N	Y N	
2. Neighbors	Y N	Y N	
Safety			
1. Indoor	Y N	Y N	
2. Street	Y N	Y N	
3. Car/school bus	Y N	Y N	
Health			
1. Doctor	Y N	Y N	
2. Dentist	Y N	Y N	
Other settings			
1. Hair salon/barber	Y N	Y N	
2. Photographer	Y N	Y N	
Holidays			
1. Birthday	Y N	Y N	
2. Halloween	Y N	Y N	
3. Winter holidays	Y N	Y N	
School community			
1. Assemblies	Y N	Y N	
2. Fire drills	Y N	Y N	
3. Field trips	Y N	Y N	

IV. COMMUNICATION SKILLS CHECKLIST

A. Basic communicative functions	Skill Yes/No	Generalized Yes/No	Target three objectives
Request needs			
1. More	Y N	Y N	
2. Preference (when given a choice)	Y N	Y N	
3. Food/drink	Y N	Y N	
4. Object/toy	Y N	Y N	
5. Favorite activity	Y N	Y N	
6. End an activity ("All done")	Y N	Y N	
7. Help	Y N	Y N	
Respond to others			
1. Responds to name ("Huh," "What," "Yeah")	Y N	Y N	
2. Refuses object	Y N	Y N	
3. Refuses activity	Y N	Y N	
4. Responds to greetings	Y N	Y N	
5. Responds to play invitations	Y N	Y N	
6. Affirms to agree/accept ("Okay," "Yes")	Y N	Y N	
7. Responds to personal questions ("What's your name?")	Y N	Y N	
8. Responds to others' comments	Y N	Y N	

DO-WATCH-LISTEN-SAY: Social and Communication Intervention for Children with Autism
by Kathleen Ann Quill © 2000 Paul H. Brookes Publishing Co.

IV. COMMUNICATION SKILLS CHECKLIST *(continued)*

A. Basic communicative functions *(cont.)*	Skill Yes/No	Generalized Yes/No	Target three objectives
Comment			
1. Comments on the unexpected ("Oops," "Uh-oh")	Y N	Y N	
2. Names object/character	Y N	Y N	
3. Labels own possessions	Y N	Y N	
4. Names familiar people	Y N	Y N	
5. Describes actions	Y N	Y N	
6. Describes location	Y N	Y N	
7. Describes attributes	Y N	Y N	
8. Describes past events	Y N	Y N	
9. Describes future events	Y N	Y N	
Request information			
1. Attention (calls person's name)	Y N	Y N	
2. Information about object ("What?")	Y N	Y N	
3. Information about person ("Who?")	Y N	Y N	
4. Information about actions ("What's _____ doing?")	Y N	Y N	
5. Information with a yes/no question	Y N	Y N	
6. Information about location ("Where is _____ ?")	Y N	Y N	
7. Information about time ("When?")	Y N	Y N	
8. Information about cause ("Why?")	Y N	Y N	

DO-WATCH-LISTEN-SAY: Social and Communication Intervention for Children with Autism
by Kathleen Ann Quill © 2000 Paul H. Brookes Publishing Co.

IV. COMMUNICATION SKILLS CHECKLIST *(continued)*

B. **Socioemotional skills**	Skill Yes/No	Generalized Yes/No	Target three objectives
Express feelings			
1. Requests a break when upset	Y N	Y N	
2. Requests a calming activity when upset	Y N	Y N	
3. Indicates need to use relaxation procedure	Y N	Y N	
4. Likes/dislikes	Y N	Y N	
5. Angry/mad	Y N	Y N	
6. Happy/sad	Y N	Y N	
7. Calm/relaxed	Y N	Y N	
8. Hurt/sick/tired	Y N	Y N	
9. Proud ("I did it!")	Y N	Y N	
10. Silly	Y N	Y N	
11. Afraid/nervous	Y N	Y N	
12. Confused ("I don't know")	Y N	Y N	
Prosocial statements			
1. Requests more social game/interaction	Y N	Y N	
2. Requests affection (hugs, kisses)	Y N	Y N	
3. Asks someone to play	Y N	Y N	
4. Politeness ("Thank you," "Excuse me")	Y N	Y N	
5. Shares (gives own food/drink/object)	Y N	Y N	
6. Assertiveness ("Go away," "Don't do that")	Y N	Y N	
7. Gives affection ("I love you")	Y N	Y N	
8. Gives help	Y N	Y N	
9. Offers a choice ("Want that or this?")	Y N	Y N	
10. Gives comfort when someone feels sad, hurt, etc.	Y N	Y N	

DO-WATCH-LISTEN-SAY: Social and Communication Intervention for Children with Autism
by Kathleen Ann Quill © 2000 Paul H. Brookes Publishing Co.

IV. COMMUNICATION SKILLS CHECKLIST *(continued)*

C. Basic conversational skills	Skill Yes/No	Generalized Yes/No	Target three objectives
Verbal			
1. Initiates by gaining person's attention/calling name	Y N	Y N	
2. Terminates conversation with a routine script	Y N	Y N	
3. Maintains conversation by sharing information with a routine script	Y N	Y N	
4. Clarifies or persists by repeating message	Y N	Y N	
5. Maintains conversation when the partner structures the interaction	Y N	Y N	
6. Initiates conversation with routine scripts	Y N	Y N	
7. Maintains conversation by providing feedback ("I know," "Uh-huh," "Okay")	Y N	Y N	
8. Maintains conversation in novel contexts	Y N	Y N	
9. Maintains conversation using appropriate topics	Y N	Y N	
Nonverbal			
1. Attends/orients to speaker	Y N	Y N	
2. Maintains natural proximity to speaker	Y N	Y N	
3. Discriminates appropriate and inappropriate touching during a conversation	Y N	Y N	
4. Modulates volume of voice for the setting	Y N	Y N	
5. Watches/waits for listener confirmation (nod, smile) before continuing message	Y N	Y N	

DO-WATCH-LISTEN-SAY: Social and Communication Intervention for Children with Autism
by Kathleen Ann Quill © 2000 Paul H. Brookes Publishing Co.

V. ASSESSMENT SUMMARY SHEET

Review the assessment checklists, and do the following:

1. Identify all items in the "Target three objectives" column.

2. Select up to three target objectives from each general skill area.

3. Transfer the objectives to the spaces provided, and write them as behavioral objectives.

CORE SKILLS

Nonverbal social interaction	Imitation	Organization
1.		
2.		
3.		

SOCIAL SKILLS

Play	Group skills	Community social skills
1.		
2.		
3.		

COMMUNICATION SKILLS

Basic communicative functions	Socioemotional skills	Basic conversational skills
1.		
2.		
3.		

Appendix B

Glossary of Terms for the Assessment of Social and Communication Skills for Children with Autism

Attention ability to focus on relevant contextual and/or social information

Behavior any observable action; responses to internal states or external events; expressions of knowledge and feelings (*see also* Behavior challenge; Self-stimulatory behavior; Spontaneous behavior)

Behavior challenge any behavior that concerns others; behavior problems

Choral activity group activity during which everyone is doing the same thing at the same time; sharing, waiting, and turn-taking are not required; language comprehension and use are required

Clarify conversation request additional information from the listener during a conversation

Closed-ended activity activity in which the toys or materials are used in specific ways and/or there is a fixed sequence of steps; can be solitary or social; examples: books, hopscotch, art project with a predetermined final product

Closed-ended cooperative play cooperative play with an organized set of rules and outcomes; example: musical chairs

Closed-ended functional play functional activity in which the toys or materials are used in specific ways and/or there is a fixed sequence of steps; examples: puzzles, board games

Comment message conveyed for the purpose of sharing information or observation; generally elicits a social response; examples: sharing interests, sharing feelings

Communication an interactive exchange between two or more people to convey needs, feelings, and ideas (*see also* Communication initiation; Nonverbal communication; Spontaneous communication; Verbal communication)

Communication initiation convey a spontaneous message after a pause in the interaction

Communicative function purpose or reason to communicate (*see also* Comment; Communicative request for self; Request for information)

Communicative means form of communication utilized; any nonverbal or verbal behavior used to interact with others

Communicative request for self message conveyed to have personal wants and needs met; generally elicits a tangible response; examples: requesting a drink, requesting help

Community skills social skills required in the community; expectations to match the skills of same-age peers

Context-specific setting social or communicative behavior that occurs in a specific location, at a specific time, or with a specific person

Conversation interactive exchange between two or more people; requires that all partners take into account context and listeners' perspectives (*see also* Clarify conversation; Initiate conversation; Nonverbal communication; Terminate conversation; Verbal conversation)

Cooperative play play during which children share a common activity and/or work together toward a common goal; requires sharing and interaction (*see also* Closed-ended cooperative play; Open-ended cooperative play)

Creative play play that involves pretending that an object or oneself is something or someone else; creating imaginative persons or objects or attributes that are not present (*see also* Creative play with objects; Creative play with self; Creative symbolic play; Imaginative creative play)

Creative play with objects   play in which a toy or an object is used as if it is something else; example: using blocks as a road

Creative play with self   play that involves pretending to be someone or something else; examples: talking for a doll, taking the role of a firefighter

Creative symbolic play   play that is novel and/or varied (*see also* Creative play)

Delayed echolalia   exact or partial repetition of speech that is produced at a significantly later time after originally heard; may serve a variety of communicative and noncommunicative functions; may or may not be contextually relevant; examples: repetition of segments from books, songs, or videos, or re-enactment of a prior experience (*see also* Echolalia)

Delayed imitation   repetition of actions and/or speech at a significantly later time after initially being seen or heard; contextually meaningful; means to practice and reenact former experiences

Discussion   language-based group activity with no social predictability; requires sharing, turn-taking, and waiting

Echolalia   exact repetition of speech (*see also* Delayed echolalia; Delayed imitation; Immediate echolalia)

Functional play   play in which toys are used in a conventional manner (*see also* Closed-ended functional play; Open-ended functional play; Single-act functional play)

Generalization   presence of a skill in five or more settings and with at least one adult and one peer

Group activity   joint participation with others; varies in complexity from parallel to cooperative and in terms of expectations to share, take turns, and interact (*see also* Choral activity; Discussion; Structured nonverbal turn-taking; Structured verbal turn-taking; Unison activity; Unstructured play)

Imaginative creative play   play that creates an absent person or object or an attribute that is not present; examples: pretending to drink from an empty cup, pretending a toy stove is hot

Immediate echolalia   exact repetition of speech that is produced immediately after heard; may serve a variety of communicative and noncommunicative functions

Initiate conversation   convey a spontaneous message after a pause in an interaction

Language   a formal symbol system that has structural qualities—specifically, phonology, morphology, semantics, and syntax; examples: speech, sign language, written language

Motivator   any person, place, or thing of interest to a child; may or may not be socially desirable from the perspective of others; examples: tickling and balloons (appropriate), spinning objects or twirling ribbons (inappropriate)

Motor imitation   ability to copy the actions of others, including gross motor actions, fine motor actions, and actions using toys or objects

Nonverbal communication   use of physical proximity, gestures, facial expressions, eye gaze, or vocalizations to convey a message

Nonverbal social interaction   interactive exchange between two or more people using physical proximity, gestures, facial expressions, eye gaze, or vocalizations

Novel contexts   any new person, environment, or activity to which the child has had limited or no exposure

Open-ended activity   activity in which toys or materials are used in a variety of ways; involves no sequence of steps or predetermined outcome; can be solitary or social; examples: playing in a sandbox, using blocks or dolls, playing dress-up, art with no predetermined final product

Open-ended cooperative play   cooperative play that has no established agenda; those involved determine the sequence of events and outcome

Open-ended functional play functional activity in which the toys or materials are used in a conventional manner but there is no fixed sequence or outcome; examples: playing musical instruments, making a building with blocks

Organization ability to plan, arrange, organize, coordinate, and regulate oneself and one's physical surroundings; the ability to remain calm, focused, and purposeful

Parallel play play that takes place independently alongside other children, involves sharing space and/or toys, may or may not involve watching others

Perseverative play excessive and persistent repetition of motor actions or verbalizations during play; examples: lining up miniature figures in a row repeatedly, acting out a few lines from a movie repeatedly

Perseverative speech persistent repetition of a spontaneous or echoed message; may serve communicative or noncommunicative functions (*see also* Delayed echolalia; Echolalia)

Play active engagement in pleasurable activity (*see also* Cooperative play; Creative play; Functional play; Parallel play; Social play; Solitary play; Symbolic play)

Prosocial skill any verbal or motor acts done to meet the needs of others; examples: sharing a toy or food, giving a compliment

Reciprocal interaction mutual social-communicative exchange; turn-taking interaction

Request for information message conveyed for the purpose of obtaining new information or clarification

Ritualistic behavior restricted, repetitive, and stereotypic patterns of behavior that include but are not limited to motor mannerisms, object use, language use, and adherence to nonfunctional routines

Ritualistic play restricted, repetitive, and stereotypic patterns of play behavior

Routine script fixed sequence of familiar steps (verbal or nonverbal) that a child says or does; may or may not be meaningfully linked to the context

Routine symbolic play script play that involves a predictable sequence of symbolic play acts linked logically by a theme

Self-stimulatory behavior persistent repetition of an action that is inconsistent with the context; using body or objects to perform an act repeatedly

Shared attention social-communicative behavior used to share a focus of interest with others; the use of eye gaze, gestures, and/or speech to initiate and maintain shared interest

Single-act functional play play that only requires repetition of a single action with one toy; examples: riding a bike, playing catch

Social attention the ability to focus on relevant contextual and social information and to respond to others

Social play play with others; can be cooperative or parallel; can be functional, creative, open-ended, or closed-ended (*see also* Cooperative play; Parallel play)

Social regulation social-communicative behavior used to influence the responses of others; may or may not be conventional; examples: screaming, pointing (both serve as a means to request an object or to request that someone leaves)

Socioemotional communication message conveyed to express feelings about self or others

Solitary play play that does not require sharing space or materials, watching others, or interaction

Speech one expression of verbal language; can be communicative or noncommunicative (*see also* Perseverative speech)

Spontaneous behavior self-generated behavior that occurs in the absence of discrete prompts or cues

Spontaneous communication   self-generated, unprompted message

Structured nonverbal turn-taking   group activity with predictable turn-taking; waiting is required; language comprehension and use are not required

Structured verbal turn-taking   group activity with predictable turn-taking; waiting is required; language comprehension and use are required

Symbolic play   play that involves using toys and objects in a variety of conventional ways or pretending the items are something else (*see also* Creative symbolic play; Routine symbolic play script)

Terminate conversation   end conversation to complete a communicative exchange

Unison activity   group activity during which everyone is doing the same thing at the same time; sharing, waiting, or turn-taking are not required; language comprehension and use are not required

Unstructured play   group activity with no social predictability; sharing, turn-taking, waiting, and language may be required

Verbal communication   using speech, signs, photographs, pictographs, a voice output system, or written language to convey a message

Verbal conversation   using speech, signs, photographs, pictographs, a voice output system, or written language to have an interactive exchange

Verbal imitation   the ability to copy the speech (sounds or words) of another

Verbal rituals   restricted, repetitive, and stereotypic language patterns that may or may not serve a communicative function (*see also* Delayed echolalia; Echolalia; Perseverative speech)

chapter 4

Designing Intervention

Kathleen Ann Quill

Social and communication deficits are the central symptoms of autism. Because social and communication skills encompass virtually every aspect of daily life, efforts to build these skills in children with autism can be an overwhelming task for educators and parents. Social and communication intervention is further complicated by the ritualistic behaviors characteristic of autism.

The purpose of this chapter is to provide a framework for designing social and communication intervention for children with autism. There are seven steps in this intervention plan:

1. Target goals and objectives that reflect critical milestones in typical development.

2. Use the Assessment of Social and Communication Skills for Children with Autism to prioritize goals and objectives.

3. Construct a framework for core skills intervention.

4. Use the new DO-WATCH-LISTEN-SAY framework to construct opportunities for social skill enhancement.

5. Construct motivating opportunities for communication skill enhancement.

6. Understand the function of social and communicative ritualistic behaviors.

7. Monitor the acquisition and generalization of skills.

The intervention plan focuses on the importance of building social skills and does not specifically discuss treatment of challenging behaviors (for excellent behavior management resources, see Durand, 1990; Koegel, Koegel, & Dunlap,1996; Schopler & Mesibov, 1994; and Smith, 1990). Many challenging behaviors, however, serve social and/or communication purposes. Therefore, intervention to build social and communication skills indirectly affects problem behaviors. As social and communication skills are acquired, there is a decrease in problem behaviors and an increase in a child's adaptive behaviors and social competence (Carr et al., 1994).

The intervention plan emphasizes the importance of building functional communication skills and makes a clear distinction between language and communication development. *Language* is a formal symbol system that has structural qualities—specifically, phonology, semantics, and syntax. Language systems include speech, sign language, written language, and other graphic symbols. Intervention to build language is primarily aimed at expanding vocabulary and grammatical complexity. In contrast, *communication* is a social exchange. Language is one vehicle used to communicate. Nonverbal messages such as eye gaze, gestures, facial expressions, and other expressions of affect are equally important vehicles of communication. Effective communication can exist in the absence of language, as shown by the communication behaviors of infants. Furthermore, language can exist in the absence of communication, as is often observed in children with autism.

PROGRAM PLANNING: TARGET GOALS AND OBJECTIVES

The first step in designing an intervention plan for supporting social and communication development in children with autism is to establish clear and specific goals. It is critical to discern what skills need to be taught. Objectives should be based on an individual child's current abilities as determined by the Assessment of Social and Communication Skills for Children with Autism (see Chapter 3). Appendix A provides examples of objectives for a child at the beginning stage of social-communication development and examples of objectives for a child at an advanced stage of social-communication development. The specific objectives comprising a child's intervention plan can be selected from the nine areas of social and communication development addressed within the assessment tool:

- Core skills: nonverbal interaction
                          imitation
                          organization
- Social skills: play skills
                          group skills
                          community social skills
- Communication skills: basic communicative functions
                          socioemotional skills
                          basic conversational skills

It is important to remember that these lists of skills in the assessment should not be viewed as a fixed developmental hierarchy; rather, assessment information should be used in a flexible way for program planning. The target objectives should be highly individualized and consist of those skills that have been identified as priorities for intervention.

When selecting objectives from the nine social and communication areas, target skills that

- Maximize the child's social and communicative competence
- Mirror the social and communication skills of same-age peers
- Increase spontaneity
- Build generalization

Maximize the Child's Social and Communicative Competence

It is preferable for children with autism to have age-appropriate, functional social and communication skills that will be used in multiple contexts and for many years. In the area of socialization, it is preferable for a child to develop a wide range of play interests that can be done alone or shared with same-age peers. Activities such as roller skating, bike riding, putting together puzzles, and using a computer will remain useful throughout a child's life.

Careful consideration must be given to the appropriateness of selecting developmental play activities that require creativity and imagination. These play skills are difficult for some children with autism and, after the preschool years, lose their utility in social peer groups. In the area of communication, it is better for a child to develop a wide range of communicative functions using one word than to develop multiple means for a single function. For example, instead of a child only working on building his request repertoire from "(single-word item)" to "want (item)" to "I want (item)" to "I want (item), please," it is more helpful for the child to have one conventional gesture, sign, symbol, or word for each of the many different functions. This range of communication skills will increase social-communicative competence and decrease the usual precursor to challenging behaviors—frustration. A careful review of the child's social profile is necessary to target objectives that are both developmentally and functionally useful.

Mirror the Skills of Same-Age Peers

Identify the social behaviors that are most important by observing how the activity or situation naturally occurs in same-age peers. For example, social acceptability among young children is often linked to similar interests. In preschool, popular toys related to television and movie characters often signal acceptability. In elementary school, interests in sports, video games, and computers often signal acceptability. Target play skills that mirror the interests of same-age peers.

Second, look at the basic communication behaviors of typically developing children. Among typical preschoolers, nonverbal interaction is primary and conversational exchanges among peers are secondary. In elementary school, there is a gradual shift to peer–peer conversations, although many activities do not require conversation. The communication messages taught to children with autism should mirror the social-communicative behaviors used by typically developing children. For example, typically developing 4-year-old children do not say "(Peer's name), do you want to play?" but, rather, "Come here," or "Look at this." Typically developing 8-year-old children do not say "Hello, how are you today?" Instead, they might give a high-five or say "Hey." In addition, examine the common questions and comments expressed by other children in the setting to target communication goals and messages. For instance, during snack time, there are opportunities to request or refuse items, to request assistance, to comment when handing items to a peer, and to indicate when finished. While building blocks, a child might request an action, label the building materials, comment on his or her action, or call attention to his or her building. Target the specific communicative functions (e.g., request a toy from a peer, comment on action) to be included within the activity routine and the means (e.g., word, phrase, communicative behavior) of expression.

Target Objectives to Increase Spontaneity

Examine the degree to which the child requires social prompts, and, as needed, target objectives to increase spontaneity. Many social and communication skills are only mastered once a child uses them spontaneously. For example, there is a significant difference between a child who can answer the question "What do you want?" and a child who can spontaneously request a desired item. Similarly, there is a sizeable distinction between a child who can answer the question "What is it?" and a child who can spontaneously label things of interest. The role of the child as a responder versus the role of the child as an initiator must be clear when designing target objectives in many skill areas.

Target Objectives to Build Generalization

Children often demonstrate a specific social or communication skill when interacting with adults, but not when interacting with peers. For instance, a child may take turns with an adult but not with a peer, or a child may make requests of adults but not make the same requests to peers. If a skill is only demonstrated with adults, the target objective should be generalization of the skill to interactions with peers. It is important to note that some skills from the assessment tool, such as organizational skills or solitary play, are independent of partners. Other skills in the assessment, specifically group skills, include the size of the group in the criteria instead of specific adult or peer partners. These differences are indicated in the assessment tool and need to be specified in the target objective.

Children frequently demonstrate specific social or communication skills in certain contexts but do not generalize the skills across multiple settings. Examples include a child who engages in functional solitary play with the same two toys every time or a child who communicates his or her need for help at mealtimes but not during other activities. Many times, a child only displays a skill in the contexts in which it was learned, not in novel contexts. If a skill is only demonstrated in specific contexts, the target objective needs to be the generalization of the skill in multiple environments.

Skill Mastery

Skill mastery is defined by the following conditions:

- Acquisition of the skill: the presence of the skill without adult prompts
- Generalization of the skill across adults, peers, and different social groupings
- Generalization of the skill across multiple familiar and novel contexts

FRAMEWORK FOR DESIGNING CORE SKILLS INTERVENTION

Nonverbal social-communication deficits, along with imitation deficits, are the most important diagnostic indices of autism (Baron-Cohen et al., 1992; Osterling & Dawson, 1994). Nonverbal social-communication and imitation develop quickly and naturally in typically developing infants and toddlers during the first 2 years of life and lay the foundation for later social, communication, and emotional development. Given the importance of these core skills, successful intervention in these areas is critical to social and communication development of children with autism.

Nonverbal Social-Communicative Interaction

During the first year of life, infants acquire the ability to use and respond to eye gaze, gestures, and facial expressions in social interactions. Infants develop nonverbal social-communication skills to initiate social interactions, to engage in reciprocal turn-taking, to make basic requests, and to share interests with others. They also nonverbally respond to the social initiations, requests, and comments of others. The development of nonverbal social-communicative behaviors is marked by the increasing capacity to coordinate eye gaze, gestural communication, and social turn-taking.

Another important aspect of nonverbal interaction is the measure of intentionality on the part of the child. *Intentionality* is defined as an awareness of the effect that a communicative behavior will have on others and the ability to persist in that behavior until the desired effect is obtained (Bates, Benigni, Bretherton, Camaioni, & Volterra, 1979). The development of social interaction begins when others infer intentionality from a child's nonverbal behaviors. For example, intent is inferred when the child reaches toward something and continues until someone responds or gazes at an object and cries until someone gives him the object. Intentionality on the child's part is observed when the child directs nonverbal behaviors toward others. For instance, the child reaches for a person's hand to be tickled, pulls a person's hand toward the desired location, or points at something of interest and then looks toward the person for acknowledgment. These behaviors are used by the child to sustain interaction with others (i.e., reciprocal interaction), influence the responses of others to meet one's needs (i.e., social regulation), and share interests (i.e., shared attention).

Children with autism, however, often do not demonstrate conventional means of intentionality, or their style of interaction is expressed in unconventional ways, as illustrated in the following examples:

Jordan is 4 years old and nonverbal. He does not direct gestures or other nonverbal behaviors toward others to seek help. If Jordan has difficulty opening a cookie container, he bites it, bangs it, cries, and eventually disregards it. These behaviors occur even when an adult is sitting next to him. Jordan's behaviors, in this context, reflect an absence of communicative intentionality.

Leigh is 3 years old and verbal. She recites the alphabet and quotes from favorite books and movies. She also makes statements to regulate her own behavior but not the behavior of others. For example, she will walk into the kitchen and say "Do you want some juice?" even if no family members are nearby. Her message has meaning and she is seeking a specific outcome, but there is an absence of communicative intent.

What Skills to Teach

To determine what nonverbal social interaction skills to select for a particular child, examine the Assessment of Social and Communication Skills for Children with Autism (Chapter 3, Appendix A). It is essential that these issues be addressed in *both* children with and without language skills. Language use without social interaction skills is common in children with autism, as reflected in the previous examples. Target skills in the following areas:

- Social attention: looking at person or object when directed
- Reciprocal interaction: repeating own behavior to maintain interaction
- Social regulation: using one or more nonverbal means to request
- Shared attention: using one or more nonverbal means to share interests

Target skills that the child is lacking or displays in limited contexts. Keep in mind that this list is not a hierarchy of skills; rather, all areas should be addressed systematically and simultaneously. The intervention plan should include goals to

- Expand the repertoire of nonverbal social interaction skills
- Expand the ability to combine two or more nonverbal communicative behaviors
- Expand the ability to persist with communication until satisfied
- Generalize skills to interactions with both adults and peers
- Generalize skills across multiple contexts

Nonverbal social interaction encompasses a wide range of gestural and affective means of expression. Eye gaze, gestures, and facial expressions can be expressed in isolation (e.g., reach for an object) or in combination (e.g., combine eye gaze and a gesture to indicate desire for an object). The ability to coordinate attention among oneself, social partners, and an object (i.e., joint attention) is more complex than the ability to use one nonverbal means in isolation. It involves the ability to follow another person's visual line of attention, the ability to coordinate eye gaze and gesture with another person, and the ability to use eye gaze and gestures to direct another person's attention to events or objects. The child becomes effective in social interactions when he can combine social behaviors in an effort to be understood by others and achieve an intended goal. The ability to combine multiple nonverbal means of communication is central to the development of effective social-communicative reciprocity.

Building Nonverbal Social Interaction Skills

Intervention to build nonverbal social interaction must take into account the child's level of motivation and assume that every moment is an opportunity to facilitate these core skills. The following fundamental principles for building nonverbal social interaction skills are summarized in Figure 4.1:

- Encourage the child to use single nonverbal means before combining multiple non-verbal means within social interactions.
- Provide interesting opportunities for interaction.
- Assign intentionality to the child's idiosyncratic behaviors.
- Contrive contexts for interaction whenever the child is unmotivated.
- Create natural opportunities for social interaction whenever possible.

Detailed intervention guidelines for expanding nonverbal social interaction are provided in Chapter 6, along with detailed instructional strategies outlined in Chapter 5. The next vignette is one example of how to build nonverbal social interaction.

> *Seven-year-old Keith is looking at an ABC chart on the wall. At first, he points to the letters and recites them alone. One of Keith's teachers sits next to him and holds her hand over his finger. They point to the letters together and, engaging in reciprocal interaction, take turns saying them. After a few turns, Keith begins to anticipate his teacher's turn and looks at her in anticipation. Shortly thereafter, Keith points to the next letter, names it, and looks at his teacher with a smile for acknowledgment (combining multiple means with communicative intent).*

Imitation

Imitation is a critical milestone in the development of social and communication skills. During the first year, typically developing children progress from repeating motor and

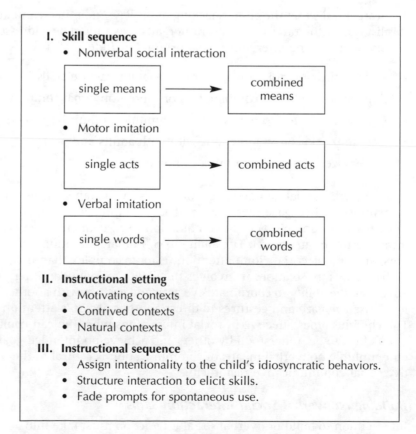

Figure 4.1.   Framework for building core skills.

vocal actions within their repertoire to imitating novel actions. By 1 year of age, they imitate social acts such as waving "bye-bye" and multiple play actions with toys. By age 2, children imitate a sequence of novel actions, invisible acts (i.e., actions they cannot see themselves do), and actions observed in others at an earlier time (i.e., deferred imitation).

Children with autism vary significantly in their ability to imitate others. In the absence of social attention, imitation does not occur. In addition, sequencing a series of motor actions (i.e., motor planning) can be challenging for some children (Hanschu, 1998). Furthermore, there is often a significant difference between a child's ability to imitate spontaneously in natural contexts and a child's ability to imitate elicited actions in structured contexts.

What Skills to Teach

To determine what imitation skills to select for a particular child, examine the Assessment of Social and Communication Skills for Children with Autism. Target skills in both motor imitation and verbal imitation. Target skills that the child is lacking or displays in limited contexts. In the area of motor imitation, developmental milestones should be considered when prioritizing goals. For example, it is easier for a child to imitate a single action with a toy than to use his body to imitate a fine motor action, such as clapping. Similarly, it is easier for a child to imitate large motor movements, such as running, than to imitate fine motor actions. With these developmental considerations in mind, priority goals should include the child's ability to

- Imitate actions with toys
- Imitate a sequence of motor actions with toys
- Imitate spontaneously in natural contexts
- Generalize skills across multiple *novel* contexts
- Generalize skills to interactions with both adults and peers

Unlike motor imitation that can be prompted, verbal imitation is more difficult to elicit. Therefore, in the area of verbal imitation, priority goals should include the child's ability to

- Imitate vocal acts initiated by the child and then imitated by the adult
- Imitate vocalizations/verbalizations in highly motivating contexts
- Spontaneously imitate in highly familiar, motivating contexts
- Generalize skills across multiple *familiar* contexts
- Generalize skills to interactions with both adults and peers

Building Imitation Skills

Intervention to build imitation must take into account the child's level of motivation and assume that every moment is an opportunity to facilitate this core skill. Given the important role of imitation skills to later development, current treatment emphasizes teaching imitation either discretely (Lovaas, 1977) or developmentally (Greenspan & Wieder, 1998). (See Chapter 5 for a detailed discussion.) Some children are able to apply imitation skills to natural contexts, while others show considerable variability in spontaneous imitation. Use the following fundamental principles for building imitation:

- Create fun, natural opportunities for imitation whenever possible.
- Encourage imitation in the context of highly motivating activities.
- Encourage imitation in the context of movement activities.
- Encourage imitation in the context of music activities.
- Imitate the child's vocal actions to encourage verbal imitation.

- Imitate the child's motor actions to encourage motor imitation.
- Elicit and prompt motor imitation in contrived situations.
- Structure play to elicit and prompt motor imitation in a meaningful way.

Detailed intervention guidelines for expanding imitation are provided in Chapter 6, along with detailed instructional strategies outlined in Chapter 5. The next vignette is one example of how to build imitation:

> Ayden is 4 years old and enjoys music. Motor and vocal imitation were elicited in the context of structured music games with her teacher. Ayden was seated across from her teacher for the activity. For each song, the teacher and Ayden had one toy to move. They shook a bell for song one, raised a pom-pom up and down during song two, and put a puppet on and off their knees during song three. Ayden was required to attend to the teacher and imitate the one action with one toy during each song. Interest motivated Ayden's successful imitation.

FRAMEWORK FOR DESIGNING SOCIAL INTERVENTION

Social activities are complex, dynamic, and constantly changing. Social skills require the ability to understand the meaning of multiple contextual, language, and socioemotional events. The requirements of social interaction sharply contrast with the learning patterns associated with autism, characterized by impaired abilities to understand and use social information in a flexible manner. This limits the development of dynamic social relationships and creates a paradox for building social skills in children with autism.

Figure 4.2 represents the dynamics of social activities for typically developing children. Most social activities require children to

- DO and
- WATCH and
- LISTEN and
- SAY

This DO-WATCH-LISTEN-SAY framework correlates with the following capacities:

1. Cognitive—the ability to know what to DO
   Children actively use toys, objects, and materials in the physical environment. Exploration contributes to an understanding of how things are related.

2. Socialization—the ability to WATCH others
   Children observe others. Observation skills contribute to an understanding of how to imitate; share physical space, toys, and materials; and take turns. Social observation contributes to understanding others' nonverbal social behaviors, such as gestures and emotional displays.

3. Language—the ability to LISTEN
   Children listen to others. They assign language meaning to the objects in the environment, their own activities, and the activities of others. They also assign meaning to and respond to the verbal and nonverbal behaviors of others.

4. Communication—the ability to know what to SAY
   Children initiate and maintain reciprocal interactions. They communicate messages that are relevant to the social context and others.

As this list and Figure 4.2 demonstrate, virtually every social activity with others requires the ability to DO-WATCH-LISTEN-and-SAY. Typically developing children flexibly engage in these four domains of social activities. The next examples illustrate how this capacity is observed in social play and a community outing.

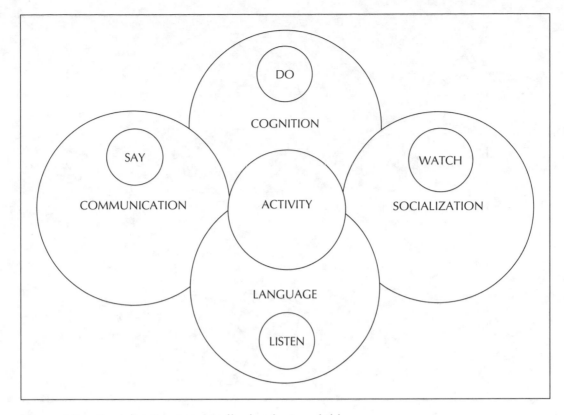

Figure 4.2. Socialization in typically developing children.

1. Social play: Behaviors that would be observed in a typically developing preschool child who is building blocks with peers

   • DO—use the blocks in exploratory, functional, or creative ways

   • WATCH—observe peers' play, observe peers' socioemotional behaviors, share blocks, take turns, and/or cooperate on a joint building project

   • LISTEN—listen to what is said during the activity; respond to the verbal requests and comments of peers; and respond to the nonverbal requests, comments, and behaviors of peers

   • SAY—initiate and maintain reciprocal communicative interactions

2. Community outing: Behaviors that would be observed in a typically developing child who is going trick-or-treating on Halloween

   • DO—complete the steps of the activity, including putting on a costume, carrying a plastic pumpkin, walking from house to house, ringing the doorbell, and putting candy in the pumpkin

   • WATCH—observe the activity of others, stay with the group, wait as needed, take turns ringing the doorbell, and accept candy that is given

   • LISTEN—listen to information given to the group, respond to nonverbal social messages, and respond to questions and directions (verbally or nonverbally)

   • SAY—know what to say and when, including "trick-or-treat," "thank you," and "bye" (verbally or with a gesture)

Figure 4.3 represents the challenge of social activities for children with autism. It is more difficult for them to integrate what to DO, who to WATCH, how to LISTEN, and what to SAY. Because of cognitive and social processing constraints, children with autism show

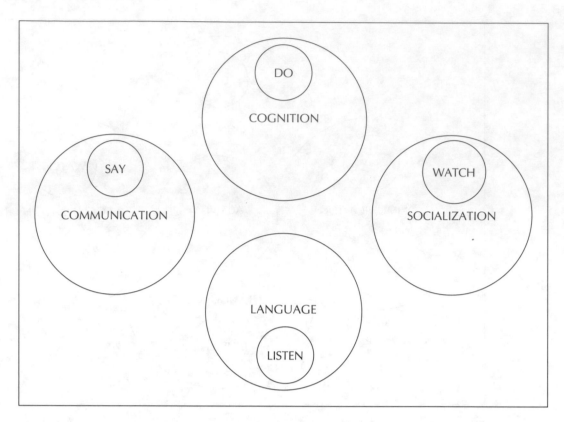

Figure 4.3. Socialization in children with autism.

less social flexibility and more fragmented social behaviors. In social settings, they are more likely to focus their attention on one of the domains and struggle when shifting from one domain to the other. For example, they may focus their attention only on what to DO or what to SAY and demonstrate difficulty combining cognitive, language, social, and communication elements. Often, their acquisition of social skills progresses from one element to the next in a linear fashion. Children with autism often

- DO then/or
- WATCH then/or
- LISTEN then/or
- SAY

The following examples illustrate social play in four different children with autism. They have mastered different elements of the social activity involved but are unable to integrate the cognitive, social, language, and communication requirements of social play:

Jeremy is 3 years old and verbal. He rarely observes the activities of others, and he does not imitate others. When Jeremy plays with blocks, he focuses all of his attention on the properties of the blocks with complete disregard for others. He lines up the blocks (DO), counts them repeatedly, and becomes upset whenever another child interrupts his play.

Brenda is 4 years old and verbal. She observes peers' play in highly motivating situations. Brenda enjoys blocks. When alone, she builds elaborate structures. When in the block area with peers, however, Brenda spends most of the time watching the play of others (WATCH). She collects blocks and waits for a peer to request one from her (LISTEN). Although she talks about her play activity when alone, Brenda is quiet when with peers. She can only focus her attention on the social behaviors of others and cannot coordinate their behavior and her own.

Ned is 4 years old and nonverbal. He observes and imitates adults and peers from time to time during play. When Ned is playing blocks with peers, he builds towers (DO), intermittently watches peers, and shares toys and space (WATCH), but he does not respond to the verbal or nonverbal bids of others. He ignores other children when they call his name, ask a question, or indicate that they want him to join their play.

Tyler is 4 years old and verbal. He frequently observes and imitates peers during play. Whenever Tyler is playing blocks with peers, he builds a structure (DO), joins his peers in building the structure, shares, takes turns, and imitates (WATCH). Tyler also nonverbally replies to the requests of his peers, such as responding when they ask him to play or when they ask him for another block and joining in their laughter (LISTEN). Although he can engage in verbal interactions with adults, he is unable to initiate or respond verbally with his peers.

As these examples illustrate, children with autism can possess various levels of social mastery in an activity. *Social mastery* is defined as the ability to DO-WATCH-LISTEN-and-SAY within a specific social context. An understanding of these four aspects of every social activity is useful for planning social skills intervention.

Figure 4.4 outlines the framework for planning social skills intervention. First, skills needed in a social activity can be categorized into the domains of DO-WATCH-LISTEN-SAY. Planning for skill acquisition can be organized in this general sequence; that is, the child first learns what to DO and/or who to WATCH, then how to respond to others (LISTEN), and then how to initiate communication (SAY). This framework can be applied to each individual social activity.

Second, there is a general hierarchy of skills within each of the four domains. For example, within the domain WATCH, a child first learns to share space, then share toys and materials, and then take turns. Within the domain LISTEN, the child first responds to nonverbal gestural messages of others, then to nonverbal prosocial behaviors, and finally to verbal messages. Using this framework, the four children described previously would have different target objectives. The objective for Jeremy would be functional use of blocks (DO); the objective for Brenda would be turn-taking while building a structure (WATCH); the objective for Ned would be responding to the nonverbal initiatives of his peers (LISTEN); the objective for Tyler would be talking with peers (SAY).

Third, it is important to consider social partners when planning social skills intervention. It is common for children with autism to master social skills with adult partners before generalizing the skills to peer partners. This distinction is largely due to the social partner's ability to understand the social efforts of the child with autism and to adapt the interaction to enhance success. Planning for social success with peers needs to take into account activities for which the child demonstrates mastery with an adult partner.

Finally, planning social skills intervention must take into account the child's core skill abilities in the environment. The presence or absence of social observation skills, imitation skills, and organizational skills dictates the selection of strategies. For instance, a child who observes and imitates would benefit from modeling, whereas a child who does not observe or imitate would require alternative prompting techniques. A child who is organized in a particular setting may benefit from traditional instructional strategies, whereas a child who is not organized would probably require special instructional supports.

The design of intervention for solitary play, social play, group skills, and community activities can be built on this basic framework. This concept is explored in the following

I. General skill sequence

DO → WATCH → LISTEN → SAY

II. General skill hierarchy within each domain

DO
- Functional, closed-ended activities
- Functional, open-ended activities
- Creative activities (optional)

WATCH
- Share physical space
- Share toys and materials
- Take turns

LISTEN
- Respond to gestural messages of others
- Respond with nonverbal prosocial behaviors
- Respond to verbal messages of others

SAY
- Initiate nonverbal prosocial messages
- Initiate nonverbal requests, comments
- Initiate verbal prosocial messages
- Initiate verbal requests, comments
- Maintain conversational exchange

III. Social partners

ADULT → PEERS

IV. Child's characteristics to consider

CORE SKILLS
- Social observation
- Imitation
- Organization

Figure 4.4. Framework for planning social skills intervention.

sections, with detailed instructions and strategies outlined in Chapter 5 and more in-depth intervention guidelines provided in Chapter 7.

Solitary Play

Teaching children with autism to engage in fun, meaningful, and socially acceptable solitary activities is central to program planning. The plan to expand a child's repertoire of solitary play activities must include decisions about what play activities to select and how to teach them.

What Solitary Play Skills to Teach

To determine what solitary play skills to select for a particular child, examine the child's play interests, play skills, and level of independence. The child's skills and level of independence can be determined by administering the Assessment of Social and Communication Skills for Children with Autism. His or her play interests can be obtained by using the Play Interest Survey (Chapter 7, Appendix A). Select solitary play skills that build on the child's play interests, play skills, and level of independence.

First, solitary play skills can be increased by building on a child's play interests. Play interests and motivation are intimately linked to the child's understanding of how to use various toys and materials. Information obtained from the assessment tool and the Play Interest Survey provides insight into which types of toys or activities the child finds meaningful. The assessment includes a list of the child's favorite toys and activities and unique interests. It gathers additional information about the child's activity level, exploratory style, and particular sensory sensitivities. The Play Interest Survey gathers more in-depth information about the child's play repertoire and helps in the selection of new play activities.

Toys and activities typical of young children's interests are organized into ten categories on the Play Interest Survey. The first eight categories list activities useful for building solitary play skills:

1. Exploratory toys and activities (e.g., a sandbox, cause-and-effect toys)
2. Physical toys and activities (e.g., bicycles, the playground)
3. Manipulative toys (e.g., puzzles, pegboards)
4. Constructive toys (e.g., blocks, train tracks)
5. Art activities (e.g., paint, playdough)
6. Literacy activities (e.g., books, computers)
7. Music activities (e.g., singing, instruments)
8. Sociodramatic play activities (e.g., dress-up, doll play)
9. Games (e.g., board games, card games)
10. Social games (e.g., chase, Hide-and-Seek)

Introduce play activities from categories in which the child has shown interest. For example, if he enjoys puzzles, introduce other manipulative activities. If a child likes using playground equipment, introduce additional physical activities. If a child has a limited repertoire of interests, examine the qualities of the child's activity preferences and introduce activities that provide the same visual, auditory, tactile, or movement feedback. For instance, play activities that provide visual feedback (e.g., a marble run, ball play, beanbag toss) would likely interest a child who enjoys watching objects move.

Second, expand solitary play by building on the child's current skills. Play skills are intimately linked to the child's understanding of what to do with toys or materials. Therefore, the child's ability to use toys and materials functionally or creatively helps determine the selection of solitary play activities.

Toys and activities can be inherently structured (i.e., closed-ended) or unstructured (i.e., open-ended). *Closed-ended play* consists of toys and activities that are used in one functional way. Some common closed-ended activities include

- Exploratory toys and activities (e.g., cause-and-effect toys, a kaleidoscope)
- Physical toys and activities (e.g., bicycles, roller skates, swings)
- Manipulative toys (e.g., puzzles, pegboards)
- Constructive toys (e.g., Lego models, train tracks)
- Art activities (e.g., stencils, paint-by-number)
- Literacy activities (e.g., books, computers)

Closed-ended activities are inherently organized. The materials have a distinct purpose and/or the activity has a clear completion. The complexity of closed-ended activities varies according to the number of materials and steps involved. For example, looking at books requires one material and one step, whereas constructing Lego models requires multiple materials and a sequential series of steps. Closed-ended activities are often the easiest play skills to teach children with autism because the activity's purpose is clear and predictable. Thus, if a child for whom an intervention is planned does not use toys in a purposeful, functional manner, select activities from each category that have a clear purpose and can only be used in one way.

Open-ended play consists of toys and activities that can be used in a variety of ways. Common open-ended play activities include

- Exploratory toys and activities (e.g., sand table, water table)
- Constructive toys (e.g., blocks, Legos)
- Art activities (e.g., collage materials, playdough)
- Sociodramatic play activities (e.g., dress-up, doll play)

Open-ended activities involve toys and materials that can be used in multiple ways. Most toys and activities lend themselves to creative use. Open-ended activities are not predictable or sequential. For example, the sandbox, blocks, dolls, and playdough can all be used in various ways. If a child has some functional play skills but lacks the ability to play creatively, introduce open-ended activities in a structured way to clarify how the toys and materials are to be used. Other factors to consider include the number of materials, whether the purpose of the materials is clear, the number of steps in the activity, and if the activity has a clear completion.

Third, expand the child's solitary play by targeting independence as a goal. Solitary play is most defined by the child's ability to sustain attention for a specified period of time. Motivation and understanding of what to do largely determine his or her level of independence. Involvement with toys and activities that are both fun and meaningful to that particular child increases independence.

Solitary Play Intervention

A variety of approaches—ranging from highly structured teaching to naturalistic intervention—are available to teach solitary play. A child's specific learning characteristics must be considered when planning intervention. Other factors that need to be considered are the child's social observation skills, motor imitation skills, organizational skills, and ritualistic behaviors. Information about these core skills and ritualistic behaviors can be obtained from the Assessment of Social and Communication Skills for Children with Autism. The steps taken to build solitary play skills are driven by this information, as the child's core abilities to observe others, imitate others, and remain organized determine the selection of strategies. For example, naturalistic approaches, such as modeling, can be used to expand play skills if the child demonstrates core skills. As this is the most natural way to build play skills, it is also the easiest. If the child does not demonstrate one or more core skills or exhibits ritualistic behaviors with new toys and materials, structured and systematic supports are needed. These include organizational supports, social supports, and visually cued instruction, all of which are detailed in Chapter 5. The following summary list suggests how to enhance solitary play in a way that is tailored to a child's specific abilities:

- If the child demonstrates social observation skills and social imitation skills, emphasize modeling strategies.
- If the child lacks social observation or social imitation skills or engages in ritualistic play, emphasize structured teaching and systematic supports.
- Limit the use of verbal instruction when teaching solitary play skills.

The following examples describe how solitary play skills were taught to three different children with autism. Each child required different systematic supports for the acquisition of solitary play skills.

Jeff was 4 years old and lacked most necessary skills for sustained solitary play. He engaged in numerous ritualistic behaviors, did not possess social observation and imitation skills, and had poor organizational skills. Closed-ended solitary play tasks were selected, and independence was taught with organizational supports. A spe-cific area at home was identified for solitary play. Individual activity materials were organized in see-through boxes and labeled with pictures. For example, one box contained a pegboard and pegs; another contained a tape player, a book, and a book on tape; and a third box contained pages from a coloring book and crayons. A picture sequence of the different toys was placed on a circular "choice board." Jeff was taught to make a choice, get the correct box, open the box, complete the play activity, put the materials and the picture back in the box, and then select another activity from the choice board. Jeff's choice board grew from two to eight activities, and his length of independent play time increased from 2 minutes to 20 minutes.

Louis was 6 years old. He had excellent social observation skills but lacked imita-tion skills. He also had a number of functional play skills but was very disorga-nized and engaged in ritualistic behaviors when presented with open-ended toys and materials. Louis was taught new play skills through the use of adult modeling and visual cues. His teacher developed a simple picture book that depicted the various ways certain activity materials could be utilized. She read the book and modeled the activity in a fixed, sequential order. After watching his teacher read and model the activity daily, Louis acquired the skill with minimal adult prompt-ing and used the book to guide his activity. Through this method, Louis acquired a new open-ended play activity each month. Gradually, with his own mastery of the materials, his play behavior shifted from play scripts to flexible toy use.

Teddy was 8 years old. He enjoyed reading and playing with manipulatives, although his ability to sustain attention was limited. The solitary play activities chosen for Teddy were Lego models, color-by-number paintings, word-find books, and books on tape. A special place was organized for Teddy to play, and a written checklist of choices was provided for him. A timer was used to specify the length of his independent play time. After 20 minutes of independent play, he was re-warded with time to watch a video. This incentive, as well as the use of organiza-tional supports, helped Teddy engage in solitary play for extended periods of time.

Social Play

Teaching children with autism to interact with peers is critical for social success. The abil-ity to participate in social interactions depends on understanding peers' verbal and non-verbal social-communicative behavior. Intervention that maximizes their ability to ob-serve others' social behavior and share toys and materials is a critical beginning. The ability of children with autism to respond to the verbal and nonverbal overtures of peers is equally important. The plan to expand a child's repertoire of social play activities must include decisions about what activities to select and how to teach the social skills within the domains of WATCH and LISTEN (see Figure 4.4).

Intervention to foster social play in children with autism must take into account the critical elements of social play observed in typically developing children. Key points to keep in mind are

- Social experiences should focus on mutually enjoyed toys and activities to foster peer acceptance.

- Social intervention should emphasize rule-based play activities that allow for parallel participation.

- More emphasis should be given to teaching social responsiveness to peers rather than to promoting initiations.

- More emphasis should be given to teaching the use of nonverbal social behaviors with peers rather than the use of verbal ones.

What Social Play Skills to Teach

To determine what social play skills to teach, assess a child's play interests and social play skills. Information about the child's social play skills can be gathered by conducting the Assessment of Social and Communication Skills for Children with Autism. The child's play interests can be determined by utilizing the Play Interest Survey.

First, social play should focus on activities that are mutually enjoyed by the child and others. The child must understand what to DO before being placed in the social situation. That is, she should demonstrate appropriate solitary play with the toys and materials. A level of familiarity with the toys and materials of an activity is an important consideration when selecting social play activities. Second, assess the child's social play skills with adults as compared with peers. Activities that the child has mastered with adults present opportunities to enhance peer interactions. This is because social skills are typically acquired through interactions with adults before the child is able to generalize the skills to peer play. Finally, use the assessment information to target specific social objectives in the domains of WATCH or LISTEN.

In the domain of WATCH, the first goal is to support the child in sharing physical space with others. In activities requiring this skill, the child first has his own set of materials and plays in proximity to peers. The second goal is to support the child in sharing materials. Parallel play activities are structured so that the child understands what specific toys and materials to share with peers. Later, cooperative play activities are organized to facilitate sharing. The third goal is to support the child in turn-taking. Acquisition of turn-taking skills begins within the context of structured, closed-ended play activities and proceeds to open-ended activities. Then, activities are selected that require turn-taking with others.

In the domain of LISTEN, the primary objective is for the child to respond to the overtures of his peers. Comprehending the nonverbal qualities of peer interactions is important for social success. Fostering nonverbal social behaviors and nonverbal communication skills should be the primary social intervention goals. Verbal interactions with peers should be secondary. In addition, more emphasis should be placed on teaching social responsiveness to peers rather than initiating social interactions. Several studies have reported success in teaching positive social behaviors—such as giving toys, giving nonverbal compliments, and responding to peers' overtures—to children with autism (Strain & Kohler, 1998; Strain & Odom, 1986; Wolfberg, 1995). This is accomplished by targeting clear goals, organizing the play environment, modeling social behaviors, and coaching the peer partners.

Social Play Intervention

As with solitary play, a variety of both highly structured and naturalistic approaches are available for teaching social play. Figure 4.5 outlines the dimensions of social play that need to be considered when designing teaching opportunities. As indicated in the figure, there are three factors to consider when determining how to design social play: the dimensions of the play activity, the child's core skills, and the skills of the social partners.

First, a child's ability to participate in social play is influenced by the structure of the activity, the organization of toys and materials, and the social and language requirements during play. Closed-ended play activities are inherently more organized and, thus, contribute to greater success. Increased participation occurs when play activities are organized so that the child clearly understands what to DO, when to take a turn, and what materials to share. Both the number of peers and the social complexity of the group (see the section "Group Skills") contribute to the child's understanding and participation. Finally, play activities that require language comprehension and use for participation will be the most challenging for children with autism.

To build successful social skills and facilitate interactions with others, examine the requirements of the activity. A distinction needs to be made between activities that require a specific skill and activities in which the use of that skill is optional. For example, all play activities may include conversation but not all activities require conversation. Similarly,

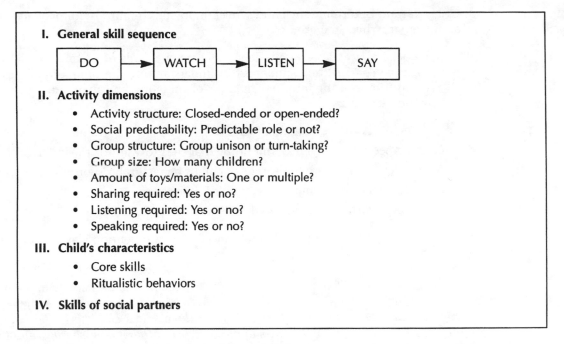

I. General skill sequence

DO → WATCH → LISTEN → SAY

II. Activity dimensions
- Activity structure: Closed-ended or open-ended?
- Social predictability: Predictable role or not?
- Group structure: Group unison or turn-taking?
- Group size: How many children?
- Amount of toys/materials: One or multiple?
- Sharing required: Yes or no?
- Listening required: Yes or no?
- Speaking required: Yes or no?

III. Child's characteristics
- Core skills
- Ritualistic behaviors

IV. Skills of social partners

Figure 4.5. Framework for designing social play.

sharing may be an option but may not be required in a particular play activity. Social play activities range in complexity according to the aforementioned social, language, and communication features. The easiest social play activities only require the child to DO something near others, whereas the most complex ones require the child to DO-WATCH-LISTEN-and-SAY.

The easiest play activities

- Are closed ended
- Utilize limited toys and materials
- Involve one partner
- Separate toys and materials for each child
- Require no sharing, turn-taking, or waiting
- Require no listening or language

The most complex play activities

- Are open ended
- Are unpredictable
- Utilize multiple toys and materials
- Involve a large group
- Require sharing, turn-taking, and waiting
- Are language based

Successful participation in social play also depends on the child's core skill abilities. The ability to observe others, imitate others, and remain organized needs to be examined in each play context as follows:

- Shared attention: Determine the child's ability to observe peers.
- Imitation: Ascertain the child's ability to imitate peers.

- Organization: Determine the child's level of organized, purposeful play activity when alone versus when in a group.

Successful social play is also highly dependent on the skills of a child's social partners. Peers need to be coached and supported in understanding the unique qualities of their friend with autism and modify their manner of initiating and maintaining interactions with their friend.

- Encourage peers to use nonverbal cues to gain the child's attention.
- Encourage peers to use verbal and nonverbal cues to wait for the child's response.
- Support peers in trying to interpret the child's behavioral responses.
- Encourage peers to respond to the child's initiatives.
- Provide peers with reminders of what to do and say to help the child succeed.

The following two examples illustrate social play intervention plans for children with autism who have different skills and abilities.

Andy is in kindergarten and possesses a limited capacity to participate in open-ended or unstructured social play. He only watches his peers intermittently in highly structured activities and never imitates them. His social intervention plan consists of a hierarchy of activities to promote peer observation, sharing, and turn-taking (WATCH) and includes 1) partner interactions requiring no waiting (e.g., sharing rides on a wagon, carrying buckets of toys and materials together), 2) partner interactions requiring sharing but no turn-taking (e.g., coloring with shared crayons or markers, sharing playdough), 3) partner interactions requiring simple turn-taking (e.g., pushing and pulling a friend in a wagon, throwing and catching a ball), 4) partner interactions requiring complex turn-taking (e.g., board games), 5) simple group interactions involving no materials (e.g., choral singing, playing chase), and 6) simple group interactions involving a toy (e.g., parachute games, listening to a story).

Brendan is in first grade. He has a wide range of interests, solid core skills in a variety of settings, and an interest in peers. Nonetheless, Brendan requires social predictability in order to participate in social play. Thus, the focus of his social play instruction is to refine his skills in structured situations by encouraging him to respond to peer initiatives (LISTEN). Peer activities used for Brendan's intervention include 1) structured games at recess, 2) cooperative games indoors, and 3) adult-facilitated play with a partner once a day in a quiet room. Peer coaching is central to this plan.

Group Skills

Teaching children with autism to participate in group activities is critical to social success. The ability to participate in groups depends on an understanding of group expectations and the role of each group member. Successful participation in a group requires the ability to attend and respond to relevant verbal and nonverbal cues.

The plan to expand the repertoire of group skills for a child with autism must include decisions about what group skills to teach, what group activities to select, and how to teach the group skills.

What Group Skills to Teach

Group skills are generally defined as

- The ability to attend to adults and peers
- The ability to wait

- The ability to take turns
- The ability to follow group directions

To determine what group skills to teach a particular child, assess the child's current group skills in various settings. This information can be obtained by using the Assessment of Social and Communication Skills for Children with Autism. A child's ability to demonstrate specific group skills is influenced by two basic factors: the group dynamic and the child's core skills in various group settings.

Group Skills Intervention

There are two factors to consider when determining how to teach group skills: the structure of the social group and the child's social, cognitive, and language skills. A child's ability to participate in a group activity is influenced by the predictability of the group setting and the social and language requirements of the group activity.

First, the predictability of the group activity, regardless of size, can vary. When the group is doing the same thing at the same time, for example, expectations are clear. In contrast, when children in the group are doing different things (even with the same toys or materials), less clarity exists regarding what is to be done. In addition, some group situations require waiting and others do not. No waiting is necessary during activities that occur in unison, such as working on an art project or academic task next to others. Some group activities require waiting for an unknown amount of time, such as group discussion. Others require waiting for a specific amount of time, such as sequential turn-taking while playing a structured board game. Any group situation that necessitates waiting also means that the child must observe the social behaviors of others and share space and materials. Furthermore, the language requirements of group activities vary. Some group activities require comprehension of language in order to participate, while others do not.

The degree to which children are able to participate successfully in a group situation is linked to these three factors. Using these three factors, it is possible to categorize group activities into six different types, listed next from easiest to most difficult:

1. Unison
2. Choral
3. Structured nonverbal turn-taking
4. Structured verbal turn-taking
5. Unstructured play
6. Discussion

See Table 4.1 for further information on these types of group activities.

The group type should be used as the primary criterion for determining the level of supports needed to enhance a child's social participation. As with social play, the level of social predictability, activity expectations (i.e., what to do), and language expectations (i.e., language complexity) contributes to the child's ability to attend, wait, take turns, and follow directions in a group. For example, if the learning objective for a particular child is group attending, it is easier for him or her to attend when the group activity format is unison or choral rather than unstructured play or discussion. If the learning objective is turn-taking, the child will have less difficulty taking turns during a group activity that is highly structured with predictable turn-taking opportunities.

The requirements of the group activity need to be evaluated in relation to a child's core skills. As with social play, the child's ability to observe others, imitate others, and remain organized in a group setting contributes significantly to the intervention planning. The child's ability to observe others, imitate others, and remain organized will also vary with the group type and environment. Children who lack social observation skills in spe-

Table 4.1. Group activities, their characteristics, and examples of each

Type of activity	Characteristics	Examples
Unison	Everyone doing the same thing at the same time No language understanding or use required Minimal to no waiting	Movement activities: aerobics, Ring Around the Rosie Art: activities where everyone has own set of materials Play: everyone has own set of toys
Choral	Everyone is doing the same thing at the same time Language understanding and use is required Minimal to no waiting	Storytime: listening to and/or choral reading of a book Music time: listening to and/or choral singing Circle/meeting times: reciting, reading from a chart, choral responses
Structured nonverbal turn-taking	Social predictability No language required Waiting required	Cafeteria: waiting in line for lunch Social games: playing catch, hopscotch Passing out or collecting work and/or toys and materials Play: activities that require sharing toys and materials
Structured verbal turn-taking	Social predictability Language required Waiting required	Adult-directed group activity where children share verbal information in a predictable order Structured indoor games such as board games Cooperative learning groups in which children take turns sharing ideas
Unstructured play	No social predictability Language may or may not be required Waiting usually necessary	Recess Free play Cooperative play
Discussion	No social predictability Language required Waiting required	Conversation Group discussion

cific types of group settings should not be expected to participate in these groups without a significant amount of individual supports.

The requirements of the group activity need to be evaluated in relation to a child's current cognitive and language skills. For instance, one child may participate in activities that require no language but not attend during language-based activities. A second child may follow routine verbal directions but not novel directions because of limited language comprehension. A third child may follow only specific verbal directions due to an inability to use social cues to follow the lead of the group. Yet another child may not follow verbal directions in group situations because he or she does not understand the meaning of the group directive, "Everybody, do _____ (activity)." Many children with autism are accustomed to responding to directions prefaced by their name and may not understand that the word *everybody* includes them.

Community Outing

Teaching children with autism to participate with family and friends in the community is often the biggest intervention challenge. Children with autism benefit from structure, predictability, and organization—elements that are typically lacking in community environments. In the community, there is a greater reliance on participating in physical environments that are busy and unstructured and social settings that involve large groups with unpredictable social behaviors. Children with autism, particularly those who exhibit sensitivities to various sensory stimuli or are fearful of changing situations, struggle in these settings.

What Community Social Skills to Teach

To establish what community social skills to teach a child, begin with information obtained from the Assessment of Social and Communication Skills for Children with Autism. The assessment provides basic information about the presence or absence of social skills and challenging behaviors in specific community situations. Identify the community situations that are intervention priorities by determining whether the child has the necessary social skills to participate in a particular community activity. That is, does the child have the skills within the domains of DO-WATCH-LISTEN-SAY necessary for the community situation? Next, determine whether the child has any challenging behaviors in the community setting that interfere with his or her participation. The procedures for designing a community skills intervention plan will assist in determining the function of the challenging behaviors. For most children with autism, challenging behaviors are directly linked to a lack of social and communication skills. The intervention plan is designed to teach the child social skills and appropriate replacement behaviors.

Community Social Skills Intervention

A number of steps can be taken to organize an intervention plan for building social skills in the community. They include the following:

- Assess the social and behavioral needs

- Target specific social skills and/or replacement behaviors

- Develop an intervention plan with instructional supports

Table 4.2 provides a framework for designing community skills intervention. As indicated on the table, intervention begins with a questionnaire that addresses four critical

Table 4.2.   Framework for planning community skills intervention

Assess the social and behavioral needs.	What preparation is given to the child prior to the activity?
	Are there aspects of the setting that may be uncomfortable for the child?
	What typically occurs in the setting?
	How do others interact with the child in the setting?
Target social skills and replacement behaviors.	What skills observed in typical peers need to be taught?
	DO
	WATCH
	LISTEN
	SAY
	What adapted skills could be taught in the setting?
	Alternative things to do
	Augmentative and alternative communication
	Relaxation procedures
Develop an instructional plan.	Develop a plan based on the identified social and behavioral needs.
	Prepare and preview the activity.
	Plan how the child will relax and maintain self-control in the setting.
	Target consistent skill expectations.
	Develop a consistent plan of responding to the child's problem behaviors.
	Develop a plan that includes instructional supports.
	Organizational supports
	Social supports
	Visually cued instruction
	Augmentative and alternative communication supports

issues: preparation given to the child prior to the activity, aspects of the setting that may be uncomfortable for the child, what the child is expected to do, and how others interact with the child in the setting.

The next step of the intervention plan is to identify social skills for instruction. As indicated previously, children first learn what to DO and who to WATCH, next learn interactive skills in the domain of LISTEN, and, last, learn what to SAY. Selection of specific social skills depends on the child's level of understanding and current social and communication behaviors. For example, social skills that the child demonstrates in other settings could be targeted for generalization to a particular community setting. Similarly, the communication skills that the child demonstrates in specific settings can be targeted for generalization to the community. Use the skills and behaviors of typical peers as a guide and target realistic skills for this child's participation and adapted skills to teach in the setting.

The final step of formulating the intervention plan is to identify the instructional supports that will be used to assist the child's acquisition of skills in the community. See Chapter 5 for detailed material on organizational supports, social supports, visually cued instruction, and augmentative and alternative communication (AAC) supports. Specific procedures for designing community skills instruction are described in Chapter 7.

The following cases provide two examples of community intervention plans:

Zoe was a very active 4-year-old. Her mother found it impossible to manage Zoe during trips to the grocery store. Using the questions to identify Zoe's social and behavioral needs, it was determined that Zoe 1) did not understand when the activity would be finished, 2) became overstimulated in the dairy aisle because she liked cheese, and 3) had maintained inappropriate behavior because she was once given an ice cream bar after she began screaming in the store. The intervention plan included 1) previewing a picture book that showed where she was going and what her mother was buying, 2) using a timer to indicate when the activity was finished, 3) providing an ice cream bar upon arrival, and 4) giving her a backpack containing a favorite toy while waiting in the cashier line. The length of time for which Zoe behaved appropriately in the grocery store was gradually increased from 2 minutes to 20 minutes.

Bret was 8 years old and screamed uncontrollably at the doctor's office. By asking the questions on Table 4.2, it was determined that Bret understood what was expected of him (i.e., what to DO) but was afraid of the experience and very sensitive to touch. Bret's intervention plan involved 1) having him watch a video about going to the doctor's office, 2) having him practice doctor visits by attending the school nurse's office, and 3) teaching him a relaxation procedure. After employing these strategies over the course of a few months, Bret was more able to visit the doctor's office calmly.

FRAMEWORK FOR DESIGNING COMMUNICATION INTERVENTION

Social-communicative interactions are complex, dynamic, and constantly changing. The requirements of social-communicative interactions sharply contrast with the learning patterns associated with autism. Social communication is unpredictable, unstructured, and requires the integration of multiple contextual, language, and socioemotional cues. Formulating responses and messages while simultaneously engaging in an activity, watching and listening to others, sharing attention with others, and understanding others' socioemotional perspectives—all of which are difficult for children with autism—are necessary for social-communicative interactions. These challenges for children with autism must be respected in order to design communication intervention.

It is essential to separate language abilities from communication abilities when planning interventions for children with autism. Language abilities can exist in the absence of communication. This phenomenon is common in children with autism, whose language may not be directed to others or may be used as a means of self-regulation. This use of language differs from communication, which is inherently social. Communication involves the use of either conventional or unconventional means to interact with others. For example, screaming to make a request or hitting someone to protest are clear (although generally unconventional) forms of communication. Eye gaze, facial expression, and gestures are conventional forms of nonverbal communication that occur with or without language. Table 4.3 summarizes the key features of communication that need to be considered when designing communication intervention for children with autism. Communication intervention must target the child's ability to

- Be motivated to communicate

- Have a means to communicate

- Communicate for a variety of social functions

- Take the interactive roles of both initiator and responder

- Engage in basic conversation

These features of communication provide a framework for designing communication intervention.

Motivation to Communicate

The degree of social motivation varies among children with autism. Some children demonstrate a desire to interact with others but do so in atypical ways. Their motivation to communicate can be used to build and expand social-communication skills. Other children with autism are motivated to communicate in order to have their own needs met but are not motivated to communicate about shared experiences. Still others rarely interact socially. It appears that many of these children often do not understand the basic social construct that interactions are meaningful and serve multiple purposes. Lack of motivation to communicate appears to come from this inability to understand the purpose of social interactions; even basic nonverbal communicative behaviors are typically lacking. Simultaneously, adults often perceive such children as noncommunicative and ignore their idiosyncratic interaction efforts (Koegel & Koegel, 1995a). Adults then anticipate

Table 4.3. Key features of communication

Motivation to communicate (desire)	Personal interests Social interests
Means of communication	Gestures Speech Augmentative and alternative system
Social functions of communication	Requests for needs Requests for information Comments Uses prosocial skills Expresses feelings
Basic roles	Initiates Responds
Elements of conversation	Initiates Maintains Repairs Terminates

and respond to the children's needs without expecting communicative attempts. This creates a cycle of the children's decreased motivation and increased self-reliance.

Increasing Motivation to Communicate

Because many children with autism display little motivation to communicate, efforts to increase motivation must emphasize natural contexts and systematic arrangement of the physical and social environments (Koegel & Koegel, 1995a; Quill, 1995a). An intervention plan should use the following key components to increase motivation:

- Arrange the physical environment to increase the child's need to communicate.
- Use the child's toy, object, and activity interests as opportunities to initiate communicative interactions.
- Use the child's social interests as opportunities to initiate communicative interactions.
- Reinforce all attempts to communicate; accept any and all communicative means.
- Make sure that the naturally occurring activity or interaction employed is pleasurable.
- Identify adults or peers who have successful interactions with the child and utilize their interactive strategies.
- See every moment as a potential opportunity to build communicative interactions.

To design an intervention plan to increase a child's motivation, examine the results from the Assessment of Social and Communication Skills for Children with Autism. Specifically, Section I of the assessment includes three sources that aid in identifying motivational components: 1) the inventory of motivators, 2) the inventory of exploratory behavior, and 3) information about the conditions under which the child communicates. Thus, preferred foods, toys, and activities can be structured into communication opportunities. Knowledge about the child's exploratory style can also be used to select new toys and activities (e.g., a child who seeks movement may enjoy wagon rides and learn to request more); in turn, all activities can be organized to provide communication opportunities. Furthermore, the child's social preferences (e.g., favorite people and social games) provide information about the type of interaction that motivates his or her communication. This is illustrated in the next case:

> Six-year-old Aaron's interests guide the direction of his social interaction. His list of interests includes actions such as swinging, jumping, tickling, and hugging as well as toys and materials such as cars, puzzles, sand, and water. Knowledge of Aaron's likes and dislikes hastens the beginnings of early communication. Each interest is made into an interactive game with numerous opportunities to request the object, the activity, or the action or to comment on the toys and the actions (e.g., "zoom, zoom" when moving a toy car). The activities are structured so that multiple communication exchanges occur.

Means of Communication

To be an effective communicator, it is necessary to use both verbal and nonverbal conventional means of communication. (Table 4.4 summarizes the range of nonverbal and verbal means of communication.) Children with autism who have speech need to learn to combine speech with nonverbal communicative behaviors. Children with autism who do not have speech need to use an AAC symbol system and learn to combine their alternative communication system with nonverbal communicative behaviors. The ultimate goal is the child's social-communicative competence.

Table 4.4. Communicative means

Nonverbal means	Verbal means
Physical proximity	Photographs
Eye gaze	Pictographs
Moving person's hand/face	Sign language
Reaching	Voice output system
Pushing/pulling person	Written language
Giving objects	Computer
Moving object toward/away	Speech
Contact point	
Open palm request	
Distal point	
Wave	
Head shake/nod	
Smile/frown	

Selecting a Means of Communication

Table 4.5 summarizes the attributes of various AAC systems and the basic criteria for selecting a communication system for a child with autism. As indicated in the table, the options are sign language; low-tech systems, such as pictures and pictographs; and high-tech systems, such as voice output systems and computers. Each system has clear advantages and disadvantages. These features are discussed in detail next.

Sign language is a formal language system with a complete grammar. Like speech, sign language is a temporal system. It requires face-to-face interaction and attention to fluid social interaction. Attention to others' signed messages also requires rapid and immediate processing of the symbols. A child must be able to retrieve the symbol from memory without any external cues. In addition, motor planning skills, motor imitation skills, and fine motor abilities are necessary for sign language. Even if all of these skills are present, it is important to remember that the child's signed messages will only be understood by limited partners.

Low-tech systems, such as the Picture Exchange Communication System (PECS; Frost & Bondy, 1994) or communication boards, place fewer social demands on the communicator. The communication is a simple, concrete exchange that is slow paced. Low-tech systems typically use photographs or pictographs. This allows the child to focus attention on a symbol for as long as necessary in order to understand its meaning. The picture or pictographic symbols do not require recall memory; rather, they serve as reminders of what to say. Low-tech systems have minimal requirements; the child only needs to show some evidence of interest in two-dimensional pictures or photographs. Their messages are

Table 4.5. Augmentative and alternative communication systems

Attributes	Sign language	Low-tech communication boards	High-tech voice output aids
Social	Face-to-face	Exchange	Exchange
Interaction	Fluid	Slow	Slow
Modality	Visual-temporal	Visuospatial	Visuospatial
Grammar	Required	Not required	Varies
Messages	Unlimited	Limited	Varies
Memory	Recall	Recognition	Recognition
Motor	Complex	Simple	Simple
Portability	Unlimited	Moderate	Limited
Partners	Limited	Universal	Universal

generally understood by everyone; however, low-tech systems limit the number of communication messages that a child can generate.

High-tech AAC systems, such as voice output systems and computers, have many of the same attributes of low-tech systems with some added advantages and disadvantages. Speech output devices can be programmed for children using pictures, pictographs, or printed words. One of the advantages of most high-tech systems is that the child can generate a broader repertoire of messages. Some systems use written language, giving the child access to a formal language. The advantage of speech output systems is that they give the child "a voice" and can make the power of communication more salient. High-tech systems, like computers, can also be more intrinsically motivating. Some disadvantages of high-tech systems are that they are less portable, more costly, and can have the same problems as any technological device.

With these systems' features in mind, the following questions should be considered when selecting an AAC system for a child with autism:

- What is the child's level of motivation to communicate?
- What is the child's repertoire of nonverbal communicative behaviors?
- Does the child show an interest in the symbol system?
- What is the child's cognitive level?
- What communication system best matches the child's learning style?
- Does the child have the skills required to use the system?
- What appears to be the easiest system for the child to learn?
- What appears to be the most functional system for the child to use?
- What is the probability that the child will use the system across multiple settings?
- Does the child have any problem behaviors that need to be considered in the selection of the communication system?

There is often confusion or disagreement about when and which AAC system to select for a particular child, as these multiple child variables, as well as the family's preference, contribute to the decision process. In the case of autism, however, it is especially important to examine the child's learning style and level of social motivation. One must remember that the primary goal for providing the child with an AAC system is to expand the child's functional communication abilities. Although this fact is obvious, it can be easily overlooked in program planning. Thus, if the child has a range of unconventional means of communication (i.e., challenging behaviors that serve communication purposes), an AAC system is imperative. In addition, if the child has a limited repertoire of symbols in his current system, another system should be explored.

There are two general ways to approach the selection of an AAC system for a child:

- Select one communication system based on the child's characteristics, or
- Systematically teach multiple messages using multiple systems in order to identify the best system for the child. For example, target three words in sign language and three other words using a low-tech system. Then compare the child's rate of acquisition using each system.

For comprehensive resources on AAC intervention, see Beukelman and Mirenda (1998), Glennen and DeCosta (1997), and Light and Binger (1998).

Communicative Functions

An effective communicator understands that gestures and language can be used for a variety of social purposes. The social functions of communication include responses to others and initiations that convey various requests, ideas, and feelings. Before the emergence of language, typically developing children use nonverbal means to express a range of communicative functions. Once language is present, they combine verbal and nonverbal means to express the full range of communicative functions across structured and unstructured contexts (Wetherby & Rodriquez, 1992).

Children with autism show significant differences in their functional use of nonverbal and verbal means of communication. First, they possess a more limited repertoire of communicative functions. Both preverbal and verbal children with autism typically request and refuse, but they rarely spontaneously comment on items of interest, express feelings, or use prosocial statements (Wetherby, 1986; Wetherby & Rodriquez, 1992). Second, children with autism demonstrate more unconventional social-communicative behaviors. Challenging behaviors can serve social functions, and language behaviors can be noninteractive. Challenging behaviors often serve communicative functions, for example, screaming to make a request. Noninteractive language use is also common, for instance, self-stimulatory or self-regulatory speech without any apparent social purpose. Echolalia, a common characteristic in many verbal children with autism, is used for both social and noninteractive purposes (Prizant & Duchan, 1981; Prizant & Rydell, 1993). As a result, the evaluation of a child's social intent and communicative function is difficult to discern. For example, a child who says "Put it away?" may be requesting to finish an activity, whereas others may perceive the communicative function to be asking a question. Similarly, a child who says "Time to go home?" may be asking to leave a stressful situation, whereas others may perceive the message as a request for information. The function of the child's speech can be judged by considering the context and observing the nonverbal actions that occur prior to, during, and after the message. The degree to which the child directs the message to others, waits for a response, and persists with the communication attempts assists in evaluating communicative function.

Expand Functional Communication

A major portion of the Assessment of Social and Communication Skills for Children with Autism is devoted to evaluating the range of communicative functions used by a child. More than 50 different specific functions are listed in the section for assessing communication skills in the following general categories:

- Requests for personal needs
- Responses to others
- Comments
- Requests for information
- Expressions of feelings
- Prosocial statements

These skills do not represent a developmental social-communicative hierarchy or a linear progression of target goals. Rather, the assessment of a child's functional communication is intended to provide a framework for making intervention decisions.

Successful communication requires the child to use conventional verbal or nonverbal means for a variety of social purposes, with multiple partners, and across a variety of contexts. Thus, intervention must emphasize the child's functional skills within social-communicative interactions. The intervention plan should include goals to

- Expand the range of communicative functions
- Communicate age-appropriate messages
- Communicate with both adults and peers
- Communicate across multiple contexts

The ultimate goal is for the child to be able to convey all of the communication functions with at least one verbal message. The goal to expand functional communication should supersede attempts to expand language. For example, if a child's repertoire of functional communication is limited to single-word requests for food and objects, the intervention goal would be to build additional functions, such as labeling or asking someone to play. Efforts to expand the child's language from a single-word request (e.g., "cookie") to an elaborate request (e.g., "I want cookie, please") should be secondary.

It is important to select messages that mirror the communication of same-age peers. Carefully examine the interactions of typically developing peers and identify the essential elements of social acceptability. For example, most typically developing children ask a friend to play by gesturing or saying "Come here." Teaching a child with autism to say, "(Peer's name), I want to play (name of activity)" may be more difficult for the child and may also add to her social difference. Most young children are likely to say "Again" or "Do it again" to get another push on the swing. Teaching children with autism to request actions by saying "Push more, please" stigmatizes them further.

In addition, it is useful to target words and messages that can be used in multiple settings. Generalized terms (e.g., "do," "go," "this," "that," "it," "here," "there") can be taught contextually and used in a variety of settings for a variety of functions. Phrases such as "Do this," "Go there," and "Want that" help expand communication without the need for expanded language.

Furthermore, it is important to consider the social partners when planning communication skills intervention. As with social skills, it is common for children with autism to master communication skills with adult partners before generalizing them to peer partners. Again, this distinction is largely due to the adult social partner's ability to understand the communication efforts of a child with autism and to adapt the interaction to enhance success. Planning for communication success with peers needs to consider those interactions in which the child demonstrates mastery with adults.

Table 4.6 outlines the general framework for planning intervention to expand functional communication. (Detailed instructional strategies are provided in Chapter 5, with in-depth intervention guidelines for expanding functional communication in Chapter 8.) The key aspects of communication intervention are

- Target specific social contexts to practice communication skills.
- Target specific communicative functions, and teach social use across multiple social contexts.
- Use every possible opportunity to build functional communication.
- Teach generalization and functional application of skills in a systematic fashion.

Figure 4.6 further explores designing communication intervention. In Plan I, a specific communicative function is targeted and the child is given multiple opportunities to

Table 4.6.　Framework for planning functional communication intervention

Select specific social contexts for communication enhancement.	Identify the specific social setting.
	Identify what the child needs to SAY.
	Select messages that mirror same-age peers.
	Practice using messages with an adult.
	Generalize using messages to peer interactions.
	Program generalization to novel contexts.
Select a specific communicative function and systematically practice it across multiple social contexts.	Target a specific communicative function.
	Target a specific communicative means.
	Target contexts in which to practice using the message.
	Program generalization to novel contexts.
Use every possible opportunity to interact.	Target moments when the child is motivated.
	Replace nonconventional means with conventional means.
	Create activity routines.
	Modify interaction patterns.
	Plan for generalization systematically.

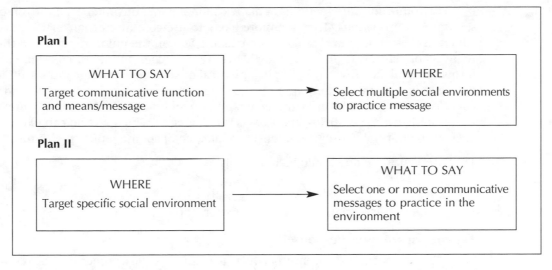

Figure 4.6. Designing communication intervention. Plan I: Begin with targeted communication goals. Plan II: Begin with a targeted social environment.

practice the skill. In Plan II, a specific setting is identified and the child practices a variety of communicative functions. The first approach provides for more systematic instruction and an easier means of assessing skill acquisition. The communication intervention guidelines described in Chapter 8 follow this format. The second approach provides more program flexibility. Using that approach means there is less specificity and accountability for skill acquisition but greater opportunities to build a range of communication skills simultaneously. The next profile illustrates expanding communicative functions through the use of Plan I:

> *Derek was 8 years old when he was taught to ask a novel question. Before then, Derek did not understand that other people could be a source of information. He would ask the same questions repeatedly in order to get predictable answers, but he had never generated a novel question. Therefore, the target function was asking a question, and the target message was "What is it?"; the target settings included multiple natural or contrived contexts. Using a cue card with a pictographic symbol for the target message, Derek was taught to ask "What is it?" during a lotto game, during show and tell, when given a present, when looking at novel pictures, and in many other situations. In the initial context, the adult working with Derek needed to pair the graphic cue with a verbal model, but she quickly faded the verbal prompt. Derek used the cue card in novel situations until he gradually learned the meaning of the question; that is, "When I see something new and want to know the name, ask the question!" Although Derek did not learn that other people were a source of information, he acquired a means to communicate his own curiosity.*

Basic Communicative Roles

An effective communicator also understands that communication is a reciprocal social exchange. This includes the basic roles of responding to others and initiating interaction with others.

Spontaneous initiations require an ability to extract relevant information from a social context in order to decide what to say. There are an infinite number of potential messages that can be conveyed in any situation, so the decision about what to say is determined by making a mental assessment of internal and external factors. One's thoughts, feelings, ideas, and perceptions of the physical and social environments are considered.

The communication patterns of many children with autism reflect more difficulty with spontaneous initiations. They are more likely to use communication that is prompted by concrete cues and has a clear and immediate effect on the environment, and their use of requests or refusals is linked to tangible contextual cues and adult consequences. Many forms of echolalia are cued by explicit physical or social events. In contrast, difficulty initiating communication may be linked to the absence of explicit physical and/or social cues. The children have difficulty generating novel information without contextual cues (Ozonoff, Pennington, & Rogers, 1991). The degree to which a child can extract relevant cues in the natural contexts influences the degree of spontaneous communication.

The intervention plan should include goals to

- Respond within social-communicative interactions
- Initiate within social-communicative interactions

Expand Meaningful Responses

There is a significant difference between teaching a child a repertoire of responses and teaching the child meaningful social-communicative interaction. Keep in mind the "M&Ms" of intervention: *motivating and meaningful* interactions. Communicative messages not taught within the context of functional use risk becoming a series of patterned responses devoid of meaning, as shown in the following case study:

> Devon, who was 5 years old, had been taught to answer the question "How are you?" with the response "I'm fine, thank you." One day, he looked sick. His teacher asked, "How are you?" Devon replied, "I'm fine, thank you," and then proceeded to become violently ill. This social exchange was not only unrealistic for a 5-year-old, but also created a meaningless response on Devon's part.

Expand Initiations

In order to expand spontaneous initiations, the intervention plan should include goals to

- Expand communication in the absence of verbal cues and prompts
- Expand communication in the absence of other social cues and prompts

Spontaneous initiations can be facilitated by changing adult–child interaction patterns, particularly by shifting interaction away from a directive style of asking questions to a facilitative style of commenting. Explicit verbal prompts, specifically questions and directives, limit opportunities for spontaneous communication. Spontaneous initiations can also be facilitated by decreasing the use of social cues and prompts and increasing the use of explicit physical cues. For example, organize the physical environment to stimulate interest and spontaneous requesting instead of simply asking "What do you want?" This type of change facilitates the essential task of decreasing the child's reliance on explicit verbal prompts. In addition, spontaneous initiations can be expanded by increasing the use of AAC supports. A wallet containing photos of favorite activities or a communication board may assist a child in making choices about what to say and can foster his or her spontaneous communication with peers. These strategies, described in greater detail in Chapter 5, are illustrated by the next example:

> Rachael, 4 years old, attended an inclusive preschool. She silently sat with three peers during art class each day. Efforts to prompt comments about the activity were too vague for her, and she inconsistently imitated adults and peers. Two modifications were made to the setting to increase Rachael's spontaneous comments. One was that at the end of the activity, each child displayed his or her artwork, and the other children took turns saying one nice thing about it. The second change was that a communication board was made for Rachael that included four

different things she might say about her friends' artwork: IT'S NICE, I LIKE IT, PRETTY, or IT'S . . . (followed by a list of colors). Rachael gradually decreased her reliance on the communication board and increased her imitation of the peers' comments.

Elements of Conversation

To participate in a conversation, it is necessary to possess communicative intent, motivation to communicate, a means to communicate, and an understanding of both communicative function and basic communicative roles. The minimum requirements for a conversation are the ability to maintain reciprocal interactions, repair conversations, and terminate conversations. Conversation requires the ability to

- Attend to multiple aspects of the speaker's message
- Process multiple aspects of the speaker's message
- Interpret the intent and meaning of the speaker's verbal, nonverbal, and affective behaviors
- Understand the speaker's message in relation to the social context
- Understand the partner's mental state (i.e., what the partner knows, understands, and feels)
- Monitor the relevance of the conversation for the other person
- Organize ideas relevant to the topic of conversation
- Retrieve information relevant to the topic, partner, and context
- Use appropriate proximity, affect, and body language
- Continually adapt to the ongoing, changing social dynamic

Enhancing Conversational Abilities

For most children with autism, an intervention plan to build conversation skills should have three basic goals: to initiate, repair, and terminate interactions with adults and peers using routine messages. The conversational abilities of same-age peers should be considered when targeting specific messages. Samples include

- Initiation (nonverbal): proximity to the partner, tapping partner's arm, showing an object, giving a high-five
- Initiation (verbal): saying a friend's name, "Hi," or "Know what?"
- Repair (verbal): saying "What?" or "I don't know"
- Termination (nonverbal): waving, putting away conversation referent
- Termination (verbal): saying "Bye," "Gotta go," or "See you later"

The complex, ongoing adjustments and modifications inherent in conversations challenge even those children with autism who are socially motivated. As a result, conversations often involve routine scripts, situation-specific topics, or repetitive and perseverative questions. Teaching children with autism to become attuned to the multiple dimensions of social-communicative interaction is a formidable task, and the responsibility largely lies with the conversational partner to adjust his or her interaction patterns to accommodate the child. Conversations generally need to be structured around a particular activity or event with familiar dialogue. In addition, games and activities can be designed to practice individual conversational rules. Conversation can be enhanced through preview, review, and practice. Finally, conversation can be fostered with the use of AAC supports. (These strategies are detailed in Chapter 5, and sample procedures for building conversation skills are described in Chapter 8.) The following vignettes exemplify intervention plans to build conversation skills:

Every day, 7-year-old Sean approached other children on the playground and said, "What color is your car?" Sean needed some explicit cues to remind him what else he could say to his friends, so each weekend Sean's family organized a wallet containing photos of his recent activities to use in school. Sean was taught to approach peers and say "Hi," and his peers were coached to ask to see his wallet. The photos gave both Sean and his peers conversation cues.

Terry is 8 years old. She has been successful with one-to-one peer interactions but unable to converse in groups. Terry practices "what to DO, who to WATCH, who to LISTEN to, and what to SAY" in group situations by watching videos of her friends playing and talking in familiar situations. Terry and her teacher generate lists of how to get the group's attention and how much to say. To ensure the intervention's success, Terry's family practices the basic skills at home with her. In addition, Terry's peer group has been coached to be aware of her efforts, to acknowledge her attempts to get their attention, and to wait for her to finish talking.

For additional resources on building conversational skills in children with autism, see Freeman and Dake (1996) and Twatchman (1995).

FRAMEWORK FOR UNDERSTANDING RITUALISTIC BEHAVIORS

All behaviors exist for a reason. Behaviors reflect knowledge, communication abilities, and emotional states; they occur in response to external events and internal states. Ritualistic patterns of behavior occur for the same reasons. They may represent a limited understanding about what to DO and what to SAY. The intensity of ritualistic patterns may reflect the level of comfort and/or understanding at any point of time. States of excitement, anxiety, boredom, and confusion all have the potential of triggering ritualistic behaviors. In addition, ritualistic behaviors can occur as a result of underlying medical conditions.

The phenomenon of ritualistic behavior dominates the social and communication patterns of children with autism to a greater degree than that of typically developing children. The form and intensity of ritualistic behaviors vary significantly among children with autism. As presented in Chapter 1, there are four theories regarding the origin of ritualistic behavior in autism: impaired sensory modulation (Hanschu, 1998), anxiety (Muris, 1998), impaired cognitive functions (Ozonoff et al., 1991), and poor inhibition (Maurer & Damasio, 1982).

It is likely that these four factors interface in complex ways that are not fully understood. It is also probable that intervention for the treatment of ritualistic behaviors may often need to be a combination of educational and medical treatment. Figure 4.7 provides a framework for understanding and planning intervention for social and communication rituals. To understand and support children with ritualistic behavior, it helps to assume that the behaviors derive from multiple sources and may be a manifestation of two or more of the following:

- Enjoyment: sensory stimulation

- Discomfort: sensory overstimulation, changes in routine, limited choices, loss of control

- Confusion: novel situations, misunderstanding the social context, ineffective social skills (not understanding what to DO), ineffective communication (not understanding what to SAY), learning disability (inability to shift mental focus)

- Medical: an anxiety disorder, other

The Assessment of Social and Communication Skills for Children with Autism can be used to identify a child's ritualistic patterns and to begin understanding possible causes. The specific portions of the assessment tool that yield this material are located in Section I, the Inventory of Social and Communication Behavior.

First, the inventory of social behavior provides information about the presence and form of self-stimulatory behaviors and ritualistic and perseverative play. Second, the inventory of communicative behavior provides information about the presence and form of

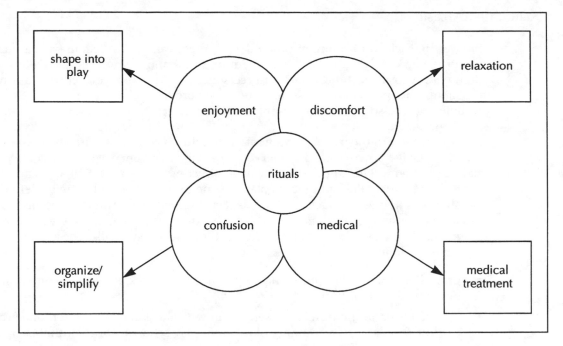

Figure 4.7. Planning intervention for ritualistic behaviors.

self-stimulatory, perseverative, and ritualized communication patterns. Third, the child's exploratory behavior provides insight into sensory preferences and aversions. The active child generally seeks sensory stimulation, whereas the passive child generally avoids sensory stimulation. Information about the child's fears and intense interests, as well as what best calms the child, also provides insight regarding the source of ritualistic behaviors. Keep in mind that it is useful to examine the physical and social contexts in which there is an absence of ritualistic behaviors and to identify the conditions under which the child is calm and interactive. These contexts and conditions can, in turn, be used to promote success in intervention plans.

The goal of educational intervention is to increase the child's comfort and understanding by providing supports that decrease discomfort and confusion and, thus, rituals. Although these supports are detailed in Chapter 5, specific ones to remember when responding to ritualistic behavior are

- Organize the physical environment.
- Organize and simplify social experiences.
- Teach alternative social and communication skills.
- Teach relaxation.
- Provide comforting toys and activities.
- Respect the child's emotional needs.

Intervention must be approached from a sympathetic point a view. An understanding of and respect for the complexity of issues facing children with autism is the cornerstone of successful intervention.

PROGRAM ACCOUNTABILITY: MONITORING PROGRESS

A cornerstone of successful intervention is measurement of a child's progress. Ongoing evaluation of a child's skill acquisition is important because it documents program effectiveness and guides future intervention decisions. Due to the inherent complexity of social and communication development, both quantitative and qualitative measures are necessary.

Quantitative Measures

Progress in social and communication development can be defined, in part, as mastery of the discrete skills listed in the Assessment of Social and Communication Skills for Children with Autism. Although one must recognize the limitations of a curriculum-based assessment, this particular assessment tool does provide a quantitative measure for the complexities of social and communication challenges specific to children with autism spectrum disorders.

In addition to the initial assessment, it is useful to collect ongoing data on the specific target objectives in the child's intervention plan. Different social and communication skills lend themselves to different forms of direct measurement. Solitary play skills may be defined by the child's number of play schemas, social play skills may be defined by the number of activities in which a specific skill is observed, communication skills may be defined by the number of settings in which the skill is observed, and conversation may be defined by the presence of various reciprocal interaction subskills. These direct measures can take the following forms:

- Checklists: the level of prompting required for skill, task analysis of community skills, or communication samples
- Frequency data: the number of settings in which a skill occurs, the number of different imitation skills, the number of different play schemas, or the number of different means to convey one communicative function
- Time sample data: the length of attention during solitary play or the length of attention to a group activity

The appendixes to Chapters 6, 7, and 8 contain a variety of data collection forms.

Qualitative Measures

Progress is defined as changes in the level of motivation, exploration, flexibility, engagement, and socioemotional comfort. These critical variables are more difficult to measure but represent the core aspects of social and communication success. This is because qualitative data capture the "real-world" application of target skills and, thus, presents the best picture of a child's social and communication development. Keeping a child portfolio is recommended to monitor social and communication progress. *Child portfolios* are an accumulation of meaningful products that are collected over an extended period of time to verify a child's progress. The items for the child portfolio might be collected on a quarterly basis to accompany progress reports. A child portfolio might include (but is not limited to)

- Audiotaped conversations
- Videotapes of social play or adult–child interactions
- Anecdotes of family outings
- Narratives about after-school activities with peers
- A homemade rating scale that assesses the child's level of anxiety or intensity of ritualistic behaviors

SUMMARY

Very detailed planning is necessary to ensure that intervention matches the needs of children with autism. Effective intervention requires specific attention to their social and communication skills. This chapter provides general guidelines for designing social and communication intervention, understanding ritualistic behaviors, and monitoring intervention progress. These frameworks can be used by parents and professionals to evaluate and maintain an effective intervention plan.

Appendix A
Sample Target Goals and Behavioral Objectives

Sample target objectives for a child at the beginning stage of social-communicative development.

All behavioral objectives need to specify conditions; for example, 80% of opportunities presented, with adult/peer, in specific/novel contexts.

Goal area: Nonverbal social-communicative interaction skills

1. _____ will look at objects when directed
2. _____ will repeat own behavior to maintain social interaction

Goal area: Imitation

1. _____ will imitate single actions with a toy
2. _____ will imitate single words during familiar songs

Goal area: Organization

1. _____ will keep toys/materials in designated areas
2. _____ will transition to the next activity when directed

Goal area: Solitary play

1. _____ will demonstrate functional play using one action with a toy
2. _____ will play independently for 10 minutes

Goal area: Social play

1. _____ will play in proximity to others using own set of toys/materials
2. _____ will respond to nonverbal invitations to play

Goal area: Group skills

1. _____ will attend to structured, choral group activities
2. _____ will follow nonverbal group directions to stop activity

Goal area: Community skills

1. _____ will demonstrate age-appropriate skills while riding in the car/school bus
2. _____ will demonstrate age-appropriate skills on the playground

Goal area: Communication skills

1. _____ will respond to greetings
2. _____ will initiate requests for desired toys/objects

Goal area: Socioemotional skills

1. _____ will request a break when upset
2. _____ will share own food/toys with others

Goal area: Conversation

1. _____ will gain a person's attention prior to communicating a message
2. _____ will attend/orient to others who get his/her attention

DO-WATCH-LISTEN-SAY: Social and Communication Intervention for Children with Autism
by Kathleen Ann Quill © 2000 Paul H. Brookes Publishing Co.

Sample objectives for a child at an advanced stage of social-communicative development.

All behavioral objectives need to specify conditions; for example, 80% of opportunities presented, with adult/peer, in specific/novel contexts.

Goal area: Nonverbal social-communicative interaction skills
1. _____ will attend to novel activities for 30 minutes
2. _____ will point out interests to others to maintain social interaction

Goal area: Imitation
1. _____ will imitate others' actions, when appropriate
2. _____ will demonstrate verbal imitation during all activities

Goal area: Organization
1. _____ will transition when an unexpected change occurs
2. _____ will share toys and materials with others

Goal area: Solitary play
1. _____ will demonstrate creative play
2. _____ will play independently when directed

Goal area: Social play
1. _____ will play structured group games
2. _____ will engage in cooperative play in unstructured group contexts

Goal area: Group skills
1. _____ will participate in group discussions
2. _____ will follow school rules for assemblies and field trips

Goal area: Community skills
1. _____ will demonstrate age-appropriate skills at birthday parties
2. _____ will demonstrate age-appropriate skills at Halloween

Goal area: Communication skills
1. _____ will request information about cause ("Why?")
2. _____ will describe a past event

Goal area: Socioemotional skills
1. _____ will indicate when confused ("I don't know")
2. _____ will offer help to others

Goal area: Conversation
1. _____ will maintain conversations by providing intermittent feedback ("Uh-huh," "Okay")
2. _____ will modulate voice volume to the setting

DO-WATCH-LISTEN-SAY: Social and Communication Intervention for Children with Autism
by Kathleen Ann Quill © 2000 Paul H. Brookes Publishing Co.

DO-WATCH-
LISTEN-SAY

chapter 5

Strategies to Enhance
Social and Communication Skills

Kathleen Ann Quill

The task of building social and communication skills in children with autism is a formidable one. The purpose of this chapter is to present an eclectic balance of strategies for enhancing social and communication development. The discussion incorporates methods that are based on the principles of applied behavioral analysis with developmental practices that are essential to social and communication growth. The recommended strategies synthesize a broad range of clinical research and clinical practices for children with autism into a continuum of intervention options.

The emphasis on a continuum of intervention strategies reflects both the complexities of social and communication development and the significant diversity that is found among children with a diagnosis of autism. The acquisition of social skills and communication requires, by nature, social motivation and meaningful relationships. There is an obvious need, then, to create motivating, meaningful activities in natural environments to promote spontaneous social and communication skills. At the same time, a significant amount of specialized supports is needed to compensate for the social, communication, and behavioral challenges characteristic of children with autism. Thus, the level of support in the natural environment will vary according to the specific social, emotional, and behavioral needs of each individual child. Recognizing that the task of building social and communication skills in children with autism is a difficult one, this discussion of strategies is offered as a set of guidelines and is not intended to be definitive or dogmatic.

The intervention strategies outlined in this chapter focus on compensatory strategies to support social and communication development. The rationale for compensatory strategies is based upon a respect for the social and communication struggles experienced by children with autism. That is, given that autism is characterized by social and communication impairments, intervention must incorporate strategies that compensate for these central issues while at the same time supporting their development. The four compensatory strategies, or *social bridges*, discussed in this chapter are

1. Organizational supports: organizing the physical environment to compensate for the child's perception of a socially disorganized environment (e.g., choice board)

2. Social supports: modifying the social environment to compensate for the child's social-communicative impairment (i.e., modifications made by others to maintain meaningful and mutually beneficial reciprocal interactions with a child)

3. Visually cued instruction: providing visual cues and prompts to assist the child in his understanding of language and social meaning (e.g., activity schedule, play script, social story, cue cards)

4. Augmentative and alternative communication (AAC) supports: providing AAC supports to assist with the child's acquisition of spontaneous social and communication skills (e.g., cue cards, communication board, conversation book)

Representative examples of various supports are provided at the end of this chapter in Appendix A.

Particular attention is given to making child-specific treatment decisions. As autism spectrum disorders represent a heterogeneous syndrome, it is unlikely that one method or strategy will work equally with all children. It is necessary to consider a child's level of social motivation, core skill abilities, and degree of challenging behaviors, particularly ritualistic behaviors, when planning social and communication skills intervention. These issues are also explored in detail within the chapter, concluding with an examination of the emotional needs of the child.

The implicit message of this chapter is to understand the child's needs and to listen to your intuition. The importance of forming a relationship with a child in order to optimize social and communication development must be inferred; this fundamental belief should not be forgotten. With this in mind, Chapter 5 bases intervention to build social and communicative competence in children with autism on the following principles:

• Social and communication development is complex and dynamic.

• Social skills are acquired in the context of naturally occurring events.

• Communication skills are acquired in the context of naturally occurring reciprocal interactions.

• Relationships are necessary to optimize a child's social and communication development.

• Intervention should be individualized.

• Intervention strategies should be used flexibly.

• Specific strategies may or may not work with a particular child.

• Every moment is a learning opportunity for social and communicative growth.

• The child is the ultimate teacher.

This information is intended as a resource to be applied critically and flexibly, because the idea of a social and communication skills intervention guide minimizes the complexity and richness of these developmental areas. It is essential that this intervention guide not be used too rigidly with the diverse group of young children that it is intended to help.

BEST PRACTICES DEBATE

The primary goal of intervention for children with autism should be to enhance their social and communication development. Although there is an understanding of the complexity of social and communication skills intervention, there is uncertainty regarding how to approach this daunting task. A polarity of viewpoints exists among the professional community as to how to achieve this objective. Intervention approaches range from traditional adherence to principles of applied behavioral analysis—through the use of massed discrete trial training—to developmental practices in inclusive settings.

Comparative reviews of intervention programs for children with autism show that different treatment models, ranging from traditional behavioral approaches to developmental approaches in inclusive educational settings, are demonstrating similar outcomes (Dawson & Osterling, 1997). Independent of methodology, programs are reporting "success" for half of the children in these programs. Measures of success, however, are generally defined in terms of academic achievement, not social and communication development. Given that impaired social and communication development is the hallmark of autism, a true understanding of the "best" means to support social and communication development in children with autism has not been empirically studied and, therefore, is unknown. An understanding of best practices to enhance social skills and communication in children with autism, it seems, is just beginning.

The Behavioral-Developmental Debate

The two highly debated treatment approaches are the *traditional behavioral approach* (Lovaas, 1981) and the *relationship-based developmental model* (Greenspan, 1992). These two opposing methods are described in detail next and are summarized in Table 5.1.

Traditional Behavioral Approach: Discrete Trial Training

The traditional behavioral model of discrete trial training is based on learning theory principles. Intervention entails specificity of purpose, goals, and activity structure. Skill acquisition reflects the mastery of a series of discrete subskills. The model emphasizes preci-

Table 5.1. Characteristics of traditional behavioral and relationship-based developmental intervention approaches

Procedural variables	Traditional behavioral: Discrete trials	Relationship-based developmental: Floor time
Target objective	Specific response	General
Context	Structured one-to-one instruction	Variety of social groupings
Setting	Artificially designed and predetermined by the adult	Naturally occurring and motivating
Activity and materials	Selected by the adult	Selected by the child
Teachable moment	Adult-directed	Continuous; follows the child's lead
Instructions	Series of single teaching units (i.e., trials) Adult-initiated Verbal instruction	Reciprocal interactions Child-initiated Contextual, language, and socioemotional information
Prompts	Verbal, gestural, and physical	Verbal, gestural, and contextual supports
Accepted child responses	One discrete target response	All behaviors are social-communicative
Adult response to child	Immediate Not linked to meaning of child's behavior	Immediate; scaffolded Linked to meaning of child's behavior
Reinforcement	Artificial Predetermined consequence	Social Continuation of the activity
Repetition	Exact	Determined by the child's interest
Measure of success	Child's correct target response	Quality of socioemotional interactions Interactive

Sources for traditional behavioral approach: Lovaas (1981) and Maurice, Green, & Luce (1996); source for relationship-based developmental approach: Greenspan & Wieder (1998).

sion and organization during instruction. This includes complete adult control over the arrangement of the learning environment; the use of prompting and shaping techniques; and attention to immediate, reinforcing feedback contingent on the child's production of the correct target response. The rationale for using discrete trials to teach children with autism is the belief that they are unable to learn in natural contexts due to their specific learning and behavioral characteristics (Lovaas, 1981; Maurice, Green, & Luce, 1996). This approach assumes that children with autism

- Lack social motivation
- Lack the ability to learn in natural contexts
- Learn when adults control all elements of activities
- Learn through exact repetition of discrete skills

See Table 5.1 for characteristics of the instructional model for discrete trial training (from Lovaas, 1981; Maurice et al., 1996).

Discrete trial approaches may be useful for the acquisition of academic or language skills but counterproductive for the acquisition of *spontaneous*, self-initiated social and communication skills (Koegel & Koegel, 1995b). The difficulties associated with using a traditional behavioral model to enhance social and communication skills include the artificial nature of the instructional setting, an emphasis on specific child responses to adult-directed interactions, and the lack of a clear link between instruction and the social use of a skill (Quill, 1995a). As a result, social and communicative spontaneity is compromised. Furthermore, skills acquired in an artificial context often do not generalize to natural social contexts.

Relationship-Based Developmental Model: Floor Time

The relationship-based developmental model is framed within the study of typical child development. Intervention emphasizes the development of skills through active exploration and positive social interactions. The model is based on the belief that children acquire skills through social interactions. Thus, it emphasizes naturally occurring situations as the context for instruction, child-directed activities, and the adult's role in facilitating development. The child's internal motivation and socioemotional qualities propel active engagement, and the responses of others to the child's initiations and interests lay the foundation for this developmental process. Intentionality and meaning are assigned to all of the child's behaviors. The rationale for using this developmental approach to enhance development in children with autism is based on the belief that the fundamental process of learning is the same for all children, so children with autism are able to learn in natural contexts (Greenspan, 1992; Greenspan & Wieder, 1998). The developmental approach assumes that children with autism

- Are capable of social and emotional flexibility
- Have core challenges in sensory processing
- Use behaviors to communicate and interact
- Learn through active engagement in natural contexts
- Learn through reciprocal social interactions

See Table 5.1 for specific characteristics of the intervention model (from Greenspan & Wieder, 1998), which uses a floor-time approach.

Drawbacks of the relationship-based model for children with autism relate to the open-ended quality of the instructional environment and reliance on the child's initiations to guide social-communicative interactions. Children who lack core skills such as joint attention and imitation or who have severe ritualistic and challenging behaviors may be less responsive to this model (Quill, 1995a).

Comparing the Two Models

As indicated by the previous discussion, the behavioral and developmental approaches share common beliefs about intervention goals but have quite divergent views about the process of learning communication and social skills, as well as how it translates into treatment for children with autism. For example, the initial goal of both behavioral and developmental intervention is to foster shared attention and imitation skills, which comprise the foundation for social and communication development. Nonetheless, the procedures used to accomplish these goals are significantly different. The following descriptions of traditional behavioral discrete trial procedures to build core attention and imitation skills (Maurice et al., 1996) and transactional floor-time procedures to build these same skills (Greenspan & Wieder, 1998) highlight the differences between these two approaches.

Discrete Trial Procedures

Instructions include eliciting eye contact from the child in response to his name:

> Sit in a chair across from the child. State the child's name and simultaneously prompt eye contact by bringing an edible reinforcer or small tangible reinforcer to your eye level. When the child makes eye contact with you for 1 second, immediately give reinforcer to the child. Over sessions, say the child's name and delay your prompt. . . . Throughout teaching sessions, provide positive reinforcement if child looks at you spontaneously. . . . Repeat procedure but sustain eye contact for 5 seconds. (Maurice et al., 1996, p. 74)

Discrete trial procedures for gross motor imitation are as follows:

> Sit in a chair facing the child and establish attending. Present the instruction "do this" while simultaneously modeling a gross motor movement. Prompt the child to perform the action and reinforce the response. Fade prompts over subsequent trials. . . . Eventually, only reinforce correct, unprompted responses. (Maurice et al., 1996, p. 75)

The child's ability to sit in a chair when directed is the prerequisite skill for teaching motor imitation. The specific gross motor movements that are targeted during this procedure include tapping the table, clapping hands, waving, putting arms up, stomping feet, and nodding head (Maurice et al., 1996).

Floor-Time Procedures

These instructions recommend joining the object of the child's attention to elicit eye contact:

> If she's playing with a ball, hold the ball in your mouth so she'll have to take it from you. Make a funny noise as she grabs it, then open your mouth and gesture for her to put it back. Make another funny noise when she puts it back in. Make "ball in, ball out" a funny cooperative game. . . . If she is mushing food and putting it in her mouth, put some of the mushed food on your face. Smile and laugh and call her name, then encourage her to take the food from your face as well as from the table. (Greenspan & Wieder, 1998, p. 142)

This next floor-time procedure suggests taking cues from the child to elicit imitation:

> If your child is jumping up and down, jump alongside her and sing "We are jumping up and down" to the tune of "Wheels on the Bus." If she allows you, take her hands so that she can jump higher or hold her so she can jump "to the sky". . . . If your child is making funny noises, hold an echo microphone in front of his mouth so he will hear his sounds amplified. Try imitating his sounds. (Greenspan & Wieder, 1998, p. 141)

Successful acquisition of core social and communication skills is defined by the child's ability to share attention, engage in nonverbal social interaction, imitate others in meaningful ways, initiate and respond to others, and use these skills spontaneously in social contexts. Thus, it is important to consider whether these or other methods provide opportunities for a particular child to acquire key social-communicative abilities.

Table 5.2. Characteristics of methods that balance behavioral and developmental factors

Instructional variables	Characteristics
Target objective	Specific but flexible within each activity
Context	Varies with target goal and child's abilities
Setting	Organized
Activities	Meaningful, age-appropriate, and motivating
Teachable moments	Continuous
Instruction/interaction	Alternate between adult-directed and child-directed teaching opportunities; make instruction and interactions meaningful
Prompts	Systematic use of contextual, verbal, visual, gestural
Accepted child responses	Limit the range of response options to behaviors meaningfully linked to activity and/or context
Response to child	Acknowledge and/or scaffold naturally
Reinforcement	Meaningfully linked to context
Repetition	Use naturally, not in a fixed sequence
Measure of success	Quantify and qualify success

RATIONALE FOR COMBINING
BEHAVIORAL AND DEVELOPMENTAL APPROACHES

The ongoing debate regarding a traditional behavioral approach versus a relationship-based developmental approach to enhance social and communication skills in children with autism is unfortunate and largely unnecessary. Both approaches argue that their approach is the "intervention of choice," thereby limiting the complexity and diversity within the spectrum of autism disorders. Discrete trial training is only one practice within the field of applied behavior analysis and does not represent the diverse field of contemporary behaviorism. Similarly, floor time is only one practice within the field of developmental intervention and does not represent the diverse field of developmental intervention. Although both methods have merit with some children, no treatment approach should be used exclusively with all children.

There is growing recognition that these two approaches represent extreme positions and that there is a continuum of options that interfaces the best elements of each approach (see Prizant & Wetherby, 1998, for a review). Therefore, intervention strategies that combine the beneficial components of behavioral technology with developmental principles seem to be the logical way to enhance social and communicative competence in children with autism. Approaches that combine behavioral and developmental principles incorporate specificity of goals and objectives, promote the child's level of motivation and interest, use developmental activities, use instructional cues and prompts in a systematic manner, and emphasize meaningful interactions within the context of adult-structured, organized learning environments. This negates the obvious problems in applying either traditional behavioral or relationship-based developmental approaches exclusively with all children by building in greater flexibility. The procedural variables of combined approaches are summarized in Table 5.2.

This blend of behavioral and developmental principles to enhance social and communication skills is described in many popular approaches used for children with various developmental disabilities and/or children with autism. Some methods that fall within this continuum of options are

- Incidental Teaching (Hart & Risley, 1982)

- Interaction Routines (Quill, 1995a)

- Joint Action Routines (McLean & Synder-McLean, 1978)
- Natural Language Paradigm (Koegel & Koegel, 1995a)
- Picture Exchange Communication System (PECS; Frost & Bondy, 1994)
- TEACCH (Treatment and Education of Autistic and related Communications Handicapped Children; Schopler & Mesibov, 1985, 1986)
- Visually Cued Instruction (Quill, 1998)

These methods make an important contribution to the enhancement of skills and, to various degrees, draw from both behavioral and developmental learning principles. Some procedures designed to promote social-communicative interaction across all contexts and for all children are Interaction Routines, Incidental Teaching, Joint Action Routines, and the Natural Language Paradigm. Other procedures emphasize the use of specific instructional cues to support learning. For instance, TEACCH and Visually Cued Instruction emphasize the use of visual prompts to support language comprehension, social understanding, and organizational skills across all contexts. In some cases, a procedure was designed to elicit specific skills for a particular subgroup of children. For example, the PECS is an AAC system specifically designed to enhance spontaneous communication in nonverbal children. These procedures represent a positive shift toward diverse models of intervention in autism, and they can be used in combination with each other as needed for specific children.

In addition to using approaches that draw from the best of behavioral and developmental principles, the selection of intervention strategies must take into account the diversity of target goals and social contexts, as well as the characteristics of a particular child. To do this, one must consider the appropriateness of a particular approach for facilitating a particular skill. More important, it is necessary to consider each child's level of motivation, attention, and organization in each environment and to adjust the approach to his behavioral state and skills moment to moment. This approach to social and communication enhancement requires ongoing decision making. The methodological variables that need to be considered for each target objective are

- Degree of structure in the environment
- Social context (group size)
- Range of learning opportunities
- Activity and materials
- Level of control (adult-directed or child-directed)
- Prompts (contextual, verbal, gestural, visual, or physical)
- Response to the child's behaviors
- Type of reinforcement (artificial or natural)
- Measure of success (quantitative or qualitative)

In each social context, the child variables that need to be considered are

- Motivation
- Level of comfort with the sensory environment
- Social attention
- Imitation skills
- Organizational skills
- Challenging behaviors

The information presented in the remainder of this chapter assists in developing and designing unique intervention strategies for individual children. This eclectic approach, in which

Table 5.3. Where to build social and communication skills

Setting
  Every moment at school and home is a teachable moment.
  Consider the most natural setting for acquisition of target skills.
  Orchestrate opportunities for interaction whenever possible.

Social context
  Skills are generally acquired with adults and generalized to peers.
  Social communication is more likely to occur in one-to-one interactions.
  Group expectations (not size) determine the probability of success.

Activities

Motivating	Fun
Meaningful	Organized
Natural	Age-appropriate

methods vary within and across children according to intervention goals and child-specific factors, seems to be the most logical solution to build socialization and communication.

TEACHING OPPORTUNITIES

Every setting, social context, and activity has the potential to include opportunities that enhance social and communication skills (see Table 5.3). Nevertheless, one must formulate a systematic plan that takes into account how various natural and structured activities will be organized to create maximum opportunities to address targeted skills. There is also a need to look at the temperament and abilities of an individual child when deciding where the objectives will be addressed.

Setting

It is essential that the setting of intervention be distinguished from the methodology. That is, the issue of *where* instruction occurs is separate from *how* instruction occurs. To date, there are no cross-sectional studies that have systematically examined the effects of different methods in a variety of settings. Therefore, decisions about where intervention will occur must take into account both the target objective and child variables.

The first key to successful intervention for social and communication skills is to recognize that every moment is a teachable moment. In addition, social or communication skills will have greater meaning and be acquired more rapidly if learned in natural settings. All settings can be structured and orchestrated to create opportunities for acquiring these skills. Furthermore, it is important to recognize that intervention must occur at school and at home. All of the skills addressed in this book require ongoing intervention and practice by everyone who interacts with the child.

Child variables to consider when selecting the best setting for acquisition of skills are linked to the child's temperament and core skill abilities, specifically the following:

- Sensory sensitivities: The setting must match the conditions under which a child is most calm. For example, if the child has difficulty participating because of sensory sensitivities to a noisy, active setting, he may require a quieter learning environment.

- Anxiety: The setting must take into account the conditions under which rituals and other expressions of anxiety are least likely to occur.

- Challenging behaviors: The setting must take into account the conditions under which challenging behaviors are least likely to occur.

- Social motivation: The setting must take into account the child's interest in peers. For example, children who watch or imitate other children need peer models in their learning environment.

- Shared attention: The setting must take into account the conditions under which the child is most attentive. For example, examine the child's ability to attend in adult–child interactions, peer–child interactions, and structured and unstructured settings.

- Imitation: The setting must take into account the conditions under which the child is most imitative. For example, examine the child's ability to imitate one or more adults and peers in structured or unstructured settings.

- Organization: The setting must take into account where the child demonstrates organized, purposeful skills. For example, examine how the level of structure or the number of people in the environment influences the child's ability to maintain organized, purposeful social and communication skills.

The following three vignettes show how individual temperaments and core skill abilities—not cognitive or language capacities—should be used to determine the appropriateness of a child's intervention setting.

Tommy is 3 years old. He is a passive child with no severe challenging behaviors. Tommy does, however, demonstrate an absence of core skills: There is no shared attention or response to adult directions, and there are no observation or imitation skills. He is extremely sensitive to sound. He says some words while playing alone, and his solitary play consists of perseverative and inappropriate use of toys. He generally uses simple gestures to make requests. When working with his parents and a therapist at home, Tommy is able to engage in functional play activities and is beginning to make requests with intent. He imitates some actions during familiar, frequently practiced songs and fingerplays, and he looks at books with an adult. When placed in an inclusive preschool, the trained therapist was unable to engage Tommy in the same activities that were successful at home. Episodes of crying dramatically increased in school, and Tommy frequently climbed into one of the classroom cabinets when it became noisy.

Caroline is 5 years old and nonverbal. She has frequent tantrums in response to adult directions and is more likely to respond to her siblings and neighborhood friends. She demonstrates shared attention and watches peers, but she does not imitate them. She has no sensory sensitivities or intense rituals. Caroline used to attend a self-contained classroom until her parents requested some inclusion opportunities; thus, Caroline and her tutor now attend kindergarten. In her kindergarten class, Caroline responds to the play invitations of peers, imitates peers during structured classroom projects, initiates use of her communication board when the peers show interest, and does not have tantrums. Caroline's parents report that she sleeps better and seems happier since starting kindergarten.

Philip is 5 years old and highly verbal. He is able to do second-grade academic work. He is also able to have simple conversations with adults about his interests, and he demonstrates creative solitary play linked to his favorite movies and books. Philip has severe tactile sensitivity and becomes easily upset when there are changes in his physical environment. At one point, Philip's educational program was composed of a self-contained small class in the morning and an inclusive kindergarten in the afternoon. After 4 months of intense effort, however, Philip's family decided to discontinue the inclusive program. Philip was displaying panic responses to kindergarten by crying, "Please, I don't like the kids" every day. His sleep and eating patterns became disrupted as well. The large social group appeared to be too stressful for Philip. He preferred having one kindergarten friend come to his classroom or home to play.

Social Context

Given that social misunderstandings and communication difficulties are central to autism, another question to be addressed is whether intervention should occur in one-to-one interactions or in small social groups. In addition, it is important to consider the dynamics of each social group when planning for social and communication intervention. See Table 5.3 for social context information to consider when making decisions for a particular child's intervention plan. Children with autism generally demonstrate specific social and communication skills with adults first and then generalize the skills to peer interactions. In addition, social and communication skills are also more likely to occur during one-to-one interactions. For example, if the goal is interactive play, interaction with one person is usually easier than cooperating in a group. Similarly, if the goal is communication, it is probable that interaction with one person will be more successful than sharing information in a group.

The group dynamic strongly affects successful participation as well. Participation in groups is less influenced by the size of the group than by the expectations of each member of the group. The ability to participate in a group activity is determined by three factors: social expectations, language expectations, and waiting expectations.

Social expectations are defined by the levels of clarity and predictability that exist in the group. For example, when all of the children are doing the same thing at the same time, there is clarity with regard to social expectation. In contrast, when children in the group are doing different things, even with the same toys or materials, there is less clarity about what to do.

Some group activities require comprehension of language in order to participate, while other group situations do not require an understanding of the language in order to participate. For example, even though children talk during mealtime, an understanding of language is not required in order to participate in the group. On the other hand, a group discussion that occurs during storytime necessitates an understanding of language in order to participate.

An expectation to wait varies across group activities, too. Most group situations require waiting for an unknown amount of time (e.g., waiting to take a turn during an activity). Some group situations require waiting for a specific amount of time (e.g., turn-taking while playing a structured board game). Still other group situations require no waiting at all (e.g., completing an art project next to others who are doing the same thing). Any group situation that requires a child to wait also expects the child to observe the social behaviors of others and to share space and materials. For instance, if the group consists of two children who are taking turns, then the child is expected to observe his peer 50% of the time and participate the other 50% of the time. If the group consists of four children who are each taking turns, then the child is expected to observe others 75% of the time. If the group consists of 10 children who are taking turns, then the child is expected to observe others 90% of the time. For children who are unable to observe the social behavior of others, waiting may be viewed as confusing or as useless time.

The degree to which children are able to successfully participate in a group setting is linked to these three factors. As a result, it is important to consider the requirements of different group contexts. The criteria of social predictability, language expectations, and waiting vary across different group activities. As discussed in Chapter 4, the six general types of group activities include unison, choral, structured nonverbal turn-taking, structured verbal turn-taking, unstructured play, and discussion (see Table 4.1). Identify the social group in which the child is most successful. What type of social group is it—unison, choral, predictable nonverbal turn-taking, or other? These will be the group contexts in which social and communication intervention goals should be addressed. If the child is not successful with any of the group contexts, then one-to-one instruction is required.

In addition to ascertaining the social, language, and communication expectations of a group activity, one must take into account an individual child's abilities in each group setting to determine its usefulness as a context for learning. Variables to consider for each child are

- Social attention: Examine the child's ability to observe others in various group situations.

- Imitation: Examine the child's ability to imitate others in various group situations.

- Language comprehension: Examine the language expectations of the group activity in relation to the child's language comprehension abilities.

- Communication: Examine the communication expectations of the group activity in relation to the child's communication abilities.

- Organization: Examine the child's level of organized, purposeful activity in various group situations.

The following two cases show how core skill abilities determine the appropriateness of various social groups for children.

> Four-year-old Joseph attends a specialized program for children with autism spectrum disorders. He is able to engage in parallel play when he has his own set of toys and materials; he does not observe his peers during these play activities. Joseph is able to participate in group activities when all of the children are doing the same thing at the same time and there is no waiting. During these unison and choral groups, he observes his peers and imitates everyone in the group. His ability to observe and imitate peers is linked to the level of social predictability in the group activity.

> Samantha, 5 years old, spends half of her school day in a kindergarten classroom. She observes and imitates peers during structured art projects and at work centers when everyone is doing the same thing at the same time. She communicates with peers during mealtimes and with one friend during structured activities. Samantha can attend while her teacher reads the class a story but loses focus when the group talks about the story. She also has difficulty during group meeting times that involve discussion and random turn-taking. In addition, Samantha isolates herself during recess and free play. Her ability to interact with peers is linked to the level of social predictability and the level of language complexity in the group activity.

Activities

Given the nature of social and communication development, every activity has the potential to include opportunities to enhance social and communication skills. Regardless of the target social or communication goal, skills will have greater meaning and be acquired more rapidly if taught during naturally occurring, fun, age-appropriate activities. All activities can be structured and orchestrated to create opportunities for acquiring these skills. The M&Ms of intervention—using activities that are *motivating and meaningful*—need to be incorporated into plans for building social and communication development. Organization also is an important consideration. These three important qualities, summarized in Table 5.3, are described in detail next.

Motivating

Motivating activities are likely to elicit positive opportunities for social engagement and communication. A child's interests are a window into what makes sense to the child; that is, he engages in activities that provide stimulation and meaningful information. It is helpful to examine a child's interests and begin using these activities as opportunities to support social participation and communication.

Many children with autism show interest in the alphabet, numbers, books, computers, and maps. These activities are organized, predictable, and patterned and involve visual materials. It is probable that children who enjoy these activities are seeking organization, predictability, patterns, and learning through the visual modality. For such children, activities providing these elements are opportunities for social engagement and communication.

Some children with autism are interested in videos. Watching videos allows them to review unchanging social scenarios and interactions repeatedly. Unlike natural social interactions, which never occur the same way twice, videos present identical reenactments over and over again. It is likely that children who show interest in videos are seeking social predictability. Video instruction may be an excellent means to assist them with social understanding and communicative competence (see later section on visual supports in this chapter).

In addition, examine a child's intense interests and obsessions and assess whether they may be opportunities for learning. Nonetheless, one must be cautious in using obsessive interests as part of an intervention plan. The following vignettes demonstrate the possible positive or negative results:

> Seven-year-old Robert is fascinated by the Muppets and talks about them incessantly. His second-grade teacher channeled this intense interest in positive ways. First, she used Muppet stickers as rewards. Second, she arranged one activity a day when Robert and one classmate could create an art project or write a story about the Muppets. The most positive interactions and conversations occurred as Robert and his peers worked together on these projects. By the end of the school year, the class had generated a Muppet encyclopedia.

> Eight-year-old Don is extremely interested in soda machines; he talks nonstop about the one in school. Initially, Don was given opportunities each day to fill the soda machine with one of his friends; however, he became increasingly more anxious while waiting for his next opportunity to do this. Don's inability to control this obsession resulted in a dramatic increase of his running out of the classroom to the soda machine, which then escalated into tantrums. Therefore, access to and discussion about the soda machine had to be completely eliminated. The teachers wrote a story for the class about the soda machine's being for teachers only, a "Do Not Enter" sign was placed on the room with the soda machine, and a new behavior contract with different rewards was designed for Don.

Meaningful

Meaningful activities are essential to social and communication success. The ability to sustain attention and to participate spontaneously in an activity is linked to its meaningfulness for the child. The challenge of intervention is to select age-appropriate, meaningful activities and then superimpose elements of structure and organization into them. The activity should be naturally reinforcing whenever possible. Remember also that structured, organized, predictable, and somewhat repetitious activities can be both meaningful and fun.

The following examples demonstrate how target social and communication objectives that are often addressed in artificial contexts can instead be structured during meaningful activities:

1. Objective: Imitation

   A meaningful, fun way to teach imitation skills is to sit across from the child, put on a music tape, give the child a musical instrument (e.g., bells), and sing a song about actions that can be done with the instrument (e.g., "This is the way we clap, clap, clap . . . shake, shake, shake . . . go up and down, up and down") while modeling and prompting the contextually meaningful actions.

2. Objective: Labeling

   A meaningful, fun way to foster labeling is to sit with a child, share a storybook, and take turns pointing to and labeling the objects in the book in a structured, predictable way. Using this technique, the adult initially goes through the entire book, pointing to and labeling one item per page. Next, the adult and child together point to the items named by the adult. Then, a turn-taking routine is established so that the adult and child take turns naming one item on each page. For example, using a book about animals, the adult points to one animal on page 1 and says "(name of animal)." Then he points to an animal on the next page and waits for the child to label or comment. Prompts are used as needed, and labeling occurs within the context of a developmentally appropriate, meaningful social activity.

Organization

As previously discussed, social activities can be open-ended or closed-ended. Open-ended activities generally lack specific rules, allow for the creative use of toys and materials, and have no set sequence of events or final product. Closed-ended activities have a clear purpose, organization, and a final product or clear completion point. The lack of organization inherent in open-ended activities is often problematic for most children with autism. (See Chapter 4 for additional information about open-ended and closed-ended activities.)

Activities that lack organization can be confusing for most children with autism and often are not the best opportunities to facilitate social and communication skills. The children will vary in their ability to participate in open-ended activities in purposeful and flexible ways. The presence or absence of core skills—specifically, shared attention, imitation, and organization—will directly affect the child's success or difficulty with open-ended activities. Considering a child's core skill abilities can assist in determining the degree to which a particular closed-ended or open-ended activity is a viable opportunity for social interaction and communication enhancement. In general,

- An absence of core skills generally translates into a need for closed-ended activities.

- The presence of core skills generally translates into the ability to participate in open-ended activities more flexibly.

Nevertheless, all activities, open- or closed-ended, can be organized and structured to create greater predictability. This is the focus of the next section.

ORGANIZATIONAL SUPPORTS

Children with autism are confronted with a world of social confusion, communication difficulties, and sensory sensitivities. This is compounded by their inherent drive for rituals and feelings of anxiety. Imagine the stress for a young child experiencing social chaos and communicative frustrations. Intervention must therefore be approached from a sympathetic point of view, based upon an understanding, respect, and empathy for the child's struggles. In turn, intervention to support social and communication success must emphasize the use of compensatory strategies. These compensatory strategies build social bridges for the child in order to maximize opportunities for social and communication success.

The first set of intervention strategies are termed *organizational supports*. Organizational supports compensate for a child's confusion with the social environment. Table 5.4 indicates that the qualities of the physical environment contrast sharply with the inherent qualities of the social world. Unlike social events, the physical world is predictable and organized. The physical world is concrete and, as such, generally allows an individual to focus attention on details or take as long as needed to examine the physical elements. As discussed in previous chapters, the cognitive strengths and learning preferences associated with autism mirror the qualities of the physical world. (This is the logical outcome of the social impairments characteristic of autism.) Children with autism focus on physical details to make sense of their environment; therefore, providing an organized environment that compensates for their confusion is a logical way to support their understanding of and success in the social world.

Table 5.4. Contrasting physical and social environments

Physical	Social
Concrete	Abstract
Organized	Unorganized
Predictable	Unpredictable
Ordered	Flexible
Patterned	Random
Static	Changing

This section discusses three types of organizational supports:

- Concrete cues to organize the physical environment
- Predictable routines to organize activities
- Behavioral strategies to organize instruction

The criteria for organizing the physical environment, creating activities with predictable routines, and using structured teaching procedures lie in the social behavior of the child. The simple criteria listed next can help determine if a child is organized and when a child needs the support of external organizers, routines, and structure.

The organized child

- Is calm when alone
- Sustains purposeful attention to an activity
- Intermittently observes others' behaviors
- Initiates contact with others to interact
- Demonstrates communicative intent
- Makes changes when directed

The disorganized child

- Is overly active or extremely passive
- Is distractible
- Engages in ritualized behaviors
- Lacks social observation skills
- Uses unconventional means to interact with others
- Engages in ritualized interactions
- Engages in challenging behaviors

Most children with autism are organized some of the time and disorganized at other times. They demonstrate some level of internal organization in some settings and not others. Still, there are some children with autism whose challenges are so complex that they are disorganized most of the time. It is important to remember, however, that the ability to be calm, sustain attention, observe others, communicate with intent, and make changes varies within and across children. A child's level of organized behavior typically correlates with level of comfort, an understanding of the social events, and an understanding of what to do in a given situation. That is, when an experience is meaningful, a child is more likely to behave in an organized manner. In contrast, when an event is experienced as chaotic, overwhelming, or uncomfortable, a child is more likely to behave in a disorganized manner. This point is illustrated by the following examples:

Four-year-old Perry continuously runs around his preschool—which is full of exciting toys, activities, and children—during playtime. He is calm and focused and watches his peers during snack time, storytime, and art. Perry's level of organization varies with the activity's level of organization.

Six-year-old Adam begins each school day by straightening all of the books, papers, and materials in his classroom. He focuses on his academic work and interacts with his peers until distracted by what he refers to as "a mess." Messes included losing one of his pencils or markers, a change in his therapy schedule, or missing an opportunity to share during circle time. All of these messes create disorganization for him and result in his inability to have calm, focused interactions with others.

Both of these children demonstrate varying degrees of organization. The use of organizational supports, activity structure, and routines should therefore vary across settings, activities, and expectations based upon the child's level of organization at the moment. Each of the three organizational supports is described in detail next.

Organize the Physical Environment

The first strategy to support success is to establish organization within the physical environment to compensate for confusion in the social environment. Whenever the child appears disorganized, the first step is to establish more organization in the physical environment. Children with autism naturally focus on details in their physical environment in order to know exactly what to do in a particular social situation. The purpose of organizing the physical environment is to clarify expectations and decrease the child's reliance on making decisions through social information. Every aspect of the physical environment can be organized in order to clarify social expectations. Table 5.5 lists the aspects of organizing the physical environment that assist the child in understanding where to be, what toys or materials to use, what toys or materials to share, what to do, with whom, for how long, when the activity is done, and how to make changes flexibly. These aspects of organization can be embedded in all social activities. Organizers are used in the physical environment with the following goals in mind:

- Clarify expectations.
- Increase the child's attention to the relevant details.
- Increase the child's purposeful activity.
- Increase the child's independence.
- Increase the child's ability to observe others.
- Increase the child's social interaction.
- Enable the child to anticipate and make changes flexibly.

Table 5.5. Organizational supports

Organize	Help the child understand
Space	Where to be
Choices	What toys or materials to use
Possessions	What is mine or shared
Expectations	What to do
Social setting	With whom
Time	For how long
Self	How to stay calm and focused
Transitions	When done

The physical environment can be organized to increase solitary play, enhance social play, enhance group participation, and improve social skills in the community.

Organize Solitary Play

Efforts to increase a child's purposeful solitary play can be enhanced by organizing space, choices, social and activity expectations, and transitions. Some ideas are described next.

Organize space: where to be
- Play at a table.
- Play inside a small tent.
- Play while sitting on a beanbag.
- Play while sitting on a specific rug.
- Play in an area with boundaries marked by colored tape.
- Play outside within a fenced area.
- Play outside within an area marked by little red flags.
- Play at the playground and stay within visually marked boundaries.

Organize choices: what toys or materials to use
- Limit the number of toys in one area.
- Provide only the exact materials needed for a particular activity.
- Place toy pieces or materials that go together for a single play activity in individual activity boxes or transparent containers.
- Label toys and materials on shelves or in transparent containers.
- Provide a checklist of play activities that includes the maximum number of daily opportunities to play with each item (e.g., videos = one time, Nintendo = two times, computer = three times, books = five times). The child makes a selection and checks it off the list.

Organize activity expectations: what to do
- Provide a specific number of toy containers in the designated area.
- Provide a specific number of toys or materials for one activity (e.g., a container that contains playdough, four cookie cutters, a roller, and a display card showing the steps for making playdough cookies).
- Provide a list of the two or more activities/toy containers for play.
- Provide a list of play options.

Organize social expectations: with whom
- Place a photo of the child in the area to clarify that this is time alone, in contrast with showing the child photos of his play partners during other times of social play.
- Use a specific space to indicate that it is time to play alone.

Organize time: how long
- Use a timer to indicate length of solitary play time.
- Use a music tape to indicate length of play time (i.e., play until the music is finished).
- Define completion of the play activity by the number of toy pieces (e.g., string together 20 beads).
- Define completion of the play activity by its finished product (e.g., complete a 50-piece puzzle).

- Visually specify what to do when the materials do not clarify completion (e.g., put a sticker on each of the five pages to be completed in a coloring book).

- Visually depict time using a time board. A Velcro strip of numbers or letters in the child's name or a set of duplicate pictures that symbolize *play* is presented to the child, and items are added (or removed) one by one so the child can see the passage of time.

- Visually depict the current and next activity using "First, Then" in picture or written form, especially when the next activity is highly preferred.

Organize transitions: when done

- Include solitary play time on a daily visual schedule.

- Select a particular location where the child puts completed play projects.

- Use a familiar "transition song" with the child.

- Use a verbal countdown to prepare for transition (e.g., "10, 9, 8 . . .").

- Have the child bring the finished play project to show and tell.

- Provide the child with a visual reminder to communicate when done (e.g., an *I'm done* card at the bottom of the time board).

The following vignette demonstrates how some of these strategies can be used to increase solitary play:

> Four-year-old Carla has difficulty remaining in the designated play center in preschool; she also often moves toys and materials out of that area. To assist Carla, her teacher used different colored tape to mark spatial boundaries in each play area, organized toys into small bins to define use more clearly, and provided Carla with a photo choice board that she uses to select and sequence her play choices.

Organize Social Play

Organizing the physical environment becomes essential when supporting the child's ability to engage in parallel or interactive play with others. Most of the examples given for solitary play should apply to social play contexts. Some additional ideas for organizing the physical environment for social play are described next.

Organize space: where to be

- Apply ideas discussed for organizing space during solitary play.

- Limit the number of peers in a particular area (e.g., use hooks for the children to place their name tags in an area).

- Place the child's name on his chair or provide a special mat.

- Use colored tape to indicate where to stand or wait during a game.

Organize choices: what toys or materials to use

- Select toys and activities that the child has mastered in solitary play.

- Apply ideas discussed for organizing choices to increase solitary play.

- Provide a box of objects that specify activity choices and how many children can participate in each activity (e.g., a box containing three paintbrushes for three children to select art, four small blocks for four children to select the block area, three bookmarks for three children to select the book area, two hats for two children to select the dress-up area).

- Select play activities that have an equal amount of toys or materials available for each child.

- Organize materials so that each child has his own set.

- Emphasize physical activities, structured games, or activities that allow parallel participation.
- Select activities that are organized and predictable (e.g., projects or games with clear outcomes).
- Have the child and his peers plan in advance what to use.

Organize possessions: what is mine and what is shared

- Select activities in which each child has his own set of materials.
- When activities require sharing materials, provide spatial boundaries to indicate personal possessions versus shared possessions (e.g., use trays in the block area to clarify that the blocks on the child's tray belong to him, the blocks on each peer's tray belong to that peer, and the blocks not on any tray can be shared).
- When activities require sharing materials, group children with play partners to limit the amount of sharing needed.
- Use different colored containers to divide materials among the children (e.g., the child with autism always uses the items in the blue box).

Organize activity expectations: what to do

- Select activities that the child has mastered in solitary play.
- Apply ideas discussed for organizing activity expectations during solitary play.
- Clarify whether the expectation is parallel play with his own set of materials, parallel play with shared materials, or interactive play.
- Use the previously listed physical organizers for space, choices, and possessions to facilitate sharing during social play.
- For interactive play, select activities that allow for clear turn-taking (e.g., putting together a train track with one peer).
- Use cue cards to remind all children what to do and who to watch.

Organize social expectations: with whom

- Have the children select partners before the play activity begins.
- Have the child select one or more peer partners from an array of photos.
- Limit the number of children permitted in a play area (e.g., place a limited number of chairs or mats in a particular area).

Organize time: for how long

- Apply ideas discussed for organizing time during solitary play.
- If waiting is required in the social play activity, provide the child with an object to hold while waiting or a card that reminds him to wait during the social play activity.

Organize transitions: when done

- Apply ideas discussed for organizing solitary play transitions.
- Share responsibility for cleanup with a friend.
- Have one partner with whom the child makes transitions (the child can select a different peer each day).

Some of these suggestions for enhancing solitary play are illustrated in the next vignette:

Five-year-old Barry ran aimlessly around the room during free play in his kindergarten classroom. He had a number of solitary play interests at home but was un-

able to make independent choices, sustain attention, or interact with peers during playtime in school. Barry's teacher set up two activity choice boards for him, one containing play choices and the other containing photos of his favorite classmates. At the beginning of free play, Barry selected two friends (who had the option to say yes or no) and two play activities. Initially, the activities were manipulative materials or art projects that allowed for parallel play. The space, time, and materials were organized for the children. Gradually, Barry and his friends were doing activities that required sharing and turn-taking. To organize sharing, Barry was given a blue box to hold those things that he did not want his friends to touch and was reinforced for occasionally exchanging items in his box with one of his peers' toys. To organize turn-taking, Barry was given a reminder card to wait for his turn. Clarifying space, materials, partners, and expectations dramatically organized Barry's ability to engage in social play.

Organize Group Participation

As indicated previously, the dynamic of a group situation contributes greatly to a child's ability to participate successfully. The six types of group activities (i.e., unison, choral, nonverbal turn-taking, verbal turn-taking, unstructured play, and discussion) demand different levels of social awareness. The more complex the group setting, the more important it is to provide physical organizers to enhance group participation. Most of the examples given for solitary play and social play apply to group contexts. Some additional ideas for organizing the physical environment to enhance group participation follow.

Organize space: where to be
- Apply the previous ideas for organizing space for solitary and social play.
- Have a designated location for all group activities.
- Place a card with the child's name at his location.
- Place a taped "X" on his place to stand in the group.
- Have the child select a partner to sit or stand with in the group.
- If the activity involves taking places in a line, always allow the child to be first or last.

Organize choices: what toys or materials to use
- Apply the previous ideas for organizing solitary and social play choices.
- Allow the child to hand out or collect group materials as often as possible.
- Use different color-coded folders for each subject/activity area.
- Provide color-coded index cards with lists of materials needed for each group activity.

Organize possessions: what is mine and what is shared
- Apply the previous ideas for organizing possessions during social play.
- Use color-coded folders and boxes for each subject's or activity's work and materials.

Organize activity expectations: what to do
- Apply the previous ideas for organizing activity expectations during solitary and social play.
- Make a list of the group rules (e.g., watch, wait, raise your hand, share, take turns, listen); cue the child in the group as needed.
- Organize small groups (less than five children) whenever waiting is required.
- Position the child in the group to maximize his ability to observe others.
- Target one peer for the child to watch in order to remember what to do.

- Provide a visual cue to clarify who the child is expected to watch or listen to (e.g., a colorful stick is held by the adult or peer who is talking).
- Provide a list of the group activity's sequence of events.
- Provide an outline of the sequence of events discussed in the group.

Organize social expectations: with whom

- Minimize social confusion and random turn-taking whenever possible.
- Use an object or colored cue to designate multiple small groups (e.g., work at the red rug area).
- In cooperative learning group activities, organize the sharing of ideas so that children take turns in a circle and the speaker holds something that signifies he is the speaker (e.g., a plastic microphone).

Organize time: how long

- Apply the previous ideas for organizing time during solitary and social play.
- Use more physical organizers as the group gets larger and group expectations become more complex.

Organize transitions: when done

- Apply the previous ideas for solitary and social play transitions.
- Use nonverbal cues for group transitions (e.g., turn down lights, have all of the children raise their hand).

The following example shows how organizing the physical environment can assist a child in successful group participation:

> Eight-year-old Tammy participates in group activities during which everyone does the same thing at the same time, but she has difficulty understanding the rules of turn-taking and watching peers in group situations. Tammy understands the information conveyed by language but is unable to follow the social events. In her classroom, she frequently calls out questions or comments; on the playground, she wanders aimlessly. Several physical organizers are being used in the classroom to assist Sarah: 1) her teacher writes down the main discussion ideas as the group is talking, 2) the teacher has Sarah sit near her, 3) the teacher and the children hold a feather when they speak so that Tammy always knows who to watch, and 4) the teacher places a reminder card on the board that says, "Raise your hand." For outside, 1) plans for organized games are made with peers prior to recess time and 2) Tammy and a friend draw a map—which is meaningful because Tammy enjoys drawing—of the school playground equipment that she uses to organize her own recess activities.

Organize Community Experiences

Applying these principles of organizing the physical environment to community settings is quite a challenge. Community settings present the child with such difficulty because they are, by nature, the least socially predictable. The physical setting and social expectations of community situations—such as visiting relatives, going to the doctor, or going to someone's birthday party—generally lack organization and are therefore very difficult for the child. Furthermore, it is not possible to organize many aspects of the physical environment in most community situations. Although the physical surroundings may remain chaotic from the perspective of a child with autism, establishing the child's understanding of what to do in the community is the major goal. The purpose of organizing community activities is to assist the child in understanding where to be, what toys or materials to use (and not to use), what can be shared (and not shared), what to do, with whom, for how long, how to stay calm and focused, and when the activity is done.

The following vignettes provide some insight into how to organize community settings for a child with autism. These issues are discussed in greater detail in Chapter 7 on social intervention.

> *Eight-year-old Toby is terrified of the doctor's office and historically has required multiple adults to hold him for an examination. A plan was generated to organize the experience for him. The emphasis was placed on the organizational elements of what to do, for how long, how to stay calm, and when the visit would be done. To assist Toby in understanding what to do, 1) a video was made about going to the doctor that Toby watches daily, 2) Toby practices what to do by visiting the school nurse's office each day, 3) he was given a special alphabet sticker book and places the letters on the board one by one to mark the passage of time, 4) a tape of his favorite music plays while he practices going to the doctor, and 5) a special high-five is used to mark the end of the event. His first visit consisted of a quick hello between Toby and his doctor, Toby using his sticker book in the waiting room, and Toby and his mother leaving after they shared the special high-five. Gradually, the procedure has evolved so that now Toby can receive his physical examination without incident.*

> *Shane, age 8, demonstrates many social skills with peers in organized settings at home and school, but he has difficulty maintaining self-control at parties. A plan was developed that focuses on the organizational elements of where to be and with whom and how to stay calm. Shane had all of the individual skills of what to do and how to share but was unable to use these skills in social contexts that included unfamiliar children. The plan consisted of 1) Shane visiting the location of the birthday party prior to the event and making a list of where he would be for the different parts of the party, 2) reviewing a list of friends who were attending the party, 3) picking two friends to play with for the entire time, and 4) selecting a quiet location where he could use his pocket calculator for a few minutes when given a warning to calm himself. With these preparations in place, the next party was a success for Shane and his friends.*

Organize Activity Routines

Once the physical setting is organized, the second strategy to support social and communication success in children with autism is to establish predictable activity routines. Establishing social routines throughout the day is an essential aspect of intervention. Routine activities consist of three simple elements:

- A consistent beginning
- A consistent sequence of events within the activity
- A consistent ending

Most social events and social interactions typically do not have a predictable sequence of events and often do not have an obvious outcome. Thus, the inherent struggle for children with autism is that their desire for routine and predictability conflicts with the dynamic and ever-changing aspects of social events and social interaction.

For a child with autism, routines are familiar activities in which he understands explicitly what to do and for how long. Familiar routines assist the child in two important ways. First, familiar activities allow the child to anticipate what is next, thereby increasing purposeful activity and decreasing confusion. Second, familiar routines decrease the child's reliance on the challenge of social flexibility. The difficulty with activity routines is that they have the potential to create rigidity in children who are already driven to routines. Therefore, it is important to use the child's own level of organized behavior across settings to determine when using predictable activity routines is necessary.

Solitary Play Routines

Children with autism who develop the core skills of shared attention and imitation are less likely to need their play organized into predictable activity routines. For those children who lack these core skills, it is often necessary to create predictable play routines for direct instruction. As indicated previously, it is important to select closed-ended play activities whenever possible, as these activities have a natural sequence of steps and a definitive outcome.

Nonetheless, activity routines can be established for most open-ended play activities. This is a critical strategy for supporting functional play in many children with autism. When creating activity routines using open-ended play materials, the objective is to create an artificial sequence of events using the play materials. Play routines can be designed in one of two ways:

1. *Multistep play acts*, which are done in a fixed sequence and for which the sequence can be repeated multiple times

2. *Repetitive play acts*, which are gradually *scaffolded*, or combined, into more elaborate play schemas and for which the different play acts can be done in various combinations

Although the ultimate goal is for the child to use the play materials in more flexible ways, he is first taught to use the play materials in a predictable way. All play routines clarify for the child what to do, how much to do, and when the activity is complete. The following examples show how multistep activity routines for open-ended play activities were created for children who did not demonstrate core skills. For multistep activity routines, a child is taught the complete sequence from the onset with gradual fading of adult prompts. The key to success is to impose routine within open activities without restricting the child's spontaneity.

> Six-year-old Dennis enjoys the sandbox but continuously sifts the sand through his fingers. Efforts to teach him to use different sand toys have failed to change his play behavior. An activity routine was implemented for Dennis that consists of hiding pieces of an ABC puzzle that he enjoys, along with other puzzle pieces, in the sandbox. Dennis has been taught to search for the puzzle pieces in the sand and to complete the ABC puzzle. Once the puzzle is finished, his sand play is finished.

> Eight-year-old Jack enjoys playing with playdough but obsessively lines up little pieces in a row. Jack was taught an activity routine of making playdough cookies that consists of the following sequence repeated multiple times: roll the playdough, use a cookie cutter to make a cookie, and put the cookie on the tray. Jack's play area was organized with one box containing the playdough, five cookie cutters, the roller, and a cookie tray. In addition, because Jack likes books, he has been taught the play sequence not only through physical prompting but also through the use of a homemade playdough cookies "cookbook," which contains one step of the play sequence per page. Once the book is finished, the activity is finished.

The next vignettes describe how repetitive play acts are scaffolded into elaborate play routines. With scaffolded play routines, one element of the play activity is done repetitively until it is mastered by the child. Then, a second repetitive play act is added (i.e., scaffolded) until it is mastered; finally, a third repetitive play act is added until it is mastered. The play activity gradually becomes increasingly complex. The key to scaffolding play is to design play routines that allow each element to be done repetitively. Notice how each element of the play activity in the following examples consists of multiple repetitions of a single action. There is no limit to the expansion potential when play routines are designed in this fashion.

> *Eight-year-old Kurt's play with trains consists of lining them up in a row. His teacher has designed a play routine that is taught through scaffolding. As one play act is mastered by Kurt, the next play act is introduced. His play is systematically becoming more complex and gradually developing into the following eight play acts: 1) put 20 train track pieces together; 2) hook a set of 12 train cars together; 3) ride the train around the circular track multiple times with a stop sign at one point; 4) put a miniature person in each of the train cars; 5) have each person say "good-bye" as they get on the train; 6) put together the pieces of a miniature train station next to the track; 7) take the people off of the train and put them in the train station; and 8) have the people say "All done; that was fun" when they get off the train.*

> *Five-year-old Jason likes toy animals, although his play consists of staring at them, one at a time. His teacher has designed a play routine that is taught through scaffolding. As one play act is mastered by Jason, the next play act is introduced. His play is becoming more complex and gradually developing into the following four play acts: 1) walk the animals into the back of the truck; 2) ride the truck along a colored tape road; 3) walk the animals off of the truck and into a barn; and 4) walk the animals out of the barn to eat, where each animal has a small bucket for food.*

Social Play Routines

Establishing play routines becomes more essential when supporting the child's ability to engage in parallel or interactive play with others. All closed-ended play activities that a child has mastered during solitary play can be done in proximity to peers or shared with peers in an organized manner. Begin with closed-ended play activities that allow for parallel participation and provide specific toys and materials for each child. Gradually, closed-ended play activities can be set up to require turn-taking and/or waiting skills. It is useful to select games and activities that focus on what to do and to minimize the need for conversational exchanges. These include

- Art projects completed with a partner
- Building projects completed with a partner
- Sharing a computer game with a partner
- Shared reading with a partner
- Board games, such as lotto
- Outdoor games, such as throw and catch

For children who demonstrate more advanced skills, structure open-ended play into activity routines with peers. Activity routines that a child has mastered during solitary play can be shared with one or more peers, or dramatic play can be structured into activity routines such as

- Acting out a familiar storybook
- Acting out a script written by the children (e.g., a script about going to the grocery store)
- Assigning the child a specific role in a dramatic play area (e.g., the cashier at a pretend restaurant)
- Planning a finished product before beginning play (e.g., plans to use blocks to build a neighborhood with four houses)

The next two vignettes illustrate how some of these techniques can be used to create social play activity routines.

Harry, age 4, enjoys arranging his toy cars in a specific order. Anticipating that others will touch his cars, Harry becomes upset when other children want to play near him. His preschool teacher therefore has organized the car area in three ways: cars are divided into three different colored boxes, two taped areas representing roads have been made available, and all children make toy choices at the beginning of the play activity. The children have been taught to trade (i.e., exchange) toys from their boxes. As long as Harry understands that he will always have a certain number of cars, he is happy to play next to his friends.

Tasha's kindergarten teacher organizes the classroom's dramatic play area around a specific theme each month. The teacher selects or makes a storybook about the theme that contains a script that can be acted out by the children. She reads the story at circle time and later participates with the children in the dramatic play area. The teacher directs the basic sequence of the play but allows for individual child creativity. For example, using the theme about Native Americans, the activity sequence consists of the seven following events: 1) select Native American costumes; 2) select pretend food to plant in the garden area; 3) enter the tent, select instruments, and sing songs about the harvest; 4) collect the food; 5) cook a meal; 6) eat; and 7) clean up by removing the costumes and putting everything back in its place. Tasha, who watches and interacts with peers only in structured contexts, is an active part of the group during these structured dramatic playtimes.

Group Activity Routines

Group activities vary in social complexity. As indicated previously, some group activities require waiting, others require random turn-taking, and still others require flexible social observation skills. To enhance the group participation abilities of children with autism,

- Maximize the use of group activities where everyone is doing the same thing at the same time.

- Emphasize activities that occur in unison and that allow for choral responses.

Such group activities are socially predictable and, thus, the most successful group routines for children with autism. More complex group activities require the physical setting to be organized (see previous section on suggestions for organizing the physical environment). If a child still appears disorganized during group activities, review the expectations of the group and determine if the child understands the four basic group rules: 1) listen to the group directions, 2) wait when directed, 3) look at the speaker, and 4) share (i.e., take your turn). To clarify these basic group rules, consider utilizing the following suggestions for embedding routines within group activities:

- Use the same verbal group direction consistently to get everyone's attention (e.g., "Everybody, _____"), but keep in mind that children with autism often need to be taught to respond to "everybody" because they may have only learned to respond to directions that are preceded by their own name.

- Use a cue card or consistent nonverbal cue for *wait* (e.g., a pictographic symbol for *wait*).

- Use the same verbal or nonverbal routine to end a group activity (e.g., a closing song).

The next vignette describes how routines can enhance a child's ability to participate in group activities:

Michael had a tutor to help him in his first-grade classroom. Although he was doing well academically in this inclusive setting, Michael always seemed to need verbal prompting from his tutor to follow group directions. The teacher would give a direction to the group. Then Michael's tutor would repeat the direction, starting it with Michael's name. Michael had always been in an inclusive setting with a tutor, and he always complied with his tutor's directions. It seems that Michael never learned, however, that he was required to follow group directions. Through a simple Simon Says game with a small group one day, Michael's teacher taught him to respond to directions beginning with "everybody." This standard group direction was then used in all classroom activities. After one day of silent prompting from his tutor, Michael consistently followed group directions prefaced by "everybody."

Community Routines

As discussed previously, children with autism struggle with the low degree of social predictability inherent in community situations. Although the community events and the social behaviors of others may remain chaotic from the perspective of a child with autism, child-centered routines can be embedded within community situations. Activity routines, like physical organizers, clarify where to go, what to do, with whom, for how long, how to stay calm and focused, and the activity's completion.

Activity routines allow a child to use concrete information to understand his role and expectations in the community. Routines provide structure and meaning in otherwise chaotic and confusing situations. Some examples of such routines include

- Clarify where to go by associating objects or pictures with the community activity (e.g., a special shopping bag to hold while going to the grocery store, a photo of the school bus to hold while waiting for the school bus).

- Clarify what to do by having the child carry a backpack of special toys that are only used in the community as needed (e.g., a tape player and headphones, a special book, toys that are appropriate to "fiddle").

- Clarify what to do by having the child follow a sequence of events presented in picture or written form.

- Clarify what to do by having the child first practice elements of the community routine at home or school.

- Clarify what to do by having the child view a videotape of the community activity prior to participating in it.

- Organize the community activity so that the child always has one person to stay with, watch, or find.

- Clarify the length of the community activity through the use of time organizers (see previous discussion on organizing community activities).

- Help the child remain calm by identifying calming toys or objects that the child can hold during the community event (e.g., a security blanket).

The following examples provide some insight into planning child-centered community routines, including the point that routines sometimes require later adjustments:

Paul, age 8, did not like going to the barber. His behavior was so upsetting to his parents that they had resorted to cutting his hair while he slept. His teacher and parents designed a routine around haircuts that included the following steps: 1) a homemade storybook was created about going to the barber; 2) a photo of the barber shop was included on Paul's Saturday schedule so that he and his father could visit the barber to say hello each Saturday; 3) a commercial video about going to the barber was shown to Paul frequently; 4) Paul did many art activities that included cutting; and 5) Paul's visits to the barber gradually included sitting in the chair, listening to his favorite music, and using a chart that indicated how long he needed to sit. With all of these mini-routines put into place, one by one, Paul now tolerates haircuts.

Annette is 6 years old and nonverbal. She comes from a large family and lives in a neighborhood full of children. Annette's family wants her to participate in Halloween activities, but this has been a terrible experience for both Annette and her family in the past. Annette's teacher designed a trick-or-treat routine in school for Annette. Each day, Annette and some of her peers would dress in their costumes, review a picture activity schedule of the trick-or-treat steps, and practice the routine in school by going door to door. Annette mastered all of the "what to do" steps in school. The big test came on Halloween night when Annette went trick-or-treating with her family, picture schedule in hand. Annette's parents later reported that she participated with her siblings and did "almost perfectly" until no one answered the door at one house. That social glitch was omitted from the activity routine and created confusion for Annette. Because Annette has very limited language comprehension, her Halloween schedule needs to be adjusted next year to account for this situation.

Organize Instruction

Once the physical environment is organized and routine activities are selected as opportunities for social and communication experiences, the third strategy to support social and communication success in children with autism is to apply basic behavioral sequences during instruction and interactions. The precise use of cues, prompts, and consequences is necessary for effective learning. The application of basic behavioral sequences to all social activities and social interactions is an essential part of the intervention plan.

There is a wealth of useful resources that discuss behaviorally based instructional methods in detail (the reader is encouraged to review references provided in the Resources section). This section summarizes three basic behavioral strategies: cues, prompts, and consequences. These strategies are based upon principles of applied behavior analysis that have been well documented with regard to their utility in teaching children with autism. At the same time, it is essential to remember that these instructional principles can be applied across all settings in a multitude of ways. These principles can be applied in natural interactions, in incidental teaching, or during activity-based instruction—they can be applied anywhere!

Cues

A *cue* is anything that triggers a response. Cues can be environmental or social, and they can be natural or contrived.

A *natural environmental cue* is anything in the physical environment that triggers a response. These cues are visual, auditory, tactile, or other sensory events that signal a reaction. For example, a curb at the end of a street triggers a response to stop before crossing. In order to respond to natural cues, it is necessary to scan the environment, notice what is relevant, and understand the meaning of the natural cues. Attending to relevant natural cues and understanding their meanings are problematic for many children with autism. To extend the previous example, a child who does not stop before crossing a street may not notice the curb, may not understand the purpose of the curb, or may not understand what to do at the curb.

A *contrived environmental cue* is anything that is added to the physical environment to assist a child in attending to relevant information and in understanding the meaning of the physical setting. The strategies for organizing the physical environment presented previously in this chapter are examples of contrived environmental cues. For children with autism, the physical environment is made more salient through the use of contrived cues.

A *natural social cue* is anything that a person says or does that triggers a response. The words, gestures, touches, and facial expressions that occur during natural interactions trigger responses. In order to respond to natural cues, it is necessary to attend to others, notice what is relevant, and understand the meaning of the natural social cues presented. Children with autism struggle with attending to relevant social cues and understanding their meanings. Again, the inability to attend to multiple social cues and to understand the intent and meaning of others' behaviors lies at the heart of autism.

A *contrived social cue* is any adaptation that a person makes (in words or in actions) to increase a child's social attention and comprehension of social meaning. The concept of establishing social modifications is the focus of this chapter's next major section, entitled "Social Supports."

When using cues during instruction and interaction, it is important to make environmental and social information as clear as necessary. The child's ability or inability to focus attention on relevant natural cues at any moment determines whether more salient environmental and social cues need to be provided. It is essential to remember that children with autism often have difficulty attending to relevant cues, focus their attention on the wrong cue, and/or have difficulty attending to multiple cues simultaneously. These characteristics are exemplified by the next vignettes.

> Seven-year-old Noah was walking down the hallway at school to deliver a message to the office when a group of older students started heading toward him. Noah walked right through the crowd, bumping the students with a complete disregard for their presence. The relevant social cues of the situation eluded him.

> Six-year-old Donna likes watching cartoons on television. In one cartoon episode, there was a fire, and the television character said, "This is serious." Now, whenever Donna sees steam (e.g., from food cooking on the stove) or smoke in any context, that environmental cue triggers her to say, "This is serious." She attended to the wrong cues to determine the meaning of the phrase "This is serious."

> Will is 4 years old and easily distracted, even in the most structured social contexts. Even when the physical setting and activity routines were organized for solitary play, Will continued to lose attention. He also lost attention when reinforcement was used. It became obvious that Will is unable to attend to multiple cues simultaneously. Only when verbal cues are eliminated from the social context and he is allowed to focus his attention on only one relevant cue (i.e., the toy) can Will maintain purposeful attention to the play activity.

Prompts

Anything that is added after the cue to help the child understand the meaning of the social context and to make the correct response is defined as a *prompt*. Like cues, prompts can be social or environmental. There are four general types of social prompts and one general environmental prompt. The five general types of prompts, starting with the one that provides the child with the most assistance, include

- *Physical prompts*: manually guiding the child to make the correct response
- *Gestural prompts*: gesturing (e.g., pointing, touching) to indicate the correct response
- *Verbal prompts*: verbally directing the child to the correct response
- *Modeling*: demonstrating the correct response
- *Environmental prompts*: visual or auditory cues in the physical environment that direct the child to the correct response

The selection of prompts depends on the child's core abilities, the child's degree of rigidity or flexibility, and the target social or communication skill. First, the selection of prompts to be used for a child depends on the presence or absence of two core skills, the ability to share attention and the ability to imitate.

- If the child demonstrates shared attention and imitation, maximize the use of modeling paired with environmental cues.
- If the child does not demonstrate shared attention and imitation, maximize the use of physical, gestural, and verbal cues paired with environmental cues.

Second, the selection of prompts must take into account the particular learning patterns of most children with autism. This learning style lends itself to acquiring skills in a manner that is identical to the way the information is presented. Nevertheless, children with autism vary in the degree to which they make rigid associations among cues, prompts, and responses. As a result,

- Do not prompt in the exact same way every time.
- To ensure success and to eliminate a pattern of routine errors, offer the child optimum support by fading prompts from the most assistive to the least assistive.
- Maximize the use of environmental prompts to fade the child's reliance on social prompts.

Third, the selection of prompts depends on the desired response. The desired response is either an action or a communication; that is, something that the child will do or say. It is far easier to prompt nonverbal responses (i.e., what to do) in social situations than to prompt spoken verbal responses (i.e., what to say). The ensuing lists provide recommendations for prompting nonverbal social skills, communication through speech, and communication through an AAC system.

When prompting a nonverbal social skill,

- Use the child's visual attention to determine when to prompt (e.g., if physically assisting a child to play who stops looking at the toys, continue holding his hand, stop the activity, say nothing, and wait for the child to focus again before continuing to prompt).
- Limit the use of verbal prompting because many children with autism develop the routinized behavior of waiting for the verbal prompt before acting.
- Provide enough prompts to ensure the child does not make a mistake (e.g., if the child is playing with playdough and begins to put it in his mouth, say nothing and prompt the child to the correct use of the material).
- Be aware of the effect that physical prompting may have on children with tactile sensitivities.
- Give the child time to process and respond to the cue.
- Replace social prompts with environmental prompts to decrease the child's reliance on others.

When prompting communication using speech,

- Maximize the use of verbal modeling.
- Limit the use of verbal prompts in the form of a question.
- Pair verbal prompts with a social prompt or an environmental prompt so that the verbal prompts can be faded.
- See the section titled "Social Supports" for greater detail.

When prompting communication using an AAC system

- Model how to use the child's system.
- Limit verbal prompts phrased as questions.
- Use physical, gestural, and/or verbal means to prompt the child's use of the AAC system.
- Pair verbal prompts with nonverbal prompts so that the verbal prompting can be faded.

Social prompts should be faded systematically to decrease the child's reliance on others and, thus, to foster independence. Prompt fading is most effective when the child is initially given the maximum support to ensure success and then prompts are faded to those offering the least amount of assistance. Given that the ultimate goal is the child's use of spontaneous social acts and spontaneous communication, it is important to fade the use of social prompts and to maximize the use of environmental prompts.

Five-year-old Alex has been learning to play with closed-ended manipulative toys. He is able to play with the toys in a purposeful manner only when an adult is present to intermittently give verbal prompts to continue. In the absence of verbal prompts, Alex begins throwing the toys. In order to fade the adult from the situation, an audiotape was made of Alex's mother giving him verbal reminders while he played. This 15-minute audiotape, which randomly presents messages such as "You're playing nice" and "Get another one," was enough to please Alex and allow him to gradually learn to play independently without throwing toys for 15 minutes.

Nathan was taught at 7 years old to play a board game with a friend. He learned the game but still needs verbal prompts for each step of the game. If an adult does not give him a verbal prompt, he will say the prompt to her (e.g., "Nathan, spin it"). For Nathan, the prompt is part of the sequence of events that occur during the game, and he is unable to continue until the verbal prompt is given. To resolve this prompt dependency, the present adult pairs the verbal prompt with a hand-over-hand point to a color-coded list of game rules. The adult quickly fades the verbal prompt and gradually fades pointing to the list. This fade results in Nathan's using the list of game rules as a reminder and allows for independence when playing board games with his friend.

Karen, age 6, has been taught to initiate play with a peer through a sequence of verbal directions and prompts. Her teacher gives the verbal direction, "Go ask (peer's name) to play." Then she uses the verbal prompt, "Say, '(peer's name), do you want to play?'" Karen imitates the sentence while standing next to her teacher and the peer. Next, she is verbally reinforced by her teacher's saying the phrase "Nice talking." Karen only asks a peer to play under these prompted conditions, however; when she is not verbally prompted, Karen looks at her teacher and states, "Say, do you want to play, nice talking." Thus, Karen has learned the sequence of instructions and prompts without understanding the meaning of her response or seeing a clear link between her message and the outcome. The instruction has therefore been changed to a nonverbal tap to get the peer's attention during specific play situations. At the same time, Karen's teacher stands behind Karen while verbally modeling and pointing to a written cue card prompt that says, "Wanna play?" Karen then directs the message to her peer and is reinforced by the peer, who says, "Yeah" and takes Karen's hand to go play. First, the verbal model is faded, then the visual cue card is quickly faded, and gradually the adult's touch is faded until a peer in special contexts becomes the natural cue for Karen to say, "Wanna play?"

Consequences

Events, both environmental and social, that occur in direct response to a child's behavior are *consequences*. In traditional behaviorism, there is a strong reliance on using artificial consequences (in the form of verbal or tangible reinforcers) that are not linked to the meaning of a child's behavior. Examples include rewarding a child's correct actions by commenting, "Good building," or by presenting tangible rewards (e.g., food, tokens) that are not related to the child's activity. Similarly, children's communication efforts are typically rewarded by phrases such as "good talking" or "good boy (or girl)" and are not linked to the meaning of the child's communication efforts.

When using consequences to support social skills and communication skills, utilizing natural consequences as much as possible is key. Given that social and communication behaviors are intimately linked to social motivation and interest, it is essential that motivation and meaning drive social behaviors, not artificial responses. To do this,

- Embed motivators into new social experiences rather than using them as reinforcers.
- Make social experiences fun.
- Use social experiences that are meaningful, thereby making the activity a natural reinforcer.
- Continue a fun social activity so that it becomes a natural reinforcer.
- Remember that the child's mastery of the social activity becomes a natural reinforcer.
- Acknowledge the child's communicative efforts as a natural reinforcer.
- Communicate in a way that is meaningful for the child for natural reinforcement.

When using social reinforcers, keep in mind that

- Verbal reinforcement should be naturally linked to what the child is doing.
- Nonverbal reinforcement should mirror the child's emotional state.
- Verbal responses to the child's communication should acknowledge him by repeating the message or adding new and relevant information to the child's message.
- Nonverbal responses to the child's communication should be linked to the communicative intent of the child's message.

In addition to the strategies outlined here, many other excellent resources describe organizational supports. See Dalrymple (1995); Hodgdon (1995); Janzen (1996); McClannahan and Krantz (1999); and Schopler, Mesibov, and Hearsey (1995) for more information.

SOCIAL SUPPORTS

A major challenge for children with autism is to extract meaning from what others are saying, doing, and feeling (Shah & Wing, 1986). There is an obvious lack of congruence between their abilities and the demands of naturally occurring interactions. Children with autism experience confusion with the dynamic and unpredictable quality of typical social interaction. The outcome is a fragmented understanding of social-communicative experiences and the use of ritualistic or context-specific social-communicative skills. Understanding, respect, and empathy for their struggles form the rationale for the second set of intervention strategies, social supports.

Social supports are defined as any modifications made by others to maintain meaningful and mutually beneficial reciprocal interactions with a child. Social supports serve as a means to structure and enhance understanding, engagement, and participation in social-communicative interactions. Social supports are a natural means to compensate for the social and communication impairments of children with autism. This section includes five ways to provide social supports:

- Understand the child's communicative intent.
- Establish reciprocal interaction routines.
- Balance directive and facilitative interaction styles.
- Modify interaction patterns.
- Act as an interpreter to facilitate peer interactions.

These forms of social supports, summarized in Table 5.6, are explored in detail next.

Table 5.6. Social supports

Understand the child's communicative intent.

Establish reciprocal interaction routines.
  Focus on contexts that require joint focus and turn-taking.
  Establish a predictable pattern of messages.
  Organize messages so the child can anticipate what to say or do.
  Repeat the same message at predictable times.
  Limit the number and variety of interactive turns.
  Scaffold:
    Systematically add a new message to the routine.
    Systematically add a new message when the child initiates any purposeful
      nonverbal or verbal behavior during the interaction.
    Systematically modify familiar messages in the routine once the child
      understands and uses the originally established interaction.

Balance directive and facilitative interaction styles.
  Balance adult-directed and child-directed interactions.
  Respond to the child's level of focused, purposeful behavior at the moment.
  Modify the child's partially successful initiations.
  Shape the child's partially successful initiations.
  Imitate and expand on the child's successful initiations.

Modify interaction patterns.
  Maintain close proximity to the child.
  Establish joint attention.
  Simplify language complexity.
  Use augmentative and alternative communication supports as needed.
  Make nonverbal cues more explicit.
  Give the child time to respond.
  Use rhythmic language when appropriate.

Act as an interpreter to facilitate peer interactions.
  Coach peers.
  Shadow and prompt the child.

Understand Communicative Intent

Communicative intent is the purpose of a child's social-communicative behavior. Nonverbal behaviors (e.g., eye gaze, facial expression, gestures) as well as verbal behaviors (e.g., speech, signing) can be used to communicate intent. *Communicative function* is the actual effect that a child's verbal and nonverbal behaviors have on others and is based on an interpretation of the child's intent and meaning. There is usually a clear relationship between the communicative intent of a typically developing child and how his message is interpreted by others. For instance, based on context and the nonverbal behaviors (e.g., pointing to the door) of a typically developing child, an adult correctly interprets the child's message "Go bye-bye?" as a request to go home. Nonverbal and verbal behaviors can generally be inferred as serving a social-communicative function when messages are directed to a person or object, the message is relevant to the ongoing activity or social context, the child waits for a response, and the child reacts to the person's response.

Interpreting the intent and function of nonverbal and verbal behaviors of children with autism poses a unique challenge. Sometimes their nonverbal and verbal behaviors serve a social-communicative function; sometimes they are not interactive. Nonverbal behaviors and verbal messages often function as noninteractive, self-stimulatory rituals or a means to regulate oneself. Even when a child's behaviors are intended to be communicative, there can be a discrepancy between what the child says and what the child means.

The nonverbal and verbal behaviors of children with autism are often misinterpreted by others due to

- Differences in their use of nonverbal skills, specifically difficulty with eye gaze, joint attention, and combining multiple nonverbal and verbal behaviors in a single message

- Differences in their use of verbal skills, specifically immediate and delayed patterns of echolalia

- Differences in their social perceptions, specifically, misinterpretations of language and social meaning

- Ritualistic patterns of behavior

- Challenging behaviors that serve communicative functions

These situations are further illustrated by the following vignettes:

Three-year-old Andy's nonverbal behaviors are often misinterpreted. For instance, he indicates his desire for food or toys by looking at the item intently. When this staring is not interpreted by others as a request for the item, he begins to cry. Andy lacks the ability to use attention-getting gestures or to shift eye gaze from the object to the adult to make his request.

Eight-year-old Laura uses delayed echolalia for a variety of communicative functions, although her intent is easily misinterpreted. Until her education team learned the intended meaning of her echolalic messages, Laura was often frustrated by her inability to be understood by others. For example, Laura would say "Chocolate milk today" to ask if she could get milk at lunchtime, but her message was misinterpreted as a comment. If she did not get the desired response from adults, she persisted with her question and her frustration escalated into a tantrum. Laura would also say "You're okay" in an upset voice to ask peers to go away. When her message was misinterpreted by her peers and they did not leave, she would persist with the same message and ultimately hit them.

Robin, 7 years old, often makes interesting statements that are the result of associations she has formed between events seen on video and her own social experiences. For example, Robin says "It's beautiful" to ask for a hair ribbon or "This is a problem" to indicate when she feels sick. Without adults and peers who understand the intent of Robin's messages, her language is easily misinterpreted.

Nine-year-old Eugene talks incessantly. He repeats segments from television commercials, books, and videos that are not linked to the social situation, or he talks himself through his activities. Other times, his language is used for interaction with others: He makes requests, shares interests, and expresses feelings. Often, Eugene uses the same phrase to regulate himself and to interact with another person. For example, he might say "Time to go home" (to himself) while organizing his backpack to go home and later say "Time to go home" to an adult to indicate he is ready to leave school.

Caitlyn, 6 years old, has two challenging behaviors that others misinterpret. She has developed a ritual of making faces in the mirror that escalates into self-injurious behavior. She also stares at adults and makes faces, but whenever her behavior is misinterpreted as social—and, thus, an adult imitates her—Caitlyn begins her self-injurious behavior. Similarly, she has a ritual of reciting a section from her favorite book. Whenever an adult attempts to join Caitlyn in her recitation, she begins to scream. In both of these situations, her intent is noninteractive, so social responses create problems.

To support a child's social success, it is important to determine the communicative intent and function of his verbal and nonverbal behaviors. Judge intention and whether the child's behaviors are interactive or noninteractive by focusing on the social context and the child's nonverbal behaviors before, during, and after the communicative message. A child's verbal and nonverbal behaviors can generally be inferred as serving a social-communicative function when two or more of the following qualities are present:

- Eye gaze, body orientation, or gesture is directed to a person or object.
- Behaviors/messages are relevant to the ongoing activity.
- Behaviors/messages are relevant to the ongoing conversation.
- The child waits for a response.
- The child reacts to others' responses to his message (e.g., persisting when the message is misunderstood).

The ability of others to determine the communicative intent and function of the child's messages is largely dependent upon the child's nonverbal social-communicative skills. The presence or absence of these core nonverbal skills determines the ease with which communicative intent and function can be inferred by others. Thus, these non-verbal interaction skills are central to conveying one's intent accurately to others.

Establish Reciprocal Social Routines

Child language acquisition studies have demonstrated the importance of interactive routines between adults and children as the framework within which language and communication are acquired (Bruner, 1975; Ratner & Bruner, 1978). A *reciprocal social routine* is an interaction pattern that follows a logical sequence and has a predictable set of communicative exchanges between an adult and a child (Snyder-McLean, Solomonson, McLean, & Sack, 1984). Social routines include a predictable set of contextually meaningful messages that are shared between adult and child. The communication messages can be verbal or nonverbal. Social routines are important because they enable children to learn through adult modeling that is highly organized, predictable, and socially salient. Through consistent experiences with a social routine, a child assigns meaning to the language and communicative behaviors used within the interaction. As the child acquires an understanding of the meaning of the social routine, he can anticipate and insert one or more communicative messages. Once the child can participate in an established routine, expansion and flexibility are introduced into the social interaction. This ongoing expansion (i.e., scaffolding) systematically builds meaningful social exchanges between the adult and the child.

Basic Social Routines

There are a series of steps to be taken in the design and implementation of basic social routines for children with autism:

- Emphasize contexts that require joint focus and turn-taking.
- Emphasize contexts in which the child is motivated to communicate.
- Establish a pattern of messages (verbal or nonverbal) that predictably occur at set times during the interaction and activity.
- Organize messages so that what the adult says or does is equally appropriate for the child to say or do in the same situation.
- Organize messages so that the child can link a message with a tangible nonverbal or contextual event in order to anticipate what to say or do in that specific situation.
- Repeat the same message at predictable times.
- Limit the number and variety of interactive turns.

Scaffolding

Social routines are valuable because they provide a framework for systematically introducing new elements to the context. The most critical element in social routines is the ongoing process of expansion. The child's level of engagement is the primary criterion for determining when to expand the social routine. Children are typically engaged when they are motivated and understand the purpose and meaning of the social interaction. When a child does not understand the meaning behind the messages and events in the situation, the routine needs to be clarified and/or simplified.

Once a child masters the basic routine—as reflected by increased participation and spontaneity—familiar messages are modified and new messages are introduced. This process of *scaffolding*, which links new information to familiar information and builds on existing successes in a meaningful way, is central to supporting a child's communication development. Methods of scaffolding include

- Adding a new message to the routine once the child understands and uses the originally established interaction

- Adding a new message when the child initiates any purposeful nonverbal or verbal behavior during the interaction

- Modifying familiar messages in the routine once the child understands and uses the originally established interaction

The following profiles present various scaffolding approaches. The first, involving Eddie, demonstrates a nonverbal interactive routine. The vignette about Betsy exemplifies scaffolding a play behavior. Larry's vignette illustrates a sample verbal interactive routine. The final vignette shows how conversation was scaffolded to assist in Garret's communication development.

Eddie is 3 years old and enjoys hiding under blankets. Eddie's mother played a four-step Peekaboo game with him that involved 1) covering his head, 2) counting to five, 3) taking off the blanket, and 4) giving him a kiss. This pattern was established until Eddie initiated putting the blanket on and off on cue and shared kisses. Then his mother put the blanket on her head, counted to five, and prompted Eddie to take it off; when he did so, they kissed. Soon the game alternated back and forth from Eddie's mother putting the blanket on Eddie to him putting the blanket on her. Eddie maintained the routine with his mother. Once this social routine was established, Eddie's mother added another element to the game: kissing different facial features. They shared this exchange, with Eddie gradually giving his mother kisses on the nose, head, ear, and lips.

Five-year-old Betsy is learning to imitate play actions. She is learning to imitate a sequence of related actions, one at a time, using playdough: First, press the playdough, then use cookie cutters, then roll, and so forth. When Betsy masters one step, her teacher adds a second, and then a third. All of the actions that Betsy imitates are related in a meaningful way. Play has become a logical sequence of imitated actions that carry meaning. This process contrasts sharply with teaching children to imitate a sequence of unrelated single actions with toys out of context.

Four-year-old Larry and his mother were singing a song with puppets. When the song was finished, Larry and his mother took turns putting the puppets in the box using set phrases. His mother said, "In goes the puppet" as she put one puppet in the box, waved good-bye, and said, "Bye-bye." Next, it was Larry's turn. His mother prompted Larry through gestures to put the other puppet in the box, to say, "In goes the puppet," to wave, and to say, "Bye-bye." Larry's mother then took another turn. Next, she prompted Larry to put the puppet in the box and said, "In goes the. . . ." Larry looked at her and said, "Puppet," then imitated his mother waving and said, "Bye-bye." After his mother took another turn, Larry spontaneously tried to put the puppet in the box; his mother waited before waving, and Larry spontaneously smiled at his mother and said, "In goes the puppet; bye-bye." Once this basic social routine was established, Larry's mother continued to add one new phrase at a time to the ever-expanding puppet game. The phrases were both linked to their actions and arranged for systematic turn-taking.

For 6-year-old Garret, shared reading time is an opportunity to engage in a conversation, composed of predictable turns, with his teacher. They each take turns describing a page of a book. Garret's teacher describes the first page, Garret describes the next page, and so forth. The complexity and variety of comments are linked to Garret's current language repertoire, and attempts are made to build new commenting functions into his repertoire. This process contrasts with teaching a child to answer a series of questions about a storybook by expecting him to give specific answers to questions asked about each page. That technique encourages passivity and cue dependency, but Garret is learning to be spontaneous and flexible through an interactive routine.

Balance Directive and Facilitative Interaction Styles

The level of social and communicative behaviors in children with autism varies significantly in response to different styles of interaction. Two primary types of adult interaction styles have been studied: directive and facilitative. The *directive style* is associated with a behavioral approach to adult–child interaction, whereas the *facilitative style* is associated with a developmental approach to adult–child interaction. The characteristics and benefits of each style are listed in Table 5.7. When using either a directive or facilitative style, keep in mind whether the target objective is to elicit a specific response from the child or to promote spontaneous social behaviors and communication.

When using a directive style, the adult controls the focus and direction of the interaction and structures the child's contribution to the ongoing interaction. The adult's verbal interaction style is dominated by the use of questions, directions, commands, and verbal prompts to elicit specific responses. Nonverbal gestures or physical prompts are also used to elicit a specific response. When a facilitative style is used, the child controls the focus and direction of the interaction and is encouraged to contribute to the interaction

Table 5.7. Comparison of directive and facilitative interaction styles

Directive interaction

Characteristics	The adult initiates the interaction.
	The adult controls the interaction.
	The adult structures the child's response.
	The adult uses questions, directions, and commands.
	The adult prompts the target response.
Outcomes	Increase the child's organization.
	Increase simple turn-taking.
	Increase the child's responses to adult initiations.

Facilitative interaction

Characteristics	The child initiates the interaction.
	The child leads the direction of the interaction.
	The adult uses imitation, elaborations, and expansions.
	The adult uses pause times and conversational lags.
Outcomes	Increase reciprocal interaction.
	Increase spontaneous communication.
	Increase ability to maintain a conversation.

in a variety of ways. The adult's interaction style is dominated by conversation related to topics introduced by the child; comments that acknowledge or elaborate upon the child's nonverbal and verbal behaviors; and long, silent pause times.

Both directive and facilitative styles have a noticeable effect on the social engagement of children with autism. Directive styles increase a child's ability to be focused and organized; they also increase the social responsiveness of a child who lacks imitation skills. Facilitative styles rely heavily on the child's ability to engage in purposeful activity; therefore, they increase social behaviors in children who have shared attention and imitation skills.

Directive and facilitative styles also influence the communication patterns of children with autism who possess verbal abilities. Directive styles enhance a child's ability to engage in simple turn-taking involving questions and answers, and they increase responses to adult initiatives. Facilitative styles foster a child's spontaneous communication and his ability to maintain more elaborate conversation exchanges. Adults support the conversation with comments and elaborations. These qualities encourage more child initiations than when adults direct the conversation through questions (i.e., use a directive style). In fact, a directive style that obliges the child to respond in a specific manner has been shown to increase echolalic responses (Curcio & Paccia, 1987; Rydell & Mirenda, 1991, 1994).

Samples of both styles are provided next. This first conversation between an adult and a child who are looking at a book of children playing exemplifies the directive style:

Adult: Who is it? (points)
Child: A boy.
Adult: Look—what is he doing?
Child: Blocks.
Adult: Say, "He's building blocks."
Child: He's building blocks.
Adult: What color? (points)
Child: Red.
Adult: Say, "Red blocks."
Child: Red blocks.

In this next case, an adult and a child are engaged in the same activity, but the conversation occurs in a facilitative style:

Adult: This is a boy, and . . . (points)
Child: This is a girl.
Adult: He's building, and . . . (points)
Child: A doll.
Adult: Playing with the doll.
Child: A bottle.
Adult: Yes, eating; yum.
Child: Yum-yum.
Adult: (points)
Child: Blocks, 1-2-3-4-5.
Adult: Five blocks; he's building.
Child: Building blocks, 1-2-3-4-5.

Combining the Directive and Facilitative Styles

Directive and facilitative interaction styles represent the polarity of interaction possibilities, and the most reasonable approach is a combination of both. The combined approach, called *the dance of interaction* (Quill, 1995a), entails choosing when to be directive and when to be facilitative based on the child's nonverbal and verbal behaviors. There are two factors that help determine how to balance the use of both directive and facilitative styles with a child: 1) the child's core social-communicative abilities at the moment and 2) whether the target objective is to elicit a specific response or facilitate spontaneous communication.

Most children with autism vary in the degree to which they are able to demonstrate social observation skills and imitation skills. They vary, moment to moment, in their ability to focus attention, observe, imitate, and/or remain organized during a social interaction. Abilities at the moment are also influenced by how easily the child becomes frustrated in loosely structured activities, is confused by unanticipated social-communicative messages, and becomes uncomfortable in particular settings. Other contextual factors that influence their ability to remain focused and organized include unpredictable social contexts, confusing transitions, difficult tasks, uncomfortable sensory stimuli, and situations that cause fear or anxiety.

The presence or absence of core nonverbal social interaction skills is central to determining when an adult should be directive versus facilitative. One must determine a particular child's

- Social observation skills at the moment
- Level of joint attention at the moment
- Ability to imitate (acts or words) at the moment
- Level of organization (i.e., if he is calm)

Verbal directive approaches, particularly questions, should be used infrequently as a means to foster reciprocal social interaction. Questions close or end an interaction and place the child in the role of a passive responder. Nonverbal directive approaches, however, are useful when a child is disorganized, lacking shared attention and/or motor or verbal imitation skills at the moment. All other contexts are opportunities for using a facilitative approach during interaction. Facilitative approaches are useful when a child is focused, sharing attention and/or displaying motor or verbal imitation skills at the moment. Second, determine whether the objective of the interaction is to elicit a specific response or to facilitate spontaneous communication. The goal in many social situations is for the child to demonstrate a specific social behavior, such as playing with a toy in a particular functional way or playing a game with rules. Sometimes the goal of instructional settings is for the child to answer a specific question. When the target goal is a specific response, more directive approaches can be used. The objective for many social situations, however, is for the child to demonstrate spontaneity and creativity within a social context, and the primary goal of communication enhancement is to foster spontaneous communication. Spontaneity, which is essential to socioemotional regulation and communicative competence, is more likely to occur through the use of facilitative techniques. Nonverbal and verbal communication is considered to be *spontaneous* when

- Messages occur without any obvious contextual or social cues (e.g., discussing a future event with no cues or prompts)
- Messages occur without any specific contextual or social cues (e.g., naming an object or event without explicit cues)
- Messages occur in response to specific contextual cues (e.g., labeling a picture in a book during shared reading)
- Messages occur in the presence of a delay in conversation (e.g., changing the topic)
- Messages occur in the absence of specific instructional prompts (Koegel & Koegel, 1995a)

The Dance of Interaction

The dance of interaction requires an understanding of each child's idiosyncratic interaction style as well as a willingness to be flexible. In particular, it also necessitates that adults

- Balance adult-directed and child-directed interactions
- Respond to the child's level of focused, purposeful behavior at the moment
- Modify the child's unsuccessful initiations
- Shape the child's partially successful initiations
- Imitate and expand on the child's successful initiations

Although this style of interaction is complex and dynamic, the adult can generally make one of three choices:

- Direct the interaction of the moment.
- Follow the child's unsuccessful attempts by redirecting the interaction of the moment.
- Follow the child's successes of the moment through imitation and scaffolding.

(It is important to remember *not* to follow the child's lead when he is engaged in inappropriate behaviors, nonverbal or verbal. Always teach meaningful social and communication replacement behaviors.)

These guidelines are illustrated through profiles involving both nonverbal and verbal interactions. In this first sample interaction, a child and his preschool teacher are playing next to each other at the sandbox. The child is nonverbal, so the interaction described is completely nonverbal:

Child:	Sifts sand through his fingers.
Adult:	Physically prompts scooping.
Child:	Scoops sand into bucket.
Adult:	Fades prompt, mirrors the child's action using another shovel.
Child:	Scoops sand.
Adult:	Scoops sand and says, "In the bucket."
	This is repeated multiple times.
Child:	Drops the shovel and pats the sand.
Adult:	Pats the sand and says, "Pat, pat, pat."
Child:	Sifts sand through his fingers.
Adult:	Prompts scooping again.

This next example demonstrates the dance of interaction during conversation. A 6-year-old child and her teacher are looking at a picture book of children playing. The teacher balances direct questions with facilitative comments and silently points at items in the book to cue the child to share additional information. This child is verbal, so a conversation ensues:

Adult:	What are the children doing?
Child:	Playing.
Adult:	Playing with trains. (points)
Child:	Playing with dolls.
Adult:	Playing with puzzles. (points)
Child:	Playing with blocks.
Adult:	Building with blocks.
Child:	(loses focus)

Adult:	Look.
Child:	(looks at picture)
Adult:	What color is this?
Child:	Blue.
Adult:	This is a blue block. (points)
Child:	A green block.
Adult:	This block is red. (points)
Child:	Red.

Modify Interaction Patterns

Successful interactions require ongoing, moment-to-moment adjustments. Adults continuously fine-tune their interaction patterns in order to be understood and to elicit information from children. For children with autism, it is largely the responsibility of adults (and peers given adult guidance) to adapt their styles of interaction to improve and maintain social-communicative exchanges. Bernard-Opitz (1982) found that parents and educators familiar with a child with autism were significantly more successful at maintaining interactions with the child during play than other professionals who were unfamiliar with the child. An analysis of the factors that influenced positive social-communicative interactions revealed that familiar adults continually modified their interaction patterns in response to the child's behaviors and response patterns. This modified input included syntactic simplicity, redundancy, and exaggerated nonverbal cues, as well as references to objects, activities, and events in the child's immediate environment. By modifying interaction patterns in such a way, others can increase the child's understanding and use of language and enhance participation in the social dynamic. Table 5.8 summarizes steps for modifying reciprocal interactions. These steps are more fully explored in the following section.

Maintain Close Proximity to the Child

The most effective interactions occur when one is near a child with autism. Squat or sit at the child's eye level. Children with autism can be easily startled, however, so it is helpful to approach them gently, observe their behavior for a moment in silence, and then convey a message.

Establish Joint Attention

It is significantly easier to share attention when a concrete referent is available. When a child is not attending, it is important to determine whether he is distracted or does not understand the events occurring at the moment. When a child does not understand the meaning behind the messages and events in the situation, information needs to be clari-

Table 5.8.   Steps for modifying interaction patterns

Maintain close proximity to the child.

Establish joint attention.

Simplify language complexity.

Use AAC supports as needed.

Make nonverbal cues more explicit.

Give the child time to respond.

Use rhythmic language when appropriate.

Act as an interpreter for others.

fied and/or simplified. Assume that the child is doing the best he can at the moment, and help the child. Remember that shared attention to the person, object, or action is more important than a vacuous eye gaze. To establish joint attention,

- Silently point to a concrete referent.
- Take the child's finger and point to the referent (i.e., use physical prompting).
- Place a salient cue (e.g., a ribbon) on the finger used for pointing.
- Use a predictable phrase to gain the child's attention (e.g., "[Child's name], look here").
- Touch the child gently and wait.

Simplify Language Complexity

The complexity of adult language needs to reflect the comprehension abilities of the child. Simple, activity-related language reduces the child's processing load and aids comprehension. In addition, language should be paired with concrete referents to enhance comprehension. Objects, photos, pictures, or written information may assist the child in understanding information regarding past and future events. Furthermore, using familiar messages in familiar activities increases appropriate interactions.

The complexity of adults' language has been shown to affect the language and communication performance of children with autism (Charlop, 1986; Paccia & Curcio, 1982; Quill, 1995a; Rydell & Prizant, 1995). Complex language can cause patterns of echolalia and difficulties responding. Thus, information presented in grammatically simple sentences elicits better responses than complex sentence forms. In addition, questions posed in sentence-completion form draw out better responses than "wh-" and yes/no questions. For example, the fill-in-the-blank question "The cat is where?" is more likely to produce a correct response than the standard form, "Where is the cat?" Simplified language involves:

- Simple sentences rather than complex grammatical forms
- Grammatically correct phrases or sentences
- Concrete language information
- Language linked to ongoing activity
- Familiar phrases used in similar situations
- Information paired with concrete referents

Use Augmentative and Alternative Communication Supports as Needed

One's language system must mirror the language system used by a child with autism. If the child uses gestural communication, others need to make their nonverbal gestural cues the most salient aspect of the interaction. If the child uses speech, adults must pair spoken language with multiple nonverbal cues to enhance understanding and use. If the child uses sign language, others need to use total communication (i.e., signing plus speech). If the child uses a communication board or other aided communication device, one must model use of the communication system all of the time.

Make Nonverbal Cues More Explicit

The adult's role is to make all of the subtle elements of conversation more explicit. Nonverbal elements of conversation include tone of voice, facial expression, gesture, affect, and pace. Making the nonverbal components of conversation salient clarifies the verbal message and increases the likelihood that a child with autism will extract meaning. The quality of interactions can be characterized as "a slow-motion video." Some children with autism respond to dramatic personalities, appearing to understand the social dynamic best when exaggerated. Others appear to respond best to individuals who speak slowly, calmly, and in a highly predictable manner. In either case, the clarity and pace with which information is presented are key elements for aiding comprehension. Overall, cues provided in a slow-motion video may include

- A slow pace
- A melodic tone of voice
- Dramatic facial expressions
- Exaggerated gestures
- Animation
- Sound effects
- Nonverbal cues fixed in space and time
- The use of pauses

Give the Child Time to Respond

A child with autism often struggles to integrate the context, social cues, and meaning behind verbal and nonverbal messages. Communication partners can help children make sense of the material presented by pausing after delivering a message. Pausing gives the child time to organize the information. Silent pauses within a conversation are also opportunities for the child to initiate an exchange. Furthermore, multiple repetitions of a message, especially when paraphrased, can be overwhelming and confusing for a child with autism.

Use Rhythmic Language

Interactions that involve rhythmic language and repetition help many children with autism participate in social interaction. Rhythmic language includes counting, reciting, and music and can be utilized in the following manners:

- To calm and refocus the child (e.g., singing a familiar song or repeating a familiar message each time the child appears anxious)
- To mark the length of a "nonpreferred" activity (e.g., singing the ABC song while the child is brushing his teeth)
- To mark transition time (e.g., counting to 10 to indicate the amount of time the child has to change his clothes)
- Embedded into simple social games (e.g., tickling)
- As part of traditional social games (e.g., Ring Around the Rosie)
- To increase participation in play (e.g., singing, "This is the way we build with blocks")
- Paired with any game involving repetition (e.g., Hide-and-Seek paired with the song "Where is _____? Where is _____? Here I am!")

Act as an Interpreter to Facilitate Peer Interactions

Studies of peer relationships have found a significant difference in the frequency and complexity of social-communicative interactions between children with autism and their peers as compared to adults (Hauck, Fein, Waterhouse, & Feinstein, 1995; Stone & Caro-Martinez, 1990). Children with autism initiate less often, and their interactions are more routinized. Low rates of peer interaction and spontaneous communication are especially apparent in unstructured, natural contexts. These studies concluded that the predictability of an adult's interactions allows for increased communicative effectiveness in children with autism, as compared with peers, who are less likely to adapt their communication style. Therefore, intervention to enhance the development of peer relationships includes both 1) peer-mediated procedures (i.e., coaching peers) and 2) modeling procedures (i.e., shadowing the child with autism).

Coach Peers

Peer-mediated procedures have been found to increase interactions between children with autism and their peers (Goldstein & Strain, 1988; Roeyers, 1996). Peer interactions are facilitated when peers modify their patterns of initiating, persisting, and responding to their friends with autism. Peer coaching strategies focus on the peer's understanding of the child's communicative attempts, the peer's ability to initiate and respond to the child, and the peer's ability to maintain an interaction with the child. Peers are encouraged to initiate and persist in trying to establish interactions, and they are taught how to react to possible challenging behaviors. Peer coaching can be done through role-playing sessions prior to the peer–child activities or by modeling during the peer–child activities. Through peer coaching, significant increases have been found in the responses of children with autism to peers and continuation of interactions, although not in initiations by children with autism. "The first step still has to be made by the nonhandicapped child" (Roeyers, 1996, p. 317).

Through role playing, peers are taught how to get a friend's attention and maintain an interaction. Depending on the particular needs of a child with autism, the peer practices what to do, such as stand close, point to or give/take an item, take the child's hand, tap the child's arm, or show the child an item. Teaching peers what to say focuses on talking about their own actions or the actions of their friend, repeating themselves, repeating what their friend says, and requesting clarification. Peers are shown how to persist if a friend does not respond, how to wait for a response, and how to ignore certain behaviors. The range and complexity of the instruction are contingent on the targeted social and communication goals for the child with autism.

Modeling gives explicit support to peers during their interactions with children with autism. Modeling takes the form of demonstration or verbal support. Demonstration is easiest when the adult acts as a co-participant. If a peer receives little feedback from a child with autism, an adult should provide ongoing reinforcement for the peer's efforts. Charts or cue cards can be used to preview, summarize, and review techniques with the peers. The ultimate goal is to promote social-communicative interactions that are mutually enjoyable and beneficial for all of the children.

Shadow the Child with Autism

Peer interactions can also be facilitated by modeling and prompting the child with autism. When modeling for the child, it is important to make the role of the adult explicitly clear. A clear distinction must be made between the adult interacting with the child and the adult modeling for the child. For example, if the adult is face to face with the child with autism and prompts the child to direct a message to a peer, the child with autism often will repeat the message to the adult, not to the peer. In contrast, if the adult stands behind the child with autism, uses an explicit nonverbal cue that indicates "I will help you," and verbally prompts the child to direct a message to a peer, the child with autism is more likely to understand to whom to direct the message. The following two examples clarify this important distinction, with the second one describing the more efficient means to facilitate interaction between a child with autism and one of his peers.

> Five-year-old Jacob is playing with trains while his teacher sits across from him. A peer arrives at the train area to play. The peer picks up one of the trains, so Jacob yells. The teacher says, "Jacob, say, 'That's mine.'" Jacob looks at his teacher and says, "That's mine." His teacher points to the peer and says, "Jacob, look." Jacob looks at the train that his peer is holding. The teacher verbally prompts, "Say, 'That's mine.'" Jacob looks back at his teacher and says, "That's mine." This exchange does not result in the peer's giving the train back to Jacob and is not an effective means to support the peer–child interaction.

Five-year-old Jacob is again playing with trains, and his teacher is sitting across from him. He yells when one of his peers comes to the train area and picks up one of the trains. His teacher stands up and walks behind Jacob. She places her hand on his shoulder and points to the peer. Jacob looks toward his peer. Next, the teacher says, "That's mine," and physically prompts Jacob to hold out his hand. Jacob holds out his hand to the peer and says, "That's mine." The peer then gives Jacob the train. By shadowing Jacob from behind and using explicit prompts, the teacher successfully facilitates the peer–child interaction.

Children with autism who have more language skills can be assisted in understanding the social-communicative behaviors of their peers and in expanding their communicative repertoires through an adult's use of modeling along with interpreting peer behavior (Twatchman, 1995). Examples include

- Pointing out a peer's social behavior (e.g., "Mary's confused because she doesn't understand the math problem")
- Prompting how to respond to peers' behavior (e.g., "John didn't hear you; you can tell him again")
- Encouraging perspective-taking (e.g., "Joe is making a face because he doesn't like that")
- Acknowledging feelings (e.g., "You are angry because Matt took the ball; tell Matt . . . ")
- Pointing out feeling in peers (e.g., "Debbie is crying because her knee hurts")
- Prompting how to respond to peers' feelings (e.g., "Mike is afraid; get the stuffed bear for him and maybe he will feel better")

These social supports serve as a means to structure and enhance understanding, engagement, and participation in social-communicative interactions. Modifications made by others are a natural means to compensate for the social and communication impairments of children with autism. Nonetheless, even when the physical environment is organized and the social environment is adapted, some children with autism require additional prompts and cues to acquire social competence. The next strategy, the use of visually cued instruction, fills this need for many children.

VISUALLY CUED INSTRUCTION

The ability of a child with autism to engage in shared attention, demonstrate imitation skills, comprehend oral language, and understand the process of social-communicative interaction varies across settings and people. Often, the use of organizational supports and social supports is not enough to build social skills. Organizational supports clarify the physical environment and social supports simplify social interaction; however, the child is still expected to identify the most salient aspects of the social setting and the most salient aspects of another person's language and nonverbal information. Given the learning style of children with autism, it is common for them to misinterpret verbal and nonverbal social information. They often attend to irrelevant or less salient aspects of the social environment or misunderstand the meaning of verbal information. It is common for them to become confused and overwhelmed in social situations. They are less able to focus or understand verbal and social information during these times. Therefore, many children need additional prompts and cues.

Visually cued instruction is the use of visual cues—objects, photographs, pictographs, written language, or video—to prepare, preview, prompt, and review social expectations (Quill, 1997). Information presented in visual form clarifies social and language information, so visually cued instruction is another means of assisting children with autism in attending, organizing, and understanding social expectations more readily. *Visual cues* are concrete, tangible referents that can support a child's ability to extract relevant language, social, and affective information. The rationale, benefits, uses, and types of visually cued instruction are summarized in Table 5.9.

Rationale for Visually Cued Instruction

Visually cued instruction compensates for a child's difficulty integrating social and language information, and it uses the child's strengths in processing visual information. Children with autism are better able to attend to, process, and remember visuospatial material than language or social material (Minshew, Goldstein, Muenz, & Payton, 1992). Children with autism can sustain attention to graphic information in the same way as typically developing peers do (Garretson, Fein, & Waterhouse, 1990), but they are unable to quickly shift attention in order to gain meaning from transient language and social cues. Sustained attention to concrete visual cues highlights relevant social and language information and, thus, can enhance a child's attention to and understanding of social and language messages. Because visually cued instruction provides children with a concrete reminder of what to do or say, it decreases their reliance on verbal and social prompts, thereby increasing independence. Visually cued instruction also augments independence because it allows a child to gain access to cues as needed and to fade them with mastery.

An increasing number of studies are validating the use of visually cued instruction as a catalyst for building social skills and fostering independence (see Quill, 1998, for a review). Visual cues are recommended in social contexts in which verbal prompts have not been effective. Boucher and Lewis (1988) studied the effect of visual cues on skill acquisition and found that the difficulty with spoken and modeled instructions was remedied

Table 5.9. Visually cued instruction

Rationale for visually cued instruction	Provides tangible, concrete information
	Highlights relevant social information
	Provides a concrete reminder of what to do or say
	Decreases reliance on verbal/social prompts
	Increases independence
	Gives the child access to cues as needed
	Allows the child to fade cues with mastery
Visually cued instruction is beneficial when	The child is identified as a visual learner
	The child is disorganized
	The child demonstrates difficulty with verbal language
	The child lacks joint attention
	The child lacks imitation
	Other strategies have not been successful
Use visually cued instruction to	Prepare (organize expectations)
	Preview (teach skills prior to the social activity)
	Prompt (provide instructional cues during a social activity)
	Review (teach skills through review after the social activity)
Types of visually cued instruction include	Schedules
	Cue cards
	Social scripts
	Social stories
	Video modeling
	Sociobehavioral displays
	Visual imagery
	Relaxation cues
	Social encyclopedias

with written instructions. Various forms of visual cues are recommended in contexts in which a child has become dependent on adult prompts and cues. Pierce and Schreibman (1994) found that acquisition, maintenance, and generalization of independent skills increased with the use of pictographic instructions. Social stories have helped many children with language and reading competencies understand social situations (Gray, 1993, 1995; Gray & Garand, 1993). Video modeling has been used as a highly motivating way to build imitation skills and communication skills (Quill & Shea, 1999), solitary play (Schwandt, Keene, & Larsson, 1998), and social skills in the community (Whalen & Schreibman, 1998). Furthermore, using visual cues to prepare, preview, prompt, and review social expectations is an option in social contexts that create anxiety or problem behaviors in some children. In these situations, the child is less likely to respond to verbal or physical prompting. Concrete, tangible visual cues—which can be used alone or combined with other prompts—provide clarification through indirect means, as opposed to more direct adult prompts. Once a child feels independent and comfortable in a particular social situation, he naturally disregards the visual cues.

When Visually Cued Instruction Is Beneficial

Visually cued instruction should be considered whenever a child appears disorganized and is not responsive to social prompts. It is also a good strategy to consider for children who lack the core skills of joint attention and imitation and are less likely to respond to social prompts. Visually cued instruction is useful for children at most levels of cognitive development. Children at a presymbolic developmental level generally require the use of object cues. A basic level of symbolic understanding is necessary for the other visual cues. For example, a child who is interested in books or computers is more likely to learn the meaning of photo or pictographic messages than a child who does not show any interest or ability to understand information in picture form. A child who is able to match or sort photos or pictures is also more likely to benefit from picture or pictographic instruction than a child who shows no understanding of graphic information. Given these basic requirements, many of the following strategies may not be appropriate for children at a presymbolic developmental level. The use of video modeling, however, is beneficial for any child who shows an interest in videos or television (Quill & Shea, 1999).

Visual cues are also helpful whenever the child is demonstrating difficulty responding to verbal language instruction. The content and complexity of the visual material presented, however, should mirror the child's level of oral language comprehension. Similarly, strategies that require the use of written language instruction should only be used with children who demonstrate interest in or understanding of written language. Children can more easily extract meaning from verbal information when it is accompanied by visual cues.

Uses of Visually Cued Instruction

Visually cued instruction can be applied in four ways: 1) to prepare a child for activities by clearly outlining expectations, 2) to preview and teach skills prior to a social activity, 3) to prompt during instruction, and 4) to review a social situation after the activity is complete.

Prepare

Visual cues can outline and organize expectations. Daily schedules, displays of activity sequences, and lists of work expectations (see subsequent section on types of visually cued instruction) clarify expectations and decrease the need for a child with autism to make social judgments or to follow social cues. In addition to this guide, many other excellent resources describe the use of visual cues to organize social situations. See Dalrymple (1995), Hodgdon (1995), Janzen (1996), McClannahan and Krantz (1999), and Schopler et al. (1995) for more information.

Preview

The majority of visual cues can be used as instructional tools for a child before he enters a social situation. Social scripts, social stories, video modeling, conversational books, social encyclopedias, sociobehavioral displays, visual imagery, and relaxation techniques (see subsequent section on types of visually cued instruction) provide an opportunity to learn about the relevant features of a social situation and to acquire social and communication skills through preview and practice prior to the situation. Given that social contexts can often be confusing for children with autism, strategies that allow for preview are often more successful than strategies that are implemented in context.

Prompt

Some of the visual cue strategies incorporate items that can be used as visual instructional prompts during the social situation. The visual cues are presented by an adult or are available for the child to use as reminders. These nonverbal prompts are invaluable during social situations. For many children who have difficulty with generalization, contextualized prompts are often more successful than preview strategies.

Review

All visual cues provide the child with an opportunity to review the social expectations after the activity is complete. The concrete, tangible cues allow for clarity and repetition of information. This is especially important for reinforcing desired social behaviors, reviewing alternatives to inappropriate social behaviors, and teaching replacement behaviors.

When using visually cued instruction, it is generally recommended to prepare, preview, prompt, *and* review social expectations as much as possible.

Types of Visually Cued Instruction

Table 5.9 outlines the nine types of visually cued instruction. This section explores how these nine strategies can be used to enhance understanding of social expectations. Each of the nine techniques is illustrated by a vignette involving a 6-year-old child named Billy.

Schedules

The main function of visual schedules is to clarify the sequence of social events. Schedules specify where to go, what to do next, and for how long and are typically presented in linear order. Visual schedules can be made with photos, pictures, pictographs, or written language. Some schedules can even be made with concrete objects. Schedules clarify expectations and can increase independence in solitary and social activities. Sample schedules include

- Daily schedules (i.e., the sequence of daily activities)
- Transitional objects (i.e., a specific object linked to an activity to prepare where to go)
- Play schedules (i.e., sequence of play activities)
- Activity lists (i.e., sequence of game or activity substeps)
- Outlines of group discussions
- Time boards (i.e., a visual representation of time in sequence or puzzle form)

Sample schedule for Billy: Billy benefits from schedules in new situations. His parents find time boards a particularly useful way to clarify time for him. As Billy likes letters, his time board consists of a card that has the letters of his name on a Velcro strip. As time passes, another letter is put on the card. When his name is complete, it is time to go.

Cue Cards

The main function of cue cards is to remind the child what to do. Cue cards, which can contain one or more pieces of information, replace verbal or other social prompts. They silently refocus a child's attention, thus making them less intrusive than other forms of prompts. Cue cards are particularly useful in situations where the child is disorganized and/or anxious. (Multiple examples were provided in the previous section on organizational supports.) Some additional ways to present cue cards include the following:

- Card with a single message in pictograph or written form
- Dry-erase board
- Wristband worn by adult that contains key directions
- Lists of reminders
- Index card with social rules (e.g., share, take turns, wait)

Sample cue cards for Billy: Billy has his own tutor in his first-grade classroom who often prompts Billy using cue cards. For example, his tutor writes key words on a dry-erase board to visually cue Billy during group discussions. When given these silent reminders, Billy attends better in group activities. Another cue card used for Billy is a STOP and GO sign on the classroom door. Prior to using the cue card, Billy often ran out of the classroom to see the fish tank in the hallway. Billy was taught when he can leave the classroom (i.e., when the sign says GO) and when he cannot (i.e., when the sign says STOP). In addition, STOP and GO signs are used throughout the classroom to clarify what activities are available or unavailable for his use.

Social Scripts

The main function of social scripts is to clarify choices in social situations. Social scripts present the child with two or more options of what to do in a social situation. They simplify open-ended social situations by providing limited options. Like schedules, social scripts can be made with photos, pictures, pictographs, or written language. Unlike schedules, however, social scripts provide more flexibility, and the information depicted on social scripts should not be presented in a linear sequence. Left-to-right presentations, numerical lists, and outlines often prompt a child to do activities in the order presented. Social scripts should be presented in arbitrary ways. Sample social scripts include

- Circular board of different solitary or social play choices
- Play script; that is, a visual depiction of play options within an open-ended activity that can be presented on a circular board or as a series of individual cards held together by a key ring
- Checklist of activities that will occur in random order
- Story about an upcoming event that includes what to do options

Sample social script for Billy: Using play scripts helps Billy expand his repertoire of play skills for open-ended activities in the playdough and dress-up areas. A series of cards that present different things to do were organized on a key chain. The playdough script, for example, contains eight different cards that depict using a roller and cookie cutters, as well as making playdough balls, snakes, gingerbread men, and so forth. He reviews the choices, practices each play schema, and then has the social scripts available at playtime. Billy's peers use the scripts to cue him when he "gets stuck."

Social Stories

Social stories are short stories that clarify expectations for a particular social situation. The main function of social stories is to teach social perspective-taking. Stories include information that is descriptive and directive and explains perspective. They describe what occurs in a social situation and why, point out the relevant features of a situation, list desired social behaviors, and describe the reactions of others in the target situation (Gray, 1995). The complexity of information must mirror a child's language comprehension abilities; for children who do not read, social stories can be audiotaped and/or include illustrations.

Sample social story for Billy: For group activities, Billy has learned to raise his hand but becomes upset when he does not get a turn. Agitation and verbal outbursts are common. A short, simple storybook about emotions was made for Billy. It is pre-

viewed each day and reviewed after each time he becomes upset. Billy's teacher verbally prompts Billy in group using the same words from the story. Gradually, Billy is using the words of the story to regulate himself when he is agitated. He has learned to say, "Sometimes you get a turn; sometimes you don't. I can stay calm."

Video Modeling

The main function of video modeling is to teach specific social and communication skills. The child learns what to DO-WATCH-LISTEN-and-SAY (see frameworks in Chapter 4). Videos can be developed to highlight salient social cues and specific social and communicative behaviors. As video instruction allows a child to view natural social events in precisely the same way repeatedly, it is the easiest way for him to preview and review social events. Video instruction can be used along with other visual strategies. Video modeling has unlimited applications, but some examples are

- Teaching motor imitation (e.g., the child watches other children doing actions to music or other movement activity)
- Teaching solitary play (e.g., the child watches a peer engaged in a specific solitary play sequence)
- Teaching social play (e.g., the child watches peers taking turns during a specific activity)
- Teaching community expectations (e.g., the child watches a peer going to the dentist)
- Teaching replacements to challenging behaviors (e.g., the child watches self engaged in appropriate behavior)
- Teaching specific communication messages (e.g., the child watches others express one message in a variety of contexts)
- Teaching discourse skills (e.g., the child watches videotapes of same-age peers engaged in simple conversations)

Video modeling can be specifically used for social and communication skills intervention. To develop a video for social skills or communication skills instruction,

1. Identify the social setting.
2. Identify the target social behavior or communicative message.
3. Videotape familiar adults or peers engaged in the target behavior or using the communicative message.
4. Make the social cues, target social behavior, or communicative message the most salient aspects of the video.
5. Limit the amount of verbal information on the video.

There are some basic ideas to keep in mind when using video modeling for instruction. These are as follows:

- Show the video to the child daily (or more often if the child is interested).
- Preview the video just prior to the actual activity, when appropriate.
- Pair the video model with a second visual cue (e.g., schedule, cue card, social script).
- Use the second visual cue as an instructional prompt in the natural social situation.
- Assess skill acquisition.
- Continue practicing the target social skill through the use of video and other visual cues as needed.
- Gradually fade the frequency of video preview until the skill is mastered.

Sample video modeling for teaching Billy appropriate social behaviors: Billy does not like to visit the dentist. He begins to scream as he nears the dental office building. His reaction is so extreme that two adults need to hold him for a routine exam. He does not want anyone to touch his teeth, as he associates dentists with toothaches. A video was made about a dentist visit. The video includes Billy's sister going to the dentist for a checkup. Billy's favorite music accompanies the otherwise silent "movie." The dentist slowly checks the girl's teeth and gums with instruments. She stays calm and receives Billy's favorite treat after leaving the dentist's office. An activity schedule is paired with the video. Billy watches the video daily for 2 weeks. From then on, he carries his activity schedule and video to the dentist's office. Each visit has become easier for him.

Sample video modeling to teach Billy specific communication skills: Billy does not like it when his classmates borrow materials from his desk. He is extremely vigilant about protecting his possessions, and this distracts him from his schoolwork. When a peer does ask to borrow something, Billy usually yells. Efforts to cue him to communicate in an alternative way were not successful until his mother tried video modeling. On the video, his classmates act out multiple scenes of saying "No, they are mine" when peers want to borrow materials. The video consists of six friends and ten different settings. Billy enjoyed watching the video at home and used the message in the classroom perfectly within 2 days.

Sociobehavioral Displays

Most classrooms display a list of classroom rules that outlines social expectations to which the teacher refers when communicating expectations to the children. Sociobehavioral displays are similar. The main function of sociobehavioral displays is to clarify rules and desirable social behaviors. Putting rules in visual form ensures that adults will be clear and consistent. A display can also refocus a child's attention and provide a concise and simple prompt when the child exhibits undesirable behaviors. Displays can depict one or more rules, and they can be presented in picture, pictographic, and/or written form. They can be used alone or in combination with other nonaversive behavior management procedures. Sociobehavioral displays should

- Clearly specify the desired behavior
- State rules in positive terms
- State rules in concrete, observable terms
- State rules in clear and concise terms

  Sample sociobehavioral display for Billy: Billy has difficulty sharing toys with his peers; yelling and grabbing toys often occurs during social play activities. Therefore, a pictographic and written display was created for Billy that lists two rules: use a quiet voice and play with friends. Billy reviews the rules daily and has practiced sharing with adults. This display is now in the play area, and it is used by adults and peers to prompt Billy.

Visual Imagery

The main function of visual imagery techniques is to teach self-control strategies. Visual imagery focuses on stressful events that are known to trigger problem behaviors and supports a child in learning alternative self-control strategies. Groden and LeVasseur (1995) developed an imagery procedure that uses repeated practice of desired social behaviors by presenting the event in visual form. A scene of a stressful situation is depicted as a sequence of pictures that is paired with a simple verbal script. The scene concludes with desired behaviors and positive outcomes. The scene and script are reviewed with the child multiple times each day. Once the child demonstrates familiarity with the scene, the scene is rehearsed before, during, or after the actual stressful situation. The goal is for the child to demonstrate the desired behaviors in the natural setting by using the visual and verbal images as cues.

> *Sample visual imagery procedure for Billy: Billy has significant difficulties on the school bus. It was determined that the difficulties are triggered by the noise on the bus. A pictorial scene of five photographs was developed that depicts the stressful event and what to do: 1) Billy gets on the bus, 2) Billy sits on the bus, 3) children talk and laugh loudly, 4) Billy puts on his Walkman to listen to music, and 5) Billy gets off the bus and receives a hug from his mother. In situations in which others are loud, Billy practices putting on his headphones. The pictorial scene is reviewed during quiet times of the day. It is also practiced before and after the bus ride. Gradually, Billy's challenging behaviors on the bus have been replaced by his self-control strategy: listening to music.*

Relaxation Cues

A relaxation cue is any form of visual cue that prompts a child to relax. Relaxation cues are an effective means to prompt a child nonverbally when he appears stressed. These cues can also be an effective way to prompt a child nonverbally from engaging in ritualistic behaviors. The cues can be objects, pictures, pictographs, or written language that represent a relaxing location, object, activity, or procedure. A specific area of the classroom, a box of "fidget toys," a display of activity choices, or a relaxation checklist are other examples of relaxation cues. The information can also be presented in the form of a cue card or social script. Relaxation cues can visually cue the child to

- Go to a particular location to take a break
- Use a particular object to relax
- Select a particular activity to relax
- Use a particular sequence of relaxation procedures

> *Sample relaxation procedures for Billy: Billy often engages in noncommunicative delayed echolalia. He repeats scenes from a favorite movie. This seems to increase during stressful situations. Billy is now cued to relax in two ways. First, the rocking chairs in the book area of his classroom and in his bedroom are identified as places to relax. A rocking chair pictograph is used to cue Billy to go to the area. Gradually, Billy has learned to hand the card to the adult to request a break. Second, Billy has been taught a series of relaxation techniques (Groden, Cautela, & Groden, 1989) that include deep breathing and counting. This relaxation procedure is visually displayed on a portable card that can be used anywhere.*

Social Encyclopedia

For children with more advanced cognitive and language abilities, social understanding can be enhanced by developing an individualized social encyclopedia. A *social encyclopedia* is a social map of the child's life, a journal of personal experiences that are organized into categories to teach social understanding. The concept of a social encyclopedia derives from Grandin (1995a), whose teachings emphasize the need to use logic (not emotion) to explain social meaning to children with autism. The feelings and behaviors of others need to be framed within the context of the child's own experience. All explanations must use perceptual, concrete, and observable criteria. This approach to social understanding compensates for the child's social misunderstanding of mental states. Therefore, although social encyclopedias can be organized in multiple ways, it is essential to organize the information into categories that help the child to see the similarities between related social

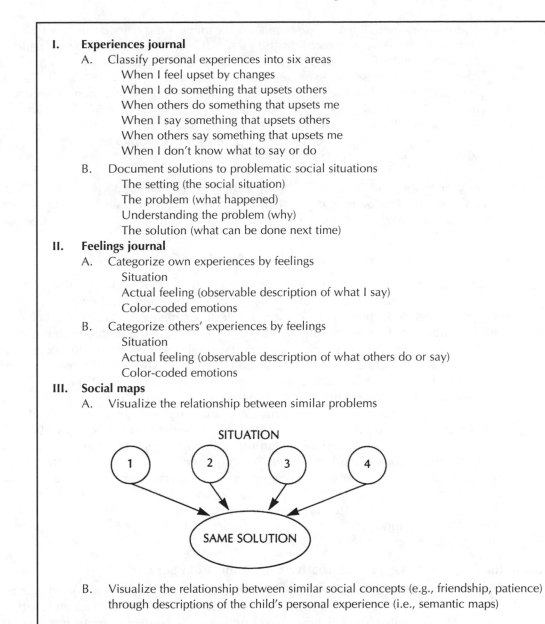

I. **Experiences journal**

    A.   Classify personal experiences into six areas

         When I feel upset by changes

         When I do something that upsets others

         When others do something that upsets me

         When I say something that upsets others

         When others say something that upsets me

         When I don't know what to say or do

    B.   Document solutions to problematic social situations

         The setting (the social situation)

         The problem (what happened)

         Understanding the problem (why)

         The solution (what can be done next time)

II. **Feelings journal**

    A.   Categorize own experiences by feelings

         Situation

         Actual feeling (observable description of what I say)

         Color-coded emotions

    B.   Categorize others' experiences by feelings

         Situation

         Actual feeling (observable description of what others do or say)

         Color-coded emotions

III. **Social maps**

    A.   Visualize the relationship between similar problems

SITUATION

1   2   3   4

SAME SOLUTION

    B.   Visualize the relationship between similar social concepts (e.g., friendship, patience) through descriptions of the child's personal experience (i.e., semantic maps)

Figure 5.1. Social encyclopedias.

events. Unlike other types of visually cued instruction, the social encyclopedia supports generalization of social concepts. Figure 5.1 shows various ways of organizing a social encyclopedia. For instance, a child and two friends make a list of favorite television shows. Each writes information about the shows they like and why. The child with autism can review his friends' interests and use these interests as conversation topics. This also helps the child begin to see similarities and differences in interests.

> *Sample social encyclopedia for Billy: Information about Billy's experiences and feelings is recorded daily. It includes a list of his daily activities and how he felt. For example, music = happy, math = angry, fire drill = afraid, and reading = happy. His encyclopedia also includes a set of short, simple stories about each emotion with photos of himself in various situations that are associated with the emotion. Billy has a happy story, a sick story, a mad story, and an afraid story.*

> *These stories help him to begin to link the meaning of the emotion terms to his own behavior. A second section of Billy's social encyclopedia is used to expand his conversational skills. Billy attends a social skills group each week with two friends. The therapist uses exercises from Freeman and Dake's (1996) book, Teach Me Language, and also organizes discussions to highlight the children's likes and dislikes. For example, each child makes a list of his favorite television programs, toys, and activities. By looking at a list, Billy is actually able to see similarities and differences. The lists are later used to help Billy generate topics of conversation with peers that are related to their interests.*

Combining visually cued instruction with organizational supports and social supports can enhance the development of social understanding and social skills. The next section describes similar strategies for enhancing communication through the use of AAC supports.

AUGMENTATIVE AND ALTERNATIVE COMMUNICATION SUPPORTS

Augmentative and alternative communication (AAC) is the term used to describe any form of language other than speech that assists a child in social-communicative interactions. *Augmentative* refers to the process of enhancing speech; *alternative* refers to the process of providing a substitute for speech (Glennen & DeCosta, 1997). Augmentative communication systems are created to expand the communication abilities of children with speech, and alternative communication systems are created for children who have limited or no speech. Thus, AAC builds communication skills in children with and without speech.

Because of the wide range of AAC supports available and the diversity of children, it is essential that an individual specializing in assistive technology and a team of relevant professionals and parents evaluate AAC options. Once the best options have been determined, the team needs to develop a plan that sets up situations that encourage the child to initiate use of the system for a variety of communicative functions. In determining the appropriateness of any communication system, certain criteria need to be examined and may include the age of the child, motivation to communicate, learning style, cognitive abilities, motor abilities, literacy, communication needs, behaviors, and family preferences. The uses and types of AAC supports, summarized in Table 5.10, are described in further detail next.

Rationale for Augmentative and Alternative Communication Supports

The rationale for using AAC supports for nonverbal children is obvious. In the absence of a conventional means of communication, children who do not speak often resort to unconventional, challenging behaviors to communicate their needs and feelings. For them, then, an AAC system is the primary means of social-communicative interactions with others. It is the responsibility of every person in the child's environment to model the use of the AAC system. The child learns about communication through exposure to other adults and peers using the system. It is also important to clarify communication expectations in each social context. If a child is using more than one system—for example, both

Table 5.10. Augmentative and alternative communication (AAC) supports

AAC should be considered for children who	Types of AAC supports
Are nonspeaking	Picture Exchange Communication System (PECS; Frost & Bondy, 1994)
Lack verbal imitation skills	
Depend on verbal prompting to communicate	Sign language
Demonstrate difficulty with spontaneous initiations	Interactive communication boards
	Communication cue cards
Have difficulty communicating in stressful situations	Conversation books
	Voice output communication aids

sign language and interactive communication boards—determine which message (i.e., sign or picture) is to be used in which contexts and for what purpose. For example, a child may more easily use an interactive board at meals and tabletop activities while using signs in active play contexts. However, a child only needs one symbolic means to convey a single message. For instance, if a child has a repertoire of signs and graphic symbols to communicate, he does not need to sign both DRINK and also point to the graphic symbol of *drink* on the communication board. The expectation to use multimodal communication systems for a singular message can place an unnecessary burden on the child and easily confuse many children with autism. Thus, there is a need to continually reevaluate and adapt a child's AAC system according to his functional use of the system across multiple contexts. (See Chapter 4 to review the criteria for selecting an alternative communication system for a nonverbal child.)

There is also strong backing for using AAC supports for verbal children with autism. First, children who demonstrate difficulty with spontaneous initiations may be unable to bring to mind things to say voluntarily (Boucher, 1981). They often use repetitive and ritualistic language when unable to recall relevant things to say during social interactions. AAC supports are a concrete means to remind children what to say and to expand their repertoires of communication skills. AAC systems should be considered for any child with speech who demonstrates a low level of spontaneous initiations and relies on verbal or nonverbal social prompts to communicate. Second, the concrete nature of AAC supports helps children with autism understand the meaning and purpose of communication. Studies have demonstrated that AAC supports build basic communicative functions (i.e., requests, negation) when spoken language is highly noncommunicative (Reichle & Wacker, 1993). Third, studies have demonstrated that AAC supports expand social-communicative functions (Quill, 1997). Both comments and expressions of feelings emerged in a group of young children when graphic AAC supports were used as retrieval cues. Thus, augmentative communication supports are an important means to facilitate spontaneous, functional communication in many children with autism who have speech. The ultimate goal is to fade the use of the AAC system as the child becomes a more effective communicator.

There are multiple benefits of using AAC for children with and without speech, as they

- Enable the child to attend to communicative interactions
- Clarify the meaning of spoken language
- Provide a means of communication
- Expand the range of communicative functions
- Provide a retrieval cue about what to say (children with speech)
- Decrease reliance on verbal prompts (children with speech)
- Increase spontaneity

Types of Augmentative and Alternative Communication Supports

The different types of AAC supports for children with autism include both traditional forms of AAC and innovative technologies to enhance functional communication. This section is limited to a review of the most common AAC supports used in intervention for children with autism:

- Picture Exchange Communication System (PECS; Frost & Bondy, 1994)
- Sign language
- Interactive communication boards
- Communication cue cards
- Conversation books
- Voice output communication aids

Picture Exchange Communication System (PECS)

PECS was developed as a procedure to develop spontaneous communication in nonverbal children with autism. The main function of PECS is to teach a child that communication is an exchange. In particular, the child is taught to make spontaneous initiations by delivering a pictorial message. To do this, the child hands a picture to a person in exchange for receiving the desired effect. The program begins with highly motivating toys, food, and activities to build requesting, and it expands to labeling. Bondy and Frost (1994) reported impressive outcomes when PECS was used with 85 nonverbal preschool children with autism. In this study, 95% of the children learned to use picture symbols for communication and 76% used a combination of speech and picture symbols to make requests and label items after 6 months of training. Therefore, PECS served as a means to teach the process of communication and to facilitate the emergence of speech in the majority of young children studied.

Other studies have demonstrated the importance of using this procedure to encourage spontaneous initiations in verbal children (Quill, 1994, 1997). Children who relied on echolalia and lacked functional communication were taught communication skills through the use of PECS. PECS was shown to be an effective method for teaching nonverbal ways to gain a listener's attention prior to conveying a message. In addition, reciprocal eye gaze and communicative gestures increased through the PECS program. Once children mastered these skills, the PECS system could be faded.

The four basic steps for implementing the PECS system are

1. Teach the basic process of exchange. Do not use verbal prompts; instead, involve two adults, one who physically assists the child and one who receives the message.

2. Systematically expand the distance that the child needs to travel to locate a person and convey a message.

3. Systematically expand the time that the child needs to persist in getting a person's attention in order to convey a message.

4. Systematically teach discrimination of two or more visual symbols to expand single-word functional vocabulary.

After a child has mastered these early phases, the PECS training includes procedures to expand vocabulary and sentence structures to build requesting and labeling in multiple settings (Frost & Bondy, 1994). The early phases of the PECS system can also be used to expand additional communicative functions. As noted previously, children should have a large repertoire of single words (i.e., symbols) to convey most communicative functions (i.e., requests, negation, comments, feelings, prosocial communications) before expanding sentence structure (Quill, 1998). PECS is beneficial in teaching verbal and nonverbal children to hand an adult a symbol to request a break, indicate frustration, indicate fear (e.g., symbol for "too loud"), ask a question, and say "thank you," among numerous other social functions (Quill, 1998). Some benefits of PECS for nonverbal children are illustrated in the following example:

> Jessie, who is nonverbal, demonstrates many challenging behaviors. He had limited success when intervention focused on his use of sign language. At age 6, his communication consisted of two signs: MORE and EAT. Recognizing that Jessie has excellent matching skills, the PECS program was introduced to him. Within 3 months of using PECS, his vocabulary grew to include 50 words. Jessie was able to convey eight communicative functions: requesting food, help, and favorite activities, as well as indicating ALL DONE, NO, YES, NEED A BREAK, and FEEL MAD. As Jessie's communication increases, his challenging behaviors decrease.

Sign Language

There are two different sign language systems: American Sign Language (ASL) and Signed Exact English. ASL is a complete language system with its own phonology, morphology, semantics, and syntax. ASL, the dominant language system used by the Deaf community, differs significantly from Signed Exact English. Signed Exact English is a system that matches the grammatical features of oral and written language.

Sign language for nonverbal children with autism received research attention in the early 1980s (Konstantareas, Webster, & Oxman, 1980; Layton, 1987, 1988). These studies reported that some children acquired the sign language system they were taught. Yet later reports indicated that even after intensive training with signs, the majority of children had gained only a small repertoire of functional signs (Layton, 1987, 1988). Although there is an absence of research comparing the effectiveness of ASL and Signed Exact English for children with autism, Signed Exact English is commonly used because it clearly matches the spoken language (Layton, 1987).

Total communication strategies—that is, the combined use of speech and sign by others—model the same language structure in two modalities for a child. Nonverbal children using sign language must be exposed to total communication across all settings. This requires a commitment from home and school community.

Total communication can be an effective AAC support for some verbal children with autism. Signs serve as a visual reference to highlight word meanings and enhance language comprehension. They also can improve social attention and serve as a prompt in social contexts. Signed cues can expand expressive communication by reminding a child what to say. Given that the goal is spontaneous communication, however, it is important to systematically fade both verbal and signed prompts. The five basic steps for implementing a sign language system are

1. Consider the complexity of the sign position and movement when selecting early vocabulary: Signs that are stationary (e.g., *eat, more*) are easier than signs that move and/or require each hand to do a different movement (e.g., *jump, done*).

2. Exaggerate signs when using total communication by utilizing slow movements and exaggerated position and by holding the position longer.

3. Physically prompt the child to sign if he does not imitate motor movements; use two adults to do this, one who physically assists the child and one who receives the message. Systematically fade physical assistance.

4. Avoid using total communication prompts to elicit requests; this often leads to echolalic signing.

5. Remember that the goal is spontaneous communication.

This next profile demonstrates one child's use of sign language:

Tiffany, age 6, has good social attention and motor imitation skills. Her family feels more comfortable using sign language than other AAC systems. Through exposure to total communication at school and home, Tiffany's communication has grown from echolalic signing to generative signed phrases. Tiffany has successfully acquired an array of modified signs to spontaneously convey numerous communicative functions.

Interactive Communication Boards

Interactive communication boards contain visual symbols—pictures, pictographs, or written words—organized by topic. Communication boards can be created in different sizes and formats for different activities and environments. They can be combined into a complete portable system or organized so that only one board is used in one location. When selecting interactive communication boards as an AAC system, it is essential that use of the communication system is modeled by adults and peers at all times. (See Beukelman & Mirenda, 1998, for detailed information about the design of communication boards; see Goosens', Crain, & Elder, 1992, for detailed information about engineering the environment for interactive communication using AAC systems.) Sample interactive communication boards include

- A series of single messages on a ring
- A wallet with multiple messages
- A single board with multiple messages
- A folder, book, or binder with multiple topic boards

Communication boards need to be portable, durable, and always available. Ambulatory children must have boards that are easy to carry and readily available at all times. They can be attached to clothing, put in a fanny pack, placed in a pocket, or put in a book with a shoulder strap.

The goal of the communication system is to enhance spontaneous, functional communication. If boards are too limited, children will not be able to communicate their range of needs and ideas effectively. The selection of symbols and communication boards should be both compact and comprehensive.

The selection and organization of symbols should enhance motivating, functional communication. Boards are generally created by topic (i.e., setting or activity). Vocabulary needs to be selected to allow for ease of requesting and commenting in that particular context. This way, the child and others can use the board to interact. The selected vocabulary is organized from left to right so that the child and others can generate a phrase or sentence in the person-verb-descriptive-noun format. Pronouns and people are in the left column, verbs in the second column, and so forth. Miscellaneous terms such as *yes* or *no* and symbols indicating phrases such as "It's not on my board" are placed in the far right column. The number of words on a board increases with time, but this basic format should be used from the onset. A sample communication board is shown in Figure 6 in the Appendix.

Communication boards can be used with nonverbal children who understand how to gain a person's attention to convey a message and demonstrate an understanding of the symbol meaning, whether pictures, pictographs, alphabet, or written words. The use of interactive communication boards can also be an effective AAC support for expanding the repertoire of some verbal children, as the visual symbols can remind the child what to say. Vicker (1991) reported that pictographic communication boards expanded the incidence of spontaneous communication in a preschool child with emerging language, and Quill (1997) found a decrease in echolalia and an increase in spontaneous commenting in 10 preschool children who had access to communication boards. Communication boards can be used with verbal children who are inconsistent verbal imitators or are verbally prompt dependent and lack spontaneous communication. There are five basic steps for using a communication board:

1. Interact with the child by touching key words on the board while talking. Use a hand-over-hand point if the child does not demonstrate shared attention to the board.

2. Limit verbal prompting to elicit the child's communication.

3. Encourage the child to take your hand and point if there is poor shared attention.

4. Acknowledge the child's communicative attempts by imitating and expanding on the child's message. For example, when a child points to the symbol for *bubbles*, the adult says (and points) "Bubbles, blow bubbles," emphasizing the *blow* symbol on the board.

5. Remember that the goal is spontaneous communication.

The following example demonstrates how interactive boards can be used to enhance the communication skills of children with autism:

Vince is extremely verbal, but his speech is predominantly noncommunicative. At age 8, he was an inconsistent imitator. Through PECS, Vince learned the purpose of communication. Once he was able to seek out a person to convey a verbal message, his communication continued to be limited to simple requests. A series of topic communication boards were designed for him. Through use of the interactive boards, Vince's communication expanded to commenting and other social functions. There was a dramatic increase in his level of spontaneous communication in contexts with access to communication boards.

Cue Cards

Cue cards are an AAC support used primarily with verbal children. They can be used for two purposes: 1) to remind the child what to say and 2) to provide the child with an alternative means of communication. Cue cards—which contain one or more messages in picture, pictographic, or written form—replace verbal prompts and are particularly useful for children who are prompt dependent.

Cue cards have been shown to enhance specific communicative functions in children with autism, particularly messages that a child needs to express in stressful situations. Successful use of pictographic cards for teaching the functions of commenting on one's action and asking "wh-" questions to a group of children with autism have been reported. Generalization of the targeted communicative functions was maintained across familiar and novel social contexts. Cue cards are also helpful for stressful situations in which a child is unable to verbalize and may need an AAC system to communicate his or needs and feelings. Messages such as "I don't want it" to express refusal, "I need a break to relax" to interrupt work, and "I feel _____" to express emotion can be communicated verbally and/or by pointing to a cue card.

Other studies report successful use of cue cards to increase peer interactions and conversational skills in children with autism. Wolfberg and Schuler (1993) used cues to teach young children to smile, clap, or give a high-five to a friend. Krantz and McClannahan (1993) used pictographic and written cues to increase peer initiatives. Both of these studies found that the skills were maintained once the cues were faded, and generalization to novel settings was observed in three of the four children studied. Freeman and Dake (1996) described a procedure for using cue cards to support conversation with peers. The cards contain the basic rules for starting, maintaining, and ending a conversation. The following example describes the use of cue cards to build conversational skills. The procedure is an adaptation of strategies outlined by Freeman and Dake (1996).

Cue cards are used to preview, review, and prompt conversational rules with Clark, who often interacts with his peers in awkward ways. Three different colored cards were made for Clark: one for conversation openers, one for conversation fillers, and one for conversation enders. The card for openers includes a choice of "Hi," "Hey," or "What's up?" Cards regarding fillers remind Clark to answer questions or to say "I don't know" as well as to listen and to say "Wow," "Really," and "Yep" sometimes. For enders, Clark's card gives the choices "Bye," "I gotta go now," and "See you later." Clark practices using these phrases during conversations with adults. The conversation cue cards have helped increase Clark's peer interactions, especially in situations that are stressful for him.

Conversation Books

A *conversation book* is a pictorial, pictographic, or written summary of conversation topics for augmenting conversational abilities (Hunt, Alwell, & Goetz, 1993; Quill, 1998). The conversation topics can be organized in an actual (small) book, in a wallet, or other portable means. The conversation book is used as a focus of conversation with an adult or peer partner. Conversation books can be used by both verbal and nonverbal children.

To design and use a conversation book for a child, first select age-appropriate topics of conversation. Topics also need to be meaningful, so choose photographs (the best for young children), pictographs, and/or accompanying written phrases of favorite people and things, as well as recent activities. Be sure to vary the content of the conversation book as experiences and interests change. Sample books and topics that can be used for most children with autism include

- A series of photographs and/or pictographs that tell a story about a recent event or outing

- A series of photographs and/or pictographs that summarize the day's school activities (to share with family)

- A wallet with photographs of family and friends

- A wallet with photographs of the child playing with favorite toys

Conversation books organize the conversation by providing a concrete, visual means to share and maintain topics. Encourage adults and peers to ask the child to share his conversation book to initiate an interaction. The nonverbal child and his partner can look at the book and *point* at the photographs, pictographs, and accompanying written phrases to maintain a conversational exchange. The books give a verbal child with autism additional reminders of things to say. In addition to the previous examples, conversation books for children having more advanced skills can contain other reminders:

- A list of general conversation rules

- Suggested conversation openers, fillers, and endings

- Lists of situation-specific topics (e.g., what to say at the library)

- Lists of person-specific topics (e.g., what to say to the minister)

The example that follows shows how a conversation book can be employed to assist a child with autism in communicating with her family:

> Alexa, who is nonverbal, shares information about her kindergarten school day with her parents through a conversation book. Alexa's teacher made a one-page form that contains photographs of her classmates and pictographs of school toys and activities. After each activity is finished, Alexa and her teacher look at the form together. They circle the activity and draw a line from the pictured activity to the classmate who participated with Alexa. Each activity is circled in a different color. Alexa takes the form home and shares it with her parents. Using the photos, pictographs, and color cues, Alexa can "tell" her parents what she did in school that day and who played with her in each activity.

Voice Output Communication Aids

The advantage of speech output devices is that they give nonverbal children a "voice." There are a wide variety of high-technology communication devices available (see Glennen & DeCosta, 1997, for a comprehensive review). The technology is constantly changing and improving to create newer, faster, smaller, and lighter devices. Subsequently, devices can become obsolete quickly. Because of the wide range of devices available and the diversity of the individuals, it is essential to consult an individual specializing in assistive technology when evaluating technology options. Once the best technology options have been determined, a child's education team needs to develop a plan to help with issues such as appropriate vocabulary selection, size of symbols, layout, organization, and the best way to set up situations that encourage the child to use the system for a variety of communicative functions. The process is ongoing and should be flexible as a child changes and grows. As most children with autism are ambulatory, a device also needs to be small and lightweight. Given their size and weight, many available high-technology devices are not appropriate for use in the community; they may, however, be useful in a classroom. Some of these devices are described next. (Detailed information about each product is listed in the Resources section at the end of the book. Neither this list nor the ensuing discussion is meant to be comprehensive or endorse any particular tool.)

There are simple devices for children who do not understand visual symbols, although one must have an understanding of cause–effect to use these simple devices. The child learns to press a switch or button to activate a prerecorded message. It is best for another child of the same age and gender to record the messages. These devices include the BIGmack (manufactured by AbleNet) and even small tape recorders. A single-message device helps a child gain an adult's attention, such as a device that says "Please come here." A preprogrammed voice message can also be used in a specific social setting, such as a device that says "Happy birthday!"

A growing number of programmable devices with speech output are available for children who understand visual symbols, whether pictograph or printed words. Interactive communication boards can be placed on a voice output system. The devices range from those that contain four messages—such as Cheap Talk (manufactured by Enabling Devices)—to fully featured, computerized systems that contain an unlimited number of messages and allow for keyboarding—such as the DynaMyte (manufactured by DynaVox Systems, a division of Sunrise Medical). There are also many computer software programs that can be used to facilitate communicative interactions. When choosing a system, one needs to take into account a child's abilities and interests: As with all other AAC systems, the child's use of the device as a means of functional communication is the primary consideration.

There are potential problems when children with autism use voice output systems. First, the durability of the device must be considered for children with challenging behaviors. Many of the devices are not durable yet are expensive. Second, a child needs access to his communication system at all times; some systems (e.g., computer-based ones) are not portable. Third, some children enjoy exploring the device to hear a voice repeatedly and, thus, may use the device without communicative intent. It is beneficial to model the correct use of these devices and to assess the functionality of a device for a child who uses it in a perseverative manner.

This next profile illustrates one young child's use of a voice output system:

Four-year-old Ian is a master on the computer. He is nonverbal but highly motivated to communicate. Because of his language and communication abilities, Ian quickly outgrew PECS and communication boards. Thus, a voice output system and keyboarding were chosen as a means for Ian to converse with his family and peers. There are problems with this AAC device, however: Ian prefers to have the voice be very loud (especially when he wants to emphasize his point), and his spelling abilities exceed that of his peers.

The combined use of organizational supports, social supports, visually cued instruction, and AAC supports enhances the development of social understanding, social skills, and social-communicative interactions in children with autism. Nonetheless, the management of ritualistic behaviors that interfere with social and communication flexibility is another intervention challenge. Intervention for ritualistic play and communication is addressed in the next major section of this chapter.

INTERVENTION FOR PLAY AND COMMUNICATION RITUALS

Ritualistic behaviors dominate the social and communication patterns of children with autism to a greater degree than those of children with typical development do. Ritualistic behaviors are observed in a multitude of ways; this discussion is limited to ritualistic play and repetitive verbalizations. Ritualistic behaviors can be a manifestation of the child's limited understanding about what to do or say or part of a learned chain of events. States of excitement, anxiety, boredom, and confusion can trigger rituals. In addition, ritualistic behaviors can occur as a result of underlying medical conditions. (For more information, see the section "Rituals in Autism" in Chapter 1.) Intervention to decrease ritualistic behaviors must take into account the reason for the behavior, which varies from child to child. The goals are to carefully monitor a child's ritualistic behavior patterns, increase the child's level of understanding and comfort, and teach replacement social and communication skills.

Table 5.11 summarizes intervention for ritualistic play and communication. The three main steps for intervention are 1) assess the ritual's function, 2) respond to the ritual according to its function, and 3) employ different ways to engage a child who has ritualistic patterns. The ensuing sections explore these three steps further.

Why Is the Child Engaged in the Ritual?

The first step is to assess why a child is engaged in ritualistic behavior. Determining the meaning of the ritual for the child (i.e., the function of the behavior) requires inquiry into the ritual's antecedent as well as careful observation of other accompanying behaviors and the child's emotional state.

First, observe the child's behavior to determine why the child started the ritual. What happened before the ritual began? Common antecedents are an uncomfortable sensory experience, something or someone of intense interest, an unexpected change, a disorganized environment, a difficult task, a social intrusion, or contact initiated with others. It is important to separate rituals that are solitary in nature from rituals that reflect a child's atypical attempt to interact.

Second, examine what else the child is doing while engaged in the ritual. Behaviors that accompany the ritual provide additional insight into the reason for the behavior. They can include ignoring all other people and events, looking at others for a reaction, persisting with the ritual until acknowledged, or engaging in another appropriate activity while performing the ritual. It is important to separate rituals that appear nonproductive from those that may be used by the child to self-regulate or interact with others. This is partic-

Table 5.11.   Intervention for ritualistic play and communication

Assess the function of the ritual.
Why is the ritual occurring (i.e., possible causes)?
What happened before the ritual began?
What other behaviors accompany the ritual?
What is the child's emotional state?
Develop an intervention plan according to the function of the ritual.
Shape the ritual into a replacement skill.
Teach an alternative play or communcation skill.
Organize the physical environment to decrease confusion.
Modify the environment to increase the child's comfort.
Provide social supports.
Engage a child who has ritualistic patterns by modifying the interaction.
Use nonverbal redirection.
Use gentle interaction.
Present a motivating distraction.
Offer a comforting activity.
Create a predictable, patterned response.
Establish rules about when the ritual can occur, if feasible.

ularly relevant when assessing the function of verbal rituals, such as some forms of delayed echolalia, perseverative questions, and ritualized conversations. See Rydell and Prizant (1995) for a detailed assessment of the function of verbal rituals.

The third and most important step for assessing the function of a ritual is to observe the child's affect while he is engaged in the play or verbal ritual. As rituals are often observed as a response to an emotionally arousing situation, the child's emotional expression will help determine if the ritual is triggered by enjoyment/excitement, discomfort, or confusion. Other ritualistic behaviors may not be an expression of emotion but, rather, a learned pattern or an indication that a child lacks a specific skill. Finally, ritualistic behaviors can be a manifestation of a neurological disorder and can occur without clear environmental antecedents. Brief sketches of seven children illustrate each of these possibilities:

- **Excitement:** Earl likes to spin things. Whenever he finds something round and shiny, he spins it. While he is spinning an object, Earl ignores everyone around him and laughs aloud.

- **Discomfort:** Michael twirls ribbons. His twirling behavior is more likely to occur when his classroom is noisy. Although he often tries to perform this ritual in a hiding place, Michael looks at adults when he twirls to convey to them his discomfort.

- **Confusion:** Lena recites segments of storybooks to herself. Her verbal ritual occurs whenever there is an unexpected change during activities. She ignores others and re-organizes the items on her desk while reciting.

- **Lack of skills:** Sally is motivated to interact with peers. However, she initiates inter-action by perseverating on the same question: "What color is your house?" Sally becomes agitated when her peers do not answer and persists in asking the question louder and faster.

- **Learned play pattern:** Rose learns a play activity and then insists that the toys and materials be used in the exact same way each time. She is happy and interactive when she can anticipate the sequence and engage in the ritual with others.

- **Learned conversation:** Louis enjoys maps and interacts with others by asking "Where do you live?" and then describing the roads in that town. Louis associates a particular person with a specific address and becomes agitated if someone has moved. He insists that the conversation follow the same sequence of exchanges.

- **Medical:** No clear environmental antecedents have been identified for Henry's habit of tapping his chest, which is cyclic in nature. The behavior will occur for a few weeks every few months. His tapping is accompanied by a decreased ability to attend to fa-miliar activities. Henry's parents indicate that his sleep patterns, eating patterns, and level of agitation change during these cycles as well.

Intervention for Ritualistic Play Behaviors

The intervention plan to modify ritualistic play behaviors should reflect the function of the behavior for the child. Ritualistic play can be immediately redirected, shaped, or re-placed. Ritualistic play can also be ignored while changes are made in the physical or so-cial setting. Once the setting is organized, the child can then be redirected. If the behav-ior is pleasurable for the child, shape the ritual into other appropriate play skills that provide similar sensory stimulation. When the ritual is an expression of discomfort or fear, redirect the child to an alternative comfort toy, modify the environment, and limit verbal interaction. If the ritual results from confusion, provide organizational supports to increase understanding and limit verbal interaction. For a ritual that is an expression of anxiety, redirect the child to a calm setting or activity and limit verbal interaction. When the ritual reflects limited skills, teach a variety of alternative play skills. When the ritual appears cyclic in nature, redirect the child to a calm setting or activity and monitor the patterns over time.

Intervention for Ritualistic Verbal Behaviors

Responses to verbal rituals are also determined by the function of the behavior. Some verbal rituals serve an interactive communicative function, some are used to regulate one's own actions, and others are noninteractive emotional responses. If the verbal rituals are noninteractive, use nonverbal redirection to another activity or setting that is calming, more organized, and familiar. Organizational supports can be used to clarify expectations, decrease confusion, and lessen the intensity of noninteractive verbal rituals. When verbal rituals are the child's way of talking himself or herself through a meaningful activity, it is important to allow the child to use the ritual. All children talk themselves through various activities. Self-regulatory verbal rituals typically fade away naturally as the child masters the activity. When the child engages in verbal rituals to interact with others, respond by acknowledging the child's intent and prompt him to use an alternative message to achieve the same result. Prompts can be made verbally or through an AAC device. It is important to respond to the inferred function of the verbal ritual, not the exact meaning of the verbal message. The child may or may not understand the meaning of the verbal message. Focus on teaching the child more effective ways to communicate in these contexts.

Strategies to Engage a Child Who Is Ritualistic

Once one understands the cause of a child's rituals, additional steps can be taken to actively engage the child. Most of the organizational, social, visual, and AAC supports that have been discussed in this chapter will decrease the frequency and intensity of ritualistic behaviors. The following list provides some additional guidelines for interacting with a child who is engaged in play or verbal rituals:

- Acknowledge the child's intent, verbally or nonverbally.
- Use nonverbal redirection (silence is key).
- Be gentle; simplify and slow down the pace of interaction.
- Present another highly motivating activity to distract or calm the child.
- Create a predictable, patterned response to draw the child's attention away from his ritual and/or prepare the child for the interruption (e.g., silently count to 5 by holding up one finger at a time, then redirect the child).
- Imitate the ritual, create joint attention, then redirect or expand the interaction into more appropriate play or communication (see the discussion on scaffolding in this chapter's section "Social Supports").
- Establish a turn-taking interaction involving the ritual and then expand it into more appropriate play or communicative interaction (see the discussion on activity routines in this chapter's section "Social Supports").
- For a play ritual, remove the object and indicate "First _____, then (the desired object)" using verbal, visual, and/or gestural prompts for appropriate play.
- If a verbal ritual is noninteractive, establish a rule for when and where the ritual can occur (e.g., a visual cue that indicates the time and place for a child to talk about the ritualized topic).
- Establish logical rules for why the ritual must stop (e.g., if a child is perseverating on turning the couch cushions around, show him the fabric tag and state the rule, "The cushion tag goes in the back").
- Establish a precise rule for why a ritual must stop (e.g., if the child is perseverating on a question, establish the rule "Ask one time"); this may not be effective when the ritual is an expression of discomfort, confusion, or anxiety.
- Model and reinforce alternative play or communicative behavior. Focus on teaching replacement skills.
- Be selective about responding to some rituals and ignoring others.

The next two vignettes show how certain steps can be taken to intervene for ritualistic behavior:

Six-year-old Jenny lines up books and audiotapes in a certain order and protests whenever someone touches them. To interrupt this pattern and to promote an expanded interaction with Jenny, her teacher uses counting to prepare Jenny for the interruption. The teacher then takes one of the book tapes. She immediately prompts Jenny to gesture "It's mine" and rewards Jenny by handing back the tape. Intermittently, Jenny's teacher takes a tape, prompts the desired communication, and returns the tape. Jenny's screaming has been replaced with her gesturing and saying "It's mine." At this point, the solitary ritual has been replaced with an interaction that can be further expanded through the use of joint activity routines.

Five-year-old Connor was lining up Lego blocks in a ritualistic manner. His mother introduced a new activity without removing the Legos. She sat next to Connor and began to play with a marble run. No directions were given to Connor. His mother simply handed Connor a marble, which he put on the run before returning to his Legos. Gradually, Connor and his mother took turns putting the marble down the run. His mother commented about the game and slowly moved the activity away from the Lego blocks. A joint activity routine was created, and the Lego ritual terminated.

A Word of Caution

Rituals reflect a child's emotional state. Some rituals are an emotional response to external events, but many rituals reflect internal states that are independent of environmental factors. As indicated in Chapter 1, a growing body of medical research links autism spectrum disorders with anxiety disorders, obsessive-compulsive disorders, movement disorders, and other neurological impairments. Intervention to decrease ritualistic behaviors must include careful monitoring of treatment effects. Efforts to redirect, replace, or stop rituals can at times worsen the problem, as shown in the following examples:

Four-year-old Oliver suddenly began a ritual of tapping objects three times before picking them up. When Oliver was redirected, the ritual escalated into aggression. Careful assessment revealed that Oliver's father started a new job and was not home every night. Oliver was anxious about the change. When Oliver was given a photographic schedule and other visual cues to indicate when he would see his father, he gradually stopped the ritual.

Six-year-old John engages in a high frequency of noninteractive talk about Sesame Street. A program was designed to give John different times during the day when he can talk with an adult of his choice about Sesame Street—as long as he refrains from this talk at other times. John understands these expectations and tries hard to withhold his verbal rituals. His efforts to stop himself have resulted in crying and pushing his mouth closed, leading to self-injurious behavior of his mouth. The program has been discontinued and medical intervention sought to resolve the problem.

As the second vignette indicates, intervention plans often require ongoing discussion with the child's physician and help ensure that educational and medical services are integrated. The treatment of ritualistic behaviors must come from a sympathetic point of view that recognizes the complexity of the disorder.

CHILD VARIABLES TO CONSIDER FOR INTERVENTION

Autism spectrum disorders represent a heterogeneous syndrome. It is unlikely that one method will succeed equally with all children. Strategies will vary within different social contexts as well as from child to child. Therefore, it is necessary to consider the specific characteristics of an individual child when planning social and communication skills intervention. It is also important to recognize that a child's abilities and comfort level will vary in different social contexts. In each social context, individual child variables that need to be considered are

- Social motivation
- Level of comfort
- Joint attention skills
- Imitation skills
- Organizational skills
- Challenging behaviors

Social Motivation

Motivation can be defined as an inner desire to explore and learn or a desire to maintain a positive feeling of mastery. Readers of this book, for example, are motivated by a desire to improve the quality of their relationships with children with autism. If the information in this book brings them greater success with children who have autism, the readers will be motivated to read more as a result of their feelings of mastery.

This same principle applies to social motivation. *Social motivation* can be defined as an inner desire to interact with another person, as well as an understanding of social interaction. Social motivation is influenced by social understanding and the emotions associated with the social experience. It is the by-product of meaningful experiences and positive socioemotional interactions.

To understand what factors may contribute to an individual child's level of motivation, information obtained from the Inventory of Social and Communication Behavior section of the Assessment of Social and Communication Skills for Children with Autism (Chapter 3) can be helpful. For each child, examine the following:

- Motivators: the child's interests and preferred activities
- Exploratory behavior: the child's activity level
- Communication behavior: the influence of others' interaction styles on the child's quality of engagement
- Social behavior: the qualities of those interactive partners to whom the child best responds

A child's social motivation can be increased by involving the child in activities that are particularly meaningful to him and appeal to his social understanding and emotional state.

Motivating Activities

Motivation is intimately linked to understanding a particular social context or activity. Therefore, social interactions are more likely to occur in the context of purposeful and meaningful activities. When the child understands what to DO in any situation, it increases the likelihood that he will interact with others. The assessment tool's Inventory of Social and Communication Behavior includes information about motivating activities. Look at the list of activities in which the child is most successful and ask the following questions:

- Are there opportunities for social-communicative interaction within the child's preferred activities?
- Are the child's preferred activities open- or closed-ended?

- Does the structure of the activity influence the child's social participation?
- Does movement foster more interaction or create more disorganization?

Next, use motivating activities as opportunities to build social and communication skills. Be sure to

- Engage in activities that are calming and comfortable for the child.
- Include the child's interests.
- Employ the child's preferred activities.
- Utilize activities that are fun and age-appropriate.
- Use meaningful solitary play activities that can serve as contexts for social interaction (not self-stimulatory play).
- Use social activities that the child has mastered with adults and that can be done with peers.
- Pair new activities with preferred objects or people to enhance motivation.
- Pair new activities with calming objects to enhance social motivation.

Social Understanding

Social motivation is naturally linked to an understanding of the social interaction. This seems obvious, but it is often overlooked. Misunderstanding the intentions and behaviors of others is central to the social struggles in children with autism. Social motivation can be influenced by the type of activity, the size of the group, and the complexity of the social interaction. Social motivation and participation occur when the social environment is meaningful and pleasurable for both the child and others. Using the information from the assessment tool's Inventory of Social and Communication Behavior, list the adults and peers with whom the child is most interactive and consider the following questions when designing the intervention plan:

- In what situations is the child most interactive with adults?
- What are the stylistic characteristics of adults who successfully interact with the child?
- In what situations is the child most interactive with peers?
- What are the stylistic characteristics of peers who successfully interact with the child?

Use this information to adopt the settings, activities, and interactive styles that "work" for the child. The intervention plan can include the type of activities in which the child is most successful as opportunities for building social and communication skills, as well as the stylistic patterns of the adults and peers with whom the child is most interactive.

Emotional State

Third, and most important, motivation is linked with emotional states. The child's social interactions at any moment in time are influenced by his desire to gain pleasure or avoid confusion. Using material gathered from the assessment tool's Inventory of Social and Communication Behavior, take the following steps when forming the child's intervention plan:

- Use motivating activities as opportunities for social interaction.
- Determine whether socioemotional interaction improves during active or passive activities.
- Ascertain the influence of affect on the child's socioemotional interactions (i.e., Does interaction improve when others use exaggerated emotions or when they express emotions calmly and gently?).
- Use the emotional qualities of those adults and peers who interact most successfully with the child.

Comfort

Children with autism vary significantly in their ability to stay calm and organized in various settings. As indicated in previous chapters, both sensory sensitivities and anxiety play critical roles in the life of most children with autism. These issues manifest themselves in the degree to which a child is active, passive, anxious, and/or ritualized at any moment in time. Both activity level and the degree of ritualized behaviors may be an expression of comfort level. These essential factors should be considered when designing intervention. To discern what factors may contribute to a particular child's level of comfort, review the Inventory of Social and Communication Behavior section of Chapter 3's assessment tool. Then, as with the social motivation domain, examine the following areas:

- Motivators: the child's interests and preferred activities
- Exploratory behavior: what the child seeks and avoids
- When the child engages in ritualized behaviors
- What the child does to calm himself or herself
- Communication behavior: the influence of others' interaction styles on the child's quality of engagement
- Social behavior: the qualities of those interactive partners to whom the child best responds
- When the child engages in ritualized social interactions

This material can be used to determine how a child's interests, activities, and style of social-communicative interaction influence his level of comfort, level of activity, and ritualized behavior. Intervention must take into account the settings, activities, and interactive partners that offer positive social experiences for the child. The characteristics of these positive aspects need to be duplicated across as many social contexts as possible to enhance comfort and, thus, to facilitate social-communicative competence.

The characteristics of the setting that may contribute to level of comfort include social dynamic (i.e., size and make-up of the group), physical environment (i.e., organized or open-ended), and activity (i.e., active or quiet; predictable or creative). The characteristics of the interactive partners that may contribute to a child's level of comfort include style (i.e., simple or complex language use; animated or calm; use of prompts and cues) and timing (i.e., slow paced or quick).

In the absence of comfort, children with autism are more likely to engage in challenging behaviors. Social contexts in which they are unable to focus or participate generally result from their feeling either confused by the activity or by the social expectations. Again, ritualistic behaviors that interfere with social interactions generally reflect:

- Not understanding the activity or what to do
- Not understanding the social situation or what to do or say
- Feeling uncomfortable
- Seeking a means to calm oneself

It is useful to view activity level and ritualistic behaviors as the child's expression of discomfort and/or disorganization. Strategies to assist the child with focus, organization, and comfort are needed at this time, including organizational supports, social supports, and visually cued instruction.

Core Skills: Joint Attention and Imitation

All retrospective studies of intervention for children with autism highlight the importance of two basic core skills as measures of long-term success: the ability to engage in joint attention and the ability to imitate others (Dawson & Osterling, 1997; Greenspan & Wieder, 1998; Lovaas, 1987). The ability to coordinate eye gaze and other nonverbal means of communication between people and objects and the ability to coordinate a sequence of motor and/or verbal acts to imitate others in natural contexts are essential to social and communication development. An understanding of these core skills is critical to successful intervention. The degree to which these core skills are present or absent largely determines the approach to social and communication enhancement for children with autism.

Figure 5.2 presents the continuum of strategy options as reflective of core skill abilities. As indicated in the figure, if joint attention and imitation are absent, intervention must include more highly structured activities, more organization of the physical environment, more adult-directed activities, and more systematic use of physical, gestural, and visual prompts. If joint attention and imitation skills are present, intervention can include less structured activities, more child-directed activities, and greater use of modeling. For most children, these core skills will vary across settings. Therefore, the presence or absence of these core skills in different settings and with different social partners will influence the degree to which structure, organizers, adult direction, and instructional supports will be provided to the child at any point in time.

If a child does not demonstrate shared attention in a particular activity, instructional supports are needed. These include, but are not limited to, organizational supports, social supports, and visually cued instruction. If a child does not have motor imitation in a particular activity, instructional modifications are needed. These include, but are not limited to, increased use of physical prompting, organizational supports, and visual cues. If a child does not have verbal imitation in a particular activity, AAC supports are generally needed. See Chapter 6 for more detail.

Organizational Skills

The organized child is calm, sustains attention to solitary activities, attends to others, initiates communication, and makes changes. Information about a child's level of organizational skills can be obtained from the Assessment of Social and Communication Skills for Children with Autism. Again, it is important to recognize that the presence or absence of organizational skills varies from setting to setting and from person to person. The continuum of intervention options is largely determined by the child's level of organization at the moment.

Core skills are so critical to social and communication success that an entire chapter has been devoted to intervention for these issues. Chapter 6 provides detailed descriptions of activities and strategies to build social attention, joint attention, motor imitation, verbal imitation, and organization.

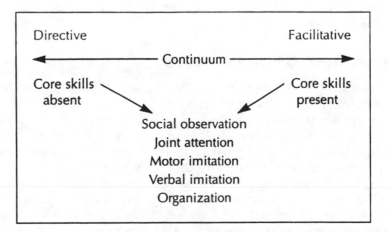

Figure 5.2. Influence of core skills on adult interaction style.

Challenging Behaviors

The challenging behaviors of children with autism are complex and can create a great degree of frustration and confusion for professionals and families. Challenging behaviors often reflect the level of a child's social and communication impairment. Although some challenging behaviors occur for other reasons (e.g., medical), the majority of behaviors reflect

- Social misunderstanding
- Communication frustrations
- Discomfort in the physical environment
- Anxiety
- Intense preoccupations or interests

In turn, most challenging behaviors indicate that the child

- Does not understand what is expected
- Does not understand what to do
- Understands what to do, but there is no meaning in it for him
- Does not understand the social situation
- Does not know what to say
- Understands what to say, but there is no meaning in it for him
- Finds the situation is uncomfortable
- Feels anxious or overwhelmed
- Feels "driven to distraction"

It is not the intent of this book to address intervention for challenging behaviors directly. (For specific information about managing challenging behaviors in a manner that is not aversive, there are numerous excellent resources. See Durand, 1990; LaVigna & Donnellan, 1986; Reichle & Wacker, 1993; and Schopler & Mesibov, 1994.) It is assumed that most challenging behaviors are the child's means of social-communicative interaction or a means to create order and comfort amid social chaos and disorganization. Given this assumption, all intervention strategies that focus on the development of specific social and communication skills should produce positive changes in other behaviors. As noted previously, the acquisition of social and communication skills will replace many challenging behaviors. Intervention that supports the development of social skills and communication skills will have a positive influence on the child's self-control and emotional well-being.

THE EMOTIONAL NEEDS OF THE CHILD

Although it is very tempting to outline a course of strategies for the teaching of social and communication skills to children with autism, it is unreasonable to assume that the path of intervention will be straight or easy. The development of socialization and communication is ultimately driven by meeting the child's emotional needs. Socialization and communication are the products of relationships. This chapter concludes with some perspectives on the emotional life of children with autism.

The basic emotional needs of all children include forming attachments and experiencing consistency, affection, respect, empathy, comfort, compromise, safety, success, and joy. A child's emotional well-being must always be considered during intervention. In order to meet the emotional needs of children with autism, it is essential to understand their uniqueness. This is not an easy task. It is often difficult to interpret their emotional signals. Unlike typically developing children, there is sometimes a mismatch between their behaviors and feelings. For example, a child may repeatedly ask a question that appears merely to be a perseverative inquiry. Nonetheless, the accompanying behavior actually indicates that the child is feeling an intense amount of anxiety and is unable to communicate his feelings in another way. Only through careful observation and sensitive listening can a child's emotional needs be understood over time. (Greenspan, 1995, is an excellent resource for more detailed information on this topic.) Specific areas important for a child's emotional well-being are discussed next.

- **Attachments:** Children with autism are often asked to work and play with many different adults in many different settings. This usually exceeds what is expected of a typically developing child. The number of people and settings in the child's life, as well as the impact this has on the child's level of comfort, need to be examined. Relationships take time.

- **Consistency:** Consistency is a core element of healthy emotional development in all young children. Children with autism seek greater consistency in their physical world to compensate for social confusion. Clarity and organization help provide consistency.

- **Affection:** There are many ways of communicating affection to a child. It can be expressed through touch, a song, or a smile. Children with autism sometimes respond to affection in unusual ways. A child who seeks a hug one minute may pull away from one in the next minute. It is important to note the types of social feedback the child enjoys. A match between the child's personal preferences and the way in which affection is expressed will enhance his social relationships.

- **Respect:** Respect can be expressed through careful observation, astute listening, and flexibility. Acknowledge all of a child's efforts, even those that lack "appropriateness." Respect the child by offering choices whenever possible. Respect that some social situations are very difficult for the child by providing modifications. Balance the day's activities between those that build self-esteem and those that are difficult. Realize that more intervention is not always better on a particular day.

- **Empathy:** Empathy is expressed by focusing on a child's strengths, establishing realistic expectations, and understanding the source of his confusion and discomfort. Empathy is expressed by including emotional needs in the functional analysis of behavior and by teaching peers to be sensitive to the child. In addition, empathy is expressed by accepting that children do the best they can at the moment.

- **Comfort:** Children learn in situations where they are comfortable. Intervention that diminishes the chaos will comfort children with autism. They are further comforted when their feelings are acknowledged and labeled. In addition, providing the children with a private place to relax supports and comforts them.

- **Compromise:** Imagine the life of a child with autism for one minute. Imagine the perceived confusion, the overwhelming fear. Imagine not understanding the perspective of adults who control the day's activities. Imagine not understanding how to ask them to stop. Imagine it for just for a moment. It is essential to learn how much to push, when to balance the needs of the child with the needs of others, and when to compromise expectations. Compromise is possible when intervention is approached from a sympathetic point of view.

- **Safety:** Safety gives a child the guarantee "I will not let you hurt yourself or others" and "I will only use physical prompting if necessary." It also provides reasonable rules and boundaries.

- **Success:** Feelings of mastery contribute to emotional well-being. It is important to balance the day between pleasurable, mastered activities and challenging situations. All small successes and efforts need to be acknowledged and praised. There are a thousand ways to praise a child. It is important to avoid the habit of empty praise; instead, use praise that is genuine and natural. Social success is also defined by social acceptance. Teach peers altruistic behaviors. Find opportunities for the child to give and be thanked by others. Encourage relationships with peers that are mutually satisfying.

- **Joy:** What makes a particular child with autism happiest? Allow him moments of joy that are independent of social "appropriateness" every day. Communication, social, and emotional development will then continue.

SUMMARY

This chapter attempts to provide a comprehensive, although not complete, guide to building social and communication skills in children with autism. It is clear that autism is not a singular disorder for which there is not a singular solution. It is obvious that social and communication intervention for children with autism is a formidable task. This book's remaining chapters provide detailed activities and suggestions for working with a child on specific goals and objectives. Although this material is organized into isolated skills, it is necessary to address multiple skills across multiple contexts in a flexible way. This will increase the quality of social and communication skills in children with autism. In sum, remember the following regarding intervention for children with autism:

1. *Every moment is a teaching opportunity* for building social and communication skills.

2. *Developmental* principles are absolutely necessary to build successful interactions, *and* the precision provided by *behavioral* approaches is absolutely necessary to build successful interactions.

3. Select a method, but *be flexible with your approach.*

4. If you think a method is working, define what "working" means. For example, in the case of social and communication development, a program is working when the child is *spontaneous* across familiar and novel situations.

5. Strategies that worked in the past do not necessarily need to be used in the present; constantly reevaluate *why* a specific procedure is being used.

6. Develop an acute *sensitivity* regarding the effect others' behaviors have on a child's social and communication efforts.

7. *Acknowledge* each social and communication attempt a child makes.

8. Make social activities *fun and meaningful.*

9. *A positive emotional experience* is the ultimate motivator for social and communication success.

Appendix A
Graphic Displays

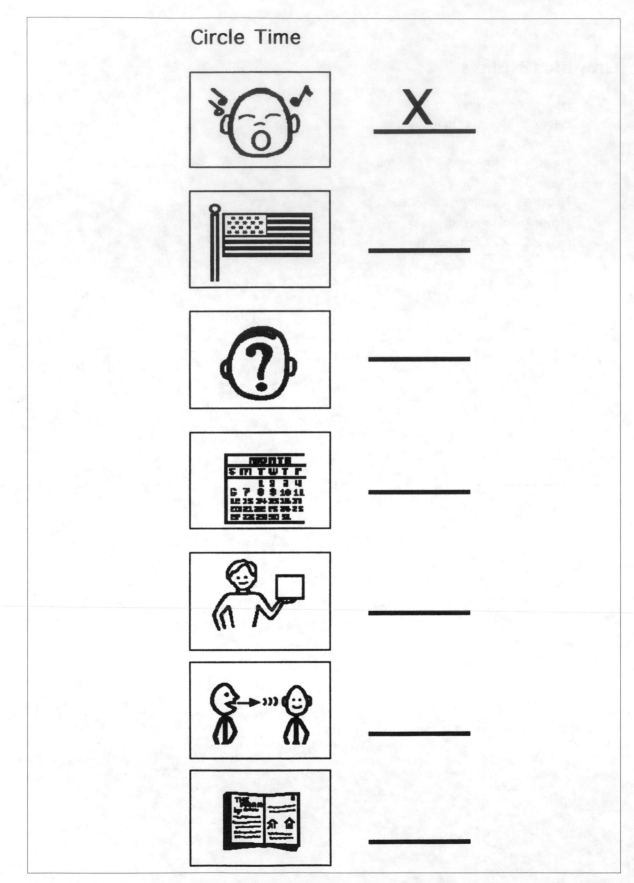

Figure 1. Sample activity schedule. This schedule helps clarify what will happen during group time. Review it with the child before the activity begins. The child can check off each step of the activity when complete. (The Picture Communication Symbols ©1981–2000 Mayer-Johnson Co. are used with permission.)

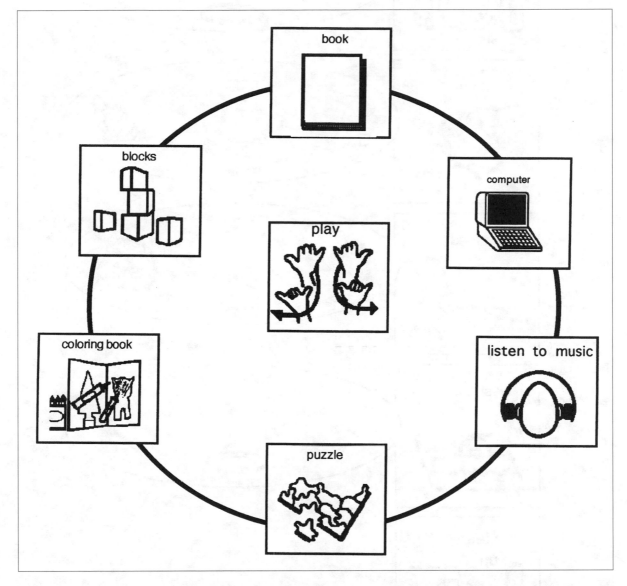

Figure 2. Sample solitary play choice board. This visual display organizes free play choices. When making the display, place choices in a circle to encourage flexible choice making. When choices are displayed in a linear format, a child may make choices from left to right or top to bottom. (The Picture Communication Symbols ©1981–2000 Mayer-Johnson Co. are used with permission.)

Figure 3. Sample play script. This visual display represents the general play sequence and the choices within each step. The sequence of steps is linear, whereas the choices within each step are presented in a circular format. This allows for organization, choice, and flexibility. (The Picture Communication Symbols ©1981–2000 Mayer-Johnson Co. are used with permission.)

My hair is getting long. _____ cuts my hair. She uses lots of tools.

She has scissors, a comb, a brush, and a hair dryer.

First, _____ helps me sit in the chair. I need to sit still.

Next, she cuts my hair and sings to me. I can sing too.

Next, she dries my hair with the hair dryer. The hair dryer is loud.

If it's too loud, I can take a deep breath and count to ten.

When I am done, my mom will take me for ice cream.

Figure 4. Sample story about a community event. This story is read to the child before, during, and after the activity to prepare for and review the experience. (The Picture Communication Symbols ©1981–2000 Mayer-Johnson Co. are used with permission.)

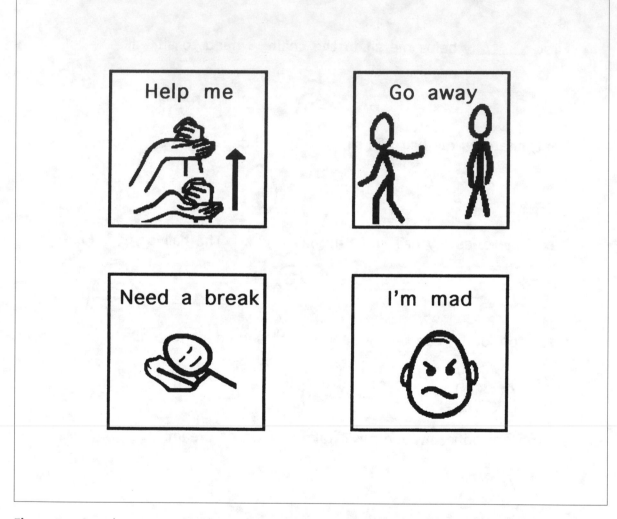

Figure 5. Sample communication cue cards. These cue cards encourage communication in stressful situations. The cards should be available at all times. (The Picture Communication Symbols ©1981–2000 Mayer-Johnson Co. are used with permission.)

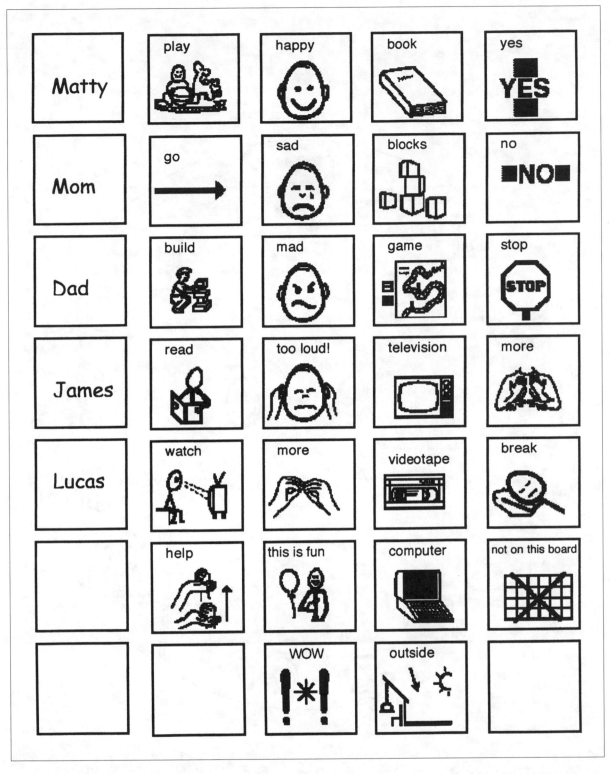

Figure 6. Sample communication board. (The Picture Communication Symbols ©1981–2000 Mayer-Johnson Co. are used with permission.)

Figure 7. Sample page from a conversation book. This display enhances a child's ability to talk about school events at home. (The Picture Communication Symbols ©1981–2000 Mayer-Johnson Co. are used with permission.)

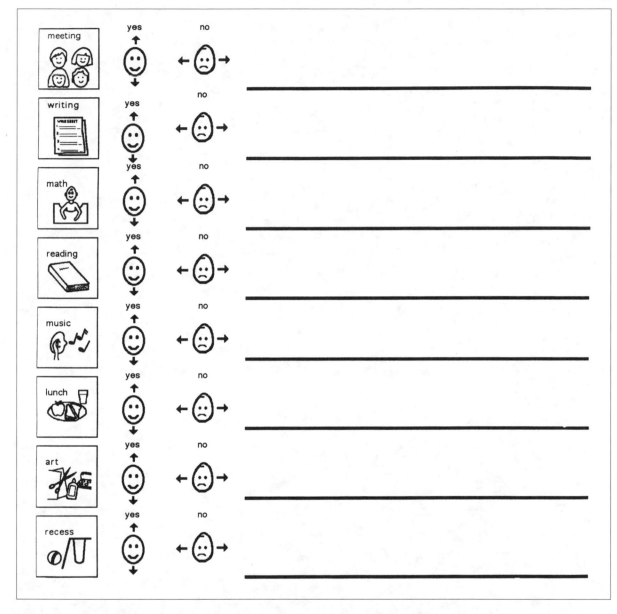

Figure 8. Sample page from a conversation book. This is a worksheet for a child with higher language abilities to enhance the child's ability to talk about school events at home. The child indicates whether he completed the activity and writes a brief statement about it. (The Picture Communication Symbols ©1981–2000 Mayer-Johnson Co. are used with permission.)

chapter 6

Core Skills Curriculum

Julie Ann Fiore

Core skill development is fundamental for the emergence of all social and communication skills. Without nonverbal interaction, imitation, and organizational skills, children lack the ability to observe, understand, and functionally utilize social information. Children first acquire nonverbal means of interaction, such as gestures and eye gaze. Success eventually leads to an emergent understanding and use of language as a tool for social interaction. Verbal as well as nonverbal communicators need to be firmly grounded in all core skill areas. Core skills foster social awareness, which is key to higher interactive skills such as conversation, social play, and participation in community outings. To be available for the complex task of social interaction, children need to feel organized and motivated.

This chapter focuses on intervention to enhance three primary core skill areas: **nonverbal social interaction, imitation,** and **organization.** It contains a set of activity sheets that correspond to each item in the Core Skills Checklist of the Assessment of Social and Communication Skills for Children with Autism. The activity sheets provide suggested activities and intervention strategies to enhance these core skills. Natural settings are the primary focus of intervention. The skills should be taught and reinforced across all activities and environments. The suggested interventions focus on structured social games as the primary means to achieve nonverbal interaction and imitation skills and structured physical environments as the primary means to achieve organizational skills. The adult's role is to organize the physical environment, respect the child's motivation, and continually expand new social behaviors in a way that engages the child. It is important to observe and understand the child before deciding on a strategy or style of interaction. Always remember that beyond the markers of autism, the child will only become socially engaged if he finds the physical environment meaningful and the interaction enjoyable.

TARGETING CORE SKILL OBJECTIVES

In determining core skill objectives, refer to the Core Skills Checklist in the assessment tool as well as the list of priority objectives that have been established for the child on the Assessment Summary Sheet. Target objectives should reflect skills that were

- Not observed or never demonstrated by the child
- Only observed when prompted
- Only demonstrated in specific contexts
- Only demonstrated with adults

The activity sheets are not presented as a linear hierarchy of skill acquisition. A child can simultaneously work to build nonverbal social interaction, imitation, and organizational skills.

Once child-specific objectives have been selected, refer to the corresponding activity sheets in this chapter for intervention strategies and interactive games. They are suggestions to encourage skill mastery and are not intended to be practiced in isolation. The child, not the arbitrary boundaries of a specific activity, should shape the interaction. Respect the child's preference, motivation, and interest when planning which strategies to adopt.

USING THE ACTIVITY SHEETS

The format of each activity sheet is organized similarly. The general goal area (e.g., Nonverbal Social Interaction) tops the activity sheet, followed by the general objective (e.g., Social Attention) and the specific skill (e.g., Stops an activity/looks at person in response to name), which correspond to the items in the assessment tool. The specific skill can be written as a criterion-based objective (samples are given in Table 6.1). Lists of strategies appear on all activity sheets. These suggestions can serve as a springboard to develop other ideas of interest to a particular child. Vignettes describing nonverbal interaction and imitation strategies are provided for further clarification.

The nonverbal social interaction activity sheets describe sample strategies and interactive games meant to generate ideas for encouraging the target objective. Most activities focus on creating fun and motivating exchanges between a child with autism and an adult play partner. They emphasize the need to tap into the child's interests and become a necessary and reinforcing component of his play. The activity sheets also list techniques to facilitate generalization to peers. The sheets conclude with a set of questions that help identify when a child may need additional compensatory supports (e.g., strategies).

There are two domains within the imitation section: motor imitation and verbal imitation. The sample strategies and activities outlined in the imitation activity sheets are based on a more comprehensive spectrum of behavioral and developmental strategies. Approaches to teaching imitation have long been split along developmental and behavioral lines. In theory, the two approaches are often in discordance, but in practice, blending the two elicits the better result. Table 6.2 describes the continuum of behavioral, behavioral/developmental, and developmental strategies used to build social/motor imitation skills. The table applies the different strategies to a sample art activity. Effective intervention does not rely on any one strategy but combines and moves among many. The child will indicate which strategy is necessary at any given point during an interaction. When teaching imitation, three choices present themselves:

- *Prompt:* Give a new action.
- *Shape:* Shape inappropriate behaviors into purposeful actions.
- *Scaffold:* Build on what the child presents.

Table 6.1. Sample criterion-based objectives

Nonverbal social interaction

Objective: The child gives a toy/object to share interests in 80% of the opportunities presented.

    During specific contexts with prompts

    During specific contexts without prompts

    During novel contexts with prompts

    During novel contexts without prompts

Imitation

Objective: The child imitates a single body action in 80% of the opportunities presented.

    During specific contexts with prompts

    During specific contexts without prompts

    During novel contexts with prompts

    During novel contexts without prompts

Organization

Objective: The child completes an activity by putting away the materials in 80% of the opportunities presented.

    During specific contexts with prompts

    During specific contexts without prompts

    During novel contexts with prompts

    During novel contexts without prompts

Objective: The child attends to an activity until it is completed in 80% of the opportunities presented.

    During specific contexts with prompts

    During specific contexts without prompts

    During novel contexts with prompts

    During novel contexts without prompts

The Activities portion of the imitation activity sheets outlines both adult–child and small group activities that draw on varying levels of prompting, shaping, and scaffolding. The Strategies section completes each activity sheet with reminders to follow the child's lead (if purposeful) and make all behavior and action meaningful.

There is one organization activity sheet each for each of the seven organization domains: space, choices, time, expectations, transitions, possessions, and comfort. The organization activity sheets outline a series of suggested strategies and compensatory supports. Each activity sheet lists the general objective (e.g., Organization of space) and the specific skills associated with the objective. This is followed by detailed strategies. The strategies should help the child understand *where* he is supposed to be, *what* the activity is or choices are, *how long* the activity will be, *when* he will be done, *what he is expected* to do or say, *whose* items are whose, and *how* to stay calm and focused. (See Chapter 5 for additional examples.)

MONITORING PROGRESS

Monitoring a child's progress with each target skill is useful in determining mastery. Progress reflects changes in the child's level of motivation, exploration, flexibility, engagement, and socioemotional comfort. Skill mastery is defined by

- Acquisition of the skill: the presence of the skill without prompts
- Generalization of the skill across adults, peers, and different social groupings
- Generalization of the skill across multiple familiar and novel contexts

Table 6.2. The behavioral/developmental continuum: Comparing approaches to build imitation in a coloring/drawing activity

Developmental 1: *Simultaneous imitation*—imitate simultaneous action following child's initiation

Give the child a crayon, and sit him before the easel. Wait to see what the child does. When he begins scribbling, imitate his strokes. Stop when the child stops coloring. Keep your activities in unison with the child's. Do not give direction or instruction to the child. Follow the child's lead throughout the activity. Any verbal input should be limited to commenting on the child's actions.

Developmental 2: *Turn-taking imitation*—imitate child's one/multiple action(s)

Give the child a crayon, and sit him before the easel. Wait to see what the child does. After he marks the paper, wait until he stops. Then, imitate his stroke. Continue to take turns scribbling on the paper with the child. Any verbal input should be limited to commenting on the child's actions, then your own.

Behavioral/Developmental 1: *Shaping*—shape child's initiations into purposeful action

Give the child a crayon, and sit him before the easel. Wait to see what the child does. As he scribbles on the paper, follow his lead, but shape his actions into more purposeful or desired strokes. If the child scribbles in a circular motion, interrupt his circular stroke after one rotation to form a circle. Label the shape formed (e.g., "It's a circle," "You made a circle"). Then, take turns forming circles. You can also use sound effects to shape scribbling into more purposeful drawing: Attach a reinforcing noise to the action and a "stop" sound effect to end the stroke. For example, roll your tongue as you make circular strokes; then make a braking noise when you end the stroke.

Behavioral/Developmental 2: *Scaffolding*—imitate child and scaffold into expanded actions

Give the child a crayon, and sit him before the easel. Wait to see what the child does. As he scribbles on the paper, follow his lead, but use modeling to extend the scribbles into strokes (or any drawing element being targeted for teaching). For example, if the child draws two vertical lines on the paper, imitate him. Then, model, drawing circular scribbles on top to form a tree. The difference between shaping and scaffolding is that scaffolding extends the action into another action, whereas shaping simply forms targeted actions from already existing ones.

Behavioral/Developmental 3: *Prompted simultaneous movement*—prompt child to move simultaneously during structured adult-directed activity

Seat the child before the easel, but do not give him a crayon. Gain the child's attention and model, drawing vertical strokes. Make it playful by using sound effects and/or an animated affect. Hand the child a crayon; then, prompt him to imitate the stroke. Continue prompting the child to draw vertical lines as you draw them at the same time.

Behavioral/Developmental 4: *Prompted turn-taking*—establish a turn-taking routine using toys, and prompt multiple repetitions of one or more actions during structured adult-directed activity

Seat the child before the easel, but do not give him a crayon. Gain the child's attention and model, drawing vertical strokes on the paper. Make it playful by using sound effects and/or an animated affect. Then, stop drawing, give the child the crayon, and prompt him to imitate the strokes. Continue to take turns.

Behavioral 1: *Prompted instruction*—use video instruction paired with prompting prior to an activity

Create a videotape detailing the steps necessary to draw targeted strokes. Go through each step with a simple verbal direction coupled with a corresponding action. If you are teaching the child to draw a tree, the instructional video should present the following: "First, pick up your crayon" while the person in the video models picking up the crayon. "Then, draw a line down" while the person in the video models drawing a line down. "Next, draw another line down" while the person in the video models drawing a second vertical line. "Finally, draw a circle on top" while the person in the video models drawing a circle above the two vertical lines. Show the child the video; then, prompt him through the targeted skill using the same instructional language.

Behavioral 2: *Discrete trial*—direct child to do multiple repetitions of an action in an artificial context

Sit across from the child at a table. Establish attending. Model, drawing a vertical stroke while presenting the verbal instruction "Do this." Prompt the child to imitate the stroke. Reinforce the child. Repeat trials until the child makes the vertical stroke upon direction.

The Assessment of Social and Communication Skills for Children with Autism can be used to monitor progress in the areas of nonverbal social interaction, imitation, and organization. Sample forms for monitoring verbal and motor imitation skills are provided in Appendix A. The two forms are designed to generate qualitative lists of verbal messages and motor actions that a child spontaneously imitates and check for the presence and consistency of those skills across adult and peer partners. Intermittent videotaping of the child is a complementary means of monitoring the acquisition of these core skills.

Activity

A. Nonverbal Social Interaction

Social Attention 1. Stops an activity/looks at person in response to name

Activities: Adult–Child

Call the child's name. Pick up the item with which he is engaged, place it in front of the child's face, then lead it to your face. The child should visually track the object and transfer his gaze to you.

Call the child's name. Take the child's hands and touch them to your face.

Call the child's name. Make a stimulating and/or reinforcing noise (e.g., finger snap, clap, drum fingers, whistle). When the child turns toward the noise, catch his gaze and reinforce his eye gaze.

Create a simple cause-and-effect game in which the child's name is called during a tabletop play activity (e.g., puzzle, pegboard). When the child looks up from the task, engage in reinforcing play (e.g., tickling). Redirect the child back to the play activity and intermittently interrupt. The play activity becomes just a backdrop for the real game—eliciting the eye gaze. Remember to praise the child for looking at you, and alter the reinforcement.

Play simple Peekaboo games. Call "Peekaboo, I see (child's name)." Prompt the child to look up and call "Peekaboo, I see (play partner's name)."

Engage in simple Hide-and-Seek games in which you call the child's name during seeking (i.e., "Where's [child's name]?").

Engage the child in anticipatory stop-and-go games. For example, set up a simple gross motor activity (e.g., marching in line, hopping away from you, crawling under obstacle). Call the child's name. Have the child stop the activity and look at you. Reinforce the child for stopping and looking, then redirect him back to the motor activity.

Generalization to Peers

1. Shadow the child with autism from behind, nonverbally moving him through the activity and supporting all communicative interactions toward a peer.
2. Teach peers how to interpret the child's behaviors and respond to the child's initiatives.
3. Coach the peers through interactions, modeling strategies that are successful between adults and the child.

Strategies

To help compensate for the inherent complexity and unpredictability of social interaction, organizational and/or social supports may be necessary.

*   When the child is not attending, ask yourself the following questions:
    1. Is the activity organized?
    2. Does the child understand the expectations of the activity?
    3. Does the language match the child's level of comprehension?
    4. Are there distractions in the environment?
    5. Is it a motivating activity?

*   When the child is difficult to engage, ask yourself the following questions:
    1. Is the child's communicative intent understood and reflected in the interaction?
    2. Do reciprocal social routines need to be established?
    3. Is there a balance between directive and facilitative interaction styles?
    4. Do interaction patterns need to be modified for the child?

DO-WATCH-LISTEN-SAY: Social and Communication Intervention for Children with Autism
by Kathleen Ann Quill © 2000 Paul H. Brookes Publishing Co.

Activity

A. Nonverbal Social Interaction

Social Attention 2. Looks at objects when directed

Activities: Adult–Child

Move your finger from the child's face to the object with the direction "Look."

Move your finger, and lead the child's point to the object by placing your hand over the child's. Use an animated tone to label the object.

Use a laser pointer or flashlight to direct attention to targeted objects.

Have the object make physical contact with the child in a way that is not invasive or disorienting. For example, fly a toy plane into the child's belly accompanied by reinforcing tickles or walk a spider puppet up the child's leg while singing "Itsy Bitsy Spider."

Place the targeted object in front of the child's face to gain attention, then lead the object back to its original location. Prompt the child to orient to it by labeling the object or attaching a reinforcing sound effect or noise to it.

Attach a silly and/or motivating noise to the targeted object. For example, if you want the child to look at a car, roll the car back and forth in front of the child while making car noises (e.g., *brrrmm*, screeching stop noises).

Play simple I Spy games. Lay out a number of motivating objects, and take turns pointing out what you see. For verbal children, say, "I spy (object name)." For nonverbal children, the play partner can say the "I spy" part, and the child can fill in the object by pointing or using a board with I, SPY, and pictographs of the objects. This can also be generalized to any environment with a number of objects to label.

Engage in Hide-and-Seek games using objects. Cue the child to find an item in a field of multiple objects with the prompt "Where's the (object name)?" The game can also be generalized to hiding single objects under boxes or cloth covers and having the child point to which one it is under.

Generalization to Peers

1. Shadow the child with autism from behind, nonverbally moving him through the activity and supporting all communicative interaction toward a peer.
2. Teach peers how to interpret the child's behaviors and respond to the child's initiatives.
3. Coach the peers through interactions, modeling strategies that are successful between adults and the child.

Strategies

To help compensate for the inherent complexity and unpredictability of social interaction, organizational and/or social supports may be necessary.

- When the child is not attending, ask yourself the following questions:
  1. Is the activity organized?
  2. Does the child understand the expectations of the activity?
  3. Does the language match the child's level of comprehension?
  4. Are there distractions in the environment?
  5. Is it a motivating activity?

- When the child is difficult to engage, ask yourself the following questions:
  1. Is the child's communicative intent understood and reflected in the interaction?
  2. Do reciprocal social routines need to be established?
  3. Is there a balance between directive and facilitative interaction styles?
  4. Do interaction patterns need to be modified for the child?

Activity

A. Nonverbal Social Interaction
Social Attention 3. Attends to one-to-one
familiar activity for _____ minutes

Activities: Adult–Child

Slowly increase the amount of materials for a given task. For example, start by building with 5 blocks, then increase to 10 blocks.

Use sequence boards to add to the number of steps within an activity, lengthening the overall time it takes to complete the activity.

Use time boards to extend the length of time the child is expected to attend.

Increase the number of turns during a turn-taking task. Make a game of it by letting the child pull a number out of a hat that will indicate the number of turns he needs to complete to be "all done" with the target activity.

Over time, once tasks have been mastered, increase the complexity of the target activity. For example, once a child has mastered two puzzles separately, give the child both puzzles to do at the same time with the pieces mixed together.

Manipulate the child's desire to be "all done" to increase attention to an activity. First, teach the child to request "all done" prior to terminating an activity. Initially reinforce each "all done" with immediate termination. Once the child understands the function of "all done," then only intermittently reinforce with immediate termination. For example, if the child is coloring a house and requests to be "all done," tell him, "First color the roof, then all done." If the child wants to end play with playdough, tell him, "Okay, 1 more minute, then playdough will be all done."

Experiment with the speed of a given activity. Sometimes racing through it quickly becomes a motivating game that the child will request to repeat immediately following the initial completion. For example, during circle time, sing a familiar song quickly to gain the child's attention, then repeat it slowly with the child's participation. The same can be done with building and crashing towers, assembling manipulatives, feeding baby dolls, and so forth.

Generalization to Peers

1. Shadow the child with autism from behind, nonverbally moving him through the activity and supporting all communicative interaction toward a peer.
2. Teach peers how to interpret the child's behaviors and respond to the child's initiatives.
3. Coach the peers through interactions, modeling strategies that are successful between adults and the child.

Strategies

To help compensate for the inherent complexity and unpredictability of social interaction, organizational and/or social supports may be necessary.

- When the child is not attending, ask yourself the following questions:
  1. Is the activity organized?
  2. Does the child understand the expectations of the activity?
  3. Does the language match the child's level of comprehension?
  4. Are there distractions in the environment?
  5. Is it a motivating activity?

- When the child is difficult to engage, ask yourself the following questions:
  1. Is the child's communicative intent understood and reflected in the interaction?
  2. Do reciprocal social routines need to be established?
  3. Is there a balance between directive and facilitative interaction styles?
  4. Do interaction patterns need to be modified for the child?

DO-WATCH-LISTEN-SAY: Social and Communication Intervention for Children with Autism
by Kathleen Ann Quill © 2000 Paul H. Brookes Publishing Co.

Activity

A. Nonverbal Social Interaction
Social Attention 4. Attends to one-to-one
novel activity for _____ minutes

Activities: Adult–Child

All of the strategies suggested for increasing attending skills during familiar activities can be applied to increasing attention during novel activities with modifications.

Teach the novel activity as an extension of a familiar, mastered task. For example, introduce playmobile people during block building, or read a familiar story such as *The Very Hungry Caterpillar* and then make a caterpillar and his food out of playdough.

Break up a novel activity with familiar, motivating activities. For example, seat the child at the table for a new task, such as stringing beads. After each bead, roll the car to him with a new bead. If rolling the car is a mastered and motivating activity, it will increase the child's interest in retrieving the next bead to string.

Use "First, Then" language to focus the child on completing the novel task so he can gain access to a more reinforcing activity.

Play with silly voices and verbal directions to prompt waiting, taking one more turn, looking, and staying seated. The animated affect, if motivating to the child, can help him attend to the novel activity.

Use the target activity as a means of gaining access to gross motor play. For example, if the target activity is to identify numbers, write them on large pieces of paper, place them on the floor, and direct the child to find a number. When the child hands it to you, spin him around, squish him in pillows, toss him in the air, or engage in some other motivating interaction. Over time, increase how many numbers the child needs to identify before getting reinforced.

Generalization to Peers

1. Shadow the child with autism from behind, nonverbally moving him through the activity and supporting all communicative interaction toward a peer.
2. Teach peers how to interpret the child's behaviors and respond to the child's initiatives.
3. Coach the peers through interactions, modeling strategies that are successful between adults and the child.

Strategies

To help compensate for the inherent complexity and unpredictability of social interaction, organizational and/or social supports may be necessary.

- When the child is not attending, ask yourself the following questions:
    1. Is the activity organized?
    2. Does the child understand the expectations of the activity?
    3. Does the language match the child's level of comprehension?
    4. Are there distractions in the environment?
    5. Is it a motivating activity?

- When the child is difficult to engage, ask yourself the following questions:
    1. Is the child's communicative intent understood and reflected in the interaction?
    2. Do reciprocal social routines need to be established?
    3. Is there a balance between directive and facilitative interaction styles?
    4. Do interaction patterns need to be modified for the child?

DO-WATCH-LISTEN-SAY: Social and Communication Intervention for Children with Autism
by Kathleen Ann Quill © 2000 Paul H. Brookes Publishing Co.

Vignettes

Social Attention Vignettes

Jillian

Jillian often engaged in solitary play with a number of preferred toys. During this play, she was frequently unresponsive to her mother's call. Her mother would try to get her attention before calling her name by interrupting Jillian's play or placing her hands over Jillian's toy. This frequently caused Jillian to become agitated and further withdraw from interaction by trying to covet the toys her mother was not holding. Subsequently, Jillian's mother tried to draw Jillian's attention by tapping Jillian's nose and then drawing Jillian's finger toward her face. This strategy worked when Jillian was seated at the table but not when she was playing on the floor or in other less structured settings. Jillian's teacher recommended that her mother try snapping when calling Jillian's name. Jillian was highly motivated by auditory input and found silly noises amusing. When her mother tried it, Jillian readily oriented to the noise. She reinforced Jillian for looking and, over time, faded the snapping.

Tyler

Often during play, Tyler would focus on the fibers in the rug rather than on the toys presented to him. His teacher tried prompting him to attend by telling him "Look," coupled with a finger point. Tyler's response was inconsistent, so his teacher began to play with the toy car herself, rolling it back and forth in front of Tyler while making animated car noises. Once he began to orient to the noise, Tyler's teacher rolled the car over his leg and stopped it in front of him. Tyler looked at the car, and the teacher drove it again. Each time he referenced the object, the teacher drove it up and over his leg in a highly motivating, playful manner.

Noah

Noah flitted from activity to activity during free play time. He would race through puzzles and other mastered activities quickly and without much attention to the task. To increase his time at the table, Noah's teacher first taught him to request "All done" prior to leaving the activity and then made him clean up. While cleaning up, Noah would inadvertently complete some activities, such as puzzles. His teacher then made the tasks more difficult by mixing up two puzzles or adding additional pegs to a pegboard. Finally, she added a 1-2-3-4-done time board to the activity. Noah would pull off a number every few minutes until the board was empty, thus indicating the activity's termination.

Sam

Although Sam attended nicely to familiar activities, he became anxious and flicked his fingers on the tabletop when a novel task was introduced. His teachers tried using a First/Then board to motivate him to try new activities. They used his favorite toy, the marble run, as a follow-up to completing a novel task. Even though Sam was adept at using First/Then boards during snack time and with two familiar activities, it did not help relieve his anxiety over the unfamiliar task. One of Sam's teachers decided to break down a novel activity, feeding a baby doll, into smaller pieces and bring it into his play with the marble run. First, she sat the baby near Sam. Once he became comfortable with its presence, the teacher intermittently used the baby to drop a marble down the run. Eventually, Sam's teacher modeled feeding the baby a marble and soon after substituted the baby's play food for the marble. Sam needed to become familiar with the new toy in a situation that was reinforcing and nonthreatening prior to engaging in play with the baby doll. Once the doll became familiar, Sam's teacher added new play actions as he was ready with minimal anxiety or resistance.

Activity

A. Nonverbal Social Interaction

Reciprocal Interaction 1. Uses eye gaze to maintain social interaction

Activities: Adult–Child

During gross motor play, intermittently stop the action. When the child orients to you, reengage in the play activity.

Set up simple turn-taking games in which you wait for the child to orient to you before you take your turn.

Interrupt the child's play by physically getting in his way or taking away a play object. Pretend not to notice the child but make a stimulating and/or reinforcing noise (e.g., finger snap, drum fingers, tongue cluck, whistle). When the child turns toward the noise, catch his gaze. Move out of the child's way or return the play item to reinforce the child for looking at you.

Create a simple cause-and-effect game in which the child receives a motivating response after he orients to you. When the child looks at you, engage in reinforcing play (e.g., tickles, high-five).

Play simple Peekaboo games. Call "Peekaboo, I see (child's name)." Prompt the child to look up and orient to you.

Engage in simple Hide-and-Seek games. When the child finds you, wait for him to orient to you before acknowledging that you have been found.

Generalization to Peers

1. Shadow the child with autism from behind, nonverbally moving him through the activity and supporting all communicative interaction toward a peer.
2. Teach peers how to interpret the child's behaviors and respond to the child's initiatives.
3. Coach the peers through interactions, modeling strategies that are successful between adults and the child.

Strategies

To help compensate for the inherent complexity and unpredictability of social interaction, organizational and/or social supports may be necessary.

- When the child is not attending, ask yourself the following questions:
    1. Is the activity organized?
    2. Does the child understand the expectations of the activity?
    3. Does the language match the child's level of comprehension?
    4. Are there distractions in the environment?
    5. Is it a motivating activity?

- When the child is difficult to engage, ask yourself the following questions:
    1. Is the child's communicative intent understood and reflected in the interaction?
    2. Do reciprocal social routines need to be established?
    3. Is there a balance between directive and facilitative interaction styles?
    4. Do interaction patterns need to be modified for the child?

DO-WATCH-LISTEN-SAY: Social and Communication Intervention for Children with Autism
by Kathleen Ann Quill © 2000 Paul H. Brookes Publishing Co.

Activity

A. Nonverbal Social Interaction

Reciprocal Interaction 2. Repeats own behavior to maintain interaction

Activities: Adult–Child

Set up simple cause-and-effect games in which the child has to perform a certain action to receive a desired response from the play partner. For example, the child raises his hands to be swung around.

Clap and/or cheer following a behavior you want the child to repeat. Remember to choose praise that the child finds reinforcing and amusing.

Pretend to go to sleep. Emphasize yawning and stretching before lying down next to the child. After he wakes you up wait for the child to imitate your yawn or stretch to request continuance of the game. Repeat the going to sleep sequence.

Play a modified version of Simon Says. Eliminate verbal directions and have the child's imitation be the prompt to continue the game.

Engage in a Peekaboo game in which the child pulls down a sheet covering your face or taps your hands to get you to "peekaboo."

Engage in simple Swat the Fly or Catch the Spider games. Walk your fingers toward the child, drumming your nails. Prompt the child to swat your hand before it reaches him. Pull away quickly as the child swats.

Modify simple tag games. Ignore the child until he tags you. Once tagged, chase and catch the child. Repeat the exchange.

Generalization to Peers

1. Shadow the child with autism from behind, nonverbally moving him through the activity and supporting all communicative interaction toward a peer.
2. Teach peers how to interpret the child's behaviors and respond to the child's initiatives.
3. Coach the peers through interactions, modeling strategies that are successful between adults and the child.

Strategies

To help compensate for the inherent complexity and unpredictability of social interaction, organizational and/or social supports may be necessary.

- When the child is not attending, ask yourself the following questions:
  1. Is the activity organized?
  2. Does the child understand the expectations of the activity?
  3. Does the language match the child's level of comprehension?
  4. Are there distractions in the environment?
  5. Is it a motivating activity?

- When the child is difficult to engage, ask yourself the following questions:
  1. Is the child's communicative intent understood and reflected in the interaction?
  2. Do reciprocal social routines need to be established?
  3. Is there a balance between directive and facilitative interaction styles?
  4. Do interaction patterns need to be modified for the child?

DO-WATCH-LISTEN-SAY: Social and Communication Intervention for Children with Autism
by Kathleen Ann Quill © 2000 Paul H. Brookes Publishing Co.

Activity

A. Nonverbal Social Interaction
Reciprocal Interaction 3. Repeats action with toy to maintain social game

Activities: Adult–Child

Design play activities in which the child needs to interact with a toy or hand over a play object to continue the game. For example, create obstacle courses with stopping points. At each stop, the child must perform a designated action with a toy to continue the course. You could also embed it in social play in the form of handing a ticket to get on a train or putting a block on a block tower to continue building.

Engage in play that is fundamentally reciprocal, such as tossing or kicking a ball back and forth.

Set up play in which receipt of a preferred object or toy is contingent on repeating a designated play action. For example, gather a pile of the child's favorite action figures. Model rolling the dump truck and placing one action figure in the truck before rolling it back. For the child to get all of his action figures, he must roll the truck to you.

Generalization to Peers

1. Shadow the child with autism from behind, nonverbally moving him through the activity and supporting all communicative interaction toward a peer.
2. Teach peers how to interpret the child's behaviors and respond to the child's initiatives.
3. Coach the peers through interactions, modeling strategies that are successful between adults and the child.

Strategies

To help compensate for the inherent complexity and unpredictability of social interaction, organizational and/or social supports may be necessary.

- When the child is not attending, ask yourself the following questions:
    1. Is the activity organized?
    2. Does the child understand the expectations of the activity?
    3. Does the language match the child's level of comprehension?
    4. Are there distractions in the environment?
    5. Is it a motivating activity?

- When the child is difficult to engage, ask yourself the following questions?
    1. Is the child's communicative intent understood and reflected in the interaction?
    2. Do reciprocal social routines need to be established?
    3. Is there a balance between directive and facilitative interaction styles?
    4. Do interaction patterns need to be modified for the child?

Vignettes

Reciprocal Interaction Vignettes

Julianna

During group chase games, Julianna would run to a specific area in the room and stop. She would not look at her peers or continue with the chase game. Her teacher tried prompting the peers to reengage Julianna with minimal success. In one-to-one work sessions, she worked to increase Julianna's eye gaze through some tickle games in which the receipt of tickles was dependent on Julianna looking at the teacher. Once Julianna connected eye gaze with the continuance of a reinforcing activity, her teacher reintroduced the group chase game. Before Julianna reached her "stop spot," her teacher physically blocked her and prompted Julianna to orient to her. Once Julianna did this, her teacher tickled her, turned her around, and directed her back into the game. Soon after, Julianna's teacher replaced herself with a peer.

Lily

Lily loved to play Peekaboo, but when her teacher altered the game by replacing her hand with hiding behind a blanket, Lily turned away and left the interaction. Her teacher pulled her back and prompted Lily to tug on the blanket. As soon as Lily touched the blanket, her teacher dropped it and said "Peekaboo" in a highly animated manner. After a number of turns, Lily independently pulled on the blanket with anticipation.

Justin

Justin typically left play situations after completing a solitary action with a toy. He would roll a car away from him, then move on to playing with blocks. His teacher decided to extend Justin's play by creating some reciprocal exchanges. First, she began by quickly rolling the car back to Justin after he pushed it away. She made animated car noises to draw his attention back. Then she substituted a ball for the car. Justin's teacher rolled it back and forth. Once reciprocity was established, she moved on to throwing and kicking the ball back and forth.

Activity

A. Nonverbal Social Interaction
Social Regulation 1. Gestures: Pushes/pulls/manipulates person to request

Activities: Adult–Child

Arrange the child's environment so he will need to use an adult to gain access to what he wants (e.g., put items out of reach, lock doors, put covers on too tight).

Become a physical barrier to the child. Shape this into simple interactive games in which the child has to move you to reach a desired item. For example, blow bubbles with the child. After a few minutes, sit on top of the wand and shape the child's attempts to get the wand into an interactive "move you out of the way" game.

Lie on the floor and prompt the child to help you up. Initially teach him to pull you up by your hands but then increase the complexity of the task by requiring the child to get you in the correct position to be pulled up (i.e., knees bent, feet on the floor). For example, lie on your back with your feet up and have the child put your legs down, bend your knees, and pull you up.

Create simple gross motor games in which the child has to move you to a designated spot to get a desired reinforcer. For example, if the child wants to be lifted into the air for a "blastoff" game, he needs to pull you into the space designated for that game and then gesture *up* to be lifted.

Engage in a turn-taking art activity during which you and the child take turns directing each other as to where to paint, color, or glue on a shared canvas. For example, give a chunky paint marker to the child. Quickly point to different sections of the paper and prompt the child to dot in those spots. Then, switch and have the child direct you. The interaction should be fast paced and somewhat silly, using exaggerated intonation and simple direction (e.g., use the command "Here" with a point, but alter vocal pitch with each "Here").

Prompt the child to gain your attention by tapping your wrist or shoulder.

Generalization to Peers

1. Shadow the child with autism from behind, nonverbally moving him through the activity and supporting all communicative interaction toward a peer.
2. Teach peers how to interpret the child's behaviors and respond to the child's initiatives.
3. Coach the peers through interactions, modeling strategies that are successful between adults and the child.

Strategies

To help compensate for the inherent complexity and unpredictability of social interaction, organizational and/or social supports may be necessary.

- When the child is not attending, ask yourself the following questions:
  1. Is the activity organized?
  2. Does the child understand the expectations of the activity?
  3. Does the language match the child's level of comprehension?
  4. Are there distractions in the environment?
  5. Is it a motivating activity?

- When the child is difficult to engage, ask yourself the following questions:
  1. Is the child's communicative intent understood and reflected in the interaction?
  2. Do reciprocal social routines need to be established?
  3. Is there a balance between directive and facilitative interaction styles?
  4. Do interaction patterns need to be modified for the child?

DO-WATCH-LISTEN-SAY: Social and Communication Intervention for Children with Autism
by Kathleen Ann Quill © 2000 Paul H. Brookes Publishing Co.

Activity

A. Nonverbal Social Interaction
Social Regulation 2. Gestures: Gives/manipulates object to request

Activities: Adult–Child

Practice following the direction "Give me" across multiple activities including play, snack time, and self-care tasks.

During cleanup, have the child hand to you the objects he is putting away so you can put them in their containers.

Give the child a puzzle he has mastered. Using a second puzzle the child has mastered, mix up the pieces and give half of them to the child. From your pile, pick a piece that belongs to the child's puzzle and hand it to him. Prompt the child to hand you the pieces that go in your puzzle. If the child reaches to put the piece in himself, interrupt and prompt the child to place the piece in your hand so you can place it in the puzzle.

During coloring, hold on to the crayons and have the child trade the crayon he is using to get a new crayon.

Play Hopscotch with the child. When the child reaches the square where the beanbag lands, have the child hand you the beanbag before he continues jumping to the end.

Play Trot Trot to Boston. Have the child hand you a ticket to begin the song and ride.

Generalization to Peers

1. Shadow the child with autism from behind, nonverbally moving him through the activity and supporting all communicative interaction toward a peer.
2. Teach peers how to interpret the child's behaviors and respond to the child's initiatives.
3. Coach the peers through interactions, modeling strategies that are successful between adults and the child.
4. Establish a simple game where the child is directed to give objects to two different play partners. Hand the child an object. Then, direct him to give it to a play partner. Physically orient and gesture the child to establish expectation. The game should be fast paced and could be shaped as a race or likewise contest.
5. Label a number of objects with pictures of the play partners those objects belong to. Have him seek out and give the object to the appropriate person.

Strategies

To help compensate for the inherent complexity and unpredictability of social interaction, organizational and/or social supports may be necessary.

- When the child is not attending, ask yourself the following questions:
  1. Is the activity organized?
  2. Does the child understand the expectations of the activity?
  3. Does the language match the child's level of comprehension?
  4. Are there distractions in the environment?
  5. Is it a motivating activity?

- When the child is difficult to engage, ask yourself the following questions:
  1. Is the child's communicative intent understood and reflected in the interaction?
  2. Do reciprocal social routines need to be established?
  3. Is there a balance between directive and facilitative interaction styles?
  4. Do interaction patterns need to be modified for the child?

Activity

A. Nonverbal Social Interaction
Social Regulation 3. Points to object to request

Activities: Adult–Child

Hold a motivating cause-and-effect toy. Prompt the child to point at it, then make the toy respond.

Pretend to lose a motivating object by placing it in a silly location, such as on your head. Ask the child, "Where's the (object name)?" Look wherever the child points, exaggerating your responses to keep the child engaged.

Give the child a choice of two objects, one highly preferred and one not as desirable. Ask the child to show you which one he wants.

Play a favorite music tape, and dance with the child. Shut the music off and have the child point to the tape player to play the music again.

Sit with the child at the computer. Start a motivating computer game, and prompt the child to point to the desired object on the screen. In response to the child's point, move the mouse to click on the indicated object.

Create an obstacle course that splits into two directions. Stop the child, and have him point to the path he wants to take.

Hold a preferred toy or object away from the child. Ask him, "What do you want?" Prompt the child to point to the desired object.

With books, set up a reciprocal I Spy game using the verbal cue "I spy (object name)" accompanied by pointing to the object.

During wagon rides around the community or shopping cart trips, stop and have the child point out something he sees. Label it, then resume moving. Stops should be playful with some element of anticipation. A verbal cue such as "Look, it's a (name of object) " or "What do you see?" can be added to support the child pointing out an object.

Generalization to Peers

1. Shadow the child with autism from behind, nonverbally moving him through the activity and supporting all communicative interaction toward a peer.
2. Teach peers how to interpret the child's behaviors and respond to the child's initiatives.
3. Coach the peers through interactions, modeling strategies that are successful between adults and the child.

Strategies

To help compensate for the inherent complexity and unpredictability of social interaction, organizational and/or social supports may be necessary.

- When the child is not attending, ask yourself the following questions:
    1. Is the activity organized?
    2. Does the child understand the expectations of the activity?
    3. Does the language match the child's level of comprehension?
    4. Are there distractions in the environment?
    5. Is it a motivating activity?

- When the child is difficult to engage, ask yourself the following questions:
    1. Is the child's communicative intent understood and reflected in the interaction?
    2. Do reciprocal social routines need to be established?
    3. Is there a balance between directive and facilitative interaction styles?
    4. Do interaction patterns need to be modified for the child?

DO-WATCH-LISTEN-SAY: Social and Communication Intervention for Children with Autism
by Kathleen Ann Quill © 2000 Paul H. Brookes Publishing Co.

Activity

A. Nonverbal Social Interaction

Social Regulation 4. Combines eye gaze and gesture to request

Activities: Adult–Child

Swing the child in a blanket. Stop swinging, and wait for the child to look at you. Verbally reinforce the child for looking, and ask if he wants "more blanket" with a gesture (e.g., point to the blanket, sign for MORE). Prompt the child as needed to complete the gesture and resume swinging.

Lie on the floor and have the child lie on your legs. Lift the child up, supporting him by the shoulders. When the child looks up at you, gesture *down,* then lower the child. Quickly, raise him back up and wait for the child to look and gesture *down.*

To begin an interactive game needing a partner, such as chase, have the child look and gesture *come here.*

Have the child gesture *come play* prior to following him into any activity. First shape this around highly motivating interactions, then generalize it as an overall expectation.

Arrange the environment so the child will need to request help to gain access to preferred items. For example, keep the door to the toy cabinet locked, twist the lid on the snack jar tightly, or place favorite toys on high shelves.

During wagon rides, stop and wait for the child to look at you. Then, ask him which way he wants to go using a direction point. Once the child points, follow his lead.

Engage in "I'm gonna get you" chase games or modified Freeze Tag. To initiate being chased or to free himself from being "frozen," have the child orient to his play partner and make an appropriate gesture.

Generalization to Peers

1. Shadow the child with autism from behind, nonverbally moving him through the activity and supporting all communicative interaction toward a peer.
2. Teach peers how to interpret the child's behaviors and respond to the child's initiatives.
3. Coach the peers through interactions, modeling strategies that are successful between adults and the child.

Strategies

To help compensate for the inherent complexity and unpredictability of social interaction, organizational and/or social supports may be necessary.

- When the child is not attending, ask yourself the following questions:
    1. Is the activity organized?
    2. Does the child understand the expectations of the activity?
    3. Does the language match the child's level of comprehension?
    4. Are there distractions in the environment?
    5. Is it a motivating activity?

- When the child is difficult to engage, ask yourself the following questions:
    1. Is the child's communicative intent understood and reflected in the interaction?
    2. Do reciprocal social routines need to be established?
    3. Is there a balance between directive and facilitative interaction styles?
    4. Do interaction patterns need to be modified for the child?

DO-WATCH-LISTEN-SAY: Social and Communication Intervention for Children with Autism
by Kathleen Ann Quill © 2000 Paul H. Brookes Publishing Co.

Vignettes

Social Regulation Vignettes

Josephine

Josephine loved to color but often used the activity to isolate herself from the busyness of the classroom. Her teacher tried to interrupt and join Josephine in the activity with minimal success. Josephine typically pushed her away, agitatedly repeating "All done." Her teacher decided to back up and try to engage Josephine prior to her starting coloring. All of the crayons were placed out of reach. Josephine's teacher prompted her to request them by pulling Josephine to the shelf before she could go to the easel. After Josephine became proficient at requesting, Josephine's teacher lay on the floor and prompted Josephine to help her up so the teacher could get the crayons. Josephine had to push the teacher's legs down and then pull her up by the hands. Over time, the teacher made the interaction longer and the process of helping her up more intricate. Once Josephine began to establish interaction prior to coloring without agitation, her teacher slowly incorporated herself into the coloring activity. She animatedly made marks on Josephine's paper in imitation of her strokes until turn-taking was established.

Maggie

Maggie was a very independent child who frequently resisted assistance. Her self-care skills were strong and highly reinforcing. Maggie's teacher tried to teach her the "Give me" direction throughout her daily activity, but Maggie was usually unresponsive and somewhat resistant when made to hand items to her teacher arbitrarily. The teacher decided to capitalize on Maggie's self-care abilities to begin encouraging her to hand objects to a partner. During cleanup, Maggie's teacher held the toy bin. As Maggie moved to put the individual toys in the bin, her teacher took them from Maggie and placed them in the bin herself with an animated "Goodbye (toy name)." Initially, Maggie struggled to get the bin from her teacher. Maggie's teacher neutrally continued cleanup, and Maggie eventually followed the new routine and began handing the toys to her teacher to be put away.

Henry

Despite Henry's interest in toys, he rarely pointed or gestured to play items. He would look toward toys of interest and cry when he needed help. Noisy cause-and-effect toys held a particular fascination for Henry. His teacher noticed that Henry always sought out the bumble ball during free play time. If a teacher did not turn it on or it stopped shaking, Henry would kick the bumble ball to make it go. Henry's teacher prompted him to point at the bumble ball, then she turned it on. She repeatedly turned it off, prompting Henry to point in order to turn it back on. After Henry began to show some independence in pointing at the bumble ball, his teacher took the ball and hid it under a blanket. She prompted Henry to point to the blanket to reveal and receive the bumble ball. She generalized hiding the bumble ball under a number of classroom objects and Henry followed along nicely.

Eliot

Eliot loved to play chase games. He would often run around proximal to peers but not in co-operation. Eliot was unaware that he had to request a peer to chase him or establish shared involvement in the play. His teacher decided to modify the game slightly to encourage Eliot to stop, orient to his play partner, and gesture to continue the game. Instead of tagging Eliot to get him to chase her, the teacher would catch him and hold Eliot facing her until he oriented and gestured for her to run. Once Eliot mastered the response, his teacher taught him to approach her and gesture "come" for her to chase him.

Activity

A. Nonverbal Social Interaction
Shared Attention 1. Alternates gaze between toy/object and person

Activities: Adult–Child

Throughout daily activity, draw attention to objects in the environment with an animated verbal "Look." When the child looks at the object, draw his attention back to you to provide the object's name.

Set out a number of familiar objects. Have the child give them to you upon request. Mix them up to force the child to scan the objects.

Hide an object in a hat or box. Ask the child to find the object. Once the child is proficient at the game, ask him to find an object that is not in the container so the child will have to look back to you to seek more information or tell you the object is not in the container.

Place a number of objects in the tub or a sink full of water. Show the child a picture of the object you want him to catch in the water. As the child tries to retrieve the slippery object, have him reference the picture you are holding to remind him of what he is trying to catch.

Give the child a familiar object with a piece missing. Hold on to the missing piece where the child can see it. After the child examines the object and begins searching for the missing piece, draw his attention to you. Repeat with a variety of objects until the child begins referencing you independently when he notices something out of place.

Once the child is engaged in play, watch his actions and pick one that is repeated often in his manipulation of the toy he is using. Every time the child does that action, make a relevant but distracting noise or say a contextually appropriate phrase in an animated manner. Be sure the child finds the verbal amusing, engaging, or otherwise motivating so he draws his attention to you each time you say it. Eventually the child should orient to you in anticipation of the action.

Generalization to Peers

1. Shadow the child with autism from behind, nonverbally moving him through the activity and supporting all communicative interaction toward a peer.
2. Teach peers how to interpret the child's behaviors and respond to the child's initiatives.
3. Coach the peers through interactions, modeling strategies that are successful between adults and the child.

Strategies

To help compensate for the inherent complexity and unpredictability of social interaction, organizational and/or social supports may be necessary.

- When the child is not attending, ask yourself the following questions:
    1. Is the activity organized?
    2. Does the child understand the expectations of the activity?
    3. Does the language match the child's level of comprehension?
    4. Are there distractions in the environment?
    5. Is it a motivating activity?

- When the child is difficult to engage, ask yourself the following questions:
    1. Is the child's communicative intent understood and reflected in the interaction?
    2. Do reciprocal social routines need to be established?
    3. Is there a balance between directive and facilitative interaction styles?
    4. Do interaction patterns need to be modified for the child?

Activity

A. Nonverbal Social Interaction
Shared Attention 2. Gives toy/object to share interests

Activities: Adult–Child

During show-and-tell, have the child pass his object to each of the children in the circle.

During snack time, have the child share his snack with a peer.

After an art activity, direct the child to give his project to a teacher who did not help him during the activity.

Create simple treasure hunt games in which the child seeks a hidden object. When he finds it, prompt him to give it to his play partner. Model for the child by saying "I found (object name)" as he passes it to the partner.

Read a book with the child. Pass the book back and forth to establish turn-taking. Read the first page, then pass the book to the child to read or point out a picture on the next page. Continue throughout the book.

Generalization to Peers

1. Shadow the child with autism from behind, nonverbally moving him through the activity and supporting all communicative interaction toward a peer.

2. Teach peers how to interpret the child's behaviors and respond to the child's initiatives.

3. Coach the peers through interactions, modeling strategies that are successful between adults and the child.

4. During circle time, present to the group a treasure box or hat filled with objects. Have each child pull out an item and hand it to a peer. You can model for the children by saying "Look, it's a (name of object)" or other relevant phrases.

5. Engage in a modified version of Hot Potato in which the child passes an object back and forth.

Strategies

To help compensate for the inherent complexity and unpredictability of social interaction, organizational and/or social supports may be necessary.

- When the child is not attending, ask yourself the following questions:
  1. Is the activity organized?
  2. Does the child understand the expectations of the activity?
  3. Does the language match the child's level of comprehension?
  4. Are there distractions in the environment?
  5. Is it a motivating activity?

- When the child is difficult to engage, ask yourself the following questions:
  1. Is the child's communicative intent understood and reflected in the interaction?
  2. Do reciprocal social routines need to be established?
  3. Is there a balance between directive and facilitative interaction styles?
  4. Do interaction patterns need to be modified for the child?

DO-WATCH-LISTEN-SAY: Social and Communication Intervention for Children with Autism
by Kathleen Ann Quill © 2000 Paul H. Brookes Publishing Co.

Activity

A. Nonverbal Social Interaction
Shared Attention 3. Points to toy/object to share interests

Activities: Adult–Child

Point to pictures in a book within a turn-taking routine.

Pretend to lose a motivating object by placing it in a silly location, such as on your head. Ask the child, "Where's (object name)?" Look wherever the child points, exaggerating your responses to keep the child engaged.

Play a favorite music tape, and dance with the child. Intermittently stop dancing. Prompt the child to point to the tape player, and then begin dancing again. After a number of trials, wait for the child to spontaneously point the tape player out to you before dancing.

During wagon rides around the community or shopping cart trips, stop and have the child point out something he sees. Label it, then resume moving. Stops should be playful with some element of anticipation. A verbal cue such as "Look, it's a (name of object)" or "What do you see?" can be added to support the child's pointing out an object.

Generalization to Peers

1. Shadow the child with autism from behind, nonverbally moving him through the activity and supporting all communicative interaction toward a peer.
2. Teach peers how to interpret the child's behaviors and respond to the child's initiatives.
3. Coach the peers through interactions, modeling strategies that are successful between adults and the child.
4. Following the building of a block tower, have the child tap a play partner and point to the completed project. If the child is verbal, he can pair the point with the verbal "look." Do not let the child knock the tower over until he shows it to his play partner.

Strategies

To help compensate for the inherent complexity and unpredictability of social interaction, organizational and/or social supports may be necessary.

- When the child is not attending, ask yourself the following questions:
    1. Is the activity organized?
    2. Does the child understand the expectations of the activity?
    3. Does the language match the child's level of comprehension?
    4. Are there distractions in the environment?
    5. Is it a motivating activity?

- When the child is difficult to engage, ask yourself the following questions:
    1. Is the child's communicative intent understood and reflected in the interaction?
    2. Do reciprocal social routines need to be established?
    3. Is there a balance between directive and facilitative interaction styles?
    4. Do interaction patterns need to be modified for the child?

Activity

A. Nonverbal Social Interaction

Shared Attention 4. Gains attention prior to sharing interests

Activities: Adult–Child

Engage in a highly motivating activity, such as tickling, blowing bubbles, or supported jumping. After a few turns, turn your head away from the child. Support him in gaining your attention (e.g., an arm tap, a verbal call), then return to the activity.

During show and tell, have the child walk around the circle and tap, shake hands, or give a high-five to his peers prior to displaying his show and tell item.

While cooperatively reading a book, have the child tap your arm before pointing to a picture.

When the child is done with an art activity, have him ring a bell or shake a maraca to prompt an adult who was not engaged in helping him look at his finished project.

During snack time, go around the table and have the children show a peer or another adult what they brought. Support the child in raising his hand, waiting for the peer or adult to respond, and pointing to his snack item.

Generalization to Peers

1. Shadow the child with autism from behind, nonverbally moving him through the activity and supporting all communicative interaction toward a peer.
2. Teach peers how to interpret the child's behaviors and respond to the child's initiatives.
3. Coach the peers through interactions, modeling strategies that are successful between adults and the child.

Strategies

To help compensate for the inherent complexity and unpredictability of social interaction, organizational and/or social supports may be necessary.

- When the child is not attending, ask yourself the following questions:
    1. Is the activity organized?
    2. Does the child understand the expectations of the activity?
    3. Does the language match the child's level of comprehension?
    4. Are there distractions in the environment?
    5. Is it a motivating activity?

- When the child is difficult to engage, ask yourself the following questions:
    1. Is the child's communicative intent understood and reflected in the interaction?
    2. Do reciprocal social routines need to be established?
    3. Is there a balance between directive and facilitative interaction styles?
    4. Do interaction patterns need to be modified for the child?

DO-WATCH-LISTEN-SAY: Social and Communication Intervention for Children with Autism
by Kathleen Ann Quill © 2000 Paul H. Brookes Publishing Co.

Vignettes

Shared Attention Vignettes

Billy

Once engaged in play, Billy would not look up from his toy or notice anyone playing around him. His older brother tried to get Billy to play with him, often by pushing objects or toys into Billy's lap in an effort to get Billy to notice him. Billy's mother would play with both boys, passing objects back and forth between them, but Billy only focused on the toy, not his mother or brother. As Billy loved to be tickled, his mother established a game in which she would walk her fingers up Billy's arm, over his head, and down to tickle his belly. After she got him to look at her and then follow her fingers, she began to walk her fingers from Billy's brother's head over to Billy's. Once Billy began to notice his brother as a part of this play, Billy's mother introduced more cooperative games in which Billy's brother would direct Billy to give him objects or pass him toys. This built up Billy's ability to share his attention between his toys and his brother.

David

In kindergarten, David struggled through show and tell. He refused to pass his show-and-tell item around the circle. Often, he would leave it in his backpack and peek inside when it was his turn to show his toy. David's teacher tried pulling it out of the bag herself and showing the group, which typically led to David's yelling and grabbing for his show-and-tell item. Given his resistance, David's teacher introduced a new treasure hunt game at circle time. She brought in her own backpack and filled it with reinforcing play objects. Each child took a turn pulling an item out of the backpack and passing it to peers. David spontaneously followed the model to take the item out of the backpack. He needed support to pass it to peers in the form of a First/Then board. "First, give the object to our friends, then give the object back to David." Following his turn, David held the play object until the game was completed. Eventually, the skill was generalized to show and tell.

Patrick

After completing projects, Patrick loved to quickly break them apart. He would tear up paper, break apart puzzles, and knock over block structures. His teacher tried to get him to show his finished projects to his teachers and peers, but Patrick was more interested in the reinforcement he received from breaking them down. She decided to shape this by making the destroying contingent on showing. She scooped Patrick in a deep pressure hug and prompted him to point to the finished project; then she quickly released him so he could knock it down. She made the hug a reinforcing exchange, so Patrick began to seek it before moving to break apart his project. Eventually, he spontaneously came to his teacher and pointed to the project, and they cooperatively broke it apart.

Reese

Although Reese could comment on her behavior and activity, she often stood in the middle of the classroom and made undirected pronouncements, such as "I'm all done coloring" or "It's the letter A." She never sought her teacher's attention before making such statements. Reese's teacher began to teach attention-seeking skills with simple gross motor games. She then generalized the expectation to gain attention prior to interaction across all classroom activity. As Reese loved bubbles, her teacher would blow bubbles, then stop and turn away from Reese. Reese's teacher ignored her requests for more bubbles. She subsequently modeled tapping and calling Reese's name to gain attention. Once Reese gained her teacher's attention, she was prompted to make the request again and received the bubbles. After Reese acquired this requesting skill, her teacher began to play reciprocal commenting games. She would point to items of interest and comment, "Reese, it's a (object in the environment)." She then modeled for Reese, "(Teacher's name), it's a (object in the environment)." Soon the teacher faded her verbal prompt to a wrist tap and only gave Reese her attention once Reese appropriately gained her attention. Throughout the day, when Reese would make her pronouncements, a teacher would intermittently ask Reese who she was talking to, thus calling attention to the fact that Reese's language needed an audience.

Activity

B. Imitation

Motor Imitation 1. Imitates an action with a toy

Activities: Adult–Child

Give the child a toy and sit across from him with an identical toy. Model a single action with the toy, then prompt the child to imitate with his toy.

Set up situations in which you quickly model a single play action and stop with an alerting, relevant noise. For example, roll a car quickly in front of the child and stop with a screech. Repeat the action until the child is engaged. Hand the child the car and prompt him to imitate. Continue in a turn-taking manner.

Do an action to the child and then imitate that action with a toy. Once the child is engaged, give him the toy and prompt imitation of the modeled action. For example, give the child a kiss, then give the doll a kiss. Hand over the doll and prompt the child to give it a kiss.

Activities: Small Group

Isolate a single action from a familiar story or song. Give each child in the group an object that corresponds to the targeted action. Have the children imitate the action at the appropriate point in the story or song. For example, give each child in the group a toy monkey. Sing "Five Little Monkeys" and have the children jump the monkeys up and down each time the song says "jumping on the bed."

Give each child a musical instrument. Have all of the children shake the instruments at the same time.

Seat the children in a circle. Model an action with a toy, then pass it around the circle, having each child imitate the action. Attach a simple phrase to label the action, and repeat it in an animated, sing-song manner during each child's turn.

Strategies

When teaching imitation, you have three choices:

1. Build on what the child gives you (scaffold).
2. Give a new action (prompt).
3. Shape inappropriate behaviors into purposeful actions (shape).

The choice of strategy and level of prompting used is made moment to moment based on the child's attention, understanding, and interest.

Follow the child's lead if purposeful. If the child is unfocused or not engaging in purposeful activity, provide appropriate modeling to cue targeted actions.

When the child's behavior is meaningful to the context, reference and shape it into the target actions.

If the child is difficult to engage or keep focused, ask the following questions:

1. Is the activity organized?
2. Is the activity meaningful to the child?
3. Is the activity motivating for the child?
4. Do you have the child's attention?
5. Is the child comfortable in the environment?
6. Can you interrupt the child's rituals?

DO-WATCH-LISTEN-SAY: Social and Communication Intervention for Children with Autism
by Kathleen Ann Quill © 2000 Paul H. Brookes Publishing Co.

B. Imitation
Motor Imitation 2. Imitates a single body action

Activities: Adult–Child

Engage in a social game in which the child must imitate a single body action to receive a desired response, such as tickles or squeezes.

Pretend to be animals, and have the child imitate one body action for each animal seen in a book or on flashcards.

Engage in a chase-and-capture game. Once the child is caught, he must imitate a single body action to free himself.

Build a train or use a wagon. Have the child imitate a single body action to board the vehicle.

Each week choose a different attention-seeking action, such as raising a hand or tapping the table. At appropriate times during the day (e.g., lunch, snack time, circle time), model the body action for the child and have him imitate it to gain attention.

Activities: Small Group

Play modified versions of Simon Says in which actions are isolated and repeated.

Engage the group in songs with isolated body actions. Have the group imitate the action simultaneously at the appropriate point in the song.

Set up movement groups in which individual body actions are targeted.

Create a turn-taking game in which each child, in turn, stands up in the circle and models a single body action. Have the other children imitate from their chairs.

Silently repeat an action in front of the group. Have another adult imitate you. When the children begin doing the action simultaneously with you, focus all of your attention and praise on them. Each child who begins to imitate the action gets your praise and attention shifted to him. Ignore the children who are not engaged. Eventually, all of the children should join in imitating the action. For example, clap your hands continuously until all of the children in the group are imitating by clapping their hands.

Strategies

When teaching imitation, you have three choices:

1. Build on what the child gives you (scaffold).
2. Give a new action (prompt).
3. Shape inappropriate behaviors into purposeful actions (shape).

The choice of strategy and level of prompting used is made moment to moment based on the child's attention, understanding, and interest.

Follow the child's lead if purposeful. If the child is unfocused or not engaging in purposeful activity, provide appropriate modeling to cue targeted actions.

When the child's behavior is meaningful to the context, reference and shape it into the target actions.

If the child is difficult to engage or keep focused, ask the following questions:

1. Is the activity organized?
2. Is the activity meaningful to the child?
3. Is the activity motivating for the child?
4. Do you have the child's attention?
5. Is the child comfortable in the environment?
6. Can you interrupt the child's rituals?

Activity

B. Imitation

Motor Imitation 3. Imitates a sequence of two actions

Activities: Adult–Child

Engage the child in play with a familiar toy. Once the child has repeatedly executed a mastered play action with the toy, model a second action. The new action should logically follow the first action in sequence. For example, if the child kisses a baby doll, prompt him to follow the kiss by putting the doll to bed.

Model a two-step sequence and attach simple verbal directions to cue the target actions (e.g., "Yawn, go to sleep," "Jump up, jump down," "Block in, roll truck"). Repeat the directions in an animated, sing-song manner during your modeling and prompting of the child through the actions.

Use a First/Then board to chain two familiar actions together or add a novel action to a familiar one. Be sure the less motivating or new action is first followed by the preferred choice.

Create flashcards representing individual body actions. Set out two cards and prompt the child through the illustrated actions.

Activities: Small Group

Isolate two actions from a book. Give each child props representing the targeted actions. Model the actions in conjunction with the story, and prompt the children to imitate.

Tape squares on the floor or lay out two Hula-Hoops. Each square or hoop represents a different action. Have each child step from square to square imitating the action attached to that space.

Strategies

When teaching imitation, you have three choices:

1. Build on what the child gives you (scaffold).
2. Give a new action (prompt).
3. Shape inappropriate behaviors into purposeful actions (shape).

The choice of strategy and level of prompting used is made moment to moment based on the child's attention, understanding, and interest.

Follow the child's lead if purposeful. If the child is unfocused or not engaging in purposeful activity, provide appropriate modeling to cue targeted actions.

When the child's behavior is meaningful to the context, reference and shape it into the target actions.

If the child is difficult to engage or keep focused, ask the following questions:

1. Is the activity organized?
2. Is the activity meaningful to the child?
3. Is the activity motivating for the child?
4. Do you have the child's attention?
5. Is the child comfortable in the environment?
6. Can you interrupt the child's rituals?

DO-WATCH-LISTEN-SAY: Social and Communication Intervention for Children with Autism
by Kathleen Ann Quill © 2000 Paul H. Brookes Publishing Co.

Vignettes

Simple Motor Imitation Vignettes

Jason

Jason loved to play in the pool. Swimming was both calming and focusing for Jason. His teacher decided to use the activity as a means of introducing toys. Jason's teacher first brought a doll into the pool. She splashed it in the water with an animated "Splash," then handed the doll to Jason. Jason's teacher repeated the verbal "Splash" and prompted Jason to imitate splashing the doll. Following his imitation, they continued taking turns with the doll.

Michael

Regardless of the context, Michael struggled to imitate motor actions. His teacher decided to forego typical modeling and tried to shape actions Michael was already demonstrating independently. She sat in front of Michael and walked her fingers up his legs. She made the animated, anticipatory sound effect "dun, dun, dun" as she inched her fingers toward Michael's belly and then rolled her tongue with increased pitch as she tickled his thigh. After she had Michael engaged, his teacher pulled away her hand before reaching the tickle spot. Michael tried to catch her hands by slapping at his knees. When his hands were on top of hers, she slapped his knees and praised him for "good slapping" of his knees. The tickles then followed Michael's slapping his knees. His teacher faded the finger walking as Michael became more responsive to the direction to slap his knees.

Jeremy

Although Jeremy quickly mastered imitation of single body actions, he was unable to combine two actions. His teacher tried chaining only mastered single actions, but Jeremy continually got stuck on the first action and could not process the second one. Jeremy's teacher engaged his class in a motor sequencing game in which she used Hula-Hoops to segregate the floor space into two distinct circles. In each hoop, she placed a flashcard of the action to be done in that area. Jeremy quickly mastered doing one action in the first hoop, then moving to the second. Jeremy's teacher modified the game in the classroom. First she added a sing-song direction to the actions (e.g., "First we clap, then we jump"). Then she moved the two action flashcards to one hoop. Accompanied by the song, Jeremy was able to complete the two actions in sequence within the single hoop. Eventually, Jeremy was able to imitate multiple body actions without the structure of the game.

Activity

B. Imitation

Motor Imitation 4. Imitates a sequence of three or more actions

Activities: Adult–Child

Create videos modeling a sequence of play actions. First have the child watch the videos, then model the play with the child.

Attach simple songs containing action cues to common routines like bath time, cleanup, or transitions.

Use a schedule board to map a sequence of play actions. Reference each picture before modeling the next action in the sequence.

For cooking activities, make simple cookbooks. Have each page represent a step in the cooking sequence.

Activities: Small Group

Engage in multistep obstacle courses that have some elements of body imitation mixed in with moving through equipment.

Set up movement sequences that imitate daily events. For example, pretend to get in a toy car, drive to a gas station, and pump gas.

Strategies

When teaching imitation, you have three choices:

1. Build on what the child gives you (scaffold).
2. Give new action (prompt).
3. Shape inappropriate behaviors into purposeful actions (shape).

The choice of strategy and level of prompting used is made moment to moment based on the child's attention, understanding, and interest.

Follow the child's lead if purposeful. If the child is unfocused or not engaging in purposeful activity, provide appropriate modeling to cue targeted actions.

When the child's behavior is meaningful to the context, reference and shape it into the target actions.

If the child is difficult to engage or keep focused, ask the following questions:

1. Is the activity organized?
2. Is the activity meaningful to the child?
3. Is the activity motivating for the child?
4. Do you have the child's attention?
5. Is the child comfortable in the environment?
6. Can you interrupt the child's rituals?

DO-WATCH-LISTEN-SAY: Social and Communication Intervention for Children with Autism
by Kathleen Ann Quill © 2000 Paul H. Brookes Publishing Co.

Activity

B. Imitation

Motor Imitation 5. Imitates a novel act during a familiar activity

Activities: Adult–Child

Set up the child in a familiar activity. Follow his lead until you establish shared attention. Introduce a new action into the play using the materials with which the child is already engaged. Intermittently repeat the same action until the child begins to observe you, then prompt him to imitate the novel action.

Teach the child to recognize a card representing concepts such as *change* or *something new.* During familiar play, show the child the card and model a new action. Prompt the child to imitate the novel action before returning to the familiar activity.

Join the child in a familiar play routine in which turn-taking has already been established. Replace one of the toys that is already part of the activity with a novel toy. First use the toy to imitate a familiar action. Once the child accepts the new toy, change the action being imitated.

Activities: Small Group

Within the routines of familiar songs and movement games, add novel actions to the preset sequence of the activity.

Establish simple imitation games with a consistent phrase that groups the activity together. Change the action, but use the same phrase to introduce the novel action.

Initiate a passing game in which you pull a toy out of a box and pass it around the group. For each toy, the children take turns performing a relevant action. First use toys or objects related to mastered actions. Mix novel toys into the game, and model the novel action that corresponds with the new toy.

Strategies

When teaching imitation, you have three choices:

1. Build on what the child gives you (scaffold).
2. Give a new action (prompt).
3. Shape inappropriate behaviors into purposeful actions (shape).

The choice of strategy and level of prompting used is made moment to moment based on the child's attention, understanding, and interest.

Follow the child's lead if purposeful. If the child is unfocused or not engaging in purposeful activity, provide appropriate modeling to cue targeted actions.

When the child's behavior is meaningful to the context, reference and shape it into the target actions.

If the child is difficult to engage or keep focused, ask the following questions:

1. Is the activity organized?
2. Is the activity meaningful to the child?
3. Is the activity motivating for the child?
4. Do you have the child's attention?
5. Is the child comfortable in the environment?
6. Can you interrupt the child's rituals?

Activity

B. Imitation

Motor Imitation 6. Imitates in novel contexts

The key to encouraging imitation in novel contexts is to carry over familiar prompts, cues, or items that provide the child with a framework for ordering and gaining access to the novel information.

Activities: Adult–Child

Bring familiar toys or objects into novel contexts.

First target mastered body actions in novel contexts, then branch into imitating novel, context-related actions.

Attach consistent visuals to individual actions. Use the visuals to link the expectations of the new context with those of familiar contexts.

Set up the child in the novel context, and watch what the child does. Build on the child's actions, and use familiar songs and cues to prompt the child to imitate novel actions relevant to the context.

Videotape novel situations and show them to the child prior to the activity.

Highlight familiar aspects of novel environments before arriving. Once there, connect the child to something consistent and comfortable before prompting the child to imitate a novel action.

Activities: Small Group

Begin a novel activity with a familiar song.

Partner the child with a familiar peer. Have the peer walk the child through the new activity before incorporating him into the larger group.

Strategies

When teaching imitation, you have three choices:

1. Build on what the child gives you (scaffold).
2. Give a new action (prompt).
3. Shape inappropriate behaviors into purposeful actions (shape).

The choice of strategy and level of prompting used is made moment to moment based on the child's attention, understanding, and interest.

Follow the child's lead if purposeful. If the child is unfocused or not engaging in purposeful activity, provide appropriate modeling to cue targeted actions.

When the child's behavior is meaningful to the context, reference and shape it into the target actions.

If the child is difficult to engage or keep focused, ask the following questions:

1. Is the activity organized?
2. Is the activity meaningful to the child?
3. Is the activity motivating for the child?
4. Do you have the child's attention?
5. Is the child comfortable in the environment?
6. Can you interrupt the child's rituals?

DO-WATCH-LISTEN-SAY: Social and Communication Intervention for Children with Autism
by Kathleen Ann Quill © 2000 Paul H. Brookes Publishing Co.

Activity

B. Imitation

Motor Imitation 7. Imitates actions from a previous play activity (delayed)

Spontaneity is not necessarily a teachable skill. It is highly dependent on how an individual child uses environmental and situational cues. Encouraging delayed imitation of play actions and fostering spontaneity centers around increasing a child's knowledge of play sequences and his awareness of environmental and/or situational cues. The following examples show how to teach the child to recognize cues and recall play and body actions relevant to the particular situation being referenced.

Activities: Adult–Child

Use pictures or repeated refrains/phrases from familiar books, songs, or videos to cue the child into a practiced play sequence connected with the specific medium.

Reconstruct a preferred scenario established in the song, book, or video by laying out relevant props, toys, or materials necessary to reenact the scene's action.

While the child is reading a book or watching a video, label the action using simple verb phrases. Then imitate the action with the child using the same language. Later observe the child playing independently. When the child performs an action tied to the practiced sequence, label it with the same language used to comment on the corresponding book or video.

When teaching play sequences, clear the play area and only set out the toys relevant to the targeted play. Once the play sequence is mastered, randomly set up the area for the child, and leave him to play alone. The toys will act as the prompt.

Activities: Small Group

Attach consistent initiation phrases to social group games such as Tag; Duck, Duck, Goose; or Mother, May I. Prompt peers to initiate game play using the established initiation phrase.

Strategies

When teaching imitation, you have three choices:

1. Build on what the child gives you (scaffold).
2. Give a new action (prompt).
3. Shape inappropriate behaviors into purposeful actions (shape).

The choice of strategy and level of prompting used is made moment to moment based on the child's attention, understanding, and interest.

Follow the child's lead if purposeful. If the child is unfocused or not engaging in purposeful activity, provide appropriate modeling to cue targeted actions.

When the child's behavior is meaningful to the context, reference and shape it into the target actions.

If the child is difficult to engage or keep focused, ask the following questions:

1. Is the activity organized?
2. Is the activity meaningful to the child?
3. Is the activity motivating for the child?
4. Do you have the child's attention?
5. Is the child comfortable in the environment?
6. Can you interrupt the child's rituals?

Vignettes:

Complex Motor Imitation Vignettes

Eric

It took Eric a long time to begin imitating play actions. Because he was a child who understood information in a very concrete manner, most play was irrelevant and not motivating. When his teacher began to target the sequencing of multiple play actions, she found Eric very difficult to engage and keep on task. She wrote home to Eric's mother to find out which activities he found interesting in the community or during the course of his day at home. Eric's mother reported that he loved to go to the grocery store and help with chores at home. Eric's teacher made up a simple three-action social story highlighting the three primary actions of grocery shopping—putting the food items in the cart, paying for them, and putting them in bags. The teacher had Eric's mother show Eric the story and recount the three main actions while shopping. His teacher then made a 1-2-3-4-done board for school with the three actions and modeled pretending to grocery shop in the kitchen area during free play time. Eric keyed into the familiar visuals and eventually began imitating his teacher's lead. He readily recalled the shopping script reinforced by his mother and, with minimal support, generalized it into play.

Catherine

During circle time, Catherine did well with familiar routines but had difficulty with new songs and activities. She would pull out the old circle materials and independently script the old routines. When ignored, Catherine yelled over the group until she had to be removed from the circle. Catherine's teacher tried to have her sit for the first few minutes of each novel activity with the intention of building up Catherine's tolerance over time. When forced to sit, Catherine's tantrum behaviors escalated. Her teacher established a blanket routine around all circle-time activities and adopted an "It's new" concept card to indicate a novel activity. Once Catherine understood the blanket routine and cued into the "It's new" card, she became calmer and more available to imitate novel songs and activities.

Grant

Grant was invited to his first birthday party. His mother was both thrilled and nervous. Because the whole experience was new to Grant, his mother targeted one party game to teach him. At the party, she would then reference the other novel activities around the familiarity of Pin the Tail on the Donkey, eating cake, and singing "Happy Birthday." Grant's mother created a videotape illustrating how to play Pin the Tail on the Donkey. First the video displayed the materials needed for the activity (e.g., tail, donkey picture, blindfold). Grant's mother then filmed two peers, who were going to be at the party, playing the game. She labeled each step verbally as each child took a turn on the video. She made an accompanying social script for Grant detailing the game sequence. She let Grant watch the video a number of times before reading him the story, and they practiced Pin the Tail on the Donkey a number of times at home before the party. At the party, when Grant was disoriented or overwhelmed, his mother pointed out the cake, singing, and Pin the Tail on the Donkey.

Tony

Tony loved to watch videos. When he watched The Lion King, Tony would act out scenes with corresponding action figures of Simba, Timon, and Pumba. However, Tony never picked up the toys spontaneously or repeated the sequences when the video was not on. Tony's mother tried reenacting the play sequences with minimal success. On the recommendation of Tony's teacher, she audiotaped sections of the video Tony would act out. She then played the audio without the video, drawing Tony's attention to his action figures. As she imitated Tony's play with identical toys, his mother repeated key phrases from the audiotaped sequences. Eventually, Tony's mother faded the audiotape and Tony spontaneously began to imitate the familiar play sequences when presented with only the action figures.

Activity

B. Imitation
Verbal Imitation 1. Imitates mouth movements/vocalizations

Activities: Adult–Child

Create simple cause-and-effect games involving mouth movements or vocalizations. For example, get the child's attention, then touch your head. As you touch your head, stick out your tongue. Repeat, then have the child touch your head and stick out your tongue. After a number of trials, touch the child's head and prompt the child to stick out his tongue.

Imitate the child's vocalizations. Once turn-taking is established, add new sounds to vocal play. For example, if the child spontaneously vocalizes *ooo,* imitate the *ooo*. Once turn-taking is established, add *eee*. The child will then imitate *ooo eee.*

Throughout play, add silly sounds or singsong labels to activities or during transitions.

Use your hands to squeeze your face and create specific mouth movements (e.g., fish face, stretched mouth). Then help the child squeeze his face to imitate your mouth movements.

Create a see-through or cutout mirror. First imitate the child's expressions and mouth movements. Once reciprocity is established, model novel mouth movements and prompt the child to imitate.

Pretend to eat something that is inedible, smell the child's feet, or interact with some other object you would find unpleasant. Overexaggerate your "yuck" reaction with distinct facial grimaces or by sticking out your tongue. Repeat the action to establish shared attention, then turn the "yucky" object on the child so he will imitate the "yuck" reaction you previously modeled.

Activities: Small Group

Sing a simple animal song. For each animal, model the sound that the children make and prompt the group to imitate.

Blow bubbles, dandelions, or pinwheels.

Build a block tower and prompt the children to blow it down or, if they are knocking it down with their feet or hands, attach a simple sound effect to the action (e.g., *eeeum crash*).

Sing simple songs with repeated sound effects, such as "Old MacDonald Had a Farm."

Present the group with pictures of faces representing defined emotional states (e.g., surprised = mouth formed in a puckered *O,* happy = big smile).

Strategies

When teaching imitation, you have three choices:

1. Build on what the child gives you (scaffold).
2. Give a new action (prompt).
3. Shape inappropriate behaviors into purposeful actions (shape).

The choice of strategy and level of prompting used is made moment to moment based on the child's attention, understanding, and interest.

Follow the child's lead if purposeful. If the child is unfocused or not engaging in purposeful activity, provide appropriate modeling to cue targeted actions.

When the child's behavior is meaningful to the context, shape it into the target actions.

If the child is difficult to engage or keep focused, ask the following questions:

1. Is the activity organized?
2. Is the activity meaningful to the child?
3. Is the activity motivating for the child?
4. Do you have the child's attention?
5. Is the child comfortable in the environment?
6. Can you interrupt the child's rituals?

DO-WATCH-LISTEN-SAY: Social and Communication Intervention for Children with Autism
by Kathleen Ann Quill © 2000 Paul H. Brookes Publishing Co.

Activity

B. Imitation

Verbal Imitation 2. Imitates word(s) during songs, fingerplays, stories, social routines, movement activities, and, eventually, all activities

Activities: Adult–Child

Hold a preferred item out of the child's reach. When the child points or otherwise indicates a desire for the item, label the item. Prompt the child to imitate the label first with the whole word, then with a phonetic cue.

Verbally label items in the environment and couple with a sign or pictographic representation. When prompting the child to imitate the label, use the visual as a means of cuing the child to say the word.

Create repetitive verbal constructs around activities with a fill-in-the-blank component, such as "I see _____" or "I want _____." Say the whole phrase with the targeted word, then repeat the phrase, replacing the word with an anticipatory pause. Prompt the child to imitate the novel word.

Engage in reinforcing motor play in which the word elicits an immediate, reinforcing action, such as *up* to get lifted up or *me* to get tickled.

Activities: Small Group

Once the children are familiar with a song, intermittently pause to allow them to fill in the missing word.

Read a familiar story, preferably one with a repeated line or refrain. When you come to the repeated phrase, pause so the children can fill in the phrase.

Attach consistent songs to cue the beginning and end of an activity. Following the song, tell the children "It's time for/to _____." Repeat the phrase and prompt the children to fill in the blank.

During circle time, create consistent routines in which the children identify peers, weather, or other daily items. Once the routine is familiar, add in novel words (e.g., new peers, weather variations) and prompt the children to imitate them within the familiar structure.

Set up a treasure chest or grab bag filled with familiar and novel items. Go around the circle and have each child pick an item and tell the group "It's a (object name)." First label the item, then have the children imitate to get the item.

Strategies

When teaching imitation, you have three choices:

1. Build on what the child gives you (scaffold).
2. Give a new action (prompt).
3. Shape inappropriate behaviors into purposeful actions (shape).

The choice of strategy and level of prompting used is made moment to moment based on the child's attention, understanding, and interest.

Follow the child's lead if purposeful. If the child is unfocused or not engaging in purposeful activity, provide appropriate modeling to cue targeted actions.

When the child's behavior is meaningful to the context, reference and shape it into the target actions.

If the child is difficult to engage or keep focused, ask the following questions:

1. Is the activity organized?
2. Is the activity meaningful to the child?
3. Is the activity motivating for the child?
4. Do you have the child's attention?
5. Is the child comfortable in the environment?
6. Can you interrupt the child's rituals?

DO-WATCH-LISTEN-SAY: Social and Communication Intervention for Children with Autism
by Kathleen Ann Quill © 2000 Paul H. Brookes Publishing Co.

Activity

B. Imitation

Verbal Imitation 3. Imitates word(s) upon request

Eliciting speech on demand is rarely as successful as encouraging speech occurring in natural contexts. A child is more likely to imitate language if it is meaningful. Be sure that the requested verbal is immediately followed by a relevant and natural response. The child should understand the function of the phrase and find it useful or motivating. The following activities provide more natural cues as substitutes for the "Say _____" prompt.

Activities: Adult–Child

Hold the child up on a swing and wait until he begins squirming to be released. Direct the child to tell you "Let me go" or a comparable phrase. When the child imitates the phrase or an approximation of it, let him go. Repeat the exchange until the phrase is imitated without the direction.

Use a pictograph of SAY + "(TARGETED WORD)." First fade the SAY pictograph. Then fade the word pictograph once the child knows the expected response.

Use a sign or gesture to represent a requested phrase. Fade the verbal prompt and use the gesture to cue the target response.

Other verbal constructs to replace *say* include "It's a _____," "Look, I see a _____," or "Tell me _____."

Activities: Small Group

Seat the children in a circle. Read a favorite book and have the children repeat the predictable words within the story. Encourage choral responses.

Seat the children in a circle. Sing a familiar song that contains repetitive lyrics. Encourage choral singing.

Strategies

When teaching imitation, you have three choices:

1. Build on what the child gives you (scaffold).
2. Give a new action (scaffold).
3. Shape inappropriate behaviors into purposeful actions (shape).

The choice of strategy and level of prompting used is made moment to moment based on the child's attention, understanding, and interest.

Follow the child's lead if purposeful. If the child is unfocused or not engaging in purposeful activity, provide appropriate modeling to cue targeted actions.

When the child's behavior is meaningful to the context, reference and shape it into the target actions.

If the child is difficult to engage or keep focused, ask the following questions:

1. Is the activity organized?
2. Is the activity meaningful to the child?
3. Is the activity motivating for the child?
4. Do you have the child's attention?
5. Is the child comfortable in the environment?
6. Can you interrupt the child's rituals?

Activity

B. Imitation

Verbal Imitation 4. Repeats words from a song, book, or play activity (delayed)

Children often use delayed echolalia as a means of regulating behavior or talking themselves through daily activities. Children with autism often engage in verbal scripts without regard for context or situational relevance. Delayed verbal imitation is not necessarily a teachable skill, but encouraging the connection of verbal scripts to appropriate contexts is possible. The following strategies show how to encourage children to make verbal imitation relevant and meaningful.

Activities: Adult–Child

When a child engages in a verbal script, begin acting it out with the child or follow the directions expressed in the script. To begin attaching definitions to words, respond to all verbal language as if it were relevant.

Interrupt the child when he verbally acts out routines from daily activities in which he is not currently engaged. Remind the child of the activity in which he is supposed to be engaged, then begin scripting the action of that activity for the child. For example, if the child verbally imitates circle-time routines during snack time, interrupt him. Remind the child "It's snack time," and begin talking about information relevant to snack time.

While the child is reading a book or watching a video, label the action using simple verb phrases. Then imitate the action with the child using the same language. Later observe the child playing independently. When the child performs an action tied to the practiced sequence, label it with the same language used to comment on the corresponding book or video.

Activities: Small Group

Attach consistent initiation phrases to social group games such as Tag; Duck, Duck, Goose; or Mother, May I. Prompt peers to initiate game play using the established initiation phrase.

When the child verbally imitates information from a known video, book, or play action, encourage peers to join the child's talk by adding information relevant to the verbalized script.

Strategies

When teaching imitation, you have three choices:

1. Build on what the child gives you (scaffold).
2. Give a new action (prompt).
3. Shape inappropriate behaviors into purposeful actions (shape).

The choice of strategy and level of prompting used is made moment to moment based on the child's attention, understanding, and interest.

Follow the child's lead if purposeful. If the child is unfocused or not engaging in purposeful activity, provide appropriate modeling to cue targeted actions.

When the child's behavior is meaningful to the context, reference and shape it into the target actions.

If the child is difficult to engage or keep focused, ask the following questions:

1. Is the activity organized?
2. Is the activity meaningful to the child?
3. Is the activity motivating for the child?
4. Do you have the child's attention?
5. Is the child comfortable in the environment?
6. Can you interrupt the child's rituals?

DO-WATCH-LISTEN-SAY: Social and Communication Intervention for Children with Autism
by Kathleen Ann Quill © 2000 Paul H. Brookes Publishing Co.

Vignettes

Verbal Imitation Vignettes

Eddie

Whenever Eddie's teacher tried to get him to imitate vocal play, he would close his eyes and try to turn away from her. She decided to pull back from her imitation drills and listen to the sounds he was making spontaneously. When Eddie was engaged in play, she would repeat his sounds without looking at him. Intermittently, Eddie's teacher would position herself in front of him. She took his hands, placed them on her mouth, and silently formed the sounds she repeated earlier. Once Eddie became comfortable with the face-to-face game, his teacher added the sounds to the mouth movements. Eventually, she imitated his sounds in a turn-taking exchange. New sounds were intermittently added to the turn-taking game.

Frankie

Frankie was having difficulty focusing during a structured motor imitation session in which he was seated in a chair across from his teacher. He continually laid his head down on her knee and tried to squirm onto the floor. The teacher decided to switch her focus to his verbal imitation goals. She followed Frankie's lead and pretended to get sleepy. She made an exaggerated yawn, stretched her arms out, and announced that she was tired. She then draped her body over Frankie's, closed her eyes, and pretended to snore as if she were asleep. When Frankie began to push against her, she told him to say "Up" as she gestured up. As soon as Frankie vocalized "Up," his teacher jumped up, exclaimed "You woke me up," and tickled his belly. She repeated the game shaping the word up into the phrase "wake up."

Sam

Although Sam would babble spontaneously when alone and could imitate some mouth movements, Sam's teacher could not get him to imitate words upon request. She would set up trials with the direction "Say _____" using visual supports, such as objects and flashcards. Sam typically began to make unrelated sounds as a response to his teacher's prompt. His teacher decided to engage in some of Sam's favorite motor play—swinging on the swing and riding in the wagon. She would imitate his babbling when he was in motion, building up the vocal tone until she would suddenly stop with an animated "Stop." She then told him to say a relevant phrase to resume movement, such as "Let's go" or "Push me." Once the expectation to speak to gain a desired response was established, Sam's teacher changed the verbal turn-taking to commenting games. When she stopped the swing or wagon, Sam's teacher pointed to an object in the environment and said, "Look, it's a (object name)." She then repeated the first part of the phrase and Sam filled in the targeted word.

Pam

During free play time, Pam would sit facing the wall and verbally imitate circle-time routines and songs. Her teacher tried to engage her in play, but Pam quickly returned to her scripts and pulled away from peers when they approached. Trying to replace her calming and somewhat reinforcing scripting with nonpreferred play turned into a power struggle often ending with Pam holding her ears and singing louder. One day during free play, a peer model approached Pam while she was singing "Itsy Bitsy Spider." He began singing with her and handed her the spider puppet. He then got the alligator puppet and began singing "Five Little Monkeys." She quieted and watched him. The peer then made his alligator eat Pam's spider while saying "Chomp, chomp. Yum, yum. That was delicious." Pam imitated his language in a turn-taking exchange for about 5 minutes. Later that week when Pam began singing "Itsy Bitsy Spider," her teacher handed her the spider and alligator puppets. Pam independently replayed the sequence she had engaged in earlier with the peer model.

Activity

C. Organization

Space 1. Prepares for activity by locating area/materials (e.g., chair, coat)

Strategies

Define the spatial boundaries for the child by

- Reducing clutter
- Limiting environmental choices
- Establishing predictable locations for items
- Separating large spaces into smaller, defined areas
- Taking out a single toy, activity, or play set at a time

Designate a place for the child to hang up his coat and store personal items. Use the child's photograph and name to identify this space.

Place the child's photograph and name on his chair.

Label dresser drawers with representative photographs or pictographs and written labels to indicate the location of the child's clothing items.

Have a specific place mat, with an outline of a place setting and the child's name and photograph, associated with eating across all settings.

Section off classroom centers by marking boundaries on the floor with colored masking tape.

Segregate floor play space by assigning each child a carpet square and directing the child to play on his own carpet square.

Label shelves and toy boxes with representational labels (pictographs or written labels) to identify the toys or items contained in those spaces.

Color-code toys that belong in a respective area by marking their bins with colored circles that correspond to an identically colored circle marking placement on a shelf, on the floor, in a closet, or in a drawer.

Use different color-coded folders for each subject area.

Separate toys into bins. Group the toys into individual play sets or closed-ended play activities. Examples: 1) a car, enough blocks to build a small tower or house, and a few play people; 2) a baby doll, spoon, plate, cup, and two or three toy foods; 3) a puzzle with all of its pieces. All of the pieces necessary to complete a specific play activity or schema should be contained in the bin.

Cover items not in use, or use stop signs to represent items that are not a choice.

Activity

C. Organization
Space 2. Keeps toys/materials in designated locations

Strategies

Define the spatial boundaries for the child by

- Reducing clutter
- Limiting environmental choices
- Establishing predictable locations for items
- Separating large spaces into smaller, defined areas
- Taking out a single toy, activity, or play set at a time

Designate a place for the child to hang up his coat and store personal items. Use the child's photograph and name to identify the space.

Label dresser drawers with representative photographs or pictographs and written labels to indicate the location of the child's clothing items.

Have a specific place mat, with an outline of a place setting and the child's name and photograph, associated with eating across all settings.

Section off classroom centers by marking boundaries on the floor with colored masking tape.

Segregate floor play space by assigning each child a carpet square and directing the child to play on his own carpet square.

Color-code toys that belong in a respective area by marking their bins with colored circles that correspond to an identically colored circle marking placement on a shelf, on the floor, in a closet, or in a drawer.

Use different color-coded folders for each subject area.

Separate toys into bins. Group the toys into individual play sets or closed-ended play activities. Examples: 1) a car, enough blocks to build a small tower or house, and a few play people; 2) a baby doll, spoon, plate, cup, and two or three toy foods; 3) a puzzle with all of its pieces. All of the pieces necessary to complete a specific play activity or schema should be contained in the bin.

Activity

C. Organization

Space 3. Completes activity by putting away materials

Strategies

Define the spatial boundaries for the child by

- Reducing clutter
- Limiting environmental choices
- Establishing predictable locations for items
- Separating large spaces into smaller, defined areas
- Taking out a single toy, activity, or play set at a time

Label dresser drawers with representative photographs or pictographs and written labels to indicate the location of the child's clothing items.

Have a specific place mat, with an outline of a place setting and the child's name and photograph, associated with eating across all settings.

Label shelves and toy boxes with representational labels (pictographs or written labels) to identify the toys or items contained in those spaces.

Color-code toys that belong in a respective area by marking their bins with colored circles that correspond to an identically colored circle marking placement on a shelf, on the floor, in a closet, or in a drawer.

Separate toys into bins. Group the toys into individual play sets or closed-ended play activities. Examples: 1) a car, enough blocks to build a small tower or house, and a few play people; 2) a baby doll, spoon, plate, cup, and two or three toy foods; 3) a puzzle with all of its pieces. All of the pieces necessary to complete a specific play activity or schema should be contained in the bin.

DO-WATCH-LISTEN-SAY: Social and Communication Intervention for Children with Autism
by Kathleen Ann Quill © 2000 Paul H. Brookes Publishing Co.

Activity

C. Organization

Choices 1. Makes choices within an activity

Strategies

Clearly establish the child's choices by

- Limiting the number of choices offered
- Not adding to choices once they have been presented to the child
- Presenting choices visually as well as verbally

Present the child with two objects, one preferred and one nonpreferred. Ask the child if he wants object A or object B. Prompt the child to point to or touch the object he desires.

Line up the child's play choices on the top of a shelf. Cover the rest of the shelving with a sheet to block other toys from view. Have the child pick a toy from the field presented.

Use linear choice boards: Visually present choices to the child in a linear pattern. Use pictographic or photographic representations of the choice items labeled with the written word. Have the child point to or pull off to exchange the pictograph of the item he desires.

Use circular choice boards: Visually present choices to the child in a circular pattern. Use pictographic or photographic representations of the choice items labeled with the written word. Have the child point to or pull off to exchange the pictograph of the item he desires.

Place choice boards on room doors, dresser drawers, closet doors, refrigerator doors, cabinets, toy boxes, and surfaces of any enclosed container space. The boards represent the choices available in those areas.

Activity

C. Organization

Choices 2. Makes choice between two objects/activities

Strategies

Clearly establish the child's choices by

- Limiting the number of choices offered
- Not adding to choices once they have been presented to the child
- Presenting choices visually as well as verbally

Present the child with two objects, one preferred and one nonpreferred. Ask the child if he wants object A or object B. Prompt the child to point to or touch the object he desires.

Line up the child's play choices on the top of a shelf. Cover the rest of the shelving with a sheet to block other toys from view. Have the child pick a toy from the field presented.

Use linear choice boards: Visually present choices to the child in a linear pattern. Use pictographic or photographic representations of the choice items labeled with the written word. Have the child point to or pull off to exchange the pictograph of the item he desires.

Use circular choice boards: Visually present choices to the child in a circular pattern. Use pictographic or photographic representations of the choice items labeled with the written word. Have the child point to or pull off to exchange the pictograph of the item he desires.

Place choice boards on room doors, dresser drawers, closet doors, refrigerator doors, cabinets, toy boxes, and surfaces of any enclosed container space. The boards represent the choices available in those areas.

At the beginning of choice or free play time, hand the child a key with his name and photograph on it. Direct the child to choose a play area. Have the child place his key on a hook in the chosen play area to indicate the space in which he chose to play. You can also use the keys to represent available play areas/activities and have the child choose from a field of keys on a choice board. In either case, have a set number of hooks in each play space for keys. When all of the hooks are full, the play space is full and no longer a choice.

Place stop signs or "X"s on items that are not a choice or play spaces that are closed.

Create a board with photographs of all of the children in the class. Prior to transitions and/or any activity conducive to partnering, have the child choose a play partner from the photographic choices. Once a child is chosen as a partner, his photograph is moved to a *taken* or *not a choice* section of the board.

Activity

C. Organization

Choices 3. Makes choice among multiple objects/activities

Strategies

Clearly establish the child's choices by

- Limiting the number of choices offered
- Not adding to choices once they have been presented to the child
- Presenting choices visually as well as verbally

Line up the child's play choices on the top of a shelf. Cover the rest of the shelving with a sheet to block other toys from view. Have the child pick a toy from the field presented.

Use linear choice boards: Visually present choices to the child in a linear pattern. Use pictographic or photographic representations of the choice items labeled with the written word. Have the child point to or pull off to exchange the pictograph of the item he desires.

Use circular choice boards: Visually present choices to the child in a circular pattern. Use pictographic or photographic representations of the choice items labeled with the written word. Have the child point to or pull off to exchange the pictograph of the item he desires.

Place choice boards on room doors, dresser drawers, closet doors, refrigerator doors, cabinets, toy boxes, and surfaces of any enclosed container space. The boards represent the choices available in those areas.

At the beginning of choice or free play time, hand the child a key with his name and photograph on it. Direct the child to choose a play area. Have the child place his key on a hook in the chosen play area to indicate the space in which he chose to play. You can also use the keys to represent available play areas/activities and have the child choose from a field of keys on a choice board. In either case, have a set number of hooks in each play space for keys. When all of the hooks are full, the play space is full and no longer a choice.

Place stop signs or "X"s on items that are not a choice or play spaces that are closed.

Create a board with photographs of all of the children in the class. Prior to transitions and/or any activity conducive to partnering, have the child choose a play partner from the photographic choices. Once a child is chosen as a partner, his photograph is moved to a *taken* or *not a choice* section of the board.

DO-WATCH-LISTEN-SAY: Social and Communication Intervention for Children with Autism
by Kathleen Ann Quill © 2000 Paul H. Brookes Publishing Co.

Activity

C. Organization

Time 1. Attends to an activity until completed

Strategies

Clarify for the child the length of time he is expected to remain engaged in a task or activity by defining time as a series of events rather than temporal units (e.g., minute, hour).

At the beginning of an activity, present the child with a visual time board.

- Use a 4-3-2-1-done board: Have the child pull off a number to mark the passage of a specific time period (e.g., 1 minute, 2 minutes). Once all numbers have been taken off, the activity is done.
- Use a name board: Have the child place a letter of his name on a board to mark the passage of a specific time period (e.g., 1 minute, 2 minutes). When his name is spelled, the activity is done.
- Use a puzzle board: Have the child place a piece of a picture on a board to mark the passage of a specific time period (e.g., 1 minute, 2 minutes). Once the picture is complete, the activity is done.
- Use a 1-2-3-4-done board: Have the child place an "X" in a numbered square to mark the passage of a specific time period (e.g., 1 minute, 2 minutes). Once all of the "X"s fill in the boxes, the activity is done.

Fill a box with a number of familiar, mastered, closed-ended toys/activities. The child takes out one activity at a time, completes it, puts it aside, and then retrieves another. Once the box is empty, the play session is over. The child puts the toys/activities back into the box, cleans up the play area, and transitions to the next activity.

Create consistent routines around play activities. Have the child retrieve a desired toy/activity/play set, bring it to the appropriate/designated play area, play, clean up, and return the item before transitioning to a new activity. If an item is not a closed-ended task (e.g., puzzles, manipulatives, books), define for the child a sense of what needs to be done for that activity to be completed.

Set a timer at the beginning of an activity or when you direct the child to wait. When the timer goes off, the task is complete or the waiting period is over, and the child can move on to the next activity.

Have the child count to or sing a set of songs to himself. Once the child completes the established count or songs, he is finished waiting and can move on to the next activity, return to the activity in progress, or receive the item for which he is waiting.

Use a digital clock with the child. Create time cards to indicate when an activity is to occur. When the time on the card matches the time on the clock, it is time for the awaited activity.

Activity

C. Organization

Time 2. Waits when directed

Strategies

Clarify for the child the length of time he is expected to remain engaged in a task or activity by defining time as a series of events rather than temporal units (e.g., minute, hour).

Present the child with a simple toy or manipulative to play with while he waits.

Have chairs set up in a designated area in the classroom. Between transitions, have the child sit in a chair and give him a waiting toy.

When the child is directed to wait in public places, teach the child to hold on to a consistent object (e.g., mother's purse, shopping cart) as a tactile cue to wait.

Place circles on the floor of areas in which a child is expected to wait (e.g., line to the bathroom, door to outside, in the garage next to the car). Teach the child to stay on the circle until it is his turn or time for him to make the transition.

Set a timer at the beginning of an activity or when you direct the child to wait. When the timer goes off, the task is complete or the waiting period is over, and the child can move on to the next activity.

Have the child count to or sing a set of songs to himself. Once the child completes the established count or songs, he is finished waiting and can move on to the next activity, return to the activity in progress, or receive the item for which he is waiting.

Use a digital clock with the child. Create time cards to indicate when an activity is to occur. When the time on the card matches the time on the clock, it is time for the awaited activity.

DO-WATCH-LISTEN-SAY: Social and Communication Intervention for Children with Autism
by Kathleen Ann Quill © 2000 Paul H. Brookes Publishing Co.

Activity

C. Organization

Expectations 1. Is independent with familiar activities

Strategies

Clearly define for the child the expectations of a presented activity by

- Defining the directions, rules, process, and/or sequence of the activity
- Establishing consistent and predictable routines around familiar activities
- Using familiar tools to plan and visually identify for the child the sequence/steps required to complete the activity; using visual cues with familiar commands and learned directions

When setting up a child to play, line up the items in the order they will be used or needed for the activity.

Have the sequence of a task visually mapped using a 1-2-3-4-done board. The board should be divided into five squares. The first four will be numbered *1, 2, 3,* and *4* with spaces for pictographs of each activity or step in the task sequence. The fifth will be for the *all done* pictograph.

Create social scripts to describe the sequence and expectations of an activity. Present the task, outline the sequence of steps necessary to complete the activity, and define the termination point or expected completed project.

Prior to infrequent events (e.g., holidays, vacations, doctor visits), create a simple social script describing the event and what the child is expected to do during the event. Ground the description in tangible objects and rituals. Practice any parts of the event that can be practiced beforehand (e.g., mock trick-or-treating, playing doctor).

DO-WATCH-LISTEN-SAY: Social and Communication Intervention for Children with Autism
by Kathleen Ann Quill © 2000 Paul H. Brookes Publishing Co.

Activity

C. Organization
Expectations 2. Follows directions during novel activities

Strategies

Clearly define for the child the expectations of a presented activity by

- Defining the directions, rules, process, and/or sequence of the activity
- Using familiar tools to plan and visually identify for the child the sequence/steps required to complete the activity; using visual cues with familiar commands and learned directions

When setting up a child to play, line up the items in the order they will be used or needed for the activity.

Have the sequence of a task visually mapped using a 1-2-3-4-done board. The board should be divided into five squares. The first four will be numbered *1, 2, 3,* and *4* with spaces for pictographs of each activity or step in the task sequence. The fifth will be for the *all done* pictograph.

Clearly verbalize what comes next, and repeat it often to the child prior to engaging in a new activity.

Create social scripts to describe the sequence and expectations of an activity. Present the task, outline the sequence of steps necessary to complete the activity, and define the termination point or expected completed project.

Assemble a series of directions and rules that the child uses on a daily basis. For each direction or rule, create a simple rule card using a pictorial representation and a written word. When presenting a novel activity, use the cards specific to the task to cue the child to the expected demands of the activity. The cards represent familiar directions and learned rules, so they allow a measure of familiarity in an unfamiliar situation.

Prior to infrequent events (e.g., holidays, vacations, doctor visits), create a simple social script describing the event and what the child is expected to do during the event. Ground the description in tangible objects and rituals. Practice any parts of the event that can be practiced beforehand (e.g., mock trick-or-treating, playing doctor).

Activity

C. Organization

Transitions 1. Makes transitions to the next activity when directed

Strategies

Prepare the child for upcoming transitions by

- Clearly defining what comes next for the child
- Establishing the sequence of activities
- Employing consistent cues to forewarn the child of transitions

Use transition objects: Find a reinforcing, motivating, and/or comforting object that the child can carry with him between activities and places.

Have a consistent auditory stimulus (e.g., bell, "all done" song, whistle) to indicate the termination of one activity and the move to the next.

Incorporate a transition routine between activities. Following the termination of one activity, have the child return to a fixed location and go through an established sequence of simple actions (e.g., basic motor imitation, songs, counting) before moving on to the next activity.

Use First/Then boards: Place two photographs of activities the child is expected to complete on a small board divided into two sections. Always put the more motivating activity second and couple with the verbal "First _____, then _____."

To prepare the child for who will be picking him up from school, use a simple home transportation visual that contains a photograph of the family member who will be picking up the child. The visual can also be coupled with a place board that indicates the location of other family members (e.g., Dad = work, Sister = school, Mom = home).

Have photographs of places commonly visited in the car to show the child the destination prior to arriving.

Map out the child's daily routine using schedule boards. For nonreaders, use pictographs; for readers, use written words.

Prior to beginning the day or leaving for an outing, have the child map out the itinerary on a dry-erase board or notepad. After completing each activity, let the child cross it off the board or pad. For older children or children moving away from rigid schedules, put activities in random order.

DO-WATCH-LISTEN-SAY: Social and Communication Intervention for Children with Autism
by Kathleen Ann Quill © 2000 Paul H. Brookes Publishing Co.

Activity

C. Organization

Transitions 2. Accepts when an activity is interrupted to make a transition

Strategies

Prepare the child for upcoming transitions by

- Clearly defining what comes next for the child
- Employing consistent cues to forewarn the child of transitions
- Creating a repertoire of objects or prompts that remain consistent despite inconsistency in sequence or changes in daily routine

Use transition objects: Find a reinforcing, motivating, and/or comforting object that the child can carry with him between activities and places.

Have a consistent auditory stimulus (e.g., bell, "all done" song, whistle) to indicate the termination of one activity and the move to the next.

Incorporate a transition routine between activities. Following the termination of one activity, have the child return to a fixed location and go through an established sequence of simple actions (e.g., basic motor imitation, songs, counting) before moving on to the next activity.

Use First/Then boards: Place two photographs of activities the child is expected to complete on a small board divided into two sections. Always put the more motivating activity second and couple with the verbal "First _____, then _____."

Have photographs of places commonly visited in the car to show the child the destination prior to arriving.

Prior to beginning the day or leaving for an outing, have the child map out the itinerary on a dry-erase board or notepad. After completing each activity, let the child cross it off the board or pad. For older children or children moving away from rigid schedules, put activities in random order.

Activity

C. Organization

Transitions 3. Makes transitions when an unexpected change occurs

Strategies

Prepare the child for upcoming transitions by

- Clearly defining what comes next for the child
- Establishing the sequence of activities
- Employing consistent cues to forewarn the child of transitions
- Creating a repertoire of objects or prompts that remain consistent despite inconsistency in sequence or changes in daily routine

Use transition objects: Find a reinforcing, motivating, and/or comforting object that the child can carry with him between activities and places.

Have a consistent auditory stimulus (e.g., bell, "all done" song, whistle) to indicate the termination of one activity and the move to the next.

Incorporate a transition routine between activities. Following the termination of one activity, have the child return to a fixed location and go through an established sequence of simple actions (e.g., basic motor imitation, songs, counting) before moving on to the next activity.

Write stories about spontaneously occurring situations that disrupt daily routines, such as fire drills, snow days, illness/accidents, car breakdowns, or computer freezes.

Attach a consistent catch phrase to indicate unexpected changes in a routine (e.g., "Oh no," "It's different," "Surprise," "Oh my"). The phrase becomes the familiar, understood factor to cue the child to what comes next, even if that event or activity is novel or disruptive.

DO-WATCH-LISTEN-SAY: Social and Communication Intervention for Children with Autism
by Kathleen Ann Quill © 2000 Paul H. Brookes Publishing Co.

Activity

C. Organization
Possessions 1. Recognizes personal belongings (mine)

Strategies

Make distinct the separation between the child's possessions and others' by

- Marking the child's space and materials
- Clearly defining community space and materials
- Identifying shared space and materials

Designate spaces for personal belongings (e.g., coat hook, chair, cubby, shoe rack, table area, work materials) using the child's photograph and name.

Create personal tags with the child's name and photograph to label items the child owns or is using.

Define possession by color-coding objects in the environment. For example, all of the items with red circles belong to the child. Items with purple circles belong to peer A. Items with blue circles belong to the teacher. The child does not have free access to items not marked by red circles. Mark common materials with multicolored dots.

Give the child a box. Prior to free play time, have the child fill it with his toys of choice. All items in the box belong to the child. Any items not in the box belong to others.

Set up a joint tabletop activity (e.g., playdough, art project, puzzle, simple building task) with shared materials. Give each child a small bin. Divide the materials between the child and his play partner by filling their bins. Define for the child that the items in his bin are his and the items in the play partner's bin belong to the play partner. If the child wants an item that is not his, prompt the child to identify who has it and direct his request to that person.

Give each child a place mat colored or labeled (with the child's photograph and name) to indicate his personal play space. Present play materials in one centrally placed box. The items placed on the child's mat are his, the items on the play partner's mat belong to the play partner. Materials in the box are shared.

Use woven place mats with two colors to represent a shared play space.

Engage the child in show-and-tell activities. Have the child bring in a personal item to show and describe to his peers. When other children bring in items, have the child identify which items belong to whom.

Activity

C. Organization

Possessions 2. Recognizes the belongings of others (yours)

Strategies

Make distinct the separation between the child's possessions and others' by

- Marking the child's space and materials
- Clearly defining community space and materials
- Identifying shared space and materials

Designate spaces for personal belongings (e.g., coat hook, chair, cubby, shoe rack, table area, work materials) using child's photograph and name.

Create personal tags with the child's name and photograph to label items the child owns or is using.

Define possession by color-coding objects in the environment. For example, all of the items with red circles belong to the child. Items with purple circles belong to peer A. Items with blue circles belong to the teacher. The child does not have free access to items not marked by red circles. Mark common materials with multicolored dots.

Give the child a box. Prior to free play time, have the child fill it with toys he has chosen to use. All items in the box belong to the child. Any items not in the box belong to others.

Set up a joint tabletop activity (e.g., playdough, art project, puzzle, simple building task) with shared materials. Give each child a small bin. Divide the materials between the child and his play partner by filling their bins. Define for the child that the items in his bin are his and the items in the play partner's bin belong to the play partner. If the child wants an item that is not his, prompt the child to identify who has it and direct his request to that person.

Give each child a place mat colored or labeled (with the child's photograph and name) to indicate his personal play space. Present play materials in one centrally placed box. The items placed on the child's mat are his, the items on the play partner's mat belong to the play partner. Materials in the box are shared.

Use woven place mats with two colors to represent a shared play space.

Engage the child in show-and-tell activities. Have the child bring in a personal item to show and describe to his peers. When other children bring in items, have the child identify which items belong to whom.

DO-WATCH-LISTEN-SAY: Social and Communication Intervention for Children with Autism
by Kathleen Ann Quill © 2000 Paul H. Brookes Publishing Co.

Activity

C. Organization
Possessions 3. Recognizes shared belongings (ours)

Strategies

Make distinct the separation between the child's possessions and others' by

- Marking the child's space and materials
- Clearly defining community space and materials
- Identifying shared space and materials

Designate spaces for personal belongings (e.g., coat hook, chair, cubby, shoe rack, table area, work materials) using the child's photograph and name.

Create personal tags with the child's name and photograph to label items the child owns or is using.

Define possession by color-coding objects in the environment. For example, all of the items with red circles belong to the child. Items with purple circles belong to peer A. Items with blue circles belong to the teacher. The child does not have free access to items not marked by red circles. Mark common materials with multicolored dots.

Give the child a box. Prior to free play time, have the child fill it with toys he has chosen to use. All items in the box belong to the child. Any items not in the box belong to others.

Set up a joint tabletop activity (e.g., playdough, art project, puzzle, simple building task) with shared materials. Give each child a small bin. Divide the materials between the child and his play partner by filling their bins. Define for the child that the items in his bin are his and the items in the play partner's bin belong to the play partner. If the child wants an item that is not his, prompt the child to identify who has it and direct his request to that person.

Give each child a place mat colored or labeled (with the child's photograph and name) to indicate his personal play space. Present play materials in one centrally placed box. The items placed on the child's mat are his, the items on the play partner's mat belong to the play partner. Materials in the box are shared.

Use woven place mats with two colors to represent a shared play space.

Engage the child in show-and-tell activities. Have the child bring in a personal item to show and describe to his peers. When other children bring in items, have the child identify which items belong to whom.

DO-WATCH-LISTEN-SAY: Social and Communication Intervention for Children with Autism
by Kathleen Ann Quill © 2000 Paul H. Brookes Publishing Co.

Activity

C. Organization

Comfort 1. Can be comforted

Strategies

Simplify language and auditory input.

Create and maintain a relaxing set of activities specific to the child's needs.

Determine child's motivators, preferred activities, and self-calming mechanisms.

Reduce environmental stimuli.

Limit or eliminate choices.

Emphasize rhythm and rituals in calming activities.

Use muted lighting and neutral colors. Restrict bright fluorescent lighting and busy wall patterns.

Use a clear, neutral vocal tone. When child is overstimulated, revert to gestural or pictographic cues.

When child appears disorganized or overstimulated, eliminate choices, clarify the child's options, and refrain from question-and-answer exchanges. Rely on simple commenting and short directives to focus and organize the child.

Intersperse gross motor activity throughout the day with clear sensory components (e.g., roll the child in blankets, squish him between pillows, swing, hang him upside down, jump, play chase games).

Create a break space in a quiet corner of the environment. Use pillows, blankets, ball pits, and/or enclosed tents to form a contained, darkened enclave so the child can enwrap himself.

Have a repertoire of simple songs with motor components to engage the child. Emphasize songs with repetitive rhythms.

DO-WATCH-LISTEN-SAY: Social and Communication Intervention for Children with Autism
by Kathleen Ann Quill © 2000 Paul H. Brookes Publishing Co.

C. Organization
Comfort 2. Can calm self

Strategies

Create and maintain a relaxing set of activities specific to the child's needs.

Determine child's motivators, preferred activities, and self-calming mechanisms.

Teach the child to request breaks and use break spaces.

Emphasize rhythm and rituals in calming activities.

Allow the child to listen to white noise or classical or preferred music.

Provide the child with a fanny pack filled with squeeze balls, rubbing fabric pieces, or other calming fidget toys for him to use when he is anxious, overstimulated, or otherwise in need of calming.

Intersperse gross motor activity throughout the day with clear sensory components (e.g., roll the child in blankets, squish him between pillows, swing, hang him upside down, jump, play chase games).

Create a break space in a quiet corner of the environment. Use pillows, blankets, ball pits, and/or enclosed tents to form a contained, darkened enclave so the child can enwrap himself.

DO-WATCH-LISTEN-SAY: Social and Communication Intervention for Children with Autism
by Kathleen Ann Quill © 2000 Paul H. Brookes Publishing Co.

Appendix A
Core Skills Progress Sheets

Verbal Imitation Progress Sheet

Child's name:_____   Date:_____

Directions: 1. Record spontaneous imitation that occurs in natural contexts.
2. Indicate whether imitation occurred in response to an adult (A) or a peer (P).

	Verbal message	Partner	
1		A	P
2		A	P
3		A	P
4		A	P
5		A	P
6		A	P
7		A	P
8		A	P
9		A	P
10		A	P
11		A	P
12		A	P
13		A	P
14		A	P
15		A	P
16		A	P
17		A	P
18		A	P
19		A	P
20		A	P

DO-WATCH-LISTEN-SAY: Social and Communication Intervention for Children with Autism
by Kathleen Ann Quill © 2000 Paul H. Brookes Publishing Co.

Motor Imitation Progress Sheet

Child's name:_____ Date: _____

Directions: 1. Record spontaneous imitation that occurs in natural contexts.
2. Indicate whether imitation occurred in response to an adult (A) or a peer (P).

	Motor action	Partner
1		A P
2		A P
3		A P
4		A P
5		A P
6		A P
7		A P
8		A P
9		A P
10		A P
11		A P
12		A P
13		A P
14		A P
15		A P
16		A P
17		A P
18		A P
19		A P
20		A P

DO-WATCH-LISTEN-SAY: Social and Communication Intervention for Children with Autism
by Kathleen Ann Quill © 2000 Paul H. Brookes Publishing Co.

chapter 7

Social Skills Curriculum

*Maria E. Fair, Kathleen Ann Quill,
and Kathleen Norton Bracken*

Virtually every social situation requires the ability to watch, listen, and/or communicate with others while engaged in an activity. Social activities are complex and constantly changing. Social skills intervention should help children with autism coordinate what to DO, who to WATCH, how to LISTEN, and what to SAY in a variety of social situations.

This chapter describes interventions to enhance three general aspects of social development: **play skills, group skills,** and **social skills** needed in community settings. There is a set of activity sheets that corresponds to the play and group items within the Social Skills Checklist of the Assessment of Social and Communication Skills for Children with Autism. The activity sheets list suggested activities and strategies for building solitary play, social play, and group participation. In addition, there is a detailed planning guide for building social skills in the community.

The design of intervention for solitary play, social play, group skills, and community activities is built on the basic DO-WATCH-LISTEN-SAY framework. It is assumed that the child first learns what to do, then who to watch, then how to interact with others. For example, solitary play begins with simple actions with one toy and develops into multiple actions with open-ended activities. In social play, the child first learns to observe others by sharing space, then learns to take turns and later cooperate with others. In group activities, the child first learns to attend to one person, then watch others in the group, and finally interact in structured and unstructured situations. The community planning guide is also based on this fundamental framework.

It is generally understood that social skills are required in every context, and every moment is an opportunity to build social competence. Therefore, instruction in natural contexts should be the primary focus of intervention. The ideas provided in this chapter should be viewed as a starting point for designing social intervention across the child's entire day. The suggested activities and strategies focus on structured environments as the primary means to achieve social success. The child's motivation and level of social understanding are respected while social skills are continually expanded and shaped through the use of organizational supports, social supports, and visually cued instructional supports. It is important to observe and understand the child's behaviors before deciding on a strategy. Always remember that beyond the markers of autism, the children will only socially participate if they find the situation motivating and meaningful.

TARGETING SOCIAL OBJECTIVES

In determining social skills objectives, refer to the Social Skills Checklist in the assessment tool as well as the list of priority objectives that have been established for the child on the Assessment Summary Sheet. Target objectives should reflect skills that are

- Not observed or never demonstrated
- Only observed when prompted
- Only observed with limited partners (when applicable)
- Only observed in limited contexts
- Not observed due to challenging behaviors

The intervention plan should include objectives to build solitary play, social play, group skills, and specific social skills in target community settings. Once child-specific objectives have been selected, reference the corresponding activity sheets for sample activities and strategies to build play and group skills. The activity sheets for play and group skills are suggestions to encourage skill mastery and are not intended to be implemented in isolation. The child, not the arbitrary boundaries of a specific activity or strategy, should shape the child's social development.

See the Community Planning Guide to design an individualized intervention plan for specific community settings. The Community Planning Guide is an outline to assist in the development and implementation of a social skills intervention plan in the community. The planning guide is organized to elicit information that is child specific and setting specific, and it can be used to design a social skills plan for any social situation. The goal of social intervention is for the child to acquire a variety of social skills across a range of situations.

USING THE ACTIVITY SHEETS

The format of each activity sheet is organized similarly. The general area (e.g., Play) tops the activity sheet, followed by the general objective (e.g., Social Play: Cooperative) and the specific skill (e.g., Shares materials) that corresponds to the items in the assessment tool. The specific skill can be written as a criterion-based objective (samples are given in Table 7.1). The play activity sheet begins with suggested criteria for selecting play activities and describes a sample activity. This is followed by a list of fun ideas to enhance play. Emphasis is placed on using the child's motivation, interests, and style of exploration to find creative ways to expand play (see examples in Table 7.2 and Table 7.3). The group skills activity sheets contain criteria for selecting group activities and offer a series of suggestions to foster group skills. *Group skills* are defined as the ability to attend to adults and peers, wait, take turns, and follow group directions. The activity sheets include a sample group activity that describes how to apply the recommended strategies. The basic assumption is that the characteristics of a group contribute to the child's success (see Chapter 4). The easiest group activities occur in unison; have limited toys and materials; and require no waiting, turn-taking, or language comprehension. In contrast, the most difficult groups involve watching others in unstructured situations, random turn-taking, waiting, and verbal discussion.

USING THE COMMUNITY PLANNING GUIDE

Teaching children with autism to participate with family and friends in the community is often the biggest intervention challenge. Children with autism benefit from structure, predictability, and organization, but these elements are typically lacking in community settings.

Table 7.1. Sample criterion-based objectives

Objective:	The child demonstrates functional play using open-ended activities in 80% of the opportunities presented. During specific contexts with adult prompting During specific contexts with visual supports During specific contexts independently During novel contexts independently
Objective:	The child participates in parallel play with sharing in 80% of the opportunities presented. During specific contexts with adults During specific contexts with peers During novel contexts with adults During novel contexts with peers
Objective:	The child plays structured group games in 80% of the opportunities presented. During specific contexts with prompts During specific contexts without prompts During novel contexts with prompts During novel contexts without prompts
Objective:	The child demonstrates the skills necessary to get a haircut in 80% of the opportunities presented. During specific contexts with prompts During specific contexts without prompts During novel contexts with prompts During novel contexts without prompts

Community settings are busy and unstructured and often involve large groups whose behaviors are unpredictable. These environments pose the greatest challenge for the children.

MONITORING PROGRESS

Monitoring a child's progress with each target skill is necessary to determine skill mastery. Progress reflects changes in the child's level of independent play, level of social participation in play and other group situations, and level of social participation and self-control in community settings. Skill mastery is defined by

- Acquisition of the skill—the presence of the skill without adult prompts
- Generalization of the skill across adults, peers, and different social groupings
- Generalization of the skill across multiple familiar and novel contexts
- Reduction of challenging behaviors

The Assessment of Social and Communication Skills for Children with Autism can be used to monitor progress in the areas of play and group skills. Intermittent videotaping of the child in various social contexts is recommended as a complementary means of documenting the acquisition of functional social skills. In addition, a number of sample reproducible forms are provided (see Appendixes A, B, C, and D) to monitor a child's progress. The data forms provide additional information about a child's play and group skills, and they can be used to systematically assess ongoing social progress and adapt the social intervention plans.

Appendix A: Play Interest Survey

The Play Interest Survey can help you monitor the child's solitary play skills and rate the child's interests. Data on the child's motivation and interests can be used to expand play skills. The data can also be used to select appropriate activities for social play. This survey is organized into 10 categories of play activities: exploratory play, physical play, manipulatives, constructive play, art, literacy, sociodramatic play, games, music, and social games.

Appendix B: Social Play Task Analysis

The Social Play Task Analysis lists the cognitive (DO), social (WATCH), and communicative (LISTEN and SAY) dimensions of social play. Twenty sample social play activities, two from each of the ten categories of play activities, are task-analyzed. The social play task analysis can be used to monitor a child's social play skills. The format of the task analysis can be duplicated for all other social play activities.

Appendix C: Social Skills Progress Sheets

Three data sheets are provided to measure progress in solitary play, social play, and group skills. These forms record observations over an extended period of time. The Solitary Play Progress Sheet asks you to list the child's solitary play activities and level of independence. The Social Play Progress Sheet asks you to list specific social play activities, coding the child's ability to watch, share, take turns, and respond to adults and peers. The Group Skills Progress Sheet asks you to list specific group activities, coding the child's ability to attend, wait, take turns, and follow directions during the activity.

Appendix D: Community Planning Guide

The Community Planning Guide can assist in the design and implementation of a child-specific, setting-specific intervention plan to build social skills in the community. The planning guide is divided into three parts. Part I is a survey completed by the child's caregiver to identify the child's social and behavioral issues in the targeted community setting. To begin, identify the community setting that is problematic for the child. Next, answer the set of specific questions to assist in developing an intervention plan. Part II targets specific goals and objectives. Using the information from the survey, identify the skills to be addressed in the target setting. Part III helps determine an intervention plan. Using the information from the survey, design strategies to prepare the child for the target setting and to help the child compensate for environmental overstimulation and understand social and communication expectations. The plan also includes intervention for "the unexpected" in the community. Two completed examples of the Community Planning Guide follow the activity sheets.

Table 7.2. Creative ways to expand play interests (for a child interested in spinning)

Fun ways to spin your body

Dancing	Gymnastics equipment	Sit 'n Spin
Hula-Hoop	Music audiotapes with movement	Tumbling
Parachute games	Spinning shaped into an interactive game	Cartwheels
Tossing balloons	Hokey-Pokey	Exercise video
Merry-go-round	Ring Around the Rosie	Kite
Amusement park rides	Bubble wand	

Fun toys and activities that spin or have spinning parts

Top	Whirl and Twirl	Audiotapes
Music boxes	Transparent ball with twirling objects	Sandwheel
See 'n Say	Small figures that twirl	Jack-in-the-box
Videos about vehicles	Spin-Rattle-Roll	Yo-yo
Computer games with rotating figures	Round-and-Round Miniature Road Race	Toy helicopter
Record player	Pet hamster on his wheel	Toy trains
Waterwheel	Marble run	Dreidel
Pop-up books with spinning parts	Pinwheel	Rotating water sprinkler
Board game spinner	Spin art	Gears
Kaleidoscope	*Fantasia* (Disney)	Star-filled "magic wand"
Toy cars and trucks	Tornado bottle	Cooking mixer

Table 7.3. More creative ways to expand play interests (for a child interested in letters and numbers)

Select toys and activities that contain numbers or letters of the alphabet, especially those that can be used in multiple ways.

Magnets	Calendar activities	Alphabet or number rubber stamps
Floor puzzles	Toy vehicles with words or numbers on them	Activity pads
Sponge shapes in a water table or bath	Dress-up hats with words or numbers on them	Hopscotch
Magnetic letters in a rice or sand table	Flannel board activities with words or numbers	Boggle Jr.
Beanbag toss into an alphabet or a number frame	Play music by following a numbered music sheet	Dot-to-dot puzzles
Letter- or number-shaped cookie cutters for playdough	Captioned videos	Writing
Vinyl clings for windows	Large piece of chalk for drawing and writing outside	Keyboarding
Coloring books with alphabet or number themes	Spelling items during any game or activity	Playing cards
Lotto games	Spell or count during any social interaction	Music with alphabet songs
Scrabble Junior	Stickers	Alphabet 1-inch blocks
Tracing	Box puzzles	Clocks
Computer games	Books	Money games
Alphabet cards by theme	Paint-by-number	Name cards
Board games	Stencils	Recipes in a play kitchen
Books with alphabet and number themes	Miniature piano with numbers on the keys	Cooking at home
Calculators		Sorting activities
String beads by a color and number pattern		Matching activities
		Magna Doodle
		Count items while playing

Activity

A. Play

Solitary Play 1. Functional: Uses one action with one toy

Selecting Activities

Select toys that can be used in only one conventional manner.

Select toys that allow for repetition of a single action.

Match toy selection to the child's exploratory style. Use Part I of the assessment tool to determine the child's exploratory style.

- If the child's exploratory style is visual, teach him to play with a kaleidoscope.
- If the child's exploratory style is auditory, teach him to play with a musical instrument.
- If the child's exploratory style is tactile, teach him to fingerpaint.
- If the child's exploratory style is kinesthetic, teach him to play on the trampoline.

Select activities that provide the same sensory feedback as the child's self-stimulatory behaviors.

- If the child throws, teach him to throw a ball.
- If the child spins objects, teach him to play with See 'n Say.
- If the child spins himself, teach him to play on the Sit 'n Spin.

Match toy selections to the child's interests. Identify child motivators from Part I of the assessment tool. Embed motivators within a novel activity when the child is resistant.

- If the child is interested in Disney characters, teach him to look at Disney books.
- If the child is interested in running, teach him to roller skate.

Introduce new activities within preferred play categories according to the completed Play Interest Survey (Appendix A).

Sample Activity: Kaleidoscope

Pair the kaleidoscope with a highly preferred toy or social motivator. Model or prompt use of the kaleidoscope. Intermittently present a second preferred toy or social motivator to sustain the child's attention. For example, if the child enjoys tickling, hold the kaleidoscope up to the child's eye as you tickle him. Repeat the sequence many times in the same manner, lengthening the amount of time the child looks through the kaleidoscope.

Other Play Ideas

Exploratory:	Tornado bottle, spinning top
Manipulatives:	Jack-in-the-box, wind-up toys
Literacy:	Books, computer
Music:	Videos, audiotapes, karaoke
Constructive:	Not applicable
Physical:	Bicycle, roller skates
Art:	Not applicable
Dramatic:	Not applicable
Games:	Not applicable
Social Games:	Not applicable

DO-WATCH-LISTEN-SAY: Social and Communication Intervention for Children with Autism
by Kathleen Ann Quill © 2000 Paul H. Brookes Publishing Co.

Activity

A. Play
Solitary Play 2. Functional: Closed-ended activities

Selecting Activities

Select toys that can be used in only one conventional manner.

Select toys for which there is a fixed sequence of steps.

Match toy selection to the child's exploratory style. Use Part I of the assessment tool to determine the child's exploratory style.

- If the child's exploratory style is visual, teach him to use Lite-Brite.
- If the child's exploratory style is auditory, teach him to listen to music audiotapes.
- If the child's exploratory style is tactile, teach him to sequence the alphabet on a flannel board.
- If the child's exploratory style is kinesthetic, teach him how to play hopscotch.

Select activities that provide the same sensory feedback as the child's self-stimulatory behaviors.

- If the child throws, teach him to play beanbag toss.
- If the child spins objects, teach him to use spinning tops.
- If the child spins himself, teach him to follow an exercise video.

Match toy selections to the child's interests. Identify child motivators from Part I of the assessment tool. Embed motivators within a novel activity when the child is resistant.

- If the child is interested in Thomas the Train, teach him to put train tracks together and use Thomas vehicles.
- If the child resists using a pegboard and likes a Barney doll, have Barney hand each peg to him.

Introduce new activities within preferred play categories according to the completed Play Interest Survey (Appendix A).

Sample Activity: Train with connected tracks

Organize a box with a few trains and track pieces. Place only the pieces the child is expected to use in the box. Use modeling and prompting to connect the train tracks. Use tangible or social reinforcement intermittently to sustain the child's attention. Encourage the child to push the train around the track. Slowly increase the number of train track pieces and the length of time the child is expected to play. For example, pair the activity with an audiotaped song about trains. The activity is complete when the music tape ends.

Other Play Ideas

Exploratory:	Not applicable
Manipulatives:	Puzzles, marble run, Mr. Potato Head
Literacy:	Books on tape
Music:	Sing-along videos, exercise videos
Constructive:	Pop beads, train tracks, Lego models
Physical:	Hopscotch, miniature golf, beanbag toss
Art:	Dot-to-dot puzzles, playdough press, stencils
Dramatic:	Not applicable
Games:	Lotto, ring toss
Social Games:	Not applicable

DO-WATCH-LISTEN-SAY: Social and Communication Intervention for Children with Autism
by Kathleen Ann Quill © 2000 Paul H. Brookes Publishing Co.

Activity

A. Play
Solitary Play 3. Functional: Open-ended activities

Selecting Activities

Select activities in which the toys and materials are used in a conventional manner but there is no fixed sequence or outcome.

Match toy selection to the child's exploratory style. Use Part I of the assessment tool to determine the child's exploratory style.

- If the child's exploratory style is visual, teach him to use hand-held computer games.
- If the child's exploratory style is auditory, teach him to play the game Simon.
- If the child's exploratory style is tactile, teach him to play in the sandbox.
- If the child's exploratory style is kinesthetic, teach him to use playground equipment.

Select activities that provide the same sensory feedback as the child's self-stimulatory behaviors.

- If the child throws, teach him to play basketball.
- If the child spins objects, teach him to do spin art.
- If the child spins himself, teach him to use a Hula-Hoop.

Match toy selections to the child's interests. Embed motivators within a novel activity when the child is resistant.

- If the child is interested in Arthur, have him color in an Arthur coloring book.
- Place costumes of favorite movie characters in the dress-up area.

Introduce new activities within preferred play categories according to the completed Play Interest Survey (Appendix A).

Sample Activity: Coloring with crayons

Initially, organize the activity so the child has an outlined figure to color. For example, when coloring a picture of Santa, color-code the outline of Santa's mittens, coat, and boots in green, red, and black. Prompt the child to follow the outline. Gradually decrease the number of color-coded items to increase the child's flexibility and creativity.

Other Play Ideas

Exploratory:	Float boats and/or scoop plastic fish into a bucket at the water table.
Manipulatives:	Group pegs by color and/or make patterns with pegs using a pegboard.
	Make a pattern with parquetry blocks and/or build with parquetry blocks.
Literacy:	Use point-and-click computer games with multiple response options.
	Sequence letters and/or make words with magnetic letters.
Music:	Use musical instruments to play along with a tape and/or play a song.
	Sing own song and/or sing along with a music tape into a microphone.
Constructive:	Hit nails with a hammer and/or unscrew screws at the play tool bench.
	Build a block tower and/or build a bridge.
Physical:	Throw a ball through a hoop and/or hit a ball with a bat.
	Roll a Hula-Hoop across floor and/or jump in and out of the hoop.
Art:	Use crayons in a coloring book; draw pictures and/or write name.
	Play with playdough using a press, cookie cutters, and/or a rolling pin.
Dramatic:	Set the table and/or wash dishes in the kitchen area.
Games:	Match Dominoes and/or build a Domino house.
	Use Boggle Jr. to match letters to word cards and/or alphabetize letters.
Social Games:	Not applicable

DO-WATCH-LISTEN-SAY: Social and Communication Intervention for Children with Autism
by Kathleen Ann Quill © 2000 Paul H. Brookes Publishing Co.

Activity

A. Play
Solitary Play 4. Symbolic: Routine scripts

Selecting Activities

Select activities that involve familiar toys, objects, and actions used in either conventional or creative ways.

Select activities that can include routine scripts—a sequence of symbolic play acts that are linked logically by a theme and occur in a predictable, sequential manner.

Match activity selection to the child's exploratory style. Use Part I of the assessment tool to determine the child's exploratory style.

- If the child's exploratory style is visual, teach him to paint by number.
- If the child's exploratory style is auditory, teach him to listen to a book on audiotape.
- If the child's exploratory style is tactile, teach him how to make playdough cookies.
- If the child's exploratory style is kinesthetic, teach him to follow an aerobics videotape.

Select activities that provide the same sensory feedback as the child's self-stimulatory behaviors.

- If the child throws, teach him to play Frisbee games.
- If the child spins objects, teach him marble games.
- If the child spins himself, teach him to dance to music videos.

Match toy selections to the child's interests. Embed motivators within a novel activity when the child is resistant.

- If the child is interested in Sesame Street characters, teach him doll play using a Big Bird doll. Introduce new activities within preferred play categories according to the completed Play Interest Survey (Appendix A).

Sample Activity: T-ball

Clarify the steps of playing T-ball by using a visual display to preview the activity. Model or prompt the sequence of putting the ball on the tee, picking up a bat, and hitting the ball with a bat. Use visual cues, hand-over-hand prompting, or modeling as needed. Repeat the sequence many times in the same manner. Once the child is hitting the ball successfully, repeat the previous sequence for Step Two and then for Step One until the child is independent for the entire sequence.

Other Play Ideas

Exploratory:	Build a sandcastle following a book that displays the steps.
	Find magnetic letters in the rice table to complete the alphabet.
Manipulatives:	Use Colorforms to make a scene following a book display of the steps.
	Recreate a face on Mr. Potato Head from a picture model.
Literacy:	Act out a story sequence from a book using miniatures, or retell a favorite story into a tape player.
Music:	Follow a choreographed dance to a video.
	Play musical instruments by following a diagram on a song card or music sheet.
Constructive:	Build a structure at the tool bench by following a visual display of the steps.
	Build a block structure following a visual display of the steps.
Physical:	Follow an obstacle course using a visual display of the steps.
Art:	Complete an art project using a visual display.
	Use watercolors to copy a character or scene from a favorite book.
Dramatic:	Establish a script when playing dress-up: choose a character, gather the clothing and accessories, then dress in costume.
Games:	Not applicable
Social Games:	Not applicable

DO-WATCH-LISTEN-SAY: Social and Communication Intervention for Children with Autism
by Kathleen Ann Quill © 2000 Paul H. Brookes Publishing Co.

Activity

A. Play
Solitary Play 5. Symbolic: Creative

Selecting Activities

Select activities that involve familiar toys, objects, and actions used in either conventional or creative ways.

Select activities that encourage using a toy or object as if it is something else; pretending to be someone or something else; or creating an absent person, object, or attribute.

Match toy selections to the child's interests. Identify child motivators from Part I of the assessment tool. Embed motivators within a novel activity when the child is resistant.

- If the child is interested in Pokémon, create dramatic play activities around Pokémon characters.

Introduce new activities within preferred play categories according to the completed Play Interest Survey (Appendix A).

Sample Activity: Playdough

Organize toys and materials to create a pretend snack using playdough. Include favorite dolls or figurines, plates, and cookie cutters. Model how to make playdough cookies to place on the snack table and to feed the dolls or figurines. Encourage the child to continue the activity until all of the playdough has been used.

Other Play Ideas

Exploratory:	Use blocks in the sandbox as vehicles driving in the sand.
	Pretend to go fishing at the water table.
Manipulatives:	Create a design with parquetry blocks.
	Make jewelry with beads and laces.
Literacy:	Generate a story about a personal experience.
	Create a novel story using flannel props at the flannel board.
Music:	Listen to Disney songs, and act out different scenes of the movies from which the songs come.
	Pretend toys or objects are musical instruments while singing.
Constructive:	Create various structures with Lincoln Logs.
	Create vehicles with Legos.
Physical:	Pretend that a scooter board is a vehicle that the child is driving.
	Pretend to be an animal climbing on the climbing structure.
Art:	Create different "foods" from playdough.
	Use collage materials in creative ways.
Dramatic:	Reenact personal experiences at the dollhouse.
	Use dress-up clothing and accessories to take on different character roles.
Games:	Not applicable
Social Games:	Not applicable

Activity

A. Play

Solitary Play 6. Plays independently for ___ minutes

Selecting Activities

Match toy selections to the child's interests. Identify motivating activities from the Play Interest Survey.

Sample Activity: Sand play

Fill the sand table with toys the child has mastered and finds interesting. Prepare a "time board" that contains four Velcro pictographs of *sand table* and one pictograph of *all done*. Go to the sand table and show him the visual display. Point to each item on the time board, and place it in his view at the sand table. Remove the first *sand table* pictograph shortly after the child begins playing. Do not talk to or interact with the child. Remove one pictograph every minute or so, until the four *sand table* pictographs are gone. Then show the child that he is "all done" and praise him for remaining at the activity. As the child begins to understand that the pictographs determine the length of the activity, gradually increase and vary the amount of time between the removal of each pictograph. As the child's understanding increases, leave the area and only return every few minutes to silently remove a pictograph.

Strategies

Organizational Supports (to clearly define the activity's length)

- Use a timer to indicate length of solitary play time.
- Verbally count to 10 to indicate completion.
- Use a musical tape to indicate length of play time (play until the music ends).
- Base completion of the play activity on the number of toy pieces.
- Base completion of play activity on its finished product.
- Use a visual time board.

Social Supports

- Ignore negative behaviors and silently redirect child back to desired task.
- Limit verbal language.
- Initially require the child to remain on task for a very short time period; gradually increase the time.
- Fade prompting as quickly as possible to avoid prompt dependence.

DO-WATCH-LISTEN-SAY: Social and Communication Intervention for Children with Autism
by Kathleen Ann Quill © 2000 Paul H. Brookes Publishing Co.

Activity

A. Play
Social Play 1. Parallel plays with own set of toys/materials

Selecting Activities

Select activities that allow the child to play independently beside an adult or peer with his own set of materials.

Select activities that the child has already mastered in solitary play (DO).

Select activities that allow for, but do not require, observations and imitation (WATCH).

Select activities that are reinforcing and motivating to the child.

Select closed-ended activities.

Sample Activity: Legos

Choose an adult or a peer model to work with the child. Seat the partners at the same table. Place a mat in front of each child that is colored to represent that child's belongings or area. Then give each child an individual bin filled with identical sets of Legos. Instruct the children to use their Legos on their designated mats for a set amount of time.

Other Play Ideas

Art:	Each child colors on his own paper with his own set of crayons.
Circle Time:	Each child has a miniature calendar and number stamps to imitate what the teacher is doing.
	Each child has his own chair or rug square marked by his color, photograph, or name.
Constructive:	Each child has his own road rug and set of cars.
	Each child has his own colored place mat and set of blocks.
	Each child has his own container that holds train tracks and a set of trains; he plays on his own rug square.
Dramatic:	Each child has his own basket in the kitchen area.
	Each child chooses dress-up clothes and accessories for his own bin.
	Place multiple dolls and accessories on a section of the floor that has been taped off with the child's specific color.
	Reenact a birthday party: Each child has his own cookie to decorate on his own colored tray with all of the necessary frosting and decorations.
Exploratory:	Each child has a set of water toys of a specific color to use at the water table.
	Each child has his own wand and container of bubble mix.
	Each child has his own bucket and sand toys of a specific color at the sandbox.
Literacy:	Each child has his own pencil box that contains necessary materials at the writing table.
	Each child has his own rug square or chair in the reading area marked by color, photograph, or name.
	Each child has his own set of flannel props in an individually marked container.
Manipulatives:	Each child has a place at the table marked with a colored place mat and a corresponding bin of the same color that holds his puzzles.
	Each child has his own bin of math manipulatives for an activity in the math center.
Music:	Each child has his own set of headphones, and audiotapes are in a bin marked by his color, photograph, or name.
Physical:	Each child is assigned his own ball for a basketball game.
	Bicycles and roller skates are marked with the child's name.
	Each child has his own hopscotch form.

DO-WATCH-LISTEN-SAY: Social and Communication Intervention for Children with Autism
by Kathleen Ann Quill © 2000 Paul H. Brookes Publishing Co.

Activity

A. Play
Social Play 2. Parallel plays with organized toys/materials

Selecting Activities

Select activities that allow the child to play independently beside an adult or peer.

Select activities in which toys and materials are clearly organized to clarify when and how sharing occurs

Select activities that the child has already mastered in solitary play (DO).

Select activities that allow for, but do not require, observation and imitation (WATCH).

Select activities that are reinforcing and motivating to the child.

Select closed-ended activities.

Sample Activity: Dramatic play

Choose an adult or a peer model to work with the child. Set up partners at the art table with a pile of playdough cookies on a plate. Give instructions for each child to decorate the "birthday cookies" on his plate. Place a tray full of accessories in the center of the table for the partners to share and use for decorating their cookies.

Other Play Ideas

Art:	Use markers to color. Create a marker holder for the center of the table by placing markers cap-first in hardening clay. Once the clay hardens, children select and return markers to their nonremovable covers. Each child has his own construction paper for an art project; markers, scissors, paste sticks, and glitter are organized in bins to be shared by the group.
Constructive:	Children build blocks in pairs. Assign a color to each child. Weave place mats in various two-color combinations. A child can place blocks on any mat that contains his color.
	Each child has a colored mat on which he can build blocks; the blocks are shared.
	One container holds all of the train track pieces; each child has a separate marked area to build his own track.
	Provide one shared set of tracks; each child has his own bin of trains.
Dramatic:	Each child has his own doll; the bin of doll clothes is shared.
	Each child uses his own set of farm animals in one barn that everyone shares.
Exploratory:	Each child has his own bucket and net for "fishing" at the water table.
	Each child has a large bubble wand; the bucket of bubble mix is shared.
Literacy:	Each child has a specific area in which he sits in the book corner; the books on the shelf are shared.
	Each child has his own set of headphones; one book on tape is shared among them.
Manipulatives:	Each child has his own Mr. Potato Head; all of the accessory pieces are hidden in the rice table for sharing.
	Each child has his own puzzle form; all of the pieces are mixed together in one shared bin.
Physical:	The children play in a ball pit.
	The children share a platform swing.
	The children share a ride in the wagon.

Activity

A. Play

Social Play 3. Participates in choral/unison group activity

Selecting Activities

Select activities in which the children are doing or saying the same thing at the same time.

Select activities that do not require waiting, turn-taking, or sharing.

Select activities that the child has already mastered in a one-to-one setting (DO).

Select activities that allow for, but do not require, observation and imitation (WATCH).

Select activities that are reinforcing and motivating to the child.

Sample Activity: Music with rhythm sticks

Seat the children in a semicircle around you. Each child should be able to see you clearly and have room to move. Have assistants behind the children, ready to silently prompt movement of nonimitators. Wear a "do" pictograph around your neck to which you can silently point. Say "Sticks up" while you hold the sticks over your head. Keep repeating the directive and action until all of the children are doing this in unison with you. Stop, and as soon as everyone stops, repeat with the same or a new action. Continue until you have reached the predetermined end of the activity, (e.g., a bell rings, five actions and then stop). Vary the complexity of the task from positional to movement. You can go from performing a single action or movement to a sequence or pattern or add music as the children improve.

Other Play Ideas

Art:	All art projects in which each child has his own set of materials are opportunities for participating in a group without waiting, turn-taking, or sharing.
Games:	Play games such as Ring Around the Rosie or Hokey Pokey in unison.
Circle Time:	Respond chorally to questions or recite a poem chorally.
	Do fingerplays in unison.
Literacy:	Each child has his own copy of a book to follow a book on tape.
	Read or respond chorally during a book reading.
Music:	Sing or use musical instruments chorally.
	Listen to an audiotape or watch music videos.
Physical:	Play Follow the Leader.
	Participate in group activities such as swimming, ice skating, or roller skating indoors.
	Jog or do aerobics together in gym.

DO-WATCH-LISTEN-SAY: Social and Communication Intervention for Children with Autism
by Kathleen Ann Quill © 2000 Paul H. Brookes Publishing Co.

Activity

A. Play

Social Play 4. Turn-taking with one partner with predictable turns

Selecting Activities

Select closed-ended activities.

Select activities in which the children share a common activity and/or work together toward a common goal.

Select activities in which there is a common focus on play and materials.

Select activities that the child has already mastered in a one-to-one setting (DO).

Select activities that are reinforcing for and motivating to the child.

Select activities that allow for but do not require observations and imitation (WATCH).

Select activities that emphasize the child's ability to nonverbally respond to others; limit requirements for verbal interaction.

Sample Activity: Playing at the computer

Prepare the computer station with two chairs and two mouse pads that match the specified colors for the children participating in the activity. Load the chosen game into the computer. Place the mouse on the pad of the child who will be going first and a *wait* pictograph on the mouse pad of the other child. Place a kitchen timer where both students can see it. Have the children sit in front of their color mouse pads. Show them that you are setting the timer for 5 minutes. Have the first child begin playing once the timer is set. If the other child is having a hard time waiting, use simple language to remind him "It's _____'s turn; you have to wait." Refer him to the pictograph, or show him that the timer is moving backward. When the bell rings, say "_____'s turn is all done. Now it's _____'s turn." Have the children exchange the mouse and the pictograph, and reset the timer for 5 minutes. You may be able to leave and only come back to reset the timer once the children become familiar with the routine. Some children may even learn to reset the timer independently. The time period can be made shorter or longer according to the children's skill levels. Remember to have a predetermined, alternate method to clearly show termination of the activity.

Other Play Ideas

Art:	Two children playing with playdough take turns using the playdough press. When one child's playdough has been pressed, he gives it to the other child. Use visual pictographs to structure the activity and make it predictable.
Constructive:	Two children share a bin of blocks. They take turns building a block tower on one mat, which is woven from both children's assigned colors. Use visual cues to structure the activity and make it predictable. Continue play until the bin is empty.
	Set up train tracks with one train to be shared by two children. Stand one child on either side of the train table. The first child pushes the train around until it reaches the other child (use visual cues as necessary). The second child then pushes the train to his partner. Continue until the predetermined end of the activity (e.g., timer goes off, the train goes around the track five times, a music tape stops).
	Two children roll a car back and forth to each other.
Exploratory:	A child blows bubbles and then hands the bubble wand and mix to his partner. Play continues until a predetermined end of the activity.
	A child winds a mechanical toy, then hands it to his partner to wind. Play continues until a predetermined end of the activity.
Literacy:	Two children take turns choosing a book and tape at the listening center.
	Two children share a book while sitting at a table. The child on the right points to or says something that is on the right page of the book, then the child on the left

points to or says something that is on the left page and turns the page. Continue until the book is finished. Use visual cues as necessary.

Two children take turns sequencing flannel props from a familiar story to retell the story on a flannel board.

Two children take turns following the musical pattern of the game Simon. They switch turns when one child makes a mistake and the game buzzes.

A child uses a microphone to sing along with a song on tape, then gives the microphone to his partner.

Physical: One child pushes his partner on the swing for a predetermined number of pushes. The children switch places when that number is reached.

Two children alternate shooting a basketball at the basket.

Two children play catch.

Two children take turns going down the slide.

Activity

A. Play
Social Play 5. Turn-taking in group game with predictable turns

Selecting Activities

Select closed-ended activities.

Select activities during which children share a common activity and/or work together toward a common goal.

Select activities in which there is a common focus on play and materials.

Select activities that the child has already mastered in a one-to-one setting (DO).

Select activities that are reinforcing for and motivating to the child.

Select activities that allow for but do not require observation and imitation (WATCH).

Select activities that emphasize the child's ability to nonverbally respond to others; limit requirements for verbal interaction.

Sample Activity: Candy Land

Arrange four chairs at a small table away from any distractions. Make three *wait* pictographs and one *my turn* pictograph. Lay the pictographs in front of the places at the table. Use a visual board of the game's directions to serve as a reminder to the children. Set up the game. Call the game players together and assign them their colors. Bring them to the table, and have them pick up their pictograph. The child with the *my turn* pictograph goes first. He uses the visual directions to turn a card and move his piece. He then swaps his *my turn* pictograph for the *wait* pictograph of the child sitting next to him. Play continues until someone reaches the candy castle and the game is over.

Other Play Ideas

Art:	Place a large cutout of a Christmas tree and all necessary decorating materials in the art center. Each child uses a clear visual schedule of turns to add something to the tree, one at a time.
Circle Time:	Post a visual order of the children's turns for show and tell.
	Children pass a microphone around the circle and take turns saying their names into it before passing it to the next child.
Constructive:	A group of children roll one car back and forth to each other for a predetermined amount of time.
	A group of children take turns placing marbles down the marble run, one at a time.
Games:	Four children sit around a table with the game Kerplunk set up in the center. Children use visual cues as necessary and take turns pulling the sticks out one at a time until all of the marbles fall down the shoot.
	Play Don't Break the Ice, Ants in the Pants, Jenga, Topple, Dominoes, and lotto games.
Literacy:	Children take turns filling in the blank when reading a familiar story at storytime. Turns are indicated by a talking stick, cards with the children's names, or simply going in order of the seating arrangement.
	Set up a number dispenser (like those used at the deli counter in a grocery store). Each child picks a number. Number one goes to the computer first for a predetermined amount of time. When his turn is over, number two is called. Continue until all children have had a turn.
	Hand out one flannel board prop to each child. The children place the props on the flannel board in the sequence of a story as it is being read.
Music:	The children pass a ball around in a circle while music is playing.
Physical:	Line up four chairs by an obstacle course. Use a visual to show the children the order in which they will complete the course. Once the first child finishes the last part of the course, the next child in line may go. Continue for a predetermined amount of time.
	The children take turns running underneath a parachute before it comes down on top of them.

DO-WATCH-LISTEN-SAY: Social and Communication Intervention for Children with Autism
by Kathleen Ann Quill © 2000 Paul H. Brookes Publishing Co.

Activity

A. Play
Social Play 6. Shares materials

Selecting Activities

Select activities in which materials are shared by *all* children.

Select activities that the child has already mastered in a one-to-one setting (DO).

Select activities in which the child has demonstrated parallel play with shared materials.

Select activities that are reinforcing for and motivating to the child.

Select activities in which the child demonstrates the ability to observe others (WATCH).

Select activities that emphasize the child's ability to nonverbally respond to others; limit requirements for verbal interaction.

Sample Activity: Dramatic play; kitchen area

Completely organize the kitchen area. Have all of the play food kept in clearly marked bins. Place utensils in another clearly marked bin and plates and glasses on clearly marked shelves. Also keep pots and pans in a clear, designated spot. Make sure all materials are accessible to the children and that the children can clearly see where they belong. Limit the number of children who are allowed in the area. The children can use the materials and return them to their places when finished. Children must share use of the sink, the refrigerator, the stove, or other accessories that are limited.

Other Play Ideas

Art:	Place different colored playdough and all materials in clearly marked bins at the table's center. The children share all materials and return them to their proper bins when finished.
Constructive:	Clearly mark the block shelves with the shape of the block that belongs on each shelf. The children use all blocks and return them to their proper shelves when finished.
	Keep Legos in color-coded bins on a clearly labeled shelf. The children must share all of the Legos and return them to their correct bins when finished.
	Keep vehicles near the road rug, in clearly labeled bins on well-marked shelves. All children share all vehicles when using the road rug and return them to their labeled bins when finished.
Dramatic:	Label four dinosaurs with the number 4 on a visual chart to remind children they may use only four toy dinosaurs at a time. When finished, the children return the dinosaurs to their labeled bins (beside the sandbox) for another child to use.
	Fill only one basket with dress-up clothes. The children must share the clothes that are available.
	Set up the toy grocery store so that every item has a clearly marked place and the children can easily reach all materials independently. When finished with an item, they must return it to its place so another child may use it.
	Label two dolls with the number 2 to show the children that they may only use two dolls at a time in the dollhouse area.
	Keep the toy animals and farm in the same place. The children must divide the animals among themselves and use the barn together.
Exploratory:	Place all water-table toys in a bin labeled with every child's name or color. This represents that the toys belong to everybody and that anyone may use them at the water table.

DO-WATCH-LISTEN-SAY: Social and Communication Intervention for Children with Autism
by Kathleen Ann Quill © 2000 Paul H. Brookes Publishing Co.

Activity

A. Play
Social Play 7. Cooperative play with one partner

Selecting Activities

Select activities for which the child understands what to DO, who to WATCH, and how to respond to others (LISTEN).

Select activities that the child has already mastered in a one-to-one setting (DO).

Select activities in which materials are shared by *all* children.

Select activities that emphasize the child's ability to nonverbally respond to others; limit requirements for verbal interaction.

Select play during which children share a common activity and/or work together toward a common goal.

Select activities that are reinforcing for and motivating to the child.

Sample Activity: Puzzles

Place a chair on either side of a small table or desk. Put two empty puzzle boards in front of one chair and the puzzle pieces in front of the other chair. Prompt the child to choose a partner. Direct the child and his partner to the table. Encourage the child sitting in front of the puzzle pieces to give them to his partner, one at a time, until the first puzzle is completed; then have the children switch roles to complete the second puzzle.

Other Play Ideas

Art:	Two children create a collage using one large piece of paper and various art materials.
Constructive:	Two children build a Lego model using a visual sequence. Each child takes half of the Legos for building.
	Two children take blocks from labeled shelves and build a block structure on a tray that is labeled with both of their colors or names.
	Two children take several pieces of train track and build a train track together.
	Two children take pieces of the marble run and work together to build it.
Dramatic:	One child is a grocery store cashier and the other is the shopper (use previously mastered scripts).
	One child is a doctor and the other is the patient (use previously mastered scripts).
Exploratory:	Place the water wheel in the empty water table; set a six-pack of bottled water next to it. One child stands by the water table and gives the bottled water to his partner. The partner dumps the water over the water wheel. Play continues until all six bottles of water have been used; the children then switch places and use another six pack of water.
Games:	Two children play Connect Four.
	Two children play tic-tac-toe.
Manipulatives:	Two children share a Colorforms house and pieces and decorate the house together.
	Two children work together to complete one floor puzzle.
	Two children are given a karaoke machine and keyboard to record a song.
Physical:	One child holds a football for the other child to kick.
	Two children work together to make the seesaw go up and down.

DO-WATCH-LISTEN-SAY: Social and Communication Intervention for Children with Autism
by Kathleen Ann Quill © 2000 Paul H. Brookes Publishing Co.

Other Opportunities: Two children are assigned a short report and visual to present to the class.

One child places the order at a fast-food restaurant, and the other child pays for it.

Two children share math manipulatives and complete a series of problems together

Two children use several photographs of themselves to write a language experience story.

Two children take the attendance sheet to the office every morning. A days-of-the-week chart is used to alternate the days that each one carries the attendance sheet.

One child reads a shopping list at the school store, and the other child collects the items.

Activity

A. Play
Social Play 8. Cooperative play in structured groups

Selecting Activities

Select activities for which the child understands what to DO, who to WATCH, and how to respond to others (LISTEN).

Select activities that the child has already mastered in a one-to-one setting (DO).

Select activities in which materials are shared by *all* children.

Select activities that emphasize the child's ability to nonverbally respond to others; limit requirements for verbal interaction.

Select closed-ended games and activities.

Select activities during which children share a common activity toward a common goal.

Select activities in which there is a common focus on play and materials.

Select activities that are reinforcing and motivating to the child.

Sample Activity: Simon Says (variation)

The children stand in a circle. You and classroom assistants can stand next to children who have weaker imitation skills or need help staying on task. The leader wears a *do* pictograph around her neck to which she can silently point. The target child stands in the middle of the circle. Explain to the children that you are going to say and perform an action. They are to copy you. Further explain that when the child in the middle performs the action, everyone is to clap and cheer for that child. Substitute your own name for Simon and begin with "_____ says clap." Perform the action as you are saying it. Begin clapping and praising the child when he performs the action. Repeat with the same or a new action. You can then have the child in the middle switch with another child or have him clap for everyone else for the next action. Continue until the predetermined end of the activity (e.g., a bell rings, five actions and then stop) is reached. You can vary the complexity of the task from positional to movement or by going from a single action or movement to a sequence or pattern. The children take turns being Simon as they improve.

Other Play Ideas

Circle Time:	The children sit in a circle to play Duck, Duck, Goose. One child is "it" and taps each child on the head, saying, "Duck." When the child who is "it" says "Goose," he is chased by the person he tapped. Whichever child is left without a seat becomes "it."
	Play Hide-and-Seek with items used to complete circle-time activities, such as the attendance sheet, calendar, and schedule. Hide the items and have the children search for them. When a child finds an item, he receives that job to do at circle time.
Constructive:	The children build a single marble run from a large pile of joint pieces.
	The children play a block tower game, such as Jenga.
Exploratory:	Have a scavenger hunt at the sand table: The children are given one treasure map to follow to find hidden items.
	The children "fish" at the water table.
Physical:	The children play kickball.
	The children run relay races.
Games:	The children play card games, such as Uno or Old Maid.
Music:	The children play Musical Chairs.
	The children play Hot Potato with a beanbag.
Literacy:	The children play Boggle Jr. or another "word jumbler" game.

DO-WATCH-LISTEN-SAY: Social and Communication Intervention for Children with Autism
by Kathleen Ann Quill © 2000 Paul H. Brookes Publishing Co.

Activity

A. Play
Social Play 9. Cooperative play in unstructured groups

Selecting Activities

Select activities for which the child understands what to DO, who to WATCH, and how to respond to others (LISTEN).

Select activities that the child has already mastered in a one-to-one setting (DO).

Select activities in which the child has mastered sharing materials.

Select activities in which the child has demonstrated the ability to verbally or nonverbally respond to others.

Select activities that are reinforcing and motivating to the child.

Sample Activity: Making a class mural

Tape a large piece of mural paper to a table. Set out various art materials, such as paint, paintbrushes, markers, glue, glitter, stickers, stencils, and tissue paper. Limit the number of each medium so the children are required to share and take turns. Have bowls of warm water or wet paper towels readily available for children who do not like to get their hands messy. Give a smock to every child. Tell the children that they are going to make a class mural relating to a theme. Give them a few ideas (e.g., St. Patrick's Day, Spring, All About Me, The Farm). The children must share the materials and work together to complete the mural. Work on the mural continues until the predetermined end of the activity (e.g., a bell goes off, all of the materials are used up, the paper is filled) is reached. The children then work together to put away the materials and clean up any mess.

Other Play Ideas

Art:	The children use playdough to make the "food" for a pizza party.
Constructive:	The children work at the tool bench to build a cage for the class pet.
	The children work together to build a block zoo for miniature animals.
Dramatic:	The children reenact a story using miniatures.
	The children dress up as favorite characters and act out a familiar story.
	The children put on a puppet show.
Exploratory:	Place a bucket on each corner of the water table; fill the table with plastic fish. Each child uses his own fishnet to scoop fish into a bucket.
Games:	Play Twenty Questions.
Literacy:	The children use flannel props to tell their own stories.
	The children work together to compile a class photograph album.
Manipulatives:	The children work together to complete a giant floor puzzle.
	The children jointly follow a visual sequence to make a Lite-Brite picture.
Music:	Each child plays an instrument as part of a marching band.
Physical:	The children all work together, flapping a parachute, to keep balls on top of it.
	The children run relay races.
Other Opportunities:	The children complete a cooking project using a visual recipe.

DO-WATCH-LISTEN-SAY: Social and Communication Intervention for Children with Autism
by Kathleen Ann Quill © 2000 Paul H. Brookes Publishing Co.

Activity

B. Group Skills
Attending 1. Attends during meals

Selecting Activities

When preparing the child for a group activity, consider the following:

- Has the child mastered the group activity in a one-to-one setting?
- Does the child understand what to do and for how long in the group activity?
- Does the child imitate peers in a group?
- Does the child understand the language used in the group?

Sample Activity: School lunch

Use a concrete means to clarify the length of the lunch period and increase the child's ability to remain with the group until mealtime is completed. This may include a time board with removable numbers (i.e., lunch is finished when all of the numbers are removed), a color-coded minute timer that rings when lunch is finished, or other organizational supports to clarify time.

Strategies

Organizational Supports

- Organize the space so the child clearly understands exactly where he needs to sit.
- Organize the materials so it is clear to the child exactly what he needs to use.
- Organize the meal to clarify when it is complete.

Social Supports

- Target a peer coach for the child to watch in order to remember what to do.

Visual Supports

- Provide a visual sequence of events for the group activity.
- Make a visual list of the group rules: watch, wait, listen, raise your hand, take turns.

Activity

B. Group Skills

Attending 2. Attends during structured projects

Selecting Activities

When preparing the child for a group activity, consider the following:

- Has the child mastered the group activity in a one-to-one setting?
- Does the child understand what to do and for how long in the group activity?
- Does the child imitate peers in a group?
- Does the child understand the language used in the group?

Sample Activity: Art

Increase the child's attending during structured group projects by organizing the activity so the child can clearly see what to do and for how long. Organize all materials needed for art projects to clarify what is for personal use and what is shared. Also organize the materials to correspond with each step of a specific activity. Place a visual schedule of a project's substeps near the child. Place the same activity schedule in the front of the room so the teacher can point (e.g., using a flashlight pointer) to relevant information as group directions are given.

Strategies

Organizational Supports

- Position the child so he can see the group leader.
- Organize the space so it is clear to the child exactly where he needs to sit.
- Organize the materials so it is clear to the child exactly what he needs to use.
- Organize the activity so the child is clear when it is complete.

Social Supports

- Use nonverbal attention-getting devices to refocus (e.g., whistling, a funny noise).
- Use exaggerated facial expressions and rhythmic language when speaking.
- Target a peer coach for the child to watch in order to remember what to do.
- Allow the child to be an *active* participant in the group (e.g., hand out or collect papers).

Visual Supports

- Provide a visual sequence of events for the group activity.
- Make a visual list of the group rules: watch, wait, listen, raise your hand, take turns.
- Instruct the child to look at whomever is wearing the colored ribbon.
- Use props to maintain attention (e.g., a funny hat, a clown nose).
- Use a light pointer to keep the child focused on charts, pictures, or words.

DO-WATCH-LISTEN-SAY: Social and Communication Intervention for Children with Autism
by Kathleen Ann Quill © 2000 Paul H. Brookes Publishing Co.

Activity

B. Group Skills
Attending 3. Attends during listening activities

Selecting Activities

When preparing the child for a group activity, consider the following:

- Has the child mastered the group activity in a one-to-one setting?
- Does the child understand what to do and for how long in the group activity?
- Does the child imitate peers in a group?
- Does the child understand the language used in the group?

Sample Activity: Listening to storybooks

Increase the child's attending during group listening activities by ensuring that the complexity of language matches the child's comprehension abilities. If needed, present all language information visually. Use pictures, graphics, and/or flannel board figures to highlight the information within the story. Use routine group directions (i.e., "Everybody, _____") to get and maintain everyone's attention. Establish a predictable routine for the beginning and end of storytime. Provide a checklist of the storybook choices. Use a special *It's new* symbol on the checklist to prepare the child for unfamiliar stories. If necessary, allow the child to leave the group before a discussion of the story begins.

Strategies

Organizational Supports

- Position the child so he can see the group leader.
- Organize the space so it is clear to the child exactly where he needs to sit.
- Organize the materials so it is clear to the child exactly what he needs to use.
- Organize the activity so the child is clear when it is complete.

Social Supports

- Use nonverbal attention-getting devices to refocus (e.g., whistling, a funny noise).
- Use exaggerated facial expressions and rhythmic language when speaking.
- Target a peer coach for the child to watch in order to remember what to do.

Visual Supports

- Provide a visual sequence of events for the group activity.
- Make a visual list of the group rules: watch, wait, listen, raise your hand, take turns.
- Instruct the child to look at whomever is wearing the colored ribbon.
- Instruct the child to look at whomever is holding the "talking stick."
- Instruct the child to look at whomever is holding the microphone.
- Use props to maintain attention (e.g., a funny hat, a clown nose).
- Use a light pointer to keep the child focused on charts, pictures, or words.

Activity

B. Group Skills
Attending 4. Attends during structured games

Selecting Activities

When preparing the child for a group activity, consider the following:

- Has the child mastered the group activity in a one-to-one setting?
- Does the child understand what to do and for how long in the group activity?
- Does the child imitate peers in a group?
- Does the child understand the language used in the group?

Sample Activity: Pin the Tail on the Donkey

Create a videotape of two peers taking turns playing Pin the Tail on the Donkey. Use the video to preview the activity with the child. Verbally label each step of the game, and make an accompanying social script of the game sequence (i.e., get the tail, put the blindfold on, walk to the donkey picture). Show the video to the child a number of times prior to playing the game in a group situation. In the group situation, be sure to use the exact language and vocabulary used in the video.

Strategies

Organizational Supports

- Position the child so he can see the group leader.
- Organize the space so it is clear to the child exactly where he needs to be.
- Organize the materials so it is clear to the child exactly what he needs to use.
- Organize the activity so the child is clear when it is complete.

Social Supports

- Use nonverbal attention-getting devices to refocus (e.g., whistling, a funny noise).
- Use exaggerated facial expressions and rhythmic language when speaking.
- Target a peer coach for the child to watch in order to remember what to do.
- Allow the child to be an *active* participant in the group (e.g., assign the child the role of helper).

Visual Supports

- Provide a visual sequence of events for the group activity.
- Make a visual list of the group rules: watch, wait, listen, raise your hand, take turns.
- Instruct the child to look at whomever is wearing the colored ribbon.
- Instruct the child to look at whomever is holding the "talking stick."
- Use props to maintain attention (e.g., a funny hat, a clown nose).
- Use a light pointer to keep the child focused on charts, pictures, or words.

DO-WATCH-LISTEN-SAY: Social and Communication Intervention for Children with Autism
by Kathleen Ann Quill © 2000 Paul H. Brookes Publishing Co.

Activity

B. Group Skills
Attending 5. Attends during play activities

Selecting Activities

When preparing the child for a group activity, consider the following:

- Has the child mastered the group activity in a one-to-one setting?
- Does the child understand what to do and for how long in the group activity?
- Does the child imitate peers in a group?
- Does the child understand the language used in the group?

Sample Activity: Recess

Increase the child's ability to watch peers during play by selecting two or three peers to serve as "buddies." Each buddy wears a colorful ribbon on his clothing. Prompt the child to look for the peers who are wearing ribbons and to join them. If the child needs additional support, a designated adult can also wear the ribbon and serve as a model during recess.

Strategies

Organizational Supports

- Organize the space so it is clear to the child exactly where he needs to be.
- Organize toys and materials so it is clear to the child exactly what he needs to use.
- Organize the activity so the child is clear when it is complete.

Social Supports

- Target a peer coach for the child to watch in order to remember what to do.
- Allow the child to watch peers before joining the activity.

Visual Supports

- Provide a visual sequence of events for the group activity.
- Make a visual list of the group rules: watch, wait, listen, raise your hand, take turns.
- Instruct the child to look at whomever is wearing the colored ribbon.
- Use props to maintain attention (e.g., a funny hat, a clown nose).
- Use a video to preview the play activity.

DO-WATCH-LISTEN-SAY: Social and Communication Intervention for Children with Autism
by Kathleen Ann Quill © 2000 Paul H. Brookes Publishing Co.

Activity

B. Group Skills

Attending 6. Attends during discussion activities

Selecting Activities

When preparing the child for a group activity, consider the following:

- Has the child mastered the group activity in a one-to-one setting?
- Does the child understand what to do and for how long in the group activity?
- Does the child imitate peers in a group?
- Does the child understand the language used in the group?

Sample Activity: Show and Tell

Attending during discussions is often challenging for children with autism and requires the use of multiple organizational, social, and visual supports. For example, have the child choose a preferred toy to use as his item for show and tell. Make written or pictographic cue cards with the child to represent what he will say about his toy. Practice show and tell several times in a one-to-one setting. Make a visual chart of which children will share and in what order. Show the chart to the child before he joins the group. Have each child wear a colorful ribbon while it is his turn. Prompt the child to watch whomever is wearing the ribbon. Keep referring to the chart to help the child prepare for his turn. Use the cue cards to facilitate the child's communication during his turn.

Strategies

Organizational Supports

- Position the child so he can see the group leader.
- Organize the space so it is clear to the child exactly where he needs to sit.
- Organize the materials so it is clear to the child exactly what he needs to use.
- Organize the activity so the child is clear when it is complete.

Social Supports

- Use nonverbal attention-getting devices to refocus (e.g., whistling, a funny noise).
- Use exaggerated facial expressions and rhythmic language when speaking.
- Target a peer coach for the child to watch in order to remember what to do.
- Allow the child to be an *active* participant in the group (e.g., hand out or collect papers).

Visual Supports

- Provide a visual sequence of events for the group activity.
- Make a visual list of the group rules: watch, wait, listen, raise your hand, take turns.
- Instruct the child to look at whomever is wearing the colored ribbon.
- Instruct the child to look at whomever is holding the "talking stick."
- Instruct the child to look at whomever is holding the microphone.
- Use props to maintain attention (e.g., a funny hat, a clown nose).
- Use a light pointer to keep the child focused on charts, pictures, or words.

DO-WATCH-LISTEN-SAY: Social and Communication Intervention for Children with Autism
by Kathleen Ann Quill © 2000 Paul H. Brookes Publishing Co.

Activity

B. Group Skills
Waiting 1. Sits for group activity

Selecting Activities

When preparing the child for a group activity, consider the following:

- Has the child mastered the group activity in a one-to-one setting?
- Does the child understand what to do and for how long in the group activity?
- Does the child imitate peers in a group?
- Does the child understand the language used in the group?

Sample Activity: Morning meeting

Make a pictographic time board with five symbols for *sit* and one symbol for *all done.* Velcro the pictographs to the board. Show them to the child, pointing and saying, "Sit, sit, sit, sit, sit, all done." Place the time board in front of the child as he sits with the group. Remove the first *sit* pictograph after a predetermined amount of time, and point and say, "Sit, sit, sit, sit, all done." Repeat in this manner until all of the *sit* pictographs are removed. The child may then leave the group. Initially keep the time between the removal of pictographs very short. As the child's understanding increases, gradually lengthen the time between removal and the time he must remain sitting with the group.

Strategies

Organizational Supports

- Give the child a specific object to hold that signifies that he has to wait.
- Use a timer to indicate the length of time to wait.
- Play a music tape the entire time the child is waiting.
- Give the child a small toy to hold while waiting.
- Designate a chair for the child to sit in while waiting.
- Use a portable visual chart that specifies "First sit, then (photo of next activity)."

DO-WATCH-LISTEN-SAY: Social and Communication Intervention for Children with Autism
by Kathleen Ann Quill © 2000 Paul H. Brookes Publishing Co.

Activity

B. Group Skills

Waiting 2. Raises hand for a turn

Selecting Activities

When preparing the child for a group activity, consider the following:

- Does the child observe peers in a group?
- Does the child imitate peers in a group?
- Does the child understand the language used in the group?
- Does the child follow group attention-getting directions?

Sample Activity: Circle time

Make a visual symbol that states the rule "Raise your hand to get a turn." Wear the pictograph around your neck during situations that require the rule. Only call on children who raise their hands. Every time you call on a child, praise him for raising his hand, and point to the pictograph around your neck. Completely ignore any child who calls out without raising his hand, but point to the pictograph around your neck. If needed, have another adult stand behind the targeted child and prompt him to raise his hand. Immediately call on and praise the child while pointing to the pictograph.

Strategies

Visual Supports

- Use a cue card that specifies "First raise your hand, then wait for your name."
- Make a visual list of the group rules: watch, wait, listen, raise your hand, take turns.
- Preview and review a social story about group rules.

Activity

B. Group Skills
Waiting 3. Stands in line

Selecting Activities

When preparing the child for a group activity, consider the following:

- Does the child understand what to do and for how long in the group activity?
- Does the child observe peers in a group?
- Does the child imitate peers in a group?
- Does the child understand the language used in the group?
- Does the child follow group attention-getting directions?

Sample Activity: Going to the library

Make up a story that tells the child it is time to line up at the door whenever he hears the song "Follow the Leader." Record the song, and use the audiotape to signal that it is time to line up. Gradually fade the use of the tape, and have the group sing the song while lining up. Silently prompt the child to the door while signing the song. Continue to use the silent, physical prompting as long as necessary.

Strategies

Organizational Supports

- Give the child a specific object to hold while in line.
- Place footprints, numbers, or names on the floor by the classroom door.
- Give the child the role of door holder.
- Have the group hold on to a rope.

Social Supports

- Always allow the child to be first or last in line.
- Have the child hold hands with one partner.
- Assign a peer helper to bring the child to the line.
- Direct the children to line up and place one hand on the shoulders of the person in front of them.
- Use a routine phrase or song to line up.
- Use a consistent phrase to get the group's attention to line up.

DO-WATCH-LISTEN-SAY: Social and Communication Intervention for Children with Autism
by Kathleen Ann Quill © 2000 Paul H. Brookes Publishing Co.

Activity

B. Group Skills
Turn-Taking 1. During structured activity

Selecting Activities

When preparing the child for a group activity, consider the following:

- Does the activity have an organized sequence of predictable steps?
- Does the child demonstrate turn-taking with an adult?
- Does the child watch others taking their turns?
- Does the child understand the language used in the group?
- Does the child understand what to do and for how long in the group activity?

Sample Activity: Cooking project

The most important element for successful turn-taking is to clarify when it is a child's turn. List a recipe's steps using words and pictographs. Number each step of the sequence. Write a child's name next to each step of the recipe. Make one copy of the recipe for every child and highlight his name to specify his turn. Every child follows his copy of the recipe as the project progresses.

Strategies

Organizational Supports

- Organize the group activity so the children are preassigned a turn.
- Base turn-taking on the order in which the children are seated.
- Define the length of a turn by using a visual timer or an auditory timer.

Visual Supports

- Provide a list of the order of the children's turns.
- Use a visual chart to specify whose turn is next.
- Have the child hold a *wait* cue card when it is not his turn.
- Have the child hold a *my turn* cue card when it is his turn.

DO-WATCH-LISTEN-SAY: Social and Communication Intervention for Children with Autism
by Kathleen Ann Quill © 2000 Paul H. Brookes Publishing Co.

Activity

B. Group Skills
Turn-Taking 2. During unstructured activity

Selecting Activities

When preparing the child for a group activity, consider the following:

- Does the child demonstrate turn-taking with an adult?
- Does the child watch others taking their turns?
- Does the child understand the language used in the group?
- Does the child understand what to do and for how long in the group activity?
- How can the activity be organized for more structure and organization?

Sample Activity: Recess

Assist the child with taking turns in unstructured situations by choosing from three important strategy options. First, all of the strategies used for waiting apply to teaching turn-taking in unstructured activities. Second, all of the strategies for organizing time can be used for turn-taking in unstructured activities (see Chapter 6). Third, coaching peers as role models can assist the child with turn-taking during unstructured activities. For example, preview a social script about the rules of recess before the children go outside. Remind them of four simple steps: 1) stop, 2) look, 3) wait, and 4) go. These steps can be written on a cue card that a child wears on his belt. Use a visual choice board to have the children decide where they are going to play before going outside. Use time organizers to limit the amount of time children may spend on one piece of equipment and to indicate how long recess will last. Finally, utilize peer models as much as possible.

Strategies

Organizational Supports

- Define completion of a turn by the finished product (e.g., two ideas shared in a discussion group, one paragraph read aloud in a reading group, a turn on the swing to the count of 50 at recess).
- Define completion of a turn by a countdown (i.e., "10, 9, 8 . . .").
- Provide a small toy for the child to hold while he waits for a turn.

Social Supports

- Pair the child with one peer buddy during unstructured activities.
- Provide the peer models with reminders of how to help their friend take turns.

Visual Supports
- Write a social story about taking turns.
- Use a cue card that specifies "First . . ., then my turn."

DO-WATCH-LISTEN-SAY: Social and Communication Intervention for Children with Autism
by Kathleen Ann Quill © 2000 Paul H. Brookes Publishing Co.

Activity

B. Group Skills
Following Group Directions 1. Nonverbal directions

Selecting Activities

When preparing the child for a group activity, consider the following:

- Does the child attend to the adult in the group?
- Does the child follow the nonverbal directions in a one-to-one situation?
- Does the child understand the nonverbal directions used in the group?
- Does the child follow the lead of peers when confused?

Sample Activity: Group instruction

Design a social story about following group directions. The story should describe one or more types of nonverbal directions and explain what to do. For example, it is time to stop and look at the teacher when the lights flick on and off. Read the story to the class several times a day. Silently flick the lights whenever it is time to give group directions. Wait for all of the children to stop what they are doing and look at you before giving any verbal directions. If the children have not stopped, have another adult silently stop them and point them in your direction. Fade the silent, physical prompting as soon as possible.

Strategies

Organizational Supports

- Turn the lights on and off.
- Ring a timer.
- Ring a bell.
- Snap to a beat.
- Have everyone raise their hands and put a finger to their lips.
- Clap to a rhythm.

Social Supports

- Use similar nonverbal group directions across the day.
- Use exaggerated gestures.
- Target a peer coach for the child to watch in order to remember what to do.
- Assign a peer partner to assist the child.

Visual Supports

- Make a visual list of the group rules: watch, wait, and listen. Cue the children as needed.
- Provide individual cue cards that specify the group rules.
- Preview and review a social story about group rules.

DO-WATCH-LISTEN-SAY: Social and Communication Intervention for Children with Autism
by Kathleen Ann Quill © 2000 Paul H. Brookes Publishing Co.

Activity

B. Group Skills

Following Group Directions 2. Attention-getting directions

Selecting Activities

When preparing the child for a group activity, consider the following:

- Does the child attend to the adult in the group?
- Does the child follow the directions in a one-to-one situation?
- Does the child understand the verbal directions given to the group?
- Does the child follow the lead of peers when confused?

Sample Activity: Simon Says

Carrier phrases are very effective for helping children follow group directions. Carrier phrases include "Everybody, _____" or "Boys and girls,_____." Teach these carrier phrases in a fun Simon Says game. Begin by playing Simon Says as a structured small group game. Then use it in the classroom at random times, saying "Simon says put your hands on your head." Praise those who follow the direction, and prompt those who do not. Once the children begin responding consistently, use "Simon says" as a means to get the group's attention in natural contexts, such as "Simon says go to the reading area." Use silent prompting by another adult when necessary.

Strategies

Organizational Supports

- Use a consistent carrier phrase.
- Use the carrier phrase "Everybody."
- Use the carrier phrase "Get ready."
- Use the carrier phrase "Simon says."
- Use the carrier phrase "Boys and girls."
- Use the carrier phrase "Okay, look up here."
- Use the carrier phrase "It's time to listen."
- Count as a carrier phrase (e.g., count to three before giving a direction).

Social Supports

- Use similar attention-getting group directions throughout the day.
- Use exaggerated gestures.
- Target a peer coach for the child to watch in order to remember what to do.
- Assign a peer partner to assist the child.
- Have the child practice responding to the carrier phrase in an activity with one or two partners.

Visual Supports

- Make a visual list of the group rules: watch, wait, and listen.
- Provide individual cue cards that specify the group rules.
- Preview and review a social story about group rules.

DO-WATCH-LISTEN-SAY: Social and Communication Intervention for Children with Autism
by Kathleen Ann Quill © 2000 Paul H. Brookes Publishing Co.

Activity

B. Group Skills
Following Group Directions 3. Routine verbal directions

Selecting Activities

When preparing the child for a group activity, consider the following:

- Does the child attend to the adult in the group?
- Does the child follow the directions in a one-to-one situation?
- Does the child understand the verbal directions given to the group?
- Does the child follow the lead of peers when confused?

Sample Activity: Gym

Increase the child's ability to follow group directions in gym by using predictable, routine phrases that the child understands in one-to-one situations. Use these phrases consistently during the group activity. For example, clearly state "It's time to line up," "Everybody, stand up," or "Come here." Always use a clear carrier phrase first to get the group's attention. The routine verbal directions can be paired with nonverbal cues (e.g., clapping hands) or visual cues (e.g., a red flag).

Strategies

Organizational Supports

- Generate a list of specific phrases to use in specific group situations, such as "It's time to _____," "Look up here," or "Clean up."

Social Supports

- Use simple, routine phrases consistently.
- Use a consistent carrier phrase before giving the direction.
- Pair routine phrases with exaggerated gestures.
- Target a peer coach for the child to watch in order to remember what to do.
- Assign a peer partner to assist the child.
- Have the child practice responding to the carrier phrase in an activity with one or two partners.

Visual Supports

- Make a visual list of the group rules: watch, wait, and listen.
- Provide individual cue cards that specify the group rules.
- Preview and review a social story about group rules.

DO-WATCH-LISTEN-SAY: Social and Communication Intervention for Children with Autism
by Kathleen Ann Quill © 2000 Paul H. Brookes Publishing Co.

Activity

B. Group Skills
Following Group Directions 4. Verbal directions in familiar contexts

Selecting Activities

When preparing the child for a group activity, consider the following:

- Does the child demonstrate attending skills in the group?
- Does the child follow the directions in a one-to-one situation?
- Does the child understand the language used in the group?
- Does the child follow the lead of peers when confused?

Sample Activity: Art

Increase the child's ability to follow verbal directions during a familiar group art activity by creating a chart that depicts the sequence of steps to be completed. Place one activity schedule at the front of the room for the entire group, and give a second copy to the child. Prompt the child to refer to the activity schedule if unclear about the teacher's instructions during the art activity.

Strategies

Organizational Supports

- Use activity schedules that depict the sequence of events.
- Organize materials to clarify what is needed for each step of the activity.

Social Supports

- Use a consistent carrier phrase before giving the direction.
- Limit the complexity of verbal directions.
- Wait a few seconds before repeating directions.
- Target a peer coach for the child to watch in order to follow what to do.
- Assign a peer partner to assist the child.
- Have the child practice responding to the phrases in an activity with one or two partners.

Visual Supports

- Make a visual list of the group rules: watch, wait, and listen.
- Provide individual cue cards that specify the group rules.

DO-WATCH-LISTEN-SAY: Social and Communication Intervention for Children with Autism
by Kathleen Ann Quill © 2000 Paul H. Brookes Publishing Co.

Activity

B. Group Skills
Following Group Directions 5. Verbal directions in novel contexts

Selecting Activities

When preparing the child for a group activity, consider the following:

- Does the child demonstrate attending skills in the group?
- Does the child follow the directions in a one-to-one situation?
- Does the child understand the language used in the group?
- Does the child follow the lead of peers when confused?
- Is the child comfortable in the new setting?

Sample Activity: Schoolwide assembly

Novel group activities are often challenging for children with autism and require the use of multiple organizational, social, and visual supports. For example, increase the child's ability to follow verbal directions during an assembly by pairing him with a peer who is wearing a red ribbon (i.e., a concrete cue). Teach the child to look for and imitate his buddy. Prompt the child to do what the peer does. Second, use familiar verbal directions when the child is in a new setting. Always begin group instructions with carrier phrases such as "Class" or "Everyone." Be sure the child has had ample practice listening for these carrier phrases in familiar contexts. In addition, prompt the child nonverbally with cue cards that list the group rules for following carrier phrases and imitating a peer. Use the cue card every time the child needs support during the novel activity.

Strategies

Organizational Supports

- Determine whether the child is comfortable in the group situation.
- Use activity schedules that depict the sequence of events.
- Organize materials to clarify what is needed for each step of the activity.
- Allow the child to carry a toy or an object that he associates with comfort.

Social Supports

- Use a consistent carrier phrase before giving the direction.
- Limit the complexity of verbal directions.
- Increase the use of explicit nonverbal gestural cues.
- Wait a few seconds before repeating directions.
- Target a peer coach for the child to watch in order to follow what to do.
- Assign a peer partner to assist the child.
- Have the child practice responding to the phrases in an activity with one or two partners.

Visual Supports

- Make a visual list of the group rules: watch, wait, and listen.
- Provide individual cue cards that specify the group rules.
- Preview and review a social story about group rules.
- Use a video to preview the novel context.

DO-WATCH-LISTEN-SAY: Social and Communication Intervention for Children with Autism
by Kathleen Ann Quill © 2000 Paul H. Brookes Publishing Co.

Community Planning Guide
Example 1

Child's name: _____ *Quinn* _____ **Date:** _____ *January 20* _____

Directions:

1. Part I: Have the child's caregiver complete the survey, answering all of the questions.
2. Part II: Identify specific goals and objectives.
3. Part III: Design an intervention plan with instructional strategies and supports.

Part I: Community Survey

A. Describe the setting:

The grocery store

B. In a brief narrative, describe what the child typically does in that setting:

We get to the store, and immediately Quinn says he wants books. He bolts from the car into the store. I grab him and direct him to the grocery cart, and I give him the choice of whether he wants to sit in the grocery cart or walk. He says he wants the grocery cart, but once I lift him in, he yells that he wants to walk. So, I take him out of the grocery cart and he bolts to the books section. I chase him to the book section; he's laughing as I grab him and bring him back to the grocery cart. I repeatedly tell him, "First shopping, then books." Then, I hold his hand and try to push the grocery cart while he displays tantrum behavior. He cries the entire time, until we get to the deli counter. Once there, he gets his usual piece of cheese. I tell him, "You're doing a good job. We're almost done, then books." He bolts to the books section again, and I let him stay there while I finish the last of my shopping. As I get in line to pay, I tell him we are all done and it's time to go. Immediately he starts screaming that he wants books. I tell him books are all done and he throws himself on the floor, so I tell him he can stay until I'm done paying for the groceries. When I go back to get him, he starts to have a tantrum again, so I say, "Time to go; if you do a good job, we'll go to McDonalds." Sometimes that works; other times I have to buy the book or offer him something else.

C. To identify the source of the problem and what skills the child needs to learn, review questions:

1. What preparation is the child given prior to the activity?
   a. Does the child understand where he is going prior to arrival?

   Yes, we go every Thursday after school.

   b. Has the child been prepared for what is expected of him in that setting?

   Yes, I tell him first shopping, then books.

   c. Does the child understand when the activity will be over?

   Yes, we always leave after he has had time in the books section.

2. Does the child have any environmental sensitivities that would keep him from being successful in this setting?
   a. Are you aware of anything in the setting that will make the child afraid or uncomfortable?

   No, nothing bothers him.

   b. Is there anything in the setting that will be distracting to the child?

   The book section.

3. Does the child understand what is expected of him in the setting?
   a. Does the child understand where he is supposed to be in that setting?

   Yes, he needs to be walking next to me with the grocery cart.

   b. Does the child understand what he is supposed to do in that setting?

   First shopping, then books.

   c. Does the child understand what to say to others, as needed, in that setting?

   Yes, he asks the deli man for cheese and tells me he wants books.

   d. Does the child understand how to wait, as needed, in that setting?

   No.

4. Does the child have the necessary communication skills?

   a. Does the child have the skills to gain attention, if needed?

   Yes, he yells my name.

   b. Does the child have the skills to make requests?

   Yes, he does; he tells me he wants books, very clearly.

   c. Does the child have the skills to ask for help, if needed?

   He can, but he doesn't need to in this situation.

   d. Does the child have the skills to follow simple directions associated with the setting?

   Yes, he knows exactly what I am saying; he just wants his own way.

5. Is there a plan for the unexpected in that environment?

   I never thought about it. We do the same thing every time we go. If the book section were gone, there wouldn't be a problem.

6. Does the child have a way to calm or occupy himself in that setting?

   The books and the cheese are calming to him.

D. During the target activity, is the child able to

	Yes	No	Priority
1. Wait		X	2
2. Attend to the activity through completion		X	4
3. Make a transition to the next activity when directed	?		6
4. Accept interruptions or unexpected change		X	5
5. Follow directions		X	1
6. Make choices when necessary	X		
7. Calm self and be comforted	X		
8. Make needs known in an appropriate manner		X	3

Part II. Goals and Objectives

A. Using the information from the survey, identify the skills to be addressed in the target setting.

   1. List the skills that need to be taught for success in the target setting.

   Follow directions

   Wait

   Make needs known in an appropriate manner

   2. Identify any environmental factors that can cause overstimulation.

   There were no overstimulating environmental factors, but the books were a distraction.

Part III. Intervention Plan

A. To assist the child in the community, design instructional strategies in the following areas:

   1. Strategies to prepare the child prior to the target activity

   a. Strategies to help the child understand where he is going prior to arrival

   As soon as you get in the car, show Quinn a pictograph of the grocery store.

   b. Strategies to prepare the child for what is expected of him in that setting

   Read Quinn a social script about going to the grocery store before getting out of the car. Have a prepared pictograph schedule of "first Mommy shops, then cheese, then books, then Mommy pays, then shopping is all done." Hand Quinn his pictographic shopping list in the car. Verbally reinforce during the ride, "Quinn, we hold on to the grocery cart in the grocery store."

   c. Strategies to clarify for the child when the activity will be over

   Verbally reinforce from the social script the shopping sequence:

   First Mommy shops, then cheese, then books, then Mommy pays, then shopping is all done.

DO-WATCH-LISTEN-SAY: Social and Communication Intervention for Children with Autism
by Kathleen Ann Quill © 2000 Paul H. Brookes Publishing Co.

2. Strategies to compensate for environmental overstimulation

    a. Strategies to desensitize the child to stimuli that are fearful or discomforting

        N/A

    b. Strategies to keep the child focused on the target activity

        Reference back to the visual sequence board, and verbally remind him in simple language what events remain in the shopping trip. For example, if you are at the deli counter, say, "It's not time for books. First cheese, then books." Keep Quinn focused on his shopping list.

3. Strategies to help the child understand what is expected of him in the target activity

    a. Strategies to help the child understand where he is supposed to be in that setting

        Verbally remind him in simple language, "Quinn, we hold onto the grocery cart in the grocery store." If Quinn chooses not to hold onto the grocery cart, hand-over-hand place his hand on the grocery cart with the repeated verbal reminder to hold onto the grocery cart.

    b. Strategies to help the child understand what he is supposed to do in that setting

        Prior to arriving at the store, arrange the items on his shopping list in the order of the aisles in which you are going to shop. Have Quinn look for one item in each aisle while you complete your shopping for that aisle. Once he retrieves the item, he puts it in the carriage, removes the pictograph from the list, holds the grocery cart, and waits for Mom. This sequence will be detailed in his social script.

    c. Strategies to help the child understand what he needs to say to others in that setting

        Target situations in the grocery store in which Quinn is expected to interact verbally with others. Script what he needs to say in each situation; for example, at the cheese counter he says, "Cheese please," or a variation of the request.

    d. Strategies to help the child wait, as needed, in that setting

        Target situations in the grocery store in which Quinn is expected to wait. Devise natural waiting interactions. For example, make a game of naming each item as it is scanned at the checkout counter. Continually reinforce appropriate waiting.

4. Strategies to provide the child with the necessary communication skills for the targeted activity

    a. Strategies to teach the child how to gain attention, if needed

        Do not respond to his yelling until he has gained your attention in an appropriate manner; for example, "Excuse me, Mom" in an indoor voice. Do not make eye contact until he has appropriately gained your attention.

    b. Strategies to teach the child how to make requests appropriately

        Do not respond to screaming and yelling, but cue his language by continually signing I WANT. *Honor appropriate requests whenever feasible. Acknowledge inappropriate requests by stating, in simple language, "It's not time for _____."*

    c. Strategies to teach the child how to ask for help, if needed

        Do not respond to screaming and yelling, but cue his language by continually signing HELP.

    d. Strategies to help the child follow simple directions associated with the setting

        Reference the social script.

        Use visual cues (pointing, pictographs, signing) to support verbal directions.

        Use rule cards attached to your wrist.

B. To compensate for the unexpected, design intervention strategies in the following areas:

Strategies to help the child remain calm when unexpected events occur during the target activity

Use the "uh-oh" strategy.

Strategies to provide the child with a means of occupying himself during the target activity

Utilize a relaxation technique, such as counting to 10 or deep breathing.

Bring a favorite, calming fidget toy.

Bring headphones to listen to a preferred story or music.

DO-WATCH-LISTEN-SAY: Social and Communication Intervention for Children with Autism
by Kathleen Ann Quill © 2000 Paul H. Brookes Publishing Co.

Community Planning Guide
Example 2

Child's name: _____ Claire _____ **Date:** _____ June 10 _____

Directions:

1. Part I: Have the child's caregiver complete the survey, answering all of the questions.
2. Part II: Identify specific goals and objectives.
3. Part III: Design an intervention plan with instructional strategies and supports.

Part I: Community Survey

A. Describe the setting:

The movies

B. In a brief narrative, describe what the child typically does in that setting:

We recently tried to take Claire to the movies for the first time to see "Mighty Joe Young." We thought this would be a good choice for a couple of reasons. First, her favorite movie at home is "Mary Poppins." She always seems to prefer live action over animation. Second, she loves gorillas and monkeys. Her favorite books are about them, and whenever we go to the zoo, she watches them for hours. We got to the movies early. Claire was fine getting the tickets and popcorn. We were ready to get our seats before the theater got too crowded, so she wouldn't feel overwhelmed by all of the people. She sat fine, and we talked about the movie coming on soon and used her communication board to tell her that she was going to see gorillas, just like at the zoo. When the previews began, she became agitated and covered her ears. We tried to calm her by commenting on what we saw and reminding her she was going to see gorillas. At that point she settled a bit, although she still periodically covered her ears. Midway through the second preview, she began requesting gorillas with her communication board. We told her she had to wait, but she became more upset and began to cry and scream. We told her she had to be quiet, which just upset her more. At that point, we tried distracting her with the popcorn. When the lights went out for the movie, she screamed and hit me. I told her that hitting is not allowed and that she needed to be quiet or the movies would be all done. She couldn't calm down, so we ended up leaving.

C. To identify the source of the problem and what skills the child needs to learn, review the following questions:

1. What preparation is the child given prior to the activity?

   a. Does the child understand where she is going prior to arrival?

   We used her communication board to show her that we were going to the movies to see gorillas. We thought she understood because she knows what movies are at home on television.

   b. Has the child been prepared for what is expected of her in that setting?

   We used her communication board to show her that she would have to sit and watch the movie quietly.

   c. Does the child understand when the activity will be over?

   She was told that when the movie was all done, we would go home. At home she always knows when her movies are done and will do nothing until they are.

2. Does the child have any environmental sensitivities that would keep her from being successful in this setting?

   a. Are you aware of anything in the setting that will make the child afraid or uncomfortable?

   We know that crowds are overwhelming and that loud, unexpected noises startle her. We weren't aware that the movie would be so loud. The lights took us by surprise. She has never been afraid of the dark.

DO-WATCH-LISTEN-SAY: Social and Communication Intervention for Children with Autism
by Kathleen Ann Quill © 2000 Paul H. Brookes Publishing Co.

     b.   Is there anything in the setting that will be distracting to the child?

        No. Movies are her most reinforcing activity.

   3. Does the child understand what is expected of her in the setting?

     a.   Does the child understand where she is supposed to be in that setting?

        Yes, sitting with me.

     b.   Does the child understand what she is supposed to do in that setting?

        Yes, watch quietly.

     c.   Does the child understand what to say to others, as needed, in that setting?

        She can get her basic needs across with her communication board, and there were no expectations for her to communicate while watching the movie.

     d.   Does the child understand how to wait, as needed, in that setting?

        Yes, she typically waits well when directed, and we keep her occupied while waiting for the movie to begin.

   4. Does the child have the necessary communication skills?

     a.   Does the child have the skills to gain attention, if needed?

        Usually, but sometimes she forgets that we need to see her board to understand her.

     b.   Does the child have the skills to make requests?

        Yes, as above.

     c.   Does the child have the skills to ask for help, if needed?

        Yes, as above.

     d.   Does the child have the skills to follow simple directions associated with the setting?

        Yes, she can sit and wait.

   5. Is there a plan for the unexpected in that environment?

        No, we didn't think of anything like that ourselves.

   6. Does the child have a way to calm or occupy herself in that setting?

        No. At home, movies tend to be a calming activity.

D.   During the target activity, is the child able to

	Yes	No	Priority
1. Wait	X		
2. Attend to the activity through completion	At home		
3. Make a transition to the next activity when directed	X		
4. Accept interruptions or unexpected change		X	2
5. Follow directions	X		
6. Make choices when necessary	X		
7. Calm self and be comforted		X	1
8. Make needs known in an appropriate manner		X	3

Part II. Goals and Objectives

A.   Using the information from the survey, identify the skills to be addressed in the target setting.

   1. List the skills that need to be taught for success in the target setting.

     Accept interruptions.

     Make needs known in an appropriate manner.

2. Identify any environmental factors that can cause overstimulation.

Loud noises and unexpected changes in lighting

Part III. Intervention Plan

A. To assist the child in the community, design instructional strategies in the following areas:

1. Strategies to prepare the child prior to the target activity

   a. Strategies to help the child understand where she is going prior to arrival

   Social stories

   Picture sequences

   Mock visit to the movie theater

   b. Strategies to prepare the child for what is expected of her in that setting

   Social story

   Cue cards

   c. Strategies to clarify for the child when the activity will be over

   Social story

   First/Then card (First lights on, then movie's all done.)

2. Strategies to compensate for environmental overstimulation

   a. Strategies to desensitize the child to stimuli that are fearful or discomforting

   Go early to avoid crowds.

   Wear earmuffs, headphones, or a hat to muffle the sound.

   Prepare the child for the lights going off during the movie.

   b. Strategies to keep the child focused on the target activity

   N/A

3. Strategies to help the child understand what is expected of her in the target activity

   a. Strategies to help the child understand where she is supposed to be in that setting

   N/A

   b. Strategies to help the child understand what she is supposed to do in that setting

   Social stories and cue cards

   c. Strategies to help the child understand what she needs to say to others in that setting

   N/A

   d. Strategies to help the child wait, if needed, in that setting

   Cue cards, if necessary

   Sign WAIT to remind her.

4. Strategies to provide the child with the communication skills necessary for the target activity

   a. Strategies to teach the child how to gain attention, if needed

   Tap an adult before using her communication board.

   b. Strategies to teach the child how to make requests appropriately

   She had the skills to request, but, due to being overstimulated, she was unable to do so in the environment. Therefore, acknowledge her communicative intent rather than her behavior. Shape her behavior into a familiar and appropriate means of communication.

   c. Strategies to teach the child how to ask for help, if needed

   As above

   d. Strategies to help the child follow simple directions associated with the setting

   Cue cards

B. To compensate for the unexpected, design intervention strategies in the following areas:

1. Strategies to help the child remain calm when unexpected events occur during the target activity

   Teach her a catch phrase to indicate an unexpected change in the routine (e.g., uh-oh, oh well).

   Social scripts

2. Strategies to provide the child with a means of occupying herself during the target activity

   Bring calming toys or transition objects.

   Bring headphones for noise.

   Utilize her sensory diet (e.g., hugging, deep pressure squeezes, fidgets).

   Teach her a calming script or song.

   Teach deep breathing.

Appendix A
Play Interest Survey

Play Interest Survey

Child's name:_____ Date:_____

Directions: 1. Rate the child's play interest on a scale of 1–3.

        1 = Does not like   2 = Shows some interest   3 = Likes a lot

        Leave the rating column blank if there has been no opportunity.

    2. Check each toy or game if age-appropriate solitary play is observed.

    3. Check each toy or game if age-appropriate social play is observed.

Exploratory play	Rate	Solitary	Social
Bubbles			
Bumble ball			
Busy bead mazes			
Cause-and-effect toys			
Handheld arcade games			
Kaleidoscope			
Macaroni bin			
Mirrors			
Paint bags			
Remote-control vehicles			
Sandbox			
Tops			
Tornado bottle			
Water table			
Wind-up toys			

Physical play	Rate	Solitary	Social
Ball			
Basketball and hoop			
Beanbags			
Bicycle			
Bowling			
Exercise equipment			
Hopscotch			
Hula-Hoops			
Jump rope			
Playground equipment			
Roller/ice skates			
Seesaw			
Sit 'n Spin			
Swing			
Trampoline			

Manipulatives	Rate	Solitary	Social
Beads and laces			
Build-and-stack sets			
Colorforms			
Lite-Brite			
Lock and latch board			
Magnetic mazes			
Marble run			
Mr. Potato Head			
Nesting dolls			
Parquetry blocks			
Pegboards			
Puzzles			
Sewing cards			
Shape sorter			
View Master			

Constructive play	Rate	Solitary	Social
Bristle blocks			
Building blocks			
Duplos			
Erector sets			
Gears building set			
Legos models			
Legos			
Lincoln Logs			
Magnablocks			
Popbeads			
Snap blocks			
Tinker Toys			
Tool bench and tools			
Train and connecting tracks			
Vehicles and roads			

DO-WATCH-LISTEN-SAY: Social and Communication Intervention for Children with Autism
by Kathleen Ann Quill © 2000 Paul H. Brookes Publishing Co.

Art	Rate	Solitary	Social
Bingo daubers			
Chalk			
Collage materials			
Coloring books			
Cutting and gluing			
Dot-to-dot			
Drawing materials			
Finger paints			
Magna Doodle			
Mazes			
Paint-by-number			
Painting materials			
Playdough			
Stamps			
Stencils			

Literacy	Rate	Solitary	Social
ABC stickers			
Activity books			
Books			
Books on tape			
Computer programs			
Flannel boards			
Language experience stories			
Magazines			
Magnetic letters			
Make-a-word picture puzzles			
Photo albums			
Sequence cards			
Sorting/matching activities			
Talking books			
Word finds			

Sociodramatic play	Rate	Solitary	Social
Barn and animals			
Birthday party			
Cars and garage			
Doctor			
Dollhouse and miniatures			
Dress-up			
Feeding the baby			
Grocery store			
Hair and makeup			
Kitchen toys			
Miniature people/animals			
Puppets			
Stuffed animals			
Telephone			
Tent			

Games	Rate	Solitary	Social
Barnyard bingo			
Boggle Jr.			
Candy Land			
Chutes and Ladders			
Connect Four			
Dominoes			
I Spy			
Kickball			
Lotto			
Memory			
Ring toss			
Scrabble Junior			
Tic-Tac-Toe			
Uno			

Music

	Rate	Solitary	Social
Dancing			
Exercise video			
Fingerplays			
Karaoke machine			
Keyboard			
Marching band			
Microphone			
Musical instruments			
Musical toys			
Rain stick			
Rhythm sticks			
Sing-along video			
Songs			
Tape recorder			
Tapes and CDs			

Social games

	Rate	Solitary	Social
Catch			
Chase/tag			
Dog, Dog, My Bone Is Gone			
Duck, Duck, Goose			
Hide-and-Seek			
London Bridge			
Mother, May I			
Musical Chairs			
Parachute play			
Peekaboo			
Red Light, Green Light			
Rough and tumble			
Simon Says			
Tickle games			
Twenty Questions			

Other preferences

	Rate	Solitary	Social
Spins objects			
Throws objects			
Sifts objects through fingers			
Watches objects fall			
Shakes objects for noise			
Smells objects			

Other interests

	Rate	Solitary	Social

Favorite solitary activities

Favorite social activities

DO-WATCH-LISTEN-SAY: Social and Communication Intervention for Children with Autism
by Kathleen Ann Quill © 2000 Paul H. Brookes Publishing Co.

Appendix B
Social Play Task Analysis

A social play task analysis is a list of discrete subskills for one social play activity. The subskills are divided into four categories:

- Group content (G)
- Toy use (T)
- Social skills (S)
- Communication skills (C)

The task analyses determine the presence or absence of adult or peer play (G), functional or creative toy use (T), social skills (S), and communication skills (C) across multiple social play activities, applying the DO-WATCH-LISTEN-SAY framework. Twenty sample social play task analyses are provided. They can be used to clarify the four dimensions of social play, assist with program planning, and monitor skill acquisition. More detailed information about the child's toy use, and generalization of social skills, communication skills, and social play with adults and peers can be determined by using the task analyses. However, given the complexity of social play, it is important to view the skills listed under each category as examples. Rigid adherence to teaching the listed subskills is not recommended.

Social Play Task Analysis

Directions:

1. Observe the child's social play in the specific activity.
2. Check all subskills (or related subskills) from the four categories observed.

Exploratory Play: Sandbox

___ G.1 Interacts with adult
___ G.2 Interacts with one peer
___ G.3 Interacts with multiple peers

___ T.1 Fills containers repeatedly during sand play
___ T.2 Fills and dumps containers and/or buries people and/or uses sand wheel
___ T.3 Uses shovel to fill bucket, then turns bucket over, and then lifts bucket up to make a sand castle
___ T.4 Imagines that pile of sand is a house and puts miniature people inside

___ S.1 Plays at sand table with others but does not interact
___ S.2 Takes turns dumping sand into the sand wheel
___ S.3 Shares limited sand toys with others
___ S.4 Jointly builds a sand structure with others

___ C.1 Responds to partner during play
___ C.2 Requests desired sand toy
___ C.3 Comments on others' play
___ C.4 Maintains a conversation during play

Exploratory Play: Bubbles

___ G.1 Interacts with adult
___ G.2 Interacts with one peer
___ G.3 Interacts with multiple peers

___ T.1 Pops bubbles
___ T.2 Waves wand, catches bubbles, and/or dips wand in bubble solution
___ T.3 Dips wand in container and then blows bubbles
___ T.4 Imagines that radiator blower is a giant mouth and holds wand over it to make bubbles

___ S.1 Plays with bubbles at same time with others but does not interact
___ S.2 Takes turns dipping wand into bubble container
___ S.3 Shares bubble solution with play partner
___ S.4 Blows bubbles to a partner to pop

___ C.1 Responds to a partner during play
___ C.2 Requests a turn to use bubble wand
___ C.3 Comments on others' play
___ C.4 Maintains a conversation during play

DO-WATCH-LISTEN-SAY: Social and Communication Intervention for Children with Autism
by Kathleen Ann Quill © 2000 Paul H. Brookes Publishing Co.

Constructive Play: Blocks

__ G.1 Interacts with adult
__ G.2 Interacts with one peer
__ G.3 Interacts with multiple peers

__ T.1 Stacks blocks repeatedly during play
__ T.2 Builds bridges for cars to drive under, builds towers, and/or knocks down blocks
__ T.3 Builds a tower and then knocks it down
__ T.4 Imagines that block is a car and drives it under a block bridge

__ S.1 Plays at blocks with others, but builds own structures and does not interact
__ S.2 Takes turns knocking down a tower
__ S.3 Shares limited blocks with play partner
__ S.4 Jointly builds a block structure with a partner

__ C.1 Responds to partner during play
__ C.2 Requests desired block
__ C.3 Comments on others' play
__ C.4 Maintains a conversation during play

Constructive Play: Trains

__ G.1 Interacts with adults
__ G.2 Interacts with one peer
__ G.3 Interacts with multiple peers

__ T.1 Pushes a train
__ T.2 Puts people on the train, builds a track, and/or pushes train around the track
__ T.3 Puts people on the train and then pushes it around the track
__ T.4 Uses train to bring materials from one play area to another

__ S.1 Plays at the train table at same table as others but does not interact
__ S.2 Takes turns pushing the train around the track
__ S.3 Shares trains with partner
__ S.4 Jointly designs and builds a train track with partner

__ C.1 Responds to partner during play
__ C.2 Requests a turn to push the train
__ C.3 Comments on others' play
__ C.4 Maintains a conversation during play

DO-WATCH-LISTEN-SAY: Social and Communication Intervention for Children with Autism
by Kathleen Ann Quill © 2000 Paul H. Brookes Publishing Co.

Literacy: Book Share with *Brown Bear, Brown Bear*

__ G.1   Interacts with adult
__ G.2   Interacts with one peer
__ G.3   Interacts with multiple peers

__ T.1   Turns pages of the book
__ T.2   Points to pictures, fills in the blank when read, and/or uses props to tell the story
__ T.3   "Reads" the story and then hangs props in sequential order
__ T.4   Uses pattern of dialogue to name different objects

__ S.1   Looks through own copy of book while others are acting out the story
__ S.2   Takes turns filling in the blanks while reading the story with a partner
__ S.3   Shares props with play partners
__ S.4   Acts out story with a partner

__ C.1   Responds to partner during play
__ C.2   Requests desired prop
__ C.3   Comments on others' play
__ C.4   Maintains a conversation during play

Literacy: ABC Stickers

__ G.1   Interacts with adult
__ G.2   Interacts with one peer
__ G.3   Interacts with multiple peers

__ T.1   Labels letters
__ T.2   Sequences alphabet, puts stickers on paper, and/or makes word associations with letters
__ T.3   Picks out letters of name and sticks them on paper in order
__ T.4   Imagines that the letters he has put down form a story and reads it

__ S.1   Plays at writing center with others but does not interact
__ S.2   Takes turns placing stickers on paper
__ S.3   Shares stickers with play partner
__ S.4   Jointly "writes" a story with play partner

__ C.1   Responds to partner during play
__ C.2   Requests a specific sticker
__ C.3   Comments on others' play
__ C.4   Maintains a conversation during play

DO-WATCH-LISTEN-SAY: Social and Communication Intervention for Children with Autism
by Kathleen Ann Quill © 2000 Paul H. Brookes Publishing Co.

Physical Play: Ball Play

__ G.1   Interacts with adult
__ G.2   Interacts with one peer
__ G.3   Interacts with multiple peers

__ T.1   Bounces ball repeatedly
__ T.2   Kicks the ball, throws the ball through a hoop, and/or hits the ball with a bat
__ T.3   Catches ball and then rolls it toward partner
__ T.4   Imagines that a ruler is a baseball bat and uses it to hit ball

__ S.1   Plays ball near others but does not interact
__ S.2   Takes turns throwing ball through basketball hoop
__ S.3   Shares ball with partner
__ S.4   Plays catch with a partner

__ C.1   Responds to partner during play
__ C.2   Requests a turn to throw the ball
__ C.3   Comments on others' play
__ C.4   Maintains a conversation during play

Physical Play: Scooter Board

__ G.1   Interacts with adult
__ G.2   Interacts with one peer
__ G.3   Interacts with multiple peers

__ T.1   Sits on scooter and uses feet to move it
__ T.2   Lies down on scooter and crawls, sits on scooter, and/or uses scooter to go around obstacles
__ T.3   Lies down on scooter and then uses feet to push self through an obstacle course
__ T.4   Imagines that the scooter is a vehicle

__ S.1   Uses scooter in gym with others but does not interact
__ S.2   Takes turns being pulled on the scooter
__ S.3   Shares scooters with partner
__ S.4   Makes a "train" by holding on to partner's feet and moving scooters while connected

__ C.1   Responds to partner during play
__ C.2   Requests a turn to use the scooter
__ C.3   Comments on others' play
__ C.4   Maintains a conversation during play

DO-WATCH-LISTEN-SAY: Social and Communication Intervention for Children with Autism
by Kathleen Ann Quill © 2000 Paul H. Brookes Publishing Co.

Art: Playdough

___ G.1   Interacts with adult
___ G.2   Interacts with one peer
___ G.3   Interacts with multiple peers

___ T.1   Repeatedly presses playdough flat
___ T.2   Rolls playdough in hands, uses cookie cutters, and/or uses playdough press
___ T.3   Rolls playdough into a pizza
___ T.4   Imagines that playdough is a pizza

___ S.1   Uses playdough at table with others but does not interact
___ S.2   Takes turns putting playdough into and squeezing playdough press
___ S.3   Shares rolling pin and playdough press with partner
___ S.4   Jointly rolls out playdough and makes "cookies" with a partner

___ C.1   Responds to a partner during play
___ C.2   Requests a specific cookie cutter
___ C.3   Comments on others' play
___ C.4   Maintains a conversation during play

Art: Gluing

___ G.1   Interacts with adult
___ G.2   Interacts with one peer
___ G.3   Interacts with multiple peers

___ T.1   Uses a paintbrush to spread glue on paper
___ T.2   Places materials on to glue, squeezes glue bottle, and/or glues two objects together
___ T.3   Squeezes glue on paper and then shakes glitter over glue
___ T.4   Imagines that cotton balls glued together form a rabbit

___ S.1   Sits at art table with others but does not interact
___ S.2   Takes turns shaking glitter on the glue
___ S.3   Shares glue bottle with partner
___ S.4   Jointly makes a large collage mural with various objects

___ C.1   Responds to partner during play
___ C.2   Requests a turn to use the materials
___ C.3   Comments on others' play
___ C.4   Maintains a conversation during play

DO-WATCH-LISTEN-SAY: Social and Communication Intervention for Children with Autism
by Kathleen Ann Quill © 2000 Paul H. Brookes Publishing Co.

Music: Microphone

___ G.1   Interacts with adult

___ G.2   Interacts with one peer

___ G.3   Interacts with multiple peers

___ T.1   Sings into microphone

___ T.2   Sings along with a tape, dances while singing, and/or holds microphone up to tape to make it louder

___ T.3   Turns on microphone, then turns on tape, and then sings along with the tape

___ T.4   Imagines that a hairbrush is a microphone and sings into it

___ S.1   Uses microphone while others are in the music center but does not interact

___ S.2   Takes turns saying names into the microphone

___ S.3   Shares the microphone with a partner

___ S.4   Sings a duet with a partner using the microphone

___ C.1   Responds to a partner during play

___ C.2   Requests a tape be put on for sing-along

___ C.3   Comments on others' play

___ C.4   Maintains a conversation during play

Music: Song

___ G.1   Interacts with adult

___ G.2   Interacts with one peer

___ G.3   Interacts with multiple peers

___ T.1   Sings a song

___ T.2   Points to words of song, uses props while singing, and/or does finger motions with the song

___ T.3   Takes out song props, then uses them to sing song, and then puts them away

___ T.4   Imagines he is the character from a Disney song and acts out its actions during it

___ S.1   Sings at music time but does not interact with others

___ S.2   Takes turns choosing a favorite song to sing

___ S.3   Shares song props with a partner

___ S.4   Jointly acts out a scene from a Disney song

___ C.1   Responds to partner during play

___ C.2   Requests a specific song be sung

___ C.3   Comments on others' play

___ C.4   Maintains a conversation during play

Manipulative Play: Mr. Potato Head

___ G.1   Interacts with adult
___ G.2   Interacts with one peer
___ G.3   Interacts with multiple peers

___ T.1   Sticks facial pieces in holes
___ T.2   Makes faces, disassembles faces, and/or constructs several Mr. Potato Heads at once
___ T.3   Looks at a model face and then recreates it with own Mr. Potato Head
___ T.4   Uses Mr. Potato Head as figure in the dollhouse

___ S.1   Uses Mr. Potato Head at the center with others but does not interact
___ S.2   Takes turns making faces with Mr. Potato Head
___ S.3   Shares facial features with partner
___ S.4   Jointly builds Mr. Potato Head with partner

___ C.1   Responds to partner during play
___ C.2   Requests a specific facial feature
___ C.3   Comments on others' play
___ C.4   Maintains a conversation during play

Manipulative Play: Marble Run

___ G.1   Interacts with adult
___ G.2   Interacts with one peer
___ G.3   Interacts with multiple peers

___ T.1   Places marbles in run
___ T.2   Drops marbles down in run, builds run, and/or watches marbles go down run
___ T.3   Builds marble run and then drop marbles down
___ T.4   Imagines run is a slide and makes cars and/or miniature people go down it

___ S.1   Uses a marble run at same time/place as others but does not interact
___ S.2   Takes turns dropping marbles down the run
___ S.3   Shares marbles with play partner
___ S.4   Jointly builds a marble run with partner

___ C.1   Responds to partner during play
___ C.2   Requests a marble to use
___ C.3   Comments on others' play
___ C.4   Maintains a conversation during play

Game Play: Candy Land

__ G.1   Interacts with adult
__ G.2   Interacts with one peer
__ G.3   Interacts with multiple peers

__ T.1   Draws cards from deck
__ T.2   Matches cards to color squares on board, moves pieces, and/or discriminates own color piece
__ T.3   Draws card and then moves piece to corresponding square
__ T.4   Imagines that cards are pieces to a road and lays them out to build a new board game

__ S.1   Uses own Candy Land board while others are playing but does not interact
__ S.2   Takes turns drawing cards and moving pieces
__ S.3   Shares playing pieces with play partner
__ S.4   Plays game to completion with partner

__ C.1   Responds to partner during play
__ C.2   Requests to be a certain color game piece
__ C.3   Comments on others' play
__ C.4   Maintains a conversation during play

Game Play: Lotto

__ G.1   Interacts with adult
__ G.2   Interacts with one peer
__ G.3   Interacts with multiple peers

__ T.1   Labels cards
__ T.2   Matches cards to board
__ T.3   Draws a card and then matches it to board
__ T.4   Uses cards as pieces to make new lotto boards

__ S.1   Uses own lotto board at same time as others but does not interact
__ S.2   Takes turns drawing cards and matching them to board
__ S.3   Shares lotto cards with play partner
__ S.4   Plays lotto game to completion with partner

__ C.1   Responds to partner during play
__ C.2   Requests to draw the card first
__ C.3   Comments on others' play
__ C.4   Maintains a conversation during play

Sociodramatic Play: Dollhouse

___ G.1 Interacts with adult
___ G.2 Interacts with one peer
___ G.3 Interacts with multiple peers

___ T.1 Makes doll figure climb the stairs
___ T.2 Puts doll in the car, makes it go down the slide, and/or sits it at the table
___ T.3 Has doll get up from table, get in the car, and drive the car around
___ T.4 Imagines that blocks are chairs and has the dolls sit on them around the table

___ S.1 Plays in dollhouse area with others but does not interact
___ S.2 Takes turns making the dolls go down the slide
___ S.3 Shares doll figures with play partner
___ S.4 Acts out play script with a partner, each having different dolls

___ C.1 Responds to partner during play
___ C.2 Requests a specific doll
___ C.3 Comments on others' play
___ C.4 Maintains a conversation during play

Sociodramatic Play: Kitchen

___ G.1 Interacts with adult
___ G.2 Interacts with one peer
___ G.3 Interacts with multiple peers

___ T.1 Puts pretend food in mouth
___ T.2 Puts food in refrigerator, washes dishes, and/or cooks food on stove
___ T.3 Takes food from refrigerator, puts it on a plate, and "eats" it
___ T.4 Imagines a spoon is a cone and places ice cream on top of it to make an ice cream cone

___ S.1 Plays in kitchen area with others but does not interact
___ S.2 Takes turns washing dishes
___ S.3 Shares food with a play partner
___ S.4 Jointly acts out play script of cooking a meal and serving it to partners

___ C.1 Responds to partner during play
___ C.2 Requests a specific play food
___ C.3 Comments on others' play
___ C.4 Maintains a conversation during play

DO-WATCH-LISTEN-SAY: Social and Communication Intervention for Children with Autism
by Kathleen Ann Quill © 2000 Paul H. Brookes Publishing Co.

Social Games: Chase

___ G.1   Interacts with adult

___ G.2   Interacts with one peer

___ G.3   Interacts with multiple peers

___ T.1   N/A

___ S.1   Takes turns being the chaser and the chased

___ S.2   Plays chase game to completion

___ C.1   Responds to partner during play

___ C.2   Requests a turn to be the chaser

___ C.3   Comments on others' play

___ C.4   Maintains a conversation during play

Social Games: Parachute

___ G.1   Interacts with adult

___ G.2   Interacts with one peer

___ G.3   Interacts with multiple peers

___ T.1   Holds on to parachute

___ T.2   Uses parachute to bounce balls

___ T.3   Holds on to parachute, walks in circle, lifts it high above head, and then brings it down

___ T.4   Imagines that the parachute is a tent and gets underneath it

___ S.1   Takes turns being the person under the parachute

___ S.2   Shares limited space at the parachute with play partner

___ S.3   Plays parachute game to completion

___ C.1   Responds to partner during play

___ C.2   Requests a specific game to play

___ C.3   Comments on others' play

___ C.4   Maintains a conversation during play

DO-WATCH-LISTEN-SAY: Social and Communication Intervention for Children with Autism
by Kathleen Ann Quill © 2000 Paul H. Brookes Publishing Co.

Social Play Task Analysis Summary Sheet

Directions:

1. Select a specific play activity.
2. Generate a list of desired social play subskills in the areas of toy use, social skills, and communication skills.
3. Observe the child's social play in the specific activity.
4. Check all subskills observed from the four categories: group context, toy use, social skills, and communication skills.

Play activity_____

Group context

— G.1   Interacts with adult

— G.2   Interacts with one peer

— G.3   Interacts with multiple peers

Toy use

— T.1 _____

— T.2 _____

— T.3 _____

— T.4 _____

Social skills

— S.1 _____

— S.2 _____

— S.3 _____

— S.4 _____

Communication skills

— C.1 _____

— C.2 _____

— C.3 _____

— C.4 _____

DO-WATCH-LISTEN-SAY: Social and Communication Intervention for Children with Autism
by Kathleen Ann Quill © 2000 Paul H. Brookes Publishing Co.

Appendix C
Social Skills Progress Sheets

Solitary Play Progress Sheet

Child's name:_____ Date: _____

Directions: 1. List the child's solitary play activities.
2. Indicate whether the child's play is independent or requires prompting.
3. If prompted, circle the level of prompting.
   P = Physical assistance
   V = Visual cue
   S = Spoken prompt

	Activity	Independent	Prompted
1			P V S
2			P V S
3			P V S
4			P V S
5			P V S
6			P V S
7			P V S
8			P V S
9			P V S
10			P V S
11			P V S
12			P V S
13			P V S
14			P V S
15			P V S
16			P V S
17			P V S
18			P V S
19			P V S
20			P V S

DO-WATCH-LISTEN-SAY: Social and Communication Intervention for Children with Autism
by Kathleen Ann Quill © 2000 Paul H. Brookes Publishing Co.

Social Play Progress Sheet

Child's name:_____ Date:_____

Directions: 1. List specific activities that the child plays with others.
              2. Circle all of the skills the child demonstrates when playing with an adult.
              3. Circle all of the skills the child demonstrates when playing with a peer.
                W = Watches
                S = Shares
                T = Takes turns
                R = Responds

	Activity	Adult	Peer
1		W S T R	W S T R
2		W S T R	W S T R
3		W S T R	W S T R
4		W S T R	W S T R
5		W S T R	W S T R
6		W S T R	W S T R
7		W S T R	W S T R
8		W S T R	W S T R
9		W S T R	W S T R
10		W S T R	W S T R
11		W S T R	W S T R
12		W S T R	W S T R
13		W S T R	W S T R
14		W S T R	W S T R
15		W S T R	W S T R
16		W S T R	W S T R
17		W S T R	W S T R
18		W S T R	W S T R
19		W S T R	W S T R
20		W S T R	W S T R

DO-WATCH-LISTEN-SAY: Social and Communication Intervention for Children with Autism
by Kathleen Ann Quill © 2000 Paul H. Brookes Publishing Co.

Group Skills Progress Sheet

Child's name:_____ Date: _____

Directions: 1. List specific group activities.
2. Check if the child independently attends, waits, takes turns, and follows directions during the group activity.

	Group activity	Attends	Waits	Takes turns	Follows directions
1					
2					
3					
4					
5					
6					
7					
8					
9					
10					
11					
12					
13					
14					
15					
16					
17					
18					
19					
20					

DO-WATCH-LISTEN-SAY: Social and Communication Intervention for Children with Autism
by Kathleen Ann Quill © 2000 Paul H. Brookes Publishing Co.

Appendix D
Community Planning Guide

Community Planning Guide

Child's name: _____ **Date:** _____

Directions:

1. Part I: Have the child's caregiver complete the survey, answering all of the questions.
2. Part II: Identify specific goals and objectives.
3. Part III: Design an intervention plan with instructional strategies and supports.

Part I: Community Survey

   A.   Describe the setting:

   B.   In a brief narrative, describe what the child typically does in that setting:

   C.   To identify the source of the problem and what skills the child needs to learn, review the following questions:

      1.   What preparation is the child given prior to the activity?

         a.   Does the child understand where he is going prior to arrival?

         b.   Has the child been prepared for what is expected of him in that setting?

         c.   Does the child understand when the activity will be over?

DO-WATCH-LISTEN-SAY: Social and Communication Intervention for Children with Autism
by Kathleen Ann Quill © 2000 Paul H. Brookes Publishing Co.

2. Does the child have any environmental sensitivities that would keep him from being successful in this setting?

   a. Are you aware of anything in the setting that would make the child afraid or uncomfortable (e.g., noise, crowds, bright lights)?

   b. Is there anything in the setting that will be distracting to the child?

3. Does the child understand what is expected of him in the setting?

   a. Does the child understand where he is supposed to be in that setting?

   b. Does the child understand what he is supposed to do in that setting?

   c. Does the child understand what to say to others, as needed, in that setting?

   d. Does the child understand how to wait, as needed, in that setting?

4. Does the child have necessary communication skills?

   a. Does the child have the skills to gain attention, if needed?

   b. Does the child have the skills to make requests?

DO-WATCH-LISTEN-SAY: Social and Communication Intervention for Children with Autism
by Kathleen Ann Quill © 2000 Paul H. Brookes Publishing Co.

c.   Does the child have the skills to ask for help, if needed?

d.   Does the child have the skills to follow simple directions associated with the setting?

5.   Is there a plan for the unexpected in that environment (e.g., fire drills, stores being closed, not having the item for which they came, novel people, change in plans)?

6.   Does the child have a way to calm or occupy himself in that setting (e.g., a backpack of favorite toys, breathing exercises, calming scripts, sensory/fidget toys)?

D.   During the target activity, is the child able to

	Yes	No	Prioritize
1. Wait			
2. Attend to the activity through completion			
3. Make a transition to the next activity when directed			
4. Accept interruptions or unexpected change			
5. Follow directions			
6. Make choices when necessary			
7. Calm self or be comforted			
8. Make needs known in appropriate manner			

Part II. Goals and Objectives

A.   Using the information from the survey, identify the skills to be addressed in the target setting:

1.   List the skills that need to be taught for success in the target setting.

2.   Identify any environmental factors that can cause overstimulation.

DO-WATCH-LISTEN-SAY: Social and Communication Intervention for Children with Autism
by Kathleen Ann Quill © 2000 Paul H. Brookes Publishing Co.

Part III. Intervention Plan

    A.   To assist the child in the community, design instructional strategies in the following areas:

        1.   Strategies to prepare the child prior to the target activity

            a.   Strategies to help the child understand where he is going prior to arrival

            b.   Strategies to prepare the child for what is expected of him in that setting

            c.   Strategies to clarify for the child when the activity will be over

        2.   Strategies to compensate for environmental overstimulation

            a.   Strategies that desensitize the child to stimuli that are fearful or discomforting

            b.   Strategies to keep the child focused on the target activity

        3.   Strategies to help the child understand what is expected of him in the target activity

            a.   Strategies to help the child understand where he is supposed to be in that setting

            b.   Strategies to help the child understand what he is supposed to do in that setting

            c.   Strategies to help the child understand what he needs to say to others in that setting

            d.   Strategies to help the child wait, as needed, in that setting

4. Strategies to provide the child with the communication skills necessary for the target activity

   a. Strategies to teach the child how to gain attention, if needed

   b. Strategies to teach the child how to make requests appropriately

   c. Strategies to teach the child how to ask for help, if needed

   d. Strategies to help the child follow simple directions associated with the setting

B. To compensate for the unexpected, design intervention strategies in the following areas:

   1. Strategies to help the child remain calm when unexpected events occur during the target activity

   2. Strategies to provide the child with a means of occupying himself during the target activity

chapter 8

Communication Skills Curriculum

Kathleen Norton Bracken

Communication is complex and socially dynamic. It requires active reciprocal interaction. To be an effective communicator, a child must be socially motivated and have a means of communication and a reason to communicate. Communication (i.e., what to SAY) is more likely to occur in those social contexts in which the child knows what to DO, who to WATCH, and how to LISTEN during an interaction.

Although there are many intervention resources available to teach the acquisition of language, most of them assume that functional communication will automatically occur. Given the nature of autism, communication skills need to be addressed systematically.

This chapter focuses on intervention to enhance three general areas of communication: **basic communicative functions, socioemotional skills,** and **basic conversational skills.** This set of activity sheets corresponds to each item in the Communication Skills Checklist in the Assessment of Social and Communication Skills for Children with Autism. The activity sheets provide suggested activities and intervention strategies to enhance these skills. It is generally understood that social-communicative interaction occurs continuously and that every moment is an opportunity to build communication. Therefore, natural settings are the primary focus of intervention. The ideas provided in this chapter should be viewed as a starting point for designing communication intervention across the child's entire day. The suggested interventions focus on structured interactions as the primary means to achieve communication skills. The child's motivation is respected while communication is continually expanded and shaped. The adult's role is to initiate interaction in a way that motivates and engages the child. It is important to observe and understand the child before deciding on a strategy or style of interaction. Always remember that beyond the markers of autism, the child will communicate only if he finds the interaction fun.

TARGETING COMMUNICATION OBJECTIVES

In determining communication objectives, refer to the Communication Skills Checklist in the assessment tool as well as the list of priority objectives that have been established for the child on the Assessment Summary Sheet. Target objectives should reflect skills that were

- Not observed or never demonstrated by the child
- Only observed when prompted
- Only demonstrated in specific contexts
- Only demonstrated with adults

The activity sheets are not presented as a linear hierarchy of skill acquisition. A child can simultaneously work to build requests, comments, expressions of feelings, prosocial skills, and basic conversational skills.

Once child-specific objectives have been selected, reference the corresponding activity sheets for strategies and interactive games. They are suggestions to encourage skill mastery and are not intended to be practiced in isolation. The child, not the arbitrary boundaries of a specific activity, should shape the interaction. Use the activities and ideas flexibly, and adapt them as appropriate for each child. Respect the child's preference, motivation, and interest when planning which strategies to adopt.

USING THE ACTIVITY SHEETS

The format of each activity sheet is organized similarly. The general goal area (e.g., Basic Communicative Functions) tops the activity sheets, followed by the general objective (e.g., Request Needs) and the specific skill (e.g., Preference when given a choice), which corresponds to the items in the assessment tool. The specific skill can be written as a criterion-based objective (samples are given in Table 8.1). The activity sheets contain suggested messages that a child may use to demonstrate the target skill, using both gestural and verbal means. This section, called Sample Means, categorizes messages into three levels:

- Communicative gestures (e.g., pushing, pointing, pulling another's hand)
- Emergent (i.e., single-word messages)
- Verbal (i.e., multiword messages)

Emergent and verbal messages can include speech, signs, photographs, pictographs, a voice output system, or written language.

Each sheet also contains two detailed descriptions of activities. One is an example of an adult–child interaction and the second describes a small-group activity. Remember that communication skills occur during adult–child interactions prior to occurring in a group setting. The activity sheets conclude with

- Contexts for Generalization (i.e., a list of interactive games), or
- Strategies (i.e., ideas to help facilitate reciprocal interaction)

The importance of increasing a child's repertoire of basic communicative functions, socioemotional skills, and basic conversational skills cannot be stressed enough. It is preferred that a child have multiple communicative functions and conversational exchanges at the single-word level rather than an expanded sentence structure for only one function or one exchange. In other words, the child who speaks in single words and is able to initiate requests, comments, and feelings as well as respond to others is a more successful communicator than the child who speaks in full sentences and communicates only one function.

MONITORING PROGRESS

Monitoring a child's progress with each target skill is useful in determining mastery. Progress reflects changes in the child's level of motivation, frequency of communicative

Table 8.1. Sample criterion-based objectives

Objective:	The child responds to name by acknowledging with a nod, "Huh," "Yeah," or "What" in 80% of the opportunities presented.
	During specific contexts with prompts
	During specific contexts without prompts
	During novel contexts with prompts
	During novel contexts without prompts
Objective:	The child indicates a preference when presented with choices in 80% of the opportunities presented.
	Objects
	Photographs
	Pictographs
	Verbal choices
Objective:	The child demonstrates assertiveness by using phrases such as "Go away" and "It's mine" in 80% of the opportunities presented.
	During specific contexts with prompts
	During specific contexts without prompts
	During novel contexts with prompts
	During novel contexts without prompts
Objective:	The child modulates tone of voice as appropriate for the emotion attempting to communicate in 80% of the opportunities presented.
	During specific contexts with prompts
	During specific contexts without prompts
	During novel contexts with prompts
	During novel contexts without prompts

attempts, variety of communicative functions, flexibility, and number of communicative partners. Skill mastery is defined as

- Acquisition of the skill: the presence of the skill without prompts
- Generalization of the skill across adults, peers, and different social groupings
- Generalization of the skill across multiple familiar and novel contexts

The Assessment of Social and Communication Skills for Children with Autism can be used to monitor progress in the areas of basic communicative functions, socioemotional skills, and conversational skills. Three sample forms are provided (see Appendix A) to monitor a child's progress. One form records a child's communication sample, coding if the message is directed to an adult or a peer, and for which function. The second form documents generalization by recording the number of social contexts in which a specific skill is observed. The third form is a record of a specific conversation between the child and one partner. Intermittent videotaping of the child is a complementary means of documenting the acquisition of functional communication.

Activity

A. Basic Communicative Functions
Request Needs 1. More

Sample Means

Communicative gestures: Looking at person, moving person's hand, reaching, pulling person's hand, giving objects, moving object toward, contact or distal pointing

Emergent: Speech, signs, photographs, pictographs, voice output system, or written language to say *More* or any vocalization

Verbal: Speech, signs, photographs, pictographs, a voice output system, or written language to convey a multiword message, such as *More marble, please*

Activity: Adult–Child

Context: Block area

Materials: Marble run or similar toy, accompanying visual supports as appropriate

Procedure: Build a marble run with the child. If the child has difficulty with such projects, build the marble run before the child becomes engaged to reduce the amount of waiting time. Place the marble in the run and watch it. Use exaggerated facial expressions, sound effects, and animation to make the interaction as fun as possible. Say "More" or "More marble" each time before placing the marble down the run. Once the child is engaged, hold the marble at his eye level, wait, and watch for the child to communicate *More*. If the child does not respond, prompt him as appropriate. Keep the interaction moving quickly. Repeat the sequence many times in the same manner. Decrease the amount of prompting as appropriate.

Activity: Small Group

Context: Games

Materials: Stack and Pop (from Discovery Toys) or any toy that provides a fun, sudden effect, accompanying visual supports as appropriate

Procedure: Demonstrate the toy a few times. Keep the interaction fun by anticipating the effect by counting to 3 and by using exaggerated facial expressions and an excited tone of voice. Say "Pop" or "More pop" each time right before the toy reacts. Pair spoken language with signed, gestural, or pictographic cues as needed. Once the children are engaged, prepare the toy but do not activate it. Wait and watch for the children to request *More pop*. Hold the toy at the children's eye level or tap the toy to get their attention. If the children do not respond, prompt them as appropriate. Keep the interaction moving quickly. Repeat the sequence many times in the same manner. Decrease the amount of prompting as appropriate.

Contexts for Generalization

- Request to continue a wind-up toy in the games area.
- Request to continue pouring water or sand into a water wheel in the sensory area.
- Request additional small pieces of a favorite food.
- Request additional trucks for play with a ramp.
- Request continued pushing on the swing at recess.
- Request to continue a fun cause-and-effect game on the computer.
- Request continued tickling by a puppet in the dramatic play area.
- Request continued spinning on a tire swing or other toy at gym.
- Request additional beads to string in the manipulative area.
- Request to continue music that suddenly stopped in the music area.
- Request during all motivating social contexts.

DO-WATCH-LISTEN-SAY: Social and Communication Intervention for Children with Autism
by Kathleen Ann Quill © 2000 Paul H. Brookes Publishing Co.

Activity

A. Basic Communicative Functions

Request Needs 2. Preference when given a choice

Sample Means

Communicative gestures: Moving person's hand, reaching, moving item toward self, contact or distal pointing

Emergent: Speech, signs, photographs, pictographs, a voice output system, or written language to say preferred item name, such as *Candy*

Verbal: Speech, signs, photographs, pictographs, voice output system, or written language to convey a multiword message, such as *I want the (item name)*

Activity: Adult–Child

Context: Music

Materials: Choice board of preferred and "nonpreferred" tapes, accompanying visual supports as appropriate

Procedure: Present the child with a choice of highly preferred and nonpreferred tapes. Hold the choices at the child's eye level. Using simple language, let the child know that he needs to make a choice. Pair spoken language with signed, gestural, or pictographic cues as needed. Wait and watch for the child to indicate a preference. If he does not respond, touch the choices or tap the table. If the child still does not respond, use hand-over-hand guidance to have the child make a choice. Give the child the item he selects, even if it is not the preferred item. If the child becomes upset, guide him hand over hand to select the preferred item and quickly give it to the child. Verbally label the item he is choosing. Keep the presentation of the choice exactly the same. Repeat the sequence many times in the same manner.

Activity: Small Group

Context: Snack time

Materials: One food that is highly preferred and another food that is not preferred—the number of choices and method of presentation (e.g., verbal, line drawings, photographs, objects) is individualized; accompanying visual supports as appropriate

Procedure: Present choices every time the children have lunch or a snack. Follow the same procedure given for the previous adult–child activity. Provide only a small amount of food at a time so the children have frequent opportunities to make a choice. Be very consistent in your presentation of each choice.

Strategies

- Hold the choices at the child's eye level.
- Experiment to find the best size and color contrast of pictographs.
- Present the choices at an angle (they can be leaned against a clear, Plexiglas picture frame).
- Maintain close proximity to the child.
- Simplify language complexity.
- Emphasize only the words you want the child to learn (e.g., say "ball" instead of "the ball").
- Give the child time to respond.
- Use natural opportunities for interactions whenever possible.
- Use the child's visual attention to determine when to prompt.
- Structure the environment so that space and materials are clearly defined.
- Offer the child maximum support to ensure success.

DO-WATCH-LISTEN-SAY: Social and Communication Intervention for Children with Autism
by Kathleen Ann Quill © 2000 Paul H. Brookes Publishing Co.

Activity

A. Basic Communicative Functions
Request Needs 3. Food/drink

Sample Means

Communicative gestures: Physical proximity, looking at person, moving person's hand, reaching, pulling person's hand, giving object, moving object toward, contact or distal pointing

Emergent: Speech, signs, photographs, pictographs, a voice output system, or written language to say the item's name or any vocalization

Verbal: Speech, signs, photographs, pictographs, a voice output system, or written language to convey a multiword message, such as *I want to eat (name of food)*

Activity: Adult–Child

Context: Dramatic play area

Materials: Shopping cart, grocery bag, empty boxes of preferred foods, cookies, candy, drinks, any other motivating props, accompanying visual supports as appropriate

Procedure: Place all pretend food on a shelf out of the child's reach but within sight. Model a shopping trip, saying the name of an item prior to removing it and putting it in the cart or bag. Exaggerate the interaction with animation, and pair spoken language with signed, gestural, or pictographic cues as needed. Next, encourage the child to go shopping. Wait and watch for the child to request out-of-reach items. If the child does not request any items, prompt him as needed. Repeat the sequence many times in the same manner, and decrease the amount of prompting.

Activity: Small Group

Context: Any activity

Materials: Fanny pack filled with preferred candy/food that is broken down easily into very small pieces (e.g., Goldfish crackers, M&M's, Skittles, Smarties), accompanying visual supports as appropriate

Procedure: Give the children some food. At the same time, slowly and clearly say the item's name. Hold the food for the children to see. Wait and watch for the children to request it. Reward any communicative attempt by immediately saying the item name and giving the children some food. If the children do not respond, prompt them as appropriate. If a child is using photographs or pictographs, attach one to your fanny pack or attach a small board to the child's waist (miniature "telephone cord" key chains are good for this). Keep the photographs and pictographs with the child throughout the entire day. Repeat many times in the same manner. Decrease the amount of prompting as appropriate.

Contexts for Generalization

- Request a food/drink item during snack time.
- Request a food/drink item during lunchtime.
- Request a food item during a cooking activity.
- Request food/drink item to feed a preferred character or puppet.
- Request a felt piece or object needed to act out a book (e.g., *The Very Hungry Caterpillar*) in the book area.
- Request food/drink during grocery store field trips.
- Request food/drink during restaurant field trips.
- Request food/drink during play in the toy kitchen.
- Request during all motivating social contexts.

Activity

A. Basic Communicative Functions
Request Needs 4. Object/toy

Sample Means

Communicative gestures: Physical proximity, looking at person, moving person's hand, reaching, giving objects, moving objects toward, contact or distal pointing, open palm request

Emergent: Vocalization or speech, signs, photographs, pictographs, a voice output system, or written language to say, for example, *Bubbles* or *Beanbag*

Verbal: Speech, signs, photographs, pictographs, a voice output system, or written language to convey a multiword message, such as *I want to play with bubbles* or *Blow bubbles*

Activity: Adult–Child

Context: Gym

Materials: Beanbag and a bell or other fun object to hit, accompanying visual supports as appropriate

Procedure: Hold a beanbag at the child's eye level and shake it. Say "Beanbag" or any appropriate word(s). Throw the beanbag at an item that creates a fun effect (e.g., a bell); experiment to determine what the child enjoys. Continue to throw beanbags. Exaggerate the interaction with animation. Once the child is engaged, wait and watch for him to request the beanbag. Reward any communicative means immediately by throwing the beanbag at the bell. If the child does not respond, prompt him as appropriate. Repeat many times in the same manner. Decrease the amount of prompting as appropriate.

Activity: Small Group

Context: Sensory area

Materials: Bubbles, accompanying visual supports as appropriate

Procedure: Blow bubbles toward the children; clearly and slowly say "Bubbles." Continue blowing and popping bubbles; experiment to determine what the children enjoy. Exaggerate the interaction with animation. Pair spoken language with signed, gestural, or pictographic cues as needed. Once the children are engaged, hold up the wand, but do not blow any bubbles. Wait and watch for the children to request bubbles. Respond to any communicative means immediately by blowing bubbles. If the children do not respond, prompt them as appropriate. Repeat the sequence many times in the same manner. Decrease the amount of prompting as appropriate.

Contexts for Generalization

- Request a favorite tape on a shelf out of reach in the music area.
- Request a favorite snack in a tightly closed jar.
- Request a favorite book in a tightly closed bag.
- Request a missing paintbrush for use with the easel during art.
- Request a missing paper towel to dry hands in the bathroom.
- Request a missing writing utensil in the writing area.
- Request a missing bead needed to string a bead sequence.
- Request control of the mouse at the computer to gain access to a motivating program.
- Request missing utensils to eat with at lunch.
- Request during all motivating social contexts.

Activity

A. Basic Communicative Functions
Request Needs 5. Favorite activity

Sample Means

Communicative gestures: Physical proximity, looking at person, pulling person's hand, giving objects, moving objects toward

Emergent: Speech, signs, photographs, pictographs, a voice output system, or written language to say preferred activity name or any vocalization

Verbal: Speech, signs, photographs, pictographs, a voice output system, or written language to convey a multiword message, such as *I want to play (name of preferred activity)*

Activity: Adult–Child

Context: Sensory area

Materials: Accompanying visual supports as appropriate

Procedure: Position a soft, thick mat beneath a low-to-the-ground chair. Sit in the chair and bounce the child up and down, opening your legs so the child falls through and lands on the mat. At the same time, slowly and clearly say "Bridge." Bounce the child up and down again. This time, suddenly lean the child backward so he is upside down and say "Waterfall." Alternate the two activities, clearly labeling them as "Bridge" or "Waterfall." Experiment to determine what the child enjoys. Exaggerate the interaction with animation. Pair spoken language with signed, gestural, or pictographic cues as needed. Bounce the child up and down, then stop. Wait and watch for the child to request *Bridge* or *Waterfall*. Reward any communicative attempt by reinforcing the child with the activity. If the child does not respond, prompt him as appropriate. Repeat the sequence many times in the same manner. Decrease the amount of prompting as appropriate.

Activity: Small Group

Context: Circle time

Materials: Beanbag, music, accompanying visual supports as appropriate

Procedure: Pass the beanbag around and play fun music while the children sit in a circle. Say "Pass the beanbag" or any appropriate word(s). Stop passing the beanbag when the music ends. Wait and watch for the children to request the activity. If the children do not respond, prompt them as appropriate. Repeat the sequence many times in the same manner. Decrease the amount of prompting as appropriate. This activity can work with a variety of actions involving beanbags (e.g., tossing, shaking). Experiment to determine what is motivating for them.

Contexts for Generalization

- Play Hide-and-Seek with ABC letters in the rice table.
- Play Ring Around the Rosie at recess.
- Blow up a balloon at circle time and then quickly let the air out.
- Dance in the music area.
- Play tunnel games in gym.
- Spin on the tire swing at recess.
- Play Pat-a-cake.
- Sing "Itsy Bitsy Spider."
- Request activities during all motivating social contexts.

Activity

A. Basic Communicative Functions
Request Needs 6. All done

Sample Means

Communicative gestures: Physical proximity, moving person's hand, moving objects away, shaking

Emergent: Vocalization or speech, signs, photographs, pictographs, a voice output system, or written language to say *All done*

Verbal: Speech, signs, photographs, pictographs, a voice output system, or written language to convey a multiword message, such as *I want to be all done with (activity)* or *I'm all done playing (name of game)*

Activity: Adult–Child

Context: Manipulative area

Materials: Variety of beads, string or laces, accompanying visual supports as appropriate

Procedure: String beads with a child. One adult covers her eyes. When the string of beads is complete, say "I'm all done." The adult uncovers her eyes and says "Wow" or "That's terrific." Provide whatever reinforcement is motivating. Repeat, then stop and wait for the child to communicate *All done* when the string of beads is finished. Reward any communicative means by reinforcing the child. If the child does not respond, prompt him as appropriate. Repeat the sequence many times in the same manner. Decrease the amount of prompting as appropriate.

Activity: Small Group

Context: Recess

Materials: Accompanying visual supports as appropriate

Procedure: Play Follow the Leader. The child or adult at the front of the line chooses an activity. Experiment to determine what the children enjoy. After 10 or 15 seconds, say "All done" or any appropriate words. Exaggerate the interaction with animation. Pair spoken language with signed, gestural, or pictographic cues as needed. Begin another activity, then stop the action. Wait and watch for the children to communicate *All done.* Reward any communicative means by stopping the activity immediately. If a child does not respond, prompt him as appropriate. Repeat the sequence many times in the same manner. Decrease the amount of prompting as appropriate.

Strategies

- Target the completion of every activity throughout the day.
- Clarify expectations.
- Use natural opportunities for interactions whenever possible.
- Do not allow the child to leave or move to another activity until he or she has indicated *All done.*
- Repeat the same message at predictable times.
- Maintain close proximity to the child.
- Give the child time to respond.
- Maximize the use of verbal modeling.

DO-WATCH-LISTEN-SAY: Social and Communication Intervention for Children with Autism
by Kathleen Ann Quill © 2000 Paul H. Brookes Publishing Co.

Activity

A. Basic Communicative Functions
Request Needs 7. Help

Sample Means

Communicative gestures: Physical proximity, looking at person, moving person's hand/face, reaching, pulling person's hand

Emergent: Vocalization or speech, signs, photographs, pictographs, a voice output system, or written language to say *Help*

Verbal: Speech, signs, photographs, pictographs, a voice output system, or written language to convey a multiword message such as *I want help* or *I need help with (activity)*

Activity: Adult–Child

Context: Art

Materials: Paint, sponges

Procedure: Paint with sponges. Place the sponges in a tightly sealed clear container. Put the container in front of the child. Wait and watch for the child to indicate *help*. If the child does not respond, prompt him as appropriate. Repeat the sequence many times in the same manner. Decrease the amount of prompting as appropriate.

Activity: Small Group

Context: Circle time

Materials: None

Procedure: Make a circle with an adult in the center. The group moves in to hug the person in the center. Everyone sings the following words to the tune of "All Around the Mulberry Bush": "This is the way we ask for help. I want help. I want help. This is the way we ask for help. I want help, please." The adult being hugged says "I want help," and the group immediately frees her. Place a child in the center and continue the game. Wait and watch for the child to request help. If the child does not respond, prompt him as appropriate. Repeat many times in the same manner. Decrease the amount of prompting as appropriate.

Contexts for Generalization

- Request help opening a food/drink container that cannot be opened at snack time or lunchtime.
- Request help putting on shoes or jacket.
- Request help placing puzzle pieces that do not fit in puzzle frame.
- Request help reaching out-of-reach favorite books in the book area.
- Request help opening locked doors when it is time to leave the room.
- Request help untwisting a favorite swing at recess.
- Request help opening a tape player that is taped shut at music time.
- Request help operating a computer that is not plugged in.
- Request toilet paper that is missing in the bathroom.
- Request help in all motivating social contexts.

DO-WATCH-LISTEN-SAY: Social and Communication Intervention for Children with Autism
by Kathleen Ann Quill © 2000 Paul H. Brookes Publishing Co.

Activity

A. Basic Communicative Functions
Respond to Others 1. Responds to name

Sample Means

Communicative gestures: Physical proximity, looking at person, waving, shaking/nodding head

Emergent: Vocalization or speech, signs, photographs, pictographs, a voice output system, or written language to say *Huh* or *Yeah*

Verbal: Speech, signs, photographs, pictographs, a voice output system, or written language to convey a multiword message, such as *What's up?*

Activity: Adult–Child

Context: Greeting

Materials: Accompanying visual supports as appropriate

Procedure: Wait at the front of the bus. Call the child's name. Pair spoken language with signed, gestural, or pictographic cues as needed. Wait and watch for the child to respond. If the child does not respond to his name, prompt the child as appropriate. Once the child responds to his name, help the child get off the bus in a fun way. Repeat many times in the same manner. Decrease the amount of prompting as appropriate.

Activity: Small Group

Context: Snack time

Materials: Motivating snack foods, accompanying visual supports as appropriate

Procedure: Sit at a table. Show a highly motivating snack. Call a staff member's name, wait for her to respond, and give her the food. Pair spoken language with signed, gestural, or pictographic cues as needed. Call the children's names one at a time. Wait and watch for each child to respond. If a child does not respond, have another staff member at the table prompt him as appropriate. Provide only a small amount of snack food and repeat the sequence many times in the same manner. Decrease the amount of prompting as appropriate.

Strategies

- Target at every opportunity throughout the day.
- Give the child time to respond.
- Try using rhythmic language.
- Use the child's visual attention to determine when to prompt.
- Maintain close proximity to the child.
- Focus on contexts in which the child is motivated to communicate.
- If the child has a nickname, be sure family and all staff use one name.
- Use appropriate adult/peer modeling if the child is an imitator.
- Use two adults: one who assists the child and one who receives the message.
- If the child has difficulty, assess the surroundings and try again in a quieter or less distracting setting.

Activity

A. Basic Communicative Functions
Respond to Others 2. Refuses object

Sample Means

Communicative gestures: Moving person's hand, moving object away, contact pointing, shaking head

Emergent: Vocalization or speech, signs, photographs, pictographs, a voice output system, or written language to say *No*

Verbal: Speech, signing, photographs, pictographs, a voice output system, or written language to convey a multiword message, such as *I don't want that*

Activity: Adult–Child

Context: Books

Materials: Favorite books out of reach (but in sight), accompanying visual supports as appropriate

Procedure: Place the child's favorite books on a shelf that is within the child's sight but out of his reach. Wait for the child to request a favorite book. Pair spoken language with signed, gestural, or pictographic cues as needed. Respond immediately to the request, but hand the child a completely irrelevant and uninteresting book. Wait and watch for the child to refuse the book. If the child does not respond, prompt him as appropriate to refuse the book. Exaggerate the refusal with facial expressions and tone of voice. Immediately give the preferred book to the child. Repeat the sequence many times in the same manner. Decrease the amount of prompting as appropriate.

Activity: Small Group

Context: Games

Materials: Lotto board, accompanying visual supports as appropriate

Procedure: Play lotto. Use lotto boards that are motivating for the targeted child (e.g., Arthur, Thomas the Train, Teletubbies). Hand the child a picture that is completely unrelated to anything on the child's board. Wait and watch for the child to refuse the card. If the child does not respond, prompt him. Take the incorrect picture back and immediately hand the child a correct picture. Keep the game fun by exaggerating facial expressions and tone of voice. Monitor the child's level of frustration and be sure to alternate presenting incorrect cards with cards that match the child's board. Repeat the sequence many times in the same manner. Decrease the amount of prompting as appropriate.

Contexts for Generalization

- Give the child a book when he is waiting for a paintbrush.
- Give the child the incorrect lunch in the cafeteria.
- Give the child the wrong jacket or backpack.
- Hide the child's preferred blocks and hand him an object that is not related to blocks.
- Play something that is not preferred when the child requests music.
- Hand the child an unrelated object when he is stringing beads.
- Give the child a computer game that is not preferred.
- Hide all of the utensils and hand the child a feather when in the writing area.
- Tell the child it is time to take a nap at an inappropriate time.
- Elicit during all motivating social contexts.

DO-WATCH-LISTEN-SAY: Social and Communication Intervention for Children with Autism
by Kathleen Ann Quill © 2000 Paul H. Brookes Publishing Co.

Activity

A. Basic Communicative Functions
Respond to Others 3. Refuses activity

Sample Means

Communicative gestures: Physical proximity, pushing activity-related object away, shaking head

Emergent: Vocalization or speech, signs, photographs, pictographs, a voice output system, or written language to say *No*

Verbal: Speech, signs, photographs, pictographs, a voice output system, or written language to convey a multiword message, such as *I don't want to work*

Activity: Adult–Child

Context: Any activity

Materials: A schedule board of the child's day, accompanying visual supports as appropriate

Procedure: Set up an individualized schedule of the child's day. (This activity is much more effective with children who are very familiar with their schedules.) After the child has checked his or her schedule, introduce the wrong activity. Wait and watch for the child to refuse the activity. If the child does not respond, prompt him, and immediately introduce the correct activity. Exaggerate facial expressions and tone of voice during the interaction. Repeat many times in the same manner. Decrease the amount of prompting as appropriate.

Activity: Small Group

Context: Games

Materials: Choice board, accompanying visual supports as appropriate

Procedure: Provide the children with choices at the games area. The number of choices should be individualized for each child. Pair spoken language with signed, gestural, or pictographic cues as needed. Once a child makes a choice, respond immediately and provide the child with an activity that is not preferred. Wait and watch for the child to refuse the activity. If the child does not respond, prompt him as appropriate. Once the child refuses the activity, immediately provide him with the correct activity. Exaggerate facial expressions and tone of voice during the interaction. Repeat the sequence many times in the same manner. Decrease the amount of prompting as appropriate.

Strategies

- Target at every opportunity throughout the day.
- Focus on contexts in which the child is motivated to communicate.
- Repeat the same message at predictable times.
- Stay near the child and work at his level during the interactions.
- Give the child time to respond.
- Use appropriate adult/peer modeling if the child is an imitator.
- Use two adults: one who physically assists the child and one who receives the message.
- Simplify language complexity.
- Use AAC supports as needed.

DO-WATCH-LISTEN-SAY: Social and Communication Intervention for Children with Autism
by Kathleen Ann Quill © 2000 Paul H. Brookes Publishing Co.

Activity

A. Basic Communicative Functions
Respond to Others 4. Responds to greetings

Sample Means

Communicative gestures: Physical proximity, looking at person, moving person's face, waving

Emergent: Vocalization or speech, signs, photographs, pictographs, a voice output system, or written language to say *Hi*

Verbal: Speech, signs, photographs, pictographs, a voice output system, or written language to convey a multiword message, such as *"Hey, what's up?"*

Activity: Adult–Child

Context: Dramatic play area

Materials: Drawstring bag, finger puppets (or any other small, motivating figures), accompanying visual supports as appropriate

Procedure: Put finger puppets in a drawstring bag. Use animation to make the interaction as fun as possible. Remove a puppet from the bag and say "Hi, (child's name)." Wait and watch for the child to respond to the greeting. If the child does not respond, prompt him as appropriate. Repeat the sequence many times in the same manner. Decrease the amount of prompting as appropriate.

Activity: Small Group

Context: Circle time

Materials: A familiar puppet, accompanying visual supports as appropriate

Procedure: Greet each child by saying "Hi, (child's name)" at circle time. Use a puppet if that helps further engage the children. Pair spoken language with signed, gestural, or pictographic cues as needed. Wait and watch for the children to respond to the greeting. If a child does not respond, prompt him as appropriate. Repeat the sequence many times in the same manner. Decrease the amount of prompting as appropriate.

Contexts for Generalization

- Respond to greetings at circle time.
- Read lift-the-flap books (e.g., *Where's Spot?*), and greet the character under each flap.
- Elicit when getting on and off of the bus.
- Explain the goal to lunchroom staff and ask for their assistance.
- Elicit during computer games such as the *JumpStart Toddler* "Peekaboo" game.
- Greet characters on television or in a video.
- Hide characters in the sensory table and, as they are found, target greetings.
- Greet during any transition time with new staff or peers.
- Greet during play with a toy telephone.
- Elicit during all motivating social contexts.

DO-WATCH-LISTEN-SAY: Social and Communication Intervention for Children with Autism
by Kathleen Ann Quill © 2000 Paul H. Brookes Publishing Co.

Activity

A. Basic Communicative Functions
Respond to Others 5. Responds to play invitations

Sample Means

Communicative gestures: Physical proximity, looking at person, reaching/pulling person's hand, giving objects, shaking/nodding head

Emergent: Vocalization or speech, signing, photographs, pictographs, a voice output system, or written language to say *Yeah* or *Sure*

Verbal: Speech, signs, photographs, pictographs, a voice output system, or written language to convey a multiword message, such as *Let's play (name of game)* or *I want to play (name of game)*

Activity: Adult–Child

Context: Sensory area

Materials: Rocking toy, doll, accompanying visual supports as appropriate

Procedure: Put a child and a doll in a rocking boat. Rock the boat, then stop. Have the doll ask the child "Let's play some more." Wait and watch for the child to respond. If the child does not answer, prompt him to respond to the play invitation. Continue the game immediately. Repeat the sequence many times in the same manner. Decrease the amount of prompting as appropriate.

Activity: Small Group

Context: Music

Materials: Accompanying visual supports as appropriate

Procedure: Sing "The Farmer in the Dell" while the children are sitting in a circle. Make the song as animated and fun as possible. Pair spoken language with signed, gestural, or pictographic cues as needed. When a child is chosen, wait and watch for his response. If the child does not respond, prompt him as appropriate to accept the play invitation. Repeat many times in the same manner. Decrease the amount of prompting as appropriate.

Contexts for Generalization

- Respond to an invitation to play a lotto game.
- Respond to an invitation to paint with a peer.
- Respond to an invitation to play ball at recess.
- Respond to a friend's invitation to go on a scavenger hunt through the school building.
- Respond to the invitation to sit next to a friend in the cafeteria.
- Respond during Duck, Duck, Goose.
- Respond to an invitation to play with a seesaw or rocker boat.
- Respond to an invitation to play Pat-a-cake.
- Respond during all motivating social contexts.

DO-WATCH-LISTEN-SAY: Social and Communication Intervention for Children with Autism
by Kathleen Ann Quill © 2000 Paul H. Brookes Publishing Co.

Activity

A. Basic Communicative Functions
Respond to Others 6. Affirms to agree/accept

Sample Means

Communicative gestures: Physical proximity, looking at person, moving person's hand/face, shaking/nodding head

Emergent: Vocalization or speech, signs, photographs, pictographs, a voice output system, or written language to say *Yeah* or *Okay*

Verbal: Speech, signs, photographs, pictographs, a voice output system, or written language to convey a multiword message, such as *Yes, I'd like that*

Activity: Adult–Child

Context: Gym

Materials: Typical gym equipment, accompanying visual supports as appropriate

Procedure: Determine a preferred activity (e.g., using the swing) for the child. Allow the child to engage in the activity and have fun. Once the child is engaged, stop the activity and say, "Do you want a push?" or any appropriate word(s). Wait and watch for the child to agree. If the child does not respond, prompt him as appropriate. Repeat many times in the same manner. Decrease the amount of prompting as appropriate.

Activity: Small Group

Context: Block area

Materials: Blocks, accompanying visual supports as appropriate

Procedure: Build a short block tower or line up blocks in a row. Hand one block at a time to each child so they all can take turns building a tower or bridge. Exaggerate the interaction with animation. Hold up a block and say, "Do you want a block?" Wait and watch for the child to respond. If the child does not respond, prompt him as appropriate to accept the block. Repeat many times in the same manner. Decrease the amount of prompting as appropriate.

Contexts for Generalization

- Hide an essential classroom item, such as the child's chair. When he looks puzzled, offer what is missing.
- Offer a preferred item, such as candy, at snack time.
- Remove items essential for completion of an activity (e.g., paintbrushes for painting) and then offer them once the child asks for help.
- Offer the child a preferred activity.
- Ask the child if he wants to participate in a preferred sensory activity, such as tickling.
- At the end of the day, ask the child if he wants to go home.
- Ask the child if he wants to eat lunch.
- Hide the child's preferred attachment item (e.g., a security blanket) and ask if he wants to hold it.
- Elicit during all motivating social contexts.

Activity

A. Basic Communicative Functions

Respond to Others 7. Responds to personal questions

Sample Means

Communicative gestures: Not applicable

Emergent: Vocalization or speech, signs, photographs, pictographs, a voice output system, or written language to respond to questions

Verbal: Speech, signs, photographs, pictographs, a voice output system, or written language to convey a multiword message, such as *I live on (street name) street*

Activity: Adult–Child

Context: Work time

Materials: Cards posing personal questions, such as "What is your name?" and "Where do you live?"; cards providing the correct responses for the targeted child (color the question cards one color and the response cards another color); accompanying visual supports as appropriate

Procedure: Choose any fun reinforcement for the child. Set up a 1-2-3-4-done board that lets the child know he needs to answer three questions before being reinforced (increase or decrease this number as is appropriate for the individual child). Ask the child a question. Pair spoken language with signed, gestural, or pictographic cues as needed. Wait and watch for the child to respond. If the child does not, prompt him as appropriate to answer the personal questions. Repeat many times in the same manner. Decrease the amount of prompting as appropriate. Watch for the child's level of frustration, and be sure to provide breaks that are motivating.

Activity: Small Group

Context: Dramatic play area

Materials: Video of a basic interview, pretend microphone, any other props the child might enjoy, accompanying visual supports as appropriate

Procedure: Watch a video of a basic interview. Point out that one person asks questions and the other person answers them. Use color-coded question cards regarding concrete features such as the children's hair colors, eye colors, clothing, and likes and dislikes. Also use color-coded response cards. Give one child the question cards and another the appropriate response cards. Have a peer ask the child questions. Wait and watch for the child to answer. If the child does not respond, prompt him to answer the questions. Repeat many times in the same manner. Decrease the amount of prompting as appropriate. Videotape the children and have them watch themselves. Make the activity fun, and do it as frequently as possible.

Strategies

- Use natural opportunities for interactions whenever possible.
- Remember that meaningful activities are the key to social and communicative success.
- Clarify expectations.
- Focus on contexts during which the child is motivated to communicate.
- Initially only ask questions that you are sure the child can answer successfully.
- Introduce one type of question at a time.
- Maintain close proximity to the child.
- Give the child time to respond.
- Simplify language complexity.
- Use two adults: one who physically assists the child and one who receives the message.

Activity

A. Basic Communicative Functions
Respond to Others 8. Responds to others' comments

Sample Means

Communicative gestures: Not applicable

Emergent: Vocalization or speech, signs, photographs, pictographs, a voice output system, or written language to respond to others' comments

Verbal: Speech, signs, photographs, pictographs, a voice output system, or written language to convey a multiword message, such as *I have the (name of object)*

Activity: Adult–Child

Context: Computer

Materials: Living Books CD-ROM, accompanying visual supports as appropriate

Procedure: Engage the child in a motivating *Living Books* CD-ROM, such as *Grandma and Me.* Allow the child to explore each page. As the object on the screen makes an action, the adult should comment by labeling the object (e.g., "Critter") and the action (e.g., "Said uh-oh"). Repeat many times so the child is very familiar with the activity. Continue the interaction, making only one comment about the object (e.g., "Critter"). Wait and watch for the child to respond with a comment. If the child does not respond, prompt him as appropriate. Repeat the sequence many times in the same manner. Decrease the amount of prompting as appropriate.

Activity: Small Group

Context: Art

Materials: Tan or white paper cut in shape of bread, yellow paper cut in shape of cheese, green paper cut in shape of lettuce, red paper cut in shape of tomato, brown paper cut in shape of meat, glue for mayonnaise, small containers for each sandwich part, clearly labeled, accompanying visual supports as appropriate

Procedure: Demonstrate how to make a "sandwich" from the pieces of paper. Be animated, and exaggerate your tone of voice as you demonstrate the procedure. After a child takes a piece to add to his sandwich, he must name the item by saying "My sandwich has tomato" or "Tomato." Pair spoken language with signed, gestural, or pictographic cues as needed. The next child responds to the comment by adding his own item. Continue so that each child says what is on his sandwich. If a child does not respond, prompt him as appropriate to comment. Repeat the sequence many times in the same manner. Decrease the amount of prompting as appropriate.

Strategies

- Consider the most natural setting for acquisition of target skills.
- Meaningful activities are the key to social and communicative success.
- Mastery of the social activity becomes the natural reinforcer.
- Maintain close proximity to the child.
- Simplify language complexity.
- Give the child time to respond.
- Balance adult-directed interactions with child-directed interactions.
- Limit the use of verbal prompts in the form of questions.
- Model using the exact same language across various settings.

Activity

A. Basic Communicative Functions
Comment 1. Comments on the unexpected

Sample Means

Communicative gestures: Looking at person, moving person's hand/face, reaching, giving objects, shaking/nodding head, shrugging

Emergent: Vocalization or speech, signs, photographs, pictographs, a voice output system, or written language to say *Oops* or *Uh-oh*

Verbal: Speech, signs, photographs, pictographs, a voice output system, or written language to convey a multiword message, such as *Uh-oh, the blocks fell down*

Activity: Adult–Child

Context: Any activity

Materials: Several large *uh-oh* cards located in each activity area of the classroom, an *uh-oh* card for each adult and child to carry or wear (the card can be placed on a ring and attached to one's belt loop, around one's wrist, or around one's neck)

Procedure: Say "Uh-oh" or any appropriate word(s) every time an unexpected change or event occurs. Experiment to determine what the child enjoys, such as knocking down blocks or putting a hat on your feet. Exaggerate all interactions with animation. Acknowledge an unexpected change with a facial expression. Wait and watch for the child to comment. If the child does not respond, prompt him as appropriate. Repeat many times in the same manner. Decrease the amount of prompting as appropriate.

Activity: Small Group

Context: Dressing time

Materials: Each child's coat, hat, mittens, backpack, and so forth; accompanying visual supports as appropriate

Procedure: Give the children the wrong coat, backpack, or other item. Pause, then say "Uh-oh" or "Oops" as you fix your mistake. Continue to make mistakes. Exaggerate the interaction with animation. Pair spoken language with signed, gestural, or pictographic cues as needed. Make a mistake, wait, and watch for the children to comment. If the children do not respond, prompt them as appropriate. Repeat many times in the same manner. Decrease the amount of prompting as appropriate. You can expand this interaction by putting items of clothing on the wrong body parts, such as a coat on your head or a boot on your nose.

Contexts for Generalization

- Put the toys from the games area in the book area during cleanup.
- Knock down a tower in the blocks area.
- Call children by the wrong names at circle time.
- Go to the wrong room after coming off the bus.
- Give each child the wrong lunch.
- Provide an empty box of food at snack time.
- Provide activities that differ from those on the child's schedule.
- Make a mistake during play, such as pushing a train backward.
- Sing nonsensical songs, such as saying "The cow says neigh" during "Old MacDonald."
- Comment on the unexpected during all motivating social contexts.
- Read a book that accents the unexpected, such as *Blue Hat, Green Hat*.

DO-WATCH-LISTEN-SAY: Social and Communication Intervention for Children with Autism
by Kathleen Ann Quill © 2000 Paul H. Brookes Publishing Co.

Activity

A. Basic Communicative Functions
Comment 2. Names object/character

Sample Means

Communicative gestures: Looking at object, moving person's hand toward object/character, contact or distal pointing

Emergent: Vocalization or speech, signs, photographs, pictographs, a voice output system, or written language to say an object or a character name

Verbal: Speech, signs, photographs, pictographs, a voice output system, or written language to convey a multiword message, such as *Look, I see Arthur*

Activity: Adult–Child

Context: Books

Materials: Book of the child's favorite characters, accompanying visual supports as appropriate

Procedure: Share a familiar and motivating book. At every page, point to a recurring character and say, "I see (character name)" or any appropriate word(s). Exaggerate the interaction with animation. Pair spoken language with signed, gestural, or pictographic cues as needed. Continue reading the story. Point to a character, then wait and watch for the child to name it. If the child does not respond, prompt him as appropriate. Repeat many times in the same manner. Decrease the amount of prompting as appropriate.

Activity: Small Group

Context: Dramatic play area

Materials: Large pot, spoon, variety of play foods, accompanying visual supports as appropriate

Procedure: Put various food items in a bag. Take out one food item at a time, hold it up at eye level, clearly say its name, and toss it into a pot of pretend soup. Stir in an exaggerated and animated manner. Continue placing one item in the pot at a time. Once the children are engaged, hold up a food item, then wait and watch for the children to name it. If they label the object, put it into the pot. If the children do not respond, prompt them as appropriate. Repeat many times in the same manner. Decrease the amount of prompting as appropriate.

Contexts for Generalization

- Name familiar characters in computer games.
- Place a picture of a familiar character for the children to name at the top of every worksheet/ coloring sheet.
- Name the parts of Mr. Potato Head.
- Hang up posters of familiar characters on the classroom walls for the children to name.
- Name items on a Colorforms or flannel board.
- Cut out, glue, and name a variety of familiar objects from magazines.
- Hide familiar objects in a bag, pull them out, and name them one at a time.
- Go on a scavenger hunt for familiar objects.
- Read a book such as *My First Word Book,* and label familiar objects.
- At mealtimes, say "One for (child's name)" as a snack is given to each child.
- Name an object or a character during all motivating social contexts.

Activity

A. Basic Communicative Functions
Comment 3. Labels own possessions

Sample Means

Communicative gestures: Reaching, moving object toward/away, touching self

Emergent: Vocalization or speech, signs, photographs, pictographs, a voice output system, or written language to say *Mine*

Verbal: Speech, signs, photographs, pictographs, a voice output system, or written language to convey a multiword message, such as *That's mine* or *It was my turn*

Activity: Adult–Child

Context: Computer

Materials: Motivating *Living Books* CD-ROMs, *my turn* card, other accompanying visual supports as appropriate

Procedure: Take turns controlling the mouse. The person holding the *my turn* card should have control of the mouse. Say "My turn" or any appropriate word(s) each time you are holding the card. Pair spoken language with signed, gestural, or pictographic cues as needed. Hand the child the *my turn* card; wait and watch for the child to indicate possession. If the child does not respond, prompt him to say "My turn." Repeat many times in the same manner. Decrease the amount of prompting as appropriate.

Activity: Small Group

Context: Any activity

Materials: Chair for each child and adult, clearly labeled with a name; accompanying visual supports as appropriate

Procedure: Each adult looks for her chair, finds it, and models pointing to it, sitting down, and saying "This is mine" or any appropriate word(s). As each child finds his chair, wait and watch for him to indicate possession. If a child does not respond by labeling his chair *mine,* prompt him as appropriate. Repeat many times in the same manner. Decrease the amount of prompting as appropriate.

Contexts for Generalization

- Give each child a job, which he labels with possession (e.g., *My job*).
- Label possessions while reading homemade books of personal possessions.
- Label possessions when lunches are mixed up.
- Label possessions when the children's coats, backpacks, and lunches are mixed up.
- Label possessions during play with lotto boards.
- Label possessions with completed artwork to take home by asking "Whose is this?"
- Label possessions during a "teddy bear picnic": Have each child bring a favorite teddy bear to the picnic, mix up the bears so they "get lost," and ask "Whose bear is this?"
- Label possessions in big show-and-tell box.
- Label possessions while looking at pictures of family by asking "Whose mom is this?"
- Label possessions during all motivating social contexts.

Activity

A. Basic Communicative Functions
Comment 4. Names familiar people

Sample Means

Communicative gestures: Physical proximity, looking at person, moving person's hand/face, reaching, pulling person's hand, distal pointing

Emergent: Vocalization or speech, signs, photographs, pictographs, a voice output system, or written language to say person's name

Verbal: Speech, signs, photographs, pictographs, a voice output system, or written language to convey a multiword message, such as *Look, it's (person's name)*

Activity: Adult–Child

Context: Work time

Materials: Pictures of familiar people (from home or school) on a ring or in a book, other accompanying visual supports as appropriate

Procedure: Look at each picture and say "(Person's name) is at home (or school)." Pair spoken language with signed, gestural, or pictographic cues as needed. Once the child is familiar with the photographs and is engaged in the activity, hold up a picture and stop. Wait and watch for the child to name the person. If the child does not respond, prompt him as appropriate. Repeat many times in the same manner. Decrease the amount of prompting as appropriate.

Activity: Small Group

Context: Snack time

Materials: Binder ring holding photographs of all of the children in the class, accompanying visual supports as appropriate

Procedure: Assign a different child each week to be snack helper. Choose a job that is motivating for the snack helper (e.g., handing out napkins, pouring juice). Show the helper a picture of a peer and say "It's (peer's name)" or "Give the napkin to (peer's name)." Continue this routine with every child in the class. Pair spoken language with signed, gestural, or pictographic cues as needed. Once the helper is familiar with the other children's names, show him a peer's picture and stop. Wait and watch for the child to name the peer. If a child does not respond, prompt him as appropriate. Repeat many times in the same manner. Decrease the amount of prompting as appropriate. This procedure can be followed in many other activities throughout the day, such as writing, giving out art materials or lunch utensils, or handing out coats and backpacks.

Contexts for Generalization

- Name familiar people while looking at photographs of peers and staff during the "hello" and "goodbye" portions of circle time.
- Name familiar peer whose photograph is photocopied at the top of a worksheet.
- Name familiar people during chase games by saying "I'm gonna get (child's name)."
- Name familiar people during Hide-and-Seek games: "(Child's name) is hiding."
- Name familiar people while reading homemade books of peers doing silly things.
- Name familiar people entering or exiting the classroom.
- Name familiar people while playing with picture puzzles: Laminate large photographs of familiar people; cut them into puzzle pieces.
- Name familiar people while playing games with photographs: Cover up photos with colored pieces of paper, remove them one at a time, and have the children guess whose photo is underneath.
- Name familiar people while watching videos from home or school: Turn off the volume and label the people.
- Name familiar people during all motivating social contexts.

DO-WATCH-LISTEN-SAY: Social and Communication Intervention for Children with Autism
by Kathleen Ann Quill © 2000 Paul H. Brookes Publishing Co.

Activity

A. Basic Communicative Functions
Comment 5. Describes actions

Sample Means

Communicative gestures: Looking/gesturing at person performing action, distal pointing, waving, acting out the action observed

Emergent: Vocalization or speech, signs, photographs, pictographs, a voice output system, or written language to say the action, such as *Rub* or *Jump*

Verbal: Speech, signs, photographs, pictographs, a voice output system, or written language to convey a multiword message, such as *Rub the lotion on my arms* or *(Peer's name) is jumping on the trampoline*

Activity: Adult–Child

Context: Sensory area

Materials: Lotion, accompanying visual supports as appropriate

Procedure: Rub lotion on the child's hands, arms, and face. Say "Rub, rub, rub," "Rub the lotion," or any appropriate word(s). Exaggerate the interaction with animation. Pair spoken language with signed, gestural, or pictographic cues as needed. Once the child is engaged, hold the lotion at his eye level and stop. Wait and watch for the child to say "Rub." If the child does not respond, prompt him as appropriate. Repeat many times in the same manner. Decrease the amount of prompting as appropriate.

Activity: Small Group

Context: Circle time

Materials: Video camera, video, VCR, television, accompanying visual supports as appropriate

Procedure: Videotape the children. Capture various activities, such as eating lunch, reading books, singing, jumping, swinging, blowing bubbles, and building blocks. Tape more than one child performing the same action. While watching the videotape, use clear language to say "(Child's name) is (name of action)." Pair spoken language with signed, gestural, or pictographic cues as needed. Watch the tape many times so the children become familiar with it. Next, turn on the videotape but leave the volume off. Wait and watch for the children to describe an action. If the children do not respond, prompt them as appropriate. Repeat many times in the same manner. Decrease the amount of prompting as appropriate.

Contexts for Generalization

* Read action books, such as *Playing* or *Daddy and Me.*
* Play Simon Says in gym.
* Use *Laureate First Verbs* or a similar computer program.
* Sing familiar songs with actions, such as "Five Little Monkeys" or "Wheels on the Bus."
* Label recess activities, such as swinging, sliding, or running.
* Make homemade books of the child's favorite activities.
* Sequence pictures of an art activity (e.g., first color, then cut, glue last).
* Use a variety of wind-up toys (e.g., ones that walk, crawl, hop, swim).
* Play with lotto boards of all actions.
* Describe actions during all motivating social contexts.

DO-WATCH-LISTEN-SAY: Social and Communication Intervention for Children with Autism
by Kathleen Ann Quill © 2000 Paul H. Brookes Publishing Co.

Activity

A. Basic Communicative Functions
Comment 6. Describes location

Sample Means

Communicative gestures: Distal pointing

Emergent: Vocalization or speech, signs, photographs, pictographs, a voice output system, or written language to say location, such as *In*

Verbal: Speech, signs, photographs, pictographs, a voice output system, or written language to convey a multiword message, such as *(Object name) is in the box*

Activity: Adult–Child

Context: Computer

Materials: *Bailey's Bookhouse* or any other computer program that hides objects/people, accompanying visual supports as appropriate

Procedure: Play *Bailey's Bookhouse,* specifically using the "Edmo" and "Houdini" sections (involving the dog, the clown, and the doghouse). Turn off the volume. If the child is literate, you may want to cover the text with paper. Label the location, such as "Edmo is in the doghouse" or "In." Exaggerate the interaction with animation. Continue playing the game, but do not label the location. Wait and watch for the child to describe the location. If the child does not respond, prompt him as appropriate. Repeat many times in the same manner. Decrease the amount of prompting as appropriate.

Activity: Small Group

Context: Recess

Materials: Giant box, accompanying visual supports as appropriate

Procedure: Encourage the children to climb in, on, under, or around the box. Say "(Child's name) is under the box," "Behind," or any appropriate word(s). Experiment to determine what the children enjoy. Exaggerate the interaction with animation. Pair spoken language with signed, gestural, or pictographic cues as needed. Continue playing. Once a child moves to a new location, stop and wait for the children to describe the location. If a child does not respond, prompt him as appropriate. Repeat many times in the same manner. Decrease the amount of prompting as appropriate.

Contexts for Generalization

- Read books such as *Where's Spot?*
- Read homemade books that depict the child in a variety of locations.
- Play with hidden puppets or stuffed animals.
- Use computer software depicting locations.
- Go on a treasure hunt.
- Play Hide-and-Seek.
- Hide fun objects in the sandbox or rice table.
- Color hidden pictures.
- Play with a jack-in-the-box.
- Describe locations during all motivating social contexts.

DO-WATCH-LISTEN-SAY: Social and Communication Intervention for Children with Autism
by Kathleen Ann Quill © 2000 Paul H. Brookes Publishing Co.

Activity

A. Basic Communicative Functions
Comment 7. Describes attributes

Sample Means

Communicative gestures: Not applicable

Emergent: Vocalization or speech, signs, photographs, pictographs, a voice output system, or written language to name an attribute, such as *Red* or *Little*

Verbal: Speech, signs, photographs, pictographs, a voice output system, or written language to convey a multiword message, such as *It's a red bird* or *I found a little car*

Activity: Adult–Child

Context: Art

Materials: Paint, paintbrushes, paper, accompanying visual supports as appropriate

Procedure: Set up paint-by-number sheets of paper. Place a large number inside of each part of the picture, and provide a code for the child (e.g., 1 = blue, 2 = black, 3 = red). Say "Thomas is blue," "Wheels are black," or any appropriate word(s) as the child is coloring that picture. As the child continues to paint, touch a color and stop. Wait and watch for the child to name the color. If the child does not respond, prompt him as appropriate. Repeat many times in the same manner. Decrease the amount of prompting as appropriate.

Activity: Small Group

Context: Books

Materials: Repetitive books that list attributes, such as *Mary Wore Her Red Dress and Henry Wore His Green Sneakers* or *Brown Bear, Brown Bear*; flannel board pieces, flannel board; accompanying visual supports as appropriate

Procedure: Read the book. As each attribute is described, place the corresponding piece on the flannel board. Once the children are familiar with the book, say part of the repeating phrase, such as "Mary wore her _____" or "I see a _____" and stop. Wait for the children to describe the attribute. If the children do not respond, prompt them as appropriate. Repeat many times in the same manner. Decrease the amount of prompting as appropriate. After the story is complete, leave the flannel board pieces up and label them one by one as they are removed. Point to one and provide an opportunity for the children to describe the attribute before removing it.

Contexts for Generalization

- Color-code each child's name at circle time.
- Hide small and large objects in the sandbox.
- Use food coloring to change the color of sensory items, such as snow, ice, and rice.
- Turn off the volume while using computer programs such as *JumpStart Toddler*.
- Hide colored shapes or other items around the classroom and search for them with a flashlight.
- Collect small and large cookie cutters, rolling pins, and other tools for use with playdough.
- Build with colored blocks.
- Make a chart or book about each child, describing his attributes.
- String beads of different colors and sizes.
- Describe attributes during all motivating social contexts.

DO-WATCH-LISTEN-SAY: Social and Communication Intervention for Children with Autism
by Kathleen Ann Quill © 2000 Paul H. Brookes Publishing Co.

Activity

A. Basic Communicative Functions
Comment 8. Describes past events

Sample Means

Communicative gestures: Not applicable

Emergent: Vocalization or speech, signs, photographs, pictographs, a voice output system, or written language to say event name

Verbal: Speech, signs, photographs, pictographs, a voice output system, or written language to convey a multiword message, such as *I played with blocks* or *I ate breakfast with Daddy*

Activity: Adult–Child

Context: Work time

Materials: Pieces of paper that list all possible activities for the day, with a *yes* and a *no* beside each activity, and a space for writing

Procedure: The child completes the sheet at the end of the day. He identifies each activity and indicates (by circling *yes* or *no*) whether he participated in it that day. If the answer is *yes,* the child must describe the activity or event (e.g., with whom he played, what he made) in the space provided. Prompt the child as appropriate. A copy of the sheet should be sent home each day so the child can practice telling his family about the day's events. Repeat daily in the same manner. Decrease the amount of prompting as appropriate.

Activity: Small Group

Context: Games

Materials: Variety of games, accompanying visual supports as appropriate

Procedure: Use a Polaroid camera to take a picture of each child playing a game. Have the children sit in a circle once the game is over. Ask each child "What did you play?" Pair spoken language with signed, gestural, or pictographic cues as needed. Wait for the children to describe the event. If they do not respond, show them the appropriate photograph, and prompt them to describe the event. Repeat many times in the same manner. Decrease the amount of prompting as appropriate.

Contexts for Generalization

- Use symbols on a calendar to mark special past events and to ask the children about the events.
- Incorporate a time for sharing news at circle time so the children can relate what they have done at home.
- Make homemade books depicting field trips and have them available for children to view.
- Use games, such as *Living Books* CD-ROMs, in which a child must relate what event just occurred.
- Require the child to tell an adult about each activity once it is completed.
- Place photographs of favorite family activities (e.g., going to the park) in a photograph album.
- Read memory books that are individualized for each child.
- Sequence strips for each activity and describe what was just completed.
- Provide recipe books for cooking to describe how a snack time food (e.g., cookies) was made.
- Describe past events during all motivating social contexts.

DO-WATCH-LISTEN-SAY: Social and Communication Intervention for Children with Autism
by Kathleen Ann Quill © 2000 Paul H. Brookes Publishing Co.

Activity

A. Basic Communicative Functions
Comment 9. Describes future events

Sample Means

Communicative gestures: Not applicable

Emergent: Vocalization or speech, signs, photographs, pictographs, a voice output system, or written language to say the name of an event (e.g., *Gym*)

Verbal: Speech, signs, photographs, pictographs, a voice output system, or written language to convey a multiword message, such as *Today, we will go to gym*

Activity: Adult–Child

Context: Circle time

Materials: Daily schedule

Procedure: Review the child's schedule upon arrival at school, and say "Today, we will (name activity)" or any appropriate word(s) for each upcoming activity. Point to the child's schedule throughout the day, and do not say anything. Wait for him to describe the day's upcoming events. If the child does not respond, prompt him as appropriate. Repeat daily in the same manner. Decrease the amount of prompting as appropriate.

Activity: Small Group

Context: Cooking

Materials: Whatever is needed to complete the cooking activity, pictures of the activity

Procedure: Cook the same recipe frequently so the children become familiar with the sequence. Use photographs, pictographs, or written text to reflect the steps of the cooking activity. Tell the children what they are going to make, and ask them to describe the upcoming sequence. If the children do not respond, prompt them as appropriate to describe the future steps. Repeat many times in the same manner. Decrease the amount of prompting as appropriate.

Contexts for Generalization

- Talk about what activity is next during transitions.
- Use a calendar to talk about future events and holidays.
- Make a choice prior to engaging in play.
- Early in the day, indicate what the child will eat for lunch.
- Indicate where this child is going or whom the child will see prior to getting on the bus.
- Gather relevant pictures to show the class prior to a field trip.
- Plan a snack menu for the week.
- Plan a cooking activity menu for the week.
- On Friday, talk about weekend plans.
- Describe future events during all motivating social contexts.

Activity

A. Basic Communicative Functions
Request Information 1. Attention

Sample Means

Communicative gestures: Physical proximity, looking at person, pulling person's hand

Emergent: Vocalization or speech, signs, photographs, pictographs, a voice output system, or written language to say person's name

Verbal: Speech, signs, photographs, pictographs, a voice output system, or written language to convey a multiword message, such as *Excuse me, (peer's name), can I play?*

Activity: Adult–Child

Context: Any activity

Materials: Multiple copies of small photographs of all adults/peers, accompanying visual supports as appropriate

Procedure: Attach photographs to all communication boards available in the classroom. Make a few boards that contain the photographs only, and be sure they are readily available within the classroom. Any time the child makes a communicative attempt, guide him to remove the picture of the individual with whom he is communicating and say that person's name. Continue this procedure throughout the day, and stop after removing the picture. Wait and watch for the child to request attention by saying the person's name. If the child does not respond, prompt him as appropriate. Repeat many times in the same manner. Decrease the amount of prompting as appropriate.

Activity: Small Group

Context: Any activity

Materials: Sticky tags, accompanying visual supports as appropriate

Procedure: Write on sticky tags the names of all adults and peers in the classroom. Attach the tags to each person's forearm or other determined location. Each time a child makes a communicative attempt, demonstrate that he is to tap the communication partner's forearm gently and say the name on the tag. It is helpful to have two adults involved so the prompting is clear. Continue this procedure as frequently as possible. Once the children are familiar with the procedure, wait for communicative opportunities and watch for any communicative means. If a child does not respond by first calling attention, prompt him as appropriate. Repeat the sequence many times in the same manner. Decrease the amount of prompting as appropriate.

Strategies

- Require the child to gain attention during all motivating social contexts.
- Use two adults: one who physically assists the child and one who receives the message.
- Clarify expectations.
- Maintain close proximity to the child.
- Use AAC supports as needed.
- Make nonverbal cues more explicit.
- Give the child time to respond.
- Ignore the child unless he gains attention.
- Teach meaningful and appropriate ways to gain attention as replacements for any inappropriate behaviors in which the child may be engaged.
- Repeat the same message at predictable times.
- Use appropriate adult/peer modeling if the child is an imitator.

DO-WATCH-LISTEN-SAY: Social and Communication Intervention for Children with Autism
by Kathleen Ann Quill © 2000 Paul H. Brookes Publishing Co.

Activity

A. Basic Communicative Functions

Request Information 2. Information about object

Sample Means

Communicative gestures: Not applicable

Emergent: Vocalization or speech, signs, photographs, pictographs, a voice output system, or written language to say *What?*

Verbal: Speech, signs, photographs, pictographs, a voice output system, or written language to convey a multiword message, such as *What is it?*

Activity: Adult–Child

Context: Sensory area

Materials: Large blanket, variety of objects, accompanying visual supports as appropriate

Procedure: Hide an object under a blanket. Say "What is under the blanket?" or any appropriate word(s). Exaggerate the interaction with animation. Continue to hide objects, but say nothing. Wait and watch for the child to request information. If the child does not respond, prompt him as appropriate to ask "What?" Repeat many times in the same manner. Decrease the amount of prompting as appropriate.

Activity: Small Group

Context: Art

Materials: Variety of objects of various textures, bag, accompanying visual supports as appropriate

Procedure: Place the objects into the bag. Reach into the bag without looking in, and feel for an object. Describe how the object feels to the children, then ask "What is it?" Wait for the children to name the item, then pull it out of the bag. Exaggerate the interaction with animation. Have each child take a turn with the "mystery bag." Prompt a child if he does not ask "What is it?" Repeat the sequence many times in the same manner, and decrease the amount of prompting as appropriate.

Contexts for Generalization

- Play lotto games and ask "What is it?"
- Hide all objects for a tea party and ask "What do we need?"
- Ask peers what they are eating for lunch.
- Play a What's Missing? game.
- Read I Spy books.
- Point to interesting items and ask "What is it?" during outside walks.
- Read books with flaps; before lifting the flap, ask "What is it?"
- Play a barrier game with two children; one must ask the other "What is it?"
- Request information about objects during all motivating social contexts.

Activity

A. Basic Communicative Functions
Request Information 3. Information about person

Sample Means

Communicative gestures: Not applicable

Emergent: Vocalization or speech, signs, photographs, pictographs, a voice output system, or written language to say *Who?*

Verbal: Speech, signs, photographs, pictographs, a voice output system, or written language to convey a multiword message, such as *Who is hiding?*

Activity: Adult–Child

Context: Games

Materials: Walkie-talkies, another adult, accompanying visual supports as appropriate

Procedure: Use walkie-talkies with the child so he understands how they work. Blindfold the child or put him in a location where he is unable to see the adults. Use the walkie-talkies, and wait for the child to ask "Who is it?" If the child does not respond, prompt him. Repeat many times in the same manner. Decrease the amount of prompting as appropriate.

Activity: Small Group

Context: Music

Materials: Large jar, pretend cookies or other fun objects, accompanying visual supports as appropriate

Procedure: Give each child a pretend cookie. One child sits in the middle of a circle, blindfolded, with his cookie behind him. Another child sneaks up, takes the blindfolded child's cookie, and hides it in the cookie jar. The group sings "Who Put the Cookie in the Cookie Jar?" The child in the center guesses who took his cookie. Watch for the child in the center to ask "Who put the cookie in the cookie jar?" If he does not respond, prompt him as appropriate. Repeat the sequence many times in the same manner.

Contexts for Generalization

- Play lotto games of people or characters.
- Play Musical Chairs or Duck, Duck, Goose and ask "Who is out?"
- Hide puppets in a bag and ask "Who is in the bag?"
- Read books such as *Have You Seen My Duckling?* to have the child guess who is being described.
- Talk about who is missing at morning circle time.
- Read stories about the children's families and ask *who* questions.
- Play games such as "Who is wearing red sneakers?"
- Read a book such as *Mary Wore Her Red Dress.*
- Request information about people during all motivating social contexts.

DO-WATCH-LISTEN-SAY: Social and Communication Intervention for Children with Autism
by Kathleen Ann Quill © 2000 Paul H. Brookes Publishing Co.

Activity

A. Basic Communicative Functions
Request Information 4. Information about actions

Sample Means

Communicative gestures: Not applicable

Emergent: Vocalization or speech, signs, photographs, pictographs, a voice output system, or written language to say *(Peer's name) doing?*

Verbal: Speech, signs, photographs, pictographs, a voice output system, or written language to convey a multiword message, such as *What is (peer's name) doing in the blocks area?*

Activity: Adult–Child

Context: Books

Materials: Homemade book about children within the classroom performing a variety of fun and silly actions/activities, accompanying visual supports as appropriate

Procedure: Read the book with the child. On every page, frequently say "What is (child's name) doing?" or any appropriate word(s). Continue reading the book daily; point to the first picture and stop. Wait and watch for the child to request information about the actions. If the child does not respond, prompt him as appropriate to ask the "What is (peer's name) doing?" question. Repeat many times in the same manner. Decrease the amount of prompting as appropriate.

Activity: Small Group

Context: Music

Materials: Accompanying visual supports as appropriate

Procedure: Sing "If You're Happy and You Know It." Have one child demonstrate an action and another child close his eyes and ask "What's he doing?" Next, all of the children continue the action. Experiment and find out what the children enjoy. Continue the game, wait, and watch for the child who is closing his eyes to request information about the action. If a child does not respond, prompt him as appropriate to ask "What's he doing?" Repeat many times in the same manner. Decrease the amount of prompting as appropriate.

Contexts for Generalization

Ask *what's he doing* questions during any of the following activities:

- Watch a silent video of classroom activities.
- Use action cards during work time.
- Use motivating puppets to perform a variety of activities in dramatic play.
- Have one child be a reporter in gym and take notes on what the class is doing.
- Read books with actions (e.g., *Animal Action ABC, Jump, Clap Your Hands*).
- Knock down blocks.
- Play with a stack and pop toy.
- Request information about actions during all motivating social contexts.

Activity

A. Basic Communicative Functions

Request Information 5. Information with a yes/no question

Sample Means

Communicative gestures: Not applicable

Emergent: Vocalization or speech, signs, photographs, pictographs, a voice output system, or written language to ask a simple question

Verbal: Speech, signs, photographs, pictographs, a voice output system, or written language to convey a multiword message, such as *Can I have the (object name)?*

Activity: Adult–Child

Context: Games

Materials: Toy characters, drawstring bag, accompanying visual supports as appropriate

Procedure: Place the characters in the bag. Take out a familiar character and have another adult ask "Is it Big Bird?" Respond, and reinforce the person asking the question. Experiment and find out what the child enjoys (e.g., having the characters jump out). Exaggerate the interaction with animation. Pair spoken language with signed, gestural, or pictographic cues as needed. Continue to play the game. Have the child take a character out of the bag. Wait and watch for the child to request information. If the child does not respond, prompt him as appropriate to ask "Is it (character name)?" Repeat many times in the same manner. Decrease the amount of prompting as appropriate.

Activity: Small Group

Context: Circle time

Materials: Fun hat for each child, Velcro, various sets of matching and motivating pictures, accompanying visual supports as appropriate

Procedure: Each child wears a hat with a picture attached to it. Each picture's match should appear on another child's hat. The children take turns removing a picture from their hats and looking for the match on another peer's hat. When they find the match they must ask their peer "Can I have the (name of object in picture)?" or any appropriate word(s). Exaggerate the interaction with animation. Pair spoken language with signed, gestural, or pictographic cues as needed. If a child does not respond by asking a yes/no question, prompt him as appropriate. Repeat many times in the same manner. Decrease the amount of prompting as appropriate.

Contexts for Generalization

- Have the classroom aide ask each child "Do you want (name of food)?" at mealtime.
- Play Go Fish.
- Play Old Maid.
- Require child to ask for permission before completing an activity.
- Have the lunch aide ask the child if he wants a hot lunch.
- Set up the dramatic play area like a restaurant to encourage the use of yes/no questions.
- Read books such as *Is Your Mama a Llama?* or *Have You Seen My Duckling?*
- For play with remote control vehicles, give the control box to an adult so the child must ask for the remote control.
- Request information with a yes/no question during all motivating social contexts.

Activity

A. Basic Communicative Functions
Request Information 6. Information about location

Sample Means

Communicative gestures: Not applicable

Emergent: Vocalization or speech, signs, photographs, pictographs, a voice output system, or written language to say *Where?*

Verbal: Speech, signs, photographs, pictographs, a voice output system, or written language to convey a multiword message, such as *Where is (object name) today?*

Activity: Adult–Child

Context: Gym

Materials: Preferred object, accompanying visual supports as appropriate

Procedure: Hide the preferred object (e.g., a Thomas the Train car) in different locations. Begin by hiding the object in your clothing (e.g., in a pocket). Move the hiding location farther away to increase the game's difficulty. Say "Where's the car?" or any appropriate word(s). Continue playing the game. Hide the object and stop. Wait and watch for the child to ask "Where is the _____?" If the child does not respond, prompt him as appropriate to request information about the location of the desired object. Repeat many times in the same manner. Decrease the amount of prompting as appropriate.

Activity: Small Group

Context: Any activity

Materials: Two identical boxes, a motivating character such as Sesame Street's Big Bird or Elmo, accompanying visual supports as appropriate

Procedure: Show the children, sitting in a circle, the two identical boxes. Place the character in one box. Pass the boxes around the circle and sing "Where is Big Bird?" to the tune of "Frère Jacques." At the end of the song, have the children open the boxes and find the character. Exaggerate the interaction with animation. Pair spoken language with signed, gestural, or pictographic cues as needed. Continue playing the game; pass the boxes and stop. Wait and watch for the children to request information about the location of the desired item. If a child does not respond, prompt him as appropriate to request "Where is Big Bird?" Repeat many times in the same manner. Decrease the amount of prompting as appropriate.

Contexts for Generalization

- Hide objects and use a flashlight to look for them.
- Play the "Peekaboo" part of certain computer games, such as *JumpStart Toddler*.
- Read books that have hidden flaps, such as *Where's Spot?*
- Sing songs such as "Where is Thumpkin?" during music time.
- Hide people in the dollhouse in dramatic play.
- Hide one or two puzzle pieces needed to complete a puzzle in the manipulatives area.
- Request the location of individuals at attendance during morning circle time.
- Hide objects in the sensory table.
- Color hidden picture worksheets.
- Request information about locations during all motivating social contexts.

Activity

A. Basic Communicative Functions
Request Information 7. Information about time

Sample Means

Communicative gestures: Not applicable

Emergent: Vocalization or speech, signs, photographs, pictographs, a voice output system, or written language to say *When?*

Verbal: Speech, signs, photographs, pictographs, a voice output system, or written language to convey a multiword message, such as *When will it be time to go home?*

Activity: Adult–Child

Context: Arrival

Materials: Schedule pictures that are not yet put in order for the day, accompanying visual supports as appropriate

Procedure: Give the child his schedule pictures one at a time. Hold up a picture at eye level and say "When is lunch?" or any appropriate word(s). Place the lunch picture on the schedule. Pair spoken language with signed, gestural, or pictographic cues as needed. Continue with many of the schedule pictures until the child is familiar with the procedure. Then hold up a schedule picture and stop. Wait and watch for any communicative means. If the child does not respond, prompt him as appropriate to ask "When?" Repeat the sequence many times in the same manner. Decrease the amount of prompting as appropriate. Repeat this activity daily.

Activity: Small Group

Context: Circle time

Materials: Calendar, symbols/pictures to signify important days for the current month, accompanying visual supports as appropriate

Procedure: Discuss the calendar each month. On the first day of the month, hold up the symbol for *birthday* and ask "When is (name of child)'s birthday?" Pair spoken language with signed, gestural, or pictographic cues as needed. The next day, follow the same procedure, asking about another special day for that month. The following day, ask a child to be the calendar helper. Hand a symbol to the child, wait, and watch for him to request information about time. If the child does not respond, prompt him to ask "When?" Repeat many times in the same manner. Decrease the amount of prompting as appropriate.

Contexts for Generalization

- Play with month and holiday lotto boards.
- Ask children about birthdays during circle time.
- Sequence a completed cooking activity.
- Talk about what activities were completed before and after each other.
- Read a book and talk about what happened first, next, and last.
- Play a lotto game about clothing and seasons.
- Play a lotto game about holidays.
- Read a book that refers to seasons, such as *I Love You, Mama, Any Time of the Year.*
- Request information about time during all motivating social contexts.

Activity

A. Basic Communicative Functions
Request Information 8. Information about cause

Sample Means

Communicative gestures: Not applicable

Emergent: Vocalization or speech, signs, photographs, pictographs, a voice output system, or written language to say *Why?* or *How come?*

Verbal: Speech, signs, photographs, pictographs, a voice output system, or written language to convey a multiword message, such as *Why does it do that?*

Activity: Adult–Child

Context: Games

Materials: Set up a lotto board of causes and effects, accompanying visual supports as appropriate

Procedure: Play lotto. Hold up a picture, such as an umbrella, and say something like "Why do we need an umbrella?" The child should find a *rain* picture on his board and match up the two pictures. Continue until the child understands the procedure and is engaged. Hold up a picture and stop. Wait and watch for the child to request information about cause. If the child does not respond, prompt him as appropriate to ask a *why* question. Repeat many times in the same manner. Decrease the amount of prompting as appropriate.

Activity: Small Group

Context: Sensory/science area

Materials: A variety of ingredients with which students can experiment, such as salt, sugar, vinegar, baking soda, corn starch, water, and food coloring (be sure everything is nontoxic); accompanying visual supports as appropriate

Procedure: Set up a station for children to experience a variety of potions. They will learn principles such as why some things dissolve and others do not. Let the children experiment and become familiar with the activity for the first day or so. Once the activity is familiar, participate with the children and begin modeling *why* questions about what they observe. Pair spoken language with signed, gestural, or pictographic cues as needed. Continue to allow the class to experiment. Wait and watch for the children to ask *why* questions about their experience. If the children do not respond, prompt them as appropriate to request information about cause. Repeat many times in the same manner. Decrease the amount of prompting as appropriate.

Strategies

* Make concrete associations, stating action + because + antecedent.
* Remember that meaningful activities are the key to social and communicative success.
* Repeat the same message at predictable times.
* Balance adult-directed interactions with child-directed interactions.
* Simplify language complexity.
* Give the child time to respond.
* Use two adults: one who physically assists the child and one who receives the message.
* Use appropriate adult/peer modeling if the child is an imitator.
* Request information about causes during all motivating social contexts.

DO-WATCH-LISTEN-SAY: Social and Communication Intervention for Children with Autism
by Kathleen Ann Quill © 2000 Paul H. Brookes Publishing Co.

Activity

B. Socioemotional Skills

Express Feelings 1. Requests a break when upset

Sample Means

Communicative gestures: Moving person's hand, reaching, pulling person's hand

Emergent: Vocalizations or speech, signs, photographs, pictographs, a voice output system, or written language to say *Break* or other appropriate word

Verbal: Speech, signs, photographs, pictographs, a voice output system, or written language to convey a multiword message, such as *I need a break, please*

Learn a Target Message to Replace Behavior(s)

Context: All settings in which the child demonstrates a high level of discomfort or frustration

Materials: A tangible symbol (e.g., object, photograph, pictograph, written message) that means *break* to the child—children with autism often lack the ability to verbalize any communication that is a replacement for problem behavior, so a tangible symbol is essential even for verbal children

Procedure: Work with the child in a setting that is challenging. Wait for the child to demonstrate some level of agitation. Present the *break* symbol to the child and silently guide him to a clearly defined break area. A break should be calming for the individual child but not reinforcing. Maintain a neutral affect and do not engage the child in any discussion. Examples might include sitting on a beanbag chair or walking in the hall. The break must have a definitive end point and the child must come back to the activity. A request for a break must never equal a request for *All done.* Continue to anticipate the child's frustration and move from picking up the symbol yourself to gesturing toward the symbol and, finally, to the child initiating that process. The final goal is for the child to request a break spontaneously, without any cuing. Repeat the sequence many times in the same manner. Initially, all of the child's communication attempts should be acknowledged, even though he may overuse this new privilege. Gradually limit the number of breaks that are available. Once the child is requesting breaks from various adults, he can also be encouraged to tell a peer.

Strategies

- Teach meaningful social and communication replacement behaviors at the moment the child is engaged in inappropriate behavior.
- Offer the child maximum support to ensure success.
- Do not prompt in exactly the same way every time.
- Limit the use of verbal prompts in the form of questions.
- Simplify language complexity.
- Use AAC supports that are consistent across various settings.
- Keep the length of breaks consistent and clearly define the end point with a timer or clock.
- Observe what situations frustrate the child.
- Ignore any of the child's attempts to engage in conversation; remain neutral.
- Clarify expectations.
- Use nonverbal reinforcement that mirrors the child's emotional state.

DO-WATCH-LISTEN-SAY: Social and Communication Intervention for Children with Autism
by Kathleen Ann Quill © 2000 Paul H. Brookes Publishing Co.

Activity

B. Socioemotional Skills

Express Feelings 2. Requests a calming activity when upset

Sample Means

Communicative gestures: Moving person's hand, reaching/pulling person's hand, moving object(s) toward

Emergent: Vocalizations or speech, signs, photographs, pictographs, a voice output system, or written language to say *Lotion* or *Squeeze*

Verbal: Speech, signs, photographs, pictographs, a voice output system, or written language to convey a multiword message, such as *I want to squeeze the ball*

Learn a Target Message to Replace Behavior(s)

Context: All settings in which the child demonstrates a high level of discomfort or frustration

Materials: Use the inventory of exploratory behavior in the Assessment of Social and Communication Skills for Children with Autism to determine a child's preferred sensory modality. Identify at least five sensory activities that are calming. Examples may include squeezing a small, squishy ball; using a weighted blanket; or holding a small preferred figurine. Use a tangible symbol (e.g., object, photograph, pictograph, written text) to depict each sensory activity. Children with autism often lack the ability to verbalize any communication that is a replacement for problem behavior, so a tangible symbol is essential even for verbal children. Make a choice board that contains two or more choices at a time, depending on the child's ability.

Procedure: Work with the child in a setting that is challenging. Wait for the child to demonstrate some level of agitation. Present the choice board to the child and wait for him to make a choice. If the child does not make a choice, use hand-over-hand guidance to help him make a choice. The calming activity (e.g., carrying a blanket, sucking a thumb) can co-occur with any activity. Take caution: If the activity interferes with or distracts the child from a task, it should be removed from the choice board. The final goal is for the child to spontaneously seek a calming activity. Repeat the sequence many times in the same manner. The child can request a calming activity any time during the day.

Strategies

- Teach meaningful social and communication replacement behaviors at the moment the child is engaged in inappropriate behavior.
- Offer the child maximum support to ensure success.
- Do not prompt in exactly the same way every time.
- Limit the use of verbal prompts in the form of questions.
- Simplify language complexity.
- Use AAC supports that are consistent across various settings.
- Clarify expectations.
- Acknowledge and label the child's feelings (e.g., "You are angry because Chris took your truck").
- Remove items that are overly distracting or interfere with a child's ability to focus on an activity.

DO-WATCH-LISTEN-SAY: Social and Communication Intervention for Children with Autism
by Kathleen Ann Quill © 2000 Paul H. Brookes Publishing Co.

Activity

B. Socioemotional Skills

Express Feelings 3. Indicates need to use a relaxation procedure

Sample Means

Communicative gestures: Moving person's hand, reaching/pulling person's hand

Emergent: Vocalizations or speech, signs, photographs, pictographs, a voice output system, or written language to say *Relax* or *Breathe*

Verbal: Speech, signs, photographs, pictographs, a voice output system, or written language to convey a multiword message, such as *I need to take a deep breath*

Learn a Target Message to Replace Behavior(s)

Context: All settings in which the child demonstrates a high level of discomfort or frustration

Materials: Determine a relaxation procedure—such as visualization, deep breathing, counting, or stretching—that works for a specific child. Make a cue card that signifies the relaxation procedure.

Procedure: Include a relaxation time in the child's daily schedule. The relaxation procedure is best taught when the child is calm; then it can be generalized to times when he is upset. Use a cue card to prompt the child to use a particular procedure to relax. Make a book for the individual child, pairing stressful contexts with the cue card for relaxation. Simple language can accompany the pictures, such as *When work makes me upset, I can shake my hands and take a deep breath.* Read the book to the child frequently throughout the day. Be sure to use the same language from the book during times when the child is actually upset. Visual imagery is also appropriate for relaxation. The main function of visual imagery techniques is to teach the child to use self-control strategies. A stressful situation is depicted as a picture sequence that is paired with a simple verbal script. The child is taught to use visual imagery to cope with the stressful situation. Any procedure should conclude with desired behaviors and positive outcomes. The procedure should be reviewed with the child multiple times daily. Once the procedure is familiar, the child rehearses before, during, and after actual stressful situations. The goal is for the child to demonstrate the desired behaviors in the natural settings by using the visual and verbal images as cues.

Strategies

- Use AAC supports that are consistent across various settings.
- Teach meaningful social and communication replacement behaviors at the moment the child is engaged in inappropriate behavior.
- Offer the child maximum support to ensure success.
- Do not prompt in exactly the same way every time.
- Limit the use of verbal prompts in the form of questions.
- Simplify language complexity.
- Clarify expectations.
- Acknowledge and label the child's feelings (e.g., "You are frustrated because this is hard").
- Consider the most natural setting for acquisition of target skills.
- Remove items that are overly distracting or interfere with a child's ability to focus on an activity.

DO-WATCH-LISTEN-SAY: Social and Communication Intervention for Children with Autism
by Kathleen Ann Quill © 2000 Paul H. Brookes Publishing Co.

Activity

B. Socioemotional Skills
Express Feelings 4. Likes/dislikes

Sample Means

Communicative gestures: Not applicable

Emergent: Vocalizations or speech, signs, photographs, pictographs, a voice output system, or written language to say *Like* or *Yuck*

Verbal: Speech, signs, photographs, pictographs, a voice output system, or written language to convey a multiword message, such as *I like gym* or *I don't like work*

Activity: Adult–Child

Context: Games

Materials: Photographs of the child performing a variety of activities (both those that are preferred and those that are not preferred), accompanying visual supports as appropriate

Procedure: Play lotto with the child. Hold up a picture and say "I like swinging" or "I don't like work." Continue presenting photographs and pairing them with appropriate phrases until the child is familiar with the game. Continue playing, present a photograph, and stop. Wait and watch for the child to express likes or dislikes. If the child does not respond, prompt him as appropriate to say "I like _____." Repeat many times in the same manner. Decrease the amount of prompting as appropriate.

Activity: Small Group

Context: Snack time

Materials: Snack items that are preferred and those that are not preferred, chart, markers, accompanying visual supports as appropriate

Procedure: Make color-coded symbols to represent *like* (e.g., yellow) and *don't like* (e.g., red). Keep a chart at the snack table. As new foods are introduced, chart which foods the child likes and which ones he does not like. Each day at snack time, present preferred and nonpreferred foods. Say "I like cookies" or "Yucky, I don't like that." Exaggerate the interaction with animation. One day, present a snack and stop. Wait and watch for the children to express like or dislike. If they do not respond, prompt them as appropriate. Repeat many times in the same manner. Decrease the amount of prompting as appropriate.

Strategies

- Acknowledge feelings (e.g., "You pushed it away because you don't like it").
- Point out feelings in peers (e.g., "Karen is smiling because she likes to play with the bus").
- Teach meaningful social and communication replacement behaviors at the moment the child is engaged in inappropriate behavior.
- Maintain close proximity to the child.
- Use AAC supports as needed.
- Make nonverbal cues more explicit.
- Give the child time to respond.
- Use dramatic facial expressions.
- Consider the most natural setting for acquisition of target skills.
- Use nonverbal reinforcement that mirrors the child's emotional state.

Activity

B. Socioemotional Skills
Express Feelings 5. Angry/mad

Sample Means

Communicative gestures: Not applicable

Emergent: Vocalizations or speech, signs, photographs, pictographs, a voice output system, or written language to say *Mad*

Verbal: Speech, signs, photographs, pictographs, a voice output system, or written language to convey a multiword message, such as *Changing my schedule makes me feel mad*

Activity: Adult–Child

(Activity applies to objectives 5–10 of "Express Feelings.")

Context: Sensory area

Materials: Mirror, accompanying visual supports as appropriate

Procedure: Encourage the child to experiment with making different faces in the mirror. Stand directly in front of the child and explain that you are going to play the mirror game. Make a mad face and say, "I'm mad." Take turns with the child, allowing him to decide which faces to make. Wait and watch for the child to express the feeling. If the child does not respond, prompt him as appropriate. Repeat many times in the same manner. Decrease the amount of prompting as appropriate. Leave a mirror out so the child can experiment with making various faces throughout the school day.

Activity: Small Group

(Activity applies to objectives 5–10 of "Express Feelings.")

Context: Games

Materials: Pictographic lotto boards of a variety of emotions or commercially available photographs of emotions, accompanying visual supports as appropriate

Procedure: Play lotto with two children. Hold up a picture and label it, such as "He's proud" or "She's happy." Pair spoken language with signed, gestural, or pictographic cues as needed. Have the children take turns. Wait and watch for the children to label the feelings. If the children do not respond, prompt as appropriate. For each emotion, encourage the children to talk about a time they felt that way. Repeat the sequence many times in the same manner. Decrease the amount of prompting as appropriate.

Strategies

- Acknowledge feelings (e.g., "You pushed it away because you don't like it").
- Point out feelings of peers (e.g., "Clara is smiling because she's happy to see her mother").
- Point out peers' social behaviors (e.g., "Mary's sad because she hurt her knee").
- Prompt how to respond to peers' behaviors (e.g., "Matt's sad; maybe you can give him his blanket").
- Encourage perspective-taking (e.g., "Look at Joe's face; he doesn't like that").
- Teach meaningful social and communication replacement behaviors at the moment the child is engaged in inappropriate behavior.
- Use AAC supports that are consistent across various settings.
- Make nonverbal cues more explicit.
- Use dramatic facial expressions.
- Consider the most natural setting for acquisition of target skills.
- Use nonverbal reinforcement that mirrors the child's emotional state.

DO-WATCH-LISTEN-SAY: Social and Communication Intervention for Children with Autism
by Kathleen Ann Quill © 2000 Paul H. Brookes Publishing Co.

Activity

B. Socioemotional Skills
Express Feelings 6. Happy/sad

Sample Means

Communicative gestures: Not applicable

Emergent: Vocalizations or speech, signs, photographs, pictographs, a voice output system, or written language to say *Sad*

Verbal: Speech, signs, photographs, pictographs, a voice output system, or written language to convey a multiword message, such as *Recess makes me feel happy*

Activity: Adult–Child

(Activity applies to objectives 5–10 of "Express Feelings.")

Context: Work time

Materials: Colored markers, accompanying visual supports as appropriate

Procedure: Color-code the activities on the child's schedule by the feeling each evokes for that child. Color-code preferred activities, such as snack time and recess, yellow, and label them *Makes me feel happy.* Color-code difficult activities, such as work time or transitions, red, and label them *Makes me feel angry.* The transition to or from the school bus might be color-coded blue and labeled *Makes me feel sad,* as the child is leaving people. (The child could also code activities on his schedule with small happy face or sad face stickers.) Each time the child checks his schedule, say "Time for lunch—lunch makes you feel happy." Continue until the child is very familiar with the routine. Wait and watch for the child to express feelings as he checks the schedule. If the child does not respond, prompt him as appropriate. Repeat many times in the same manner. Decrease the amount of prompting as appropriate.

Activity: Small Group

(Activity applies to objectives 5–10 of "Express Feelings.")

Context: Dramatic play area

Materials: The book *Glad Monster, Sad Monster;* art supplies; accompanying visual supports as appropriate

Procedure: Read the book frequently. Cut out the masks provided in the book, laminate them, and attach them to craft sticks. Use the masks to emphasize the emotions presented in the story as it is read. Have the children make their own monster faces to represent an emotion, and have them talk about what makes them feel that way. Wait and watch for the children to express feelings in this context. If a child does not respond, prompt him as appropriate. Repeat many times in the same manner. Decrease the amount of prompting as appropriate.

Strategies

- Acknowledge feelings (e.g., "You pushed it away because you don't like it").
- Point out feelings in peers (e.g., "Clara is smiling because she's happy to see her mother").
- Point out peers' social behaviors (e.g., "Mary's sad because she hurt her knee").
- Prompt how to respond to peers' behaviors (e.g., "Matt's sad; maybe you can give him his blanket").
- Encourage perspective-taking (e.g., "Look at Joe's face; he doesn't like that").
- Teach meaningful social and communication replacement behaviors at the moment the child is engaged in inappropriate behavior.
- Use AAC supports that are consistent across various settings.
- Make nonverbal cues more explicit.
- Use dramatic facial expressions.
- Consider the most natural setting for acquisition of target skills.
- Use nonverbal reinforcement that mirrors the child's emotional state.

DO-WATCH-LISTEN-SAY: Social and Communication Intervention for Children with Autism
by Kathleen Ann Quill © 2000 Paul H. Brookes Publishing Co.

Activity

B. Socioemotional Skills
Express Feelings 7. Calm/relaxed

Sample Means

Communicative gestures: Not applicable

Emergent: Vocalizations or speech, signs, photographs, pictographs, a voice output system, or written language to say *Calm*

Verbal: Speech, signs, photographs, pictographs, a voice output system, or written language to convey a multiword message, such as *I feel calm*

Activity: Adult–Child

(Activity applies to objectives 5–10 of "Express Feelings.")

Context: Any activity

Materials: Choice board, colored markers, accompanying visual supports as appropriate

Procedure: Color-code activity choices: pink for calming activities, purple for activities that are difficult but might make the child feel proud upon completion, orange for silly activities. Experiment to determine what feelings certain activities evoke from that child. Each time a choice is selected, say "Swinging makes you calm," "Listening to that tape makes you feel silly," or other appropriate words. Continue presenting choices, but stay quiet. Wait and watch for the child to express feelings. If the child does not respond, prompt him as appropriate to make a choice and express the accompanying feeling. Repeat the sequence many times in the same manner. Decrease the amount of prompting as appropriate.

Activity: Small Group

(Activity applies to objectives 5–10 of "Express Feelings.")

Context: Circle time

Materials: Homemade chart containing all of the children's and staff members' names, color-coded pictures of various emotions (e.g., blue is *sad,* yellow is *happy,* red is *angry*), accompanying visual supports as appropriate

Procedure: Read a book about emotions each morning at circle time. Ask each person to identify himself, label how he feels, and place the corresponding picture on the chart. Pair spoken language with signed, gestural, or pictographic cues as needed. If a child does not express how he feels, prompt him as appropriate. Repeat the sequence many times in the same manner. Decrease the amount of prompting as appropriate.

Strategies

- Acknowledge feelings (e.g., "You pushed it away because you don't like it").
- Point out feelings in peers (e.g., "Clara is smiling because she's happy to see her mother").
- Point out peers' social behaviors (e.g., "Mary's sad because she hurt her knee").
- Prompt how to respond to peers' behaviors (e.g., "Matt's sad; maybe you can give him his blanket").
- Encourage perspective-taking (e.g., "Look at Joe's face; he doesn't like that").
- Teach meaningful social and communication replacement behaviors at the moment the child is engaged in inappropriate behavior.
- Use AAC supports that are consistent across various settings.
- Make nonverbal cues more explicit.
- Use dramatic facial expressions.
- Consider the most natural setting for acquisition of target skills.
- Use nonverbal reinforcement that mirrors the child's emotional state.

DO-WATCH-LISTEN-SAY: Social and Communication Intervention for Children with Autism
by Kathleen Ann Quill © 2000 Paul H. Brookes Publishing Co.

Activity

B. Socioemotional Skills
Express Feelings 8. Hurt/sick/tired

Sample Means

Communicative gestures: Not applicable

Emergent: Vocalizations or speech, signs, photographs, pictographs, a voice output system, or written language to say *Sleepy*

Verbal: Speech, signs, photographs, pictographs, a voice output system, or written language to convey a multiword message, such as *My tummy hurts*

Activity: Adult–Child

(Activity applies to objectives 5–10 of "Express Feelings.")

Context: Manipulatives area

Materials: Photographs or any pictures of people who are expressing various emotions, accompanying visual supports as appropriate

Procedure: Laminate the pictures and cut them into puzzle pieces. Encourage the child to complete the puzzle. Upon completion of the puzzle, label the puzzle: "Silly," "She's sick," or any appropriate word(s). Talk about times the child has felt that way. Pair spoken language with signed, gestural, or pictographic cues as needed. Once the child is familiar with the procedure, have him complete a puzzle and wait and watch for him to label the emotion. If the child does not respond, prompt him as appropriate. Repeat many times in the same manner. Decrease the amount of prompting as appropriate. (Commercially available emotion puzzles can be used in the same manner.)

Activity: Small Group

Context: Circle time

(Activity applies to objectives 5–10 of "Express Feelings.")

Materials: A video of a variety of people acting out emotions in many situations, accompanying visual supports as appropriate

Procedure: Make a video of the children in the class, capturing different emotions. Watch the video with the volume turned off, and label the emotions. Stop labeling the emotions, and wait for the children to label them. If the children do not respond, prompt them as appropriate. Repeat many times in the same manner. Decrease the amount of prompting as appropriate.

Strategies

- Acknowledge feelings (e.g., "You pushed it away because you don't like it").
- Point out feelings in peers (e.g., "Clara is smiling because she's happy to see her mother").
- Point out peers' social behaviors (e.g., "Mary's sad because she hurt her knee").
- Prompt how to respond to peers' behaviors (e.g., "Matt's sad; maybe you can give him his blanket").
- Encourage perspective-taking (e.g., "Look at Joe's face; he doesn't like that").
- Teach meaningful social and communication replacement behaviors at the moment the child is engaged in inappropriate behavior.
- Use AAC supports that are consistent across various settings.
- Make nonverbal cues more explicit.
- Use dramatic facial expressions.
- Consider the most natural setting for acquisition of target skills.
- Use nonverbal reinforcement that mirrors the child's emotional state.

DO-WATCH-LISTEN-SAY: Social and Communication Intervention for Children with Autism
by Kathleen Ann Quill © 2000 Paul H. Brookes Publishing Co.

Activity

B. Socioemotional Skills

Express Feelings 9. Proud

Sample Means

Communicative gestures: Not applicable

Emergent: Vocalizations or speech, signs, photographs, pictographs, a voice output system, or written language to say *Proud*

Verbal: Speech, signs, photographs, pictographs, a voice output system, or written language to convey a multiword message, such as *I did it myself. I feel proud.*

Activity: Adult–Child

(Activity applies to objectives 5–10 of "Express Feelings.")

Context: Books

Materials: Photographs of the child completing activities or other accomplishments, construction paper, contact paper, binder rings, any other materials to make a book, accompanying visual supports as appropriate

Procedure: Make a social story for whatever emotion you are targeting. Use photographs of the child acting out various emotions. Put one photograph on a page and write the text—for example, "I feel proud when I (complete a certain activity)." Continue on each page with a new photograph and a new caption. Read the book as frequently as possible. Pair spoken language with signed, gestural, or pictographic cues as needed. Touch a picture and stop. Wait and watch for the child to express the emotion. If the child does not respond, prompt him as appropriate. Repeat many times in the same manner. Decrease the amount of prompting as appropriate.

Activity: Small Group

(Activity applies to objectives 5–10 of "Express Feelings.")

Context: Music time

Materials: Accompanying visual supports as appropriate

Procedure: Sing a song about emotion to the tune of the *Barney* theme song: "I feel sad, I feel sad; when I say 'bye' then I feel sad" or "I feel proud, I feel proud; when I do my work then I feel proud." Sing the song frequently, and have the children participate in deciding what makes them each feel a certain way. Use the song at the moment a child is actually experiencing the emotion. Be sure to help the child make concrete associations (e.g., "Swinging is all done, so you are mad"). When an experience occurs, wait to see if the child expresses his feelings. If he does not, prompt him as appropriate.

Strategies

- Acknowledge feelings (e.g., "You pushed it away because you don't like it").
- Point out feelings in peers (e.g., "Clara is smiling because she's happy to see her mother").
- Point out peers' social behaviors (e.g., "Mary's sad because she hurt her knee").
- Prompt how to respond to peers' behaviors (e.g., "Matt's sad; maybe you can give him his blanket").
- Encourage perspective-taking (e.g., "Look at Joe's face; he doesn't like that").
- Teach meaningful social and communication replacement behaviors at the moment the child is engaged in inappropriate behavior.
- Use AAC supports that are consistent across various settings.
- Make nonverbal cues more explicit.
- Use dramatic facial expressions.
- Consider the most natural setting for acquisition of target skills.
- Use nonverbal reinforcement that mirrors the child's emotional state.

Activity

B. Socioemotional Skills
Express Feelings 10. Silly

Sample Means

Communicative gestures: Not applicable

Emergent: Vocalizations or speech, signs, photographs, pictographs, a voice output system, or written language to say *Silly*

Verbal: Speech, signs, photographs, pictographs, a voice output system, or written language to convey a multiword message, such as *Tickling is silly*

Activity: Adult–Child

(Activity applies to objectives 5–10 of "Express Feelings.")

Context: Art

Materials: Markers, crayons, pencils, dot-to-dot sheets of various faces, accompanying visual supports as appropriate

Procedure: Provide a variety of dot-to-dot sheets with varying emotions. When the face is completed, point to it and label the emotion, such as "Oh, he is silly." Continue completing dot-to-dot sheets, then stop. Wait and watch for the child to label the feeling when the face is completed. If the child does not respond, prompt him as appropriate. Repeat the sequence many times in the same manner. Decrease the amount of prompting as appropriate.

Activity: Small Group

(Activity applies to objectives 5–10 of "Express Feelings.")

Context: Dramatic play area

Materials: Brown paper lunch bags, socks, or other items to make into puppets; art supplies such as yarn, eyes, markers, and felt scraps to decorate the puppets; accompanying visual supports as appropriate

Procedure: Make puppets with various emotional expressions. When the puppets are completed, say "He's silly," "My puppet is mad," or any appropriate word(s). Use the puppets to interact, and continue to label the emotions presented. Wait and watch for the children to express feelings using the puppets. If a child does not respond, prompt him as appropriate. Repeat many times in the same manner. Decrease the amount of prompting as appropriate. Leave the puppets in the dramatic play area for further play.

Strategies

- Acknowledge feelings (e.g., "You pushed it away because you don't like it").
- Point out feelings in peers (e.g., "Clara is smiling because she's happy to see her mother").
- Point out peers' social behaviors (e.g., "Mary's sad because she hurt her knee").
- Prompt how to respond to peers' behaviors (e.g., "Matt's sad; maybe you can give him his blanket").
- Encourage perspective-taking (e.g., "Look at Joe's face; he doesn't like that").
- Teach meaningful social and communication replacement behaviors at the moment the child is engaged in inappropriate behavior.
- Use AAC supports that are consistent across various settings.
- Make nonverbal cues more explicit.
- Use dramatic facial expressions.
- Consider the most natural setting for acquisition of target skills.
- Use nonverbal reinforcement that mirrors the child's emotional state.

Activity

B. Socioemotional Skills

Express Feelings 11. Afraid/nervous

Sample Means

Communicative gestures: Not applicable

Emergent: Vocalizations or speech, signs, photographs, pictographs, a voice output system, or written language to say *Scared*

Verbal: Speech, signs, photographs, pictographs, a voice output system, or written language to convey a multiword message, such as *That noise makes me feel nervous*

Activity: Adult–Child

Context: Music

Materials: Tape recordings of thunder, a vacuum cleaner, or any noise that frightens the child; accompanying visual supports as appropriate

Procedure: Softly play the noise that frightens the child. Demonstrate how the child can lower the sound or make it louder and that he has control of the audiotape player. Each time the child lowers the volume, say "I'm scared," "That makes me nervous," or any appropriate word(s). Pair spoken language with signed, gestural, or pictographic cues as needed. The next time the child turns down the volume, wait and watch for the child to express his fear. If the child does not respond, prompt him as appropriate to indicate his feeling afraid or nervous. Repeat many times in the same manner. Decrease the amount of prompting as appropriate.

Activity: Small Group

Context: Dramatic play area

Materials: A scary book about monsters or ghosts; flashlight, blanket, or any other appropriate prompts; accompanying visual supports as appropriate

Procedure: Turn off the lights and pull down the shades to make the room dark, and read a scary book. Use the flashlight and blanket to make the interaction fun. Say "I am afraid" or any appropriate word(s). Continue to read the story and talk about things that make people afraid or nervous. Wait and watch for the children to express fear or nervousness. If they do not respond, prompt them as appropriate. Repeat many times in the same manner. Decrease the amount of prompting as appropriate.

Strategies

- Acknowledge feelings (e.g., "That noise is loud, so you're scared").
- Point out feelings in peers (e.g., "He's holding his teddy because he's afraid").
- Point out peers' social behaviors (e.g., "Ann's throwing things because she's nervous that her mom left").
- Prompt how to respond to peers' behaviors (e.g., "Jeff's afraid; maybe you can tell him it's okay").
- Encourage perspective-taking (e.g., "Al's afraid of that noise, so he's crying").
- Use AAC supports that are consistent across various settings.
- Make nonverbal cues more explicit.
- Use dramatic facial expressions.
- Consider the most natural setting for acquisition of target skills.
- Use nonverbal reinforcement that mirrors the child's emotional state.

DO-WATCH-LISTEN-SAY: Social and Communication Intervention for Children with Autism
by Kathleen Ann Quill © 2000 Paul H. Brookes Publishing Co.

Activity

B. Socioemotional Skills
Express Feelings 12. Confused

Sample Means

Communicative gestures: Not applicable

Emergent: Vocalizations or speech, signs, photographs, pictographs, a voice output system, or written language to say *Don't know*

Verbal: Speech, signs, photographs, pictographs, a voice output system, or written language to convey a multiword message, such as *I don't know the answer*

Activity: Adult–Child

Context: Work time

Materials: Variety of pictures depicting things with which the child is familiar and those with which the child is not familiar, two boxes labeled *I know* and *I don't know,* accompanying visual supports as appropriate

Procedure: Show the familiar pictures to the child one at a time. Allow the child to label each picture, and put the pictures in the appropriate box. Then show the child the unfamiliar pictures. Say "I don't know," and put the pictures in the corresponding box. Next, mix up the pictures, and show the child one picture at a time. Wait and watch for the child to express confusion. If the child does not respond, prompt him as appropriate to indicate *I don't know.* Repeat the sequence many times in the same manner. Decrease the amount of prompting as appropriate.

Activity: Small Group

Context: Games

Materials: Uniset or Colorforms

Procedure: Play with the manipulative pieces to make a picture. Give the children simple directives that you know they can follow. Then give them a directive that is impossible to complete given the materials present. Wait for them to look confused, and say *I don't know.* Continue to give simple directives, then give one that is impossible. Wait and watch for the children to express confusion. If they do not respond, prompt them as appropriate. Repeat the sequence many times in the same manner. Decrease the amount of prompting as appropriate.

Strategies

- Acknowledge feelings (e.g., "You're confused because this is different").
- Point out feelings in peers (e.g., "He's confused because he doesn't know the answer").
- Prompt how to respond to peers' behaviors (e.g., "David's confused; can you help him finish his math work?").
- Use AAC supports that are consistent across various settings.
- Make nonverbal cues more explicit.
- Use dramatic facial expressions.
- Consider the most natural setting for acquisition of target skills.
- Use nonverbal reinforcement that mirrors the child's emotional state.
- Respond to the child's level of focused purposeful behavior at the moment.

DO-WATCH-LISTEN-SAY: Social and Communication Intervention for Children with Autism
by Kathleen Ann Quill © 2000 Paul H. Brookes Publishing Co.

Activity

B. Socioemotional Skills
Prosocial Statements 1. Requests more social game/interaction

Sample Means

Communicative gestures: Physical proximity, looking at person, moving person's hand/face, reaching, pulling person's hand, giving objects, or moving object toward/away

Emergent: Vocalizations or speech, signs, photographs, pictographs, a voice output system, or written language to say *More*

Verbal: Speech, signs, photographs, pictographs, a voice output system, or written language to convey a multiword message, such as *I want more tickle*

Activity: Adult–Child

Context: Sensory area

Materials: Accompanying visual supports as appropriate

Procedure: Sit opposite the child and hold hands. Rock back and forth, singing "Row, Row, Row Your Boat." Experiment with rate to determine what the child enjoys. Stop rocking and wait for the child to request more of the game. If the child does not respond, prompt him as appropriate. Repeat the sequence many times in the same manner.

Activity: Small Group

Context: Circle time

Materials: Castanets or finger puppets (optional), accompanying visual supports as appropriate

Procedure: Have the children sit on the floor with their legs straight out in front of them. Pretend your fingers are mice (you can also use mouse finger puppets or castanets for added effect), and place a chunk of "cheese" at the children's toes for the mice to eat. Slowly walk your fingers down the children's legs or encourage them to do so as well. Say "Creep mouse," "More creep mouse," or any appropriate word(s). Once your fingers reach the cheese, pretend a cat comes along and quickly run your fingers away. Exaggerate the interaction with animation. Experiment with speed and tickling to determine what the children enjoy. Pair spoken language with signed, gestural or pictographic cues as needed. Once the children are engaged in the game, begin to crawl your fingers down their legs and suddenly stop. Wait and watch for the children to request more of the game. If a child does not respond, prompt him as appropriate. Repeat many times in the same manner. Decrease the amount of prompting as appropriate.

Strategies

- Keep in mind that meaningful activities are the key to social and communicative success.
- Maintain close proximity to the child.
- Establish joint attention.
- Use AAC supports as needed.
- Give the child time to respond.
- Use natural opportunities for interactions whenever possible.
- Use natural, meaningful, motivating, age-appropriate, and organized activities.
- Use the child's visual attention to determine when to prompt.
- Limit the use of verbal prompts in the form of questions.

Activity

B. Socioemotional Skills

Prosocial Statements 2. Requests affection

Sample Means

Communicative gestures: Physical proximity, looking at person, moving person's hand/face, reaching, or pulling person's hand

Emergent: Vocalizations or speech, signs, photographs, pictographs, a voice output system, or written language to say *Hug* or *High-five*

Verbal: Speech, signs, photographs, pictographs, a voice output system, or written language to convey a multiword message, such as *I need a hug, please*

Activity: Adult–Child

Context: Arrival

Materials: Hug symbol or text to add to the child's daily schedule, accompanying visual supports as appropriate

Procedure: Set up a consistent morning routine. Make *Ask for a hug* the first item on the child's schedule; follow this with a highly motivating activity for that specific child. Check the schedule with the child, and prompt him to request a hug from a teacher or peer. Do this daily; one day, allow the child to check his schedule independently. Wait and watch for the child to request a hug. If the child does not respond, prompt him as appropriate. Repeat many times in the same manner. Decrease the amount of prompting as appropriate.

Activity: Small Group

Context: Dramatic play area

Materials: Motivating puppets or figures, accompanying visual supports as appropriate

Procedure: Pretend to put toy figures to bed. Set up a structured bedtime routine. Prior to putting a character to bed, have it request a hug and kiss. Continue to model the same routine with a variety of motivating characters. When the children are familiar with the routine, put the character to bed and stop. Wait and watch for the child to request affection. If a child does not respond, prompt him as appropriate. Repeat many times in the same manner. Decrease the amount of prompting as appropriate.

Strategies

- Acknowledge feelings (e.g., "You are sad; I can give you a hug").
- Point out peers' social behaviors (e.g., "He is giving his mom a hug").
- Use AAC supports that are consistent across various settings.
- Make nonverbal cues more explicit.
- Use nonverbal reinforcement that mirrors the child's emotional state.
- Keep in mind that meaningful activities are the key to social and communicative success.
- Acknowledge the child's communicative efforts as a natural reinforcer.
- Use natural opportunities for interactions whenever possible.
- Use the child's visual attention to determine when to prompt.
- Limit the use of verbal prompts in the form of questions.

Activity

B. Socioemotional Skills
Prosocial Statements 3. Asks someone to play

Sample Means

Communicative gestures: Physical proximity, looking at person, moving person's hand/face, reaching, pulling person's hand, or giving objects

Emergent: Vocalizations or speech, signs, photographs, pictographs, a voice output system, or written language to say *Play*

Verbal: Speech, signs, photographs, pictographs, a voice output system, or written language to convey a multiword message, such as *Will you play ball with me?*

Activity: Adult–Child

Context: Playtime

Materials: Accompanying visual supports as appropriate

Procedure: Send the child to an activity area that you know is another child's favorite. When the child with autism makes a choice, say "(Other child's name) is there; you can ask him to play." Wait to see if the child asks his peer to play. If he does not respond, prompt the child with autism. Continue to set up situations in which the child must ask a peer to play. Repeat many times in the same manner. Decrease the amount of prompting as appropriate.

Activity: Small Group

Context: Recess

Materials: Accompanying visual supports as appropriate

Procedure: Play a game such as The Farmer in the Dell or Duck, Duck, Goose. Teach the children to say "Goose, will you chase me?" or "Will you come in the circle with me?" Pair spoken language with signed, gestural, or pictographic cues as needed. Continue to play the game; wait and watch for the children to ask peers to play. If a child does not respond, prompt him as appropriate. Repeat many times in the same manner. Decrease the amount of prompting as appropriate.

Contexts for Generalization

- If the child gives an adult a toy, redirect him to a peer.
- Require the child to ask a peer to play lotto games.
- Refuse pushing the child on the swing; require him to ask a peer.
- Make it so the child cannot eat lunch or snack until he asks a peer.
- Make it so the child cannot go outside for recess until he asks a peer.
- Require the child to ask a peer to bounce a ball from child to child.
- Require the child to ask a peer to throw a beanbag from child to child.
- Encourage the child to ask a peer to play on a seesaw, a rocking toy, or another activity that requires two children.
- Ask someone to play during all motivating social contexts.

DO-WATCH-LISTEN-SAY: Social and Communication Intervention for Children with Autism
by Kathleen Ann Quill © 2000 Paul H. Brookes Publishing Co.

Activity

B. Socioemotional Skills
Prosocial Statements 4. Politeness

Sample Means

Communicative gestures: Not applicable

Emergent: Vocalizations or speech, signs, photographs, pictographs, a voice output system, or written language to say *Please*

Verbal: Speech, signs, photographs, pictographs, a voice output system, or written language to convey a multiword message, such as *Can I have cookies, please?*

Activity: Adult–Child

Context: Dramatic play area

Materials: Any book about manners (e.g., *Mind Your Manners, Ben Bunny*), props to act out the book, accompanying visual supports as appropriate

Procedure: Read the book to the child so he becomes familiar with the story. Set up the dramatic play area to reenact the book. Wait and watch for the child to use polite words. If the child does not respond, prompt him as appropriate. Repeat many times in the same manner. Decrease the amount of prompting as appropriate.

Activity: Small Group

Context: Circle time

Materials: Homemade video of children acting out polite situations and impolite situations, as well as the consequences of both (e.g., show a child running into a teacher, knocking her over, and sitting in time-out; show the same child saying "Excuse me" to the teacher and receiving verbal praise); accompanying visual supports as appropriate

Procedure: Watch the manners video frequently. Make many concrete associations. Keep language simple and consistent. Pair spoken language with signed, gestural, or pictographic cues as needed. Role-play the situations from the video. Watch it and wait for the children to use polite words. If the children do not use polite words, prompt them as appropriate. Repeat many times in the same manner. Decrease the amount of prompting as appropriate.

Strategies

- Use AAC supports as needed.
- Use exaggerated facial expressions and gestures.
- Use rhythmic language as appropriate.
- Give the child time to respond.
- Use the most natural opportunities for interactions whenever possible.
- Clarify expectations.
- Limit the use of verbal prompting in the form of questions.
- Teach meaningful social and communication replacement behaviors at the moment the child is engaged in inappropriate behavior.
- Acknowledge the child's communication efforts as a natural reinforcer.
- Focus on contexts in which the child is motivated to communicate.
- Shadow the child and provide scripts of what to say to peers.

DO-WATCH-LISTEN-SAY: Social and Communication Intervention for Children with Autism
by Kathleen Ann Quill © 2000 Paul H. Brookes Publishing Co.

Activity

B. Socioemotional Skills
Prosocial Statements 5. Shares

Sample Means

Communicative gestures: Moving person's hand/face, pulling person's hand, giving objects, or moving object toward another person

Emergent: Vocalizations or speech, signs, photographs, pictographs, a voice output system, or written language to say *Here* or *Share*

Verbal: Speech, signs, photographs, pictographs, a voice output system, or written language to convey a multiword message, such as *Do you want some candy?*

Activity: Adult–Child

Context: Snack time

Materials: Motivating snacks, sandwich bags or small containers, accompanying visual supports as appropriate

Procedure: Appoint the child with autism as the special helper. Give him a special crown, a badge, or any other motivating item. Exaggerate the interaction with animation. Give the child the candy; ask him to count out the snacks and to prepare a bag for each child in the room. Say "Time to share the candy," "Share," or other appropriate word(s). Continue daily, and wait and watch for the child to share his candy. If the child does not respond, prompt him as appropriate. Repeat many times in the same manner. Decrease the amount of prompting as appropriate.

Activity: Small Group

Context: Music

Materials: Prize that is wrapped or boxed in many layers, accompanying visual supports as appropriate

Procedure: Play music and pass the prize around. When the music stops, the child holding the package must unwrap the first layer. Start the music again and continue passing the prize. Repeat, consistently saying the words "Give the package to (next child's name)," "Share," or any appropriate word(s). Continue to pass the prize, but remain silent. Wait and watch for the children to continue the game by sharing. If a child does not respond, prompt him as appropriate. Repeat many times in the same manner. Decrease the amount of prompting as appropriate.

Contexts for Generalization

- Play Wonder Ball at recess.
- Organize a treasure hunt for missing art supplies; the child who finds the box must share its contents.
- Give out drinks/snacks at mealtimes.
- Have the child share snack items such as bananas or grapes with friends.
- Order a pizza and share the slices.
- Make special occasion gift bags full of goodies for all of the children; have one child help divide up the contents.
- Give one child all of the trucks; send another child to play with the garage so the first child must share.
- Share food/drink/object during all motivating social contexts.

DO-WATCH-LISTEN-SAY: Social and Communication Intervention for Children with Autism
by Kathleen Ann Quill © 2000 Paul H. Brookes Publishing Co.

Activity

B. Socioemotional Skills:
Prosocial Statements 6. Assertiveness

Sample Means

Communicative gestures: Physical proximity, looking at person, moving person's hand/face, reaching, pulling person's hand, moving object away, or shaking/nodding head

Emergent: Vocalization or speech, signs, photographs, pictographs, a voice output system, or written language to say *No* or *Mine*

Verbal: Speech, signs, photographs, pictographs, a voice output system, or written language to convey a multiword message, such as *Give it back; that's mine*

Activity: Adult–Child

Context: Any activity

Materials: Materials for the favorite activity, accompanying visual supports as appropriate

Procedure: Allow the child to engage in a favorite activity (e.g., playing with blocks). Intervene once the child is settled, and suddenly remove the block that the child was using. Another adult prompts the child to say "That's mine," "Give it back," or any appropriate word(s). Pair spoken language with signed, gestural, or pictographic cues as needed. Continue to allow the child to play, and periodically take something away. Wait and watch for the child to demonstrate assertiveness. If the child does not respond, prompt him as appropriate. Repeat the sequence many times in the same manner. Decrease the amount of prompting as appropriate.

Activity: Small Group

Context: Gym

Materials: Chairs, music, accompanying visual supports as appropriate

Procedure: Play musical chairs. Appoint one child to be the organizer for each round. That child wears a special hat and badge. When the music stops and one child is left without a chair, the organizer must say "You're out; go away." Each child should have a turn as the organizer. Keep the language consistent and pair spoken language with signed, gestural, or pictographic cues as needed. Continue playing, and wait and watch for the children to demonstrate assertiveness. If a child does not respond, prompt him as appropriate. Repeat many times in the same manner. Decrease the amount of prompting as appropriate.

Strategies

- Use AAC supports as needed.
- Shadow the child and provide scripts of what to say to peers.
- Give the child time to respond.
- Use the most natural opportunities for interactions whenever possible.
- Teach meaningful social and communication replacement behaviors at the moment the child is engaged in inappropriate behavior.
- Acknowledge feelings (e.g., "You don't like when he pushes you; tell him to stop").
- Point out peers' social behaviors (e.g., "You told Kara to give it back, and she did").
- Make nonverbal cues more explicit.

Activity

B. Socioemotional Skills
Prosocial Statements 7. Gives affection

Sample Means

Communicative gestures: Physical proximity, looking at person, moving person's hand/face, reaching, pulling person's hand, or giving objects

Emergent: Vocalizations or speech, signs, photographs, pictographs, a voice output system, or written language to say *Hug*

Verbal: Speech, signs, photographs, pictographs, a voice output system, or written language to convey a multiword message, such as *Do you need a hug?*

Activity: Adult–Child

Context: Books

Materials: Paper, markers, cardboard, rings, photographs, and any other supplies to make a social story; accompanying visual supports as appropriate

Procedure: Write a social story that describes situations in which the child can share affection with his parents, how his parents would feel, and what he would do to share affection. The complexity must mirror the child's language comprehension. Social stories may be audiotaped or may include illustrations. Use concrete and simple language. For instance, write "(Child's name) hugs his mom. His mom hugs (child's name). It feels good to hug." Read the story to the child every day as part of his routine. Send a copy of the story home and encourage the child's parents to read the story daily as well. Use the story's language for any naturally occurring situation.

Activity: Small Group

Context: Music

Materials: Favorite attachment item for each child (e.g., teddy bear), accompanying visual supports as appropriate

Procedure: Sing the *Barney* theme song. Hug and kiss an attachment item. Say "Hug Teddy," "Kiss," or any appropriate word(s). Pair spoken language with signed, gestural, or pictographic cues as needed. Continue to sing the song, but stop and wait and watch for the children to give affection. If a child does not respond, prompt him as appropriate. Repeat many times in the same manner. Decrease the amount of prompting as appropriate.

Strategies

- Use AAC supports as needed.
- Shadow the child and provide scripts of what to say or do.
- Use the most natural opportunities for interactions whenever possible.
- Acknowledge peers' feelings (e.g., "Shane is sad; you could give him a hug").
- Point out peers' social behaviors (e.g., "Brianna fell down, so she asked Mrs. Smith for a hug").
- Make nonverbal cues more explicit.
- Balance adult-directed interactions with child-directed interactions.
- Respond to the child's level of focused purposeful behavior at the moment.

Activity

B. Socioemotional Skills
Prosocial Statements 8. Gives help

Sample Means

Communicative gestures: Physical proximity, looking at person, moving person's hand/face, reaching, pulling person's hand, giving objects, or moving object toward/away

Emergent: Vocalizations or speech, signs, photographs, pictographs, a voice output system, or written language to say *Help*

Verbal: Speech, signs, photographs, pictographs, a voice output system, or written language to convey a multiword message, such as *Do you need help?*

Activity: Adult–Child

Context: Snack time or lunchtime

Materials: Motivating foods in closed containers, accompanying visual supports as appropriate

Procedure: Pretend to have difficulty opening a lunch container. Say "I need help" or any appropriate word(s). Look directly at the child and hand him the container. Pair spoken language with signed, gestural, or pictographic cues as needed. Wait and watch for the child to offer help. If the child does not respond, prompt him as appropriate. Repeat many times in the same manner. Decrease the amount of prompting as appropriate.

Activity: Small Group

Context: Music

Materials: Tape recorder, accompanying visual supports as appropriate

Procedure: Establish a routine to prepare for music time. For example, practice setting up the chairs, turning on the tape player, or adjusting the tape player's volume. Exaggerate the importance of these steps, and repeat them every day. Then begin the routine and omit a step (e.g., "Oops, I forgot the chairs; I need help"). Wait and watch for the children to initiate helping. If a child does not respond, prompt him as appropriate. Repeat the sequence many times in the same manner for various steps of the routine. Decrease the amount of prompting as appropriate.

Strategies

- Use AAC supports as needed.
- Shadow the child and provide scripts of what to say or do.
- Use the most natural opportunities for interactions whenever possible.
- Acknowledge peers' feelings (e.g., "Michael can't finish the puzzle; you could help him with that piece").
- Point out peers' social behaviors (e.g., "José can't reach his backpack, so he asked Mary to help him").
- Act as an interpreter for others.
- Clarify expectations.
- Balance adult-directed interactions with child-directed interactions.
- Respond to the child's level of focused purposeful behavior at the moment.

Activity

B. Socioemotional Skills
Prosocial Statements 9. Offers a choice

Sample Means

Communicative gestures: Giving objects, moving object toward, or contact or distal pointing

Emergent: Vocalizations or speech, signs, photographs, pictographs, a voice output system, or written language to say *Choose* or *This or that*

Verbal: Speech, signs, photographs, pictographs, a voice output system, or written language to convey a multiword message, such as *Do you want juice or crackers?*

Activity: Adult–Child

Context: Computer

Materials: Any motivating computer program, cue card

Procedure: At the computer, the adult and child alternate offering each other choices from a list of items activated in the software program. For example, the adult models "Do you want to see the _____ or the _____?" and allows the child to make a choice. Next, the child offers the adult a choice with the help of a cue card. The adult and child continue to alternate offering each other a choice. Repeat many times in the same manner. Decrease the amount of prompting as appropriate.

Activity: Small Group

Context: Snack

Materials: Two choices of preferred snack items, accompanying visual supports as appropriate

Procedure: Appoint a snack helper who asks questions such as "Do you want pretzels or Cheez-Its?" Have the snack helper ask each child in the class. Continue daily, and give the snack helper two snacks. Wait and watch for the child to offer a choice to his peers. If the child does not respond, prompt him as appropriate. Repeat many times in the same manner. Decrease the amount of prompting as appropriate. Have the same snack helper for a few days if needed.

Strategies

- Act as an interpreter for others.
- Clarify expectations.
- Balance adult-directed interactions with child-directed interactions.
- Respond to the child's level of focused purposeful behavior at the moment.
- Maintain close proximity to the child.
- Give the child time to respond.
- Use natural opportunities for interactions whenever possible.
- Structure the environment so that the space and materials are clearly defined.
- Offer the child maximum support to ensure success; fade prompts from the most assistance to the least.
- Use AAC supports as needed.
- Shadow the child, and provide scripts of what to say or do.

Activity

B. Socioemotional Skills
Prosocial Statements 10. Gives comfort

Sample Means

Communicative gestures: Physical proximity, looking at person, or reaching for/hugging person

Emergent: Vocalizations or speech, signs, photographs, pictographs, a voice output system, or written language to say *Sorry* or *You okay?*

Verbal: Speech, signs, photographs, pictographs, a voice output system, or written language to convey a multiword message, such as *Are you okay?* or *Do you feel okay?*

Activity: Adult–Child

Context: Any activity

Materials: Paper, markers, cardboard, rings, and any other supplies to make a social story; accompanying visual supports as appropriate

Procedure: Write a story about giving comfort that includes pictures and simple phrases, such as "She's hurt. Ask if she's okay" or "He's sad. Ask, 'Do you need a hug?'" Individualize the complexity of the book. Read it frequently to the child. Use the same words from the book to comment on similar naturally occurring situations. In these contexts, wait and watch for the child to give comfort. If the child does not respond, prompt him as appropriate. Repeat the sequence many times in the same manner. Decrease the amount of prompting as appropriate.

Activity: Small Group

Context: Dramatic play area

Materials: Dolls that cry (or commercially available computerized "pets" that require care), accompanying visual supports as appropriate

Procedure: Encourage the children to play with dolls. Say "Oh, you need a hug" or any appropriate word(s) whenever a child's doll cries. Exaggerate the interaction with animation. The next time the doll cries, wait and watch for the child to offer comfort. If a child does not respond, prompt him as appropriate. Repeat many times in the same manner. Decrease the amount of prompting as appropriate.

Strategies

- Act as an interpreter for others.
- Clarify expectations.
- Balance adult-directed interactions with child-directed interactions.
- Respond to the child's level of focused purposeful behavior at the moment.
- Maintain close proximity to the child.
- Give the child time to respond.
- Use natural opportunities for interactions whenever possible.
- Offer the child maximum support to ensure success; fade prompts from the most assistance to the least.
- Use AAC supports as needed.
- Shadow the child, and provide scripts of what to say or do.
- Acknowledge peers' feelings (e.g., "Sean is sad because his mother left; you could give him a hug").

Activity

C. Basic Conversational Skills

Verbal 1. Initiates by gaining person's attention/calling name

Sample Means

Communicative gestures: Physical proximity, looking at person, moving person's face, or reaching/pulling person's hand

Emergent: Vocalization or speech, signs, photographs, pictographs, a voice output system, or written language to say *Hey* or a person's name

Verbal: Speech, signs, photographs, pictographs, a voice output system, or written language to convey a multiword message, such as *Hey (person's name)*

Activity: Adult–Child

Context: Work time

Materials: A preferred toy, book, or attachment item; accompanying visual supports

Procedure: Take the child's motivating object away, and give it to someone else as the child is watching. Prompt the child to go to that other person and gain the person's attention to retrieve the desired item. Pair spoken language with signed, gestural, or pictographic cues as needed. Repeat many times in the same manner with various adults and peers. Decrease the amount of prompting as appropriate.

Activity: Small Group

Context: Any activity

Materials: Cue cards color-coded green

Procedure: Make cue cards of conversational starters, such as "Say your friend's name first," "Hi," or "What's up?" Individualize with photographs, pictographs, or written text as appropriate for the child. Use the cue cards to remind the child what to say and/or to provide the child with an alternative means of communication. Preview and practice with the cue cards in adult–child interactions prior to generalizing to group activities.

Strategies

- Offer the child maximum support to ensure success.
- Remember that meaningful activities are key to social and communicative success.
- Focus on contexts in which the child is motivated to communicate.
- Use the child's visual attention to determine when to prompt.
- Use AAC supports as needed.
- Maintain close proximity to the child.
- Give the child time to respond.
- Maximize the use of verbal modeling.
- Shadow the child, and provide scripts of what to say to peers.

Activity

C. Basic Conversational Skills

Verbal 2. Terminates conversation with a routine script

Sample Means

Communicative gestures: Not applicable

Emergent: Vocalization or speech, signs, photographs, pictographs, a voice output system, or written language to say *Bye* or *See ya*

Verbal: Speech, signs, photographs, pictographs, a voice output system, or written language to convey a multiword message, such as *I gotta go now*, *See ya,* or *Bye*

Activity: Adult–Child

Context: Any activity

Materials: Cue cards color-coded red

Procedure: Make cue cards of messages to terminate conversations, such as "Bye," "I gotta go now," or "See you later." Individualize with photographs, pictographs, or written text as appropriate for the child. Use the cue cards to remind the child what to say and/or to provide the child with an alternative means of communication. Preview and practice with the cue cards in adult–child interactions prior to generalizing to group activities.

Activity: Small Group

Context: Books

Materials: Social story

Procedure: Create a social story that includes all of the children in the class. Each page provides an example, such as "Katie says 'I gotta go now' when she is all done talking to her friend. John says 'Bye' when he is finished talking to the store clerk. Alex says 'I'll see you later' when he is all done talking to his mom." Read the social story aloud to a small group of children daily. Language used within the classroom during similar situations must be consistent with the language used in the story. Also use puppets and/or dolls and figurines to act out the story.

Strategies

- Offer the child maximum support to ensure success
- Remember that meaningful activities are key to social and communicative success.
- Focus on contexts in which the child is motivated to communicate.
- Use the child's visual attention to determine when to prompt.
- Use AAC supports as needed.
- Maintain close proximity to the child.
- Give the child time to respond.
- Maximize the use of verbal modeling.
- Shadow the child, and provide scripts of what to say to peers.

Activity

C. Basic Conversational Skills

Verbal 3. Maintains conversation
by sharing information with a routine script

Sample Means

Communicative gestures: Not applicable

Emergent: Vocalization or speech, signs, photographs, pictographs, a voice output system, or written language to say _____ *(any object from a familiar book)*

Verbal: Speech, signs, photographs, pictographs, a voice output system, or written language to convey a multiword message, such as *I see a (name of object)* or *Yesterday, I went swimming*

Activity: Adult–Child

Context: Books

Materials: Motivating books and accompanying visual supports as appropriate

Procedure: Read a motivating book. Point to various pictures on each page and say "I see a (name of item on page)." Do this routinely throughout the book. Once the child is familiar with the activity, pause while pointing to pictures in the book, and wait for the child to fill in the target word. Later point and wait for the child to fill in the entire phrase. If the child does not respond, prompt him to complete the phrase. Take turns: Make your comment first, then allow the child to comment. Repeat many times in the same manner. Decrease the amount of prompting as appropriate.

Activity: Small Group

Context: Work time

Materials: Journal for each child containing sheets structured in the following manner:

Today, I _____; Yesterday, I _____; Tomorrow, I want to _____.

Procedure: Individualize the journals for each child, using pictographs, photographs, or written text. Provide a limited choice of responses for a child who has difficulty with open-ended tasks. Pick a set time each day when the children can complete their journals (with the help of an adult, if needed). Once the journals are completed, pair two children of similar abilities to share their journals. Prompt the children to take turns sharing the information in their journals. Once the children are familiar with the format of their journals, have them share the information without reading it so it is more of a conversational exchange. For example:

Child 1: Today, I took the bus to school.

Child 2: Today, my mommy brought me to school.

Child 1: Yesterday, I went swimming.

Child 2: Yesterday, I went to the park.

Child 1: Tomorrow, I want to play with the computer.

Child 2: Tomorrow, I want to go to McDonalds.

Strategies

- Use two adults: one who physically assists the child and one who receives the message.
- Shadow the child, and provide scripts of what to say to peers.
- Remember that meaningful activities are key to social and communicative success.
- Maximize the use of verbal modeling.
- Imitate and expand on the child's successful initiations.
- Balance adult-directed interactions with child-directed interactions.

DO-WATCH-LISTEN-SAY: Social and Communication Intervention for Children with Autism
by Kathleen Ann Quill © 2000 Paul H. Brookes Publishing Co.

Activity

C. Basic Conversational Skills

Verbal 4. Clarifies or persists by repeating message

Sample Means

Communicative gestures: Not applicable

Emergent: Vocalization or speech, signs, photographs, pictographs, a voice output system, or written language to repeat the message

Verbal: Speech, signs, photographs, pictographs, a voice output system, or written language to repeat the message

Activity: Adult–Child

Context: Any activity

Materials: Accompanying visual supports as appropriate

Procedure: Give the child something other than what he requested. Say "You wanted the (object name)" as you hand the child that wrong item. Pair spoken language with signed, gestural, or pictographic cues as needed. Wait and watch for the child to repeat his message. If the child does not respond, prompt him to persist. Repeat many times.

Activity: Small Group

Context: Gym

Materials: Accompanying visual supports as appropriate

Procedure: Play Duck, Duck, Goose. When a child taps your head and says "Duck," say "Oh, goose," stand up, and begin to chase as if he had said "goose." Have another adult prompt the child to repeat his message of *duck*. Sit down and say, "Oh, you said 'duck.'" Exaggerate the interaction with animation. Pair spoken language with signed, gestural, or pictographic cues as needed. Repeat many times in the same manner, continuing to prompt the child as needed.

Strategies

- Respond to the child's level of focused purposeful behavior at the moment.
- Repeat the same message at predictable times.
- Link verbal reinforcement to what the child is doing.
- Use AAC supports as needed.
- Give the child time to respond.
- Act as an interpreter for others.
- Clarify expectations.
- Use the child's visual attention to determine when to prompt.

Activity

C. Basic Conversational Skills

Verbal 5. Maintains conversation when
the partner structures the interaction

Sample Means

Communicative gestures: Not applicable

Emergent: Vocalization or speech, signs, photographs, pictographs, a voice output system, or written language to use single words within a conversational exchange

Verbal: Speech, signs, photographs, pictographs, a voice output system, or written language to convey a multiword message within a conversational exchange

Activity: Adult–Child

Context: Telephone

Materials: Telephone, visual display

Procedure: Create a telephone conversation script with one familiar person, such as the following:

Grandma:	Hi, Ryan, it's Grandma.
Ryan:	Hi, Grandma. How are you?
Grandma:	Great. How are you?
Ryan:	Good.
Grandma:	Tell me one thing you did at school today.
Ryan:	I ate my lunch.

Give one copy of the script to Grandma and keep one by the telephone at home. Have Grandma call Ryan each night. If Ryan does not respond, prompt him as appropriate. Repeat the sequence many times in the same manner.

Activity: Small Group

Context: Cooking

Materials: Cards (individualized with pictographs, photographs, or written text) depicting each step of a familiar cooking activity (e.g., baking cookies)

Procedure: After the cooking activity is finished, give each child a card with the step he completed. Use the cards to structure the conversation about baking the cookies. Have the children say what they did. For example, one child says "I put the egg in," and another says "I used the big spoon to stir." If the children do not respond, prompt them to say what step they completed during the activity. Repeat many times.

Strategies

- Remember that meaningful activities are key to social and communicative success.
- Focus on contexts in which the child is motivated to communicate.
- Use the child's visual attention to determine when to prompt.
- Use AAC supports as needed.
- Maximize the use of verbal modeling.
- Shadow the child, and provide scripts of what to say to peers.
- Imitate and expand on the child's successful initiations.
- Balance adult-directed interactions with child-directed interactions.

DO-WATCH-LISTEN-SAY: Social and Communication Intervention for Children with Autism
by Kathleen Ann Quill © 2000 Paul H. Brookes Publishing Co.

Activity

C. Basic Conversational Skills

Verbal 6. Initiates conversation with routine scripts

Sample Means

Communicative gestures: Not applicable

Emergent: Vocalization or speech, signs, photographs, pictographs, a voice output system, or written language to say *Let's talk*

Verbal: Speech, signs, photographs, pictographs, a voice output system, or written language to convey a multiword message, such as *Hi, I'm Kathleen. What are you doing?*

Activity: Adult–Child

Context: Telephone

Materials: Telephone, visual display

Procedure: Make a cue card for the child with a telephone script, such as "Hello, this is Jason. One minute please." Accompany the text with pictures if that is appropriate for the child. Attach the cue card with Velcro next to every telephone. When the telephone rings, prompt the child to get the cue card, pick up the telephone, and follow the script. Prompt the child as appropriate, and repeat the sequence many times in the same manner.

Activity: Small Group

Context: Work

Materials: Videotape, accompanying visual supports as appropriate

Procedure: Videotape familiar adults and peers using a targeted single message in social contexts. Examples include "Hi, my name is (person's name). What is your name?" or "I'm playing (activity name). What are you doing?" Make the communicative message the most salient aspect of the video. Use video modeling for instruction by showing the video daily or even more often if the children are interested. Preview the video prior to actual social situations. Use a cue card as an instructional prompt in the actual setting, and gradually fade the frequency of video previews until the skill is mastered.

Strategies

- Offer the child maximum support to ensure success.
- Remember that meaningful activities are key to social and communicative success.
- Focus on contexts in which the child is motivated to communicate.
- Use the child's visual attention to determine when to prompt.
- Use AAC supports as needed.
- Maintain close proximity to the child.
- Give the child time to respond.
- Maximize the use of verbal modeling.
- Shadow the child, and provide scripts of what to say to peers.

Activity

C. Basic Conversational Skills

Verbal 7. Maintains conversation by providing feedback

Sample Means

Communicative gestures: Not applicable

Emergent: Vocalization or speech, signs, photographs, pictographs, a voice output system, or written language to say *Uh-huh, I know,* or *Okay*

Verbal: Speech, signs, photographs, pictographs, a voice output system, or written language to convey a multiword message, such as *Really? Wow!*

Activity: Adult–Child

Context: Any activity

Materials: Social story

Procedure: Write a social story about listening and providing feedback. Use simple language, such as "When my friend is talking, I need to say 'Uh-huh' or nod my head. I say 'Uh-huh' so my friend knows I heard him." The complexity of the story should mirror the child's level and should be individualized with pictographs, photographs, or written text. Read the social story daily. Use the same phrases from the story in all naturally occurring situations.

Activity: Small Group

Context: Games

Materials: Two sets of materials to complete an activity, cue cards

Procedure: Give two children the exact same project materials (e.g., blocks, stickers). Set up a barrier so the children cannot see each other's work area. Each child takes a turn providing a directive. For example, "Glue the circle in the middle of the page" or "Put the triangle on top of the circle." The goal is for both projects to look identical. Give each child an *Uh-huh* or *Okay* cue card. The child receiving the directive acknowledges that he heard and understood the message. If the child does not respond, prompt him to say "Uh-huh" or "Okay" with the cue card. Repeat many times.

Strategies

- Establish a pattern of messages that predictably occurs at set times during the interaction and activity.
- Remember that meaningful activities are key to social and communicative success.
- Focus on contexts in which the child is motivated to communicate.
- Use the child's visual attention to determine when to prompt.
- Use AAC supports as needed.
- Maintain close proximity to the child.
- Give the child time to respond.
- Maximize the use of verbal modeling.
- Shadow the child, and provide scripts of what to say to peers.

Activity

C. Basic Conversational Skills
Verbal 8. Maintains conversation in novel contexts

Sample Means

Communicative gestures: Not applicable

Emergent: Single words

Verbal: Multiword message

Activity: Adult–Child

Context: Work time

Materials: Words/pictures depicting common classroom vocabulary, Velcro or magnet board

Procedure: Set up a Velcro or magnet board on a clipboard or an easel. The child should be able to manipulate and rearrange the words easily. Begin novel conversation about classroom happenings by using the words on the board. Give the child time to respond. If the child does not respond, prompt him to take a turn. Repeat many times in the same manner. Decrease the amount of prompting as appropriate. Some specific ways to use a chart—beginning with an easy example—follow:

People - Do - What

Kathy - plays - blocks

Mom - plays - marbles

Dad - blows - bubbles

People - Where - Do - Say

Kathy - playground - swing - this is fun

Mom - store - buy pizza - this is for dinner

Dad - school - play with computer - wow

Activity: Small Group

Context: Games

Materials: Game board with a spinner that points to words/pictographs for *what, where, why, when, who,* and *how;* accompanying visual supports as appropriate

Procedure: Make a list of interesting topics. Write each topic on the top of a piece of paper. Take turns using the spinner. The child must ask the type of question indicated by the spinner. Write the answer on the sheet under the appropriate topic. The topic sheets can help guide conversation by providing the children with many details about that topic.

Strategies

- Offer the child maximum support to ensure success.
- Acknowledge the child's communicative efforts as a natural reinforcer.
- Repeat back the child's message, and add new and relevant information.
- Organize messages so that what the adult says or does is equally appropriate for the child to say or do in the same situation.
- Balance adult-directed interactions with child-directed interactions.
- Use AAC supports as needed.
- Maintain close proximity to the child.
- Give the child time to respond.
- Maximize the use of verbal modeling.
- Provide the child with scripts of what to say to peers.

DO-WATCH-LISTEN-SAY: Social and Communication Intervention for Children with Autism
by Kathleen Ann Quill © 2000 Paul H. Brookes Publishing Co.

Activity

C. Basic Conversational Skills

Verbal 9. Maintains conversation using appropriate topics

Sample Means

Communicative gestures: Not applicable

Emergent: Single words

Verbal: Multiword message

Activity: Adult–Child

Context: Any activity

Materials: Materials to make a conversation book (e.g., paper and pencils)

Procedure: Make a conversation book detailing topics about which the child has a lot of knowledge. Individualize the conversation book with photographs, pictographs, or written text. List topics about which the child knows a good deal of information. (Ideally, the child brainstorms to provide chosen topics ahead of time.) Also list situation-specific topics (e.g., what to say at the library or a restaurant) and person-specific topics (e.g., what to say to a minister, store clerk, or doctor). The conversation book can be organized in the form of a wallet, a small book, or any other portable means. Prior to social situations, review the book with the child. Prompt him to maintain the topic if necessary.

Activity: Small Group

Context: Any activity

Materials: Materials to make a conversation book (e.g., paper, pencils)

Procedure: Make a book that organizes topics of conversation with partners. Individualize the conversation book with photographs, pictographs, or written text. A child and two friends then make detailed lists of favorite topics (e.g., television, sports, foods). A page in the book looks like this:

Child

I like _____

Because _____

Friend 1

I like _____

Because _____

Friend 2

I like _____

Because _____

The children then use the book to review the interests of their friends prior to social situations. The book helps the children summarize conversational topics appropriate during interactions with peers. For example:

I can ask (Friend 1) about _____

(Friend 1) and I can talk about _____

I can ask (Friend 2) about _____

(Friend 2) and I can talk about _____

DO-WATCH-LISTEN-SAY: Social and Communication Intervention for Children with Autism
by Kathleen Ann Quill © 2000 Paul H. Brookes Publishing Co.

Strategies

- Offer the child maximum support to ensure success.
- Repeat back the child's message, and add new and relevant information.
- Balance adult-directed interactions with child-directed interactions.
- Use AAC supports as needed.
- Maintain close proximity to the child.
- Give the child time to respond.
- Maximize the use of verbal modeling.
- Shadow the child, and provide scripts of what to say to peers.

Activity

C. Basic Conversational Skills
Nonverbal 1. Attends/orients to speaker

Sample Means

Communicative gestures: Not applicable

Emergent: Single words

Verbal: Multiword message

Activity: Adult–Child and/or Small Group

(Activity applies to objectives 1–5 of "Nonverbal.")

Context: Any activity

Materials: Sociobehavioral display clarifying desirable social behaviors

Procedure: Individualize the display with photographs, pictographs, or written text. Use it to refocus the child's attention during social situations. The display must clearly specify the desired behaviors stated in positive, concrete, and concise terms, such as

- I will look at the person with whom I am talking.
- I can touch someone's arm gently.
- I will use my inside voice.
- First, I will start a conversation. Then, I will watch the other person. He will look at me and smile, nod, or make another positive gesture if he wants to talk to me. If the other person indicates that he wants to talk, I can keep talking.

Strategies

- Use AAC supports as needed.
- Mirror the child's emotional state with nonverbal reinforcement.
- Act as an interpreter for others.
- Shadow the child, and provide scripts of what to do during social exchanges.
- Consider the most natural setting for the acquisition of target skills.
- Make nonverbal cues more explicit.
- Use dramatic facial expressions, exaggerated gestures, and animation.
- Use the child's visual attention to determine when to prompt.

DO-WATCH-LISTEN-SAY: Social and Communication Intervention for Children with Autism
by Kathleen Ann Quill © 2000 Paul H. Brookes Publishing Co.

Activity

C. Basic Conversational Skills

Nonverbal 2. Maintains natural proximity to speaker

Sample Means

> *Communicative gestures:* Not applicable
> *Emergent:* Single words
> *Verbal:* Multiword message

Activity: Adult–Child and/or Small Group

> (Activity applies to objectives 1–5 of "Nonverbal.")
>
> *Context:* Any activity
>
> *Materials:* Accompanying visual supports as appropriate
>
> *Procedure:* Videotape familiar adults and peers exaggerating nonverbal cues (e.g., body language), both appropriately and inappropriately. Watch the video daily or even more often if the child is interested. Assist the child in identifying the nonverbal skills presented. Create a social encyclopedia to help the child visualize a relationship between social behaviors. Preview the video prior to social interactions and use a cue card as an instructional prompt.

Strategies

- Use AAC supports as needed.
- Mirror the child's emotional state with nonverbal reinforcement.
- Act as an interpreter for others.
- Shadow the child, and provide scripts of what to do during social exchanges.
- Consider the most natural setting for the acquisition of target skills.
- Make nonverbal cues more explicit.
- Use dramatic facial expressions, exaggerated gestures, and animation.
- Use the child's visual attention to determine when to prompt.

Activity

C. Basic Conversational Skills

Nonverbal 3. Discriminates appropriate and inappropriate touching during a conversation

Sample Means

Communicative gestures: Not applicable

Emergent: Single words

Verbal: Multiword message

Activity: Adult–Child and/or Small Group

(Activity applies to objectives 1–5 of "Nonverbal.")

Context: Dramatic play area

Materials: Life-size doll or stuffed animal, accompanying visual supports as appropriate

Procedure: Role-play what types of touching are acceptable during a conversation. Exaggerate the interaction with animation and make it fun. Encourage the child to role-play these situations as well. Prompt the child to describe types of touching (e.g., "Tapping a shoulder gently is okay"). Repeat many times in the same manner. Decrease the amount of prompting as appropriate.

Strategies

- Use AAC supports as needed.
- Mirror the child's emotional state with nonverbal reinforcement.
- Act as an interpreter for others.
- Shadow the child, and provide scripts of what to do during social exchanges.
- Consider the most natural setting for the acquisition of target skills.
- Make nonverbal cues more explicit.
- Use dramatic facial expressions, exaggerated gestures, and animation.
- Use the child's visual attention to determine when to prompt.

DO-WATCH-LISTEN-SAY: Social and Communication Intervention for Children with Autism
by Kathleen Ann Quill © 2000 Paul H. Brookes Publishing Co.

Activity

C. Basic Conversational Skills
Nonverbal 4. Modulates volume of voice for the setting

Sample Means

Communicative gestures: Not applicable
Emergent: Single words
Verbal: Multiword message

Activity: Adult–Child and/or Small Group

(Activity applies to objectives 1–5 of "Nonverbal.")

Context: Work time

Materials: Tape recorder, cue card

Procedure: Make a cue card that reads

> 1 = whisper
>
> 2 = okay
>
> 3 = too loud

Tape record the child, and listen to the tape together. Pair the voice on the tape player with the terms *whisper, okay,* and *too loud.* Once the child can identify whether his voice is "okay" on the tape, use the cue card to prompt appropriate voice modulation in natural contexts.

Strategies

- Use AAC supports as needed.
- Mirror the child's emotional state with nonverbal reinforcement.
- Act as an interpreter for others.
- Shadow the child, and provide scripts of what to do during social exchanges.
- Consider the most natural setting for the acquisition of target skills.
- Make nonverbal cues more explicit.
- Use dramatic facial expressions, exaggerated gestures, and animation.
- Use the child's visual attention to determine when to prompt.

DO-WATCH-LISTEN-SAY: Social and Communication Intervention for Children with Autism
by Kathleen Ann Quill © 2000 Paul H. Brookes Publishing Co.

Activity

C. Basic Conversational Skills
Nonverbal 5. Watches/waits for listener confirmation before continuing message

Sample Means

Communicative gestures: Not applicable

Emergent: Single words

Verbal: Multiword message

Activity: Adult–Child and/or Small Group

(Activity applies to objectives 1–5 of "Nonverbal.")

Context: Any activity

Materials: Writing materials and notebook

Procedure: Note each social interaction in a journal. This running log should include columns for the following information: setting, problem, and solution. Fill in the *setting* and *problem* columns. Color-code similar problems. Also note any situations the child solves on his own, and reinforce the child as appropriate. Review the log with the child at the end of the day. Brainstorm for solutions to the problems, and write them in the *solution* column. Review the previous day's log each morning, and remind the child of the solutions as well as any problems that he solved independently.

Strategies

- Use AAC supports as needed.
- Mirror the child's emotional state with nonverbal reinforcement.
- Act as an interpreter for others.
- Shadow the child, and provide scripts of what to do during social exchanges.
- Consider the most natural setting for the acquisition of target skills.
- Make nonverbal cues more explicit.
- Use dramatic facial expressions, exaggerated gestures, and animation.
- Use the child's visual attention to determine when to prompt.

Appendix A
Communication Skills Progress Sheets

Communication Sample

Child's name:_____ Date:_____

Directions: 1. Record the child's spontaneous message.
2. Indicate if the message was directed to an adult (A) or peer (P).
3. Circle the communicative function of the message.
R = Requests for self
Q = Requests for information
C = Comments
F = Expresses feelings
P = Prosocial skills

	Message	Partner	Function
1		A P	R Q C F P
2		A P	R Q C F P
3		A P	R Q C F P
4		A P	R Q C F P
5		A P	R Q C F P
6		A P	R Q C F P
7		A P	R Q C F P
8		A P	R Q C F P
9		A P	R Q C F P
10		A P	R Q C F P
11		A P	R Q C F P
12		A P	R Q C F P
13		A P	R Q C F P
14		A P	R Q C F P
15		A P	R Q C F P
16		A P	R Q C F P
17		A P	R Q C F P
18		A P	R Q C F P
19		A P	R Q C F P
20		A P	R Q C F P

Communication: Generalization

Child's name:_____ Date:_____

Directions: 1. Select a specific communicative function (e.g., request help).
2. List the different contexts in which the communicative function occurs.
3. Specify the means used (gesture, sign, speech, or other).
4. Indicate if the message was directed to an adult (A) or peer (P).

Communication objective:_____

	Context	Means	Partner	
1			A	P
2			A	P
3			A	P
4			A	P
5			A	P
6			A	P
7			A	P
8			A	P
9			A	P
10			A	P

DO-WATCH-LISTEN-SAY: Social and Communication Intervention for Children with Autism
by Kathleen Ann Quill © 2000 Paul H. Brookes Publishing Co.

Conversation Sample

Child's name:_____ Date:_____

Directions: Transcribe a conversational exchange.

Turns	Child	Partner
1		
2		
3		
4		
5		
6		
7		
8		
9		
10		
11		
12		

References

American Psychiatric Association. (1994). *Diagnostic and statistical manual of mental disorders* (4th ed.). Washington, DC: Author.

Attwood, T. (1998). *Asperger's syndrome: A guide for parents and professionals*. London: Jessica Kingsley Publishers.

Baron-Cohen, S. (1987). Autism and symbolic play. *British Journal of Developmental Psychology, 5,* 113–125.

Baron-Cohen, S. (1988). Social and pragmatic deficits in autism: Cognitive or affective? *Journal of Autism and Developmental Disorders, 18,* 379–402.

Baron-Cohen, S. (1993). From attention-goal psychology to belief-desire psychology: The development of a 'theory of mind' and its dysfunction. In S. Baron-Cohen, H. Tager-Flusberg, & D. Cohen (Eds.), *Understanding other minds: Perspectives from autism* (pp. 59–82). Oxford, United Kingdom: Oxford University Press.

Baron-Cohen, S. (1995). *Mindblindness.* Cambridge, MA: The MIT Press.

Baron-Cohen, S., Allen, J., & Gillberg, C. (1992). Can autism be detected at 18 months? The needle, the haystack, and the CHAT. *British Journal of Psychology, 161,* 839–842.

Baron-Cohen, S., Leslie, A.M., & Frith, U. (1985). Does the autistic child have a "theory of mind"? *Cognition, 21,* 37–46.

Baron-Cohen, S., Tager-Flusberg, H., & Cohen, D. (Eds.). (1993). *Understanding other minds: Perspectives from autism.* Oxford, United Kingdom: Oxford University Press.

Barron, J., & Barron, S. (1992). *There's a boy in here.* New York: Simon & Schuster.

Bates, E. (1976). *Language in context: The acquisition of pragmatics.* San Diego: Academic Press.

Bates, E., Benigni, L., Bretherton, I., Camaioni, L., & Volterra, V. (1979). *The emergence of symbols: Cognition and communication in infancy.* San Diego: Academic Press.

Bayley, N. (1993). *Bayley Scales of Infant Development* (2nd ed.). San Antonio, TX: The Psychological Corp.

Berko-Gleason, J. (Ed.). (1985). *The development of language.* Columbus, OH: Merrill.

Bernard-Opitz, V. (1982). Pragmatic analysis of the communicative behavior of an autistic child. *Journal of Speech and Hearing Disorders, 47,* 99–109.

Beukelman, D.R., & Mirenda, P. (1998). *Augmentative and alternative communication: Management of severe communication disorders in children and adults* (2nd ed.). Baltimore: Paul H. Brookes Publishing Co.

Bondy, A., & Frost, L. (1994). The Picture Exchange Communication System (PECS). *Focus on Autistic Behavior, 9,* 1–19.

Boucher, J. (1981). Memory for recent events in autistic children. *Journal of Autism and Developmental Disorders, 11,* 293–301.

Boucher, J., & Lewis, V. (1988). Memory impairments and communication in relatively able autistic children. *Journal of Child Psychology and Psychiatry, 30,* 99–122.

Boucher, J., & Warrington, E. (1976). Memory deficits in early infantile autism: Some similarities to the amnesic syndrome. *British Journal of Psychology, 67,* 73–87.

Bowers, L., Huisingh, R., Barrett, M., Orman, J., & LoGiudice, C. (1994). *Test of Problem Solving* (Rev. ed.). East Moline, IL: LinguiSystems.

Brazelton, T. (1994). *Touchpoints: Your child's emotional and behavioral development.* Reading, MA: Addison Wesley Longman.

Brigance, A.H. (1983). *Brigance Inventory of Early Development.* North Billerica, MA: Curriculum Associates.

Bristol, M., Cohen, D., Costello, E., Denckla, M., Eckberg, T., Kallen, R., Kraemer, H., Lord, C., Maurer, R., McIlvane, W., Minshew, N., Sigman, M., & Spence, M. (1996). State of the science in autism: Report to the National Institutes of Health. *Journal of Autism and Developmental Disorders, 26,* 121–154.

Brockett, S. (1998, July). *How to develop successful play activities for the child with autism.* Paper presented at the annual conference of the Autism Society of America, Reno, NV.

Bruner, J. (1975). The ontogenesis of speech acts. *Journal of Child Language, 2,* 1–19.

Bruner, J. (1981). The social context of language acquisition. *Language and Communication, 1,* 155–178.

Capps, L., Kehres, J., & Sigman, M. (1998). Conversational abilities among children with autism and children with developmental delays. *Autism, 2,* 325–344.

Carr, E.G., Levin, L., McConnachie, G., Carlson, J.I., Kemp, D.C., & Smith, C.E. (1994). *Communication-based intervention for problem behavior: A user's guide for producing positive change.* Baltimore: Paul H. Brookes Publishing Co.

Cesaroni, L., & Garber, M. (1991). Exploring the experience of autism through firsthand accounts. *Journal of Autism and Developmental Disorders, 21,* 303–313.

Charlop, M. (1986). Setting effects of echolalia acquisition and generalization of receptive labeling in autistic children. *Journal of Applied Behavior Analysis, 16,* 111–126.

Charman, T. (1997). The relationship between joint attention and pretend play in autism. *Development and Psychopathology, 9,* 1–16.

Charman, T., & Baron-Cohen, S. (1994). Another look at imitation in autism. *Development and Psychopathology, 6,* 403–413.

Charman, T., Swettenham, J., Baron-Cohen, S., Cox, A., Baird, G., & Drew, A. (1997). Infants with autism: An investigation of empathy, pretend play, joint attention and imitation. *Developmental Psychology, 33*, 781–789.

Ciesielski, K., Courchesne, E., & Elmasian, R. (1990). Effects of focused, selective attention tasks on event-related potentials in autistic and normal individuals. *Electroencephalography and Clinical Neurophysiology, 7*, 207–220.

Courchesne, E. (1991, July). *A new model of brain and behavior development in infantile autism.* Paper presented at the Autism Society of America National Conference, 25.

Curcio, F. (1978). Sensorimotor functioning and communication in mute autistic children. *Journal of Autism and Childhood Schizophrenia, 8*, 281–292.

Curcio, F., & Paccia, J. (1987). Conversations with autistic children: Contingent relationships between features of adult input and children's response adequacy. *Journal of Autism and Developmental Disorders, 17*, 81–93.

Dalrymple, N. (1995). Environmental supports to develop flexibility and independence. In K. Quill (Ed.), *Teaching children with autism: Strategies to enhance communication and socialization* (pp. 243–264). Albany, NY: Delmar Publishers.

Dawson, G., & Adams, A. (1984). Imitation and social responsiveness in autistic children. *Journal of Abnormal Child Psychology, 12*, 209–226.

Dawson, G., & Galpert, L. (1986). A developmental model for facilitating the social behavior of autistic children. In E. Schopler & G. Mesibov (Eds.), *Social behavior in autism* (pp. 237–261). New York: Kluwer Academic/Plenum Publishers.

Dawson, G., Hill, D., Spencer, A., Galpert, L, & Watson, L. (1990). Affective exchanges between young autistic children and their mothers. *Journal of Abnormal Child Psychology, 18*, 335–345.

Dawson, G., & Osterling, J. (1997). Early intervention in autism. In M.J. Guralnick (Ed.), *The effectiveness of early intervention* (pp. 307–326). Baltimore: Paul H. Brookes Publishing Co.

DeMyer, M.K. (1975). The nature of neuropsychological disability in autistic children. *Journal of Autism and Childhood Schizophrenia, 5*, 109–128.

DiGennaro, F., & McDonald, M. (1998, May). *Effects of video modeling on spontaneous play initiations and conversational speech in children with autism.* Poster presented at the annual conference of the Association for Behavior Analysis, Orlando, FL.

DiLavore, P., Lord, C., & Rutter, M. (1995). The Pre-Linguistic Autism Diagnostic Observation Schedule. *Journal of Autism and Developmental Disorders, 25*, 355–379.

Durand, V.M. (1990). *Severe behavior problems: A functional communication training program.* New York: The Guilford Press.

Eckerman, C.O., & Stein, M.R. (1982). The toddler's emerging interactive skills. In K.H. Rubin & H.S. Ross (Eds.), *Peer relationships and social skills in childhood* (pp. 41–71). New York: Springer-Verlag New York.

Eisenmajer, R., & Prior, M. (1991). Cognitive linguistic correlates of 'theory of mind' ability in autistic children. *British Journal of Developmental Psychology, 9*, 351–364.

Fein, G.G. (1981). Pretend play in childhood: An integrative review. *Child Development, 52*, 1095–1118.

Ferrara, C., & Hill, S. (1980). The responsiveness of autistic children to the predictability of social and nonsocial toys. *Journal of Autism and Developmental Disorders, 10*, 51–57.

Freeman, S., & Dake, L. (1996). *Teach me language: A language manual for children with autism, Asperger's syndrome and related developmental disorders.* Langley, Canada: SKF Books.

Frith, U. (1989). *Autism: Explaining the enigma.* Oxford, England: Blackwell.

Frith, U., & Baron-Cohen, S. (1987). Perception in autistic children. In D.J. Cohen & A.M. Donnellan (Eds.), *Handbook of autism and pervasive developmental disorders* (pp. 85–102). New York: John Wiley & Sons.

Frith, U., Happe, F., & Siddons, F. (1994). Autism and theory of mind in everyday life. *Social Development, 3*, 108–124.

Frost, L., & Bondy, A. (1994). *The Picture Exchange Communication System (PECS) Training Manual.* Cherry Hill, NJ: PECS.

Garretson, H., Fein, D., & Waterhouse, L. (1990). Sustained attention in autistic children. *Journal of Autism and Developmental Disorders, 20*, 101–114.

Garvey, C. (1977). *Play.* Cambridge, MA: Harvard University Press.

Glennen, S., & DeCosta, D. (1997). *Handbook of augmentative and alternative communication.* San Diego: Singular Publishing Group.

Goldstein, H., & Strain, P. (1988). Peers as communication intervention agents: Some new strategies and research findings. *Topics in Language Disorders, 9*, 44–57.

Goosens', C., Crain, S.S., & Elder, P.S (1992). *Engineering the preschool environment for interactive symbolic communication.* Birmingham, AL: Southeast Augmentative Communication Conference Publications.

Grandin, T. (1995a). The learning style of people with autism: An autobiography. In K. Quill (Ed.), *Teaching children with autism: Strategies to enhance communication and socialization* (pp. 33–52). Albany, NY: Delmar Publishers.

Grandin, T. (1995b). *Thinking in pictures and other reports from my life with autism.* New York: Doubleday.

Grandin, T. (1998, March). *Thinking in autism: A personal account.* Paper presented to the Institute on Autism and Pervasive Developmental Disorders, Emerson College, Boston.

Gray, C. (Ed.). (1993). *The social story book.* Jenison, MI: Jenison Public Schools.

Gray, C. (1995). Teaching children with autism to read social situations. In K. Quill (Ed.), *Teaching children with autism: Strategies to enhance communication and socialization* (pp. 219–242). Albany, NY: Delmar Publishers.

Gray, C., & Garand, J. (1993). Social stories: Improving responses of students with autism with accurate social information. *Focus on Autistic Behavior, 8*, 1–10.

Greenspan, S. (1992). *Infancy and early childhood: The practice of clinical assessment and intervention with emotional and developmental challenges.* Madison, CT: International Universities Press.

Greenspan, S. (1995). *The challenging child: Understanding, raising, and enjoying the five difficult types of children*. Reading, MA: Addison Wesley Longman.

Greenspan, S., & Wieder, S. (1998). *The child with special needs: Encouraging intellectual and emotional growth*. Reading, MA: Addison Wesley Longman.

Groden, J., Cautela, J.R., & Groden, G. (1989). *Breaking the barriers: The use of relaxation for people with special needs* [Videotape]. Champaign, IL: Research Press.

Groden, J., & LeVasseur, P. (1995). Cognitive Picture Rehearsal: A system to teach self-control. In K. Quill (Ed.), *Teaching children with autism: Strategies to enhance communication and socialization* (pp. 287–306). Albany, NY: Delmar Publishers.

Hadwin, J., Baron-Cohen, S., Howlin, P., & Hill, K. (1997). Does teaching 'theory of mind' have an effect on the ability to develop conversation in children with autism? *Journal of Autism and Developmental Disorders, 27*, 519–538.

Hanschu, B. (1998, April). *Evaluation and treatment of sensory processing disorders*. Paper presented to the Sensory Integration Consortium, Boston.

Harris, S., & Handleman, J. (1994). (Eds.). *Preschool education programs for children with autism*. Austin, TX: PRO-ED.

Harris, S., Handleman, J., & Burton, J. (1990). The Stanford-Binet profiles of young children with autism. *Special Services in the School, 6*, 135–143.

Hart, B., & Risley, T. (1982). *How to use incidental teaching for elaborating language*. Austin, TX: PRO-ED.

Hart, B., & Risley, T.R. (1999). *The social world of children learning to talk*. Baltimore: Paul H. Brookes Publishing Co.

Hartup, W. (1983). Peer relations. In P.H. Mussen (Series Ed.) & E.M. Hetherington (Vol. Ed.), *Socialization, Personality, and Social Development: Vol. 4. Handbook of child psychology* (4th ed.). New York: John Wiley & Sons.

Hauck, M., Fein, D., Waterhouse, L., & Feinstein, C. (1995). Social initiations by autistic children to adults and other children. *Journal of Autism and Developmental Disorders, 25*, 579–596.

Hermelin, B., & O'Connor, N. (1970). *Psychological experiments with autistic children*. London: Pergamon Press.

Hobson, R.P. (1989). Beyond cognition. In G. Dawson (Ed.), *Autism: Nature, diagnosis, and treatment* (pp. 22–48). New York: The Guilford Press.

Hobson, R.P. (1996). *Autism and the development of the mind*. Mahwah, NJ: Lawrence Erlbaum Associates.

Hodgdon, L. (1995). *Visual strategies for improving communication*. Troy, MI: Quirk Roberts Publishing.

Howes, C. (1987). Peer interactions in young children. *Monographs of the Society for Research in Child Development, 53* (1, Serial No. 217).

Hunt, P., Alwell, M., & Goetz, L. (1993). *Teaching conversational skills to individuals with severe disabilities with a communication book adaptation: Instructional handbook*. San Francisco: San Francisco State University.

Janzen, J. (1996). *Understanding the nature of autism: A practical guide*. San Antonio, TX: Therapy Skill Builders.

Jarrold, C., Boucher, J., & Smith, P. (1993). Symbolic play in autism: A review. *Journal of Autism and Developmental Disorders, 23*, 281–309.

Jarrold, C., Smith, P., Boucher, J., & Harris, P. (1994). Children with autism's comprehension of pretence. *Journal of Autism and Developmental Disorders, 24*, 433–456.

Johnson-Martin, N.M., Attermeier, S.M., & Hacker, B. (1990). *The Carolina Curriculum for Preschoolers with Special Needs*. Baltimore: Paul H. Brookes Publishing Co.

Johnson-Martin, N.M., Jens, K.G., Attermeier, S.M., & Hacker, B.J. (1991). *The Carolina Curriculum for Infants and Toddlers with Special Needs* (2nd ed.). Baltimore: Paul H. Brookes Publishing Co.

Kagan, J. (1994). *Nature of the child*. New York: Basic Books.

Kleiman, L. (1994). *Functional Communication Profile*. East Moline, IL: LinguiSystems.

Koegel, R., & Johnson, J. (1989). Motivating language use in autistic children. In G. Dawson (Ed.), *Autism: New perspectives on diagnosis, nature, and treatment*. New York: The Guilford Press.

Koegel, L.K., & Koegel, R.L. (1995a). Motivating communication in children with autism. In E. Schopler & G. Mesibov (Eds.), *Learning and cognition in autism* (pp. 73–87). New York: Kluwer Academic/Plenum Publishers.

Koegel, L.K., Koegel, R.L., & Dunlap, G. (1996). *Positive behavioral support: Including people with difficult behavior in the community*. Baltimore: Paul H. Brookes Publishing Co.

Koegel, R.L., & Koegel, L.K. (Eds.). (1995b). *Teaching children with autism: Strategies for initiating positive interactions and improving learning opportunities*. Baltimore: Paul H. Brookes Publishing Co.

Konstantareas, M., Webster, C., & Oxman, J. (1980). An alternative to speech training: Simultaneous communication. In C. Webster, M. Konstantareas, J. Oxman, & J. Mack (Eds.), *Autism: New directions in research and education*. New York: Pergamon.

Krantz, P., & McClannahan, L. (1993). Teaching children with autism to initiate to peers: Effects of a script-fading procedure. *Journal of Applied Behavior Analysis, 26*, 121–132.

Krug, D., Arick, J., & Almond, P. (1980). *Autism Screening Instrument for Educational Planning (ASIEP)*. Portland, OR: ASIEP.

LaVigna, G., & Donnellan, A. (1986). *Alternatives to punishment: Solving behavior problems with nonaversive strategies*. New York: Irvington Publishers.

Layton, T. (1987). Manual communication. In T. Layton (Ed.), *Language and treatment of autistic and developmentally disordered children* (pp. 189–213). Springfield, IL: Charles C Thomas Publisher.

Layton, T. (1988). Language training with autistic children using four different modes of presentation. *Journal of Communication Disorders, 21*, 333–350.

Layton, T., & Watson, L. (1995). Enhancing communication in nonverbal children with autism. In K. Quill (Ed.), *Teaching children with autism: Strategies to enhance communication and socialization* (pp. 73–104). Albany, NY: Delmar Publishers.

Leslie, A.M. (1987). Pretense and representation: The origins of 'theory of mind'. *Psychological Review, 94*, 412–426.

Leslie, A., & Frith, U. (1988). Autistic children's understanding of seeing, knowing and believing.

British Journal of Developmental Psychology, 6, 315–324.

Lewy, A., & Dawson, G. (1992). Social stimulation and joint attention in young autistic children. *Journal of Abnormal Child Psychology, 20,* 555–566.

Libby, S., Powell, S., Messer, D., & Jordan, R. (1998). Spontaneous play in children with autism: A reappraisal. *Journal of Autism and Developmental Disorders, 28,* 487–497.

Light, J.C., & Binger, C. (1998). *Building communicative competence with individuals who use augmentative and alternative communication.* Baltimore: Paul H. Brookes Publishing Co.

Lincoln, A., Couurchesne, E., Kilman, B., Elmasian, R., & Allen, M. (1988). A study of intellectual abilities in high-functioning people with autism. *Journal of Autism and Developmental Disorders, 18,* 505–523.

Linder, T.W. (1993). *Transdisciplinary Play-Based Assessment (TPBA): A functional approach to working with young children* (Rev. ed.). Baltimore: Paul H. Brookes Publishing Co.

Lord, C. (1996). Diagnosis. State of the science in autism: Report to the National Institutes of Health. *Journal of Autism and Developmental Disorders, 26,* 122–126.

Lord, C., Rutter, M., DiLavore, P., & Risi, S. (1999). *Autism Diagnostic Observation Schedule (ADOS).* Los Angeles, CA: Western Psychological Services.

Lord, C., Rutter, M., & LeCourteur, A. (1994). Autism Diagnostic Interview–Revised (ADI-R): A revised version of a diagnostic interview for caregivers of individuals with possible pervasive developmental disorder. *Journal of Autism and Developmental Disorders, 24,* 659–685.

Lovaas, I. (1977). *The autistic child: Language development through behavior modification.* New York: Irvington Publishers.

Lovaas, O.I. (1981). *Teaching developmentally disabled children: The ME book.* Baltimore: University Park Press.

Lovaas, I. (1987). Behavioral treatment and normal educational and intellectual functioning in young autistic children. *Journal of Consulting and Clinical Psychology, 55,* 3–9.

Lovaas, O.I. (1998, July). *Strengths and weaknesses in early and intensive intervention.* Paper presented at the Autism Society of America National Conference, Reno, NV.

Lovaas, O.I., Koegel, R.L., & Schreibman, L.E. (1979). Stimulus overselectivity in autism: A review of research. *Psychological Bulletin, 86,* 1236–1254.

Lowe, M., & Costello, A. (1976). *Symbolic Play Test.* Windsor, Canada: NFER.

Maurer, R.G., & Damasio, A.R. (1982). Childhood autism from the point of view of behavioral neurology. *Journal of Autism and Developmental Disorders, 12,* 195–205.

Maurice, C., Green, G., & Luce, S. (1996). *Behavioral intervention for young children with autism.* Austin, TX: PRO-ED.

Mayer-Johnson, R. (1981). *The Picture Communication Symbols book.* Solana Beach, CA: Mayer-Johnson Co.

McBride, J., & Panksepp, J. (1995). An examination of the phenomenology and the reliability of ratings of compulsive behavior in autism. *Journal of Autism and Developmental Disorders, 25,* 381–396.

McClannahan, L., & Krantz, P. (1999). *Activity schedules for children with autism: Teaching independent behavior.* Bethesda, MD: Woodbine House.

McCune-Nicolich, L. (1981). Toward symbolic functioning: Structure of early pretend games and potential parallels with language. *Child Development, 3,* 785–797.

McDougle, C.J., Price, L.H., & Goodman, W.K. (1990). Fluvoxamine treatment of autistic disorder and obsessive-compulsive disorder: A case report. *Journal of Autism and Developmental Disorders, 20,* 537–543.

McEvoy, R., Rogers, S., & Pennington, B. (1993). Executive function and social communication deficits in young autistic children. *Journal of Child Psychology and Psychiatry, 34,* 563–578.

McGee, G., Feldman, R., & Morrier, M. (1997). Benchmarks of social treatment for children with autism. *Journal of Autism and Developmental Disorders, 27,* 353–364.

McLean, J., & Snyder-McLean, L. (1978). *A transactional approach to early language training: Derivation of a model system.* Columbus, OH: Merrill.

Mercer, J.R., & Lewis, J.F. (1978). *Adaptive Behavior Inventory for Children.* San Antonio, TX: The Psychological Corp.

Michaels, A. (1998, November). *Understanding 'theory of mind': A personal account.* Workshop at the Autism Support Center, Danvers, MA.

Minshew, N., Goldstein, G., Muenz, L., & Payton, J. (1992). Neuropsychological functioning of nonmentally retarded autistic individuals. *Journal of Clinical and Experimental Neuropsychology, 14,* 749–761.

Mueller, E., & Brenner, J. (1977). The origin of social skills and interaction among playgroup toddlers. *Child Development, 48,* 854–861.

Mundy, P. (1995). Joint attention, social-emotional approach in children with autism. *Development and Psychopathology, 7,* 63–82.

Mundy, P., & Crowson, M. (1997). Joint attention and early social communication: Implications for research on intervention with autism. *Journal of Autism and Developmental Disorders, 27,* 653–676.

Mundy, P., & Sigman, M. (1989a). Specifying the nature of the social impairment in autism. In G. Dawson (Ed.), *Autism: Nature, diagnosis, and treatment* (pp. 3–21). New York: The Guilford Press.

Mundy, P., & Sigman, M. (1989b). The theoretical implications of joint attention deficits in autism. *Development and Psychopathology, 1,* 173–183.

Mundy, P., Sigman, M., & Kasari, C. (1993). Joint attention, developmental level, and symptom presentation in young children with autism. *Development and Psychopathology, 6,* 389–401.

Mundy, P., Sigman, M., Ungerer, J., & Sherman, T. (1986). Defining the social deficits of autism: The contribution of nonverbal communication measures. *Journal of Child Psychology and Psychiatry, 27,* 657–669.

Mundy, P., Sigman, M., Ungerer, J., & Sherman, T. (1987). Nonverbal communication and pay correlates of language development in autistic children. *Journal of Autism and Developmental Disorders, 17,* 349–364.

Muris, J. (1998). Anxiety disorders in children with pervasive developmental disorders. *Autism Research Review International, 12,* 2.

Odom, S.L., & Strain, P.S. (1984). Peer-mediated approaches to promoting children's social interaction: A review. *American Journal of Orthopsychiatry, 54,* 544–557.

O'Neill, M., & Jones, R. (1997). Sensory-perception abnormalities in autism: A case for more research? *Journal of Autism and Developmental Disorders, 27,* 283–294.

Ornitz, E.M. (1989). Autism at the interface between sensory and information processing. In G. Dawson (Ed.), *Autism: Nature, diagnosis, and treatment* (pp. 174–207). New York: The Guilford Press.

Osterling, J., & Dawson, G. (1994). Early recognition of children with autism: A study of first birthday home videotapes. *Journal of Autism and Developmental Disorders, 24,* 247–257.

Ozonoff, S. (1995). Executive functions in autism. In E. Schopler & G. Mesibov (Eds.), *Learning and cognition in autism* (pp. 199–220). New York: Kluwer Academic/Plenum Publishers.

Ozonoff, S., & Miller, J. (1995). Teaching 'theory of mind': A new approach to social skills training for individuals with autism. *Journal of Autism and Developmental Disorders, 25,* 415–433.

Ozonoff, S., Pennington, B., & Rogers, S. (1990). Are there emotional perception deficits in young autistic children? *Journal of Child Psychology and Psychiatry, 31,* 343–361.

Ozonoff, S., Pennington, B., & Rogers, S. (1991). Executive function deficits in high-functioning autistic individuals: Relationship to theory of mind. *Journal of Child Psychology and Psychiatry, 32,* 1081–1105.

Paccia, J., & Curcio, F. (1982). Language processing and forms of immediate echolalia in autistic children. *Journal of Speech and Hearing Research, 25,* 42–47.

Park, C.C. (1986). Social growth in autism. In E. Schopler & G. Mesibov (Eds.), *Social behavior in autism* (pp. 81–102). New York: Kluwer Academic/Plenum Publishers.

Peeters, T. (1997). *Autism: From theoretical understanding to educational intervention.* London: Whurr Publishers.

Perner, J., Frith, U., Leslie, A., & Leekam, S. (1989). Exploration of the autistic child's 'theory of mind': Knowledge, belief and communication. *Child Development, 60,* 689–700.

Phelps-Terasaki, D., & Phelps-Gunn, T. (1992). *Test of Pragmatic Language.* Austin, TX: PRO-ED.

Piaget, J. (1962). *Play, dreams and imitation.* New York: W.W. Norton & Company.

Pierce, K., Glad, K.S., & Schreibman, L. (1997). Social perception in children with autism: An attentional deficit? *Journal of Autism and Developmental Disorders, 27,* 265–282.

Pierce, K., & Schreibman, L. (1994). Teaching daily living skills to children with autism in unsupervised settings through pictorial self-management. *Journal of Applied Behavior Analysis, 27,* 471–481.

Prior, M. (1979). Cognitive abilities and disabilities in autism: A review. *Journal of Abnormal Child Psychology, 2,* 357–380.

Prizant, B.M. (1982). Gestalt processing and gestalt language in autism. *Topics in Language Disorders, 3,* 16–23.

Prizant, B.M. (1996). Brief report: Communication, language, social and emotional development. *Journal of Autism and Developmental Disorders, 26,* 173–178.

Prizant, B.M., & Duchan, J.F. (1981). The functions of immediate echolalia in autistic children. *Journal of Speech and Hearing Disorders, 46,* 241–249.

Prizant, B.M., & Rydell, P.J. (1993). Assessment and intervention considerations for unconventional verbal behavior. In S.F. Warren & J. Reichle (Series Eds.) & J. Reichle & D. Wacker (Vol. Eds.), *Communication and Language Intervention Series: Vol. 3. Communicative alternatives to challenging behavior: Integrating functional assessment and intervention strategies* (pp. 263–297). Baltimore: Paul H. Brookes Publishing Co.

Prizant, B., & Schuler, A. (1987). Facilitating communication: Language approaches. In D. Cohen & A. Donnellan (Eds.), *Handbook of autism and pervasive developmental disorder.* New York: John Wiley & Sons.

Prizant, B., & Wetherby, A. (1987). Communicative intent: A framework for understanding social-communicative behavior in autism. *Journal of the American Academy of Child and Adolescent Psychiatry, 26,* 472–479.

Prizant, B., & Wetherby, A. (1990). Toward an integrated view of early language and communication development and socioemotional development. *Topics in Language Disorders, 10,* 1–16.

Prizant, B., & Wetherby, A. (1998). Understanding the continuum of discrete-trial traditional behavioral to social-pragmatic developmental approaches in communication enhancement for young children with autism/PDD. *Seminars in Speech and Language, 19,* 329–354.

Quill, K. (1995a). Enhancing children's social-communicative interactions. In K. Quill (Ed.), *Teaching children with autism: Strategies to enhance communication and socialization* (pp. 163–192). Albany, NY: Delmar Publishers.

Quill, K. (Ed.). (1995b). *Teaching children with autism: Strategies to enhance communication and socialization.* Albany, NY: Delmar Publishers.

Quill, K. (1995c). Visually cued instruction for children with autism and pervasive developmental disorders. *Focus on Autistic Behavior, 10,* 10–22.

Quill, K. (1996, December). *Using pictographic symbols in the communication training of nonverbal preschoolers with autism.* Paper presented at the annual conference of the American Speech-Language-Hearing Association (ASHA), Orlando, FL.

Quill, K. (1997). Instructional considerations for young children with autism: The rationale for visually-cued instruction. *Journal of Autism and Developmental Disorders, 27,* 697–714.

Quill, K. (1998). Environmental supports to enhance social-communication. *Seminars in Speech and Language, 19,* 407–423.

Quill, K., & Bracken, K. (1998). *The dominance of nonverbal interactions among typically developing young children: Rationale for rethinking social-communication goals for children with autism.* Unpublished manuscript.

Quill, K., & Shea, S. (1999, May). *Video instruction as an instructional tool to build social imitation.* Paper presented at the annual meeting of the Association for Behavior Analysis, Chicago.

Ratner, N., & Bruner, J. (1978). Games, social exchange, and the acquisition of language. *Journal of Child Language, 5,* 391–401.

Reichle, J., & Wacker, D.P. (Volume Eds.) & Warren, S.F., & Reichle, J. (Series Eds.). (1993). *Communication and Language Intervention Series: Vol. 3. Communicative alternatives to challenging behavior: Integrating functional assessment and intervention strategies.* Baltimore: Paul H. Brookes Publishing Co.

Reichle, J., York, J., & Sigafoos, J. (Eds.). (1991). *Implementing augmentative and alternative communication: Strategies for learners with severe disabilities.* Baltimore: Paul H. Brookes Publishing Co.

Riguet, C., Taylor, N., Benaroya, S., & Klein, L. (1981). Symbolic play in autistic, Down's and normal children of equivalent mental age. *Journal of Autism and Developmental Disorders, 11,* 61–70.

Roeyers, H. (1996). The influence of nonhandicapped peers on the social interactions of children with a pervasive developmental disorder. *Journal of Autism and Developmental Disorders, 26,* 303–320.

Roeyers, H., & van Berkalaer-Onnes. (1994). Play in autistic children. *Communication and Cognition, 27,* 349–359.

Rogers, S., & Pennington, B. (1991). A theoretical approach to the deficits in infantile autism. *Development and Psychopathology, 3,* 137–162.

Ross, K., & Ross, H. (Eds.). (1982). *Peer relationships and social skills in childhood.* New York: Springer-Verlag New York.

Rossetti, L. (1990). *The Rossetti Infant-Toddler Language Scale.* East Moline, IL: LinguiSystems.

Rubin, K.H. (Ed.). (1980). *Children's play.* San Francisco: Jossey-Bass Publishers.

Russell, J. (Ed.). (1993). *Autism as an executive disorder.* New York: Oxford University Press.

Rydell, P., & Mirenda, P. (1991). The effects of two levels of linguistic constraint on echolalia and generative language production in children with autism. *Journal of Autism and Developmental Disorders, 21,* 131–158.

Rydell, P., & Mirenda, P. (1994). Effects of high and low constraint utterances on the production of immediate and delayed echolalia in young children with autism. *Journal of Autism and Developmental Disorders, 24,* 719–736.

Rydell, P., & Prizant, B. (1995). Assessment and intervention strategies for children who use echolalia. In K. Quill (Ed.), *Teaching children with autism: Strategies to enhance communication and socialization* (pp. 105–132). Albany, NY: Delmar Publishers.

Schopler, E., & Mesibov, G. (Eds.). (1985). *Communication problems in autism.* New York: Kluwer Academic/Plenum Publishers.

Schopler, E., & Mesibov, G. (Eds.). (1986). *Social behavior in autism.* New York: Kluwer Academic/Plenum Publishers.

Schopler, E., & Mesibov, G. (Eds.). (1988). *Diagnosis and assessment in autism.* New York: Kluwer Academic/Plenum Publishers.

Schopler, E., & Mesibov, G. (Eds.). (1994). *Behavioral issues in autism.* New York: Kluwer Academic/Plenum Publishers.

Schopler, E., Mesibov, G., & Hearsey, K. (1995). Structured teaching in the TEACCH System. In E. Schopler & G. Mesibov (Eds.), *Learning and cognition in autism* (pp. 243–268). New York: Kluwer Academic/Plenum Publishers.

Schopler, E., Reichler, R., Bashford, A., Lansing, M., & Marcus, L. (1990). *Psychoeducational Profile–Revised (PEP-R).* Austin, TX: PRO-ED.

Schopler, E., Reichler, R., & Renner, B. (1988). *The Childhood Autism Rating Scale (CARS).* Los Angeles: Western Psychological Services.

Schwandt, W., Keene, A., & Larsson, E. (1998, May). *Using videotaped models to generalize independent toy play in intensive early intervention.* Poster presented at the annual conference of the Association for Behavior Analysis (ABA), Orlando, FL.

Shah, A., & Wing, L. (1986). Cognitive impairments affecting social behavior in autism. In E. Schopler & G. Mesibov (Eds.), *Social behavior in autism.* New York: Kluwer Academic/Plenum Publishers.

Shatz, M., & Gelman, R. (1973). The development of communication skills: Modifications in the speech of young children as a function of the listener. *Monographs of the Society for Research in Child Development, 38*(5, Serial No. 152).

Siegel, J., Minshew, N., & Goldstein, G. (1996). Wechsler IQ profiles in diagnosis of high-functioning autism. *Journal of Autism and Developmental Disorders, 26,* 389–406.

Sigman, M., Kasari, C., Kwon, J., Jung-Hye, L., & Yirmiya, N. (1992). Responses to the negative emotions of others by autistic, mentally retarded, and normal children. *Child Development, 63,* 796–807.

Sigman, M., & Ungerer, J. (1984). Cognitive and language skills in autistic, mentally retarded, and normal children. *Developmental Psychology, 20,* 293–302.

Sigman, M., Ungerer, J., Mundy, P., & Sherman, T. (1987). Cognition in autistic children. In D.J. Cohen & A.M. Donnellan (Eds.), *Handbook of autism and pervasive developmental disorders* (pp. 103–120). New York: John Wiley & Sons.

Simons, J.M. (1974). Observations of compulsive behavior in autism. *Journal of Autism and Childhood Schizophrenia, 4,* 1–10.

Simpson, R. (1991). Ecological assessment of children and youth with autism. *Focus on Autistic Behavior, 5,* 1–18.

Singer, D., & Singer, J. (1990). *The house of make-believe.* Cambridge, MA: Harvard University Press.

Smith, M.D. (1990). *Autism and life in the community: Successful interventions for behavioral challenges.* Baltimore: Paul H. Brookes Publishing Co.

Snow, C. (1977). The development of conversation between mothers and babies. *Journal of Child Language, 4,* 1–22.

Snyder-McLean, L., Solomonson, B., McLean, J., & Sack, S. (1984). Structuring joint action routines: A strategy for facilitating communication and language development in the classroom. *Seminars in Speech and Language, 5,* 213–228.

Sparrow, S., Balla, D., & Cicchetti, D. (1984). *Vineland Adaptive Behavior Scales.* Circle Pines, MN: American Guidance Service.

Stone, W., & Caro-Martinez, L. (1990). Naturalistic observations of spontaneous communications in autistic children. *Journal of Autism and Developmental Disorders, 20,* 437–453.

Stone, W., Ousely, O., Yoder, P., Hogan, K., & Hepburn, S. (1997). Nonverbal communication in two- and three-year-old children with autism. *Journal of Autism and Developmental Disorders, 27,* 677–696.

Strain, P., & Kohler, F. (1998). Peer-mediated social intervention for young children with autism. *Seminars in Speech and Language, 19,* 391–405.

Strain, P., & Odom, S. (1986). Peer social initiations: Effective interventions for social skills development of exceptional children. *Exceptional Children, 52,* 543–551.

Szatmari, P. (1992). The validity of autistic spectrum disorders: A literature review. *Journal of Autism and Developmental Disorders, 22,* 583–600.

Tager-Flusberg, H., & Anderson, M. (1991). The development of contingent discourse ability in autistic children. *Journal of Child Psychology and Psychiatry, 32,* 1123–1134.

Tiegerman, E., & Primavera, L. (1984). Imitating the autistic child: Facilitating communicative gaze behavior. *Journal of Autism and Developmental Disorders, 14,* 27–38.

Tomasello, M. (1995). Joint attention as social cognition. In C. Moore & P. Dunham (Eds.), *Joint attention: Its origin and role in development* (pp. 103–130). Mahwah, NJ: Lawrence Erlbaum Associates.

Tremblay, A., Strain, P., Hendrickson, J., & Shores, R. (1981). Social interactions of normal preschool children. *Behavior Modification, 5,* 237–253.

Twatchman, D. (1995). Methods to enhance communication in verbal children. In K. Quill (Ed.), *Teaching children with autism: Strategies to enhance communication and socialization* (pp. 133–162). Albany, NY: Delmar Publishers.

Ungerer, J. (1989). The early development of autistic children: Implications for defining primary deficits. In G. Dawson (Ed.), *Autism: Nature, diagnosis, and treatment* (pp. 75–91). New York: The Guilford Press.

Ungerer, J., & Sigman, M. (1981). Symbolic play and language comprehension in autistic children. *Journal of the American Academy of Child Psychiatry, 20,* 318–337.

Uzgiris, I. (1981). Two functions of imitation during infancy. *International Journal of Behavioral Development, 4,* 1–12.

Vandell, D., & Wilson, K. (1982). Social interactions in the first year: Infants' social skills with peers versus mother. In K. Rubin & H. Ross (Eds.), *Peer relationships and social skills in childhood* (pp. 187–208). New York: Springer-Verlag New York.

VanMeter, L., Fein, D., Morris, R., Waterhouse, L., & Allen, D. (1997). Delay versus deviance in autistic social behavior. *Journal of Autism and Developmental Disorders, 27,* 557–570.

Vicker, B. (1991, July). *The minimally verbal individual with autism and the role of augmentative communication.* Paper presented at the annual conference of the Autism Society of America, Indianapolis, IN.

Vygotsky, L.S. (1964). *Thought and language.* New York: John Wiley & Sons.

Wellman, H.M. (1990). *The child's theory of mind.* Cambridge, MA: The MIT Press.

Wells, G. (1981). *Learning through interaction: The study of language development.* Cambridge, United Kingdom: Cambridge University Press.

Wenar, C., Ruttenberg, B., Kalish-Weiss, B., & Wolf, E. (1986). The development of normal and autistic children: A comparative study. *Journal of Autism and Developmental Disorders, 16,* 317–333.

Westby, C.E. (2000). A scale for assessing development of children's play. In K. Gitlin-Weiner, A. Sandgrund, & C. Schaefer (Eds.), *Play diagnosis and assessment* (2nd ed.). New York: John Wiley & Sons.

Wetherby, A.M. (1986). Ontogeny of communicative functions in autism. *Journal of Autism and Developmental Disorders, 15,* 295–315.

Wetherby, A.M., & Prizant, B.M. (1989). The expression of communicative intent: Assessment guidelines. *Seminars in Speech and Language, 10,* 77–91.

Wetherby, A.M., & Prizant, B. (1990). *Communication and Symbolic Behavior Scales (CSBS)* (Research ed.). Itasca, IL: The Riverside Publishing Co.

Wetherby, A.M., & Prizant, B. (1993). Profiling communication and symbolic abilities in young children. *Journal of Childhood Communication Disorders, 15,* 23–32.

Wetherby, A.M., & Prutting, C.A. (1984). Profiles of communicative and cognitive-social abilities in autistic children. *Journal of Speech and Hearing Research, 27,* 364–377.

Wetherby, A.M., & Rodriquez, G. (1992). Measurement of communicative intentions in normally developing children during structured and unstructured contexts. *Journal of Speech and Hearing Research, 35,* 130–138.

Whalen, C., & Schreibman, L. (1998). *Easing transitional difficulties of children with autism using video priming techniques.* Poster presented at the annual conference of the Association for Behavior Analysis, Orlando, FL.

Wiig, E.H., & Secord, E. (1989). *Test of Language Competence–Expanded Edition* (TLC-Expanded). San Antonio, TX: The Psychologial Corp.

Williams, D. (1992). *Nobody nowhere.* New York: Times Books.

Wing, L. (1988). The continuum of autistic characteristics. In E. Schopler & G. Mesibov (Eds.), *Diagnosis and assessment in autism* (pp. 93–121). New York: Kluwer Academic/Plenum Publishers.

Wing, L. (1996). *The autistic spectrum: A guide for parents and professionals.* London: Constable.

Wing, L., & Attwood, A. (1987). Syndromes of autism and atypical development. In D. Cohen, A. Donnellan, & R. Paul (Eds.), *Handbook of autism and pervasive developmental disorders* (pp. 3–19). New York: John Wiley & Sons.

Wolfberg, P. (1995). Enhancing children's play. In K. Quill (Ed.), *Teaching children with autism: Strategies to enhance communication and socialization* (pp. 193–218). Albany, NY: Delmar Publishers.

Wolfberg, P. (1999). *Play and imagination in children with autism.* New York: Teachers College Press.

Wolfberg, P., & Schuler, A. (1993). Integrated play groups: A model for promoting the social and cognitive dimensions of play. *Journal of Autism and Developmental Disorders, 23,* 1–23.

Zirpoli, T. J. (1995). *Understanding and affecting the behavior of young children.* Upper Saddle River, NJ: Prentice Hall.

Resources

ASSESSMENT TOOLS

There are a number of assessment tools that can provide a social and communication profile of children with autism. The majority of these tools either provide general diagnostic information and/or use developmental norms (see Chapter 3 for a detailed discussion about these assessment instruments). The following autism diagnostic scales, adaptive behavior scales, and pragmatic language assessments are standardized tools. The autism educational assessments, curriculum-based developmental assessments, and play assessments are informal measures. See the References for a complete listing of assessment tools of social skills and communication for children with autism.

Autism Diagnostic Scales

Autism Diagnostic Interview–Revised (ADI-R; Lord, Rutter, & LeCourteur, 1994)

Autism Diagnostic Observation Schedule (ADOS; Lord, Rutter, DiLavore, & Risi, 1999)

Childhood Autism Rating Scale (CARS; Schopler, Reichler, & Renner, 1988)

Adaptive Behavior Scales

Adaptive Behavior Inventory for Children (Mercer & Lewis, 1977)

Vineland Adaptive Behavior Scales (Sparrow, Balla, & Cicchetti, 1984)

Autism Educational Assessments

Autism Screening Instrument for Educational Planning (ASIEP; Krug, Arick, & Almond, 1980)

Psychoeducational Profile–Revised (PEP-R; Schopler, Reichler, Bashford, Lansing, & Marcus, 1990)

Curriculum-Based Developmental Assessments

Brigance Inventory of Early Development (Brigance, 1983)

The Carolina Curriculum for Preschoolers with Special Needs (Johnson-Martin, Attermeier, & Hacker, 1990)

Transdisciplinary Play-Based Assessment (TPBA; Linder, 1993)

Play Assessments

A Scale for Assessing Development of Children's Play (Westby, 2000)

The Symbolic Play Test (Lowe & Costello, 1976)

Wolfberg's informal play assessment for children with autism (Wolfberg, 1995)

Assessments of Prelinguistic Social-Communication

Checklist for Autism in Toddlers (CHAT; Baron-Cohen, Allen, & Gillberg, 1992)

Communication and Symbolic Behavior Scales (CSBS; Wetherby & Prizant, 1990)

Pre-Linguistic Autism Diagnostic Observation Schedule (PL-ADOS; DiLavore, Lord, & Rutter, 1995)

Pragmatic Language Assessments

Functional Communication Profile (Kleiman, 1994)

The Rossetti Infant-Toddler Language Scale (Rossetti, 1990)

Test of Language Competence–Expanded Edition (TLC-Expanded; Wiig & Secord, 1989)

Test of Pragmatic Language (Phelps-Terasaki & Phelps-Gunn, 1992)

Test of Problem Solving (Bowers, Huisingh, Barrett, Orman, & LoGiudice, 1994)

AUGMENTATIVE AND ALTERNATIVE COMMUNICATION DEVICES

The following is a brief list of high-tech and low-tech augmentative and alternative communication (AAC) devices that are most commonly considered for children with autism. The manufacturer's name is provided in parentheses. Please see the list of companies offering assistive technology products in the Distributors section. Decisions regarding the use of AAC devices for a particular child require comprehensive assessment by a specialist.

Sample Voice Output Devices

BIGmack: single-message switch (*AbleNet*)

Cheap Talk: available in four- or eight-message squares (*Toys for Special Children, Enabling Devices, Inc.*)

Tech/Talk: eight recorded messages with multiple levels available (*Mayer-Johnson Co., Inc.*)

Speak Easy: 12 recorded messages (*AbleNet*)

Sidekick: 24 message spaces that can be sequenced to produce unlimited words, phrases, or sentences using the Minspeak system (*Prentke Romich Company*)

Tech/Speak: 32 recorded messages with multiple levels available (*Mayer-Johnson Co., Inc.*)

Message Mate and Mini Message Mate: available to store up to 8, 20, or 40 messages in various configurations (*Words + Inc.*)

DynaMyte: easy-to-carry, full-featured, dynamic-display, digitized-communication device (*DynaVox Systems, a division of Sunrise Medical*)

DynaVox: easy-to-carry, full-featured, dynamic-display, digitized-communication device (*DynaVox Systems, a division of Sunrise Medical*)

Inexpensive Solutions

Tape recorder: single message (*Radio Shack*)

Talking Picture Frame: single-message device with one picture (*Radio Shack*)

Personal Talker: single-message device with one picture (*Attainment Company*)

Time Frame: talking picture frame programmed with one to four messages (*Speech-Language Innovations*)

Record-a-Book from Golden Books: strip with five message spaces (*commercial toy stores*)

CHILDREN'S BOOKS

This list of children's books is divided into five sections. The first section lists authors whose writing style appeals to many children with autism. The second section divides books according to five different stylistic patterns: Cumulative Repetition, Imitation, Minimal Language, Predictable, and Wordless Picture Books. The third section lists books in four different social themes: All About Me, Emotions, Community, and Holidays. In the fourth section, books used for activities in the curricula chapters are listed. The last section contains some of the most popular books among children with autism.

Recommended Authors of Children's Books

- Asch, Frank
- Carle, Eric
- Crews, Donald
- Dale, Penny
- Elhert, Lois
- Gibbons, Gail
- Hill, Eric
- Hutchins, Pat
- Isadora, Rachel
- Keats, Ezra Jack
- Martin, Jr., Bill
- Mayer, Mercer
- Neitzel, Shirley
- Spier, Peter
- Wood, Audrey

Special Suggestions by Style

Cumulative Repetition: Books that carry the text from page to page, adding one new line per page

Aardema, V. (1983). *Bringing the rain to Kapiti Plain.* New York: Penguin Books.

Adams, V. (1990). *This is the house that Jack built.* Auburn, ME: Child's Play.

Arnold, T. (1996). *No jumping on the bed.* New York: Penguin Books.

Kalan, R. (1991). *Jump, frog, jump!* New York: William Morrow & Co.

Neitzel, S. (1998). *The bag I'm taking to grandma's.* New York: William Morrow & Co.

Pizer, A. (1992). *It's a perfect day.* Reading, MA: Addison Wesley Longman.

Satin Capucilli, A. (1995). *Inside a barn in the country.* New York: Scholastic.

Schmidt, K. (1985). *The gingerbread man.* New York: Scholastic.

Seuss, Dr. (1976). *Green eggs and ham.* New York: Random House.

Wood, A. (1984). *The napping house.* New York: Harcourt.

Imitation: Books that encourage children to imitate the actions of their characters

Carle, E. (1997). *From head to toe.* New York: HarperCollins Children's Books.

Cauley, L.B. (1992). *Clap your hands.* New York: The Putnam Publishing Group.

Hague, M. (1993). *Teddy bear, teddy bear: A classic action rhyme.* New York: Morrow Junior Books.

Marzollo, J. (1997). *Pretend you're a cat.* New York: Viking Penguin.

Oxenbury, H. (1991). *Monkey see, monkey do.* New York: Dial Books for Young Readers.

Schwartz, H., & Schwartz, A. (1994). *Make a face: A book with a mirror.* New York: Scholastic.

Sheehan, N. (1996). *Animal actions.* New York: Scholastic.

Minimal Language: Books with very few words on each page

Bang, M. (1991). *Yellow ball.* New York: Scholastic.

Bunting, E. (1994). *Flower garden.* New York: Harcourt.

Canizares, S. (1998). *Who lives in the Arctic?* New York: Scholastic.

Canizares, S., & Moreton, D. (1998). *Polar bears.* New York: Scholastic.

Carle, E. (1998). *What's for lunch?* New York: Scholastic.

Crews, D. (1992). *Freight train.* New York: William Morrow & Co.

Pascoe, G. (1991). *Sand.* New York: Newbridge Educational Publishing.

Rathmann, P. (1996). *Good night, gorilla.* New York: The Putnam Publishing Group.

Schreiber, A. (1994). *Boots*. New York: Scholastic.

Stickland, P., & Stickland, H. (1997). *Dinosaur roar!* New York: Dutton's Children's Books.

Predictable: Books that repeat a word or phrase throughout the text

Carle, E. (1996). *Have you seen my cat?* New York: Simon & Schuster Children's Publishing.

Carle, E. (1997). *The very quiet cricket*. New York: The Putnam Publishing Group.

Crebbin, J. (1996). *A train ride*. Cambridge, MA: Candlewick Press.

Gale, L. (1953). *The animals of Farmer Jones*. New York: Simon & Schuster.

Jorgenson, G. (1997). *Gotcha!* New York: Scholastic.

Pinczes, E. (1993). *One hundred hungry ants*. Boston: Houghton Mifflin Co.

Root, P. (1998). *One duck stuck*. Cambridge, MA: Candlewick Press.

Rosen, M. (1997). *We're going on a bear hunt*. New York: Simon & Schuster Children's Publishing.

Ward, C. (1997). *Cookie's week*. New York: The Putnam Publishing Group.

Wood, A. (1985). *King Bidgood's in the bathtub*. New York: Harcourt.

Wordless Picture Books: Books that tell the story only through pictures

Anno, M. (1986). *Anno's counting book*. New York: HarperCollins Children's Books.

Briggs, R. (1978). *The snowman*. New York: Random House.

Carle, E. (1990). *1, 2, 3 to the zoo*. New York: The Putnam Publishing Group.

Cousins, L. (1992). *Kite in the park*. Cambridge, MA: Candlewick Press.

Crews, D. (1997). *Truck*. New York: The Hearst Book Group.

Day, A. (1985). *Good dog, Carl*. New York: Simon & Schuster Trade Division.

Elhert, L. (1989). *Color zoo*. New York: HarperCollins Children's Books.

Mayer, M. (1977). *Ah-choo*. New York: Puffin Books.

Oomen, F. (1995). *My toys*. New York: Simon & Schuster Children's Publishing.

Spier, P. (1997). *Peter Spier's rain*. New York: Bantam Doubleday Dell Publishing Group.

Special Suggestions by Theme

All About Me

Baer, E. (1992). *This is the way we go to school*. New York: Scholastic.

Carlson, N. (1990). *I like me*. New York: Puffin Books.

Dalton, A. (1992). *This is the way*. New York: Scholastic.

Hindley, J. (1999). *Eyes, nose, fingers, and toes*. Cambridge, MA: Candlewick Press.

Intrater, R.G. (1995). *Two eyes, a nose, and a mouth*. New York: Scholastic.

MacKinnon, D. (1994). *All about me*. Hauppauge, NY: Barron's Educational Series.

Markham-David, S. (1994). *Mouths and noses*. Worthington, OH: SRA/McGraw-Hill.

Martin, Jr., B., & Archambault, J. (1999). *Here are my hands*. New York: Henry Holt and Co. LLC.

Mayer, M. (1997). *This is my family*. New York: Golden Books Family Entertainment.

Roe, E. (1990). *All I am*. New York: Scholastic.

Wood, A. (1995). *Quick as a cricket*. Auburn, ME: Child's Play.

Emotions

Aaron, J., & Gardiner, B. (1998). *When I'm angry*. New York: Golden Books Family Entertainment.

Baker, K. (1998). *Sometimes*. New York: Harcourt.

Berry, J. (1996). *Let's talk about feeling afraid*. New York: Scholastic.

Berry, J. (1996). *Let's talk about feeling sad*. New York: Scholastic.

Conlin, S. (1989). *Let's talk about feelings: Ellie's day*. Seattle: Parenting Press.

Emberly, E. (1997). *Glad monster, sad monster: A book about feelings*. Boston: Little, Brown and Company.

Geddes, A. (1995). *Faces*. San Rafael, CA: Cedco Publishing.

Kachenmeister, C. (1996). *On Monday when it rained*. Boston: Houghton Mifflin Co.

Seuss, Dr. (1996). *My many colored days*. New York: Random House.

Wittels, H., & Greisman, J. (1973). *Things I hate!* New York: Behavioral Publications.

Community

Cooper, M. (1995). *I got community.* New York: Henry Holt and Co. LLC.

Heo, Y. (1998). *One afternoon.* New York: Orchard Books.

Hutchings, A., & Hutchings, R. (1993). *Firehouse dog.* New York: Scholastic.

Kalman, B. (1999). *What is a community?: From A to Z.* New York: Crabtree Publishing Co.

Loomis, C. (1995). *At the diner.* New York: Scholastic.

Loomis, C. (1995). *At the laundromat.* New York: Scholastic.

Loomis, C. (1995). *At the library.* New York: Scholastic.

Loomis, C. (1995). *At the mall.* New York: Scholastic.

Loomis, C. (1995). *In the neighborhood.* New York: Scholastic.

Holidays

DePaola, T. (1990). *My first Easter.* New York: Scholastic.

DePaola, T. (1992). *My first Thanksgiving.* New York: Scholastic.

DePaola, T. (1995). *My first Chanukah.* New York: Scholastic.

Falwell, C. (1995). *Feast for 10.* Boston: Houghton Mifflin Co.

Freeman, D. (1992). *Corduroy's Christmas.* New York: Viking Children's Books.

Freeman, D. (1995). *Corduroy's Halloween.* New York: Penguin Books.

Freeman, D. (1997). *Corduroy's birthday.* New York: Viking Penguin.

Oxenbury, H. (1996). *It's my birthday.* Cambridge, MA: Candlewick Press.

Titherington, J. (1986). *Pumpkin, pumpkin.* New York: Scholastic.

Waters, K., & Slovenz-Low, M. (1990). *Lion dancer.* New York: Scholastic.

Books Highlighted in the Curricula Chapters

Boynton, S. (1995). *Blue hat, green hat.* New York: Simon & Schuster Children's Publishing.

Carle, E. (1994). *The very hungry caterpillar.* New York: The Putnam Publishing Group.

Cauley, L.B. (1992). *Clap your hands.* New York: The Putnam Publishing Group.

Courtin, T. (1997). *Daddy and me.* New York: Grosset & Dunlap.

Emberley, E., & Miranda, A. (1997). *Glad monster, sad monster: A book about feelings.* Boston: Little, Brown and Company.

Guarino, D. (1989). *Is your mama a llama?* New York: Scholastic.

Hill, E. (1980). *Where's Spot?* New York: Puffin Books.

Lavis, S. (1997). *Jump.* New York: Dutton's Children's Books.

Martin, Jr., B. (1970). *Brown bear, brown bear.* New York: Harcourt.

Marzollo, J., & Wick, W. *I spy little book series.* New York: Scholastic.

Oxenbury, H. (1981). *Playing.* New York: Simon & Schuster.

Pandell, K., & Wolfe, A. (1996). *Animal action ABC.* New York: Dutton's Children's Books.

Peeke, M. (1985). *Mary wore her red dress and Henry wore his green sneakers.* Boston: Houghton Mifflin Co.

Smith, M. (1998). *Mind your manners, Ben Bunny.* New York: Scholastic.

Tafuri, N. (1984). *Have you seen my duckling?* New York: Scholastic.

White-Carlstrom, N., & Degen, B. (1997). *I love you, Mama, any time of the year.* New York: Simon & Schuster Children's Publishing.

Wilkes, A. (1991). *My first word book.* New York: D K Publishing.

Children's Picks (Per Request)

Arlborough, J. (1996). *It's the bear.* Cambridge, MA: Candlewick Press.

Bond, F. (1996). *Tumble bumble.* New York: Scholastic.

Carle, E. (1994). *The very hungry caterpillar.* New York: The Putnam Publishing Group.

Carle, E. (1995). *The very busy spider.* New York: The Putnam Publishing Group.

Carle, E. (1998). *Catch the ball.* New York: Scholastic.

Carter, D. (Illustrator). (1992). *Over in the meadow: An old counting rhyme.* New York: Scholastic.

Crews, D. (1984). *School bus.* New York: Greenwillow Books.

Dale, P. (1988). *Ten in the bed.* Carlisle, MA: Discovery Enterprises, Ltd.

Dodds, D. (1992). *The color box.* Boston: Little, Brown and Company.

Guarino, D. (1997). *Is your mama a llama?* New York: Scholastic.

Hutchins, P. (1993). *The wind blew.* New York: Simon & Schuster Children's Publishing.

Jorgenson, G. (1994). *Crocodile beat.* New York: Simon & Schuster Children's Publishing.

Londan, J. (1994). *Froggy gets dressed.* New York: Puffin Books.

Martin, Jr., B. (1989). *Chicka chicka boom boom.* New York: Simon & Schuster Trade Division.

Martin, Jr., B. (1996). *Brown bear, brown bear what do you see?* New York: Henry Holt and Co. LLC.

Myers, B. (1994). *Because of a sneeze.* New York: Newbridge Educational Publishing.

Neitzel, S. (1994). *The jacket I wear in the snow.* New York: William Morrow & Co.

Shaw, N. (1997). *Sheep in a jeep.* Boston: Houghton Mifflin Co.

Waddell, M. (1975). *Owl babies.* New York: Scholastic.

Wood, A. (1999). *Silly Sally.* San Diego: Red Wagon Books.

COMPUTER SOFTWARE

The following list of educational software is neither complete nor exhaustive. Although all software programs can provide opportunities for structured social-communicative interactions, these programs are particularly popular among many children with autism. The list is organized according to the companies that distribute these products. All of this software can also be purchased from Hatch's catalog. (See the Distributors section for more information.)

**Available Through
Attainment Company**

Colorful Concepts Series

Room by Room

Survival Skills Software

Towards Independence CD-ROM

WordWise Software Series

**Available Through
DK Multimedia**

My First Amazing Words and Pictures

**Available Through
Don Johnston**

Circletime Tales Deluxe

Clicker Plus

Day at Play

Early Learning Series

Five Green Speckled Frogs

Games to Play

Jokus Faces

On a Green Bus

Out and About

Picture Communication Symbols

The Rodeo

Simon Sounds it Out

Turn Taking

**Available Through
Edmark Corporation**

Bailey's Book House

Destination: Neighborhood

Words Around Me

**Available Through
Knowledge Adventure**

Chicka Chicka Boom Boom

JumpStart Kindergarten

JumpStart Phonics

JumpStart Preschool

JumpStart Toddler

**Available Through
Laureate Learning Systems**

Categories

Early Emerging Rules

First Verbs

First Words

Language Activities of Daily Living

Talk Time with Tucker

Talking Nouns

Talking Verbs

Words and Concept Series

**Available Through
MattelInteractive**

Darby the Dragon

Living Books Library

The Playroom

Reader Rabbit Series

Where in the World is Carmen Sandiego?

**Available Through
Scholastic New Media**

Wiggle Works

CHILDREN'S MUSIC

Music is an enjoyable way to engage children in social and communicative interactions. The following is a partial listing of popular records, cassettes, CDs, and music videos. The list is organized by artist as well as the companies that distribute these materials. (See the listing of general education products in the Distributors section.)

Records, Cassettes, and CDs

Favorite Artists

Gregg and Steve

Ella Jenkins

Hap Palmer

Raffi

Available Through
Early Childhood Direct/Chime Time

All-Time Favorite Dances

Good Morning Exercises

Hello Toes

Kids in Motion

Preschool Aerobic Fun

Seat Works

Available Through Kaplan School Supply

Sittercise

Toes Up, Toes Down

Available Through Kimbo Educational

Bean Bag Fun

Everybody Dance

Me and My Beanbag

Songs About Me

Available Through
Lakeshore Learning Materials

Best of Ella Jenkins (Record, Cassette, and CD Libraries)

Best of Hap Palmer (Record, Cassette, and CD Library)

The Best of Raffi (Record, Cassette, and CD Library)

Let's Get Moving (Record, Cassette, and CD Library)

We All Live Together with Gregg and Steve (Record, Cassette, and CD Libraries)

Children's Music Videos
(available through commercial retailers)

Disney Sing-Along Songs

Elmocize

Hap Palmer Baby Songs

Hap Palmer Follow-Along Songs

Shari Lewis: Lamb Chop's Play Along Do As I Do

Wee Sing in Sillyville

Winnie-the-Pooh: Sing a Song with Pooh Bear

TOYS

The Play Interest Survey (See Chapter 7, Appendix A) provides a list of common toys and activities. The following list offers additional fun and creative toys that are popular among many children with autism. It is organized by the 10 general play categories. Each toy is followed by the company that distributes the item. (See the Distributors section of the Resources for ordering information.)

Exploratory Play Toys

Rainbow Rod (*Constructive Playthings*)

Rock 'N Roll Top (*commercial toy stores*)

Shadow Play Screen (*Lakeshore Learning Materials*)

Sink or Float Exploration Kit (*Lakeshore Learning Materials*)

Stack & Pop (*Discovery Toys*)

Physical Play Toys

Balance and Movement Kit (*Lakeshore Learning Materials*)

Beanbag Learning Center (*Lakeshore Learning Materials*)

Jump-O-Lene (*Lillian Vernon Corp.*)

Little Tykes Roller Coaster (*commercial toy stores*)

Roller Racer (*Lakeshore Learning Materials*)

Manipulatives

Follow the Picture Magnetic Mazes (*Lakeshore Learning Materials*)

Gazoobo (*Lakeshore Learning Materials*)

Going Around the Town Wall Model (*Constructive Playthings*)

Sight and Sound Animal Puzzle (*Constructive Playthings*)

Simon (*commercial toy stores*)

Constructive Play Toys

Acrobat Builders (*Lakeshore Learning Materials*)

Build and Balance Activity Blocks (*Lakeshore Learning Materials*)

Classroom Clayworks Kit (*Constructive Playthings*)

Safari Gears (*Discovery Toys*)

Zolo Fun Factory (*Lakeshore Learning Materials*)

Art Materials

Dial-A-Shape Paper Punch (*Lakeshore Learning Materials*)

Dough Stampers (*Lakeshore Learning Materials*)

Magic Colors Assortment (*Lakeshore Learning Materials*)

Painting Discovery Kit (*Lakeshore Learning Materials*)

Teacher's Brew Art Recipes Box (*Lakeshore Learning Materials*)

Literacy Activities

Early Language Concept Kits (*Lakeshore Learning Materials*)

First Words Lotto (*Lakeshore Learning Materials*)

Storytelling Kits (*Lakeshore Learning Materials*)

Language Audio Card Reader (*Lakeshore Learning Materials*)

Match 'N Spell School Blocks (*Constructive Playthings*)

Sociodramatic Toys

Choosy Baby All Gone (*commercial toy stores*)

Grandma/Grandpa's Dress Up Trunk (*Lakeshore Learning Materials*)

Let's Pretend Driver (*Lakeshore Learning Materials*)

Sesame Street Talking Farm (*commercial toy stores*)

The Doll Clinic (*Lakeshore Learning Materials*)

Games

Body Bingo (*Lakeshore Learning Materials*)

Color Train (*commercial toy stores*)

Dizzy Dyer (*commercial toy stores*)

Feelings and Faces Game (*Lakeshore Learning Materials*)

Kerplunk (*commercial toy stores*)

Music Activities

Bean Bag Activities Cassette (*Constructive Playthings*)

Follow-Along Hand Bell Activity Kit (*Lakeshore Learning Materials*)

Hook-&-Loop Jingle Bells (*Lakeshore Learning Materials*)

Multicultural Rhythm Sticks & Activity Kit (*Lakeshore Learning Materials*)

Sing & Play Raffi Song Kits (*Lakeshore Learning Materials*)

Social Games

No toys needed. See the "Recommended Readings" section of the Resources for curriculum resources to build communication and socialization in children with special needs.

DISTRIBUTORS

The following is a list of recommended companies that specialize in educational materials. The list is subcategorized into six areas: General Education Products, Assistive Technology Products, Software Companies and Catalogs Specializing in Computer Software, Companies Specializing in Children's Books, Companies Specializing in Instructional Materials, and Companies Specializing in Toys.

General Education Products

ABC School Supply
3312 North Berkeley Lake Road
Box 100019
Duluth, GA 30096-9419
(800) 669-4222
www.abcschoolsupply.com

Childcraft Education Corporation
Post Office Box 3239
Lancaster, PA 17604
(800) 631-5652
www.childcrafteducation.com

Constructive Playthings
13201 Arrington Road
Grandview, MO 64030
(800) 448-1412
www.constplay.com

The Education Center
3515 West Market Street
2nd Floor
Greensboro, NC 27403
(800) 714-7991
www.theeducationcenter.com

Hawthorne Educational Services
800 Gray Oak Drive
Columbia, MO 65201
(800) 542-1673

Imagineart
307 Arizona Street
Bisbee, AZ 85603
(800) 828-1376
www.imagineartonline.com

Kaplan School Supply
Post Office Box 609
1310 Lewisville-Clemmons Road
Lewisville, NC 27023-0609
(800) 334-2014
www.kaplanco.com

Kimbo Educational
Post Office Box 477
Long Branch, NJ 07740
(800) 631-2187
www.kimboed.com

Lakeshore Learning Materials
2695 East Dominguez Street
Carson, CA 90749
(800) 428-4414
www.lakeshorelearning.com

Slosson Educational Publications
Post Office Box 280
East Aurora, NY 14052-0280
(888) 756-7766
www.slosson.com

Super Duper Publications
Department SUM 98
Post Office Box 24997
Greenville, SC 29616
(800) 277-8737
www.superduperinc.com

Thinking Publications
Post Office Box 163
424 Galloway Street
Eau Claire, WI 54702-0163
(800) 225-4769
www.thinkingpublications.com

Toys for Special Children, Enabling Devices, Inc.
385 Warburton Avenue
Hastings-on-Hudson, NY 10706
(800) 832-8697
www.enablingdevices.com

Assistive Technology Products

AbleNet
1081 Tenth Avenue SE
Minneapolis, MN 55414-1312
(800) 322-0956
www.ablenetinc.com

Access First
Post Office Box 3990
Glen Allen, VA 23058-3990
(888) 606-6769
www.accessfirst.net

Adaptivation
2225 West 50th Street
Suite 100
Sioux Falls, SD 57105
(800) 7-ADAPTD
www.adaptivation.com

AlphaSmart, Inc.
20400 Stevens Creek Boulevard
Suite 300
Cupertino, CA 95014
(888) 274-0680
www.alphasmart.com

Assistive Technology
7 Wells Avenue
Newton, MA 02459
(800) 793-9227
www.assistivetech.com

Attainment Company
Post Office Box 930160
Verona, WI 53593-0160
(800) 327-4269
www.attainmentcompany.com

DynaVox Systems, a division of Sunrise Medical
2100 Wharton Street
Pittsburgh, PA 15203
(800) 344-1778
www.dynavoxsys.com

Innocomp
Innovative Computer Applications
Suite 302
26210 Emery Road
Warrensville Heights, OH 44128
(800) 382-8622
www.sayitall.com

IntelliTools
1720 Corporate Circle
Petaluma, CA 94954
(800) 899-6687
www.intellitools.com

Mayer-Johnson Co., Inc.
Post Office Box 1579
Solana Beach, CA 92075
(800) 588-4548
www.mayer-johnson.com

Prentke Romich Company
1022 Heyl Road
Wooster, OH 44691
(800) 262-1984
www.prentrom.com

Toys for Special Children, Enabling Devices, Inc.
385 Warburton Avenue
Hastings-on-Hudson, NY 10707
(800) 832-8697
www.enablingdevices.com

Words + Inc.
1220 West Avenue J
Lancaster, CA 93534
(800) 869-8521

Zygo Industries
Post Office Box 1008
Portland, OR 97207-1008
(800) 234-6006
www.zygo-usa.com

Software Companies and Catalogs Specializing in Computer Software

Academic Communications Associates
Publication Center, Department 611
4149 Avenida de la Plata
Post Office Box 586249
Oceanside, CA 92058-6249
(760) 758-9593
www.acadcom.com

Attainment Company
Post Office Box 930160
Verona, WI 53593-0160
(800) 327-4269
www.attainmentcompany.com

DK Multimedia
95 Madison Avenue
New York, NY 10016
(877) 884-1600
www.dk.com

Don Johnston
26799 West Commerce Drive
Volo, IL 60073
(800) 999-4660
www.donjohnston.com

Edmark Corporation
Post Office Box 97021
Redmond, WA 98073-9721
(800) 691-2986
www.edmark.com

Hatch
4994-D Indiana Avenue
Winston-Salem, NC 27106
(800) 624-7968
www.hachstuff.com

Knowledge Adventure
4100 West 190th Street
Torrance, CA 90504
(800) 542-4240
www.knowledgeadventure.com

Laureate Learning Systems
110 East Spring Street
Winooski, VT 05404-1898
(800) 562-6801
www.laureatelearning.com

MattelInteractive
2850 Earhart Court
Hebron, KY 41048
(800) 358-9144
www.mattelinteractive.com

Mayer-Johnson Co., Inc.
Post Office Box 1579
Solana Beach, CA 92075
(800) 588-4548
www.mayer-johnson.com

Scholastic New Media
Division of Scholastic
555 Broadway
New York, NY 10012
(800) SCHOLASTIC
www.scholastic.com

The Speech Bin
1965 25th Avenue
Vero Beach, FL 32960
(561) 770-0007
(800) 4-SPEECH

Sunburst
101 Castleton Street
Pleasantville, NY 10570
(800) 321-7511
www.sunburst.com

Companies Specializing in Children's Books

Chinaberry, Inc.
2780 Via Orange Way, Suite B
Spring Valley, CA 91978
(800) 776-2242
www.chinaberry.com

Rigby Education
500 Coventry Lane
Crystal Lake, IL 60014
(800) 822-8661
www.rigby.com

Scholastic
Post Office Box 7505
Jefferson, City, MO 65102-9968
(800) 724-6527
www.scholastic.com

Troll Communications
100 Corporate Drive
Mahwah, NJ 07430
(800) 541-1097
www.troll.com

Companies Specializing in Instructional Materials

Academic Communications Associates
Publication Center, Department 611
4149 Avenida de la Plata
Post Office Box 586249
Oceanside, CA 92058-6249
(760) 758-9593
www.acadcom.com

Adaptive Consulting Services
253 Merritt Square Mall
Suite 642
Merritt Island, FL 32952
(800) 515-9169
www.augmentative.com

AGS Early Childhood
American Guidance Service
4201 Woodland Road
Post Office Box 99
Circle Pines, MN 55014-1796
(800) 328-2560
www.agsnet.com

Communication Skill Builders
The Psychological Corporation
555 Academic Court
San Antonio, TX 78204-2498
(800) 228-0752
www.hbtpc.com

Early Childhood Direct/Chime Time
Post Office Box 369
Landisville, PA 17538
(800) 784-5717
www.chimetime.com

Educational Activities, Inc.
1937 Grand Avenue
Baldwin, NY 11510
(800) 645-3739
www.ed-pak.com/edact.html

Great Ideas for Teaching
Post Office Box 444
Wrightsville Beach, NC 28480
(910) 256-4494
www.gift-inc.com

HELP Associates
Post Office Box 43515
Upper Montclair, NJ 07043
(973) 655-0801 (fax)
www.linkstolanguage.com

LinguiSystems
3100 Fourth Avenue
East Moline, IL 61244-9700
(800) PRO-IDEA
www.linguisystems.com

Newbridge Educational Publishing
333 East 38th Street
Eighth Floor
New York, NY 10016
(800) 867-0307
www.newbridgeonline.com

PCI Elementary Special Education
Post Office Box 34270
San Antonio, TX 78265-4270
(800) 594-4263
www.pcicatalog.com

PRO-ED
8700 Shoal Creek Boulevard
Austin, TX 78757-6897
(800) 729-1463
www.proedinc.com

Remedia Publications
10135 East Via Linda, #D124
Scottsdale, AZ 85258-5312
(800) 826-4740
www.rempub.com

The Speech Bin
1965 25th Avenue
Vero Beach, FL 32960
(561) 770-0007
(800) 4-SPEECH

Companies Specializing in Toys

Childswork/Childsplay
135 Dupont Street
Post Office Box 760
Plainview, NY 11803-0760
(800) 962-1141
www.childswork.com

Constructive Playthings
13201 Arrington Road
Grandview, IL 64030
(800) 448-1412
www.constplay.com

Discovery Toys
Post Office Box 5023
Livermore, CA 94551-5023
(800) 426-4777
www.discoverytoysinc.com

Lakeshore Learning Materials
2695 East Dominguez Street
Carson, CA 90749
(800) 428-4414
www.lakeshorelearning.com

Lillian Vernon Corp.
100 Lillian Vernon Drive
Virginia Beach, VA 23479-0002
(800) 285-5555
www.lillianvernon.com

MindWare
121 Fifth Avenue NW
New Brighton, MN 55112
(800) 999-0398
www.mindwareonline.com

Oriental Trading Company
Post Office Box 2050
Omaha, NE 68103-2050
(800) 228-2269
www.teachercentral.com

The Story Teller
308 East 800 South
Salem, UT 84653
(800) 801-6860
www.thestoryteller.com

WEB SITES

There is a staggering amount of information about autism and related disorders available on the Internet. The following list of web sites is neither complete nor exhaustive. Rather, it is a starting point for obtaining information about both autism and early childhood education.

Web Sites for Special Education and Autism

Autism National Committee: www.autcom.org

Autism Research Institute: www.autism.com/ari

Autism Society of America: www.autism-society. org

Center for the Study of Autism: www.autism.org

Discrete Trial Intervention: www.listserv@indycms. iupui.edu

Division TEACCH: www.unc.edu/depts/teacch/

The Educational Resources Information Center (ERIC): www.accesseric.org

Family Web Sites: www.canfoundation.org/ newcansite/resources/websites.html

Inclusion Press International: www.inclusion.com

Indiana Resource Center for Autism: www.isdd. indiana.edu/~irca

MAAP (More Advanced Individuals with Autism, Asperger's Syndrome and Pervasive Developmental Disorder): www.maapservices.org

National Alliance for Autism Research: www. naar.org

On-Line Asperger's Syndrome Information and Support (O.A.S.I.S.): www.udel.edu/bkirby/ asperger/

Pervasive Developmental Disorders–Frequently Asked Questions (PDD-FAQ): www.cec.sped. org/faq/pdd-faq.htm

Special Education Resources on the Internet (SERI): www.hood.edu/seri/autism.htm

Yale Child Study Center: http:/info.med.yale.edu/ chldstdy/autism

Web Sites for Early Childhood Education
Book Clubs
www.ala.org/alsc/notable97.html

www.rigby.com

www.scholastic.com

www.troll.com

Curriculum Ideas for Preschool
www.copycatpress.com

www.theideabox.com

www.themailbox.com

www.timeforkids.com/TFK/

Curriculum Ideas for Grades K–3
www.classroom.net

www.copycatpress.com

www.Disney.com

www.kconnect.com

www.themailbox.com

www.ume.maine.edu/~cofed/eceol

RECOMMENDED READINGS

The following list of recommended readings is neither complete nor exhaustive. These resources explore specific aspects of autism and intervention in greater depth.

Autism: Developmenal Overview

Attwood, T. (1998). *Asperger's syndrome: A guide for parents and professionals.* London: Jessica Kingsley Publishers.

Janzen, J. (1996). *Understanding the nature of autism: A practical guide.* San Antonio, TX: Therapy Skill Builders.

Peeters, T. (1997). *Autism: From theoretical understanding to educational intervention.* London: Whurr Publishers.

Autism: Developmental Theories

Baron-Cohen, S., Tager-Flusberg, H., & Cohen, D. (Eds.). (1993). *Understanding other minds: Perspectives from autism.* Oxford, United Kingdom: Oxford University Press.

Frith, U. (1989). *Autism: Explaining the enigma.* Oxford, United Kingdom: Blackwell.

Hobson, R.P. (1996). *Autism and the development of the mind.* Mahwah, NJ: Lawrence Erlbaum Associates.

Typical Development

Berko-Gleason, J. (Ed.). (1985). *The development of language.* Columbus, OH: Merrill.

Brazelton, T. (1994). *Touchpoints: Your child's emotional and behavioral development.* Reading, MA: Addison Wesley Longman.

Garvey, C. (1977). *Play.* Cambridge, MA: Harvard University Press.

Kagan, J. (1994). *Nature of the child.* New York: Basic Books.

Ross, K., & Ross, H. (Eds.). (1982). *Peer relationships and social skills in childhood.* New York: Springer-Verlag New York.

Wells, G. (1981). *Learning through interaction: The study of language development.* Cambridge, United Kingdom: Cambridge University Press.

Zirpoli, T.J. (1995). *Understanding and affecting the behavior of young children.* Upper Saddle River, NJ: Prentice Hall.

Autism Intervention: The Behavioral-Developmental Debate

Greenspan, S. (1995). *The challenging child: Understanding, raising, and enjoying the five difficult types of children.* Reading, MA: Addison Wesley Longman.

Greenspan, S., & Wieder, S. (1998). *The child with special needs: Encouraging intellectual and emotional growth.* Reading, MA: Addison Wesley Longman.

Lovaas, O.I. (1981). *Teaching developmentally disabled children: The ME book.* Baltimore: University Park Press.

Maurice, C., Green, G., & Luce, S. (1996). *Behavioral intervention for young children with autism.* Austin, TX: PRO-ED.

Autism Intervention to Build Communication and Socialization

Freeman, S., & Dake, L. (1996). *Teach me language: A language manual for children with autism, Asperger's syndrome and related developmental disorders.* Langley, Canada: SKF Books.

Gray, C. (Ed.). (1993). *The social story book.* Jenison, MI: Jenison Public Schools.

Greenspan, S., & Wieder, S. (1998). *The child with special needs: Encouraging intellectual and emotional growth.* Reading, MA: Addison Wesley Longman.

Hodgdon, L. (1995). *Visual strategies for improving communication.* Troy, MI: Quirk Roberts Publishing.

Koegel, R.L., & Koegel, L.K. (Eds.). (1995). *Teaching children with autism: Strategies for initiating positive interactions and improving learning opportunities.* Baltimore: Paul H. Brookes Publishing Co.

Quill, K. (Ed.). (1995). *Teaching children with autism: Strategies to enhance communication and socialization.* Albany, NY: Delmar Publishers.

Watson, L., Lord, C., Schaffer, B., & Schopler, E. (1989). *Teaching spontaneous communication to autistic and developmentally handicapped children.* New York: Irvington Publishers.

Wolfberg, P. (1999). *Play and imagination in children with autism.* New York: Teachers College Press.

Intervention to Build Communication and Socialization in Children with Special Needs

Bricker, D. (1998). *An activity-based approach to early intervention* (2nd ed.). Baltimore: Paul H. Brookes Publishing Co.

Johnson-Martin, N.M., Attermeier, S.M., & Hacker, B. (1990). *The Carolina Curriculum for Preschoolers with Special Needs.* Baltimore: Paul H. Brookes Publishing Co.

Linder, T.W. (1993). *Transdisciplinary play-based intervention: Guidelines for developing a meaningful curriculum for young children.* Baltimore: Paul H. Brookes Publishing Co.

McGinnis, E., & Goldstein, A. (1990). *Skillstreaming in early childhood: Teaching prosocial skills to the preschool and kindergarten child*. Champaign, IL: Research Press.

Schwartz, S., & Miller, J.E. (1996). *The new language of toys: Teaching communication to children with special needs* (2nd ed.). Bethesda, MD: Woodbine House.

York-Barr, J. (Series Ed.). (1996). *Creating inclusive school communities: A staff development series for general and special educators* (6 vols.). Baltimore: Paul H. Brookes Publishing Co.

Augmentative and Alternative Communication

Beukelman, D.R., & Mirenda, P. (1998). *Augmentative and alternative communication: Management of severe communication disorders in children and adults* (2nd ed.). Baltimore: Paul H. Brookes Publishing Co.

Frost, L., & Bondy, A. (1994). *The Picture Exchange Communication System (PECS) Training Manual*. Cherry Hill, NJ: PECS.

Glennen, S., & DeCosta, D. (1997). *Handbook of augmentative and alternative communication*. San Diego: Singular Publishing Group.

Goosens', C., Crain, S.S., & Elder, P.S. (1992). *Engineering the preschool environment for interactive symbolic communication*. Birmingham, AL: Southeast Augmentative Communication Conference Publications.

Johnson, J.M., Baumgart, D., Helmsetter, E., & Curry, C.A. (1996). *Augmenting basic communication in natural contexts*. Baltimore: Paul H. Brookes Publishing Co.

Reichle, J., York, J., & Sigafoos, J. (Eds.). (1991). *Implementing augmentative and alternative communication: Strategies for learners with severe disabilities*. Baltimore: Paul H. Brookes Publishing Co.

Behavior Management

Durand, V.M. (1990). *Severe behavior problems: A functional communication training program*. New York: The Guilford Press.

Koegel, L.K., Koegel, R.L., & Dunlap, G. (Eds.). (1996). *Positive behavioral support: Including people with difficult behavior in the community*. Baltimore: Paul H. Brookes Publishing Co.

LaVigna, G., & Donnellan, A. (1986). *Alternatives to punishment: Solving behavior problems with nonaversive strategies*. New York: Irvington Publishers.

Reichle, J., & Wacker, D.P. (Vol. Eds.). & Warren, S.F., & Reichle, J. (Series Eds.). (1993). *Communication and language intervention series: Vol. 3. Communicative alternatives to challenging behavior: Integrating functional assessment and intervention strategies*. Baltimore: Paul H. Brookes Publishing Co.

Schopler, E. (1995). *Parent survival manual: A guide to crisis resolution in autism and related developmental disorders*. New York: Kluwer Academic/Plenum Publishers.

Schopler, E., & Mesibov, G. (Eds.). (1994). *Behavioral issues in autism*. New York: Kluwer Academic/Plenum Publishers.

Smith, M.D. (1990). *Autism and life in the community: Successful interventions for behavioral challenges*. Baltimore: Paul H. Brookes Publishing Co.

Index

Page numbers followed by "f" indicate figures; those followed by "t" indicate tables.